# NATIONALISM

# LIAH GREENFELD

# NATIONALISM

## Five Roads to Modernity

HARVARD UNIVERSITY PRESS
Cambridge, Massachusetts
London, England

First Harvard University Press paperback edition, 1993

*Library of Congress Cataloging-in-Publication Data*

Greenfeld, Liah.
Nationalism: five roads to modernity / Liah Greenfeld.
p.   cm.
Includes bibliographical references (p.     ) and index.
ISBN 0–674–60318–4 (acid-free paper) (cloth)
ISBN 0-674-60319-2 (pbk.)
1. Nationalism—History.   I. Title.
JC311.G715   1992
320.5'4'09—dc20        92–6990
CIP

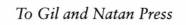

*To Gil and Natan Press*

# Acknowledgments

Today, with nationalism reinvigorated and wreaking havoc in parts of the globe where it long since has been considered a phenomenon of the past, I do not feel the need to justify my decision to write a book about it. The importance of nationalism in our world has been proven to us again, and it is imperative that we make a new effort to understand it. My interest in nationalism, however, predates its recent newsworthiness. It dates back to the fall of 1982, when I made this country my home and changed nationality for the second time. This change made me acutely aware of the constructed nature of national identity and the profound differences, reaching to every sphere of social existence, between nations defined in individualistic and civic terms—to use the categories I arrived at later—and those defined as ethnic collectivities.

I began writing this book in the fall of 1987, when a fellowship from the John M. Olin Foundation allowed me to take a year of leave and devote my undivided attention to the subject. Another year of full-time research and writing—made possible in 1989–90 by the German Marshall Fund of the United States and a stay at the Institute for Advanced Study in Princeton, financed in part by a grant from the MacArthur Foundation—allowed me to complete it.

During these years I have incurred many debts. I cannot adequately express my gratitude to my colleagues, sociologists, historians, and political scientists, who shared with me their insights and offered support and encouragement. Daniel Bell spent an entire month in effect editing the manuscript line by line. I would like him to know how touched and honored I felt by this degree of attention. I am forever in his debt. I am also indebted to Nathan Glazer for valuable comments on the original manuscript; to David Riesman for his untiring interest and for being ever willing to give advice; and to the chairman of the Harvard Department of Sociology, Aage Sørensen, for his theoretical sensitivity, intellectual tolerance, and constant personal support. Among the other colleagues at Harvard, Wallace MacCaffrey, Patrice Higonnet, and Richard Pipes read, respectively, chapters on England, France, and Russia, and shared with me their expert knowledge; David Landes found time to read the entire book and made useful suggestions. Members of the Russian Research Center, particularly the Director, Adam Ulam, have been supportive of my work since I first came to Harvard. Robert and Jana Kiely allowed me and my family to spend two relatively carefree years, during which I began this book, under the roof of Adams House.

Edward Shils, at the University of Chicago, has been a constant example of intellectual dedication and integrity. He encouraged me and made me strive for perfection. I know that the result falls short of this ideal, but I hope he will approve of what I have done.

At the Institute for Advanced Study in Princeton, where I spent one of the most productive and intellectually satisfying years of my life, I am particularly grateful to Michael Walzer for reading the entire original manuscript in a remarkably short time and providing detailed comments on it; to Clifford Geertz for making most helpful suggestions on the presentation of the argument; and to Albert Hirschman for a very sensitive, personal reading of the German chapter. Among scholars elsewhere with whom I had the privilege of discussing the subject of this book are the sociologists Bernard Barber, Peter Berger, Daniel Chirot, S. N. Eisenstadt, Peter Etzkorn, Suzanne Keller, Kurt and Gladys Lang, S. M. Lipset, and Edward Tiryakian; the scholar of English literature Heather Dubrow; the American historians John Murrin, Fred Siegel, and Richard John; the historians of Germany Jeffrey Herf, Thomas Nipperdey, and Peter Paret; and the Russian historians George Liber and Phillip Pomper. To some of them my debt is not only scholarly: they have been my friends, and their moral support and personal concern for me could not be more important. The two anonymous readers for Harvard University Press also deserve my thanks for their careful and appreciative readings and detailed comments.

I have greatly benefited from the advice of my colleagues, but in certain cases I left some very good advice unheeded. Since the author proposes and other agencies dispose, my prime consideration in preparing the manuscript for publication has been reducing its length, while preserving the integrity of the central argument. For this reason, with very few exceptions, I decided not to engage in explicit arguments with other scholars who have dealt with the subjects I treated, and refrained from spelling out the implications of my treatment for certain, rather important related areas of study. The first among these implications has to do with the theory of state-formation. If my argument regarding the nature and development of nationalism is correct, much of this theory (as a generous reader indeed remarked), so central in contemporary sociology and political science, should be subject to revision. The problem of ethnicity, and its significance in the age of nationalism, also requires greater articulation. The difference between ethnicity and ethnic nationalism is largely semantic. In nations defined in ethnic terms, every ethnic minority is considered a nationality (for this reason, the Soviet Union, for instance, never defined itself as a nation, but as a union of nations). Cultivation of ethnic identity is the form ethnic nationalism takes in civic nations; ethnicity is the name under which the latter is known in them. These subjects have been touched upon at different points in the book, but I would like to take them up independently and explore them further at a later time.

Also in the interest of saving space, I have significantly compressed the original material in the notes, limiting it to essentials and in many cases combining several references in a paragraph into one. In a few places I did the same for references spread over several paragraphs, if they referred to the same source or dealt with the same subject matter. I apologize for any inconvenience this may have caused.

These acknowledgments would not be complete if I did not mention my students. The undergraduates Ben Alpers, Phil Katz, and Justin Daniels, who worked on aspects of Russian, French, and American nationalism respectively, under my supervision, forced me to sharpen my ideas both when they followed my advice and when they disputed it. My graduate students, always willing to listen, to question, and to offer suggestions, have been a source of support in many ways. In particular, Marie-Laure Djelic and Paula Frederick were of great assistance in the final editing of the manuscript and its preparation for the publisher.

Anna Grinfeld helped in organizing the notes, and Natalia Tsarkova helped with the index. The printing-out of the final version would have been impossible without the expertise and patience of Nancy Williamson. Jacqueline Dormitzer made the copy-editing process a pleasure. Some of my earlier work on nationalism was published in *Research in Political Sociology* and *Survey*. In addition, chapter 1 incorporates portions of my paper "Science and National Greatness in 17th Century England," published in *Minerva 25* (Spring–Summer 1987); and a portion of chapter 3 appeared as "The Formation of the Russian National Identity: The Role of Status Insecurity and *Ressentiment*" in *Comparative Studies in Society and History* 32:3 (July 1990), published by Cambridge University Press. The editors of all these journals made valuable suggestions. My thanks are due to all of them.

Harvard University
January 1992

# Contents

# NATIONALISM

# INTRODUCTION

T his book is an attempt to understand the world in which we live. Its fundamental premise is that nationalism lies at the basis of this world. To grasp its significance, one has to explain nationalism.

The word "nationalism" is used here as an umbrella term under which are subsumed the related phenomena of national identity (or nationality) and consciousness, and collectivities based on them—nations; occasionally it is employed to refer to the articulate ideology on which national identity and consciousness rest, though not—unless specified—to the politically activist, xenophobic variety of national patriotism, which it frequently designates.

The specific questions which the book addresses are why and how nationalism emerged, why and how it was transformed in the process of transfer from one society to another, and why and how different forms of national identity and consciousness became translated into institutional practices and patterns of culture, molding the social and political structures of societies which defined themselves as nations. To answer these questions, I focus on five major societies which were the first to do so: England, France, Russia, Germany, and the United States of America.

## The Definition of Nationalism

The specificity of nationalism, that which distinguishes nationality from other types of identity, derives from the fact that nationalism locates the source of individual identity within a "people," which is seen as the bearer of sovereignty, the central object of loyalty, and the basis of collective solidarity. The "people" is the mass of a population whose boundaries and nature are defined in various ways, but which is usually perceived as larger than any concrete community and always as fundamentally homogeneous, and only superficially divided by the lines of status, class, locality, and in some cases even ethnicity. This specificity is conceptual. The only foundation of nationalism as such, the only condition, that is, without which no nationalism is possible, is an idea; nationalism is a particular perspective or a style of thought.[1] The idea which lies at the core of nationalism is the idea of the "nation."

### The Origins of the Idea of the "Nation"

To understand the nature of the idea of the "nation," it might be helpful to examine the semantic permutations which eventually resulted in it, as we follow the history of the word. The early stages of this history were traced by the Italian scholar Guido Zernatto.[2] The origin of the word is to be found in the Latin *natio*—something born. The initial concept was derogatory: in Rome the name *natio* was reserved for groups of foreigners coming from the same geographical region, whose status—because they were foreigners— was below that of the Roman citizens. This concept was thus similar in meaning to the Greek *ta ethne*, also used to designate foreigners and, specifically, heathens, and to the Hebrew *amamim*, which referred to those who did not belong to the chosen monotheistic people. The word had other meanings as well, but they were less common, and this one—a group of foreigners united by place of origin—for a long time remained its primary implication.

In this sense, of a group of foreigners united by place of origin, the word "nation" was applied to the communities of students coming to several universities shared by Western Christendom from loosely—geographically or linguistically—related regions. For example, there were four nations in the University of Paris, the great center of theological learning: "l'honorable nation de France," "la fidèle nation de Picardie," "la vénérable nation de Normandie," and "la constante nation de Germanie." The "nation de France" included all students coming from France, Italy, and Spain; that of "Germanie," those from England and Germany; the Picard "nation" was reserved for the Dutch; and the Norman, for those from the Northeast. It is important to note that the students had a national identity only in their status as students (that is, in most cases, while residing abroad); this identity was immediately shed when their studies were completed and they returned home. While applied in this setting, the word "nation," on the one hand, lost its derogatory connotation, and on the other, acquired an additional meaning. Owing to the specific structure of university life at the time, the communities of students functioned as support groups or unions and, as they regularly took sides in scholastic disputations, also developed common opinions. As a result, the word "nation" came to mean more than a community of origin: it referred now to the community of opinion and purpose.

As universities sent representatives to adjudicate grave ecclesiastical questions at the Church Councils, the word underwent yet another transformation. Since the late thirteenth century, starting at the Council of Lyon in 1274, the new concept—"nation" as a community of opinion—was applied to the parties of the "ecclesiastical republic." But the individuals who composed them, the spokesmen of various intraecclesiastical approaches, were also representatives of secular and religious potentates. And so the word "nation" acquired another meaning, that of representatives of cultural and political authority, or a political, cultural, and then social *elite*. Zernatto cites Montesquieu, Joseph de Maistre, and Schopenhauer to demonstrate how late this was still the accepted significance of the word. It is impossible to mistake its meaning in the famous passage from *Esprit des lois:* "Sous les deux premières races on assembla souvent la nation, c'est à dire, les seigneurs et les évêques; il n'était point des communes." [3]

### The Zigzag Pattern of Semantic Change

At this point, where Zernatto's story breaks off, we may pause to take a closer look at it. To an extent, the history of the word "nation" allows us to anticipate the analysis employed in much of the book. The successive changes in meaning combine into a pattern which, for the sake of formality, we shall call "the zigzag pattern of semantic change." At each stage of this development, the meaning of the word, which comes with a certain semantic baggage, evolves out of usage in a particular situation. The available conventional concept is applied within new circumstances, to certain aspects of which it corresponds. However, aspects of the new situation, which were absent in the situation in which the conventional concept evolved, become cognitively associated with it, resulting in a duality of meaning. The meaning of the original concept is gradually obscured, and the new one emerges as conventional. When the word is used again in a new situation, it is likely to be used in this new meaning, and so on and so forth. (This pattern is depicted in Figure 1.)

The process of semantic transformation is constantly redirected by structural (situational) constraints which form the new concepts (meanings of the word); at the same time, the structural constraints are conceptualized, interpreted, or defined in terms of the concepts (the definition of the situation changes as the concepts evolve), which thereby orient action. The social potency and psychological effects of this orientation vary in accordance with the sphere of the concept's applicability and its relative centrality in the actor's overall existence. A student in a medieval university, defined as a member of one or another nation, might derive therefrom an idea of the quarters he was supposed to be lodged in, people he was likely to associate with most closely, and some specific opinions he was expected to hold in the course of the few years his studies lasted. Otherwise his "national" identity, probably, did not have much impact on his self-image or behavior; outside the narrow sphere of the university, the concept had no applicability. The influence of the equally transient "national" identity on a participant at a Church Coun-

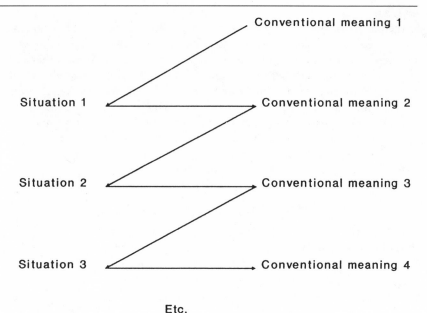

Etc.

*Figure 1*   The zigzag pattern of semantic change

cil could be more profound. Membership in a nation defined him as a person of very high status, the impact of such definition on one's self-perception could be permanent, and the lingering memory of nationality could affect the person's conduct far beyond conciliar deliberations, even if his nation no longer existed.

### From "Rabble" to "Nation"

The applicability of the idea of the nation and its potency increased a thousandfold as the meaning of the word was transformed again. At a certain point in history—to be precise, in early sixteenth-century England—the word "nation" in its conciliar meaning of "an elite" was applied to the population of the country and made synonymous with the word "people." *This semantic transformation signaled the emergence of the first nation in the world, in the sense in which the word is understood today, and launched the era of nationalism.* The stark significance of this conceptual revolution was highlighted by the fact that, while the general referent of the word "people" prior to its nationalization was the population of a region, specifically it applied to the lower classes and was most frequently used in the sense of "rabble" or "plebs." The equation of the two concepts implied the elevation of the populace to the position of an (at first specifically political) elite. As a

synonym of the "nation"—an elite—the "people" lost its derogatory connotation and, now denoting an eminently positive entity, acquired the meaning of the bearer of sovereignty, the basis of political solidarity, and the supreme object of loyalty. A tremendous change of attitude, which it later
reinforced, had to precede such redefinition of the situation, for with it
members of all orders of the society identified with the group, from which
earlier the better placed of them could only wish to dissociate themselves.
What brought this change about in the first place, and then again and again,
as national identity replaced other types in one country after another, is, in
every particular case, the first issue to be accounted for, and it will be the
focus of discussion in several chapters of the book.

National identity in its distinctive modern sense is, therefore, an identity
which derives from membership in a "people," the fundamental characteristic of which is that it is defined as a "nation." Every member of the
"people" thus interpreted partakes in its superior, elite quality, and it is in
consequence that a stratified national population is perceived as essentially
homogeneous, and the lines of status and class as superficial. This principle
lies at the basis of all nationalisms and justifies viewing them as expressions
of the same general phenomenon. Apart from it, different nationalisms share
little. The national populations—diversely termed "peoples," "nations,"
and "nationalities"—are defined in many ways, and the criteria of membership in them vary. The multiformity which results is the source of the conceptually evasive, Protean nature of nationalism and the cause of the perennial frustration of its students, vainly trying to define it with the help of one
or another "objective" factor, all of which are rendered relevant to the problem only if the national principle happens to be applied to them. The definition of nationalism proposed here recognizes it as an "emergent phenomenon," that is, a phenomenon whose nature—as well as the possibilities of its
development and the possibilities of the development of the elements of
which it is composed—is determined not by the character of its elements,
but by a certain organizing principle which makes these elements into a
unity and imparts to them a special significance.[4]

There are important exceptions to every relationship in terms of which
nationalism has ever been interpreted—whether with common territory or
common language, statehood or shared traditions, history or race. None of
these relationships has proved inevitable. But from the definition proposed
above, it follows not only that such exceptions are to be expected, but that
nationalism does not have to be related to *any* of these factors, though as a
rule it is related to at least some of them. In other words, *nationalism is not
necessarily a form of particularism.* It is a political ideology (or a class of
political ideologies deriving from the same basic principle), and as such it
does not have to be identified with any particular community.[5] A nation
coextensive with humanity is in no way a contradiction in terms. The United

States of the World, which will perhaps exist in the future, with sovereignty vested in the population, and the various segments of the latter regarded as equal, would be a nation in the strict sense of the word within the framework of nationalism. The United States of America represents an approximation to precisely this state of affairs.

### The Emergence of Particularistic Nationalisms

As it is, however, nationalism is the most common and salient form of particularism in the modern world. Moreover, if compared with the forms of particularism it has replaced, it is a particularly effective (or, depending on one's viewpoint, pernicious) form of particularism, because, as every individual derives his or her identity from membership in the community, the sense of commitment to it and its collective goals is much more widespread. In a world divided into particular communities, national identity tends to be associated and confounded with a community's sense of uniqueness and the qualities contributing to it. These qualities (social, political, cultural in the narrow sense, or ethnic)[6] therefore acquire a great significance in the formation of every specific nationalism. The association between the nationality of a community and its uniqueness represents the next and last transformation in the meaning of the "nation" and may be deduced from the zigzag pattern of semantic (and by implication social) change.

The word "nation" which, in its conciliar and at the time prevalent meaning of an elite, was applied to the population of a specific country (England) became cognitively associated with the existing (political, territorial, and ethnic) connotations of a population and a country. While the interpretation of the latter in terms of the concept "nation" modified their significance, the concept "nation" was also transformed and—as it carried over the connotations of a population and a country, which were consistent with it—came to mean "a sovereign people." This new meaning replaced that of "an elite" initially only in England. As we may judge from Montesquieu's definition, elsewhere the older meaning long remained dominant, but it was, eventually, supplanted.

The word "nation," meaning "*sovereign* people," was now applied to other populations and countries which, like the first nation, naturally had some political, territorial, and/or ethnic qualities to distinguish them, and became associated with such geo-political and ethnic baggage. As a result of this association, "nation" changed its meaning once again, coming to signify "a *unique* sovereign people." (These changes are shown in Figure 2.) The last transformation[7] may be considered responsible for the conceptual confusion reigning in the theories of nationalism. The new concept of the nation in most cases eclipsed the one immediately preceding it, as the latter

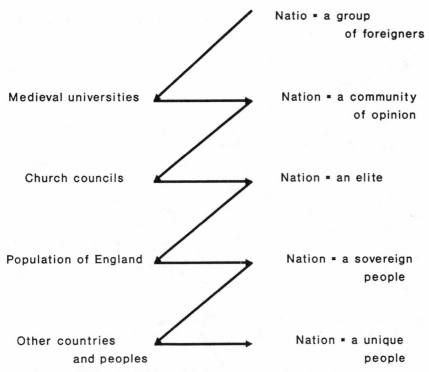

*Figure 2*   The transformation of the idea of the nation

eclipsed those from which it descended, but, significantly, this did not happen everywhere. Because of the persistence and, as we shall see, in certain places development and extension of structural conditions responsible for the evolution of the original, non-particularistic idea of the nation, the two concepts now coexist.

The term "nation" applied to both conceals important differences. The emergence of the more recent concept signified a profound transformation in the nature of nationalism, and the two concepts under one name reflect two radically different forms of the phenomenon (which means both two radically different forms of national identity and consciousness, and two radically different types of national collectivities—nations).

## Types of Nationalism

The two branches of nationalism are obviously related in a significant way, but are grounded in different values and develop for different reasons. They also give rise to dissimilar patterns of social behavior, culture, and political institutions, often conceptualized as expressions of unlike "national characters."

Perhaps the most important difference concerns the relationship between *nationalism* and *democracy*. The location of sovereignty within the people and the recognition of the fundamental equality among its various strata, which constitute the essence of the modern national idea, are at the same time the basic tenets of democracy. Democracy was born with the sense of nationality. The two are inherently linked, and neither can be fully understood apart from this connection. Nationalism was the form in which democracy appeared in the world, contained in the idea of the nation as a butterfly in a cocoon. Originally, nationalism developed *as* democracy; where the conditions of such original development persisted, the identity between the two was maintained. But as nationalism spread in different conditions and the emphasis in the idea of the nation moved from the sovereign character to the uniqueness of the people, the original equivalence between it and democratic principles was lost. One implication of this, which should be emphasized, is that democracy may not be exportable. It may be an inherent predisposition in certain nations (inherent in their very definition as nations—that is, the original national concept), yet entirely alien to others, and the ability to adopt and develop it in the latter may require a change of identity.

The emergence of the original (in principle, non-particularistic) idea of the nation as a sovereign people was, evidently, predicated on a transformation in the character of the relevant population, which suggested the symbolic elevation of the "people" and its definition as a political elite, in other words, on a profound change in structural conditions. The emergence of the ensuing, particularistic, concept resulted from the application of the original idea to conditions which did not necessarily undergo such transformation. It was the other, in the original concept accidental, connotations of people and country which prompted and made possible such application. In both instances, the adoption of the idea of the nation implied symbolic elevation of the populace (and therefore the creation of a new social order, a new structural reality). But while in the former case the idea was inspired by the structural context which preceded its formation—the people acting in some way as a political elite, and actually exercising sovereignty—in the latter case the sequence of events was the opposite: the importation of the idea of popular sovereignty—as part and parcel of the idea of the nation—initiated the transformation in the social and political structure.

As it did so, the nature of sovereignty was inevitably reinterpreted. The *observable* sovereignty of the people (its nationality) in the former case could only mean that some individuals, who were *of* the people, exercised sovereignty. The idea of the nation (which implied sovereignty of the people) acknowledged this experience and rationalized it. The national principle that emerged was individualistic: sovereignty of the people was the implication of the actual sovereignty of individuals; it was because these individuals (of the people) actually exercised sovereignty that they were members of a nation. The *theoretical* sovereignty of the people in the latter case, by contrast, was an implication of the people's uniqueness, its very being a distinct people, because this was the meaning of the nation, and the nation was, by definition, sovereign. The national principle was collectivistic; it reflected the collective being. Collectivistic ideologies are inherently authoritarian, for, when the collectivity is seen in unitary terms, it tends to assume the character of a collective individual possessed of a single will, and someone is bound to be its interpreter. The reification of a community introduces (or preserves) fundamental inequality between those of its few members who are qualified to interpret the collective will and the many who have no such qualifications; the select few dictate to the masses who must obey.

These two dissimilar interpretations of popular sovereignty underlie the basic types of nationalism, which one may classify as individualistic-libertarian and collectivistic-authoritarian. In addition, nationalism may be distinguished according to criteria of membership in the national collectivity, which may be either "civic," that is, identical with citizenship, or "ethnic." In the former case, nationality is at least in principle open and voluntaristic; it can and sometimes must be acquired. In the latter, it is believed to be inherent—one can neither acquire it if one does not have it, nor change it if one does; it has nothing to do with individual will, but constitutes a genetic characteristic. Individualistic nationalism cannot be but civic, but civic nationalism can also be collectivistic. More often, though, collectivistic nationalism takes on the form of ethnic particularism, while ethnic nationalism is necessarily collectivistic. (These concepts are summarized in Figure 3.)

It must be kept in mind, of course, that these are only categories which serve to pinpoint certain characteristic tendencies within different—specific—nationalisms. They should be regarded as models which can be approximated, but are unlikely to be fully realized. In reality, obviously, the

|  | *Civic* | *Ethnic* |
|---|---|---|
| *Individualistic-libertarian* | Type I | Void |
| *Collectivistic-authoritarian* | Type II | Type III |

*Figure 3*   Types of nationalism

most common type is a mixed one. But the compositions of the mixtures vary significantly enough to justify their classification in these terms and render it a useful analytical tool.

## Distinctiveness of National Identity

Nationalism being defined as a specific conceptual perspective, it is evident that to understand national identity one must explain how this perspective—the fundamental idea of the nation and its various interpretations—emerged. Clearly, national identity should not be confused with other types of identity which do not share this perspective, and it cannot be explained in general terms or in terms which may explain any other type of identity. This point is worth reiterating, for national identity is frequently equated with collective identity as such.

Nationalism is not related to membership in all human communities, but only in communities defined as "nations." National identity is different from an exclusively religious or a class identity. Nor is it a synonym for an exclusively or primarily linguistic or territorial identity, or a political identity of a certain kind (such, for instance, as an identity derived from being a subject of a particular dynasty), or even a *unique* identity, that is, a sense of Frenchness, Englishness, or Germanity, all of which are commonly associated with national identity. Such other identities are discussed in this book only if they influence the formation of national identity and are as a result essential to its understanding, which is not always the case. Frequently a unique identity (the character of which, depending on the source of uniqueness, may be religious or linguistic, territorial or political) exists centuries before the national identity is formed, in no way guaranteeing and anticipating it; such was the case in France and to a certain extent in Germany. In other cases, the sense of uniqueness may be articulated simultaneously with the emergence of the national identity, as happened in England and, most certainly, in Russia. It is even possible, though very unusual, for national identity to predate the formation of a unique identity; the development of identity in America followed this course. National identity is not a generic identity; it is specific. Generating an identity may be a psychological necessity, a given of human nature. Generating national identity is not. It is important to keep this distinction in mind.

In ethnic nationalisms, "nationality" became a synonym of "ethnicity," and national identity is often perceived as a reflection or awareness of possession of "primordial" or inherited group characteristics, components of "ethnicity," such as language, customs, territorial affiliation, and physical type. Such objective "ethnicity" in itself, however, does not represent an identity, not even an "ethnic" identity. The possession of some sort of "ethnic" endowment is close to universal, yet the identity of a person born in England of English parentage and English-speaking may be that of a Christian; the identity of a person born and living in France, speaking French, unmistakably French in habits and tastes, that of a nobleman; their "ethnicity" being quite irrelevant to their motives and actions, and seen, if at all noticed, as purely accidental. An essential characteristic of any identity is that it is necessarily the view the concerned actor has of himself or herself. It therefore either exists or does not; it cannot be asleep and then be awakened, as some sort of disease. It cannot be presumed on the basis of any objective characteristics, however closely associated with it in other cases. Identity is perception. If a particular identity does not mean anything to the population in question, this population does not have this particular identity.[8]

The "ethnicity" of a community (its being an "ethnic community") presupposes the uniformity and antiquity of its origins, as a result of which it may be viewed as a natural grouping and its characteristics as inherent in the population. Such inherent characteristics do regularly form the basis of the group's sense of particularity, or what has been here referred to as its unique identity. Yet ethnicity does not generate unique identity. It does not, because of the available "ethnic" characteristics only some are selected, not the same ones in every case, and the choice, in addition to the availability or even salience of the selected qualities, is determined by many other factors. Moreover, no clear line separates selection from artificial construction. A language of a part may be imposed on the entire population and declared native to the latter (or, if no part of a population has a language to speak of, it may be outright invented). An "ancestral" territory may be acquired in conquest, "common" history fabricated, traditions imagined and projected into the past. One should add to this that the unique identity of a community is not necessarily ethnic, because the community may not see any of the (allegedly) inherent attributes of the population as the source of its uniqueness, but may concentrate, for example, as was the case in France, on the personal attributes of the king or on high, academic, culture. Some populations have no "ethnic" characteristics at all, though this is very unusual. The population of the United States of America, the identity of which is unmistakably national and which undoubtedly possesses a well-developed sense of uniqueness, is a case in point: it has no "ethnic" characteristics because its population is not an "ethnic community."

National identity frequently utilized ethnic characteristics (this is obvious in the case of ethnic nationalisms). Yet it should be emphasized that "ethnicity" in itself is in no way conducive to nationality. "Ethnic" characteristics form a certain category of raw material which can be organized and rendered meaningful in various ways, thus becoming elements of any number of identities. National identity, in distinction, provides an organizing principle applicable to different materials to which it then grants meaning, transforming them thereby into elements of a specific identity.

## The Outline of the Argument

The original modern idea of the nation emerged in sixteenth-century England, which was the first nation in the world (and the only one, with the possible exception of Holland, for about two hundred years). The individualistic civic nationalism which developed there was inherited by its colonies in America, and later became characteristic of the United States.

Particularistic nationalism, reflecting the dissociation of the meaning of the "nation" as a "people" extolled as the bearer of sovereignty, the central object of collective loyalty, and the basis of political solidarity, from that of an "elite," and its fusion with geo-political and/or ethnic characteristics of particular populations, did not emerge until the eighteenth century. This happened on the continent of Europe, whence it started to spread all over the world. Collectivistic nationalism appeared first, and almost simultaneously, in France and Russia, then, close to the end of the eighteenth century and in the beginning of the nineteenth, in German principalities. While France, from many points of view, represented an ambivalent case (its nationalism was collectivistic and yet civic), Russia and Germany developed clear examples of ethnic nationalism.

When nationalism started to spread in the eighteenth century, the emergence of new national identities was no longer a result of original creation, but rather of the importation of an already existing idea. The dominance of England in eighteenth-century Europe, and then the dominance of the West in the world, made nationality the canon. As the sphere of influence of the core Western societies (which defined themselves as nations) expanded, societies belonging or seeking entry to the supra-societal system of which the West was the center had in fact no choice but to become nations.[9] The development of national identities thus was essentially an international process, whose sources in every case but the first lay outside the evolving nation.

At the same time, for several reasons, every nationalism was an indigenous development. The availability of the concept alone could not have motivated anyone to adopt a foreign model, however successful, and be the reason for the change of identity and the transformation which such fundamental change implied. For such a transformation to occur, influential actors must have been willing, or forced, to undergo it. The adoption of national identity must have been, in one way or another, in the interest of the groups which imported it.[10] Specifically, it must have been preceded by the dissatisfaction of these groups with the identity they had previously. A change of identity presupposed a crisis of identity.

Such was in fact the case. The dissatisfaction with the traditional identity reflected a fundamental inconsistency between the definition of social order it expressed and the experience of the involved actors. This could result from the upward or downward mobility of whole strata, from the conflation of social roles (which might imply contradictory expectations from the same individuals), or from the appearance of new roles which did not fit existing categories. Whatever the cause of the identity crisis, its structural manifestation was in every case the same—"anomie." [11] This might be, but was not necessarily, the condition of the society at large; it did, however, directly affect the relevant agents (that is, those who participated in the creation or importation of national identity). Since the agents were different in different cases, the anomie was expressed and experienced differently. Very often it took the form of status-inconsistency, which, depending on its nature, could be accompanied by a profound sense of insecurity and anxiety.

The specific nature of the change and its effects on the agents in each case profoundly influenced the character of nationalism in it. The underlying ideas of nationality were shaped and modified in accordance with the situational constraints of the actors, and with the aspirations, frustrations, and interests which these constraints generated. This often involved reinterpreting them in terms of indigenous traditions which might have existed alongside the dominant system of ideas in which the now rejected traditional identity was embedded, as well as in terms of the elements of this system of ideas itself which were not rejected. Such reinterpretation implied incorporation of pre-national modes of thought within the nascent national consciousness, which were then carried on in it and reinforced.

The effects of these structural and cultural influences frequently combined with that of a certain psychological factor which both necessitated a reinterpretation of the imported ideas and determined the direction of such reinterpretation. Every society importing the foreign idea of the nation inevitably focused on the source of importation—an object of imitation by definition—and reacted to it. Because the model was superior to the imitator in the latter's own perception (its being a model implied that), and the contact itself more often than not served to emphasize the latter's inferiority, the reaction commonly assumed the form of *ressentiment*. A term coined by Nietzsche and later defined and developed by Max Scheler,[12] *ressentiment* refers to a psychological state resulting from suppressed feelings of envy and hatred (existential envy) and the impossibility of satisfying these feelings. The sociological basis for *ressentiment*—or the structural conditions that are necessary for the development of this psychological state—is twofold. The first condition (the structural basis of envy itself) is the fundamental comparability between the subject and the object of envy, or rather the belief on the part of the subject in the fundamental equality between them, which makes them in principle interchangeable. The second condition is the actual inequality (perceived as not fundamental) of such dimensions that it rules out practical achievement of the theoretically existing equality. The presence of these conditions renders a situation *ressentiment*-prone irrespective of the temperaments and psychological makeup of the individuals who compose the relevant population. The effect produced by *ressentiment* is similar to that of "anomie" and to what Furet, discussing Tocqueville's argument regarding the emphasis on equality in pre-revolutionary France, calls "the Tocqueville effect." [13] In all these cases the creative impulse comes from the psychologically unbearable inconsistency between several aspects of reality.

The creative power of *ressentiment*—and its sociological importance—consists in that it may eventually lead to the "transvaluation of values," that is, to the transformation of the value scale in a way which denigrates the originally supreme values, replacing them with notions which are unimportant, external, or indeed bear in the original scale the negative sign. The term "transvaluation of values" may be somewhat misleading, because what usually takes place is not a direct reversal of the original hierarchy. Adopting values directly antithetical to those of another is borrowing with the opposite sign. A society with a well-developed institutional structure and a rich legacy of cultural traditions is not likely to borrow lock, stock, and barrel from anywhere. However, since the creative process resulting from *ressentiment* is by definition a reaction to the values of others and not to one's own condition regardless of others, the new system of values that emerges is necessarily influenced by the one to which it is a reaction. It is due to this that philosophies of *ressentiment* are characterized by the quality of "transparency": it is always possible to see behind them the values they disclaim. *Ressentiment* felt by the groups that imported the idea of the nation and articulated the national consciousness of their respective societies usually resulted in the selection out of their own indigenous traditions of elements hostile to the original national principle and in their deliberate cultivation. In certain cases—notably in Russia—where indigenous cultural resources were absent or clearly insufficient, *ressentiment* was the single most important factor in determining the specific terms in which national identity was defined. Wherever it existed, it fostered particularistic pride and xenophobia, providing emotional nourishment for the nascent national sentiment and sustaining it whenever it faltered.[14]

It is possible, then, to distinguish analytically three phases in the formation of specific nationalisms: structural, cultural, and psychological, each defined by the factor dominant in it. The adoption of a new, national identity is precipitated by a regrouping within or change in the position of influential social groups. This structural change results in the inadequacy of the traditional definition, or identity, of the involved groups—a crisis of identity, structurally expressed as "anomie"—which creates among them an incentive to search for and, given the availability, adopt a new identity. The crisis of identity as such does not explain why the identity which is adopted is *national,* but only why there is a predisposition to opt for some new identity. The fact that the identity is *national* is explained, first of all, by the availability at the time of a certain type of ideas, in the first case a result of invention, and in the rest of an importation. (It is this dependence on the idea of the nation, ultimately irreducible to situational givens and solely attributable to the unpredictable ways of human creativity, that makes national identity a matter of historical contingency rather than necessity.) In addition, *national* identity is adopted because of its ability to solve the crisis. The variation in the nature of the crises to which all specific nationalisms owe their inception explains some of the variation in the nature of different nationalisms.

The adjustment of the idea of the nation to the situational constraints of the relevant agents involves its conceptualization in terms of indigenous traditions. This conceptualization further distinguishes every national identity.

Finally, where the emergence of national identity is accompanied by *ressentiment,* the latter leads to the emphasis on the elements of indigenous traditions—or the construction of a new system of values—hostile to the principles of the original nationalism. The matrix of the national identity and consciousness in such cases evolves out of this transvaluation of values, the results of which, together with the modifications of the original principles reflecting the structural and cultural specificity of each setting, are responsible for the unique, distinct character of any one nationalism.

This bare-bones outline should be regarded as but the skeleton of a very complex story, which can be observed in such stark nakedness only when stripped of the resplendent historical flesh that covered it. As I tried to reveal the skeleton in the book—through a careful study of detail and comparison of different cases—I made every effort not to reduce the presentation to an x-ray picture. As much as was possible within the confines of one volume, I tried to allow the reader the opportunity to examine the evidence that led me to these conclusions, and thus to agree or disagree with them after reading the book.

## The Nature of the Argument

This work belongs to the long tradition of sociological inquiry which seeks to understand the nature, and to account for the emergence, of modern society. Among its founders one finds the founding fathers of the discipline of sociology: Emile Durkheim, Max Weber, Ferdinand Toennies, as well as such great proto-sociologists as Karl Marx and Alexis de Tocqueville. While I have been, no doubt, influenced by the ideas of all these great men, it is Weber's thought that I find the most congenial. I adopt Weber's definition of social reality as essentially symbolic, of social action as *meaningfully* oriented action, and share his conviction that the study of meaningful orientations, of the motivations of social actors, constitutes "the central subject" of sociology.[15] In this Weberian orientation my book differs from much of the current sociological literature on modernity as well as on nationalism, which is commonly regarded as one of the components of the latter.

The focus of the book—throughout—is a set of ideas or, rather, several sub-sets of a set of ideas, at the core of which lies the idea of the "nation," which I believe forms *the constitutive element of modernity*. In this belief, I reverse the order of precedence, and therefore of causality, which is usually, if sometimes tacitly, assumed to exist between national identity and nations, and nationalism and modernity: namely that national identity is simply the identity characteristic of nations, while nationalism is a product or reflection of major components of modernization. Rather than define nationalism by its modernity, I see modernity as defined by nationalism. The Weberian idea of the *social* provides a rationale for this view.[16]

Social reality is intrinsically cultural; it is necessarily a symbolic reality, created by the subjective meanings and perceptions of social actors. Every social order (that is, the overall *structure* of a society) represents a materialization, or objectivization, of its image shared by those who participate in it. It exists as much in the minds of people as in the outside world, and if it loses its grip on the minds of a sufficient majority, or of a minority with sufficient power to impose it on others, it cannot be sustained and is bound to vanish from the outside world as well. The essentially symbolic character of social reality has to do with the fundamental biological constitution of the human species. In general, society appears to be a necessary corollary of life at the advanced stages of biological evolution. The preservation of a species requires cooperation of its member organisms (often to the detriment of the latter). For animals, nature, in the form of instincts, provides detailed "models for"[17] any ordinary activity; their ability to cooperate, their capacity for integration in general and in particular, is inborn. The cardinal fact of human existence is that humans lack built-in "models for" behavior in groups. Social integration and cooperation are necessary for the preservation of the human species (as well as of its individual members), but there is no innate knowledge of how this should be accomplished. The lack of innate knowledge results in the need for models and blueprints, for an image of order, or *created symbolic order,* among human beings. Such symbolic order—culture—is the human equivalent of animal instincts, and is an indispensable condition for the survival of the human species as well as of individuals. The particular image of social order provided by a culture forms the constitutive element of any given society. Within the limits set by the physical and psychological parameters of human nature, symbolic orders are widely variable, which explains the variability of human societies.

The recognition that human society is the social aspect of life of a certain species, and that to study it one must acknowledge this species' specificity, its baggage of biological disabilities (such as the lack of instincts) and abilities (for instance, creativity), implies an emphasis on the cultural, subjective, meaning- and model-creating symbolic elements in social reality, and makes consideration of the concepts and ideas in the minds of people necessary for the interpretation of any social phenomenon. In other words, since men (generically speaking) happen to be reasoning beings and their reasoning is immediately related to their actions, one must take their reasoning into account and look in it for an explanation of their actions. Of course, this reasoning—the actors' ideas, volitions, motivations—is influenced by their situational constraints, and through these *specific* situational constraints is related to the structural macro-social processes. But we can discover the relevant structural factors in any given case only if we first concentrate on the actors—the creators and carriers of ideas—and ascertain the situational constraints which have a bearing on their interests and motivations.

I have no argument with the claim that structures are an extremely important component of every social action and should necessarily be considered as a part of its explanation: a structural analysis is a central part of my discussion of nationalism. This view does not imply disregard for structures. What it implies is methodological individualism and, therefore, rejection of reification, be it of structures or of ideas. For this reason it is equally opposed to strict sociological structuralism and to idealism, which are akin in their tendency to reify concepts. Social structures are relatively stable systems of social relationships and opportunities in which individuals find themselves and by which they are vitally affected, but over which most of them have no control and of the exact nature of which they are usually unaware. The essence of sociological "structuralism" consists in that structures are reified and seen as "objective" (that is, ontologically independent of individual—subjective—volitions) social forces which act through and move individuals, who are in turn regarded as their vehicles and representatives. The behavior of individuals and their beliefs, in this framework, are determined by this "objective" reality and acquire the character of epiphenomena. Idealism regards ideas rather than structures as the moving forces in history. According to it, ideas beget ideas, and this symbolic generation accounts for the phenomenon of social change. Like reified structures, ideas act through and move individuals, seen as vehicles or representatives of clusters of ideas. Neither "structuralism" nor idealism recognizes the significance of the human agency, in which culture and structure are brought together, in which each of them is every day modified and recreated, and only by—not through—which both are moved and shaped, and given the ability to exert their influence. Both ideas and social structures are only operationalized in men. Men (to quote Durkheim this time) "are the only active elements of society." [18] Neither structural constraints nor ideas can beget other structural constraints and ideas. What they can do is produce different states of mind in the individuals within their sphere of influence. These states of mind are rationalized and, if rationalized creatively, may result in new interpretations of reality. These interpretations, in turn, affect structural conditions, which then can produce other states of mind at the same time as they directly affect states of mind, and the infinitely complex process is endlessly and unpredictably perpetuated. Theories of social reality, whether past or present, which disregard the human agency can never rise above pure speculation. They belong to metaphysics.

Cultural and structural constraints always interact, and because of the creative nature of the human agency, they rarely interact in predetermined ways. In most cases one cannot know in advance which factor plays the role of a cause and which is an effect in a particular stage of social formation and change. Social action is determined chiefly by the motivations of the relevant actors. Motivations are formed by their beliefs and values, and at the same time are shaped by the structural constraints of the actors, which also affect the beliefs and values. Social action, determined by motivations, creates structures. It follows from here that the arrow of causality may point both ways. Moreover, the very same phenomenon at one phase in its development may be a result, and at another—a primary factor in the social process. Only on the basis of careful examination of all the available evidence can one establish with certainty its place in the causal chain.

Nationalism, among other things, connotes a species of identity, in the psychological sense of the term, denoting self-definition. In this sense, any identity is a set of ideas, a symbolic construct. It is a particularly powerful construct, for it defines a person's position in his or her social world. It carries within itself expectations from the person and from different classes of others in the person's surroundings, and thus orients his or her actions. The least specialized identity, the one with the widest circumference, that is believed to define a person's very essence and guides his or her actions in many spheres of social existence is, of course, the most powerful. The image of social order is reflected in it most fully; it represents this image in a microcosm. In the course of history people's essence has been defined by different identities. In numerous societies religious identity performed this function. In many others an estate or a caste identity did the same. Such generalized identity in the modern world is the national identity.

A change of the generalized identity (for example, from religious or estate to national) presupposes a transformation of the image of the social order. It may be prompted by independent structural changes—that is, the transformation of the order itself—either as a result of the accumulation of minute and imperceptible-in-isolation modifications, or of a one-time cataclysmic event—a major epidemic or war or, alternatively, a sudden emergence of great economic opportunities and even the appearance of a particularly strong-willed ruler with peculiar ideas. (The latter, as we shall see, is not merely a mad supposition: this was what started Russia on its path toward nationality.) The change in the image of social order may also reflect a desire to change an order resistant to change. In neither case does the emergent image simply mirror the transformations already ongoing: there is always a discrepancy between the image of reality and reality. Whether or not inspired and triggered by them, it represents a blueprint of a new order (a model) and, by motivating actions of individuals harboring it, causes further transformations and gradually modifies social structure in accordance with its tenets.

These assumptions—which allow for the causal primacy of ideas, without denying it to structures—are consistent with the course of historical events in the case of nationalism. Historically, the emergence of nationalism predated the development of every significant component of modernization. In interaction with other factors it helped to shape its economic forces, and stamped its cultural temper. As for the political organization and culture of modernity, its formative influence was also the controlling one. It is nationalism which has made our world, politically, what it is—this cannot be put strongly enough. Within the complex of national phenomena itself, national identity preceded the formation of nations. These social structures, a towering presence in the life of every conscious individual (and political collectivities which are the peculiar mark of modern society), owe their existence to the individuals' belief in it, and their character to the nature of their ideas. But the ideas of nationalism, which have forged social structures and suffused cultural traditions, were also produced by structural constraints and inspired by traditions that preceded them. Before nationalism was a cause of certain social processes, it was an effect of others.

## The Structure of the Book

The book is divided into five chapters, each dealing with the development of national identity and consciousness in one of the societies in the sample. The chapters are organized chronologically, according to the periods crucial for the evolution of the respective national identities, which are the sixteenth century in England, the years between 1715 and 1789 in France, the second half of the eighteenth century in Russia, the late eighteenth and early nineteenth centuries in Germany, and the late eighteenth to mid-nineteenth century in the United States of America. The discussion does not focus on these periods exclusively: the consideration of earlier history (in some cases, such as France and Germany, centuries) is necessary to understand the nature of the identity that is formed in these years; and of later events, to appreciate its effects.

The moments of the emergence of nationalism in general and of its specific types can be located in time with a fair degree of precision. The new concepts are reflected in changes of vocabulary, which may be gauged from examination of period dictionaries, legal documents, and literature. Several sections of the book include such analysis and follow the permutation and development of the relevant political and cultural discourse from its beginning until the time when national consciousness, and the respective nations (the realization that the societies in question were nations), became, in the opinion of the participants, established facts and were no longer treated by them as problematic.

The data which make it possible to pinpoint the time when these specific nationalisms emerged also allow us to identify the agents, or actual participants, in this transformation. These are, in the first place, the people who came up with, articulated, and popularized the new concepts. This explains the central role played in the emergence of national identities by intellectuals—by definition, articulators and disseminators of ideas—whether or not professional and whatever their social origins. Conversely, the role *professional* intellectuals of middle-class origin played in the formation of national identity in some societies explains the high status they have since then enjoyed in them.

The influence, if not status, of groups instrumental in bringing nationalism about was great to begin with: groups lacking influence would not be able to promulgate the new identity within the rest of society. In some cases—notably in England, where nationality from the start acquired significance for wide sectors of the population—the influence of certain groups during the formative stage was due to their numerical strength. More commonly, those were elites, social, political, and cultural (the key group in England, France, and Russia was the aristocracy, and in Germany, the middle-class intellectuals), and their influence derived from various combinations of status, power, and wealth, and/or from their control of the means of communication. This book, however, concentrates upon the formation of national identity, not its promulgation, and when it analyzes its spread, it addresses the question of the transfer of the idea of the nation from one society to another, rather than its penetration from the center of each society into its periphery. The spread of nationalism in the latter case, an important and interesting topic in itself, doubtless increased the efficacy of national identity as a force of social mobilization, but it had no significant impact on the character of specific nationalisms. The character of every national identity was defined during the early phase, which is here discussed in detail. Its effects, in the political, social, and cultural constitution of the respective nations, as well as their historical record, are attributable to this original definition which set the goals for mobilization, not to the nationalization of the masses. Even with regard to its efficiency, nationalism was a potent force already before it became a mass phenomenon, simply because it motivated the elites who held the reins of power and controlled collective resources.

The cases were chosen for several reasons. One was the undisputed centrality of each one of them in modern history. Between them they set the pattern followed by the rest of the planet, and have presided over its development. The transformations within them, which are the subject of this book, have repercussions far beyond their borders. In these five societies were shaped the destinies of our world.

The national evolution of these societies represents one coherent—though exceedingly complex—process, rather than five discrete developments. For several centuries they have shared the same social space, each being a significant other for the rest, each influencing the others' self-perception, goals, and policies. Neither Russia nor, clearly, the United States of America was present in the consciousness of sixteenth-century England, but the impact of the transformation that occurred in sixteenth-century England on both Russia and the United States is beyond question. The five nationalisms are interconnected and, with the exception of the English, none can be fully understood in isolation from the others. This interconnectedness lends substantive unity to the book, which complements its theoretical unity.

Finally, each one of the five cases has a particular analytical significance, bearing specifically on one or another aspect of the general argument, and therefore forming an indispensable element in the theoretical structure of the book. The significance of the English case is obvious. The birth of the English nation was not the birth of a nation; it was the birth of the nations, the birth of nationalism. England is where the process originated; its analysis is essential for the understanding of the nature of the original idea of the nation, the conditions for its development, and its social uses. France offers the possibility of observing the successive evolution of several unique identities within the same political entity, highlighting the specific nature of national identity. It also demonstrates the possible influences of pre-national identities on nationalism. Russia is an exemplary case of the formative influence of *ressentiment*, and therefore of external models, on national identity. The development of nationalism in Germany focuses attention on the importance of indigenous traditions which form a mold for national consciousness. All these four cases demonstrate the chronological and causal primacy of structural conditions—the state of "anomie"—in starting off the process of the transformation of identity. The American case illustrates the essential independence of nationality from geo-political and ethnic factors and underscores its conceptual, or ideological, nature. Since national identity is the original identity of the American population, which preceded the formation of its geo-political and institutional framework, the analysis of American nationalism does not focus on the conditions of its emergence, which is unproblematic, but rather on its effects, which can in this case be observed in an almost pure form. Together, the five cases create a comparative perspective which alone makes the understanding of nationalism possible.

The analysis, in each chapter, is conducted on several levels: those of political vocabulary, of social relations and other structural constraints (specifically, those affecting key groups in the formation of national identity—the importance of a group always being defined as a function of the extent of actual participation of its members in the articulation and promulgation of national consciousness), and of general educated sentiment. The aim is to explain the evolution of a particular set of ideas and to show how they permeate the attitudes of relevant actors. For this reason, certain periods in the history of a given society, or certain groups, may be considered several times from different angles, while periods and groups with no bearing on the problem, however important otherwise, are omitted from discussion. Similarly, I have focused on those regions or sections within each population whose traditions have left a particularly deep imprint on that population's national identity. This is the reason for the emphasis on the developments in Protestant as against Catholic Germany (and specifically on Prussia as against Austria), or on New England as against other regions in the United States.

My aim was not to write the histories of the five nationalisms, but to understand the major forces which have shaped our identities and destinies. Thus I have focused on the commonalities of the developments in the five cases and on the significant singularities in each that either could illuminate the nature of the phenomenon of nationalism in general or helped to determine the course of modern history and lay at the roots of the central features of modernity. The points that I emphasize include not only the interpretations of the sovereignty of the people and the relationship between the individual and the community, which influenced the fate of democracy and defined its political and social alternatives. The discussion of England, in addition, contains a section on the symbiotic relationship between the young English nationalism and science, because of which science was fostered and launched to become the mighty power it now is. A large section addresses the equally intimate connection between German nationalism and Romanticism—the basis of major political ideologies, such as Marxism, on the one hand, and National Socialism, on the other—which has for two centuries informed our notions of art and human creativity, made us clamor for openness and for freedom to develop our creative potentials, and, shaping our views of our personalities, to a large extent shaped our personalities themselves.

Obviously science, though first institutionalized in England, developed in other countries as well, and Romanticism, though German in origin, had its representatives outside Germany. The same holds true for the universalistic and individualistic liberalism which I see as the central feature of English and American nationalisms, or, for that matter, anti-Semitism, the discussion of which completes the analysis of German nationalism. I treated such "international" traditions as singular features of particular nationalisms, first, if as a result of importation a tradition was not significantly modified (for example, science) or if the modified tradition (for example, English Romanticism), in distinction from the original one, did not profoundly affect the character of modern society in general; and second, if, while it shaped and was reflected in the nature of a particular nationalism, a tradition, even though present, in other cases failed to have such a formative influence. The same tradition, metaphorically, might be a dominant gene in one case, and a recessive one in another. I am aware of "multiple continuities" in every one of the nationalisms I studied. In each, there were defeated traditions and roads not taken. I did not focus on them *because* they were not taken.

This leads me to consider one final point that must be raised in the introduction. Do the origins of a nationalism which define its nature—establishing certain traditions as dominant and suppressing others—also *completely* shape its social and political expressions? Is the conduct of a nation—its historical record—*determined* by its dominant traditions? The answer to these questions is *no*. The dominant traditions create a predisposition for a certain type of action, and a probability that, in certain conditions, such action will take place. Without them this would be impossible; ideas of a certain kind are a necessary condition for certain kinds of social action. Knowledge of the nature of a specific nationalism should lead us to expect from the nation in question certain types of behavior, for there is a developed potentiality for some types and not for others. But society is an open system, and whether or not the existing potentialities are fully realized depends on many factors entirely unrelated to the nature of these potentialities.

The scope and the conception of the work prohibited exhaustive treatment, and much fascinating detail had to be left out. Yet I tried not to oversimplify and not to generalize for the sake of generalization. My goal was not to construct a model of reality that could have been, but to explain the reality that in fact emerged. I wished my analysis to reflect its complexity, even as I dissected it, and have sought to retain in my descriptions at least some of the unique flavor of the different times and societies I was describing. I tried to get into the shoes of the heroes of my story to understand what was it like to live the lives they lived and think what they thought, for without doing so I would not know how and why their experiences were transformed into forces which affect our lives. And this necessitated immersion in historical detail.

I based my interpretation on the testimonies of the participants, left by them in laws and official proclamations, as well as in the works of literature or scholarship they produced, their diaries and private correspondence. I tried to rely chiefly on primary sources, using secondary historical analysis for orientation where my own knowledge of them was insufficient. This secondary literature sensitized me to documents of which I was unaware, and through them to certain library shelves which would guide me from then on. Occasionally I used secondary literature as a source of data, quoting obscure writers and archival or hard-to-situate materials directly from them. Wherever appropriate, I acknowledged my indebtedness to other scholars.

I was bewildered by the complexity of historical evidence and periodically discouraged by the sheer quantity of the material. At times I despaired of my ability not to sin against and yet make sense of it, and questioned the feasibility of historical sociology (either as historical or as sociology). As I struggled, buttressed by piles of dictionaries, to present and interpret my data in English, I was always acutely conscious that this splendid medium needed a much better master, and was as often frustrated by my insufficient familiarity with its resources as I was exhilarated by their evident abundance.

Yet I was sustained in my determination—by the firm conviction in the absolute centrality of nationalism in our experience and the vital importance of its understanding today; by the irresistibly fascinating nature of social processes; and by the example of people I studied, who created a whole new world, not simply wrote a book about it. From one of them, the never discouraged American Sam Patch, a lesser version of Davy Crockett, I borrowed a motto: "Some things can be done as well as others." [19]

I hope my readers will bear with me.

# God's
# Firstborn:
# England

A multitude held together by force, though under one and the same head, is not properly united: nor does such a body make *a people*. It is the social league, confederacy, and mutual consent, founded in some common good or interest, which joins the members of a community, and makes a People one. Absolute Power annuls *the publick;* and where there is no *publick,* or *constitution,* there is in reality no *mother-*Country, or Nation.

Anthony Ashley Cooper, Earl of Shaftesbury

On May 16, 1532, the English clergy formally acknowledged Henry VIII as the Supreme Head of the Church, and Sir Thomas More resigned his post as Lord Chancellor. On July 6, 1535, after being tried for treason, the great scholar and author of *Utopia* was beheaded, insisting to the last on the unity of Christendom. His fate was decided to a great extent by himself. Sir Thomas More was a Christian: he preferred to die rather than subscribe to the English king's supremacy in the affairs of the English Church, and deny the authority of the Pope. The reasons for his conduct were summarized in a letter to Thomas Cromwell—the chief engineer of England's separation from Rome—of March 5, 1534. Sir Thomas wrote: "I never neither read nor heard anything of such effect . . . that ever could lead me to . . . deny the primacy [of the Pope] to be provided by God, which if we did, yet can I nothing . . . perceive any commodity that ever could come by that denial, for that primacy is at the leastwise instituted by the corps of Christendom and for a great urgent cause in avoiding of schisms and corroborate by continual succession more than the space of a thousand year at the least . . . And therefore sith all Christendom is one corps, I cannot perceive how any member thereof may without the common assent of the body depart from the common head."

In April that year More was summoned to swear to the Act of Succession, and, refusing to conform to the denial of papal supremacy implied in the oath, was committed to the Tower. There was a sincere attempt to persuade him to give up his opinion and save himself from the royal wrath and its consequences, but it failed. Already in the Tower, referring to this attempt Sir Thomas More wrote again: "Then said my Lord of Westminster to me that howsoever the matter seemed unto my own mind, I had cause to fear that mine own mind was erroneous when I see the great council of the realm determine of my mind the contrary, and that therefore I ought to change my conscience. To that I answered that if there were no mo but myself upon my side and the whole Parliament upon the other, I would be sore afraid to lean to mine own mind only against so many. But on the other side, if it so be that in some things for which I refuse the oath, I have (as I think I have) upon my part as great a council and a greater too, I am not then bounden to change my conscience and confirm it to the council of one realm, against the general council of Christendom." [1]

Sir Thomas More was a Christian; this was his identity, and all his roles, functions, and commitments that did not derive from it (but were implied, for example, in being a subject of the king of England) were incidental to it. The view that "one realm" could be a source of truth and claim absolute sovereignty was, to him, absurd. "Realms" were but artificial, secondary divisions in the ultimately indivisible body of Christendom. It is significant that the reason for his conduct, as he himself presented it, was not the salvation of his soul. His refusal to accept the king's supremacy was based on something different from devotion to a dogma. It was based, rather, on his inability to deny what seemed to him plainly evident. Sir Thomas' perspective was that of a pre-nationalist era. He found the position of his judges incomprehensible. He failed to realize that they were already transformed, that being Englishmen, for them, was no longer incidental to their allegiances, as it was for him, but had become the very core of their being.

More than four hundred years later, his trial appears profoundly symbolic. Here were the two fundamental worldviews, the pre-nationalist and the nationalist, pitted against each other. And since these worldviews defined men's very identities, no intermediate position was possible between them; there was a cognitive abyss, a clear break in continuity. The unified world Sir Thomas More saw through his inner vision was a vanishing world, and he was a lonely figure among the growing numbers of neophytes of the new, national, faith.

The radical shift in attitude which was expressed in the application of the word "nation" to a people, and which in more than one way signified the beginning of the modern era, was already under way in the 1530s. [2] In the course of the sixteenth century this shift had affected a substantial segment of the English population, and by 1600, the existence in England of a national consciousness and identity, and as a result, of a new geo-political entity, a nation, was a fact. The nation was perceived as a community of free and equal individuals. This was at its core a Humanist notion, and it was based on several premises. Among these, the principal premise was the belief in man as an active, essentially rational being. Reason was the defining characteristic of humanity. Its possession, namely the ability to consider and choose between alternatives, entitled one to decide what was best for oneself and was the basis for the recognition of the autonomy of the individual conscience and the principle of civic liberty. Moreover, since human beings were equal in this crucial respect, in principle they had the equal right to participate in collective decisions. The fulfillment of human nature thus implied political participation, active membership in one's political community, or what we now understand as citizenship. As a result, patriotism—the civic virtue of the Renaissance and the zealous service of one's political community—came to be seen not only as a virtue, but also as a right.

The concept of the nation presupposed a sense of respect toward the individual, an emphasis on the dignity of the human being. One was entitled to nationality (membership in a nation) by right of one's humanity. Essentially, the nation was a community of people realizing their nationality; the association of such a community with particular geo-political boundaries was secondary. The love of nation—national patriotism, or nationalism—in this framework meant first and foremost a principled individualism, a commitment to one's own and other people's human rights. And so, while the exaltation of the nation would everywhere be the exaltation of oneself, in the English case it was the exaltation of oneself as a human being—a free, rational individual—and therefore, the exaltation of human dignity, humanity in general.

The correspondence between the concept of the nation and the reality was not perfect; a perfect fit is seldom the case. Not all the people of England were actually included in the nation in this first century of its existence—and many would, for a long time, remain outside it. The faculty of reason, theoretically a necessary concomitant of humanity, in practice was thought to be developed unevenly, and as a result not everyone deserved enjoyment of the rights based on this fundamental endowment to the same extent. Nevertheless, the commitment to the idea of the nation on the part of the most active and articulate segment of the English population signified a profound change in political culture and could not fail to affect reality and eventually bring the two into closer alignment.

## Reflection of the National Consciousness in Discourse and Sentiment

### Changes in Vocabulary

The evolution of the national consciousness was reflected in the changing vocabulary. In the period between 1500 and 1650 several crucial concepts altered their meaning and came into general use. These concepts were "country," "commonwealth," "empire," and "nation." The changes in meaning were concentrated in the sixteenth century. The four words became understood as synonyms, acquiring the sense which, with slight alterations, they retained later, but which differed from their separate meanings before. They came to mean "the sovereign people of England." The meaning of the word "people" was, of course, changed accordingly.

None of these crucial words appears in the 1499 edition of *Promptorium Parvulorum* (first compiled in 1440).[3] There is, however, an entry "common people," which is translated as *vulgus gineu,* and "Emperoure," translated as *imperator.* In the sixteenth-century dictionaries the situation is different. The word "country"—the initial meaning of which, according to Perez Zagorin,[4] was "county," that is, the administrative unit and the locality in which one resided, and which, he thought, changed toward the Interregnum—appears to have become synonymous with the word "nation," and acquired the connotation of *patria* already in the first third of the sixteenth century. The new meaning coexisted with the older one, but was predominant and evidently more important. Already in Thomas Elyot's Latin-English *Dictionary* of 1538,[5] *patria* is translated as "a countraye." This is also the translation of *patria* in the 1578 edition of Thomas Cooper's *Theasaurus Linguae Romanae et Britannicae* (first published in 1565).[6] *Nationes refinae* is translated there as "the countreys where resin [reason?] groweth." John Rider's 1589 analytical dictionary *Bibliotheca Scholastica*[7] gives the following meanings for the word "country" and related terms: "a Countie, or Shiere"—*comitatus;* "to do after the countrey fashion"—to behave in a rustic way; "a countrey"—*regio, natio, orbis;* "our countrey, or native soyle"—*patria;* "a lover of his owne countrie"—*Philopolites;* "countrie man, or one of the same country"—patriot, compatriot.

Literary sources, too, attest to the change of sentiment and meaning this word conveyed. "Who is here so vile that will not love his country?" Shakespeare has Brutus ask in *Julius Caesar,* while Marlowe put the same rhetorical question into the mouth of the Governor in *Tamburlaine:* "Villaine, respects thou more thy slavish life than honor of thy country?"[8] "Country" was one of the most evocative terms of the period, and it is clear from the context of numerous contemporary writings that in saying "my country," sixteenth-century Englishmen did not mean their county. They meant a great entity to which they owed supreme allegiance, *patria,* the nation.

While "country" was defined as "nation," "nation" was defined as "country." In John Rider's dictionary, the entry "nation" starts: "a Nation, or countrie," while the first meaning of the word "people," translated as *populo,* is that of "a nation." Thus the three concepts are equated. There is also an entry "the common people" there, which is translated as *plebs.* Somewhat more ambivalently Cooper's *Thesaurus* translates *natio* as "a nation," which it then defines as "a people hauyng their beginnyng in the countrey wheare they dwell." "Natio me hominis impulit, vt ei recte putarem," however, is rendered unambivalently as "The mans countrey mooued or forced me." In Elyot's dictionary, although most entries are accompanied by an explanation, *natio* is simply rendered: "a nation." Apparently, this translation is seen as unproblematic and does not call for a comment. *Populus* is translated as "people," while "commune people" is the translation of *plebs.*

The equation of a country with a nation, which, in turn, is defined as people, is significant: among other things, it leads one to reinterpret the symbolism of the pre-revolutionary conflict between Court and Country, about which we shall have more to say later. If country meant "nation," this was not a conflict between urban and rural subcultures, as was claimed,[9] but an explicitly understood conflict over sovereignty between the monarch and the people.

Such struggle over sovereignty within a polity could have happened only if the polity itself was considered sovereign. England, indeed, was already seen by many Englishmen as such. This, too, was a novel perception, and a transformation in an important concept, "empire," [10] corresponded to it. In medieval political thought, "empire" *(imperium)* was an attribute of kingship; it was the essence of being an *Imperator*. An *Imperator* possessed sovereign power within his realm in temporal matters. "Empire," therefore, was a term for such sovereign power in temporals. It has been claimed that this meaning was radically and intentionally changed in the 1533 Act of Appeals, in which the term "empire" was extended to include sovereignty in spiritual matters and employed to denote "a political unit, a self-governing state free from 'the authority of any foreign potentates' . . . a sovereign national state." While everyone agreed that "the intention and effect of the Act was to make the crown the head of the spiritual jurisdiction in an unprecedented way"—which could be justified only on the grounds that the term "empire" implied such spiritual authority—some historians believe that the evidence that the Act extended the meaning of the term was "at best equivocal." [11]

The wording of the Act, it seems, supports the former view. The Act was drawn in reaction to the appeal from Catherine of Aragon to Rome. Its intention was to render further appeals of this nature illegal, thus withdrawing spiritual authority over English subjects from the Pope and reserving it to agents within the realm. The justification for this revolutionary measure was offered in the preamble, which read: "Where by dyvers sundrie old authentike histories and cronicles it is manifestly declared and expressed that this realme of Englond is an Impire, and so hath ben accepted in the worlde, governed by oon supreme heede and King." [12] We cannot rely on the text alone, of course, since, obviously, it can be interpreted in a number of ways. But, whether the term "empire" did or did not radically alter its meaning at this particular moment, clearly in the course of the sixteenth century it was increasingly understood to mean "a sovereign [though at first not necessarily national] polity."

The fact that in the 1499 *Promptorium Parvulorum* the term "Emperoure" appears, but "empire" does not, may possibly be explained thus: it was indeed understood at the time simply as an attribute, an abstract quality of being an emperor, namely, in its medieval meaning. Elyot's dictionary does not translate *Imperium*, but defines it as "a solemne commaundemente, a preeminence in gouernaunce, autoritie royal." From this we can infer that in 1538 "empire" was not a highly significant concept. Yet, and this is highly significant, Elyot's definition does not limit *Imperium* to temporals. Later dictionaries provide some evidence of the growing currency of the term. Cooper's *Thesaurus*, while it borrows Elyot's definition of *Imperium* in its entirety, adds his own translation: "power: dominion: empyre." John Rider also includes "empire," which he too translates, as unproblematic: *Imperium, Dominium.*

As late as 1582 it was still thought advisable to articulate and stress the new meaning of the concept—ostensibly its authentic meaning—in a homily published for the benefit of the general public. The homily accused the Pope in "usurping against . . . naturall lordes the Emperours, as against all other Christian kings." It seemed to the author "more than maruaile, that any subjects would . . . hold with unnatural forraigne usurpers against their owne soueraigne lordes, and naturall countrary." The fact that they did so he explained by their ignorance of God's word, in which the Bishops of Rome kept the populace "by keeping it under the bayle of an unknowen strange tongue." By such means they "plucked" from the sovereigns "their ancient right of Empire," and concealed from the subjects what it was. "If the Emperours subjects had knowen out of Gods worde their duetie to their prince," read the homily, "they would not haue suffered the Bishop of Rome to perswade them to forsake their soueraigne lord the Emperour against the oth of fidelitie . . . Had the Emperours subjects likewise knowen, and beene of any understanding in Gods worde, would they at other times haue rebelled against their Soueraigne Lorde, . . . onely for that the Bishop of Rome did beare them in hande, that it was symonie and heresie too, for the Emperour to give any ecclesiasticall dignities, or promotions of his learned Chaplaines, or other of his learned cleargie, which all Christian Emperours before him had done without controlement[?]"[13] In short, the true and original meaning of "empire" implied both spiritual and temporal authority; this true meaning was intentionally concealed from the populace by the Bishops of Rome, who, keeping the people in ignorance of God's word, were thus able to usurp the authority in spirituals, and perverted the concept. A polity which was an empire, accordingly, in truth was a sovereign polity; in both temporal and spiritual matters it was self-sustaining, a separate entity in the sense in which no polity under the spiritual jurisdiction of the common head of all Christendom could be.

The adoption of this novel meaning of "empire," as an independent polity, which, with only slight alterations, is the meaning inherited by us, was of crucial importance in the evolution of the first nation. The concept now implied that the world was divided along political rather than confessional lines. The separatist tendency, expressed in this concept, was, incidentally, supported by the religious developments of the age. However, "empire" implied more than belonging to the true religion and opposing the heretical one; it implied that within the true religion there were totally independent separate polities, to whose destinies the lives of the people within them were tied to a much greater extent and in a much more immediate fashion than to the destinies of their coreligionists.

"Empire" never became an exact synonym of "nation." The two terms, rather, referred to different aspects of the same phenomenon. "Empire" also never became quite as current as the other closely related terms, and was generally less evocative than they. This was, probably, due to the fact that it retained the connotation of *royal* sovereignty when the idea itself was losing popularity.

"Commonwealth" was another term that came into wide use in this period. It was the exact translation of *res publica,* but the Latin term could be variously interpreted. In England of the period it became a synonym for "society." This is the meaning ascribed to the term in both Elyot's and Cooper's dictionaries. Elyot translates *respublica* as "a publike weale," and Cooper, as "a common weale; a common state." In 1531, in the *Boke Named the Governour,* Elyot interpreted "a publike weale" as "a well-governed society." "Respublica," he wrote, "is a body lyuyng, compacte or made of sondry astates and degrees of men, whiche is disposed by the ordre of equite and gouerned by the rule and moderation of reason." [14] In many other important cases, such as Sir Thomas Smith's *The Commonwealth of England,* the term was neutral. In this sense of a society, one's society, the word "commonwealth" was used interchangeably with the terms "country" and "nation." This was not, however, its initial meaning in sixteenth-century discourse; the initial meaning was that of "public good" or "common well-being." *Promptorium Parvulorum* appears to interpret *res publica* even more literally; there it is the translation of the "comowne thynge; comowne good." Later, in many instances, the manner in which the term was employed was ambiguous and could be interpreted both as "a society" and as "public good," as, for example, in *The Tree of Commonwealth,* 1509, by one of the first servants of the New Monarchy, Edmund Dudley, where he spoke of "the Commonwealth of this Realm."

It is important to note in this context that the word "state" (which, in the phrase "a common state," is offered by Cooper as a translation of *respublica*) in all the early dictionaries has none of the political connotations it will acquire later. [15] It means either "status" (Cooper explains: "the condition or state of ones life or other thing") or "estate," that is, property. This term does change its meaning toward the end of the century, when it becomes another near synonym for the "nation," but it does not have the same evocative power and is not employed with the same frequency as the other concepts discussed here.

### The Language of Parliamentary Documents

The new concepts infiltrated the language of documents gradually and inconspicuously; there was nothing revolutionary in their introduction, and as a result it seemed as if they always had been there, that the realities they referred to had always been a part of the English constitution, that the English constitution, in other words, had always been the constitution of a nation. The Parliament followed, rather than led, the shift of sentiment outside it and adopted the emerging language of national identity slowly and cautiously. Yet, in so doing, it gave it official recognition and the aura of law. These were still, in a way, only changes in vocabulary, but the vocabulary was that of the Parliament, and when, at last, it was transformed, this meant change in reality itself.

In the laws of Henry VII, England is referred to as "the realm" and, less frequently, as "the land" in a manner lacking the emotional overtones this latter term acquires later. In the Statute of Treason, 1495, the "subjects of this [King's] realm" are reminded that they should when needed participate in the "defence of [their King] and the land" of which the King is the Sovereign Lord. The monarch's rule, however, is justified—as in the 1485 Act of Succession—on the grounds that it serves "the pleasure of Almighty God, the wealth, prosperity and surety of this realm of England, and the singular comfort of all the King's subjects of the same." [16] Here the concept of the public good and common well-being is used, albeit not under the name of "commonwealth." There is also a constant appeal to and reliance on "the laws of the land." Yet the conception of the polity that comes through the documents of this reign is that of a realm or kingdom, namely of the estate of the king, the rest of the population being related to it only as occupants of the land and the king's subjects, and their stake in it being of a utilitarian and, in a sense, accidental nature.

Documents of the next reign, too, refer to England as "this realm," "this noble realm," as in the Tunnage and Poundage Act of 1510, the Act of Appeals of 1533, the Dispensation Act of 1534, and others. Yet the understanding of the subjects' relation to the land changes. The 1534 Act Annexing Firstfruits and Tenths to the Crown starts with the following assertion: "It is, and of very duty ought to be, the natural inclination of all good people, like most faithful, loving and obedient subjects, sincerely and willingly to desire to provide not only for the publick weal of their native country but also for the supportation, maintenance, and defence of the royal estate of their most dread, benign, and gracious Sovereign Lord, upon whom and in whom dependeth all their joy and wealth." The duty of the subjects to their sovereign is justified on utilitarian grounds, for, presumably, his well-being means their well-being. But while this duty calls for a justification, the "desire to provide for the publick weal of their native country" is assumed to be a natural inclination (to which the duty toward "the royal estate" indeed is represented as analogous) and does not have to be justified. Here already the relationship of the population to the land and the polity is seen as an inner attachment, and their interest in its preservation and prosperity derives from a "natural" love. It cannot be said yet that the notion of the polity as primarily the property of a king, in which the others have but a limited stake, completely disappears. The two views seem to coexist. The Third Succession

Act of 1543, referring to Henry's belligerent intentions in France, represents the conflict in purely dynastic, and even personal, terms, as a matter not directly concerning the population. "Our said most dread Sovereign Lord the King . . . intendeth by God's grace to make a voyage . . . into the realm of France against *his* ancient enemy the French King" [emphasis added]. There is also ambiguity in relation to the notion of the "commonwealth." As in the previous reign the king's authority and actions are invariably justified by their presumed contribution to the common good, and the term "commonwealth" is sometimes employed to refer to it. In some cases, however, the meaning of the term becomes ambivalent, and it is unclear whether it denotes "public good" or a "society." For example, in the Statute of Proclamations of 1539 it occurs twice in the following passage: "For an unity and concord to be had amongst the loving and obedient subjects of this [King's] realm and other his dominions, and also concerning the advancement of his common wealth and good quiet of his people . . . it is therefore thought in manner more than necessary that the King's Highness of this realm for the time being, with the advice of his honorable Council, should make and set forth proclamations for the good and politic order and governance of this his realm of England . . . for the defence of his regal dignity and the advancement of his common wealth and the good quiet of his people."[17]

The First Treasons Act of Edward VI in 1547, in distinction, certainly employs "commonwealth" in its novel meaning of a "society": "such times at some time cometh in the commonwealth that [the sharper laws are necessary]." In other Edwardian documents, the term is still used ambiguously. For example, the 1550 Act Concerning the Improvement of Commons and Waste Grounds speaks about "statutes . . . beneficial for the commonwealth of this Realm of England."[18] But evidence that this word becomes a near synonym of "realm"—which is still very frequently used—is present. The "realm" thus acquires the meaning of a polity which is a collective enterprise, rather than the king's property, a shift in perception called for by Edward's minority.

Documents of Mary's reign no more than preserve the discourse in the state it was left by her brother. There is no further development, but it is significant that the trend is not reversed. Her rule too is justified by its contribution to the "common wealth of this realm," and the use of the term "common wealth" is at times ambiguous.

Under Elizabeth the political discourse underwent a fundamental change which was clearly reflected in the writings of the period, such as Sir Thomas Smith's *Commonwealth of England* or Richard Hooker's *Laws of Ecclesiastical Polity*. "Country" was used in the same breath with "God"; it evoked religious sentiments and acquired a significance similar to that of a religious concept. The term "nation" became increasingly widespread. The word "commonwealth" was commonly used to denote the English (or any other) polity and society. The vocabulary of the Elizabethan documents, however, while it certainly was in flux, lagged behind the times. The Parliament's use of the term "commonwealth" was still at best ambiguous and at that time already archaic, as if it deliberately refused to commit—or to express its commitment—to the new concept. When new terms were used—and these included such important additions as, frequently, "state" and, rarely, "nation"—they were also used in an uncommitted fashion, not in order to make a statement, but almost as an unreflective concession to the already conventional language. The concepts and ideas with which these new terms in time came to be associated denoted a position in the contest over sovereignty within a polity. Elizabethan Parliaments, however, were more concerned about perceived external threats, and were unwilling to engage in internal strife. Their language, therefore, while vigorously anti-foreign, displayed a rather striking, by comparison, lack of determination in relation to internal political matters.

The word "state" is used in most cases as a form of "estate." The 1559 Act of Supremacy speaks of "restoring to the Crown the ancient Jurisdiction over the State Ecclesiastical and Spiritual"; in the 1571 Treasons Act the phrase "comfort of the whole state and subjects of the realm" appears, while in the 1585 Act for the Surety of the Queen's Person the same cliché has the word "estate": "the good felicity and comfort of the whole estate of this realm." In the Lay Subsidy Act of 1601, however, the meaning of the term is different. It occurs there in a preamble: "We your majesty's humble, faithful, and loving subjects being here . . . assembled . . . to consult . . . and provide . . . for all such means as are or may be necessary to preserve both you and us from those apparent dangers wherein this State may fall." Here the term is used to make a stand and is intentionally substituted for "kingdom" or "realm," which represent the polity as the personal property of the monarch. "State" here is a synonym of "commonwealth"; it denotes a depersonalized polity in which her "Majesty's humble, faithful, and loving subjects" have as much share as she does and therefore the same right of political decision. The Act, in general, was a display of Parliament's flexing its muscles; the use of the term "state" in this context was to show that they realized what their rights were and were going to stand by them. The word "nation," in distinction, is used in Elizabethan acts in a totally neutral manner. For example, the Second Treasons Act of 1571 uses it as one possible characterization in a description of persons: "All and every person or persons, of what degree, condition, place, nation, or estate soever they be." [19] This Act chiefly refers to Elizabeth's subjects, from which we may infer that "nation" here probably meant no more than a family of kin.

With the accession of James, both the tone and the vocabulary of the documents change dramatically. In this reign the Parliament was asserting its right to an equal share in the government of the country with remarkable constancy, and this assertion expressed itself in its insistence on the representative character of its position, and in its changed perception of the referent of its service. This referent, England, was no longer "his Majesty's realm" (this term lost its proprietary connotations), but "our native country," a commonwealth—*res publica*—and a nation.

This point was made clear as early as in the first, peaceful by comparison with the ones that were to come, documents of the period. The 1604 Act of Succession, which was "a most joyful and just recognition of the immediate, lawful, and undoubted succession, Descent, and Right of the Crown," told James about the "great and manifold" benefits with which "Almighty God blessed this kingdom and nation" by the union of the houses of York and Lancaster. It also reminded him that in Parliament "all the whole body of this realm, and every particular member thereof, either in person or by representation (upon their own free elections), are by the laws of this realm deemed to be personally present." [20] The 1604 Apology and Satisfaction of the House of Commons also started with a reminder to the king that the House of Commons represented the English "knights, citizens, and burgesses," and after complimenting James on his wisdom, told him, an alien in the country, that "no human wisdom, how great soever, can pierce into the particularities of the rights and customs of people . . . but by tract of experience and faithful report of such as know them." For this reason, stated the Commons, "we have been constrained, as well in duty to your royal Majesty whom we serve as to our dear native country for which we serve in this Parliament" to give advice to the king. They advised respect and attention to "the rights and liberties of this realm," which more than anything else meant recognition of the equal, or perhaps more than equal, share of the Parliament in the government of the country; justified the expressions of their discontent with James's behavior by their "duty unto your Majesty as to our country, cities and bouroughs, who sent us hither"; and in the end suggested that his Majesty be "pleased to receive public information from [his] Commons in Parliament as to the civil estate and government, for . . . the voice of the people, in the things of their knowledge, is said to be as the voice of God." [21] This ending, though somewhat specified, was a dramatic sign of the Parliament's altered perception of its own status and political reality. The documents of the end of the reign were full of similar assertions.

Interestingly, the spirit of the changing discourse permeated the king's speeches in Parliament as well. In the 1607 speech "Concerning Union with Scotland," James referred to England and Scotland as "two nations" and represented his desire for the union as an intention "only to advance the greatness of your Empire seated here in England." In the 1610 speech "Concerning Regal Power," he again justified his desires by the appeal to the "honor of England," spoke of "state of the commonwealth," "the ancient form of this State, and the laws of this Kingdom," and consented that Parliament represented "the body of the people" and was the "representative body of the whole realm." [22] Even in the 1621 letter to the House of Commons, where James expressed his discontent with the House, he wrote, certainly believing that ruling England was the exclusive prerogative of kings: "None therein [House of Commons] shall presume henceforth to meddle with anything concerning our government or deep matters of the State." In using this new and depersonalized concept of the polity, James could not have wanted to emphasize that this was indeed a shared enterprise in which many parties had stakes, but the view that a country was simply the Crown's property was already inconceivable, the political reality was not what it had been before, and new concepts were needed to express one's thoughts about it.

The parliamentary reinterpretation of political reality—which was shaping it in no less direct and material a manner than any economic or political revolution—was only continued under James's unfortunate son, Charles I. "Kingdom" and "commonwealth" were used in one breath. Whoever did something against their, or rather its, presumed good was to be "reputed a betrayer of the liberties of England, and an enemy to the same"; the Grand Remonstrance of 1641 was motivated by the desire to restore and establish "the ancient honor, greatness, and security of this Crown and nation." The king himself, in the Writ for the Collection of Ship Money, appealed to the ancient habits of the English "nation." [23]

While the conflict "betwix the king and his people" was not inevitable, the assertion of the national character of the polity, after this new perspective had developed uninterrupted for nearly a century and a half, was. The conflict triggered such assertion; it assumed the character of a civil war and was reflected in, among other things, the language of the documents of the Interregnum period. These documents are characterized by an unequivocally nationalist position in the interpretation of the polity, which was this time unambiguously defined as a nation. The word itself was used with extraordinary frequency and constancy; it became the main term for "England." The term "realm," in contrast, appeared only rarely. The synonyms of "nation" were "people" and "commonwealth"; the latter, however, was defined rather more specifically after the abolition of kingship.

The changed tone of official documents became evident immediately. In 1644 the Parliamentary Ordinance Appointing the Committee for Cooperation with Scotland spoke of the management of "the affairs of both nations in the common cause, according to the ends expressed in the late *Covenant and treaty between the two nations of England and Scotland*" (although the Covenant actually was between the two *kingdoms*). The Heads of Proposals in 1647 promised the king that, in case of acceptance and "the things here before proposed being provided, for settling and securing the rights, liberties, peace and safety of the kingdom—his Majesty's person, his Queen, and royal issue, may be restored to a condition of safety, honour and freedom in this nation." [24]

Understandably, this language was at its clearest and most vigorous in the documents of 1649: in the acts Abolishing the House of Lords, Abolishing Kingship, Establishing the Commonwealth, and Erecting a High Court of Justice for the Trial of Charles I. The House of Lords was abolished, according to the first Act, because it was "useless and dangerous to the people of England." [25] The Act Erecting a High Court of Justice for the Trial of Charles I was similarly justified. The king, it claimed, "not content with those many encroachments which his predecessors had made upon the people in their rights and freedoms, has had a wicked design totally to subvert the ancient and fundamental laws and liberties of this nation . . . [and] levied and maintained a cruel war in the land against the Parliament and Kingdom." Therefore, and "for prevention [of any further attempt] to imagine or contrive the enslaving or destroying of the English nation," it was ordained that he should be brought to trial. The Act Abolishing Kingship, passed two months later, stated that "it is and has been found by experience that the office of a King in this nation and Ireland . . . is unnecessary, burdensome, and dangerous to the liberty, safety, and public interest of the people." It therefore enacted "that the office of a King in this nation shall not henceforth" be, whereas "a most happy way [was] made for this nation . . . to return to its just and ancient right of being governed by its own representatives." The government, it proceeded to say, was "now settled in the way of a Commonwealth." "Commonwealth" here acquired a new meaning, namely that of "a republican government." There was still confusion between the several terms which were used as near synonyms of "nation." The Act Establishing the Commonwealth declared that "the people of England, and of all dominions and territories thereunto belonging, are and shall be, and are hereby constituted, made, established, and confirmed, to be a Commonwealth and Free State, and shall from henceforth be governed as a Commonwealth and Free State by the supreme authority of this nation, the representatives of the people in Parliament." [26] While "commonwealth" clearly meant "a republic" (in distinction from monarchy), it—and the state—were still equated with "the people of England." A people was certainly not a form of government, and the terms could be equated only because they all implied a new form of polity—the nation.

The conjecture that the vocabulary of the parliamentary documents was changed consciously, although it was not created by the Parliament, but existed as a part of the general political discourse, is supported by the fact that the earlier formulations returned with the Restoration. England again became a "realm" (though it was rather clear that it was not the same sort of realm it had been before), and the crucial word "nation," while it did not altogether disappear, was used inconspicuously, in contexts where it could

not convey much. The word is present, however, in its more evocative meaning in the secret letter of invitation sent to William and Mary in 1688 and in
the Bill of Rights of 1689. These facts suggest, on the one hand, that those
concerned clearly understood the philosophies the different terms implied,
and, on the other, that the partial return to the older rhetoric signified a
cosmetic rather than fundamental change in discourse: there was no return
to the pre-nationalist conception of polity.

### Early Expressions of National Sentiment

It is possible to locate the emergence of national sentiment in England in the
first third of the sixteenth century. This sentiment manifested itself in several
ways. On a popular level there was a strong anti-alien feeling. In 1517 it
found expression in a violent riot against foreign artisans resident in London, suppressed by Cardinal Wolsey. Foreign artisans represented a significant portion of London's population at that time, and Edward Hall claimed
in his *Chronicle* that their competition barely allowed native Englishmen in
the city to earn a living.[27] But it was exactly during this period that the influence of foreigners in England was diminishing, and Hall felt that the xenophobia of his compatriots was explained by the foreigners' contempt for the
English, rather than by exclusively economic factors.

Whether foreigners indeed felt any such contempt is immaterial. What
was new and important was that the English became exceedingly sensitive
and vulnerable to offenses of such nature. This sensitivity was clearly expressed in the writings of the two most prominent of the early English nationalists: John Bale and Roger Ascham. Both vehemently defended England
from the alleged slights by foreigners. Bale, in 1544, would not forgive Polydore Vergil—the first systematic English historian—whom he called "this
Romish gentleman, the pope's collector," for his lack of recognition of the
intellectual riches of England. In Bale's opinion, Polydore was "polluting
our english Chronicles most shamefully with his Romish lies and other Ital-
ish beggarys." Bale insisted there were "most excellent fresh wits" in England and, as he could not think of "a more necessary thing to be laboured to
the honour of God, beauty of the realm, erudition of the people, and commodity of other lands, next to the sacred scriptures of the Bible, than that
work would be," he urged learned Englishmen "to set forth the English
Chronichles in their right shape." [28]

It did not matter whether the offender was dead or alive. Ascham, in his
later book, *The Scholemaster,* ridiculed Cicero, whose opinion of England,
apparently, was not very flattering, for having such poor judgment. Look
here, "master Cicero," he wrote, "blessed be God, I say, that sixten hundred
yeare after you were dead and gone it may trewly be sayd, that for silver
there is more cumlie plate in one Citie of England than in four of the proud-

est Cities in all Italie, and take Rome for one of them." And in regard to learning, "beside the knowledge of all learned tonges and liberall sciences, even your owne bookes, Cicero, be as well read, and your excellent eloquence is as well liked and loued, and as trewlie followed in England at this day, as it is now, or euer was, sence your owne tyme in any place of Italie." [29]

Both Ascham and Bale constantly compared England to other societies, ancient and contemporary. Hardly any sphere of life was left out of these comparisons. "The Artillarie of England," wrote Ascham in 1545 in *Toxophilus*, "farre excedeth all other realms." Bale, in the *Examinations of Anne Askew* in 1547, compared Anne to Blandina, a martyr of "the primitive spring of . . . Christianity," described by Eusebius. He took some pains to show that Anne Askew resembled Blandina in every aspect of her martyrdom, the strength and purity of her spirit, and even her physical appearance, a proof that English martyrs were the equals of any whom Christianity produced.[30] In Bale's writings patriotism and religious zeal were curiously confused. In the *Chronicle of . . . John Oldecastell* he compared Christian martyrs to those "which have either died for their natural country, or dangered their lives for a commonwealth," and thought them equally "worthy of eternal memory." [31] Such comparisons, the equation of service to one's natural country or people with the service of the church, underlined what was common to them, in Bale's eyes, and commendable in one's behavior. Those were heroes deserving of high praise, who sacrificed their lives or comforts for the collectivity to which they belonged. Martyrdom thus was not a matter of religion proper; or, rather, religious communities were seen as a variety of what were increasingly referred to as "nations."

Cultural creativity in this period was almost invariably—and exclusively—motivated by patriotism. There was a Chaucerian revival; William Thynne collected, edited, and republished Chaucer's manuscripts, the first folio of which appeared in 1532. *Toxophilus* was written as a token of the author's love of and duty toward the king and as a sign of his zeal toward his country. For this reason too it was written "for English men . . . in the Englyshe tongue." Ascham explained: "Though to have written it in an other tonge, had been so the more profitable for my study, and also more honest for my name, yet I can thinke my labour wel bestowed, yf wt a little hynderaunce of my profyt and name, maye come any fourtheraunce, to the pleasure or commoditie, of the gentlemen and yeomen of Englande, for whose sake I tooke this matter in hande." Thomas Elyot, in the Proheme to the *Governour,* confessed: "I nothing esteme so moche in this worlde as youre royall astate [the book was dedicated to Henry VIII] . . . and the publike weale of my country." The book was written as a result of his considering the duty he owed "to my naturall contray," whereby Elyot was "violently stered to deuulgate or sette fourth some part of my studie, trustynge therby tacquite me of my duties to God, to your hyghness, and this my contray." Patriotism, in general, was replacing other forms of loyalty. Sir Thomas Wyatt, a diplomat and one of the first poets of the century, which was in England to become a century of great poets, wrote: "My King my Country alone for whom I lyve"; and Thomas Starkey, in his *Dialogue* in the 1530s, demanded that Cardinal Pole devote his life to the Commonwealth.[32]

### The New Aristocracy, the New Monarchy, and the Protestant Reformation

The English were not the first to proclaim their commitment to their political community and not the only ones to do so in the sixteenth century. Niccolo Machiavelli, a near contemporary of the first English nationalists, was more original than they when he declared that he loved Florence more than his soul, and it is evident (both from the nature of the concepts themselves and from the upbringing of their propagandists) that the English borrowed heavily from the ideas of the Italian Renaissance. But what happened to these ideas in England failed to happen at the time elsewhere. Only in England a remarkable coincidence, a string of circumstances, in whose happening there was nothing inevitable, sustained and advanced them in the course of a full century. These circumstances ensured the development and internalization of these ideas by growing numbers of people in different social strata, with the effect that by 1600 they were mere ideas no more, but became a reality with the power to breed new ideas and transform social structures. The chief among these circumstances—in the order of appearance rather than importance—were the transformation of the social hierarchy and the unprecedented increase in social mobility throughout the sixteenth century; the character and the needs of the successive Tudor reigns; and the Protestant Reformation.

History rarely provides us with one-time events which constitute a clean break from the past and to which one can trace the origins of much that happens afterward. At least some of the important circumstances which ensured the emergence of English nationalism and the nation, however, can be said to originate at Bosworth field, with the final battle in the War of the Roses and the accession of the Tudor dynasty to the English throne. If little else, this event added the symbolic finishing touch to the dissolution of the English feudal order (to whose speedy termination the two Henrys subsequently contributed) and spurred the reorganization of the social pyramid along different lines.

The assertion of the nationality of the English polity went hand in hand

with the insistence on the people's right of participation in the political process and government through Parliament. In fact, in this case nationhood,
England's being a nation, actually meant such participation. The representation of the English people as a nation symbolically elevated it to the position of an elite which had the right and was expected to govern itself, and
equated nationhood with political citizenship. Such symbolic elevation implied a thoroughly changed view of social hierarchy and the traditional class
structure.

Literary sources of the period provide abundant evidence of this change,
which specifically was reflected in new attitudes toward both the upper and
the lower strata of society. They were now treated remarkably alike. On the
one hand, English authors demanded respect toward the common people.
George Gascoigne implored the clergy: "Pray/for common people, each in
his degree," and said: "Behold him [ploughman], priests, and though he
stink of sweat/Disdain him not. For shall I tell you what?/Such clime to
heaven before the shaven crowns."[33] On the other hand, noble birth, and
descent in general, were rapidly losing their importance.[34] Nobility was now
defined not by family name, but by the individual's personal qualities and
behavior. John Bale, in the *Examination of Anne Askew*, devoted a subchap-
ter to the subject "Nobility, whereof it riseth," and in talking of Anne, defined it thus: "In Lincolnshire she was born of a very ancient and noble
stock," he wrote. "But no worthiness in the flesh, neither yet any worldly
nobleness, availeth to God-ward, afore whom is no acceptation of person
. . . Only is it faith with his true love and fear, which maketh us accept,
noble, and worthy children unto God." Marlowe's Tamburlaine declared:

> I am a lord for so my deeds shall prove
> And yet a shepherd by my parentage.

Barnabe Googe similarly extended the applicability of the term "gentleman":

> For if their natures gentell be
> Though birth be never so base
> Of gentlemen (for mete it is)
> they ought have name and place.

Many were more specific and, like George Chapman, believed that "learning makes noble." George Puttenham opposed "martial barbarity," which
had traditionally been the hallmark of nobility, to "laudable science," while
Henry Peacham considered learning "an essential part of nobility."[35]

Remarkable for its completeness in this respect was the view of Sir
Thomas Elyot, which he elaborated in the *Boke Named the Governour*.
Elyot is sometimes regarded as an advocate of a hierarchical social order,[36]
which he certainly was, and yet his view of the social hierarchy, expressed in

1531, had very little in common with the concept of the feudal social structure. For him, the basis of hierarchy was natural intelligence, which he
called "understanding" and which, according to him, could be cultivated by
learning. Understanding, he wrote, "is the most excellent gyft that man can
receive in his creation, wherby he doth approche most nyghe unto the similitude of god; it is therefore congruent, and accordynge that as one excelleth
an other in that influence [quality of understanding], as thereby beinge next
to the similitude of his maker, so shulde the astate of his person be auanced
in degree or place where understandynge may profite: which is also distributed in to sondry uses faculties, and offices, necessary for the lyuing and
gouernance of mankynde . . . they whiche excelle other in this influence of
understandynge . . . such oughte to be set in a more highe place than the
residue . . . that by the beames of theyr excellente witte, shewed throughe
the glasse of auctorite, other of inferior understandynge may be directed to
the way of vertue and commodious liuynge." Consequently, only that was a
just and reasonable society—"a publike weal"—"where, like as god hath
disposed the saide influence of understandyng, is also appoynted degrees
and places accordynge to the excellencie thereof." Elyot took to task such
persons among the nobility who, "without shame, dare affirme, that to a
great gentilman it is a notable reproche to be well lerned and to be called a
great clerke." Nobility itself was "only the prayse and surname of vertue,"
of which understanding and learning provided the foundation.[37]

Learning, indeed, considerably gained in prestige and importance. While
the picture painted by Elyot in 1531 regarding the appreciation, or rather its
lack, of learning in England was rather gloomy, just fifteen years later Roger
Ascham compared the current situation with "our fathers tyme [when]
nothing was read, but bookes of fayned chiualrie, wherein a man by redinge,
shuld be led to none other ende, but onely to manslaughter and baudrye,"
and noted that there was a significant difference. "In our tyme nowe," he
said, "euery manne is gyuen to knowe muche rather than to liue wel." It is
dubious that this was an entirely objective statement of fact, for as late as
1622 Peacham wrote his *Complete Gentleman* with an intention to "recover" young English gentlemen "from tyranny of these ignorant times and
from the common education, which is to wear the best clothes, eat, sleep,
drink much, and to know nothing." Yet there certainly was a noticeable shift
of attitudes: learning was becoming an important value and an attribute of
behavior expected of a gentleman; it was replacing other attributes by which
nobility had been defined earlier. Its name was "noble," next to the fear of
God it was considered "the fountain of all counsel and instruction," and it
fulfilled a crucial function in the nation: "Pray for the nources of our noble
realm," Gascoigne told the clergy; "I mean the worthy Universities."[38]

Literature, in this case, only reflected the tendencies clearly evident in reality. In the sixteenth century England underwent a profound social trans-

formation. The period was one of unprecedented mobility, which, owing to a series of circumstances, was sustained uninterruptedly on a very high level for a solid hundred years or so. The first of these circumstances was the extinction of the old nobility, "the over-mighty subjects of the late middle ages," [39] which was for all intents and purposes complete by 1540. It was in the interests of the monarchy, which never missed an opportunity to speed the process with an execution, a confiscation, an attainder, or a combination of these, and was on the whole due to the determined policies of the Crown.

Simultaneously with the destruction of the old nobility, a stratum destined to replace it appeared. The new—Henrician—aristocracy differed from the one it replaced both in terms of its functional basis and in terms of the social profile of its members. It was predominantly an official elite. The massive creation of peers among deserving royal servants did not commence until 1530.[40] At this time, however, it coincided with the elimination of clergy from key positions in the administration,[41] which made the Crown dependent on the services of university-trained laymen. The majority of the new creations[42] were people of modest birth but remarkable abilities and education. They were recruited from the minor gentry or even humbler strata. The aristocracy, in fact, changed its very nature and became open to talent. While the elimination of the old nobility freed important positions and made a certain mobility possible, the character of the new aristocracy virtually invited mobility.

The redefinition of nobility in the literature as a status based on merit, and not on birth, was a simple acknowledgment of this change, the transfer of authority from one elite to another, which was virtually happening before one's eyes. A fundamental transformation of this kind, however, required a rationalization and a justification which were not to be found in the acknowledgment. *It is at this juncture, I believe, that nationalism was born.* The idea of the nation—of the people as an elite—appealed to the new aristocracy, and the slowness with which the Crown before 1529 confirmed its status by the granting of titles contributed to this appeal. In a way, nationality made every Englishman a nobleman, and blue blood was no longer necessary to achieve or aspire to high positions in society. The new aristocracy was a natural aristocracy, an elite of intelligence and virtue, and its superior position was justified by the service it, being so endowed, could render the others.

By the 1530s the idea of service to the nation had entered, or at any rate was entering, the discourse, as was the concept of England as a separate entity and as a polity which was not simply a royal patrimony, but a commonwealth. These ideas are clearly present in the sources. It is certain that they were in part a modification of certain Renaissance ideals: the idiom of classical patriotism was frequently used for their expression, and the first spokesmen of the nascent nationalism were all men of "new learning." Yet this definitely was not a case of passive importation and acceptance of foreign ideas. These ideas, which were "like souls hovering in a mythological limbo"[43] all over Europe, in England found and entered a body. The need of the new elite for a view of reality that would bolster, rationalize, and lend legitimacy to their place in it was at least as important as the borrowed concepts that went into its making.[44]

Since the idea of the nation was first appreciated by the new aristocracy, the segment of the population that needed its rationalizing and legitimating power and found it appealing was constantly growing. The new aristocracy was bolstered by the wealth expropriated from the Church at the time of the break from Rome, which was given away for the benefit of the worthy servants of the Crown, or sold at prices much below the value of the property. In the 1540s, because of the financial needs of the campaign in France, more of the Church lands were sold and came into increasing numbers of hands. The majority of the new landlords came from the gentry and more prosperous yeomen, and, solidified by the new wealth, helped to create a large stratum, the squirarchy, which was to become the main pool of recruits into the ruling elite.

In turn, the squirarchy was supplemented by the winners in the process of the dissolution of the traditional rural society and the reorganization of agriculture that was happening at this time. Paternalistic relationships between the lord and his tenants, and traditional arrangements for the common use of the land, were giving way to the arrangements and relationships of the market. Common and waste lands were enclosed and farms engrossed to allow a more efficient use of the land, and as a result many people were driven off the land, creating perhaps the gravest social problem of the time and becoming the object of much of the sixteenth-century welfare legislation, while many others became landless agricultural laborers. For a smaller but still significant number, however, enclosures opened a new avenue of upward mobility; these people improved their situations, became prosperous tenants and landowners, and gradually filtered into the gentry.[45]

The gentry thus grew both in numbers and in wealth. Its growth was complemented by parallel developments among the professions, especially the lawyers and later clergy, and the merchants. Lawrence Stone characterized these parallel developments as "the central fact about English social history between 1540 and 1640, and in consequence of English political history";[46] indeed their significance was tremendous, for they amounted to the creation of what, sociologically, is defined as the middle class. Not only was this stratum literally located in the middle of the social pyramid, but it was broad, heterogeneous, and achievement-oriented. It was itself in constant flux, with people in it moving up and down, with new people coming into it from below and others rising from it into the aristocracy.

While entry from below to the gentry was through ownership of land, the professions favored the other avenue of mobility, education. Like the transfers of landed property, and perhaps even more so, education was a great equalizer. In schools, universities, and at the Inns of Court, younger sons of gentry families prepared themselves for the professions alongside sons of yeomen, merchants, and artisans. All of them intermixed there with young squires and aristocrats, since the thin upper layers of society were now expected to consist of men of learning. The aristocracy and the gentry of the sixteenth and early seventeenth centuries indeed were remarkably well educated. One example of gentry education was provided by the House of Commons of 1640, which "in terms of formal attendance of its members at an institution of higher learning," from the perspective of the 1970s, "was the best educated in English history before or since." Just how remarkable this development in England was becomes clear if one remembers that in the beginning of the sixteenth century, according to Erasmus' estimation, there were five or six *(sic!)* erudite people in London, and, according to John Leland, one "slender" library.[47]

The decline in the importance of descent and the rise in that of learning as a criterion of nobility caused a general redefinition of the social hierarchy. Upper-status categories became very broad, binding together people from what previously would have been very different walks of life. The "noble name of Knight,/ May comprehend, both Duke, Erle, lorde, Knight, Squire,/ Yea gentlemen, and every gentle borne," wrote Gascoigne. Gentlemen in England were becoming "good cheap," absorbing people from ever-widening sectors of the population. Observers noted the blurring of distinctions between previously sharply distinguished strata. "[Every] mean gentleman . . . will fare as well as beforetime were wont princes and lords . . . A mean man will have a house meet for a prince," wrote Starkey as early as the 1530s. The social structure appeared for a time remarkably open. This was a period of self-made men, a spirit of adventure characterized the age, and ambition reigned supreme. No one seemed to be content with his own station in life, and everybody aspired to a higher status. "[The] husbandsman gapeth after a degree of a yeoman, the yeoman would bee a gentleman, the Gentleman a knight, the knight a Lorde, the Lorde a Duke," noticed John Bate in 1589,[48] and many contemporary biographies testified that as nothing, apparently, could prevent one's downfall, nothing stood in one's way to success and high position in life.

The idea of the nation appealed to the constantly growing middle class, no less than it did to the new aristocracy. It justified the de facto equality between the two in many areas, as well as the aspirations of the members of the former stratum for increased participation in the political process and more power. It made them proud of their station in life whatever it was, for they were first and foremost Englishmen, and confident in the possibility of higher achievements, for being Englishmen gave them the right to be whatever they wished. Many, probably most, of the authors who developed and propagated nationalist ideas in the latter part of the sixteenth century (1540s on) came from this middle class. Its representatives, too, sat in the House of Commons. And while the increasing importance of the Parliament provided yet another proof that they were indeed representatives of a nation, their national consciousness led them to demand more power for the Parliament. The power of the Parliament and national consciousness thus fed on each other, and in the process both grew stronger.

Nationalism in England rationalized and provided legitimation to what Tocqueville later, and in a different context, called "democracy"—that is, the tendency toward equality of condition among different social strata. And though the word in application to a political regime of government by the multitude had an odious sound for the advocates and spokesmen of English nationhood, who were not at all sympathetic to the idea, political democracy was exactly what the idea of the nation implied and was eventually destined to lead toward. Yet, in the sixteenth century English nationalism mostly centered on the figure of the monarch—an important symbol of England's distinctiveness and sovereignty. The Crown, for its part, favored nationalism, occasionally bolstered it with official measures which greatly enhanced its respectability, and in general lent it the sort of support it needed to develop.

The Tudor rulers of England were time and again placed in a position of dependence on the good will of their subjects. Henry VII won the crown on a battlefield, and his authority was based on little more than the willingness of the people to have him as their ruler. He was also dependent on their purses, which were controlled by the Parliament. Whatever his inclinations, therefore, he could not play a despot and had to rule "constitutionally," that is, according to "the law of the land." He might have done this reluctantly; it was said that he used to take the advice of common lawyers "obliquely, and no otherwise than to discover how safe his own designs were, and so with less danger to vary from them." Nevertheless, it is very important that he did ask for advice and took care to represent his "deviations" in such a way "that his actions at home had still, if not their ground, yet at least their pretext from Common Law." He also took care, as we have seen in the official documents of his reign, to justify his rule by its contribution to the general welfare of his people.

Though the position of Henry VIII was stronger than that of his predecessor, it was also such as to necessitate a constantly deferential stance toward the people, its representatives, and the Common Law. It is possible that there was in him, as in his father, a desire to rule as an autocrat, but again, this desire never became a reality, at least partly for the fortuitous reason "that too much had to be done in too short a time." [49] This, above all, included the break from Rome. The separation, although it seemed to be precipitated by events of a personal, accidental nature, reflected the changing mood and reality within English society. It is generally correct to assert that "when Henry VIII nationalized the faith, he was carrying out the inarticulate wish of . . . his people desirous to preserve the essentials of their creed, and in a moment of growing national consciousness, no less anxious for riddance of the hated vestiges of foreign intervention." [50] Whether because Henry failed to realize this, or because he believed that he would gain further by explicitly representing his "great matter" as a cause of the commonwealth, he made the Parliament a party to it and ensured its active involvement in planning and carrying out the separation. He flattered his "wise, sage, politic commons," [51] and was not unsympathetic to the national sentiment growing among them. For his own reasons, he actively supported the growth of the national consciousness. Even those who refuse to view the Act of Appeals as the moment of the definitive reinterpretation of the term "empire" admit that it was indeed Henry's aim and expressed wish to imply in its application to England that England was a sovereign polity separate from the rest of Christendom. [52] Significantly, Henry wanted or, at any rate, felt compelled to seek proof of this in the English records, and commissioned historians to look into them. In this way he inaugurated the study of "English antiquities" and helped to cultivate what was to become a continuous preoccupation of the century and an important factor in the shaping of the national identity.

It was also under Henry and with his explicit permission that another factor appeared, the implications of which for both the development and the nature of English nationalism were enormous. This was the printing of the English Bible. Henry's attitude toward it, it is true, was at best ambivalent, [53] but this is beside the point. The impact of the translation was unprecedented in its character and extent, and could not be predicted or even imagined before it was experienced. Similarly to the Reformation itself, the printing of the English Bible tied Henry, or rather England, to "the back of a tiger," [54] and as in so many other cases, the extraordinary significance of his action lay entirely in its unintended consequences.

## The English Bible, the Bloody Regiment of Queen Mary, and the Burning Matter of Dignity

The great importance of Henry's break from Rome consisted in that it opened the doors to Protestantism, perhaps the most significant among the factors that furthered the development of the English national consciousness. [55] Protestantism facilitated and spurred its growth in several ways, and

had a major impact on its nature, although nationalism predated the Reformation and most likely contributed to its appeal in England.

To begin with, the Reformation rendered the break from Rome meaningful and sanctioned the development of separate identity and pride.[56] The
Protestant insistence on the priesthood of all believers reinforced the rationalist individualism in which the idea of the nation in England was grounded.
The major independent contribution of Protestantism to the development of
English nationalism, however, had to do with the fact that it was a religion
of the Book. The centrality in it of the Old Testament was of crucial significance, since it is there that one found the example of a chosen, godly people,
a people which was an elite and a light to the world because every one of its
members was a party to the covenant with God. This message was not lost
on England, and it is not coincidental that in the years of the great upheaval
that brought Englishmen to assert themselves as a nation in the Puritan Rebellion, they believed themselves to be the second Israel, constantly returning to this metaphor in parliamentary speeches and pamphlets, as well as
sermons. The Old Testament provided them with the language in which they
could express the novel consciousness of nationality, for which no language
had existed before. This language reached all levels of society and was, as a
result, far more important in its influence than the language of Renaissance
patriotism known only to a small elite.

Still, the significance of the Old Testament as the *source* of the popular
idiom for the expression of the nascent national consciousness should not
be overestimated. While they were borrowing from the Book, Englishmen
were simultaneously modifying it. There are marked differences among versions of the English Bible, but all of them are characterized by a high degree
of independence from their sources. For example, there are no exact equiv-
alents of the word "nation" (especially in its modern sense) in either Biblical
Hebrew or Greek. Yet all the English Bibles use the word. This could be
easily explained irrespective of the growth of national sentiment if the Latin
*natio* were used in the same contexts in the Vulgate, with which the translators of all English versions were well acquainted and by which some of them
(notably Miles Coverdale) were influenced. But *natio* is not used in the Vulgate in the same contexts. The Authorized Version, or King James Bible, is
particularly remarkable in this respect. To begin with, the word "nation"
appears in it 454 times, as compared with 100 for *natio* in the Vulgate.
Moreover, in the Vulgate, *natio* is invariably used in relation to communities
of kin and language; it has a limited "ethnic" connotation. In distinction, in
the English translation the word "nation" has multiple meanings, corresponding to the usages of the word in other English sources of the period. It
is used to designate a tribe connected by ties of kinship and language, and a
race, but at least as frequently it is employed as a synonym of a people, a
polity, and even a territory. The King James Bible uses "nation" as the trans-

lation of the Hebrew *uma, goi, leom,* and *am,* which in most cases are trans-lated as *populus* in the Latin version, and of the Greek *ethnos* and *genos,* to render which the Vulgate does employ *natio* but frequently uses other terms, such as *populus* and *genus* or *gens.* In one case (Isaiah 37.18) the English Bible translates as "nation" the Hebrew *aretz,* which means "land" or "country," and which is correctly rendered *terra* in the Vulgate.[57] The mean-ing of "nation" is often unmistakably political. While the use of the word in relation to communities of kin and language could come from the Latin version of the Bible, its consistent application to polities, territory, and peoples (which makes of these distinct concepts synonyms) is, clearly, a pe-culiarity of the English translation. And wherever the inspiration for it came from, it did not, could not, come from the sacred text itself. Instead, the Old Testament lent itself to a nationally inspired interpretation and helped to provide an idiom for an independently growing phenomenon.

A nationalism sanctioned by religion and a religious creed which had per-ceptible nationalistic overtones made a powerful combination, but it had to wait for another development to realize its potential. The affinity between Protestantism and the idea of the nation guaranteed no more than the lack of religious opposition to nationalism; perhaps a favorable environment within which nationalism would grow. The role of religion in the develop-ment of English nationalism, however, was much greater than that of a fa-cilitating condition, because it was owing to the Reformation, more than to any other factor, that nationalism spread as wide as it did in the sixteenth century, and a whole new stratum was added to those who could find the idea of the nation appealing.

Protestantism was able to perform this crucial *active* role in the furthering of English nationalism because it, to an unprecedented degree, stimulated literacy. Its effect was in part due to what it made people read, and to at least an equal extent resulted from the fact that it required them to read at all. It should not be forgotten that the printed English Bible was a comparatively late addition to the vernacular translations of the book. The first English translation of a part of the Bible appeared in 1525, a complete Bible ten years later, and only in 1538 was a vernacular Bible actually printed in Eng-land. In France, Italy, and Holland, for example, vernacular translations had existed much earlier;[58] in Germany the Scriptures were printed as early as 1466, and fourteen different editions of the Bible in German appeared be-tween this date and 1518. Yet nowhere did the availability of the vernacular Bible have the effect it had in England.

The reasons for the effect of the English Bible were several. It appeared in the context of the Reformation, for which literacy was essentially a religious virtue, an ability necessary for the knowledge of God and a requirement of the true faith. Secular developments—the general state of flux in the social structure in England and the change of attitude toward education—also promoted the literacy of the lower strata. Literacy was exceptionally wide-spread in sixteenth-century England; only the bottom of the social ladder remained unaffected.[59] The English, therefore, and in contrast to other societies, were not satisfied with the availability of the vernacular Bible, but actually read it. Most of them were but barely literate, and in the first half of the sixteenth century the Bible was not simply a book they all read, but the only book they read. It was the combination of these factors—the remarkably widespread literacy, its legitimation and sanctioning by the accepted religious creed, and the exceptional position of the Bible in the early, crucial period—which brought about what at first glance may seem to be the exclusive effect of the Bible.

Reading is a solitary activity. The Bible could be preached to and learned by collectivities, but it was read by individuals. Yet it was the Word, the Book, the revealed truth. And tens of thousands of, for the first time and barely literate, common individuals were actually able to read it. Moreover, they were encouraged to do so by learned and powerful men who insisted on the right and ability of these common individuals to converse with God, and claimed that this, in fact, was the only way to His Kingdom.[60] It was thus that the reading of the Bible planted and nurtured among the common people in England a novel sense of human—individual—dignity, which was instantly to become one of their dearest possessions, to be held dearer than life and jealously protected from infringement. This was a momentous development. Not only had it awakened thousands of individuals to sentiments which common people nowhere had experienced before, and gave them a position from which they were to view their social world in a new way, but it opened a new, vast terrain to the possible influence of the national idea and at once immensely broadened the population potentially susceptible to its appeal. For the newly acquired sense of dignity made masses of Englishmen a part of that small circle of new aristocrats and clergymen, the men of new learning and new religion, who were already enchanted by the idea of the people as an elite, and of themselves as members of such a people. The masses, too, would find in their Englishness the right and guarantee of the new status to which they were elevated by self-respect, and see their individual destinies as linked to the destiny of the nation. In turn, this consciousness of belonging to the English nation, the national consciousness to which the reading of the Bible made common Englishmen so receptive, reinforced the effects of reading and further strengthened the sense of dignity and respect for the individual which resulted from it.

### Martyrdom and Exile as Catalysts of National Consciousness

Hence, when this dignity and respect were infringed upon, as they were under Mary, they were nothing to toy with, and it was in part because Mary tried unadvisedly to infringe upon the dignity and self-respect of masses of common Englishmen, when these sentiments were already well developed among them, that her persecution had the effect opposite to the one she intended and further strengthened the tendencies she desired to fight.

It was her burning of Protestants which made Queen Mary's name. According to authoritative estimates,[61] between February 1555 and November 1558, a week before her death, 275 people were convicted of heresy and executed. In the light of our century's experiences and tendency to think in large numbers, Queen Mary's regiment does not seem anything so "bloody and terrible" as it evidently appeared to her contemporaries. And yet the burning of 275 Protestants had a much greater impact on the history of humanity than atrocities incomparably greater in magnitude, including the Holocaust, which took the lives of more people than in Mary's time constituted the population of England.

This impact, again, was due to the combination of factors of which the burning of Protestants was only one, rather than to its essence; or, in other words, this again was the combined effect of one particular action and the historical circumstances within which it took place. For reasons related to the nature of the groups Mary's policies discriminated against, and to no small extent due to the shortness of her reign, the effect of the persecution was to ensure a long-term identification between the Protestant and the national causes, which immensely strengthened nationalism and was, perhaps, the most important contribution of religion to its development.

Mary's anti-Protestant policies directly affected two groups. One was a segment of the new elite: university-educated, well-positioned people, who either already enjoyed all the advantages the new definition of the aristocracy by education and ability made possible, or had reasons to expect to enjoy them in the near future. These people were removed from their positions by Mary, and their expectations, which they regarded as nothing but just, were frustrated. They were accused of heresy, in their opinion an intolerable affront, and made to suffer, which only fortified their sense of rectitude. A few of the martyrs burnt at the stake and all the exiles came from this stratum. The other group, which supplied the great majority of the martyrs, consisted of simple men and women, artisans, merchants, housewives, who read the Bible and claimed to understand it, and who, under the threat of death, would not agree to relinquish their right to do so. The first group waged an ideological struggle against the Marian regime, its main tool the insistence on the interconnection between the Protestant and the national causes. When Mary died, this group provided the intellectual and official leadership in the new reign, and would spare no effort to convince the world at large about this interconnection and make it a fact. The second group, antagonized by the attitudes of Mary and her bishops toward the English Bible, indignant and unwilling to yield, found the claim advanced by the elite most appealing and provided a congenial environment for its speedy entrenchment.

The interests of the two groups, from which the martyrs and the exiles under Mary were recruited, and which in fact represented no less than the Protestant elite and rank and file, converged. For both, in their own ways, the chief issue was the preservation and guarantee of their newly acquired status, human dignity, and unhindered ability to be and do what they believed they were entitled to. At the level of the common people this issue could not be expected to be well articulated, but its centrality was clearly manifested in the pattern of behavior which led them to martyrdom. It is astonishing to realize that the reason why these people consciously and calmly went to a frightful death was their confidence in being able to think for themselves. They would not concede that as common people and laymen they were less able to interpret the law of God, to read and understand the Bible, than some others, and refused to admit any inequality in this fundamental regard between different groups of individuals. The questions of doctrine, which at their interrogations they were commanded to answer, meant nothing to them. They failed to understand their significance and regarded them as deliberate attempts to trap them. One of them, George Marsh (who was burned at Chester in April 1555), "loth to answer to the question of transubstantiation," told his questioners that much: these hard questions, he said, were but means "whereby to bring my body into danger of death and to suck my blood." The purpose of true religion was to ensure the rule of God's law in this world, they thought. What was then the justification of the "Latin service"? "What are we of the laity the better for it?" asked Roger Holland, a London merchant tailor, when questioned by Bishop Bonner. "Wherein shall a young man direct his ways but by the Word of God? and yet you will hide it from us in a tongue unknown. St. Paul had rather in the church to have five words spoken with understanding, than ten thousand in an unknown tongue." [62]

The martyrs were a peculiar sort of people: they were those for whom a principle was dearer than life. They would not betray the principle, even when, in addition to life and freedom, they were offered, as was the apprentice William Hunter, the opportunity to be set up in business, and even though the bystanders begged them to conform to save themselves. The bystanders, in distinction, were bystanders because they would and did conform. But as they watched those obstinate men and women, from their own midst and so very much like themselves, go to their deaths, "not as thieves or as ones that deserved to die," [63] but as heroes and saints, they could not but identify with them and share—vicariously and with a much lesser discomfort, but nevertheless share—their martyrdom. And so 275 bonfires continued to burn in the hearts of thousands.

The more articulate and learned among the persecuted Protestants also, though in their case consciously, avoided the controversial doctrinal questions, and emphasized the legitimacy of their belief in England. Their Protestantism was not only the manifestation of a true faith, but also the manifestation of their being Englishmen. The London preachers who, in January 1555, addressed to Mary's government a supplication protesting the persecution justified themselves as "faithful and diligent subjects" who had always acted as "the laws of God at all times and the statutes of the realm did then allow." [64] The interrogations of the martyrs from the elite group of educated and, before their fall, powerful people—among whom were such personalities as Bishop Latimer, the first one to speak of "the God of England," and Archbishop Cranmer—focused on the question of supremacy and on the legitimacy of papal authority, and therefore tied the question of doctrine to the issue of England's political independence and national interest. These martyrs were few, but the impact of their martyrdom was enormous. It was magnified by the elevated position they had previously enjoyed, as well as by their extraordinary skill and poise in parrying the attacks of their judges, and the remarkable courage and dignity with which they carried their misfortune and faced death, all of which were carefully recorded and made public knowledge. The message implied in this connection of Protestant faith with England as a sovereign polity was not forgotten.

The stories of the martyrs were collected and preserved (and were later popularized) by the exiles—those members of the displaced elite who were fortunate enough to escape martyrdom themselves and gathered abroad. A part of the Protestant elite, the exiles were sympathetic to the idea of England as a sovereign polity, an empire. They also belonged to the stratum which was the first to advance the idea of the nation, for it served its objective interest. But whatever national sentiment they had had before the exile, it was strengthened manifold in it.

The exile also led them to emphasize certain previously attenuated implications of national identity. The new Henrician aristocracy (of which the exiles were members, descendants, or which they expected to enter) was originally attracted to the idea of the nation because national identity made every fellow national a member of an elite and justified their own being the elite de facto, though they were not entitled to this by birth; and also because it extolled patriotism, or service to the nation, as the highest virtue, of which they were, obviously, the chief repository. The idea of the nation, namely the concept of a people of a certain polity as a nation, implied that a polity was not simply the patrimony of a monarch, but a commonwealth, a community and a collective enterprise of many fundamentally equal participants. The monarch was a member of the nation and received his authority to rule from it. He could not do to a nation as to his own property, and ruled not over a territory, but an elite, in the common interest. So long as the monarch did rule in the common interest, the rest of the nation owed him or her their gratitude and obedience, but if the trust was betrayed, the monarch was a tyrant, and could be deposed. It would be foolish to press this point under Henry or Edward; there was no need for this whatsoever. But the situation changed dramatically under Mary. For Mary England was not a nation; it was indeed a patrimony which she wished to rule in the interests of the Roman Catholic Church. The anti-monarchical implications of national identity, thus, had to be articulated to protect the identity itself. The exiles emphasized the possibility of unlawful rulers and, as a result, in the tracts they left, nation was for the first time explicitly separated from the Crown and represented as the central object of loyalty in its own right. John Poynet, the sometime Bishop of Winchester, who died in exile in 1556, wrote in one of the most important of these tracts: "Men ought to have more respect to their country than to their prince, to the commonwealth than to any one person. For the country and the commonwealth is a degree above the king." "Kings and princes," he added, "be they never so great are but members, and commonwealths may stand well enough and flourish albeit there be no kings." [65]

The English exiles were not the only ones who wrote anti-monarchical tracts at the time, but if they let themselves be influenced by the ideas of others, it was because the situation they were in made them exceptionally susceptible to such influences. Their place in England's changing social structure, which opened so many possibilities for men of their condition, made them receptive to Protestantism. They were Protestants and could regain the positions they had lost only if England became Protestant again. Protestantism was possible in England only if it was an empire. And it was an empire if (or rather since, for they firmly believed that) it was a nation. Mary's government seemed doubly illegitimate since it was anti-national and anti-Protestant. And the salvation they could hope for was both Protestant and national.

It was, therefore, during the short and unhappy reign of Queen Mary and largely because of her bloody and terrible regiment that the Protestant and the national causes became firmly associated and even confused. In the next half century, indeed, it would be close to impossible to tell one from the other. And yet, during Mary's reign itself the national sentiment evidently predominated over the religious one in the popular mind. Already at the time of Henry VIII, the Venetian Ambassador, Michele, had noted in a report to his government that the English "would be as Zealous followers of the Mohammedan or Jewish faith if the King professed either or commanded them to do so." The doctrinal transformations of his and the following reigns did not contribute to the religious zeal of the lay population, but rather undermined what was left of it. [66] The self-aggrandizing policies of the Protestant protectorate under Edward led to the association of Protestantism with corrupt government, with the result that the devoutly Catholic Mary was indeed, in some way, placed on the throne by "popular election." [67] The majority of her subjects accepted the return to the "most holy Catholic faith" with equanimity if not relief, repenting where necessary without undue inner strife,[68] and her House of Commons was characterized as "Catholic in sentiment." [69] While martyrs underwent their martyrdom, other Englishmen watched them—they watched them without pleasure, it is true, but this was due to their sympathy toward and admiration of the martyrs' personalities rather than to the belief in the illegitimacy of persecuting Protestants for heresy. For this reason, there was no popular protest against the burnings. It is certain that the lack of such protest can in no measure be attributed to the fear or inability of the population to voice its opinions, for on another matter they were clearly expressed.

The rebellion led by Wyatt was a direct effect of Mary's refusal to comply with the petition of the House of Commons of November 16, 1553, to marry within England, and her insistence on marrying King Philip of Spain. The appeal of the rebel leaders to those they attempted to incite and draw to their side left little place for doubt as to the nationalistic nature of their cause. "Because you be our friends," said Wyatt, "and because you be Englishmen that you will join with us, as we will with you unto death, in this behalf." "Religion was not the cause of his rising," claimed a close friend who defended Wyatt's actions in the 1590s, and Wyatt himself instructed a Protestant supporter: "You may not so much as name religion, for that will withdraw from us the hearts of many." It is clear from this instruction that he saw religion as a disuniting rather than a unifying force, and, what is more important, that national loyalty was and could already be expected irrespective of confessional affiliation. The force of five hundred Londoners sent against Wyatt deserted to the rebels, revealingly shouting: "We are all Englishmen!" The dangerous potential of the nationalist appeal for the regime was clearly recognizable. Mary tried to downplay the national issue in the rebellion and represent it as a heretical religious uprising for which "the matter of the marriage" was "but a Spanish cloak to cover their pretended purpose." At the same time she also took care to pacify the populace by promising to follow Parliament's advice and marry within the country. In spite of this, as Wyatt marched on London, the population there remained indecisive, and although the rising was eventually suppressed, "Wyatt came nearer than any other Tudor rebel to toppling a monarch from the throne." [70] The evidence that this explicitly nationalistic cause had some appeal in that age when a close-to-universal apathy and indifference could be expected in relation to political matters, and when there existed a widespread popular fear of rebellion for whatever reasons, seems far more significant than the fact that this appeal was uneven and that the rebellion proved unsuccessful. The absence of a religious agenda in it is equally remarkable. The year, after all, was just 1554.

### England as God's Peculiar People, and the Token of His Love

It so happened that the hopes of Marian exiles were realized rather soon, when a Protestant princess, Elizabeth, succeeded her sister on the throne. When the exiles returned to assume the leading positions in the new regime, they devoted themselves to the purpose of proving the connection between England's national existence and the Protestant faith inseparable and making sure that it indeed remained such. In 1559 the future Bishop of London John Aylmer took up Latimer's astonishing claim that God had nationality. In a striking passage in *A Harborowe of True and Faithful Subjects . . . ,* he declared: "God is English" and called his countrymen to thank Him "seven times a day" that they were Englishmen and not Italians, Frenchmen, or Germans. Not only was England "the land of plenty, abounding in beef and mutton, butter, cheese, and eggs, beer and ale, besides wool, lead, cloth, tin and leather," but "God and his angels fought on her side against her foreign foes." "For you fight not only in the quarrel of your country," he reminded his compatriots, "but also and chieflye in defense of hys true religion, and of his deare son Christe." [71]

The returning exiles did not restrain themselves to mere displays of eloquence. The Archbishop of Canterbury, Matthew Parker,[72] sponsored and actively aided the research and publication of English history and antiquities which made it evident that Christianity in England always had a distinct character, for the English Church was the true apostolic Church. In addition to serving as the editor-in-chief of the *Bishops' Bible,* assembling a valuable collection of historical documents, manuscripts, and books (which he bequeathed to Corpus Cristi College at Cambridge), and publishing a history of the original establishment of Christianity in Britain, Parker was the patron of several important chroniclers, among whom was the author of the *Book of Martyrs,* John Foxe.

The *Book of Martyrs* is the popular shorthand name of Foxe's monumental work *Actes and Monuments of these latter and perilous dayes, touching matters of the church, wherein ar comprehended and described the great persecutions and horrible troubles, that have been wrought and practised by the Romishe Prelates, speciallye in this Realme of Englande and Scotlande, from the yeare of our Lorde a thousand, unto the tyme nowe present. Gathered and collected according to the true copies and wrytings certificatorie as wel of the parties them selves that suffered, as also out of the Bishops Registers, which wer the doers thereof.*[73] Faithful to its title, the book was the most comprehensive and masterful circumstantial account of the sufferings of Marian martyrs, the great men and simple people alike, presented as just another expression, the most recent and obvious, of England's loyalty to the true religion for which it had suffered many times in the past and which it on numerous occasions had been called to defend against ungodly foreign assailants. The message of the book was that England was in covenant with God, had remained faithful to the true religion in the past, and now was leading the world in the Reformation, because it was favored in His sight. Being English in fact implied being a true Christian; the English people was chosen, separated from others and distinguished by God; the strength and glory of England was the interest of His Church; and the triumph of Protestantism was a national triumph. Such identification of the Reformation with Englishness led to the definition of the See of Rome as the prime national enemy, which implied the exclusion of English Catholics from membership in the nation. Yet this divisive implication was never articulated. However critical Foxe was of the behavior of his "papist" compatriots, it was to unite in the service of the nation that he called his readers in the dedicatory epistle, striking an unmistakably conciliatory note. "They that be in error," he wrote, "let them not disdain to learn . . . No man liveth in that commonwealth where nothing is amiss; but yet because God hath so placed us Englishmen here in one commonwealth, also in one church, as in one ship together; let us not mangle or divide the ship, which being divided perisheth: but every man serve with diligence and discretion in his order, wherein he is called." [74]

The status of Foxe's book, the influence it was allowed to exert on the minds of sixteenth- and seventeenth-century Englishmen, was far above that of any other work of the age, and comparable only to that of the Bible. It went through six editions during Foxe's lifetime (1554, 1559, 1563, 1570, 1576, and 1583) and was reprinted four times after his death (in 1596, 1620, 1632, and—significantly—1641). In 1570 "that full and perfect history" [75] was by order of the mayor and corporation of London read in city orphanages and the halls of city companies; and in 1571 it was decreed by convocation that a copy of it be set for general use, along with the Bible, in cathedral churches and residences of archbishops, bishops, archdeacons, deans, and resident canons. In 1577, according to William Harrison, "every office [at the royal court had] either a bible, or the bookes of the acts and monuments of the church of England, or both, besides some histories and chronicles lieng therein." [76] The popularity of the *Book of Martyrs* was immense and its authority indisputable. The "famous chieftan Sir Francis Drake" took the book to sea and colored the pictures. [77] And even the author of *Principal Navigations . . . of the English Nation*, Richard Hakluyt, who in regard to his rather specific subject "(to speak the truth) . . . [had] received more light in some respects than all our own histories could afford me in this case," thought Foxe to be an exception. [78]

The argument of the book was the most articulate statement of the identity of the English national and Protestant interests. For a time English religion and nationality were one. In a text as authoritative as *The Laws of Ecclesiastical Polity*, the Anglican apologist Richard Hooker wrote: "We hold, that seeing there is not any man of the Church of England but the same man is also a member of the Commonwealth; nor any man a member of the Commonwealth, which is not also of the Church of England; . . . so albeit properties and actions of one kind do cause the name of a Commonwealth, qualities and functions of another sort the name of a Church to be given unto a multitude, yet one and the selfsame multitude may in such sort be both, and is so with us, that no person appertaining to the one can be denied to be also of the other." [79] What had driven this point home was the example of recent martyrs, people so much like the rest that one could not help thinking that, should their lesson be forgotten, their fate could befall the others.

It was England's religious standing which was the basis of the nation's distinctiveness and uniqueness. God's favor and divine trust were evident in everything. There could be apparently no other reason for such expressions of England's prosperity as, for example, the victory over the Armada,[80] or Elizabeth's continuous good health and stable government, which defied the intrigues of her enemies. Consequently they were interpreted as signs of divine intervention. This interpretation found expression in much of the popular literature of the time. Being chosen to be constantly at the focus of God's attention, England both had the security of divine support so long as she was faithful to the covenant, and was sure to be punished the moment she relaxed. Her national existence was dependent upon her religious zeal. Roger Cotton put this argument in verse in a work entitled "The Armour of Proofe, brought from the Tower of Dauid."

> If this be true, that all God's trueth we holde,
> What neede we then of Spayne to be afrayde?
> For God, I say, hath neuer yet such solde
> To sworde of foe; but still hath sent them ayde.
> The trueth we haue, yet therein walke not wee;
> Whereof oftimes God hisseth for a bee . . .
> O Englande, then consider well thy state;
> Oft read God's worde, and let it beare chiefe sway
> Within thy hart: or els thou canst not scape
> The wrath of God; for he will surely pay . . .
> Remember then thy former loue and zeale,
> Which thou to God and to his worde didst beare,
> And let them now agayne with thee preuale:
> And so no force of forrayne shalt thou beare.[81]

*National* identity implied a totally new set of boundaries which separated England from the rest of the world. But at this period the existence of a separate entity such as a nation was not self-evident. It was problematic and needed justification and conceptualization in familiar terms. Thus it was only natural that at the time of the centrality of religion in every sphere of social existence, nascent nationalism was clothed in religious idiom. Furthermore, because of the association between the Reformation and English national identity, Protestantism not only provided the yet voiceless nationalism with a language, but also secured it a sanctuary and protection which it needed in order to mature. In short, though Protestantism cannot be said to have given birth to the English nation, it did play the crucial role of a midwife without whom the child might not have been born.

It was also through the association between Protestantism and nationalism that monarchy again became a major factor in the development of national consciousness. The crowning story of the *Book of Martyrs* was the story of Elizabeth, who became the symbol of the link and identity between the Protestant and national causes. Protestantism and nationalism united in her person. Foxe was not the only one or the first of the returning exiles to uphold this view, but through his book it was spread among the people.

The extent and the manner of Elizabeth's glorification make many of today's observers of sixteenth-century England uneasy. These observers are irritated and ashamed by what, in the light of present-day equality, may look like a language of undignified and repugnant sycophancy.[82] What they fail to see is that, eulogizing Elizabeth, the seemingly sycophantic Englishmen were in fact giving expression to their increasing self-respect. Elizabeth was a sign of God's recognition of the nation's goodness, of England's being a chosen people. The words of John Jewel, who wrote, "When it pleased God to send a blessing upon us, He gave us His servant Elizabeth to be our queen, and to be an instrument of His glory in the sight of the world," might have been the "fullest and finest expression"[83] of this belief. But the argument was favored by many authors. In the book entitled *A Progress of Piety*, John Norden, a minor author of educational and devotional literature for the common people, and a layman, included the following "Jubilant Praise for her Majesty's most Gracious Government," in which he thanked God for giving England Elizabeth:

> Rejoice, O England blest!
> Forget thee not to sing:
> Sing out her praise, that brought thee rest
> From God thy mighty King!
> Our God and mighty King
> Our comforts hath renewed
> Elizabeth, our Queen, did bring
> His word with peace endu'd . . .
> She brings it from his hand;
> His counsel did decree,
> That she, a Hester in this land,
> Should set his children free.

> None ruleth here but she;
> Her heavenly guide doth shew
> How all things should decreed be
> To comfort high and low.
> Oh, sing then, high and low!
> Give praise unto the King
> That made her queen: none but a foe
> But will her praises sing.
> All praises let us sing
> To King of kings above!
> Who sent Elizabeth to bring
> So sweet a taste of love.[84]

This poem demonstrates the triple identification of the nation, godliness, and the queen. God is praised, significantly, for being good to England, to whom he gave Elizabeth as a sign of recognition and special favor. But neither God nor Elizabeth is praised for His or her own sake! Both the religious sentiments of Englishmen at the end of the sixteenth century and their devotion to their monarch are unmistakably nationalistic.

John Phillip, in stanzas from "A friendly Larum, or faythfull warnynge to the trueharted subiects of England," appealed to God with the following request:

> Our realme and queen defend, dere God,
> With hart and minde I praie;
> That by thy aide hir grace may keepe
> The papists from their daie.
> Hir health, hir wealth, and vitall race,
> In mercy longe increase;
> And graunt that ciuill warre and strife
> In England still may cease.[85]

God thus was asked to do service to Elizabeth so that she might be able to serve England.

Elizabeth was perceived as the symbol of England's chosenness in the eyes of God. "She was the golden pipe, through which great Jove/ Deriv'd to us his blessings manifolde:/ She was the token of his tender love." [86] And yet, in retrospect, this godly queen was remembered for peculiarly mundane achievements, achievements that were political in nature and increased the this-worldly glory of England. When Michael Drayton characterized her reign in *Poly-Olbion,* this is what he had to say:

> Elizabeth, the next, this falling Scepter hent;
> Digressing from her Sex, with Man-like government
> This Island kept in awe, and did her power extend
> Afflicted France to ayde, her owne as to defend;

Against the 'Iberian rule, the Flemmings sure defence:
Rude Ireland's deadly scourge; who sent her Navies hence
Unto the Either Inde, and so to that shire so greene,
Virginia which we call, of her a virgin Queen:
In Portugall gainst Spaine, her English ensignes spread;
Took Cales, when from her ayde the brav'd Iberia fled.
Most flourishing in State: that all our kings among,
Scarce any rul'd so well: but two that reigned so long.[87]

Like her father, Elizabeth might not have been much of a nationalist her-self,[88] but, like him, she found it in her interests to acquiesce to and support the growing national sentiment. Indeed, without any effort on her part, she performed for it a most valuable service. For nearly half a century the person of the Virgin Queen was the chief object on which the national sentiment focused. Elizabeth was the symbol of England's uniqueness and greatness. This fact accounted for the remarkable tranquility of a regime which was judged as fundamentally unstable in retrospective analysis; it made the dominant motivation of the period—patriotism—coterminous with the devotion to the reigning monarch and ensured zealous concern for the preservation of her government. The association of the national sentiment with the person of the queen attenuated and slowed down the development of the democratic implications of English nationalism; during most of Elizabeth's reign the Parliament chose not to press its demands for equal share in the government, or at least chose not to press them aggressively. At the same time, this happy harmony and unity of interest between the Crown and the nation that it now governed, between the old and the new, the support which the traditional order gave the one that was just emerging, similarly to Protestantism, allowed national consciousness to mature and become a widely shared, legitimate way to look at the world, which at the end of the century was already a powerful force with its own momentum. It was allowed to become embedded in the English culture and could no longer be rooted out. Elizabeth's role in this development was that of an official endorsement of the English national identity, and it was to no small degree because of it that by the end of the sixteenth century England did in fact possess a full-fledged nationalism and enter the modern era.

It has been argued against the view that these attitudes signified and promoted the development of the English national identity, that the emerging identity was religious, Protestant, rather than national.[89] This argument, however, is based on the misunderstanding of the nature of nationalism and on a mistaken equation of national identity with ethnicity. English nationality at this time certainly was not defined in ethnic terms; it was defined in terms of religious and political values which converged on the rational— and therefore entitled to liberty and equality—individual. The dissident character of the Reformation and the congruence of Protestant theology accepted in England with values of rationalist individualism rendered Protestantism a perfect ally for the nascent national sentiment. Owing to unique historical circumstances, especially those of Mary's reign, the two; religion and national sentiment, became identified. The English nation, therefore, was a Protestant nation. But it is essential to realize that it is the noun and not the adjective which makes all the difference in this case. Protestant or not, England was a *nation*. It was a nation because its people was symbolically elevated to the position of an elite, and this elevation created a new type of collectivity and social structure unlike any other, and a novel, at that time unique, identity.

Toward the end of the sixteenth century, the secular nation was claiming the loyalty of already great and growing numbers of Englishmen, and religion was increasingly relegated to the periphery. Those who lived in this age were aware of that, although we must not underestimate the extent to which it was difficult to separate the issues at the time. Richard Crompton wrote in 1599: "Though we be divided for religion . . . yet I trust that we will wholly faithfully, and as we are bound . . . join together in this service of defence of our Prince and countery against the enemie." Sir Walter Raleigh appealed to all Englishmen "of what religion soever" to join him in the war against Spain, in which, according to another contemporary, people died "with joyful and quiet mind, [having] ended . . . life as [someone] that hath fought for his [note the order] countrey, Queene, religion and honour." [90] In a reader of Elizabethan devotional poetry, to which we have already resorted, we find the following dialogue between a Roman Catholic and a supporter of the Reformed religion, entitled "An Answer to a Romish Rhyme," by J. Rhodes. In it, the Protestant in a popular language, but skillfully, parries all the doctrinal propositions of his adversary, proving beyond doubt the superior reasonableness of his own position. Among other hard-to-dismiss arguments, he says:

> Our Bibles teach all truth indeede
> Which every Christian ought to reede:
> But Papists thereto will say nay;
> Because their deedes it doth bewray.
> Christ, he the twelue apostles sent;
> But who gaue you commandement
> To winne and gather anywhere?
> To bind by othe, to vowe, and sweare
> New proselytes to Popery,
> Gainst trueth, our prince, and countrey? [91]

Apparently, it went against common sense that true religion could imply anything so unparticularistic.

## The Sound of Their Voices

Whether because of the certainty in the Divine election, or because so many more people were now committed to the idea of England as a nation, the national sentiment of Elizabeth's reign asserted itself with a vigor and an ability it had not known before. It was expressed in sermons, which continued, albeit more openly and insistently, the tradition of the *Book of Martyrs*. It was also expressed in secular literature in English—a dramatic new development, which laid the foundations of the modern English culture. It is commonplace in contemporary literary history to note the remarkable, indeed striking in its omnipresence and intensity, nationalism of Elizabethan literature. This nationalism, however, is not surprising. The secular vernacular literature was the conspicuous expression of the national consciousness and identity coming of age in England. It was the realization in written form of the previously formless, new sentiments of the people "intoxicated with the sound of their own voices." [92] It was the first, expressive, act of national self-assertion.

The Elizabethans purported to realize the cultural aspirations of the first Henrician nationalists. A whole new class of people emerged whose main preoccupation was to do research and write—chronicles, treatises, poems, novels, and plays—in English about England. This class of authors and scholars drew for recruits on the peerage as well as the common people and included Englishmen from every walk of life, with the exception of the lowest strata: the urban and rural poor. [93]

Everything English became an object of attention and nourished a new feeling of national pride. The Society of Antiquaries was formed. Holinshed, Warner, Camden, and others wrote general histories of England and histories of specific periods. Playwrights—whose number included Shakespeare and Marlowe—dramatized episodes of national history. The first novelists, such as Nash, Lyly, and Deloney, and such authors as William Harrison and Sir Thomas Smith focused on English ways of life. Michael Drayton, in *Poly-Olbion,* celebrated the land of England and its rivers, an undertaking to which Spenser too gave some thought. The new feeling of patriotic love grew into a passion and was expressed in poetry with exuberance and deep lyricism heretofore reserved for the sphere of intimate personal relations. "This blessed plot, this earth, this realm, this England, . . . this land of such dear souls, this dear-dear land" [94] was extolled on all levels, inspiring the creation of many an exquisite work of art, as well as literary efforts of lesser aesthetic, but solid documentary, value.

The efflorescence of cultural creativity experienced in England in the sixteenth and early seventeenth centuries was quite unprecedented and sudden, as those who contributed to it were fully aware. Before their time there was little to speak of in the manner of English letters. Numerous literary surveys written by sixteenth-century pioneers acknowledged this. "The first of our English Poets that I haue heard of," wrote William Webbe in 1586, "was Iohn Gower . . . Chawcer was next after if not equall in time to Gower . . . [then] Lydgate . . . Since these I knowe none other tyll the time of Skelton who writ in the time of kyng Henry VIII." [95]

Yet, discouraged they were not. They were the founders of the national culture, and their awareness of this lofty role bolstered their sense of self-importance. "We Beginners," wrote Gabriel Harvey in a letter to Spenser, "haue the start and advantage of our Followers, who are to frame and con-forme both their Examples and Precepts, according to that President which they haue of vs: as no doubt Homer or some other in Greek, and Ennius or I know not who else in Latine, did prejudice, and overrule those, that fol-lowed them." [96] In addition to this, the culture they were creating showed clear signs of superiority and was destined to become the greatest. This the sixteenth-century men of letters in England believed and never grew tired of repeating. In navigation, "in searching the most opposite corners and quar-ters of the world, and, to speak plainly, in compassing the vast globe of the earth more than once," the English, thought Richard Hakluyt in 1589, "have excelled all the nations and peoples of the earth." Sir Walter Raleigh claimed that the English were much more humane than the Spaniards; Wil-liam Harrison, that the English clergy were considered the most educated. Somewhat later, Henry Peacham, in *The Complete Gentleman*, defended English composers, who, he stated, were "inferior to none in the world (how much soever the Italian attributes to himself) for depth of skill and richness of conceit." He also believed that the same could be said about English em-blems. [97]

But most praise in the sixteenth century was showered on the English au-thors. The most was made of Chaucer, whom his grateful compatriots called "our father Chaucer," "our worthy Chaucer," "Noble Chaucer." The three old masters—among whom Chaucer was the most famous and revered—were the English equivalent of the great masters of antiquity. "As Greece had three poets of great antiquity," wrote Francis Meres in the 1598 *Com-parative Discourse of Our English Poets with the Greek, Latin, and Italian Poets*, "Orpheus, Linus, and Musaeus, and Italy other three ancient poets, Liuius Andronicus, Ennius, and Plautus, so hath England three auncient poets, Chaucer, Gower, and Lydgate." To the "English Italians" who talked of "Petrarche, Tasso, Celiano, with an infinite number of others," Thomas Nash would oppose Chaucer, Lydgate, and Gower. "One thing I am sure of," he wrote, "that each of these three haue vaunted their meters with as much admiration in English as euer the proudest Ariosto did his verse in Italian." Sir Philip Sidney drew a similar parallel: "So among the Romans were Liuius, [*sic*] Andronicus, and Ennius. So in the Italian language the first that made it aspire to be a Treasure-house of Science were the Poets Dante, Boccace, and Petrarch. So in our English were Gower and Chawcer." [98]

Contemporary authors were celebrated with as much enthusiasm. There is no end to references—which were self-references in some way—to the "quick-witted Sir Thomas More, our countryman," "the miracle of our age Sir Philip Sidney," "our famous English poet Spenser"—"diuine Master Spenser, the miracle of wit," whom Thomas Nash would have "brandie line for line for [his own] life in the honor of England, gainst Spain, France, Italie, and all the worlde," "our English Homer"—Warner, and "honey-tong'd Shakespeare," whose "fine-filled phraze" would muses choose to speak if they would speak English. [99]

The English language itself was an object of passionate devotion. It was loved as "our mother tongue," but it was cultivated for what it could contribute to the nation's standing—as "our best glory." There was nothing that could not be achieved or expressed by "so copious and fluent a language as oure English tongue is." Some claimed that it was equal in everything to the other "famous and chief languages," namely Hebrew, Greek, Latin, Syriac, Arabic, Italian, Spanish, and French. Michael Drayton, in a poem from *England's Heroic Epistles,* 1598, wrote:

> Though to the Thuscans I the smoothness grant
> Our dialect no majesty doth want
> To set thy praises in as high a key
> As France, or Spain, or Germany, or they. [100]

By the majority, however, English was judged as a language far superior to any other. The consummate expression of this attitude was Richard Carew's *Epistle on the Excellency of the English Tongue* (1595–96). Carew wrote this epistle "seekinge out with what Commendations I may attire our english language, as Stephanus hath done for the French and diuers others for theirs." Such commendations, he found, were several. It was richer than other tongues, for it had borrowed from several of them: "Seeing then wee borowe (and that not shamfully) from the Dutch, the Breton, the Romaine, the Dane, the French, Italyan, and Spanyard, how cann our stocke bee other then exceeding plentiful?" And while Carew gave all other languages their due, or so he thought, he found that English was also sweeter than the others:

> The Italyan is pleasante but without synewes, as to stillye fleeting water; the French delicate but ouer nice, as a woman scarce daring to open her lipps for feare of marring her countenaunce; the Spanish maiesticall, but fulesome, running too much on the O, and terrible like the deuill in a playe; the Dutch man-like, but withall very hoarse, as one ready at every worde to picke a quarell. Now wee in borrowing from them geue the strength of Consonantes to the Italyan, the full sounde of wordes to the French, the varietye of terminacions to

the Spanish, and the mollifieinge of more vowells to the Dutch; and soe (like bees) gather the honye of their good properties and leave the dreggs to themselves. And thus, when substantiallness combyneth with delightfullness, fullness with fynes, seemlynes with portlynes, and courantnes with staydnes, howe canne the languadge which consisteth of all these sounde other then most full of sweetnes?[101]

Such a magnificent language could not but be destined to play a great role in the culture of the world. Samuel Daniel evinced this prophetic vision—shared by many—in his *Musophilus:*

> And who, in time, knows whither we may vent
> The treasure of our tongue, to what strange shores
> This gaine of our best glory shall be sent
> T'inrich vnknowing Nations with our stores?
> What worlds in th'yet vnformed Occident
> May come refin'd with th'accents that are ours?[102]

Princes, nobility, the country, and mankind in general were considered beholden to the men of letters for the service they performed. Elizabeth, Spenser's Faerie Queene, thought Francis Meres, "hath the advantage of all the queens in the world to be eternalized by so diuine a poet." Ascham was certain that the learning of Sir Thomas Elyot "in all kynde of knowlege bringeth much worship to all the nobilitie of England." Ben Jonson expressed his admiration of Camden in the following words:

> Camden, most reverend head . . .
> 　　to whom my country owes
> The great renown and name wherewith she goes.

And Peacham, referring to Sir Robert Cotton, declared that "not only Britain, but Europe herself is obliged to his industry, cost, and care in collection of so many rare [British] manuscripts and other monuments of valuable antiquity." [103]

While it gave vent to the sentiments of individual dignity and national pride accumulated over the previous decades, this literature further developed and spread them. It gave form to and thus established a whole new dimension of experience; like religion earlier, it offered a language through which national sentiment could express itself, but in this case, it was nationalism's own language, no less evocative than, but distinct from religion. It thus was another, perhaps the last, among the long string of developments which collectively led to the firm entrenchment of modern, full-fledged, mature nationalism in England already at the end of the sixteenth century. Since then a major (if not the major) factor in every significant development in English history was this nationalism itself.

## The Changing Position of the Crown and Religion
## in the National Consciousness

In the seventeenth century the supremacy of nationality was manifested in several ways, some of which, though true to the spirit of Elizabethan nationalism, differed from the manner in which it was usually expressed. Circumstances of the early Stuart reigns caused the dissociation between national and monarchical sentiments. The social and political transformations of the previous age resulted in a steady and dramatic increase in the actual wealth and power of the groups represented in Parliament, of which they were keenly aware. These groups were the vanguard of nationalism, and their national consciousness grew in proportion to this awareness. The intransigence of the Stuarts, who had the misfortune to succeed Elizabeth, and the stupidity to insist on the divine right of kings, was an intolerable affront to them. They felt entitled to a greater share in the government of their country and more respect, and received less than they were accustomed to. The policies of James and Charles, and their inability to realize the implications of England's definition as a nation, seemed to threaten the very existence of Englishmen as Englishmen, their being what they believed they were, and contradicted the people's very identity. These policies interfered with the liberty of being English, of realizing one's membership in a nation, and thus were perceived as an assault on "English liberties." It was this inability to be English in England that forced some sixty thousand people to leave the country during this period. Twenty of these sixty thousand went to North America, a momentous move whose significance was not to be appreciated until two centuries later.[104]

In a way, the early Stuarts repeated the mistake of Queen Mary's reign. They offended a significant segment of the population in its *national consciousness,* the consciousness that elevated masses of Englishmen to the position of an elite and gave to each one among them that sweet feeling of dignity which, since they had known it for but a short time, had not yet lost for them any of its taste. The reaction to this offense was, as it was under Mary, the accentuation of the anti-monarchical implications of the national idea and the reinterpretation of the nation as the only source of authority. The groups that had by this time acquired national identity still—and deeply—felt loyalty toward a political entity of which they were a part, but the king was no more the focus of this loyalty. The very existence of a monarch was rendered superfluous and menacing. The democratic and libertarian connotations of nationality were strengthened.

The policies of the Stuarts offended the specifically religious sentiments of the people as well, which was almost unavoidable since the nation whose nationality they failed to appreciate was at that time a Protestant nation. The protest against these policies, similarly to the opposition to Marian government, was therefore entangled with the religious protest and used the available idiom of the Protestant religious opposition, the Puritans. Puritanism was an Elizabethan development. The immediate reason for the emergence of the movement was probably the shortage of prestigious positions for the clergy combined with the rapidly growing numbers of university-trained, sophisticated people prepared and able to fill them.[105] The Puritan state of mind, however, was but a logical development of the national consciousness which was growing stronger each day and outgrowing the complacently monarchical clothes that had served it so well in the early years.

While Elizabeth's accession led the returning exiles to downplay the republican implications of the national definition of the English polity, these implications were not forgotten. Hooker, in *The Laws of Ecclesiastical Polity*, wrote that "where the King hath power of dominion . . . there no foreign state, or potentate, no state or potentate domestical, whether it consist of one or of many, can possibly have . . . authority higher than the King." "On the other side," he added, "the King alone hath no power to do without consent of the Lords and Commons assembled in Parliament: the King of himself cannot change the nature of pleas, nor courts . . . because the law is a bar unto him." By the end of the century the parliamentary classes were powerful and conscious of their power. Sir Thomas Smith wrote in *De Republica Anglorum* (1589) that "the most high and absolute power of the Realm of England consists in the Parliament . . . The Parliament abrogates old laws, makes new . . . changes rights, and possessions of private men . . . establishes forms of religion . . . gives forms of succession to the Crown . . . For every Englishman is intended to be there present, either in person or by procuration of attorneys of what prominence, state, dignity, or quality soever he be, from the prince to the lowest person in England."[106] This was not just a statement of desiderata, but a fairly accurate description of the current state of affairs. It was because of this that after the greatest parliamentary controversy of her reign—the debate on monopolies of 1601—the defeated Elizabeth found it appropriate to thank the Commons for saving her from error, adding that the State was to be governed for the benefit of the people and not those to whom it is committed, and appealed to the "loves" of her subjects.[107]

This fundamentally republican position was widely shared as an implicit understanding, but it took a religious faction to advocate its actual implementation within the social order. At first, this religious faction, which came to be recognized by "the odious name of Puritans,"[108] demanded a reform only of the Church according to the allegedly Scriptural model. Puritans attacked the bishops, insisted on the right and ability of every one to read and interpret the Bible, and agitated for a presbyterian Church government. Yet their adversaries were right in pointing out that Puritanism opened wide the gates for the reform of society in general, and implied nothing less

than the destruction of the established order. In the words of Thomas Cart-
wright, the leader of the faction, Archbishop Whitgift read "the overthrow
of the Prince's authority in ecclesiastical and civil matters," Bishop Aylmer
saw in Puritanism the basis for "the greater boldness of the meaner sort," [109]
and King James I summarized it all in his proverbial "no Bishop, no King."
Lawrence Stone has justly defined Puritanism as "no more than the generalized conviction of the need for independent judgment based on conscience
and Bible reading." [110] The Puritans were passionate nationalists, and Puritanism appealed to different and wide circles; that is why the great social
and political upheaval of the mid-seventeenth century bore the name of the
Puritan Rebellion. This, of course, does not at all contradict the fact that the
original Puritans were, probably, deeply religious people. It is as probable,
though, that their supporters and the members of the opposition to the
Stuarts, who were indiscriminately called and identified as Puritans later,
were not. [111] But whether or not it was at its core a religious development,
Puritanism was immensely helped by its self-presentation as a religious
movement. Religion still was the most convincing means for justifying social
change of the unprecedented magnitude which was implicit in the definition
of England as a nation. It helped to believe that whatever new reform was
pending, it was demanded by God and derived directly from the role of England in the religious struggle between the forces of light and darkness. In
November 1640, the Puritan preachers summoned by the Parliament urged
Englishmen to revolt in fulfillment of their religious responsibility. But by
this time the primacy of the political, national concerns over the religious
ones was becoming increasingly evident.

The issue of the revolution, thought Hobbes, was not religion, but "that
liberty which the lower sort of citizens under the pretence of religion, do
challenge to themselves." [112] And it was no longer religion, but the national
idea based on the liberty of the rational individual, which united people. The
switch in the relative centrality of the specifically religious and secular national loyalties had been reflected already earlier in the pliability—quite extraordinary in the sixteenth century—of the English population during the
numerous changes of faith to which they had been subjected by the turbulent history of the period. And amidst the heated public controversy, in the
very years preceding the Puritan Rebellion, the general attitude was "that it
is safest to do in religion as most do." [113]

This is not the place to engage in a detailed discussion of the causes, pre-
conditions, and course of the Revolution, all of which have been discussed
at great length, for the Revolution has been the focus of historical scholarship dealing with seventeenth-century England. At the same time, it is
obvious that the discussion of nationalism puts this event in a somewhat
different perspective and in fact necessitates a new interpretation. In this
perspective the Revolution essentially appears to be indeed the conflict be-

tween the Court and the Country, that is, a confrontation between the
Crown and the *nation*. It was the act of political self-assertion by the nation—namely all those groups which at the time were incorporated into the
political process and possessed national consciousness—and it focused on
the issue of sovereignty.

This interpretation of the English Revolution gives it a reason (a motive),
a necessary element in human action of a similar complexity. It also explains
several problematic characteristics of the Revolution. It explains, for example, the inactivity and indifference of the rural poor and the urban wage-
earners. They were passive and uninterested in the Revolution because they
were the illiterate, not yet affected by the dignifying influence of the national
identity; they were not yet members of the English nation, and could not be
concerned about the insults to nationality. It also explains the lack of a clear-
cut split within the population actively involved in the conflict. The fact that
representatives of all the participant strata could be found in both camps
reduces the plausibility of explanations in terms of existing stratification
divisions, whether of class or of status.

When analyzed in terms of national sentiments, however, the otherwise
unclassifiable divisions become intelligible. After almost a century and a half
of sustained development, the idea of the nation had been associated with
various factors which through this association acquired an evocative nationalistic connotation, and could be interpreted in several ways. For a long time
the nation was associated with, indeed personified in, the figure of the English monarch; for many, therefore, opposition to royal authority was nothing less than anti-national. The predominant view, however, defined the nation in terms of the individual dignity, or liberties, of its members, and
anything that inhibited the exercise of these liberties was anti-national. The
two interpretations were available to people in every social group, and one
chose between them sometimes against one's "objective" interest. The fact
that the rebels' view had interest to support it, while the association of the
nation with monarchy was in this sense accidental, was the reason for the
predominance of the former and for the ultimate victory of the Parliamentarian (or "patriotic," "country") cause. The definition of the English nation
without the monarchy, which in the course of its first crucially important
century consistently contributed to its development, however, was very
problematic; in the Restoration the two were linked again, although on different terms, and the crown remained an important national symbol.

Nevertheless, the Revolution helped to disentangle the issues historically
associated with the idea of the nation but not essential to it and made it clear
that nationalism was about the right of participation in the government of
the polity—it was about liberty, and not monarchy or religion.[114] These two
earlier indispensable allies were temporarily abandoned. Kingship was abolished, while religion was reinterpreted in such a way as to lose most of its

specifically religious significance. As before, it was identified with the national cause, but while earlier it was the association with religion which legitimated nationalism, now it was the association with nationalism which made religion at all meaningful. In *An Humble Request to the Ministers of Both Universities and to All Lawyers in Every Inns-A-Court*, 1656, Gerard Winstanley, the Digger, defined true religion as the possibility of national existence. "True religion," he said, "and undefiled, is to let everyone quietly have earth to manure, that they may live in freedom by their labors." Significantly, the Diggers represented the breakthrough of the national consciousness into the lowest, previously unaffected by this development, strata of society. Winstanley's understanding of nationality was unencumbered by too great a familiarity with all the complexities of traditions which went into its making; his simple vision captured its very essence. Being an Englishman, for him, meant being fundamentally equal to any other Englishman and having a right to a share in whatever the nation possessed. If nationalism of the Parliament did not mean that, it did not mean anything at all, and the Parliament was betraying the nation. "Nay, it is the bottom of all national laws," insisted Winstanley, "to dispose of the earth . . . The first Parliament law, which encourages the poor commons of England, to plant the commons and waste land, is this; wherein they declare England to be a free Commonwealth: This law breaks in pieces the kingly yoke, and the laws of the Conqueror, and gives a common freedom to every Englishman, to have a comfortable livelihood in this their own land, or else it cannot be a Commonwealth . . . the Justices cannot call these men [Diggers] vagrants . . . for by the law it is no vagrancy to dig and work . . . They are *Englishmen* upon the commons of *England*." [115]

Pronouncements of the central actors of the period may lack Winstanley's directness, but the sway of the national idea in their views is equally apparent. The nation (and the related issue of liberty), clearly, was the focus of Cromwell's concerns, and he saw no sharp distinction between the service of the nation and profession of the true faith. "The two greatest Concernments that God hath in the world," he said, "[are] the *one* is that of Religion . . . and also the Liberty of men professing Godliness (under the variety of forms amongst us) . . . The *other* thing cared for is the Civil Liberty and Interest of the Nation. Which though it is, and indeed I think ought to be, subordinate to a more peculiar Interest of God,—yet it is the *next best* God hath given men in this world . . . if anyone whatsoever think the interest of Christians and the Interest of the Nation inconsistent, or two different things, I wish my soul never enter into *their* secrets!" Religion was put first, but Cromwell's interpretation of the "interest of God" (in effect religious liberty) made it just another interest of the nation. Elsewhere Cromwell asserted: "Liberty of conscience and liberty of the subjects—two as glorious things to be contended for, as any God hath given us." In his speeches to the

Parliament he many times emphasized that it was "the liberty of England" (not religion) that he fought for; that the aim of the Revolution was "to make the nation happy." He proudly asserted his loyalty to the nation and spoke of "True English hearts and zealous affections toward the general weal of our Mother Country." "We are apt to boast that we are Englishmen," he said, "and truly it is no shame to us that we are so; but it is a motive to us to do like Englishmen, and seek the real good of this nation, and the interest of it." [116]

Whatever Cromwell's own nationalism (and it appears to have been genuine and deeply felt), it was his contribution to the strength and glory of the nation which was emphasized and for which he was praised by Dryden, Sprat, Pepys, and other contemporary intellectuals. Some three centuries after his death it seemed apt to call a monograph on Cromwell's personality and social role "God's Englishman," and choose as an epigraph his exclamation: "We are English, that is one good fact." [117]

Milton, a leader of the "new religion of patriotism," [118] is another example of the increasingly secular nationalism and the accentuation of its libertarian implications in the seventeenth century. Like many before him, Milton believed the English to be the chosen people. He appealed to the Lords and Commons of England in *Areopagitica*: "Consider what Nation it is whereof ye are, and whereof ye are the governours: a Nation not slow and dull, but of a quick, ingenious, and piercing spirit, acute to invent, suttle and sinewy to discours, not beneath the reach of any point the highest that human capacity can soar to . . . this Nation chos'n before any other . . . [When] God is decreeing to begin some new and great period . . . What does he then but reveal Himself . . . as his manner is, first to his English-men?" His notion of the nature and reasons for this election, however, underwent a significant change in the course of the years. Early in his work, in the tract *Of Reformation in England* (1641), he presented the already familiar apocalyptic conception, very much in the spirit of Foxe, of England's leadership in the Reformation. Later, arguing for different social reforms, such as the reform in marriage (*Doctrine and Discipline of Divorce*, 1643–44) and unlicensed printing (*Areopagitica*, 1644), he justified them on the grounds that these reforms were congenial to England's national character, as well as to its religious and historical destiny. In his *History of Britain* (1670) he attacked the organized Church as such, carrying to its logical conclusion the Protestant doctrine of the priesthood of all believers, and demanding full equality for his nation "so pliant and so prone to seek after knowledge." His pronouncements, full of religious fervor and still employing the authority of religious texts, became devoid of any religious content. "The great and almost only commandment of the Gospel, is to command nothing against the good of man," he wrote, "and much more no civil command, against his civil good," and: "the general end of every ordinance, of every severest, divinest, even of Sabbath, is the good of man, yea, his temporal good not excluded." Now England's peculiarity, for him, was reflected in its being "the mansion-house of liberty," the people "ever famous, and foremost in the achievements of liberty." Instead of leading other nations in religious Reformation, England led them on the way to civil liberty. In that, wrote Milton, "we have the honour to precede other Nations who are now laboring to be our followers." [119] Liberty became the distinguishing characteristic of Englishness.

The Revolution helped to conclude the process started a century earlier. It caused more people to be "drawn into political action during the revolutionary forties and fifties, and brought [them] under the more direct dominance of London . . . national consciousness [therefore] was extended to new geographical areas and lower social levels." [120] Parliamentary statutes, speeches, and pamphlets separated the issue of nationality from the issues of religion and the power of the English Crown and clarified the meaning of national identity. After the Civil War, nation as the primary object of loyalty was established and ceased to be problematic. As a self-evident fact, it no longer needed religious or monarchical justification.

The religious idiom in which initially the national ideals had been expressed was soon cast away. This does not imply that people had lost their faith in God or ceased to practice religion—this would be close to inconceivable in the seventeenth century—rather, religion lost its authority over the other fields of activity; it ceased to be the source of social values, and instead of shaping them, had to adapt to social and national ideals. The conditions which facilitated the acceptance of Protestantism and Puritanism in England were also the ones that prepared the growth of the English national consciousness, for which religion served as a lubricator. It was natural that religious creed, secondary anyway, would be pushed aside when national identity became established as fundamental and the need for justification diminished.

The fate of the monarchy was not much different. The Restoration did not restore the old relationship between the Crown and the people. Under Charles II the Parliament was intent on emphasizing its humility and peaceful nature and, as we have seen, refrained in the documents from using the word "nation" itself. Yet the fundamentally changed position of both religion and monarchy was symbolized and recorded very soon after the king's return in his *Common Prayer Book*. The version of Charles II added to the volume a whole new section of "Prayers and Thanksgivings upon several occasions," which included rain, fair weather, war and tumults, common plague and sickness; among the prayers pertaining to such uncontrollable expressions of divine wrath or favor there was a "A Prayer for the High Court of Parliament, to be read during their session." The text of the prayer was subdued; it read:

Most gracious God, we humbly beseech thee, as for this Kingdom in general, so especially for the High Court of Parliament, under our most religious and gracious King at this time assembled: That thou wouldest be pleased to direct and prosper all their consultations to the advancement of thy glory, the good of thy church, the safety, honour, and welfare of our Sovereign, and his Dominions; that all things may be so ordered and settled by their endeavours, upon the best and surest foundations, that peace and happiness, truth and justice, religion and piety, may be established among us for all generations. These and all other necessities, for them, for us, and thy whole Church, we humbly beg in the name and Mediation of Jesus Christ our most blessed Lord and Saviour. Amen[121]

The context of the prayer—the place of the Parliament among the evident expressions of God's favor and disfavor—is revealing, and it is significant that there was no such prayer for the health or well-being of the king.

## A Land of Experimental Knowledge

The sense of the cultural specificity of the nation emerged simultaneously with its political self-assertion. The tendencies of the Elizabethan age were continued in the new century. Writers as earlier stressed the merits of the English language and literature and insisted on their superiority to classical and French languages and literature, which were considered the standards of excellence at the time. The most famous expression of this literary patriotism in the seventeenth century was, probably, found in the works of John Dryden, who was convinced that English drama far surpassed the French and demanded that English poets be given "their undoubted due, of excelling Aeschyllus, Euripides and Sophocles." In *Annus Mirabilis* Dryden echoed the optimistic belief of Samuel Daniel in the future greatness of England:

> But what so long in vain, and yet unknown,
> By poor man-kind's benighted wit is sought,
> Shall in this Age to Britain first be shown,
> And hence be to admiring Nations taught.

The reason for his optimism here, however, was not the excellency of the English tongue or the promise of its literary genius, but science.[122]

Already in the early sixteenth century, as we have observed, reason—the faculty of understanding—was upheld as a supreme value in England. It was man's "diuine essence," [123] and language itself was believed to be its handmaiden. Language was reason's medium of expression, which was reason enough to cultivate it. Indeed this was the first among arguments used by Sir Brian Tuke to commend to the king Thynne's edition of Chaucer's collected works, to which he wrote an introduction in 1532.[124] For Sir Philip Sidney the kinship between language and reason proved the usefulness of poetry, and he argued in the *Apologie*: "If *Oratio* next to *Ratio*, Speech next to Reason, bee the greatest gyft bestowed vpon mortalitie, that can not be praiselesse which dooth most pollish that blessing of speech." [125]

As the notion of the English national character crystallized, "rationality" assumed a central place in it. This English intellectual disposition was reflected in the independence of thinking, a critical mind, an ability to arrive at decisions on the basis of one's own—preferably firsthand—knowledge and logical deliberation, a love of (practical) knowledge, a desire to be appealed to in a rational, not emotional and not authoritative, manner, a dispassionate temper, and a distaste for enthusiasm. From the point of view of a philosophical purist, the English outlook in the seventeenth century could be characterized as anti-rational. The distrust of reason, and its "relegation to a position subordinate to the senses," in the writings of Bacon and his followers was rightly emphasized, as was the popularity enjoyed in this period by the Skeptics.[126] But whatever its derivation and philosophical purity, this outlook led to rational conduct. Speculation, theorizing unrelated to facts, was indeed suspect, but the counterpart of the ubiquitous distrust of authority was the belief in the reason of the individual. Skeptics reconciled with authority and lacked this belief.

While the belief in individual reason made for assertiveness vis-à-vis authority, skepticism, with its emphasis on the futility of speculation, made sensory, empirical knowledge the basis for the assertion of reason. From these diverse elements sprang a unique position, philosophically impure, but thoroughly systematic in its support of the liberty of individual consciousness. Its rationalism implied the right of free thought; its skepticism discredited dogmatizing and demanded tolerance of others' opinions; its empiricism undermined the notion of intellectual aristocracy, making everyone in possession of normal human senses equally capable of acquiring the true knowledge on which the progress of humanity was thought to be dependent. This position, which came to be regarded as inherently English, both embodied and provided the conceptual foundation for the democratic tendencies of the age, and science was the epitome of this rationalist, empiricist, skeptical view.

Since Bacon, science was considered the sign of superiority of the moderns over the ancients, to whom, allegedly, it was unknown. Since Bacon, too, it was viewed as a sign of a nation's greatness, the foundation and guarantee of its strength and virtue.[127] In the battle between the ancients and the moderns, the English identified with the moderns. The ancients were foreigners with no connection whatsoever to England, but linked to Italy, France, and Spain. These three continental countries were the chief cultural competitors of England. National pride impelled England to claim equality with and even superiority to its competitors. However, in classical learning England was no match for France and Italy, and to accept the authority of the ancients would mean admitting cultural inferiority on its part. Unwilling to do so, the English espoused a primitive cultural relativism, arguing that what suited one period and society did not necessarily suit another. This freed them from competing for intellectual excellence on the arena chosen by "ruinous Athens or decayed Rome" [128] and rescued England's national dignity. Siding with the moderns enhanced it. Science was a modern activity and therefore one in which England could compete effectively. At first the sign of the cultural specificity of the English, it soon became the proof of their superiority. At the same time the importance of literary preeminence diminished, because literary accomplishment was considered less expressive of the English national genius.

The rise of modern science, announced by the foundation of the Royal Society of London, has been attributed to the influence of religion, specifically the affinity between the spirit of science and the Protestant ethic.[129] But though the infant science undoubtedly profited from the fact that it was consistent with the dominant religious belief and therefore was tolerated by religion, on the whole it owed little to the support of the latter. Its increasing authority in fact was another reflection of the waning influence of religious faith in society and the already unquestionable dominance of secular national concerns. It was the importance of science for the English national identity and the function it performed for the cultural image of England that created the state of public opinion favorable to its cultivation, encouraging to those who had the abilities to devote to it, and causing many Englishmen who knew very little about the substance of scientific knowledge to stand in reverence before expressions of scientific creativity. It was nationalism that raised science to the apex of occupational prestige and ensured its institutionalization.

The pursuit of science was a matter of national prestige. Accomplishments of English scientists were constantly used as a weapon in the cultural competition with advanced continental nations—the heirs of classical antiquity. Boastfully, John Wilkins called Bacon "our English Aristotle"; Dr. William Gilbert, the author of *De Magnete,* was "our countryman (admired by all foreigners)." [130] England's scientific leadership was evident (at least to Englishmen) very early. In 1600, in the first chapter of *De Magnete,* dealing with the history of his subject, Gilbert himself wrote: "Other learned men who on long sea voyages have observed the differences of magnetic variation [were] all Englishmen . . . Many others I pass by purpose: Frenchmen, Germans and Spaniards of recent time who in their writings, mostly composed in their vernacular languages, either misuse the teachings of others, and like furbishers send forth ancient things dressed with new names and tricked in an apparel of new words as in prostitutes' finery; or who publish things not even worthy of record." [131]

National prestige was also the main issue in the controversies over priority in scientific discoveries. John Wallis, one of the most prominent mathematicians of the age and the author of a treatise on the greatness of English mathematics, frequently raised the issue in his correspondence. He wished "that those of our own Nation; were a little more forward than I find them generally to bee (especially the most considerable) in timely publishing their own Discoveries, and not let strangers reape ye glory of what those amongst us are ye Authors." [132] This, too, was the subject of the first official letter from the Royal Society to Newton. In it, Henry Oldenburg, the secretary, informed Newton about the examination of his invention of contracting telescopes by "ye most eminent in Opticall Science and practise" and their opinion that it was "necessary to use some means to secure this invention from ye Usurpation of forreiners." In a letter written later the same year regarding Newton's discourse on light and colors, Oldenburg again urged: "This discourse should without delay be printed, there being cause to apprehend that the ingenious and surprising notion therein contained . . . may easily be snatched from you, and the Honor of it be assumed by forainers, some of them, as I formerly told you being apt enough to make shew of and to vend, what is not of the growth of their Country." [133]

The glory of the nation was also an important reason—probably the only one that competed with the personal inclinations of scientists—to proceed with scientific endeavor at all. In one of the later letters from Oldenburg, Newton was informed of the acclaim his studies enjoyed abroad, which, Oldenburg believed, should increase Newton's "vigour to prosecute and advance them to the utmost, as well as for your owne as the Nations honor." [134] Edmond Halley, himself an eminent scientist and Astronomer Royal, used the same argument upon the publication of *Principia,* to make sure that Newton would proceed with his work: "I hope you will not repent you of the pains you have taken in so laudable a Piece, so much to your own and the Nations credit, but rather . . . that you will resume those contemplations." [135]

Practicing scientists fully shared the opinion of the propagandists or apologists of science, who were not engaged in it themselves, that a major source of its legitimation was the contribution it made to the national prestige. Even Newton, in a rare letter not exclusively devoted to the technicalities of his scientific investigations, concurred in it. [136] Recommending another scientist, the geographer John Adams, to his cousin Sir John Newton, he presented his work (a geographical survey of England) as a "designe for the credit of the Nation," and thought that this explained that Adams had "hitherto met with good encouragement." [137] Robert Boyle, too, was ob-

viously concerned about England's superiority in science. He had Oldenburg translate into Latin all his works written in English immediately upon
completion, to protect them from appearing in unauthorized translations in
other European languages and being claimed by foreigners. For his part,
Oldenburg rarely failed to communicate to Boyle what he learned from the
foreign correspondents of the Royal Society about the reactions to English
science abroad. Some of his letters were almost entirely devoted to this subject. "It must be said," he would conclude typically, "that England has a
large number of learned and inquisitive men, a larger number than is to be
found in all of Europe; and what they produce is solid and detailed—the
world has, for too long, been sufficiently entertained with general theories." [138]

Such expressions of self-praise were more than matched by praise from
foreigners who acknowledged England's leadership in science and also saw
it as reflecting the greatness of the nation. A German correspondent of the
Royal Society, J. D. Major, wrote in 1664: "It seems to be a characteristic of
the remarkable English people to accomplish great things through their pen-
etrating and truly unusual ability." Another one compared England's preeminence in medical science to the glory of its navigation: "As in the past
maritime exploration has day by day added new islands to the British realm
. . . so their love of inquiry after truth led the illustrious Bacon and Digby,
with the ingenious Harvey, Boyle, Charleton, Highmore, Glisson and Wallis
to throw much new light upon medicine. What may not rightly be expected
from the concourse of so many men of such caliber, and from companions
in letters headed straight for truth's Gate!" German scientists, he promised,
would not forget their debt to England: "[If] Germany can contribute nothing else of note to your British ocean, we offer unfailing memory of benefits
received; and such as they are our writings when they appear in time to
come shall testify to the English springs from which we drank our fill." [139]

Foreign correspondents noted the pride Englishmen took in the scientific
achievements of their compatriots, the incomparably higher prestige of science in England, the value assigned to it by society, and the widespread social support it enjoyed. How strikingly different England's appreciation of
science seemed at the time, compared with that of other countries, can be
gauged from Fontenelle's famous *Eulogium to Newton*. Fontenelle clearly
believed that scientific greatness meant national greatness. In the light of this
belief, the significance of the exceptionally high prestige enjoyed by science
in England, exemplified by the nation's appreciation of Newton, was greatly
enhanced. Of the attitude of the English toward their scientists, Fontenelle
wrote:

> It was Sir Isaac Newton's peculiar happiness to enjoy the reward of his merit in
> his life-time, quite contrary to Des Cartes, who did not receive any honours 'till

after his death. The English do not respect great Genius's the less for being born amongst them; and so far are they from endeavoring to depreciate them by malicious criticism, so far from approving the envy which attacks them, that they all conspire to raise them; and that great degree of Liberty which occasions their differences in the most important points, does not hinder them from uniting in this. They are all very sensible how much the glory of the Understanding should be valued in a State, and whoever can procure it to their country becomes extremely dear to them . . . We must look back to the Ancient Greeks if we would find out examples of so extraordinary a veneration for learning.[140]

The admiration of foreigners, mixed as it was with a dose of envy, reinforced England's self-definition as the scientific nation. The spokesmen of the Royal Society used it to ensure further support for science and constantly reminded the public that science made England great. The service science performed for the nation was also evoked by the apologists of science who had to ward off its still numerous (and, incidentally, inspired by religion) enemies. Among these apologists, Thomas Sprat is particularly important. His *History of the Royal Society* was "the climax of propaganda for the new science," "the most elaborate and comprehensive defense of the Society and experimental philosophy" in the seventeenth century, and "the most significant document in all propagandist literature on behalf of the new science." In addition, it "constituted an official statement of the matter." [141] The work had been commissioned by the Royal Society, refereed by several of its prominent members, and approved by them when completed.

The sentiments to which Sprat appealed almost exclusively were national pride and loyalty. In writing the *History*, he declared, he was inspired by "the Greatness of the Design itself" and "the Zeal which I have for the Honour of our Nation." [142] Referring to the work elsewhere, he added that he was trying "to represent its [Royal Society] Design to be Advantageous to the Glory of England"; [143] revealingly, the future Bishop of Rochester did not mention religion.

Sprat was acutely aware of the English inferiority in "matters of elegance" (which included art and literature), though as a rule he presented it as an unjust allegation of foreigners and an expression of their arrogance, rather than a fact. In *Observations on Mons. de Sorbiere's Voyage into England,* a profoundly nationalist document, he wrote: "The French and the Italians . . . generally agree, that there is scarce any Thing of late written that is worth looking upon, but in their own languages. The Italians did at first endeavour to have it thought that all Matters of Elegance had never yet pas'd over the Alps: But being overwhelmed by Number, they were content to admit the French and the Spaniards into some share of their Honour. But they all three still maintain the united opinion, that all Wit is to be sought for nowhere but amongst themselves: It is their Established Rule, that Good

Sense has always kept near the Warm Sun, and scarce ever dared to come further than the Forty-ninth Degree Northward." He tried to defend the honor of English letters, but, clearly, this for him was slippery ground. ("In the first Restoration of Learning the English began to write well as soon as any, the Italians only excepted; and . . . if we may guess by what we see of the Italians at this Day, the English have continued to write well longer than they . . . We have at this Present as many Masters of true and real Wit as ever Greece produced in any Age, whose Names, though I conceal, yet Posterity shall declare.") He also tried to present the apparent deficiencies of the English culture as a sign of its actual superiority: "The Temper of the English is Free, Modest, Kind, hard to be provok'd. If they are not so Talkative as others, yet they are more Careful of what they Speak. If they are thought by Some of their Neighbours to be a little defective in the Gentleness and the Pliableness of their Humour, yet that Want is abundantly supplied by their firm and their masculine virtues: And perhaps the same Observation may be found true in Men which is in Metals, and that the Noblest Substance are hardest to be polished."

But it was England's leadership in science that Sprat cited as the incontestable proof of his country's cultural ability: "The Arts that . . . now prevail amongst us are not only all the useful Sciences of Antiquity, but most especially all the late Discoveries of this Age in the Real Knowledge of Mankind and Nature. For the Improvement of this Kind of Light the English Disposition is of all the others the fittest." [144] In comparison with such real knowledge, "the True Arts of Life," humanistic learning and literature were mere trifles. Consequently, the *History of the Royal Society* was permeated with a sense of confidence in England's future glory and prosperity: science was ingrained in the English national character, and its advancement doubly guaranteed the advancement of the nation. "If there can be a true character given of the Universal Temper of any Nation under Heaven," argued Sprat, "then certainly this must be ascribed to our Countreymen: that they have commonly an unaffected sincerity; that they love to deliver their minds with a sound simplicity . . . they ought . . . be commended for an honourable integrity, for a neglect of circumstances, and flourishes; for regarding things of greater moment, more than less; for a scorn to deceive as well as to be deceived; which are all the best indowments, that can enter into a Philosophical Mind. So that even the position of our climate, the air, the influence of the heavens, the composition of the English blood; seem to joyn with the labours of the Royal Society to render our country, a Land of Experimental Knowledge." "The Genius of the Nation itself," he claimed, "irresistibly conspires" with the inclination toward science. The success of the Royal Society was assured, because it embodied "the present prevailing Genius of the English Nation." Having asserted that, the versatile clergyman demanded: if the Church of England opposed scientific investigation, "how could it be fit for the present Genius of this Nation?" [145]

Science did not only express the English "temper"; it could actually reform minds, contribute to greater rationality, and thereby unite and strengthen the nation. Sprat thought so, and this was one of Joseph Glanvill's arguments in *Plus Ultra*, where he prophesied: "[Science] will in its progress dispose mens Spirits to more calmness and modesty, charity and prudence in the Differences of Religion and even silence Disputes there. For the free sensible knowledge tends to the altering the Crasis of mens minds and so cures the Desease at the root; and true Philosophy is a Specifick against Disputes and Divisions." [146]

Through its close identification with the English nation, science acquired great authority and assumed a central place in the national consciousness. Other practices and spheres of culture were now measured against science and had to be proved congruent with it to receive national approbation. Religion was among practices so reassessed. Enumerating the advantages which made England the happiest of societies, Sprat, after citing military strength, political power, and science, mentioned also "the Profession of such a Religion, and the Discipline of such a Church, which an impartial Philosopher would chuse, [and] which . . . has given evident Sign . . . how nearly its interest is united with the Prosperity of our Country." [147] Significantly, religion recommended itself not only by its affinity to the spirit of the nation and consistency with its interests, but also by being acceptable to "impartial Philosophers," that is, scientists. Science stood guard over the national interest, and when religious zeal was perceived as a threat to it, its spokesmen thought it their duty to attack religion, which they did with an at-the-time remarkable sense of impunity. Sprat's *History,* Glanvill's *Plus Ultra,* Dryden's *Annus Mirabilis,* besides being apologies of science, constituted a part of the offensive against the religious enthusiasm of the "Mirabilis Annus" of 1666. [148] This enthusiasm they held responsible for the troubles that had befallen England in recent years, and science was opposed to it as a cure. The general distrust of enthusiasm and religious fervor reflected a strong and explicit anti-Puritan sentiment. It was expressed in, among other things, the attack on the Puritan style of preaching which took place in the second half of the seventeenth century. [149] Scientists and scientifically inclined clergymen were among the most outspoken assailants. Central among their criticisms was the familiar egalitarian—and nationalistic—argument that heavy reliance on Latin and Greek, and the use of fancy language, of which they accused the clergy, rendered preaching intelligible only to the upper strata. The clergy were urged to improve their knowledge of plain English and use it instead.

The scientific style of preaching soon prevailed in England, and the swift

success of the attack once again demonstrated the reversal in the importance
of secular and religious concerns in English society. For a time science assumed the place in English national consciousness which had previously
been held by Protestantism. It revealed the essence of the English national
identity. One of the effects of this interconnection between the first nation
destined soon to become the mightiest of the world powers and a previously
marginal activity was the tremendous authority of science in modern society. Because of its association with English nationalism, science became a
cult object long before it could demonstrate its potential, the subsequent
realization of which only partly accounts for its semi-religious status.


The England that emerged from the civic and religious trials of the mid-
seventeenth century was a nation. Its formation in the course of the preceding century and a half represented a tremendous change in the nature and
pervasiveness of politics and the first major breakthrough toward democracy. English national consciousness was first and foremost the consciousness of one's dignity as an individual. It implied and pushed toward (though
it could not necessitate the immediate realization of) the principles of individual liberty and political equality. These notions were primary in the definition of English nationhood. The casting away of the religious idiom did
not change the principles, but only laid them bare. Men were still believed
to have reason because they were created in the image of God; the requirements of their equality and liberty, therefore, derived from the act of creation. But it was the pride in man's reason and not reverence for its source
which inspired people like Milton after the Civil War; the right of the individual conscience, the liberty of man, the autonomy of a rational being were
advocated for their own sake, as supreme values. These ideas were in no
way peculiarly English and did not originate in England. Yet in England they
were able to become the content of the people's very identity, and therefore
rooted so firmly in the consciousness, both individual and collective, and the
culture as to transform the social terrain which nurtured them itself.
    This was due to the combined support of several factors. The idea of the
nation was adopted in the first place because of the social transformation in
the course of which one elite was replaced by another, and, the old definition
and justification of the existence of aristocracy becoming obsolete, there was
a need for a new definition and justification. The intense mobility, sustained
for a remarkably long period, and the continuous regrouping of the social
structure which resulted from it brought more and more people within the
sector to whom national identity appealed. For their own reasons, the Tudors—all, with the exception of Mary—were sympathetic to it too and offered it their weighty royal encouragement. The already growing national
consciousness was strengthened manifold when it became confluent with the

Protestant Reformation. The English Bible and the unprecedented stimulation of literacy were functionally equivalent, for a great mass of common Englishmen, to the effects of the social elevation on the new aristocracy. This mass of readers, too, was elevated and acquired a totally new dignity, the sense of which was reinforced by national identity and led them to embrace it. The counter-Reformational policies of Mary were also anti-national and succeeded in antagonizing the common people as well as the elite group with a vested interest in both Protestantism and nationalism. The end of her reign, which came so soon, made this group, intent on never again allowing the frustration of its interests—which it identified with those of England— the ruling group in the country for many years to come and brought about the close association of the Protestant and national causes. This association provided the growing national consciousness with Divine sanction, represented the national sentiment as religious at a time when only religious sentiments were self-legitimating and moral in their own right, and secured it the protection of its own strongest rival. It seemed as if all the important factors in English history of the time conspired to favor this growth, while the opposition to it was virtually non-existent. Thus English nationalism had the time to gestate; it was allowed—and helped—to permeate every sphere of political and cultural life and spread into every sector of society except the lowest, and become a powerful force which no longer needed buttresses to exist. It acquired its own momentum; it existed in its own right; it was the only way in which people now could see reality and thus became reality itself. For nationalism was the basis of people's identity, and it was no more possible at this point to stop thinking in national terms than to cease being oneself.

The combination of factors which ensured the development and entrenchment of nationalism in England and made it possible for England to become a nation was, of course, unique. It could not possibly be repeated anywhere. Why, then, did nationalism spread?

# The Three Identities of France

Behind their faces I see other men and in the same realm another state. The form remains, but the interior has been renewed. There has occurred a moral revolution, a change of spirit.

Guez de Balzac

How the face of this empire has changed! how we have advanced with a giant step towards liberty! . . . at present . . . the foreigners are going to regret that they are not French. We shall surpass these English, so proud of their constitution, who ridiculed our servitude.

Camille Desmoulins

All sovereignty resides essentially in the Nation. No body, no individual can exercise authority which does not explicitly emanate from it.

Declaration of the Rights of Man and Citizen

T he unique French identity, the consciousness of being *French*, though limited to a narrow elite circle, had existed centuries before it was reinterpreted as *national* identity. Made possible by the continuity, independence, and early, albeit relative, centralization of the authority of kings who in one form or another adopted the name "French," this consciousness was from very early on articulated by clerics. In their writings, the French identity first acquired the meaning of awareness of the religious, and then of the cultural and institutional, uniqueness of the royal domain. Later, during the ministry of Richelieu, it was tied to the concept of the "state." But at all times—before the advent of nationalism in the eighteenth century—it centered on, and derived from the relationship of dependence on and loyalty to, the king. The evolution of the French identity—from a religious-Christian to a political-royalist one with only vague religious overtones, which was in turn supplanted by national identity—implied two successive changes in the ultimate bases of legitimacy or fundamental values. The divinely appointed French king replaced the Christian Church, of which he had been the eldest son, and the state (which in France eventually became coterminous with nation) replaced the French king. Each time, the new identity grew under the auspices of the old one and received its importance from association with it, yet, in favorable circumstances, it helped to bring about the neutralization, if not the destruction, of the latter. Interlinked and gradually shading one into another, the three identities can be visualized as a set of patricidal nesting dolls, with the important difference that each successive one was more inclusive—and far more insistent on its inclusiveness—than the one out of which it emerged, and evidently this was no child's play.

## I. The Development of Pre-National French Identity

### France—a Church, and the Faith of the "Fleur de Lys"

It was not until well into the eighteenth century that a consensus emerged as to the correct spelling of the word "French"—*Français*. It was originally spelled *François* and pronounced *françoue* and then *france* in Parisian French. In the seventeenth century, Racine defended the form *François;* a century later d'Alembert thought that *Frances* reflected the pronunciation most accurately, and Voltaire favored the form that was eventually adopted, *Français.*

The referent of the word *François*—that became *Français* and came to mean "French"—was, for the authors of the sixteenth and seventeenth centuries, "the Franks," those belonging to the Germanic tribe that in the fifth century A.D. moved into Roman Gaul, whose territory, roughly, was to correspond to that of France. A Frankish political identity predated the formation of France—the domain of the French kings—by several centuries, and the relationship between the two was hardly one of straightforward continuity. Later architects of German as well as of French identity could claim Charlemagne as their ancestor, and for equally sound—or unsound—reasons. In the ninth century, after the partition of the Carolingian Empire, the Eastern Franks, whose descendants were to become Germans, contested the exclusive right of the Western Franks, in the domain of Charles the Bald, to the name *Francia.* Indeed, only in the eleventh century was *Francia* reserved solely for the designation of *Francia occidentalis,* and other, in future German, parts of the Carolingian Empire abandoned their "French" aspirations and identity. A century later, on the other hand, the name applied only to the central part of the domain, the Ile-de-France of today, while *Francia tota* was used to designate the kingdom as a whole.

The consistent identification of the patrimony of a particular dynasty, that is, of the territory under its control and the polity it represented, as *Francia*—France—dates from 1254, when the title of *rex Francorum* was officially changed to *rex Franciae,* from king of the Franks to that of king of France. The kings' knowledge of the extent and the exact contours of their territory was at that time far from accurate. The name thus did not simply label an unambiguously circumscribed territorial entity, but rather defined, that is, created, an image of such an entity, and helped to shape reality.

The identity of the people was no less ambiguous than that of the territory. At the time of the modification of the royal title, the name of "Franks" commonly referred to the inhabitants of the Western part of the divided Carolingian Empire, and had been used this way for several centuries. Yet these new Franks were thoroughly mixed with, and therefore were, to an equal degree, Gauls, who had inhabited the territory before the Germanic invasion. (In later centuries the theory of the Frankish origin of the French would be contested and the Gauls—among some other, less obvious possibilities—proposed as the true ancestors of the latter. During the Revolution the idea of the Gallic ancestry of the French people would temporarily triumph, to the extent that virtuous citizens would urge casting aside the very name "France," as expressive and reminiscent of *foreign* invasion and domination.) In the eleventh century (and probably as late as the thirteenth) "Franks"—*Franci*—was the name by which the Arabs of the Holy Land referred to all Westerners. The vernacular literature of the crusades, such as the *Chanson de Roland,* was the first to glorify "sweet" France. But the *Chanson* was written in Anglo-Norman, rather than in the language of Ile-de-France which was destined to become "French," and it is unclear what the "France" it sang of was—Ile-de-France, the Frankish kingdom, or perhaps Western Christianity.[1]

Objectively speaking, the Franks were not French. But in defining their dominions vis-à-vis the great powers of the age—the Papacy and the (German) Empire—the Capetian kings appropriated and utilized the Frankish legacy. Claiming to be the legitimate descendants of the Frankish kings and Emperors, they also claimed to inherit their traditional function—that of the defenders of the Church and the Papacy. The fact that *Franci,* in the Orient, represented Christianity was interpreted as proof of the superior piety which distinguished the French and regarded as a reason for a specifically French pride. In the literature of the crusades, the *Gesta Dei per Francos* of Guibert de Nogent and the *History of Jerusalem* of Robert de Moine, the Franks *(gens Francorum)* are represented as a people who epitomize Christianity, the most Christian, "chosen by God and distinguished among the nations by the fervour of [their] faith and devotion to the Church."[2] Jacques de Vitry in the thirteenth century reiterates: "There are many Christian nations, the first among them is France, the French are pure Catholics."[3] When the *Grandes chroniques de France* (which, written at St. Denis under the auspices of the Crown, present the official definition of the collective identity, thus effectively forging it) start to appear at the end of the thirteenth century, they emphasize the Christian piety of the French and their special place within Christendom as the distinguishing characteristics of the kingdom. Ironically, French piety is older than French Christianity; "même du temps où ils étaient dédiés à l'idolâtrie, ils étaient moult observants d'icelle"[4]; even as pagans the French were characterized by an exceptional zeal.

In the twelfth and thirteenth centuries the hereditary Frankish superiority in piety was seen as an attribute of both the kingdom and the king of France, but it was the latter who eventually came to epitomize this characteristic. For that reason the French kings insisted on their exclusive right to the title of "the most Christian king"—"le roi très chrétien"—which, during most of the period in question, was applied rather indiscriminately, being a conventional form in which the See of Rome expressed its approbation of those princes of whose services it at different times might have been in particular need. Toward the end of the Middle Ages, however, the kings of France successfully arrogated to themselves the designation of "très chrétien," and it became a part of the French royal title. The relative strength of the kingdom of France in contemporary politics, the constant menace of the Empire, which tended to undermine both its own influence and that of the Papacy which it menaced, forcing the Pope frequently to seek the protection of France, led Rome to acquiesce to the claims of the Capetians and acknowledge their exceptional position within Christendom. The Papacy recognized that "God chose the kingdom of France among all other peoples" and in fact insisted on the Divine election of the French king. In the fifteenth century the papal nuncio admonished Charles VII in the following words: "To you the most Christian of kings we entrust the common salvation, for by hereditary right you are the head of the Christian army, and it is to you that the other princes look up for the salvation of all." Others concurred: "You were the first to be planted on earth by God . . . God fights on your side . . . God has inclined His face toward you, His hand is on the people he has chosen." [5]

To be French in the late Middle Ages, therefore, meant to be a particularly good Christian. Eventually, though, and starting already in this early period, the insistence on the special position of the house and the kingdom of France within the Catholic Church led, however imperceptibly, to the separation from and even rupture with the latter. The French kings used the distinction of "très chrétien" as the ground for demanding the "liberty of France" from papal and imperial intervention in its affairs, extending these demands to both temporal and spiritual matters. The exceptional Catholicism of the French was interpreted as the proof of a direct link to God that bypassed His Vicar on Earth. Glad to see the Empire challenged, the Papacy—in the person of Innocent III—affirmed that the king of France, like the Emperor, "recognizes no superior in temporal matters." Philip Augustus, however, would not be satisfied with the concession of his equality to the Emperor alone and, when Innocent interfered in his quarrel with John Lackland of England, declared: "[Feudal] matters in dispute between kings are no business of the Pope." Neither did the French Crown stop at the exclusion of Rome from interference in temporals. At the end of the thirteenth century, the conflict over matters of taxation which erupted between the Papacy and Philip IV (le Bel) led this monarch to insist on the exclusion of foreign interference altogether and therefore on his sovereignty in spirituals as well. The juridical literature of the period maintained that the French king "is the Emperor in his kingdom." [6] In the course of the next century the jurists used several arguments in defense of the "sovereign liberty" of the king: they alluded to the obvious meaning of the name "France": *Franche*—free, which could not but express the essence of the realm that bore it, and was therefore a proof that France had never suffered domination by any other power. The revival and creative interpretation of the Salic law gave rise to the view that France, since its pagan infancy, had lived by its own legislation. But the central and most persistent argument was religious. Basically, it

amounted to the assertion that the French ("the special people for the execution of God's commandments")[7] were more Catholic than the Pope. The
election of France, and the immediate relationship between the kingdom
and God, was manifested first and foremost in the king. From an exemplary
son of the universal Church, the king became the focus of a new Christian
cult, and France—a Church in its own right.

Soon this cult and this Church developed a ritual peculiar to them and
their own symbolism. Colette Beaune traces the process of the transmission
of grace to and sacralization of the king of France via the *fleur de lys*—
originally the symbol of the Virgin Mary, to whom the French monarchs
professed special devotion—which became the symbol of royal authority,
thus confounding the images of the Mother of God and the kings of France,
establishing a particular relationship between them, and enveloping the
kings in Mary's divinity. The cult of Mary and the cult of royalty fused in
the symbol of the virginal lily, which was at the same time the royal one;
both were represented by and thus identified in it. The coronation at
Rheims—*le sacre*—whose paraphernalia and instruments were believed to
be supplied from heaven in one way or another, was a sacralization by definition. It reaffirmed the direct bond of the French king with the Lord Jesus
and reinforced the awareness of it at the commencement of each reign.

This was the context of the Hundred Years' War, which, therefore, for
participants had a significance very different from the one it seems to have
for a modern observer. It was a religious conflict, rather than a conflict between two nations. For the champions of the Valois, the two claimants to
the French throne, members of the same family, did not represent different
and more or less well reasoned positions regarding the law and custom of
dynastic succession, but were, emphatically, the forces of light and darkness,
of true faith and its Satanic perversion. Only the religious perception of the
kings of France—"the most Christian" princes, marked and chosen by
God—makes it possible to account for the "patriotic" determination of
Jeanne d'Arc amidst the wavering loyalties of her compatriots, many of
whom saw nothing wrong in being ruled by the English branch of the royal
family, and for the specific nature of her mission: to ensure the king's coronation—sacralization—at Rheims.[8]

God having chosen the "house of France" for his particular care, the law
of dynastic succession also acquired religious significance. Since succession
was hereditary, the interpretation of this law implied, in the phrase of Colette Beaune, a "political theology of [the royal] blood," which was articulated simultaneously with the emergence of the cult of the blood of Christ in
Latin Christianity as a whole. God, apparently, had chosen neither a particular person nor a people or a territory over which he ruled, but a lineage;
persons, people, and territory were sanctified only by association. It was,
therefore, through blood that the sanctity of the French kings was transmit-

ted (and only in a certain way: women, for example, from the fourteenth century on, when the Salic law was reinterpreted in connection with the Plantagenet claims, were no longer members of the lineage in the full sense). Individual kings could be canonized in their own right, as was Louis IX, but it was blood, not exemplary individual virtues, that ensured the saintliness of most of the French kings. An impressive amount of effort went into elaborating what exactly made this blood so potent. It was continuous, perpetual, the same "blood" on the throne of France, even though under different names, from the Frankish kings and emperors to the Valois; exceptionally "pure" in two senses: it was of different consistency from the blood of ordinary mortals, "transparent" and luminous, rather than dark red; and it was impeccably legitimate, always sanctified by the sacrament of holy matrimony. There were no bastards by definition among the French kings. For this reason, adultery, or suspicions thereof, on the part of the queens or princesses of France and their accomplices (which was probably no more uncommon than among the womenfolk of any other ruling house) was considered both political treason and sacrilege. In general, the political and religious spheres were confounded. In the thirteenth century those who spoke against the king were accused of blasphemy and sacrilege. On the other hand, it is possible that the extensive legislation against blasphemy and sacrilege during the reigns of Philip Augustus to Louis XI was but an early stage in the development of the concept of *lèse-majesté*.[9]

The royal blood was referred to—revealingly, for our purposes—as "the blood of France," as in the expression: "At the king's side were all the blood of France, namely the grand seigneurs."[10] The princes of the blood, the topmost rank of the nobility, were "the princes of France." They were members of the sacred lineage and by "the right of blood" participants in the government of the kingdom. The princes of the blood were, however, systematically and effectively excluded from participation in the government. By the sixteenth century their imposing title amounted to little more. Theirs thus was a situation of extreme status-inconsistency, and they did not hide their frustration. It found expression in the notorious radicalism of the members of the royal family—up to the brothers of the reigning monarch—who traditionally participated in openly treasonous activities. This behavior on their part was not at all restrained, but indeed reinforced by the fact that royal blood was taboo; it could not be touched, and thus while their accomplices frequently suffered cruel torture and ultimate punishment for their crimes, the princes themselves never did.[11] They formed a group emphatically and consistently opposed to the increasingly centralized ("absolute") rule of their royal kin and were natural leaders of the more general opposition to it.

Because of the sacralization of the French dynasty, service and loyalty to the king necessarily bore religious meaning. These were matters of Christian piety. The French community was a community united—created—by a cult, and thus a Church. As it was a Christian Church of sorts, the king, in formulating and justifying his demands on the loyalty of his subjects, drew upon the Western Christian tradition. The expressions of specifically French loyalty, loyalty to the king of France and to his policies, which certainly had existed as early as the fourteenth century and appears akin to the later French patriotism, were but an extension and particularization of traditional expressions of Christian piety. Given the essentially religious perception of the French monarchy, the *defensio regni*—the defense of the kingdom, whether with goods or with life, and service to the king—was unambiguously service to God. It was also, and more directly than in other countries, a form of religious practice in accordance with the principles of Christian altruism, of *caritas,* the service of God through the service of His creatures.

Medieval *amor patriae*—patriotism, that is—was a fundamentally Christian sentiment, both, and evidently, when *patria* was interpreted as "heavens" and when it referred to the province of one's birth. (During the Middle Ages *patria* only very rarely designated the polity, the kingdom in its entirety.) Military service, in particular, was seen as a continuation of the crusading tradition. The sanctity, the piety of death for one's country was increasingly emphasized during the Hundred Years' War; the earthly *patria* was sanctified by this religious association and could—as it did—later become a realm and a source of the sacred in its own right.

The consistently pursued royal policy vis-à-vis the Papacy and the Empire, and the royal endorsement and promulgation of and participation in the Christian cult of royalty related to this policy, thus very early established France as a separate, unique entity and stimulated a specifically French identity (an awareness of belonging to this particular entity and partaking of its characteristics) and specifically French loyalty, patriotism—devotion to this entity. Essentially religious at the outset and personified by the king and the royal lineage, France gradually acquired other—cultural and institutional—characteristics and became an image, a person, in its own right, whose existence, though confounded with that of the royal lineage, was not identical with it.

The most important among the characteristics which distinguished the French, alongside their superior piety, were the French language, French superiority in learning and letters, French law, and the constitution of French society. The choice of these characteristics, similarly to the emphasis on the superior Christianity of the Franks, was not a result of simple empirical observation. To begin with, these, emphatically, were not the characteristics of either the territory or the population of France (though, since some of them, namely law and constitution, could not be seen as attributes of the king alone, they were necessarily represented as such). Yet all were within the wide range of the possible signs of French specificity, and were selected and appropriated from within this range and imaginatively reinterpreted, for they were points of actual or potential strength for the French culture, and could be of use in the relationship of France with other powers.

## Language

Expressions of pride in the French language abounded already in the thirteenth century. In the opinion of the writers of that early period, French was "the most beautiful language in the world," "the sweetest," "la plus délitable à ouir et à entendre." "The sweet French tongue," they rhapsodized, "is the most beautiful, gracious and noble language in the world, the best accepted and loved. For God made it so sweet and lovable for his glory and praise, that it can be compared to the language spoken by the angels in heaven." The fact of its technical paucity, recognized by the translators of the time, who were among its chief encomiasts, and put forward as the ground for the introduction of numerous latinisms, did not at all dampen the enthusiasm of the linguistic patriots. Eulogies of the tongue continued to appear—sometimes in Latin, as in the case of Jean de Montreuil, who linked the superiority of French over other European tongues, particularly English and German, to its purity and originality: it was impervious to foreign influences, which had corrupted the other two. French, therefore, in explicit and rather ironic distinction from German, was conceived of as an *Ur-Sprache*.

Neither were the enthusiasts dismayed by the fact that the French language they glorified was not the language of France. This language was spoken in Paris, indeed; it was the "French of Paris." Its origin was *francien*, the dialect of Francie, the territory between the Somme and the Loire, which in the tenth and eleventh centuries constituted the domain of the Counts of Paris, the progenitors of the Capetian kings. It was neither spoken nor, apparently, for a long time written in the other parts of the kingdom of France. The literary production in the vernacular, according to Suzanne Citron, was predominantly Anglo-Norman in the eleventh and twelfth centuries, and Picarde, Champenoise, and Bourguignonne in the thirteenth to fifteenth centuries, depending on the province and native dialect of the authors.

At the same time, from the twelfth century on, the French of Paris was the international language of the upper classes (which allowed some to claim that it was a language "common to all people"—"commune à totes gens"). As early as 1148 "one who [did not know] French was considered a barbarian." French was the language of the Crusader State in the Orient, and in the thirteenth century was spoken at the courts of England, Germany, and Flanders. It also became the literary medium for many writers outside France. Colette Beaune names Brunetto Latini, Martino da Canale, Marco Polo, and

Philippe de Novare as examples of Italian men of letters who wrote in French.

As the language of the upper classes, however, the French of Paris had to compete with Latin—a language of sacred texts, which for a long time remained the language of scholarship and law, as well as the medium of polite discourse. In 1444 Jean d'Armagnac preferred to negotiate with the English in Latin, for, as he confessed, he did "not know French well, especially to write." The Renaissance contributed to the prestige and appreciation of Latin, so that toward the end of the Middle Ages it seemed further than ever from being ousted by another tongue.

The linguistic policy of the Crown was not forceful enough. While Philip the Fair made French the language of royal edicts in the Northern parts of France (France du Nord), in the South the administration still used Latin. Two hundred fifty years later the Edict of Villers-Cotterets of 1539, under Francis I, extended the use of French to all official deeds. But yet another century had to pass before a Bourbon, Louis XIII, decreed in the Code Michaud of 1629 its use compulsory in the registration of baptisms, marriages, and burials.

Throughout the Middle Ages the population of France was divided into at least five linguistic groups (the speakers of langue d'oïl, langue d'oc, basque, breton, and flamand, some of which were subdivided into important dialects). This evident lack of linguistic unity, namely the conspicuous absence of the *French* language, was, paradoxically, a matter of pride rather than mortification for linguistic patriots; it was believed to be a reflection of the imposing size of the kingdom, which compared so favorably with that, for example, of laughably small England that could boast but of one native tongue.[12] This situation, however, in no way prevented the presentation and celebration of the French of Paris as the *French* language, which, beginning in the fourteenth century, and in the atmosphere of growing appreciation for "mother" tongues in general, became an object of ardent love among scholars and men of letters—the creators of symbols of collective identity—and as a result a central symbol of the French identity, and eventually an objective characteristic of French ethnicity.

### *Translatio Studii*

The claim of French cultural superiority was likewise born in the minds of a few scholarly dreamers. It was predicated on the stature of the University of Paris in medieval letters and on the related notion of *translatio studii*. The schools of Paris, which numbered among the most illustrious centers of theological studies in the West, were incorporated into a university at the beginning of the thirteenth century. The teaching was in Latin, and the students as well as professors were recruited from every part of Western Christendom. The institution was one of the most frequented; many of the higher clergy, at least as often foreign as indigenous, were educated there and later spread the fame of their *alma mater*. The notion of *translatio studii*, the transmission of learning from the centers of classical antiquity to Paris, was a reflection of the university's centrality for *respublica Christiana*. It placed Paris in a direct line of succession to Athens and Rome, and implied that it was the New Athens and New Rome. Yet, while heir to the wisdom and scholarship of the ancients, Paris was the seat of a different culture. Its province was theology rather than the philosophy and mathematics of Athens, or law—the area of Rome's excellence. The emphasis on theology (as the unique strength of the University of Paris) reinforced the collective self-perception of France as the domain of superior piety: the University reflected the nature of the kingdom within which it dwelt. Conversely, with the mounting tensions between the kings and the Papacy, the scholars tended to see the institution (and themselves) as a repository of specifically French, rather than general Christian, wisdom. Toward the end of the thirteenth century, their allegiance was unambiguously with the king, and the university was referred to as the "fille du roi." The notion of *translatio studii* thus acquired a novel significance: it no longer meant the transmission of learning from venerable but pagan antiquity to Christianity, of which the University of Paris happened to be a receptacle, but rather the transmission of the *cultural leadership* of Greece and Rome to France. Simultaneously, the definition of French culture as theology changed too, for the Italian Humanists challenged the view that modern culture was first and foremost religious learning, and defined it as poetry and rhetoric. The academics of Paris saw the world of letters through the eyes of Italian Humanists, and were eager to prove that France was anyone's equal, if not superior, in these secular spheres as well. In the fourteenth century secular letters were in their infancy. The competition French intellectuals encountered was stimulating rather than discouraging. It is true that at first they had few native talents to oppose to the Italian Dante and Petrarch, but at this barely breaking dawn of modernity, a dream of cultural superiority was a deed half accomplished, the gap between the two was nowhere as depressing as it has become since then, and to honestly desire intellectual excellence was going a long way toward actually achieving it.

### The Salic Law

The language and the leadership in letters have remained with the French until our day, elevated or transformed as they were on the way from objects of pre-national to those of national pride. The other two distinguishing characteristics of France, the territory and the subjects of the kingdom, namely the Salic law and the constitution of the realm, later lost much of their importance. The Salic law—one of the numerous Germanic laws dating back to some time between the sixth and the eighth centuries—owed its exceptional standing to the Hundred Years' War. It was known but rarely evoked until the reign of Charles V (1364–1380), when in the search for legal means to render illegitimate the claims of the English Plantagenets to the French throne—a problematic undertaking—it was reinterpreted and presented as the proof of their unlawfulness. The original law did not unequivocally exclude women from inheritance and was ambiguous as to whether it referred to royal domain at all. But it possessed several qualities which endeared it to a monarchy intent on proving its traditional independence from interference of the great powers and increasingly relying on jurists to support its position. These endearing qualities included, first of all, its ancient birth (believed to have occurred in the fifth century, during the reign of Pharamond—the first Merovingian king and founder of the French monarchy), pagan and uninfluenced by Rome, which convincingly proved the legal independence and maturity of the kingdom from its very foundation. The deference—bordering on worship—to this law also endeared it to the jurists themselves, who, in addition, tended to see in it a flattering-to-them indication of the early existence in France of a Parlement, for, in drawing it, Pharamond was believed to have been advised by a council of wise men. The fifteenth-century interpretation of the Salic law as the fundamental law of the kingdom, the law of dynastic succession and the legal foundation of the legitimacy of the sacred lineage of the French kings ("the law of France," "the royal law"), contributed immensely to its prestige. To defend the Salic law was to "fight for one's country, like a Roman soldier,"[13] the classical expression of classical patriotism.

### The Image of France

In connection with the reinterpretation of the Salic law, scholars in the fifteenth century thought in addition of the uniqueness and superiority of the constitution of the French polity *(politia nostra)*.[14] The members of this body politic—the king, the Parlement, twelve peers, and three Estates—labored in concert, under the rule of law, for the glory of God and the common good. The domain of the French kings, whose inhabitants were united in a community of worship, thus became, in the eyes of some of them, an entity with many admirable qualities of its own. These qualities were first sacralized by association with "the most Christian" royal lineage, but having been sacralized could be worshipped and adored independently. France as a special entity, the land and the polity, indeed very early became an object of tender and deeply felt devotion, though only a few partook in this sentiment. The authors of the vernacular *chansons de geste* of the twelfth century expressed their love of France in charming verse. One of them wondered how

Jesus could prefer the desert of the Holy Land as his earthly abode, when
He had the choice between it and the provinces of France:

> Merveille moi de Dieu le fil sainte Marie
> Qui chi se hebergea en ceste desertie . . .
> Miex aim d'el borc d'Arras la grant castelerie
> Et d'Aire et de saint Pol la grant caroierie
> Et de mes biaus viviers la riche pescherie
> Que tote ceste terre . . .

France was also imagined as a person, first manifested in a voice (as in
Alain Chartier's *Quadrilogue invectif*), then as a beautiful woman, "Dame
France," a blond princess clothed in garments adorned with the *fleur de lys*.
In the early fourteenth century appeared the image of France as a garden, an
earthly paradise, *le jardin de France*. This image was secularized in the
fifteenth century—or rather the nature of its sanctity was altered—and it
came to reflect the sense of the exceptional beauty and abundance of the
land. "France is the ornament of the earth," wrote in 1483 Chancellor Jean
Masselin. "The beauty of the country, the fertility of its soil and the salubrity of its air eclipse all the other countries of the earth." [15]

To be French in the fifteenth century, for a scholar, a jurist, or an occasional nobleman, already meant more than just being a subject of "the most
Christian" French king, with all the religious implications of this identity. It
also meant speaking or writing French, or at least appreciating this language; carrying on the cultural tradition of antiquity; a respect for the Salic
law and pride in the constitution of the polity based on it; and an attachment to the land of France, whose perfection, one must realize, before the
means of reliable and regular transportation became available, was imagined rather than known. The key point of allegiance, the *source* of the
French identity, however, was still the royal person, the high priest of a
unique religious cult. One became French through the relationship to the
"most Christian" king. Even when one identified with the territory, the territory was defined by the extent of the possessions of the Crown, and that
Crown had a specific religious meaning. Nothing French could conceivably
exist at this time outside of this relationship. This was not a *national* identity. In the sixteenth century things began to change.

## Heresy and Its Child

### Tradition and Change in Sixteenth-Century French Patriotism

On the face of it the new century carried on the traditions already crystallized toward the close of the old one. In its first half, it would seem, all it
added to the emerging sense of the French identity and pride in it was sheer

volume and a more confident and articulate expression, reflecting the existing sentiment in a new, specific-to-it, vocabulary. In the Middle Ages, the
Latin word *patria* lost its evocative meaning as the supreme object of loyalty
and pride of the citizens, which it had held within the classical system of
values, and was associated with this lofty import only when referring to the
heavenly Kingdom of God. In other cases it in a matter-of-fact manner denoted the province of one's birth, *pays natal*. The word was employed frequently and, with the increasing use of the French language, was frenchified
around the middle of the fifteenth century, as *patrie*.[16] In the first half of the
sixteenth century, as another example of Renaissance, *patrie* regained its
classical connotations. Denoting the polity as a whole, it again signified the
referent of the most noble devotion and, being used in this sense already in
the 1520s, by the 1540s became a regular element of discourse. The service
of the *patrie* was praised as a great and indispensable virtue. Ronsard insisted that one should put "every means . . . even one's life to help, support
and serve the *Patrie*." Joachim du Bellay, in composing his *Deffence et illustration de la langue françoyse* (1549), was moved by his "natural affection
for the *patrie*," and believed his work to be "a duty which [he owed] to the
*patrie*." [17] The Roman origins—and transparently derivative nature—of the
new value were resented by some. Charles Fontaine scolded du Bellay
around 1550: "He who has a country *(pays)* has nothing to do with *patrie*.
Which name *pays*, derived from Greek sources, all the ancient French poets
and orators used in that meaning . . . But the name *patrie* has entered
obliquely and arrived only recently, with all the other Italian corruptions.
The ancient [poets] refused to use this word, fearing Latin swindles, and
were content with what was properly their own." [18] But the champions of
the *patrie*, du Bellay among them, were as protective as their critics of the
independence and prestige of the French culture. The chief object of their
work was to persuade the world as well as themselves, and to ensure, that
this culture was at least equal in value to the culture of ancient Greece and
Rome, and to that of contemporary Italy—the natural heir of antiquity—
which at the time convincingly claimed cultural superiority.

The "patriotism" of the first half of the sixteenth century was less revolutionary than its vocabulary would make it appear. First, devotion and service to the *patrie* were tightly connected, in fact identical, with traditional
loyalty to the king. In the texts the two are frequently evoked together, often
in the same sentence, and service to the prince is usually mentioned first.
Second, defending the honor of the French *patrie*, the authors emphasized
the traditional virtues of the "most Christian" kingdom. The Renaissance
discourse thus did not reflect a new reality. The alteration in the perception
of reality, which it undoubtedly affected (for worship of the *patrie* implied
both the depersonalization of the traditional loyalty and its de-
Christianization), not made explicit and clearly realized, was therefore but

slight. And yet the reality with which this discourse coexisted was undergoing a profound transformation.

The "most Christian" monarchs of France, the eldest sons of the Catholic Church, were slowly but surely freeing themselves from the parental cares of Rome. The bonds that tied them to the *respublica Christiana*, if this was to be considered as something other than a loose federation of separate polities, were wearing thin. In 1516 the Concordat of Bologna made the king of France in fact, though not in name, the head of the Gallican Church. Turning inward, the resolute Valois determined to add to the independence from outside interference the liberty from limitations of the royal power by what their feudal subjects considered constitutional rights. The military and economic exigencies of the first two reigns of the Angoulème branch (François I and Henri II) prompted a massive reorganization of the administrative apparatus and the emergence of a professional bureaucracy. While administration in France had been relatively centralized for a long time, this centralization now increased dramatically, and the extent to which previously powerful aristocratic families could influence the formation of royal policies dramatically decreased.

In the course of this reorganization the concept of the "state"—*état*—began to acquire its modern connotations. Originally an "estate" in the sense of an order—the king representing the first of several estates composing the body of French society, according to the constitutional thought of the period, epitomized perhaps in the *Grande monarchie* of Claude de Seyssel[19]—the word was still used in this sense by François Hotman in *Francogallia* in 1572. Every estate was defined as a body of right, and since the right of the king, the royal prerogative, was the right of authority, the "state," when employed in association with the king, also denoted "authority" or "system of authority." The word was used in 1595 as an exact synonym of what Max Weber would call "a system of legitimate domination" by Charron, who, like Weber, saw in the organization of relations of authority the constitutive element of any society. "The state [*l'état*], that is, the domination, the specific order of command and obedience, is the support, the cement, and the soul of everything human. It is the vital spirit that breathes life into thousands of men, and animates all things."[20] The name of the king's council, called now the *conseil d'état*, and the titles of *secrétaires d'état*, given to four of the *secrétaires du roi* by Henri II, possibly emphasized this abstract aspect of royal authority. In this manner and by association with the king, the "state" was acquiring the meaning of "the government" and "the sphere of politics."[21]

The professional officers were gradually yet energetically supplanting the old nobility in government. Catherine de Medicis, who had control of the government during the minority of her sons, relied on the officers rather than the unruly grandees. She formalized the position of the superintendents

of finance and established that of provincial intendants, destined to become
an unparalleled source of annoyance for the traditional nobility. The status
of this nobility was in the meantime also being undermined by the sale of
offices on a massive scale, begun under François I, and by the sale of noble
titles. The nobility was in a way strengthened by the influx of *novi homines,*
but it was seen by members of the old aristocracy as an affront and became
a major cause of disaffection among them. In their minds, as in actuality, the
swelling of the ranks of the higher nobility, as a result of the royally sponsored stampede of low-born officers and men of wealth into it, was connected to the concentration of authority in the hands of the king, and they
would oppose the latter all the more because they detested the former.

Between 1494 and 1559 the attention of the general or provincial nobility
was occupied by the Italian wars: military service was not only a noble pursuit by definition, but also, for many of its members, an economic necessity.
Peace deprived them of an important source of income, and they joined the
ranks of the disaffected. By 1560 the discontent was universal. At the General Estates that and the following year, both the nobility and the Third
Estate voiced their sentiments and blamed their unhappiness on the Crown.
The opposition grew bolder. Henri II died in 1559, leaving the government
to a child (François II), who followed his father to the grave in a year's time
and left the throne to another child (Charles IX); in these circumstances
boldness involved little risk. Notwithstanding the capable diplomacy of the
Queen Mother, or perhaps because of it, power suddenly appeared to be up
for grabs.

The monarchy was in crisis, and it was exacerbated by the volatile religious situation. The general discontent made wide circles of French society
responsive to the message of the Protestant doctrine. Various sectors of the
urban population, the mainstay of Huguenotism in the beginning, after the
peace treaty of Cateau-Cambresis of 1559 were joined by large numbers of
the nobility. In 1562, two thousand Calvinist churches existed in France.
The spread of Calvinism provided other discontented people with a legitimate target of attack, a group on which they could blame their misfortunes
all they wanted and vent their frustrations. Already in the 1560s local Catholic leagues appeared, which were combined in 1576 into the Catholic Holy
League, led by the ducal family of Guise. Resentments provoked by the centralizing policies of the Crown and aggravated by the economic difficulties
of several important strata were diverted into a religious conflict. The leaders, at least, of both parties regretted the good old days of feudalism. But
instead of openly attacking the monarchy, which was as yet inconceivable,
they engaged in a savage civil war. It lasted almost forty years (1562–1598),
and both sides claimed to be defending the true interests of the Crown
against wicked advisers and clamoring for the legitimate successor. The situation, indeed, lent itself to a good deal of clamor, especially as it became

increasingly entangled in the complex issues of the nature of French identity. Two of the last three sickly Valois died one after the other, and the third one was assassinated childless, though not before he had named as his successor the leader of the Huguenots, his distant cousin, Henri de Navarre. Was France to be ruled by a Frenchman, indeed the next in the legitimate line according to the Salic law, who was not a Catholic, or by a foreigner true to the professed religion of the "most Christian" kingdom?

The Reformation and its wide appeal in France, although it might have increased the catholicity of the latter, dealt an irreparable blow to the Catholic self-image of the country. French Catholicism grew more and more idiosyncratic for centuries, and the kings, while flaunting the title of *Rex Cristianissimus,* did everything possible to separate themselves from the Universal Church and its head in Rome. Yet this determined decatholicization was never made explicit; if anything it was the Pope who was accused of being not Catholic enough. The Catholicism of France was, by definition, impeccable; France, it was said, had never known heresy. Now it knew it only too well. When the new teaching first reached France in 1519, the "most Christian" king François I rather lazily flexed his Catholic muscles. In 1521 he prohibited the publication of Lutheran texts, but he did not consider the battles of Rome his own. Still, later, when matters appeared to be getting out of hand, and anti-Catholic affiches distressed the citizens of Paris, he began persecution in earnest, and Henri II continued his father's high-handed policies. These two strong kings, unable to imagine and unlikely to have their authority assailed, believed they could tell their subjects what their true identity consisted of. The widow of Henri II, Catherine de Medicis, no longer believed so. She recognized her own and her minor sons' weakness and prudently relaxed the treatment of Huguenots. However reluctant a devotee of Dumas may be to abandon the compelling image of the poisonous queen, the instigator of the St. Bartholomew's Day Massacre, Catherine's rule was that of systematic concessions to Protestants. The Crown, in general, was unsympathetic to the Catholic reaction, and the last Valois, destined, alas, to be impotent in so many aspects of his life, dissolved the League in a vain effort to undermine its influence.

An impressive minority of French subjects in all social strata were heretics. This, as Oliver Cromwell might have said, was "one good fact." Nevertheless they were French subjects. And so, in the latter half of the sixteenth century the heretofore central—religious—element in the French identity was systematically downplayed by the Huguenots, by the Crown, by the Gallican Catholics and *politiques,* leaving the League alone to stress Catholicism at the expense of Frenchness. The *Frenchness* of the combatants was emphasized and appealed to over the differences of religion. "Frenchmen should not think of other Frenchmen as Turks," pleaded the Italian Queen Mother. "There should be brotherhood and love between them." Henri III (who had hastily returned from Poland—where he was king—upon the death of his brother to intercept a very possible usurpation of the French throne) announced: "I come with arms outstretched to receive my subjects all alike without distinction." In 1589, Henri de Navarre, the Huguenot leader, appealed to him: "In the name of all I beg peace from my Lord the King, for me, for all the French and for France," and, when already Henri IV of France, having converted for the sake of political prudence to Catholicism (he agreed that Paris was worth a Mass), he spoke to his people: "I call on you as Frenchmen. I espouse no man's passions . . . I am not blind. I see clearly. I wish members of the Faith to live in peace in my kingdom . . . not because they are of the Faith, but inasmuch as they have been loyal servants to me and to the French crown . . . We are all French and fellow-citizens of the same country." [22] The French identity was therefore redefined by default—for its previously central element had been taken out of it—and yet left undefined, for it was not clear what was to take its place.

## Mother France

The Catholic *politiques* found the position of the League preposterous. The 1593 *Dialogue du maheustre et du manant* presented it as the pinnacle of absurdity: "If it pleases God to give us a king from the French nation, blessed be his name; if from Lorraine, blessed be his name; if from Spain, blessed be his name. If he is a devout Catholic and sent by God it is a matter of indifference to us to which nation he belongs. We are not concerned with the nation but with religion." [23] For the *politiques* as for many others, the question was decidedly of the "nation," and that increasingly irrespective of religion. The word was used in the sense of "community of birth." France was defined as the progenitor of this community, and was in this quality now worshipped by patriots. They imagined it as a person, a woman and a mother whose body was lacerated and soul ravaged by the religious strife of her children, those literally born of her. Contemporary authors constantly returned to this image of France—the mother, holding them at her nourishing breast:

> France, mère des arts, des armes et des loix
> Tu m'as nourry long temps du laict de ta mamelle.[24]

Their patriotic concerns derived quite directly from this filial relation. Gérard François, the physician of Henri IV, whose profession added poignancy to the title of his *De la maladie du grand corps de la France,* wrote in the dedication to the king: "Sire, as God made me by birth and by name a true Frenchman [*vray François*] and consequently . . . most devoted to the welfare of my own Patrie . . . as I saw it so afflicted . . . I could not do anything short of offering it all the support that every child naturally owes his mother."[25]

This patriotism—which, paradoxically, assumed a form of mother-worship, and which was to some extent a result of the Wars of Religion—had little in common with nationalism as it is defined in this book. France, the devoted daughter of the Catholic Church, graduated to become the mother of her people, but was far from being a *nation*. This final transformation of identity would take place two centuries later. Yet, in some ways, the sixteenth century anticipated it.

## Doctrines of Popular Resistance

The religious conflict gave rise to doctrines, constitutional and religious, which had a distinctly nationalist flavor, for although they did not reach the conclusions that would allow one to classify them as such without reservation, they tended in the direction of defining France as a sovereign collectivity. These doctrines, fundamentally, were justifications of the opposition to the reigning monarch, and were first elaborated by Huguenots forced into such opposition. Calvinism advised passive disobedience to ungodly rulers and even allowed resistance by inferior magistrates,[26] but it is significant that the arguments advanced by the Huguenot writers were of a constitutional rather than theological nature; namely the grounds for the legitimacy of resistance they emphasized had to do with the constitution of the French kingdom, and not with ungodly rule as such.

The two most important treatises of this kind, François Hotman's *Francogallia* and *Vindiciae contra tyrannos,* attributed to du Plessis-Mornay,[27] invested the community with sovereign power and the inalienable right to oppose the unjust ruler who did not recognize or showed no respect for it. Hotman's method was historical: he reconstructed the ancient constitution of the kingdom and arrived at the following conclusions. Royal authority in France, he said, had been delegated to the Crown by the free association of Franks and Gauls, who, together, elected a king. Succession had been regulated by custom (Hotman did not think that the Salic law was of crucial importance in this respect), and therefore had always been subject to the tacit agreement of the people, and in a sense an election. The people never abrogated its sovereignty or ceded its right to control the ruler, which was, in ancient times, exercised by the council of the realm, the three Estates (the king, the aristocracy of office, and the people), which represented the community as a whole. The French polity, originally, had been constituted as a limited monarchy; the Crown's arrogation of autocratic powers was a usurpation. It was, therefore, in agreement with the French constitution to oppose an autocratic ruler (a ruler who wished to impose his will on the people without the latter's consent—an important point for Huguenots). The king was not the essential element of the community. In a manner closely resembling that of John Poynet, Hotman insisted: "A people can exist without a king . . . whereas a king without a people cannot even be imagined." [28] Yet there was a fundamental difference between the author of *Francogallia* and his English contemporary. Hotman reified—and deified—the community. For him, it was not an association of living individuals, but a being with its own will or spirit, reflected and embodied in its founding, constitutive decision. Its original state reflected its nature, and therefore was to be jealously preserved in essence if not in exact form, irrespective of the wishes of the individual members, who were incidental to it.

Mornay also urged adherence to the ancient constitution and saw rule without consent (specifically in matters of religion) as its betrayal, and therefore a tyranny, which it was a duty to resist. He postulated the existence of a double contract, first, between God and both the king and the people, which acknowledged the Divine sanction of royal power; and second, between the king and the people, which made just rule, that is, rule in accordance with the constitutional rights of the people, a condition of the king's authority. Mornay came closer to the individualist insistence of Marian exiles on the right of every subject actively to resist unjust and ungodly rule, but stopped short of it. While he invested individual magistrates, rather than the Estates, with the authority to check and oppose tyranny, this authority belonged to public officers who represented the laws of the community, rather than to private individuals. Only the community, or the corporate bodies of which it was composed, could revolt against the higher authority to which it had consented collectively. The right of private persons to revolt, on the other hand, spelled anarchy or even greater evils; were such a right recognized, "infinite troubles would ensue even worse than tyranny itself and a thousand tyrants would arise on the pretext of suppressing one." [29] In short, Protestantism alone was not enough to engender respect for the individual.

### The Divine Right of Kings

Upon the death, in 1584, of the Duc d'Alençon, another one of the unhappy Valois brothers, the Huguenot Henri de Navarre became heir apparent to the French throne. The situation for the Huguenots changed, and since then they were mainly preoccupied with proving the legitimacy of Henri's succession. At the same time, and for the same reasons, however, the situation also changed for the supporters of the Catholic League, who found themselves in imminent danger of being ruled by a heretic. The League, therefore, adopted the doctrine of popular resistance to ungodly rule at the very moment when the Huguenots abandoned it. But the Ultramontanist leanings and connections of the League, as well as the populist and frankly demagogical tactics of its leaders, served to antagonize moderate Catholic, that is, predominantly Gallican, opinion; and the League, again, found itself alone fighting for a lost cause.[30] At the close of the sixteenth century, France had no use for anything remotely resembling populism and would have no talk of resistance. Yet the idea which came to replace these subversive doctrines, and was to dominate French political thought for the next century and a half, though on the face of it diametrically opposed to any kind of popular rights theories, paradoxically also paved the way for national identity. This idea was that of the Divine Right of kings.

The theory of Divine Right was inspired by the experience of the Religious Wars and brought together in a coherent and morally compelling system several elements which had developed independently, but also were related to or at least strengthened by this experience. The mob-rousing tactics of the League and the impressive manifestation of popular appetite for a certain kind of freedom convinced many among the nobility of the desirability of strong government. The *politiques,* in general agreement with the Huguenot theorists of resistance, were growing increasingly unsympathetic to the "people" that "like a fierce and savage animal wanted to shake off the yoke of royal domination, and to replace it by God knows what imaginary liberty, which, to their utter confusion and dismay, turned out to be a tyranny more barbarous and cruel than those that were known to the miserable slaves of the heathens." [31] Not the least among the results of the firsthand experience of these popular inclinations, and the revulsion that developed as a reaction, was a new respect for educated intellect and discipline in all its forms. Another one, of direct political relevance, was the desire for "a king who would give order to all." [32]

First clearly formulated in *De l'autorité du roi* by Pierre de Belloy in 1588, the Divine Right theory drew upon the Gallican assertion of the sovereignty of the king vis-à-vis the Pope and Bodin's theory of sovereignty, which it bolstered by the immediate Divine sanction. The desire for a strong—authoritarian—government was presented as both very reasonable and highly ethical, for it agreed with political theory and demonstrated admirable obedience to the Divine order of things. The king, who received his authority directly from God, was accountable to God alone; resistance was made theoretically unjustifiable; a legitimate ruler was by definition just, and the subjects had no right but to obey. Between 1596 and 1598 the doctrine was presented in a simplified version by a number of royalist pamphletists. "It is very certain and beyond doubt," wrote one of them, "that all power comes from above, and that to resist it is to resist the commandments and orders of God . . . by this I mean a true and genuine power, a rule by the grace of God, and by a legitimate and authentic king, supported by the laws and constitutions of the realm. I intend to speak here of an absolute and full power, founded on just laws, divine as well as natural and civil, a worthy ornament of a true king, a power descended from the heavens that can't be measured by men, nor subjected to their control." From here there was no difficulty to deduce that "tout Roy de la terre est Dieu" and "que veut le Roy, si veut la loy." [33]

The emphasis on the Divine Right of kings was not new in France. The French kings for centuries, from the thirteenth century on systematically, substituted the direct bond with God to that with His Church in order to escape the limitations on their power implied in the latter allegiance. Neither was the sanctification of the royal authority and person a novelty, for this was the essence and the effect of the "religion of royalty" that—also for centuries—had been a central element of French Catholicism. By these means the French Crown had inconspicuously, but by the sixteenth century effectively, extricated itself from the jealous tutelage of Rome, at the same time tightening its religiously sanctioned absolutist grip on its subjects. The novelty of Divine Right theory lay neither in the transcendental nature of the justification of royal power nor in the appeal to direct Divine sanction. It lay in the fact that this theory, for once, dispensed with appearances. The God who authorized the sovereignty of the king was a Christian God, to be sure—what else could He be? But He was no longer the God of the Catholic Church; His divinity was, therefore, deconcretized, made abstract. The emphasis on the abstract Divine Right was a step of fundamental importance in the decatholicization of royal authority in France, and thus, paradoxically, in its secularization.

Moreover, the increasingly impersonal God of the French, apparently, had a peculiar penchant for legality. The Divine appointment of the sovereign prince took the form of birth into the legitimate line, so that his providential election was simultaneously and necessarily authorized by the Salic law. The king was divinely appointed, but he acceded according to a decidedly human, "constitutional" law of the kingdom. Neville Figgis emphasized the legalistic and *secular* character of the French variant of Divine Right theory in his comparison of the French doctrine with its seventeenth-century English counterpart. [34] In His dependence on the Salic law, God Himself was secularized. Yet this secularization had no element of *entzauberung* in it. The nature of the sacred changed, but it remained sacred. Parallel to the secularization of divinity, secular authority sanctioned by the fundamental and nevertheless human law was sacralized, and with it the law, and consequently the community of which it was an emanation. The ultimate result of the doctrine of the Divine Right of kings was the deification of the French polity.

It was left to the next century to equate the king with the polity, which in France would first be called "the state," and to the century after to transfer the loyalty from the royal person to that increasingly reified and yet impersonal body of authority of which at first he was thought to be both the source and the incarnation. But the stages in this portentous evolution were implied in the idea of the Divine Right of kings just as the conclusions of a syllogism are in its propositions. Some signs of the seventeenth-century development were already apparent in the 1590s, specifically in the thought of Charles Loyseau. In *Traité des seigneuries* (published in 1608) Loyseau represented a polity as sovereignty and the territory within and over which it was exercised *(une terre seigneuriale)*. Neither of the two could constitute a polity, a *res publica,* a social organism, without the other, but while the territory represented as it were the dead matter, sovereignty or authority provided the spirit which animated it.[35] Authority was the essence of the polity. By association with the king and his estate *(état du roi),* authority was already referred to as the "state." The reconceptualization of authority in these terms, therefore, could easily result in the parallel reification of the concept of "state" and its equation with the *res publica* or society. For the proponents of the Divine Right doctrine, the king was sovereign in the strict sense of the word: the authority of the king knew no bounds within his realm, besides God and the fundamental law, which in practice meant no bounds at all. Seventeenth-century thinkers would merely draw from this the conclusion that the king was the incarnate essence of society, that, in other words, *the king was the "state."* This radical personalization of the political community allowed the development of fervent devotion to an abstraction that by itself would not be able to claim such loyalty. But the redistribution of power (and the reorganization of social structure) that it necessarily implied bred frustrations which eventually led to a reaction against royal authority and the transfer of loyalty to the (abstract) community itself.

## The King and His State

The seventeenth century concluded the transformation of the French identity (among those who possessed it) from an essentially religious into a political one, which agreed with the lack of religious uniformity and was implicit in the concept of Divine Right sovereignty. It also laid the groundwork for further developments as the articulation of the new character of Frenchness gave rise to different ideas as to what constituted a polity. The stages of this transformation can be clearly distinguished. The substitution of the worldly allegiance for the transcendental (and of the earthly *patrie* for the celestial) took place under that great prince of the Church, Cardinal Richelieu. And in the next reign neither Pope nor Christ could challenge the supremacy of the Sun-King. This clarity is necessarily an advantage of hindsight; matters did not seem so simple to the participants. It should be remembered that religion—and in France, Catholicism—was to remain a factor of crucial importance for a long time to come. The first half of the seventeenth century witnessed a "Catholic Renaissance," which was felt in France more than in other countries. The Court partook in this revival, Louis XIII surpassing in piety all French monarchs since the time of Saint-Louis four centuries earlier. And yet, underneath it all, the relentless thrust toward the secularization of identity continued. It took a long time before Frenchmen realized that they were speaking—an essentially irreligious—prose. Since the discourse never became profane (for one category of sacred was merely replaced by another) and since, moreover, its idiom was borrowed from the Christian Catholic tradition, this change, possibly, was practically imperceptible to the participants. But there is no possibility of mistaking what was happening from our standpoint.

### The State-Building Efforts of Cardinal Richelieu

Frenchness was dissociating itself from Catholicism. This was expressed in, among other things, the self-presentation of the conflicting parties during Richelieu's ministry. Those who stood for the advancement of the particularist interests of France and the war with Spain, which led and represented the forces of international Catholicism, called themselves *bons Français*. Their opponents, who thought that religious considerations should take precedence over everything else, were *catholiques zèlés* or *dévôts*.[36] Of course, the *bons Français* never presented their position as irreligious; instead they claimed that theirs was the true Catholicism, the one that demanded unconditional loyalty and obedience to the commands of the king, for he was the vicar of God. The *bons Français* were sympathetic to Richelieu's efforts (which twentieth-century observers define collectively as "state-building") to ensure and strengthen the absolute authority of the king within the realm and impress the glory of his state on the world outside it. The Cardinal himself would side with either of the two parties, as the circumstances required, but he put the support of articulate *bons Français* (with whom the circumstances required him to side more often) to good use. The goal of the great minister in his collaboration with the *bons Français* writers was to defend his policies, whether anti-Catholic or anti-Protestant, foreign or domestic, as consistent with religion; its end-result was the establishment of the earthly polity as the ultimate good and the source of all values. After Richelieu, the existence of "reason of state" and its supremacy over all other considerations would be no longer disputed.

As Charles McIlwain rightly observed many years ago, it was the doctrine of Divine Right sovereignty which made the argument by "reason of state" possible.[37] To the *bons Français* writers who defended Richelieu's policies against the accusation of irreligion, the proof of their inherently and undeniably religious character lay in that Richelieu was the minister and champion of authority of a divinely appointed king, who was placed in his realm above law, and in the world above the universal Church, because of his direct relationship to God. The royal authority was the source of all values, as it was of all law, and loyalty to the king was supreme piety. A classical expression of this position is found in *Catholique d'estat*, an articulate apology of Richelieu's anti-Hapsburg policies and royal absolutism. "It is because of God's will and on his authority that kings reign," stated the dedicatory epistle addressed to Louis XIII; "kings are the most glorious instruments of divine providence in the government of the world. The ancients who were not flatterers called you *corporeal and living gods*, and God himself has taught men the same language and desires that you be called gods. And since he calls you this, he wishes that you be gods and detests without doubt all who seek to tie your hands, diminish your rights, deny your acts that should be venerated, and attempt to be judges and censors of Your Majesty in things where you have only God as your judge." In the body of the text, the author lamented: "Until this miserable time that has befallen us, it was never a source of blame for a Catholic to love the state in which he was born and to desire its preservation and aggrandizement. It is a monstrous thing for Christianity that it is now an insult to call a man a Catholic of state and *politique*, for whoever is not is a traitor to his country; he is a hypocrite and an enemy of God and his word . . . the enemies of our kings are the enemies of God; they should therefore be ours." [38]

As is clear from this passage, the borderline between direct Divine sanction and divinity was blurred and easily crossed. Not infrequently the idea of king as God's representative was replaced by that of king as God's earthly incarnation. One of the more innocent victims of the pitiless process of centralization of power, which pressed on in the name of God, the Maréchal de Marillac, in his parting words on the scaffold, exhorted his nephew "after God" to serve the king. A *bon Français,* Paul Hay du Chastelet, took him to task for that. What did the culpable Maréchal mean, indeed, advising his nephew to serve the king only *after* God, what but an utterly un-Christian disrespect for royal authority could hide behind thus belittling the exalted position of the king? "The service of God and the king are indistinguishable," declared Hay du Chastelet. "How should we judge a Catholic speaking of his King, reputed to be the most just, pious, and Catholic ruler ever to hold the sceptre, who recommends serving him with the proviso, 'after God'? What can we assume but that such a man had conceived a most malicious opinion of his prince's ardor and piety and that his desire to render him suspect, a secret hatred, desire for vengeance and conspiracy formed against him under the pretext of a cabalistic piety had rendered this man so verbose in death that he took pains to indicate in his last words a distinction between serving the king and serving God?" [39] Good Frenchmen wished to dissociate themselves from such "cabalistic piety." Increasingly, they served the king not after, and not even alongside, but rather as God. And as earlier superior Christianity had been the mark of Frenchness, so now to be French meant to be devoted body and soul to the principles of Divine Right and royal absolutism. "To be French and hate one's king," postulated the author of *Catholique d'estat*, "condemn him, excommunicate him, criticize his religion and that of his council, and seek to destroy his state . . . are things incompatible." To those who failed to recognize the king's infallibility quickly enough, Guez de Balzac retorted: "Is this the way to be French and a faithful servant of the king? Is it not to be ignorant of what one treats and malicious to the utmost point of extreme madness?"[40]

Sacred beings had sacred attributes; the deification of the king implied eventual deification of the king's state. The concept of the "state," originally the mark of kingship, royal authority, in the early seventeenth century was multivalent.[41] It continued to be used in the sense of royal authority, but also referred to the functions of royal government, as well as the territory—the realm—and the people over which this authority was exercised. Royal authority was guided by special laws or motives for territorial expansion and aggrandizement of status and power; these were the chief "reasons of state." Around 1625, a writer considered "majesty, sovereignty, and the government of the people [*l'Empire sur leur peuples*]" as "the most important laws of states." The king, he wrote, "should be more heedful of these laws than of his own life . . . One would not call him unjust if he extended the boundaries of his state. He should do so because of reasons of state and the laws of majesty, and because as soon as he touches the sceptre he swears a solemn oath, solely because he takes it in his hand, to devote all his strength to the preservation and growth of his rule. Whoever doubts this truth is very ignorant in politics."[42] These were principles. On a more practical level, Richelieu advised their implementation in foreign affairs: "We may think of Navarre and the Franche-Comté as belonging to us, since they are contiguous to France and easy to conquer whenever we have nothing else to do."

The state was, therefore, possessed of a special, different-from-Christian, morality. This, again, derived directly from the doctrine of Divine Right sovereignty. Since royal authority, or the king's state, was at the same time God's, the state necessarily became an end in itself and a source of moral values. God's will was inscrutable, but whatever was the interest of the state was God's will. And yet the state was clearly a mundane reality. "Man's salvation occurs ultimately in the next world," wrote the Cardinal perceptively, "but States have no being after this world. Their salvation is either in the present or nonexistent."[43] This world was no longer the antechamber to the one above; the earthly state became the incarnation of the Divine.

Everything that came in contact with the divinely appointed king was sacralized by association with him. "All who approach kings," wrote Guez de Balzac in a letter appended to *Le Prince*, "should seem to us purer and more resplendent because of the radiance that they receive from them. The respect that we give them should extend even to their livery-servants and valets, and all the more to their affairs and their ministers." [44] Balzac's own adulatory treatise (which makes the most extravagant sycophants of the Elizabethan Court look like dilettantes) acquired in his eyes the standing of a sacred text which could not be criticized or contradicted. Those who did not find his book to their taste, he said, were more enemies of his subject than of the work and "more hostile to their prince than to his spokesman": "Whoever finds my prose excessive does not understand the duty of the subject and does not have the opinion that he should have of his prince."

This irrefutable reasoning failed to ensure the popularity of Balzac's book. But the very same argument was used in relation to Richelieu's policies. The minister was not to be contradicted, for an attack on him was, *ipso facto,* an attack on the king. What added weight to this argument was that Louis XIII himself concurred in this opinion. To those who throughout the reign attacked Richelieu as the despoiler of the kingdom, who gave the king bad counsel, concealing from him the true state of affairs and otherwise deceiving him, the king answered that Richelieu's policies were his own, that he knew very well indeed what his minister was doing, and that to assume otherwise was to take him, the divinely appointed sovereign, for a fool: "It is insufferable that cowardly and infamous persons should . . . be so presumptious as to write that I am a prisoner without knowing it, which is to heap upon me the worst possible insult." [45] Richelieu's supporters among intellectuals utilized all the possibilities the royal endorsement offered and articulated its implications. "Those who attack ministers of state spare the person of the king on paper but actually censure and offend him," warned one *vieil courtisan désintéressé.* The scholar Jean Sirmond drew the ultimate conclusion: "Ministers are to the sovereign as its rays to the sun. Even the imagination has difficulty distinguishing between them." This, as was immediately recognized, made Richelieu king. [46] The process was similar to the deification of the king as a result of direct Divine sanction. Alongside the royal person a new reality was coming to existence, a reality which partook in his sacred character and like him was to be obeyed and worshipped. This new reality, the *state,* was intertwined with his being, and yet it was represented by creatures of flesh and blood that were not royal.

The diffusion of the sacred from the person of the king to "his affairs and ministers" was reflected in the extension and relative depersonalization of the concept of *lèse-majesté,* the crime of high treason. In the laws of the sixteenth and early seventeenth centuries, high treason was essentially defined as crimes against the king's person, family, and rule: "nostre personne, nos enfans et nostre posterité, [et] la république de nostre royaume." In *De la souveraineté du roy* by the jurist Cardin Le Bret, the most elaborate treatment of the crime in the legal scholarship of the Richelieu period, high treason was defined in a similar fashion. Le Bret divided crimes of *lèse-majesté* into three categories—defamation of the king, attacks on his life, and plotting against his state—which were justified by traditional arguments. Since kings were divinely appointed, slander against them was blasphemy and sacrilege: "Because sovereign princes being vicars of God, his living images, or rather gods on earth as Holy Scripture calls them, their persons should be respected by us as divine and sacred things . . . so that one may say that when one insults the king, one insults God himself." But the king's life was unlike that of any other mortal "since the prince is the spirit that animates the body of the state"; its loss would mean the destruction of the latter. Le Bret's interpretation of *lèse-majesté,* which still revolved around the person of the king, therefore already presupposed the existence of another end, an extension of the king in a sense, and inseparable from him, and yet such for the existence of which even the king himself was a means.

The Code Michaud of 1629 added to the offenses of *lèse-majesté* the publication and sale of defamatory libels on matters of state, as well as leaving the country without royal permission, contacts with foreign ambassadors, calling assemblies and entering into leagues, building fortifications, and producing or possessing more or heavier weapons than necessary for personal protection. Article 179 of the law stipulated:

> We forbid . . . all our subjects without any exception . . . to write, print or help in printing, sell, publish and distribute any books or defamatory and injurious libels and other writings, either printed or hand-written, directed against the honour and reputation of persons, including Our own person and Our counsellors, magistrates, and officers, as well as those concerning the public affairs, and the government of Our state [*estat*]. We declare all who neglect to comply with the above mentioned regulations, especially in regard to leagues and associations in and outside of the realm: raising and training of troops: building fortifications: communications with Our enemies: equipment, gathering and provision of considerable armies and canons [all subjects of Articles 170–178]: defamation of Our government and state, and Our principal officials, guilty of *lèse-majesté* [and, significantly] traitors to the *patrie*.[47]

This was the letter of the law. In practice, the definition of *lèse-majesté* became even more inclusive. In 1627 François de Montmorency, Comte de Bouteville, a nobleman of exalted standing, fought a duel in flagrant disregard of the royal edict against duels. For this, he was accused of high treason, tried, condemned to death, and executed. Several years later the definition of high treason was expanded on an ad hoc basis to include all those in any way instrumental and loyal to Gaston d'Orléans, the king's brother, and the Queen Mother, who fled the realm, demanded the deposition of Richelieu, and plotted against his government, as well as others who opposed

Richelieu's policies or were associated with those who opposed them. Charged with *lèse-majesté*, the accused were tried by special commissions, as a rule found guilty, and condemned to death.

The state, still in the sense of royal authority (necessarily an abstraction), was thus acquiring an existence separate from the king. It was something which the king, as well as everyone else, was supposed to serve. The king was essential to it, but the two were no longer identical. The state was intrinsically, fundamentally monarchical; it was impossible to oppose the king's state without opposing the king, while loyalty to the king implied loyalty to the state. The state was not as yet an independent object of loyalty, but it was a new object of loyalty nonetheless.

This emergent sphere of the sacred (this new abstract entity) was defined in a way which can only be characterized negatively. It was diametrically antithetical to the definition of "nation" as it had evolved in England. The service of the "state," it must be noted, in this framework did not primarily denote the service of the "general good." Though "public interest" might be mentioned among "reasons of state," these usually referred to the majesty, sovereignty, and glory of the king. It is those ideals that the king was supposed to serve, not the "general good," or rather, "general good" was synonymous with the majesty, sovereignty, and glory of the king. The good of the people over whom he reigned was of secondary, if any, importance; the position was the exact opposite of the one expressed half a century earlier by Hotman. Richelieu's open and complete indifference to the suffering of the people as a result of his efforts to benefit the state was striking. "The aversion of the people [*les peuples*] toward war," wrote the Cardinal, "does not deserve consideration as a reason for making . . . peace, since they are often sensitive to and complain of necessary evils as readily as those that may be avoided, and they are as ignorant of what is useful to a state as they are excitable and quick to bewail the ills that they must endure in order to avoid greater ones." War was indeed a necessary and useful evil, given the minister's definition of public utility. "The people's misery is a disadvantage that passes," advised comfortingly one of his *bons Français* supporters, Achille de Sancy; "a year of peace restores everything. But the gain that has accrued to the king in these wars is permanent. He has restored his reputation through Christendom and has brought fear of his arms to those who in the future would do him violence."[48] That misery they dismissed so philosophically was not, one should note, a temporary shortage of luxury goods or suchlike inconveniences. It was a lack of bread continuous enough to drive people to suicide; in some provinces peasants were reduced to eating grass.[49] But it is incontestable that the glory of the French state grew, and it was the glory of the state that mattered, not the diet of the rabble.

Because the king and his state were inseparable, and it was impossible to oppose the good of the state without at the same time opposing the king, those who could not stomach Richelieu's methods of serving both attempted to reinterpret the notion of the good of the state, and in so doing proposed different definitions of the state itself. The rebellious brother of Louis XIII, Gaston d'Orléans, and his supporters among the intellectuals drew attention both to Richelieu's lack of respect toward traditional relations and privileges, which they called "liberties," especially those of the nobility, and to the misery of the people, which they blamed exclusively on his policies, and seemed to see the state as the polity constituted by these traditional relations, privileges, and people. Related to this tentative redefinition of the state as a polity were the rare and timid reservations regarding absolute monarchy. Nobody questioned the Divine appointment of the king and the legitimacy of absolutism, but those who had not as yet become *bons Français* wished that the king would temper his absolute power, rather than aggrandize it, as urged Richelieu, for whom this was the chief interest of the state. On the whole, the opposition to absolutism, in this early period of its formation, had not yet received an articulate expression, but existed as an inchoate sentiment. In the seventeenth century, Richelieu's views of the state and absolute monarchy triumphed over all others. And yet it was Richelieu's invention of the state as an object of loyalty as sacred as the king and existing alongside the king which later helped to undo the absolute monarchy.

Absolute rulers, and their egotistical state, demanded absolute devotion. The political god was a deity more jealous than the God of Christians, who peacefully coexisted with scores of lesser idols (such as, among other things, kings, social orders, and corporations). The state of the absolute kings, by contrast, wished to rule in the hearts of its subjects alone (that is, the chief ministers and at least the greatest absolute ruler France was to have thought it should), and refused to share them even with religion, be it pretended reformed or the true one. Certainly it had no tolerance for the plethora of lesser loyalties and identities which constituted the fabric of traditional French society. The God of Christians had eternity at His disposal, but the state had no being beyond this world: it had to have all that was its due at once. Absolutism was an aspiring totalitarianism: absolute rule was possible only if all sources of independence—and therefore potential opposition—were rooted out, and divided loyalty bred independence.

To be a good—that is, devoted, patriotic—Frenchman was to be a good subject. To be a good subject meant to be obedient and to leave politics to the professionals. "Obedience is the true characteristic of the subject," wrote Richelieu. Balzac, who was possibly the most unreservedly euphoric of Richelieu's apologists, foresaw the imminent coming of idyllic times when "innovations will be accepted only in colors and fashions of dress. The people will leave liberty, religion, and the public good in the hands of their superiors, and from legitimate government and perfect obedience will come that felicity which political leaders seek and which is the objective of civil life."[50]

The determined expropriation of political power and of the right to participate in government from those who traditionally had enjoyed such power
and participation, which amounted to the reduction of all to the position of
subjects equal before the king in their submission, was detested and ardently
opposed, and provided the main reason for resisting Richelieu as a "tyrant."
This was the chief complaint of Gaston d'Orléans and the high nobility in
general, and the meaning of exhortations to return to the monarchy "tem-
pered by aristocracy." "Arrest his ambition, his malice, and his violence,
Great King," Mathieu de Morgues implored Louis XIII, as if royal absolutism were nothing but the whim of the upstart Richelieu. "Call to yourself
those who by natural right should be near you." [51] But absolutism consisted
exactly in that authority was to be centralized in one source, and nobody
had a "natural right" to share in it.

It was during this period that the state in the sense of royal—central—
government took shape and became a tangible reality. Gradual centralization of authority in France went back to the Middle Ages and had visibly
accelerated already in the first half of the sixteenth century. The Bourbon
rulers inherited the governmental structure built by François I and Henri II
and continued their work. By the end of the reign of Henri IV, the king,
increasingly defined as absolute, ruled with the help of what might be called
a small "central administration." [52] It consisted of several councils, or sections, which divided among themselves the extensive judicial, legislative,
and executive responsibilities of the original king's council (Conseil du Roi
or Grand Conseil). The chief personnel of these councils were the chancellor—the chief justice; the secretaries of state for foreign, military, and internal affairs; and the superintendent, the comptroller-general, and the intendants of finance. Frequently one person performed several important
functions. The central administration also included numerous lesser func-
tionaries such as councillors of state and *maîtres des requêtes,* of whom the
former participated in the discussion of policies, while the latter provided
the councils with necessary information. The members of the central administration held no entitlement to their offices, and owed them, ultimately, to
the royal favor. Among other things, this was expressed in their perception
as "creatures" of the king, who, in turn, was their "protector." [53] Their well-
being (at least in the sense of position and wealth) depended entirely on the
degree to which their services pleased the sovereign, who raised and had the
power to undo them.

Not all of the members of the king's council were thus dependent on him,
though. The great nobles—princes of the blood, cardinals, and peers—were
entitled to participate in it too. Government was their birthright. They did
not necessarily use this right, or at least did not use it systematically, possibly
because the business of government demanded application, which was not
one of the foremost noble virtues. But under Richelieu they were deprived

of the very possibility of using it. The grand nobility had independent sources of status, wealth, and, until recently, power. Its identity was formed by feudal relationships, and its loyalty to the king, who was for the nobles just *primus inter pares,* that is, the first nobleman of the realm, was voluntary. It had no sympathy for the practice of absolutism (although it came to accept its theoretical tenets, developed by the more articulate members of society, and having purely ritual meaning for the rest), and—as so many authors point out—it did not understand the concept of the "state." For most of the *grands,* as, of course, for the overwhelming majority of the people, the state as an entity in any sense separate from the king and an object of loyalty, in the first half of the seventeenth century, did not exist. The nobles had no stake in the aggrandizement of the king's authority, majesty, and sovereignty, and so long as they participated in his government, it was not actually his, and the state in this sense (of a unified central government) could not emerge. Unlike the *grands,* Richelieu, who had the ambition of a great noble, but none of the independent resources which could help to satisfy it, identified with the king's cause. Service to the king, for him, was the only way up, and he insisted that it should be so for everyone.[54] The king, naturally, was in sympathy with this view. The exclusion of the nobility as such from government was in fact an attempt to redefine a power elite as a service elite, separate from lineage and wealth (of which it could become a source, but could not be a derivative), and to create a corps of people whose personal interests would be inseparable from the interests of the royal authority. (Powerful noblemen could be a part of this elite if they renounced their independence and identified with the king—which they would never do.)

Supported by the king and never deviating from the principles of Divine Right sovereignty, Richelieu set out to realize his vision. In this he was helped by circumstances. The factious *grands,* determined to discredit themselves by intriguing against the royal authority, which had been their constant preoccupation since the assassination of Henri IV, and later specifically against Richelieu, succeeded in this undertaking and were removed from the council. Richelieu then replaced them with his "creatures," advancing his relations and friends, and the relations and friends of his friends (that is, people of similar background), to positions of influence. The "creatures" owed him their elevation, and he could count on their loyalty, which was as firm as his own devotion to Louis XIII. The administrators, linked thus into one chain of dependence, acted as one body and had one will, their sole interests being the preservation and aggrandizement of royal authority and keeping all those with different interests out of the king's sight and proximity. The nobles complained that not only were they prevented from influencing the course of the *grandes affaires,* but, in addition, that even their traditional right to attend on the king was curtailed. Richelieu's councillors stood between the monarch and the rest of the world and jealously watched over the attentions of their sovereign.[55]

The trust between Louis XIII and Richelieu, and the king's unqualified support for the tactics and policies of his favorite, resulted in a de facto transfer of certain sovereign powers to the principal minister and in an ostensible confusion of their roles. No such confusion existed either in the mind of Richelieu or in that of the king, but the impression contributed toward the collectivization of the concept of sovereignty, its further abstraction from the person of the monarch, and even the idea that it could possibly exist outside (though not without) him. To the uninitiated it might seem that there existed side by side two powers (even if these were but reflections of one), the king and his government or the "state," which was represented by the collective body of ministers with the principal minister as its spirit.

As royal government was transforming from an attribute or an activity of the king into the state, a collective bearer of sovereignty, it was also becoming a pervasive, everyday reality. To the consolidation of political power in the center corresponded the administrative centralization of the entire realm. To carry out the policies decided on by the councils, the kings, before Richelieu, relied on legions of officials, *officiers* organized in corporations, such as Parlements. *Officiers,* in distinction from the members of the councils (those who were not great nobles), enjoyed considerable independence. Since the sixteenth century, because of the practice of venality, they owned their offices, and a law introduced in 1604, the *paulette,* made the offices in effect hereditary: payment of an annual fee made it possible to bequeath them through wills. By the early seventeenth century there were about forty thousand *officiers* in France.[56] The *officiers* were commoners by birth, but already in this period numerous offices, specifically in sovereign courts, under certain conditions conferred nobility, and soon this large group was to develop into a particular category of nobility, the *noblesse de robe.*

The implementation of royal policies depended on these permanent professional officials; they were entrusted with the everyday actual work of government. But government by *officiers,* similarly to government by nobles, was not, strictly speaking, royal government. On the face of it, the *officiers* represented the royal authority, but in practice they were proprietors of a certain function. They paid for a portion of this authority and considered it theirs to keep and use with profit. Their well-being, in distinction from the well-being of members of the royal administration, depended first and foremost on the well-being of their corporations. Their loyalties were at best divided. Venality of office contradicted the principle of indivisible sovereignty on which the mental edifice of royal absolutism rested, and the *officiers* had little interest in its development.

If the "state" referred to royal government, the *officiers* were not the state.

State-building, therefore, in the French case, implied the construction of an alternative corps of officials. This is indeed what had happened. Richelieu neither inaugurated this process nor brought it to conclusion, but he advanced it so conspicuously that his ministry has been credited with (or accused of) a "revolution in government." His dramatic innovations were not intended as such; they were conceived as temporary measures and thus peacefully coexisted with formal traditionalism. But, though the new wine was served in the old bottles, it nevertheless tasted different, and the *officiers* had no difficulty realizing that its taste did not agree with them.

The twin pressures which burdened the reign of Louis XIII—the internal unrest and the conflict with the Hapsburgs—compelled Richelieu to seek ways to increase the efficiency and accountability of government. Among the methods he resorted to, most had already been tried and all were considered legitimate; what distinguished his ministry was a "spectacular" increase in the use of extraordinary measures, as a result of which they became normal. The most important and thoroughgoing of the changes that Richelieu thus, without intending to do so, introduced was the emergence of the provincial intendants as the ubiquitous representatives of central authority. Provincial intendants were originally special commissioners who served at the king's pleasure and were accountable to his council; they were chosen from councillors of state and *maîtres des requêtes* and sent to the provinces with temporary assignments: to examine the work of a certain court, to put down a revolt, to supervise and ensure the collection of a tax. It was the need for a more efficient and reliable collection of taxes due to the escalation of hostilities with Spain which led to the sharp increase in the use of intendants between 1634 and 1637. Since then, according to Roland Mousnier, the significance of the institution of the intendancy changed. Intendants effectively subordinated or even altogether replaced all financial officials and ordinary judges. Their powers, within the limits of their commissions, were absolute. Everyone owed them obedience and assistance, and their decisions could be appealed only at the king's council.[57] The *officiers* kept their offices, but lost their functions, and with these went income and sources of influence.

In general, the privileged subjects of the French king, great and small, did not like the state which, helped on its way by Cardinal Richelieu, was emerging before their eyes: it deprived them of their privileges. Only the king's power and the fear of punishment caused them temporarily to submit to this innovation, and while they did so, grumbling unceasingly, they did not lose hope of returning to the good old days. Richelieu's death, in 1642, was a cause of public rejoicing.[58] When Louis XIII followed his minister to the grave a year later, leaving as his successor a little boy, hardly five years of age, the *grands* and the *officiers* rose in revolt.

## The Fronde

The periods of minority, when authority was exercised by a Regent in the king's name, rather than by a divinely appointed king, and the government was by definition provisional, opened cracks in the otherwise impregnable wall of legitimacy which protected royal absolutism, weakened it, and exposed it to attack. The central government and its practices were dissociated from the person of the king and could be righteously opposed as a usurpation of royal authority and a perversion of just rule, without in any way implicating in these accusations the young monarch himself (whose innocence, in fact, was insisted upon), or questioning the monarchical principle. Intensified opposition to absolutism during the periods of minority, expressed chiefly in the reassertion of independence by the nobility, was a recurrent pattern in absolutist France: it happened during the minority of Louis XIII and that of Louis XIV, and again, at the beginning of Louis XV's reign. (One unintended result of this was that all these kings, who, between them, ruled France for 164 years, learned early in their childhood to recognize their enemies, and never forgot who they were, which gave these enemies all the more reason to revolt against their successors.) Ideologically, this opportunistic agitation bore the character of radical conservatism: the noble rebels called for the re-establishment of their privileges and an end to pernicious innovations. The *Fronde,* that momentous expression of aristocratic reaction during the minority of Louis XIV, differed from the other two cases only in its scale and intensity. The government temporarily lost control, all its activities were brought to a halt, and the country was plunged into a state of general turmoil, disorder, and misery. "It was the last massive rebellion against royal absolutism in the seventeenth century," says W. F. Church.[59]

If one is to believe the somewhat romanticized account of Alexandre Dumas-*père,* it must have been fun, if not entirely bliss, to be alive, and even more so, young, during those exciting times, especially if one was a member of the Parisian aristocracy. However, besides divertissement for the high-spirited nobility, the *Fronde* offerred little. The *Frondeurs* were moved by the very same particularist motives that in 1789 were to bring what their descendants, in contrast to them, already considered the "old regime" to an end. But they lacked the ideological framework which gave these motives moral luster and fueled the grand event. The *Frondeurs* had no ideal to oppose to absolutism. And thus their revolt remained but a "crusade against all discipline," "a period of impetuosity and turbulence" that had no "creative significance."[60] It was as if a group of actors, indeed predestined to give the great performance, tried to stage the French Revolution without bothering to look at the text of the play.

Yet, when the actors spoke—which happened rarely, for they were busy making merry—their words expressed truly revolutionary sentiments and could be taken from the pages of Hotman's *Francogallia* or out of the mouths of the insurrectionists across the Channel who at that very moment were putting the official seal on their *nationality*. In his *Maximes pour l'institution du roi,* said to be "the most important theoretical justification" of the *Fronde,*[61] Claude Joly expostulated: "Certain persons who are badly informed concerning the rights of the sovereign believe that the people were made for kings, whereas on the contrary it is true that kings were made only for the people. There have always been people without kings, but never kings without people." The power of kings, he insisted, "is not absolute and without limits"; "kings are bound by law," for it is by contract "formed by two equal parts . . . [that] the people submitted to [the king] only on condition that he preserve and maintain the law." The pernicious notion that kings were absolute masters of the lives and goods of their subjects was "insinuated" into their minds by wicked ministers, especially the "alien minister" Mazarin, "in order to gorge themselves with wealth, raise themselves to titles of dukes and peers, and do many other things that are entirely above their birth." These ministers usurped the authority of the kings; they tricked them into waging unnecessary wars, wishing merely "to create confusion in order to find excuses to wring taxes from the people, keep the great nobles away from court in order to be absolute masters there, cause many quick deaths so as to have many offices to fill, and rid themselves of those whom they dislike." (Thus Joly identified the chief targets of the ministers' treacheries.) They also propagated the "accursed maxims" of the "reason of state," as if royal authority had any reason for existence other than the welfare of the people, and any morality other than that of the Gospel. For Joly, the state was not identical with royal authority; nor did he use the term to refer to the institutions of government. For him it meant the community over which the king ruled and for the sake of which he was "made" king, and he bewailed the many ills that afflicted this state, and the uprisings which violently agitated it due to the criminal activities of the ministers.[62]

## Louis XIV

But in Louis XIV, *le Dieudonné,* the Sun-King and the "Grand Monarch," central authority was dramatically reunited with the royal person, and further attacks on absolutism became impossible. The king who could with some reason argue "L'Etat c'est moi" used the term "state" in a relatively (though not entirely) unambiguous sense, consistent with this pronouncement. He was a conscientious ruler, hard-working and devoted to his profession, a truly professional king, one might say, and judging by the pleasure he derived from his work, an artist of his trade.[63] In his *Mémoires* he declared that the interest of the state should always take precedence over the private pleasure of the king;[64] "public duty and private," so it seemed to him, in the case of kings, were inseparably connected. From the moment he ceased to be a child and decided to become a ruler, Louis XIV served the state, yet he was not its servant. In the spirit of Richelieu's etatism, the state was not above him; it was to him what the Holy Ghost was to God the Father. The "good of the state" implied the welfare of the king's subjects only in the last place, and mostly because a minimal degree of the latter was necessary for the pursuit of higher ideals: the grandeur, the glory, and the power, the outward reflection of the king's dignity. Glory was the ultimate "good of the state" and the end of all the king's cares; at the same time, it was the surest means for the further attainment of this end. "Reputation alone often accomplished more than the most powerful armies," noted the king with surprising sociological acumen. "All conquerors have advanced more with their names than their swords." The needs of the state, that is, of the grandeur of the king's rule, necessitated absolutism. "The interests of his [the king's] glory and *even* [emphasis added] of his subjects require," wrote Louis, "that he enforce strict obedience to himself . . . The slightest division of authority always produces the greatest misfortunes." The chief reason for that, in the opinion of the king, seemed to be "the ambition of the great [nobles]," which, if not suppressed, inevitably led to revolts, civil wars, and everyday abuses. "There is no noble," thought the august author, "who does not tyrannize over the peasants." Thus, if authority is divided, "instead of one king that the people should have, they are ruled simultaneously by a thousand tyrants. But there is this difference: the commands of the legitimate prince are always kind and moderate because they are founded on reason, whereas those of these false sovereigns are always unjust and tyrannical because they are inspired by unbridled passion."

Contemporaries of the great king, such as the churchman Bossuet or the jurist Jean Domat, articulated his position, while others, the foremost of whom was Colbert, helped to implement it. Domat's defense of absolutism was rather unorthodox. It was based on two remarkably modern premises: one, that all men were created equal; two, that they were assigned to unequal social positions for their own good, for the satisfaction of everyone's needs necessitated division of labor. The essential reason for absolutism was functional. It was, however, propped by the will of God. Social hierarchy and political power were divine institutions, while the equality of men was merely a creation of nature. In this manner, the traditional considerations of Divine Right sovereignty and the legitimacy it implied were also brought in. The logic of Domat's argument revealed a gifted legal mind: "This necessity of government over men whom nature created equal but who differ among themselves according to the diversity that God established in their conditions and professions demonstrates that government results from His ordering. As He is the only natural sovereign over men, it is from Him that all who govern hold their power and authority, and it is God himself that they represent in their functions . . . Since government is necessary for the common good and God himself established it, it follows that those who are its subjects must be submissive and obedient." [65]

Bishop Bossuet addressed Louis XIV and, apparently, all past and future monarchs in his person, as "gods of flesh and blood," and taught that "not only . . . the rights of royalty are established by His laws but the choice of rulers is an effect of His providence . . . In order to establish this power, which represents his own, God places on the foreheads of sovereigns and on their visages a mark of divinity." Some of the duties of a divinely appointed king, however, were surprisingly mundane. "Carry the glory of your name and that of France," Bossuet urged the king, "to such heights that there may be nothing for you to desire but eternal felicity."

In this framework, loyalty to the king was piety. But, for Bossuet, pious behavior in this world included more than loyalty to the king. In his *Histoire des variations des églises protestantes,* he insisted that Protestantism was "not Christian, since it is faithless to its Princes and to its Country." The *country* was becoming sacralized by association with the king. In his eulogy of patriotism, Bossuet echoed the idealists of earlier times. "Human society requires us to love the land in which we live together," he wrote in his *magnum opus, Politique tirée de l'Écriture Sainte;* "this is what the Romans called *caritas patrii soli,* love of country [*l'amour de la patrie*] . . . It is a feeling natural to all peoples." The *patrie* was defined as "the altars and the sacraments, the glory, the wealth, the peace and the security of life; in one word, the community of all divine and human things." One owed to it, in a time of need, everything one owned and one's very life. The duties toward the king were the same, because the king and the *patrie* were one. "One owes the prince the same services one owes to the *patrie* . . . the entire State is in the person of the prince. In him is the power, in him is the will of the entire people . . . A good man prefers the life of the prince to his own." [66]

The *grand siècle* indeed considered patriotism a noble sentiment. Its great poets carried on the tradition of their predecessors and extolled patriotic sacrifices. Corneille rhapsodized:

> Mon cher pais est mon premièr amour . . .
> Mourir pour le pais est un si digne sort
> Qu'on brigueroit en foule une si belle mort . . .

Without the *patrie* life was not worth living. When the *country* was in peril, one's life was a small price to pay if this ensured its continued existence. So at least thought Racine:

> Quoi! lorsque vous voyez périr votre patrie
> Pour quelque chose, Esther, vous comptez votre vie! [67]

In this poetry, too, service of the *patrie* was frequently indistinguishable from devotion to the ruler. Prince and country were often mentioned in one breath. In times of victory, in particular, French subjects readily identified with their king, whose glory was that of France, and proudly felt French. No doubt, not everyone shared in such pride, even among the educated, who were the most prone to do so. Pascal found patriotism, as it was understood in his time, absurd, and distinguished between the interests of individual subjects and those of the king. La Bruyère juxtaposed *patrie* and absolute monarchy as mutually exclusive: "There is no *patrie* under despotism, it is replaced by other things: interest, glory, the service of the prince." [68] Such things, however, were not said aloud during the greater part of the reign, although they became more common as it drew to its close. Patriotism was a gratifying sentiment in the latter half of the seventeenth century; it was a matter of consensus that the age was a *grand siècle* for France, an age of glory and grandeur; that Louis XIV was the "grand monarch"; and that the *patrie*—the common mother of the king and his subjects—and the king's "state," France and the king, were one.

As long as a polity was defined by the authority it was under, it was indeed difficult to disengage its image from that of the king who was his own first minister. Yet Louis XIV's personal government was accompanied by an accelerated development of the state apparatus, and administrative centralization found its conspicuous expression in the emergence of a disinterested (that is, lacking particular interests other than that in the smooth running of government) bureaucracy. It was by developing the bureaucracy, wrote Georges Pagès, "that the Secretaries of State at the center and the intendants throughout the realm [and, one should add, the king through them] established their power." The intendants, the "thirty *maîtres des requêtes* sent to the provinces, on whom depended their success or misfortune, their prosperity or sterility," [69] though long detested, acquired their lasting image of all-powerful agents of the central government during this period. In distinction from their predecessors at the time of Richelieu and Mazarin, when they competed with *officiers* who still retained important administrative powers, the intendants of Louis XIV dispossessed the *officiers* of their functions and took over the entire administration from the courts. They virtually controlled taxation, shared with governors of the provinces (usually the *grands*) supervision of the provincial estates, and with bishops, of the Catholic clergy, and took from the Parlements "administrative control of the armies, management of local communities, appeals from local courts, the execution of sentences imposed by royal and ecclesiastical courts, evaluation of the advisability of founding convents, primary schools, high schools, universities and reforming these institutions, the policing of religious dissidents and the newly converted, and general direction of the poor law administration, commerce, agriculture, and industry." [70] In short, they governed France, and by the same token, deprived potential opposition leaders of their influence and sources of power. On the whole, the results of the intendants' rule were beneficial. Even Pagès, generally unsympathetic to the centralization of authority, agreed that with them the realm was better administered, and "the common people gained thereby." Yet his assessment of the ethical significance of their rule is unequivocal: "It was the intendants' administration that acquainted the nation with royal *despotism*." [71]

Someone's gain is often another's loss. This was undoubtedly so in the case of French absolutism. And what someone who gained may have regarded as an unparalleled condition of civic felicity was indeed seen by many others as despotism. With Louis XIV absolutism triumphed, but in its very triumph it was (to borrow a metaphor from the turbulent history of another embattled "ism") "producing its own grave-diggers." Some of them were the victims of its forceful—victorious—imposition. The majority, however, were the beneficiaries of the exceeding self-confidence of its proponents and their mistaken notion that it did not have to be forcibly imposed in every area to reign uncontested.

The religious policy of Louis XIV inevitably resulted in the disaffection of Huguenots. The latter represented a major source of independence in France, and it is understandable why the king would wish to suppress them. Given this goal, one can only wonder whether the methods of its achievement could have been less abrasive; as it happened, they were brutal. The alienation of Huguenots was of momentous significance in the development of the French national idea. An oppressed and threatened minority, they were, as once before, during the Religious Wars of the sixteenth century, among the first to indict the system as a whole and to uphold the cause of all its victims. They represented the discrimination against them as but a specific expression of a general pattern which affected the lives of other groups as well; identified these other victims of oppression: nobility, Parlements, peasantry, even the Catholic Church; and stressed the common bond between these groups and themselves. Thus they appointed themselves spokesmen and representatives of the community—the redefined "state" and "people." The "state" was invested with a profound spiritual, in fact religious, meaning by the Crown itself. It had been a recognized sphere of the sacred since the time of Richelieu. Huguenot writers took this creation of the architects of absolutism, this corollary of the Divine Right of kings, and turned it against them. They juxtaposed the community—the victim—to the monarch, the obvious source of their own oppression and, *ipso facto*, the victimizer of the community as a whole.

A Huguenot in exile, probably Pierre Jurieu, left a famous testimony of this revolutionary transformation in the image of social order in a tract entitled *The Sighs of Enslaved France, Who Thirsts for Liberty*. The state,

France, said the author, as a result of a tyrannical rule, unprecedented in its claims on the subjects and disregard for the general good (and in comparison with which, indeed, the ministries of Richelieu and Mazarin looked benign), became undistinguishable from the plebs. The community of France became identical with "the people." "It must first be understood," he wrote, "that under the present government, everyone is of the people. We no longer recognize quality, distinction, merit, or birth. The royal authority has risen so high that all distinctions disappear and all merit is lost. From the heights to which the monarch has been raised, all humans are but dust beneath his feet. By grouping all among the people, oppression and misery have been extended even to the noblest and highest elements of the state." This, in itself, was a depressing development, but, having happened, it changed the nature of discourse and opened important possibilities for opponents of Louis XIV's policies. The "people" was ennobled by the elevated character of those whom royal disregard of privilege made its members. It received an infusion of blue blood, and was mere rabble no more. It was on its way toward sacralization. In this particular case, the de facto equation of the state with the people allowed the author to represent the misery of the people—that is, of the peasantry—as the misery of the state, which had superb potential as a rhetorical device. The policies of the Sun-King, and especially his military undertakings, took a heavy toll on the peasantry, whose prosperity even under lesser exactions rarely transcended bare subsistence. Its misery was in fact shocking. But so long as it was the misery of the peasantry alone, those who, happily for them, were not peasants were rarely shocked by it. The representation of the misery of the people as common misery transformed it into a concern for all, for it made other groups aware of what dangers all were exposed to under a government which treated all alike.

The author of the tract focused on taxation, a burden from which the peasantry suffered most and in the most convincing manner. He explained to his "dear unfortunate compatriots," who, apparently, did not realize the degree of their misfortune, how heavy and unnecessary this burden was, for the money collected in taxes (which in France, according to his estimation, far exceeded sums collected elsewhere) was used to finance the satisfaction of the king's selfish interests and the enrichment of low-born tax-collectors. Such an extortionist policy was unlawful. "Kings," argued the author, once again echoing the sixteenth-century contention, "were established by the people to preserve their persons, lives, liberty, and properties. But the government of France has risen to such excessive tyranny that the prince today regards everything as belonging to him alone. He imposes taxes at will without consulting the people, the nobles, the Estates, or the Parlements . . . in precisely the way that the Moslem princes of Turkey and Persia and the Great Moghul made themselves sole masters of all property . . . I beg you to realize where you are and under what type of government you live." In a striking passage the author decisively dissociated the king from the state. "It sometimes happens," he argued, "that princes and sovereigns exact levies that appear excessive and greatly inconvenience individuals, but are required by what are called the needs of the state. In France there is no such thing . . . The king has taken the place of the state. It is the service of the *king*, the interest of the *king*, the preservation of the provinces and wealth of the *king*. Therefore the king is all and the state nothing . . . [The king] is the idol to which are sacrificed princes, great men and small, families, provinces, cities, finances and generally everything. Therefore, it is not for the good of the state that these horrible exactions are made, since there is no more state." [72]

Two groups remained associated with the king and were also defined as "tyrants and bloodsuckers of the state." The first one was the tax-farmers and financiers. Their early criminalization in the popular consciousness was an ominous sign and did not bode well for those new groups whose status was dependent on their wealth. The second was the upstart ministers whose elevation implied the humiliation of the aristocracy of the blood, "for these newly great who rise from the dust and climb to places besides the throne," claimed the author, "serve merely to beat down and annihilate the ancient houses." The state was redefined as the people, and the good of the state came to mean, emphatically, the public good, yet, clearly, the upright champion of these lofty—and radical—ideas did not think that rising from the dust was morally defensible. It was the good old days, when everyone knew one's place, that he longed for. "Public good" referred to the preservation of vested interests. The king's chief crime was that he had no regard for either of the two. Absolutism was revolutionary, and the old order defended itself against it. But in its desire to effect a counter-revolution and turn the wheel back, it prepared a revolution in consciousness which would make return to the past impossible.

The king's misplaced zeal in the persecution of Jansenists, the tactlessness with which he pursued centralization of authority into the innermost recesses of his *orthodox* subjects' consciousness, was potentially more damaging to absolutism than the alienation of the Protestant minority. Louis's motives in this case are harder to explain. If we are to believe the Duc de Saint-Simon, who reports the following "anecdote," it was not purity of faith that the king cared about. "When M. d'Orléans was about to start for Spain, he named the officers who were to be of his suite. Among them was Fontpertius. At that name the king put on a serious look. 'What! my nephew!' he said. 'Fontpertius! the son of a Jansenist, of that silly woman who ran everywhere after M. Arnould!—I do not wish that man to go with you.' 'By my faith, Sire,' replied the Duc d'Orléans, 'I know not what the mother has done; but as for the son, he is far enough from being a Jansenist,

I'll answer for it; for he does not believe in God.' 'Is it possible, my nephew?' said the king, softening. 'Nothing more certain, Sire, I assure you.' 'Well, since it is so,' said the king, 'there is no harm: you can take him with you.'"[73]

Showing such tolerance toward atheism, the king wished his believing subjects to believe in complete servility. The obligation to sign the Formulary,[74] indiscriminately required of all clerics, had the effect of converting many of them to Jansenism and strengthened rather than weakened the influence of the teaching, contributing to the division within the Gallican Church. This was all the more detrimental to the regime, since Jansenism became associated with the insistence on the right of the lower clergy to participate in Church government. It opposed itself to the coalition of Jesuits and bishops who did not recognize such a right and treated priests as subordinates without any authority of their own, and were backed by the king. The involvement of the Jesuits was particularly compromising for the government because of their ultramontane sympathies: it was now possible to accuse the king's religion of being anti-French. A dogmatic controversy was invested with acute political significance and became a struggle over centralization of authority in religion.

The persecution of Jansenism thus led to the estrangement from the central government of a very broad and influential part of the population, and, as a result, the discontent spread far and wide. In the writings of Jansenists or of churchmen and magistrates who sympathized with Jansenists, "true Christian monarchy" was tied to the idea of "general good," while the absolute monarchy, by opposition to it, was defined as un-Christian. Fénelon, the disgraced but influential Archbishop of Cambrai, whose brand of heresy was rather different from that of the Jansenists, also equated the "true needs of the state" with the "true benefit of the people" and treated "state" and "people" as synonyms. The ominous dissociation between the king and the state, and the substitution of the state for the king as the central object of loyalty, which was to be of fateful consequence for the monarchy, was growing common.

Absolutism encroached on the *society of orders* and threatened and irritated those whose well-being was tied to it and who had a vested interest in its preservation. At the same time, in the "state," a new deity which was its creation and symbolized the new—political—universe of the sacred, absolutism provided its potential opponents with an alternative object of loyalty and focus of social cohesion. It was a lofty ideal around which they could rally and in the name of which (rather than in pursuit of their naked particularistic interests) they could fight the king's authority, while enjoying the agreeable sense of moral rectitude.

The king lived by the laws he had been taught as a child.[75] He thought it was his duty to be an absolute ruler, and sincerely believed that his grandeur and glory were indeed the good of the state. Of course, it served his interest to worship at the altar of his own, inseparable-from-his-person, authority (although many a prince would find the exactions such worship imposed on him somewhat excessive). But it also served the interest of many people who were not kings but were, rather, ambitious men with no props such as birth or riches with which to support their ambition. Absolutism was a great equalizer; it distinguished people by merit among other things and allowed such men to rise from the dust and above their birth.

But it changed the rules of the game, without changing the stakes in it or the game itself; the social structure was relatively unaffected by the radical transformation in the political sphere. The game was zero-sum: if someone gained power and influence, and through them the ultimate reward—status—someone else, by the same token, became that much poorer in this regard. As absolutism created new winners, it also created losers alongside them. Furthermore, and this was its greatest miscalculation, it put the latter in a position to feel their losses acutely and left them at liberty to ruminate over them. The most formidable opponents of the absolute monarchy were not the few articulate men who spelled out the implications of etatism, but the mass of disaffected nobility—whether of race, the sword, or the robe, increasingly recruited from among the *officiers*—whose grievances these men articulated. By wresting power away from the hands of the nobility, the kings and ministers of seventeenth-century France established absolutism de facto. But by letting the nobility be and preserving its privileged social position, they made certain that it would never be accepted willingly. Nobles were growing painfully conscious of the disconcerting imbalance of their situation. Their privileges, no longer connected to any useful function and therefore cut off from the sources of power and influence, seemed to be suspended in thin air. They felt threatened and frustrated. It was this affliction of the proudest order of the French kingdom which led many of its members to transfer their loyalty from the royal person to the state, and as the reign of the "grand monarch" drew to its close, rendered France ready to embrace the idea of the nation.

## II. The Social Bases of the Nationalization of French Identity and the Character of the Nascent National Consciousness

### Turns of the Social Wheel: The Plight of the French Aristocracy

To say that by the 1780s the nobility had become "a marginal minority in the French society, under sentence," and that "in 1789 nobles were the kingdom's Jews," as does Guy Chaussinand-Nogaret,[76] is to go too far. Although legally the second order of the kingdom, the nobility, until the very day of its abolition on August 4, 1789 (and largely on the initiative of its members), remained the first order in terms of social prestige, the unrivaled elite of the country, a stratum above the rest. Membership in it continued to be desired by every socially aspiring individual, and its ways, the model for relentless imitation by the common multitude.[77] Yet there is no doubt that in the century before the Revolution, the nobility as a whole, and most particularly its upper crust, the aristocracy, was uneasy, threatened, and losing status.

In 1707 Vauban estimated that there were 52,000 noble families in France, or 260,000 individuals. D'Hozier's *Armorial général* listed 58,000 "genealogically significant" names, including, it is generally agreed, approximately three out of every ten noblemen, whose number therefore would be 190,000 persons.[78] Half a century later, Abbé Coyer believed the nobility to be twice that large: 400,000. It represented, therefore, between 1 and 2 percent of the population of 20,000,000.[79] According to Chaussinand-Nogaret, in the course of the eighteenth century 6,500 families were ennobled, and at least as many had joined the nobility in the seventeenth century.[80] The psychological implications of such increase, both for the older nobility and for those waiting in the wings, would have been staggering, whatever estimate one subscribed to. This development certainly could not fail to be destabilizing in the highest degree for the top echelons of the order, the aristocracy, that were absorbing most of the new nobility.

Although in principle all noblemen were equal, and the order was uniformly deprived of political power, there existed within the nobility vast differences of status and wealth, and the two hierarchies crisscrossed rather than overlapped, creating an anomic and psychologically disorienting situation. Noblemen were without doubt the richest of the royal subjects, but a majority of the nobility were found among the poor, frequently desperately poor, population. The regulations for the capitation, or poll, tax established in January 1695 make it possible to form an idea of the economic profile of the nobility. These regulations divided the population, according to estimated ability to pay, into twenty-two groups, regardless of legal status. All persons in the first group, who owed in taxes 2,000 livres annually, were nobles, albeit of varied origins, some of them quite recent; they included princes of the blood alongside ministers and tax-farmers general. But there were noblemen in group nineteen as well, those without a chateau or a fief, who had to pay 6 livres, "like craftsmen in second-grade towns who have a shop and employ journeymen."[81] Paupers were exempt from the payment of the poll tax; nevertheless, we know that there was blue blood among them, too. On the basis of the capitation records, Chaussinand-Nogaret divided the nobility into five broader categories. Those paying 500 livres or more (the first four groups of the official twenty-two) and enjoying at least 50,000 livres of annual income, were no more than 250 families (1,100–1,200 individuals, or less than 1 percent), mostly residing in Paris and belonging to the immemorial as well as the newest nobility. The second category, 13 percent of the nobility, mostly provincial, had incomes of between 10,000 and 50,000 livres. Twenty-five percent of the noblemen had between 4,000 and 10,000 livres, which still made possible a comfortable life-style. Below this level frugality was necessary. Forty-one percent of the nobility lived frugally on 1,000 to 4,000 livres a year. But an additional 17 percent had less, 500 livres, and some as little as 50. The poor "gentilhomme de Bauce/Qui reste au lit pendant qu'on raccommode ses chausses" was no figment of imagination. Not included in the taxable population, in garrets and poor-houses, imprisoned for petty debts, or reduced to begging, these nobles led at least as wretched an existence as the poorest of peasants. What could they have in common with a Prince de Robecq whose food bill amounted to 58,000 livres a year and who annually spent more than 2,000 on concert subscriptions, books, and prints, or with a Mme de Matignon who paid 24,000 a year to her hairdresser?[82]

Yet in some ways these noble wretches were superior to many of their wealthy confreres. Whether rich or poor, ancient or new, the French nobility found the conditions of its existence oppressive, and it is hard to say which of the groups that composed it suffered more. While the plight of poor *hobereaux* was economic, the aristocracy, which bathed in luxury, was subjected to a most "cruel anguish of mind," [83] the torture of status anxiety. We might be unable to empathize with the importance the society of orders attached to honor. But, clearly, in that social world, status was dearer than life; otherwise it is impossible, for example, to explain the nobility's devotion to dueling. Only because it conspicuously set them off from the common multitude did the nobles insist so vehemently on their right to be killed or crippled on the slightest pretext; only because of that did they take such offense at the efforts of the Crown, which they regarded as the surest sign of despotism, to prevent them from butchering and being butchered by their equals; only because of that, the moment the government relaxed its grip, would they rush, their swords unsheathed, and resume this worthy pursuit, and value nothing more than the liberty to be in constant peril of violent death and mutilation.[84]

Not all the nobles were equally noble. To begin with, the Second Estate was divided into two "estates": the *gentilshommes* and the other nobles. Only the former were truly noble; they were defined as persons "whose ancestry [had] never included a commoner," but four generations of nobility were generally accepted as equivalent to eternity. An ennobled person became a noble but not a *gentilhomme*. This exclusive category consisted of further gradations of prestige. "At the highest point of human greatness and at the summit of the hierarchy of all who are down here on earth" [85] stood the *gentilshommes de nom et d'armes,* the truly immemorial nobility. The descendants of ennobled persons, who could in the fourth generation become *gentilshommes,* could never attain the dignity of the *gentilshommes de nom et d'armes.* Below them, but still above simple *gentilshommes,* were the *gentilshommes de quatre lignes,* persons whose ancestors of both sexes for three generations at least were *gentilshommes.* Three generations of *gentilhommerie* of the male ancestry alone were a requirement for *noblesse de race.* By the eighteenth century the immemorial nobility whose beginnings were lost somewhere before the fifteenth century represented only 5 percent of the noble population as a whole.[86] As to less illustrious *noblesse de race,* it could probably be met at least as frequently among poor *hobereaux* in the provinces as amidst the glitter of the Court.

Professional, or functional, subdivisions within the nobility were organized into another hierarchy of prestige. The significant division was between military nobility, *noblesse d'épée,* and judiciary nobility, *noblesse de robe.* In general, *noblesse d'épée* enjoyed a higher status than *noblesse de robe;* it was a truer nobility, yet the poorest sectors of the nobility belonged to the former. Both these professional divisions were hierarchies of status on their own right and each had an aristocracy of its own. The aristocracy of the military nobility was composed of the nobles of the Court, those who either lived at the Court and performed functions in the household of the king or the households of the royal family, or those who were "presented" to the king at the Court. To be "presented," one needed to prove immemorial military nobility, at least 300 years in 1732, which increased to 360 years in 1760. However, royal ministers, chancellors, and secretaries of state were exempt from this requirement, as were the marshals of France and knights of the Order of the Holy Spirit. Other persons could be "presented" if the king so desired. By 1789, in Mousnier's estimate, the Court nobility counted 4,000 families, or 20,000 individuals. Of them, apparently, only 942 families had the required proofs of ancient nobility.[87]

The absolutist Court was a creation of the seventeenth century and reached the fullness of its development in Louis XIV's Versailles. This was a truly momentous development. "The establishment of Versailles," remarked an astute historian, "was more important and had graver consequences than any of Louis XIV's wars or all his wars put together."[88] The Court nobility was the apex of the social ladder, a world above and apart from the rest; it was "another country" into which the other residents of France, who dreamed, dreamed of immigrating. But the envied residents of this Olympus led an unhappy life. "There is a country," wrote La Bruyère of it, "where the joys are conspicuous but false and the sorrows—hidden but real. Who would believe that the rush for spectacles, the laughter and the ovations at the performances of Molière and Arlequin, the banquets, the hunt, the ballet, the merry-go-rounds, cover so much anxiety, so many cares and such diverse interests, so many fears and hopes, such lively passions and such serious affairs?" [89]

The Olympians, too, were subject to minute distinctions of rank. At the very top stood the dukes and peers of France. Of course, there were distinctions between them, as well. The princes of the blood, for instance, who were peers by birth, took precedence over other peers. Originally great feudal lords, twelve in number, the group changed its character in the course of the seventeenth century. By 1715 there were fifty-five peerages, most of them new creations dating since 1600. Promotion to this exalted rank was the highest honor the king could bestow on a subject, and those promoted in this fashion usually already belonged to the highest military nobility. In 1650, to the consternation of the *grands,* the plebeian Chancellor Seguier was created a duke, and in 1651 his duchy became a *duché-pairie.* However, Providence refused to cooperate with such whims of absolutism; the Chancellor, although a peer, had no male issue, and his peerage returned to *noblesse d'épée.*[90]

Unfortunately, Providential intervention could not be counted upon at all times, and the life of a duke and peer was not easy. Peers, like the rest of the nobility, were powerless against the Juggernaut of absolutism which stripped them of their influence, leveled their dignities with those of its new creations, and seemed intent on reducing them to the rest of the human race. Before 1667 dukes and peers were members of the Conseil des Parties by right and could participate in government. Then, as Louis XIV was consolidating his personal rule, they sat at the Council only if invited. After 1673 they were never invited. The king carried his resolution to deprive his once most powerful subjects of every vestige of political influence beyond their removal from his councils. It was indeed the most exalted nobility whom he systematically deprived of all useful employment. He preferred to give positions of command to persons of "smaller consequence" (thereby increasing the latter), or to his illegitimate children, the *légitimés,* who were entirely dependent on him. The elevation of the *légitimés* incensed the princes of the blood, dukes, and peers more than anything else, and they never tired of complaining about that. "The rank of [the] illegitimate sons was placed just below that of the princes of the blood, and just above that of the peers even of the oldest creation. This gave us all exceeding annoyance; it was the greatest injury the peerage could have received, and became its leprosy and sore . . . The King was delighted with . . . everything tending to advance his illegitimate children and to put a slight upon the princes of the blood." The "world [was] scandalized" by the determination of the king to marry his illegitimate daughters to princes of the blood. When came the turn of the Duc de Chartres (the son of the king's brother and future Regent) to take one of these maidens in marriage, his father, faced by the "indignity" of this union, was "overwhelmed with shame." [91] But the king had to be obeyed. Repulsed by the shameful birth of his wife, the Duc de Chartres, so it was said, found solace in debauchery. Monsieur, his father, blamed this on his idleness at the Court, the fact that he had no important office to fulfill. He "had wished his son to serve, to keep him out of the way of these intrigues," and pleaded with the king to that effect, "but . . . his demands had been in vain." In his *L'Instruction du Dauphin,* Louis admitted: "I believed that it was not in my interest to seek men of . . . eminent station because . . . it was important that the public should know, from the rank of those whom I chose to serve me, that I had no intention of sharing my power with them." [92] Saint-Simon, therefore, had reason to conclude that "the best of conditions in France is to have none at all and to be a bastard." [93]

Under Louis XIII and Richelieu, and during the *Fronde,* the aristocracy still contested the absolute power of the Crown. Under Louis XIV it admitted defeat and focused all its energies on questions of precedence among the nobles. The irredeemable loss of political influence and standing in the eyes of the king undermined the status of the *grands,* and the obsessive preoccupation of the dukes and peers at the Court of the Sun-King, which cannot fail to appear to us petty and childish, must be interpreted as an attempt to compensate for this loss. Precedence, which in these circumstances had but a ritual value, became the only proof of the nobles' exalted position, and its order had to be adhered to at all costs. The tremendous significance attached to the order of precedence highlights the situation of the French aristocracy under absolutism in the fullness of its development. The great and proud nobles were indeed reduced to the position of children. Denied all independence and treated without respect, they were expending their pent-up energies in intriguing against each other and for the attentions of the ruler whose supreme power over them they no longer dared to contest, and in fear of displeasing him. Their exaggerated concern over formal dignities coexisted with pathetically, pitifully undignified behavior vis-à-vis the king.

Court life was not conducive to proud bearing. A manual for courtiers, Sieur de Chevigny's *La Science des personnes de la cour,* advised utter self-effacement and submission to the will of the sovereign. Among the qualities most necessary for a courtier, it recommended "patience, politeness, and no will at all; listen to everything, and tell nothing. Always appear to be content. Have a lot of friends and very few confidants"—low profile indeed, hardly compatible with the unconditional and uncalculating independence implied in the aristocratic notion of "honor." La Bruyère had good reason to remark that there is no one more enslaved than an assiduous courtier, if not a still more assiduous courtier. Saint-Simon, in the first ranks of those who "basely crouched" at the feet of the first nobleman of the realm, noted with contempt "the servile eagerness [of] the greatest people, the highest in power, and the most in favor." The degree of their obsequiousness, to say the least, is astonishing; they would go to incredible lengths in their voluntary degradation. Of one Abbé de Polignac, the diligent duke reported the following: "One day when following the King through the gardens of Marly, it began to rain. The king considerately noticed the Abbé's dress, little calculated to keep off rain. 'It is no matter, Sire,' said de Polignac, 'the rain of Marly does not wet.'"[94]

Toward the end of the *grand siècle* La Bruyère commented: "A nobleman, if he lives at home in his province, lives free but without substance; if he lives at court, he is taken care of but enslaved." He might have been mistaken in regard to provincial nobility, for there were substantial fortunes among its members, but his opinion of the Court should be trusted.[95] The experience of the Court nobility was that of an indignity as abject as its luxury was extravagant. "I confess," wrote Saint-Simon, summing the situation up, "I can scarce restrain myself when I think on the cruel state to which the late government reduced the order whence I take my life and honor."[96]

Naturally, the degraded dukes and peers had nothing but contempt for the *noblesse de robe*. The Duc de Coislin, a man "of a politeness that was unendurable" and to whose "outrageous civilities" there was no end, earned the admiration of many "people of consequence" for the following deserving action:

> M. de Coislin went to the Sorbonne to listen to a thesis sustained by the second son of M. de Bouillon. When persons of distinction gave these discourses, it was customary for the princes of the blood, and for many of the Court, to go and hear them. M. de Coislin was at that time almost last in order of precedence among the Dukes. When he took his seat, therefore, knowing that a number of them would probably arrive, he left several rows of vacant places in front of him, and sat himself down. Immediately afterward, Novion, Chief President of the Parlement [a *robin*], arrived, and seated himself in front of M. de Coislin. Astonished at this act of madness, M. de Coislin said not a word, but took an armchair, and while Novion turned his head to speak to Cardinal de Bouillon, placed that armchair right in front of the Chief President, in such a manner that he was, as it were, imprisoned, and unable to stir. M. de Coislin then sat down. This was done so rapidly, that nobody saw it until it was finished. When once it was observed, a great stir arose. Cardinal de Bouillon tried to intervene. M. de Coislin replied, that since the Chief President had forgotten his position he must be taught it, and would not budge.

Later, recounts Saint-Simon, "on every side M. de Coislin was praised for the firmness he had shown," and it was "easy to comprehend the shame and despair of Novion."[97] Noble deeds of this nature were necessary to lift the spirit of the exalted nobility, otherwise depressed into a most ignoble servility, and to divert it from the sorry spectacle of its degradation. Where else could they parade their dignity, if not in front of a President Novion who was, perhaps, even more humiliated than they?

For Saint-Simon, in the dawning eighteenth century, the judicial nobility still remained but vile bourgeoisie, the vulgar rich. The *noblesse de robe* was indeed an affluent nobility; the rank of the *robins* was defined by venal offices, whose price, as Saint-Simon rightly observed, far outstripped their yield. The nobility of the *noblesse de robe* as a group was relatively new. The edict of 1600 on the *taille* was the first to stipulate the conditions of hereditary transmission of nobility acquired with office: a grandson became a hereditary noble if his father and grandfather had both died in office, or if they had held it for at least twenty years each and while in it "lived nobly." [98]

This judicial nobility, descended from the *officiers* of the sixteenth century and as late as the Estates General of 1614 still associated with the Third Estate, did not perceive the absolutist aspirations of the Crown as detrimental to its interests until later. Indeed, it was not until later that they became detrimental to its interests. The magistracy owed its privileges, as did many newly privileged groups before it, to the determination of the monarchy to weaken the independent sources of power (that is, first and foremost the feudal nobility, but also groups which had become independent in the course of time). To achieve this goal, the Crown used the device of diffusion of functions and privileges and their redistribution among new elements. [99] It was this periodical redistribution which in the end led to the existence of two parallel and hostile hierarchies in France, one of prestige and the other of power, and to the malaise of status-inconsistency, and opposition to the central power responsible for it, among privileged groups which had been deprived of power. The creation of new layers of nobility, especially when it happened on a massive scale as in the sixteenth and seventeenth centuries, also necessarily resulted in the inflation of noble dignities, which were losing value in proportion to their proliferation. This had become evident already under Richelieu, with *titres de fantaisie*, "Baron" and above, becoming increasingly common. By the end of the seventeenth century, wrote Saint-Simon, "the titles of Count and Marquis have fallen into the dust because of the quantity of people . . . who usurp them; and . . . they have become so worthless, that people of quality who are marquises or counts . . . are silly enough to be annoyed if those titles are given to them in conversation." [100] This devaluation caused anguish to the old *noblesse*, which felt dispossessed, in fact robbed of status, but initially it benefited the officials.

The vintage nobility, however, was not the only one with problems. As soon as the unsuspecting commoner joined the Second Estate—which continued to be the common object of the *roturier* desire—he left behind whatever peace of mind he had had before. The less recent members of the stratum which he so eagerly entered begrudged him every fragrant particle of his "soap for scum," while the government to which he owed his social advancement seemed to amuse itself by keeping him constantly in fear of losing it. The recency of one's nobility weighed upon the soul of a thus-elevated person as a badge of shame which invited and justified the most outrageous abuse. Even the highest reaches of the social hierarchy could not protect the unhappy new creation from it; it is possible that there one was particularly exposed to humiliation.

The Crown unscrupulously used the dignity of the nobility as a fiscal resource in times of need. Letters of nobility had been sold in increasing numbers since the sixteenth century, but at no other time so cynically or on such a scale as under Louis XIV. When the funds obtained from the sale were spent, the new nobles ceased being a source of income for the state and instead turned into a financial liability, for they swelled the ranks of the privileged, exempt from payment of certain taxes, most notably the *taille*. The kings were always ready to correct this lamentable situation and time and again annulled recent ennoblements. The victims of this ingenious exercise, though, often were generously given the opportunity to purchase the right to keep their noble status (that is, to pay for it twice). In the seventeenth century this was a regular occurrence. In 1598 all ennoblements by purchased letters patent in the past twenty years were abolished, and then reinstituted on a second payment in 1606. A 1634 edict again revoked the ennoblements of the twenty years previous to that date. This did not affect those who had acquired their status between 1606 and 1614, and in 1638 the number of such fortunate new nobles was supplemented by those who were created nobles on the occasion of the birth of the Dauphin. Two years later, however, all ennoblements of the previous thirty years were canceled, this time affecting both the buyers of letters patent and those ennobled through other means. In 1656 all ennoblements that had taken place since 1606 were reinstituted on payment of 1,500 livres (not so minor a fortune, especially by comparison with 50 or 100 livres of annual income of some of the nobility) each. In 1664 all the enoblements of the previous thirty years, by purchase or not, were revoked (though some of those granted for merit were reconfirmed). In 1667 the effect of this revocation was extended to 1611 in most provinces. Many of those thus stripped of their nobility were reinstated in it on condition of a new payment. In 1715 all ennoblements since 1689 were annulled. But the same year, already under the Regency, the nobility of all those ennobled by letters patent between 1643 and 1715 was confirmed on payment. Under Louis XIV alone there were nine revocations; his was, admittedly, an unusually long reign, but it was not longer than a life-span of one generation.[101] A new nobleman, unless exceptionally phlegmatic by temperament, could not escape feeling insecure; this brutal teasing must have been very unnerving.

Moreover, it was in the nature of things that new nobility became old with the passage of time, and as it became old, the continued redistribution of privilege, naturally, appealed to it less and less. Soon the judicial aristocracy, as well as the military, saw new creations as an encroachment on their rights, or liberties, and an expression, perhaps *the* expression, of despotism. By the end of the seventeenth century, in spite of all the confusion which had resulted from recurrent revocations and subsequent confirmations of ennoblements, there was no doubt that the nobility of the robe, though perhaps of an inferior kind, was as true as that of the sword. Individual *robins* were ennobled as early as the thirteenth century; in the Parlement of Paris the great majority had been noble since the seventeenth century at least and many were true *gentilshommes*. In fact there were more nobles of ancient families at the Parlement of Paris (7 percent) than in the noble population as a whole.[102] The judicial aristocracy (the *haute robe* or *grands robins*)[103] was already old enough to treat ennobled bourgeois with contempt, and the Parlement became increasingly reluctant to admit them as members.

Only the rich could afford ennoblement through the purchase of an office (that of a king's secretary in the eighteenth century cost 150,000 livres), and the gentlemen of the magistracy were particularly piqued by the pretensions of the new rich. The financiers—bankers and farmers general—were blamed by the *robins,* whose wealth had been made respectable by age, for the economic difficulties of the country and, though admitted to high society, could not marry daughters of the older nobility and were considered by the aristocrats of the robe as well as of the Court as "bourgeois." [104]

Nevertheless, the *robins* did not mix with the *noblesse d'épée*. The relationship between the two aristocracies during most of the old regime was characterized by "reciprocal scorn" [105]; they did not unite until later in the eighteenth century.[106] Daughters of the great military families rarely married *robins,* however rich. La Vrillière, son of Secretary of State Chateauneuf, and himself a marquis, upon his father's death and on condition that the king would give him his father's offices, proposed to take in marriage, without dowry, a maiden of illustrious birth, but impoverished, Mademoiselle de Mailly. The king immediately agreed. The maiden, however, was less than happy. Saint-Simon, who bore witness to the incident, recalled: "There was only one person opposed to the marriage, and that was Mademoiselle de Mailly. She was not quite 12 years of age. She burst out crying, and declared she was very unhappy, that she would not mind marrying a poor man, if necessary, provided he was a gentleman, but that to marry a paltry bourgeois, in order to make his fortune, was odious to her . . . Mlle de Mailly always was sore at having been made Madame de La Vrillière." [107]

*Robins* insisted on the equal worth of judicial and military nobility and resisted the pretensions of the latter wherever possible. The antagonism between the two nobilities was dramatically manifested in the "affair of the bonnet," which concerned the grave question of whether the president of the Parlement should take off his hat while addressing a peer, and whether the latter could keep his headgear on while giving his opinion. The *parlementaires,* as could be expected, in both cases thought not.[108] The dukes and peers were "born councillors" in the Parlement, and this ostentatious display of disrespect only served to increase their dislike of the judiciary upstarts.

The *noblesse de robe* doubtless craved the acceptance of its nobler counterpart: without such recognition its own nobility lost much of its luster. For that reason magistrates added the aristocratic particle "de" to their names, took to dueling, and otherwise cultivated the habits of the Court. In 1715 the Parlement of Paris insisted: "There is only one nobility. It may be acquired differently, by military services or by those of judicature; but the rights and prerogatives are the same, for the robe has its honors no less than the sword." "There is only one sort of nobility," agreed the *grands* mockingly, "which cannot be acquired by judicial services. One may respect merit when one encounters it in magistrates, but as to birth . . . they will never be regarded as other than honorable bourgeois who enjoy the privileges of noblemen." [109]

Thus fighting on two fronts, against the snobbery of the military aristocracy and the impudence of the upstart new nobility, the nobility of the robe also suffered at the hands of the absolute monarchy. The resolute Louis XIV deprived it of the possibility of influencing legislation, reducing the right of remonstrance to that of after-the-fact complaints. In distinction from the Court nobility, however, it did retain an organizational base. It must also be added that the *robins* reacted to inevitable humiliations in a more dignified manner than the obsequious *grands*: since, as a matter of ceremony, the king did not kiss their wives, the magistrates would not appear at the Court.

By the end of the great reign, the aristocracy as a whole had not only lost its battle against absolutism, but hardly remembered that it ever had had the audacity to oppose it. It was humbled; it learned to be submissive. The king to the last piled humiliations upon it. Although exempt from the most onerous taxes, the nobles, like everyone else, had to pay the capitation and then the *dixième;* unless they were princes of the blood royal, they had to begin service in the army in one of the companies of musketeers and afterward pass "through the ordeal of being private or subaltern in one of the regiments of cavalry or infantry"; finally, they had to bear the burden of paying for the changes they wished to introduce in their apartments at the Court, for since 1700 the king refused to cover their cost. In short, to borrow a phrase from a complaint articulated somewhat later, they were "degraded and reduced to the position of other subjects, confused with the very people." [110] Yet the world of the *roture* remained completely unaware of their suffering, and there was never a dearth of volunteers to join this oppressed elite. Robbed of its influence, and threatened by the pressure of *novi homines,* it squandered its energies in squabbles over worthless dignities in a vain effort to preserve what remained of its increasingly insecure position.

It cannot be doubted that the preoccupation with status was foremost in the minds of the French aristocracy as it entered the eighteenth century, and that it was worn out by the petty jealousies which it invested with such vital significance. In 1698 Henri François d'Aguesseau painted a grim portrait of men around him: "Man is always unhappy, both because of what he desires and because of what he possesses. He is jealous of the fortune of others while he himself is the object of their jealousy, constantly envious and constantly envied . . . Such is the dominant character of our century: a general restlessness felt by all professions; an agitation that nothing can appease, inimical to rest, and incapable of work, and above all weighted down by a troubled and ambitious idleness; a universal uprising of men against their condition—a sort of conspiracy in which all are determined to get out of their selves."[111] Louis XIV completed the work of many generations of his predecessors; there was nothing new in his policies, although he pursued them more successfully. In general, as J. H. Shennan rightly pointed out, "what took place in the sixteenth and seventeenth centuries was another turn of the social wheel by which new men seized the opportunity to pursue those dignities and honours held by men who were themselves descendants of new men."[112] Only as the wheel kept on turning, the nobility was broken on it.

The unique predicament of the French *noblesse* consisted in that their increasingly problematic status was the only problem on which they were allowed to focus. They were denied the possibility of nursing other ambitions or employing their energies in pursuits that were less futile. At the Court, as well as the sovereign courts of the capital, they lived, like exotic pets, in a gilded cage, well fed and groomed, but reduced to indolence and boredom, which drove them to seek diversion in ways which they might otherwise have renounced. They felt caged. In these circumstances, the preoccupation with precedence was indeed an attempt to insist on their threatened dignity, on the fact that they were proud men, and not pets. Some asserted their independence differently: they escaped into dissipation. Denied liberty to do or to be anything in the public sphere, they enjoyed it to the full in the privacy of their bedrooms. There was a definite affinity between the rejection of the society which humiliated them and sexual license; it expressed the rejection of the norms (that is, tutelage) of this society in a sphere where audacity was guaranteed relative impunity.[113] This association of sexual freedom and opposition to absolutism had significant consequences: it was perpetuated in the values of the new society which succeeded the "old regime," and sexual freedom remained an important aspect of liberty *à la française.* Neither of these ways of coping with the problem, however, was satisfactory. It was becoming increasingly onerous—indeed ignoble—to be noble in France. By the time the great king died, the situation of the French aristocracy became insupportable, and many of its members were seeking for ways to escape it altogether. What they needed was a new identity.

## The Perilous Escape: Redefinition and Reorganization of the *Noblesse*

Whatever else nobility meant, it stood for social superiority. Yet, defined as it was by birth, the nobility was bankrupt. The time had come to reconsider the bases of status. In the eighteenth century, as the outpouring of literature on the subject testified, the intellectuals among the nobility were doing exactly that. The preoccupation with the definition of nobility, in general, was a response to the growing discomfort caused by the ambiguity of the noble identity, and an attempt to provide the nobility with a more secure basis for its status and assuage its anxiety.

The ambiguity, at least, could be dispelled in several ways. As we have seen, a perfect consensus as to what constituted nobility never existed. Yet it was possible to pretend that it did, and the primacy of the criterion of birth, however meaningless (given the constant onslaught of the new nobles born bourgeois), was never openly disputed. Birth was not entirely self-sufficient; its importance lay in that it was the source of virtue. But it might be said that virtue was generally believed to be biologically determined and, therefore, could not be found outside a certain genetic pool. This seventeenth-century view of nobility was articulated by G. A. de La Roque. Already in the beginning of Louis XIV's reign, Boileau thought virtue as such, whether or not accompanied by birth, to be the essence of nobility. Around the same time, La Bruyère reasoned in *Les Caractères:* "If nobility is virtue, anything that is not virtuous may cause its loss; and if it is not virtue, it is hardly anything at all." [114] On the whole, however, the notion that nobility was based on birth persisted.

In the eighteenth century this view came under vigorous attack, and it is worth noting that its main assailants were gentlemen of the best breeding. In the course of this attack, virtue was defined specifically as patriotic virtue, service to the state, and came to be seen as the sole foundation of the noble status. It was strongly emphasized even in those theories which defended hereditary nobility: their authors maintained the traditional view that birth was the necessary condition for a public spirit and in effect equated nobility of birth with patriotism. Henri de Boulainvilliers, an impoverished nobleman, but of impeccable birth, in the most impressive restatement of the feudal doctrine, argued that the nobility was a race, the descendants of the Franks, those of "the conquerors' blood" and the *Naissance Françoise.* This implied that true nobility could not be acquired, and that it owed nothing to the favor of princes. The justification for the preservation of the privileges of the nobility, was, however, not their blood as such, but the services they for thirteen centuries had rendered to the "state." [115]

The Chevalier d'Arc, the illegitimate son of the Comte de Toulouse, the illegitimate son of Louis XIV, in a book revealingly entitled *La Noblesse militaire, ou le patriote français,* proposed a professional definition: none but the profession of arms, the traditional basis of nobility, conferred noble dignity. For d'Arc, however, heredity alone did not suffice; active service was an indispensable prerequisite for noble status. Common officers who rose from the ranks could acquire it and be treated as equal to gentlemen of extraction; the latter, on the other hand, however highly born, lost nobility if they rejected a military career.

Clearly, neither of these positions appealed to the nobility of the office or those who owed their dignities to anything besides direct descent from Germanic invaders or the trade of a soldier. These newer nobles had their own ideas as to what constituted true nobility. The Chevalier d'Arc's book, in fact, was a response to one of their propositions, expounded in another work published in 1756, Abbé Coyer's *La Noblesse commerçante.* Unlike his opponent, Coyer did not claim that only commercial nobility was nobility worthy of its name, but he did consider commerce as noble an activity as the military, for it was as valuable a service to the state. The good of commerce was the good of France. Besides, most of the nobility, owing to its indigence, was deprived of the possibility of rendering its country any other service. Commerce was the best they could do, both for themselves and for the *patrie.* "The *patrie* expects your service," the public-minded Abbé exhorted his well-born, impecunious (but nevertheless reluctant to follow his advice) countrymen. "Become by way of commerce tutelary gods for your wives and children. Become for the *patrie* the nurturers of its lands, the life of the arts, supporters of the population, pillars of the navy, the soul of our colonies, the nerves of the state, and the instrument of the public wealth." D'Arc was incensed by this proposition: "Commerce cannot be introduced into the nobility without shaking the very foundations of monarchical government . . . the nobility cannot be made commercial without thereby offending the harmonious inequality of ranks . . . and without corrupting the state . . . French nobles, do you want to be rich? Renounce that luxury that degrades you . . . Your ancestors, your virtues, the services you render to the state—that is your true greatness." [116]

Not unexpectedly, it was the poor nobility that was most readily persuaded by the Chevalier. The *hobereaux* did not buy Coyer's argument for the simple reason that they could not afford it. The rest detested wealth in the hands of ignoble bourgeois, who had the cheek to attempt to mix with them, as if indeed money could buy pedigree, but found nothing degrading in luxury, and, it seems, did not disdain commerce, perhaps because they believed, not without reason, that rather than disrupting the harmonious inequality of ranks, commercial success combined with adequately blue blood could be most instrumental in preserving it.

At the same time, the attitude of the aristocracy toward inequality was itself changing. At the end of the old regime, nobility was unequivocally defined as a reward for service rendered to the state, "a quality that the sovereign power imprints upon private persons, so as to raise them and their descendants above the other citizens." Consequently, wrote a contemporary expert, "all citizens can aspire to nobility." [117] Some went further. As early as 1739, the Marquis d'Argenson, in *Considérations sur le gouvernement de la France,* proposed to abolish hereditary nobility altogether and substitute for it a "royal democracy." "Let all citizens be equal to each other," he urged. "We must in fact move toward a goal of equality where the only distinction between men is that of personal merit." [118] Still later, the aristocratic Comte d'Antraigues selflessly assevered: "Hereditary nobility is a scourge which is devouring the land of my birth." The Comte had an annual income of 38,068 livres, but was unable to prove immemorial nobility, and as a result was denied the right of riding in the king's carriages;[119] he was democratically inclined.

The poor nobility resisted attempts to blur the distinctions of birth most stubbornly. "This should come as no surprise," noted the Comte de Ségur, who was by no means poor, reflecting on their pathetic snobbery, "for all these people had were their titles." [120] Toward the Revolution, as is clear from the *cahiers,* even the *hobereaux* came around. But so long as the old regime lasted, the triumph of egalitarianism within the nobility, its elite as well as rank and file, was not self-evident. In fact, the development of the egalitarian ideology was accompanied by the rigidification of honorific distinctions in many areas, which has been characterized as "the feudal reaction." Sovereign courts, most notably the Parlement of Paris, refused to accept newly ennobled persons into their ranks; the royal Court became subject to new regulations which favored old nobility,[121] and commissions in the army were made the virtual monopoly of the *noblesse de race.*

The legal rigidification of lines separating different groups within the elite from each other, as well as the ideological attempts to define the noble identity, were so many responses to the fact that the traditional distinctions could no longer be maintained without legal support, that the traditional definition was becoming meaningless, and that the identity based on these distinctions and definition was in crisis. The legal measures, which necessarily irritated certain sectors within the nobility as they tried to benefit others, were too late and too little to be able to appease at least some of them. The nobility was torn by mutual, crisscrossing and conflicting, jealousies, of which every thinking nobleman was a battleground. In this situation with no solution, to throw a temper tantrum, to say "to hell with it all," was as good a solution as any. In fact, psychologically it was more satisfactory than any other solution both because of its expressive potential and because by declaring one's contempt for hereditary status, one subscribed to a most magnanimous position, thus demonstrating an unmistakable inner nobility.

This momentous change in attitude both reflected and fostered corresponding changes in the structure and composition of the nobility. After the failure of *Polysynodie,* the high nobility of the Court, with the exception of a few die-hard peers, joined forces with the nobility of the robe, speeding up the redefinition of the aristocratic elite along lines which corresponded to the characteristics of the magistracy.[122] One of these characteristics, without which one in fact could not qualify as a member of the *noblesse de robe,* was its superior education. In the eighteenth century the aristocracy appropriated education as a quality peculiar to it. It redefined itself as a cultural elite. If at the end of the seventeenth century a cultivated prince was a rarity,[123] several decades later schooling became a necessary condition for success in high society. New social frameworks, literary and political salons, dining clubs, academies, Masonic lodges, and all sorts of secret and semi-secret societies emerged, which corresponded to the thus-modified hierarchy. As these frameworks became increasingly central in the life of the aristocracy, the importance of the Court decreased proportionally. Provincial academies (with a composite membership of six thousand) were 37 percent noble, those in Paris—35 percent; fifty members of the Académie Française were "presented" at Court; almost all of the important salons were in the houses of the nobility; nobles represented 47 percent of the subscribers to the *Mercure de France* and more than half of those who subscribed to Expilly's *Geographical, Historical, and Political Dictionary of France.* This cultural revolution touched only the upper crust of the nobility. Within the order as a whole, only a small minority was culturally engaged. And yet the relative weight of this minority within the nobility was incomparably greater than the relative weight of the analogous minority within the other participating stratum, the bourgeoisie; the nobility, not the bourgeoisie, was the educated class in old-regime France. Some of the elite concerns penetrated to the rank and file of the order through the Masonic lodges in the army, where officers recruited from the petty nobility formed the largest contingent.[124] It certainly was not, as Tocqueville would have it, that middle-class intellectuals usurped the now vacant "place [the nobility] had occupied in the direction of public opinion," which they were able to do all the more easily because "the French nation was the most literary-minded of all nations and intellectually quickest on the uptake." Instead, as Chaussinand-Nogaret points out, much of the intelligentsia "were recruited from the nobility. Or rather it was more as if the nobility, in this age of doubt and self-questioning, was seeking to redefine itself as an intelligentsia in order to escape the threat of extinction and refound its existence with a new identity." [125]

The emphasis on culture as a definitive characteristic of the nobility was the cause of the social elevation of middle-class intellectuals and the incorporation of the most successful of them into the aristocracy. The *philosophes* were at least as often noble as bourgeois in actual status if not origin; 30 out of 160 authors of the *Encyclopédie* came from the old nobility. Talent became a ground for ennoblement. Middle-class intellectuals mixed with *grands seigneurs* in salons and academies. They enjoyed comfortable incomes and could marry into respectable circles. [126] They were pampered by generous pensions and "cultivated" by noble admirers: 30 percent of Rousseau's correspondents, 50 percent of Voltaire's, came from the nobility. [127] Suard, an editor of the *Gazette de France,* was a friend of the Prince de Beauvau, the Marquis de Chastellux, and Mme de Marchais; the first two sent the *philosophe* and his wife game from their hunts; Mme de Marchais provided carriages to drive the couple to dinners, where Mme Suard was well satisfied with "the rank and merit of the guests." [128] Voltaire's apotheosis during his tour of Paris in 1778—after twenty-seven years of exile—was just one conspicuous example of the changed attitudes toward men of letters. Authors, it was said, acquired "a kind of nobility." [129] The definition of the intellectuals as an aristocracy was not entirely new. Already La Bruyère thought that there were, theoretically, two aristocracies, one of birth and the other of intelligence (both of which, incidentally, he opposed to the "people," ascribing to the word an unmistakable connotation of "plebs"). [130] But in his time this must have been a truly unorthodox thought. In the eighteenth century the claim that intellectuals formed a separate elite "estate" or a part of the traditional elite became rather common. [131]

Against another intruder, however, the nobility stood firm. While it came to recognize culture as ennobling, it would not yield to money. Money could buy nobility, but it could not buy social acceptance. The hard work of "living nobly" (which in the eighteenth century implied participation in the aristocratic culture of the Enlightenment) could earn this, perhaps, but to owe one's place in the elite to wealth was a social disadvantage not likely to be forgiven. Unlike the middle-class intellectuals, the *gens de finance* were pariahs; they became the incarnation of everything that was evil and impure. Even when they were *philosophes* themselves, like Helvetius or Lavoisier, they were compromised by the filthy lucre that passed through their hands, forever marking them as vile, contemptible characters who could (and should) be used by but not admitted amidst the righteous.

Money became the focus of all the pent-up irritation of the nobility, which, having become "enlightened," it could not openly express. It became the symbol of the ignoble, of the invading hords of *roturiers,* unstoppable and closely associated with despotism. It was on money that the rich elite concentrated its wounded pride and vented its fears and frustrations. And this hatred of wealth lost none of its ardor when it happened to coexist, as it often did, with the remarkable economic acumen of the noble anti-capitalists who were busily engaged in capitalist activity.

The aristocratic contempt for vulgar riches capitalized on the long-standing hostility toward tax-collectors among the people, which elite intellectuals articulated and fueled. Works of literature, such as Jean-Baptiste Darigrand's *L'Anti-financier,* published in 1763, called financiers "blood-suckers fattening themselves off the substance of the people." A very successful play by A. R. Lesage, *Turcaret,* represented them as ruthless, unscrupulous, greedy, and, above all, plebeian characters.[132] By the time of the Revolution, tax-farmers were commonly known as "those public bloodsuckers" and considered enemies of the people, from whom they were "stealing." [133]

Out of the impotent ferment of aristocratic reaction one of the most potent revolutionary myths was born: the myth of capitalism. The word "capitalist," a French invention, was first used around 1770 in the neutral sense of a person with capital to invest.[134] It entered the discourse, however, through the work of Louis-Sébastien Mercier. In *Tableau de Paris* the term appeared several times and acquired a highly charged derogative meaning. In 1804, a dictionary, *L'Improvisateur français,* credited Mercier with the invention of the word and relied on his text for a definition. *"Capitaliste,"* it stated, is a word "known only in Paris, and it describes a monster of wealth who has none but monetary affections [*des affections métalliques*]. When people talk about land taxation the capitalist jeers at them: he has not an inch of land, so how can he be taxed? Like the Arabs of the desert who, having robbed a passing caravan, would bury their loot, out of fear of being robbed in their turn by other brigands, so our *capitalists* hide away our money." [135]

Of course, these noble sentiments were not entirely disinterested. Sometimes plain, common envy mixed with righteous indignation. The men of money were resented not only by those whom they so insolently insisted on joining, thereby degrading the very meaning of nobility, but also by those who nursed the same ambition yet lacked the means to finance their own ennoblement. After all, just the registration of the letters of merit involved the round sum of six thousand livres.[136] Moreover, the rich aristocracy, eager to malign the vulgar rich, could not restrain the rage it unleashed and sanctioned only to the wealth of others. The most vehement detractors of capitalism came from among penniless intellectuals who did not make it into the elite. And they hated the rich whose blood was blue as much as the rich whose blood was red.

In general, the intellectuals, both those who became members of the aristocracy and those who felt entitled to be considered its members, made the sympathies and antipathies of the nobility their own. The new status came with peculiar-to-it worries. The intellectuals identified with the order they joined or aspired to join. They also hated independent wealth; they also wanted an exclusive elite. The vehemence of their loathing of money, the intensity of their abhorrence, is astonishing. "The word *finance*," wrote tender-hearted Rousseau unkindly in the *Social Contract*, "is a slavish word . . . I hold enforced labor to be less opposed to liberty." In the *Government of Poland* he explicitly identified money with social degeneracy and went to some length to persuade his audience that this was so: "Rich peoples, in point of fact, have always been beaten and taken over by poor peoples." He implored: "Poles, do this for me: let the others have all the money in the world . . . Systems of finance produce venal hearts." And, with the authority and modesty becoming to a philosopher, he declared: Of all interests "that of pecuniary gain is the most evil, the most vile, the readiest to be corrupted, though also—in the eyes of one who has knowledge of the human heart (I reiterate this with confidence and shall always insist upon it)—the least important and compelling." [137]

Rousseau's concern for the well-being of the serf-owning Polish nobility was as touching as his detestation of wealth was uncompromising. Above all, the intellectuals were preoccupied with preserving the "harmonious inequality" of ranks. Fifteen pages devoted to *noblesse* in the *Encyclopédie*, as compared with two pages for *patrie*, two pages for *peuple*, and thirty-seven lines of one column for *nation*, is an eloquent example of the nature of their concerns. *Noblesse littéraire ou spirituelle* is duly acknowledged there, among *Noblesse immémoriale, Noblesse militaire*, and *Noblesse de robe*.[138] In the history of the members of the Académie Française, d'Alembert asked: "Is a great effort of philosophy necessary to understand that in society, and especially in a large state, it is indispensable to have rank defined by clear distinctions, that if virtue and talent alone have a claim to our true homage, the superiority of birth and position commands our deference and our respect . . . ? And how could men of letters envy or misconstrue the so legitimate prerogatives of other estates?" [139]

The incorporation of the intellectuals was part and parcel of the self-redefinition of the aristocracy, which was no longer satisfied with its traditional identity. Because of it, an articulate segment was added to the embattled elite, able to spell out, elaborate, and draw conclusions from the grievances in which it fully shared. Clearly, the self-redefinition of the nobility implied no intention to step down on its part. Its purpose was to re-establish its social superiority on a firmer basis and make it impregnable. Furthermore, however insecure the aristocracy felt in regard to its status, this insecurity was entirely an internal matter, an affair between nobles and nobles. It was the result of the onslaught of absolutism on the rights of the nobility and of the onrush of the new persons to partake in them; it had nothing to do with the society at large, and the libertine nobles (and near-nobles) who expressed their scorn for the system of which they, however irksome their experiences as individuals, were the chief beneficiaries as a group perceived no danger in articulating and broadcasting their ideas of its imperfections.[140] If they were intellectuals, they participated joyfully in the business of discrediting and undermining their own position; if they were not, they gave it their whole, though light-hearted, support. They found new dignity in their audacity. In a striking passage, the Comte de Ségur described their mood and their reasons:

> We deeply respected the remnants of an ancient order whose habits, ignorance and prejudices we gaily defied . . . We lent enthusiastic support to the philosophic doctrines professed by bold and witty scribblers. Voltaire won us over, Rousseau touched our hearts, and we felt a secret pleasure when we saw them attack an old structure that appeared to us gothic and ridiculous. So whatever our rank, our privileges, the remains of our former power eaten away beneath our feet, we enjoyed this little war. Untouched by it, we were mere onlookers. These battles were mere pen- or word-play which did not seem to us likely to affect the worldly superiority we enjoyed and which centuries-old possessions made us believe indestructible . . . Liberty, whatever its tones, appealed to us through its courage, and equality through its convenience. It can be pleasurable to sink so long as one believes one can rise again at will, and, heedless of the future, we tasted in one draught patrician advantages and the delights of plebeian philosophy.[141]

Enlightenment was noble in more than one sense. It was as much an expression and an instrument of the "feudal reaction" as was the attempted aristocratization of the army; only its consequences were infinitely greater.

Following the studies of Ford, Chaussinand-Nogaret, Higonnet, and most recently Simon Schama,[142] one should not be surprised that the great Revolution which abolished the nobility was the work of the nobility nevertheless, and that the aristocracy, not the bourgeoisie that remained bourgeoisie, was the truly revolutionary class. Tocqueville was mistaken in placing the blame for the Revolution (which, for him, was a calamity) on the bourgeoisie and *bourgeois* intellectuals, as were many others who saw in it a glorious, but essentially bourgeois, event. And yet Tocqueville was undoubtedly right in his analysis of the socio-psychological dynamics that led to the Revolution. Like so much of the seemingly inconsistent behavior of the nobility in the eighteenth century, the Revolution was a result of the "Tocqueville effect," aptly so called by François Furet, who recognized in this the very core of Tocqueville's argument.[143] The rapid disintegration of the traditional order threw the social system out of balance, and the strata composing the elite which were directly affected by it found themselves in a situation of status-inconsistency. The divisions of the traditional order lost their meaning, yet the outward signs of them were jealously preserved. The hierarchy of prestige no longer corresponded to the hierarchies of wealth, education, and power and bore no relation to the responsibilities of various strata toward each other. This growing inconsistency between old and new elements of the social order made its continued survival intolerable. The frustrations this structural inconsistency generated among the members of the old nobility, new nobility, and aspirants seeking, and sometimes denied, entrance into the nobility were of course different. The experience of the old *noblesse* was that of threat to its status and fear of losing what it already possessed; that of the newly ennobled and those waiting to be ennobled, in distinction, might be the fear of never getting what they could expect to possess, or not getting all of it at once, that is, the experience of relative deprivation produced by rising expectations. Nevertheless, all were affected and all alike were suffering from status-insecurity and anxiety. The abolition of the nobility by the Constituent Assembly was not at all, as Chaussinand-Nogaret claims, a sign of fusion of the old and new elites, a simple recognition of, and reconciliation with, an already existing situation. It was, rather, an act of willful destruction, an expression of unbearable irritation with a system which made such fusion at all possible—or, on the other hand, allowed only for an incomplete fusion—and thus became psychologically insupportable. It was the "Tocqueville effect" in action.

The French Revolution—that "first great revolution in modern history"—was, therefore, a child of the aristocratic reaction. There is no contradiction in this assertion; this kinship only goes to show how violent and radical indeed this reaction was. (Of course, this does not imply that the Revolution was only this. Like any child, it soon acquired a character and life of its own, and moved away from its parent, whom in this case it came to regard as an enemy.) The aristocracy tried a variety of routes in its attempt to escape its predicament. The modernization of the elite—its participation in non-traditional economic activity, its prominence in the audience and among the creators of subversive ideology, its support of ostensibly "bourgeois" values in art, literature, and philosophy—all this was an expression of its disaffection from and *reaction* against the modernizing society and absolutist state which undermined its social preeminence. Even the cult of sensibility, relying as it did on the English model, so apparently "bourgeois" and modern in character, in pre-revolutionary France was a reactionary phenomenon. The values which it opposed (the calculating, rational behavior) were those of the stilted absolutist Court and the ideal-typical man of money—the symbol of the encroaching *new men*. The values which it represented perpetuated important elements of the noble code of behavior, repressed by absolutism—the emphasis on directness, courage, contempt for consequences—behavior which was both honorable and imprudent and was epitomized in the notion of "honor." Had the events developed differently, these routes might have led France onto a different course. In the form it assumed and at the time it occurred, the Revolution was not inevitable. Had there been no fiscal crisis—which was quite independent of the crisis of identity among the elite—it might not have happened. But, in its plight, the threatened elite developed an idea that provided the inspiration for the Revolution, and none but this idea could make the Revolution what it was.

The constant threat to its status, undermined by the loss of political influence, the swelling of ranks of the nobility and the inflation of titles, which could be bought for money and made ancient nobility legally equal to a lowborn *officier* barely washed by his "soap for scum," and the contemptuous attitude of the Crown, had dire consequences for the society whose elite was affected in this manner. In the eighteenth century, the nobility was prepared to renounce the formal dignity which concealed the lack of dignity in fact, and ready to reorganize and redefine itself. In the process of such redefinition, it stumbled upon the idea of the nation. This idea was one of several devices the members of the order utilized to protect it from further assault. Once advanced, it acquired a life of its own, and its very success was to doom its noble champions. France as a nation owes its birth to the nobility, which was almost immediately sacrificed to and devoured by its ungrateful offspring. It was hardly possible to foresee that following such an enticing ideal would bring its advocates onto a suicidal path.

## The Birth of the French Nation

The malaise of the French elite was the major factor in the development of the French national consciousness and the emergence of the French nation. It made the aristocracy sympathetic to the idea of the "people" as the bearer of sovereignty and a fundamentally positive entity. This revolution in attitudes was a logical outcome of the situation in which the nobility found itself by the end of the seventeenth century. Its privileges, the significance of which lay in their exclusiveness, were becoming less and less exclusive; of political influence it had as little as any other group in the population; it perceived itself as "degraded," reduced to the "people." There were basically two ways for the nobility to reclaim the status which it was losing: to dissociate itself unequivocally from the "people," or to redefine the "people" in such a way that being of it would become an honor rather than a disgrace. The nobility never committed itself entirely to either one of these solutions, pursuing both all through the eighteenth century. But the second solution, the idea of the nation, had important advantages over the first, and it is not surprising that in the end it was the one that triumphed. It came with its own stratification, which reflected a new hierarchy of values. Within the community defined as a nation, status was based on service to the nation, merit. Unlike the conflicting criteria of birth or wealth, merit made all the groups within the nobility as well as those aspiring to enter it eligible to partake in high status, and, unlike culture, service was self-justifiable.

The realization that the idea of the nation was advantageous in the situation of the nobility brought to the surface and accelerated a subterranean process which had been going on for generations since the sixteenth century, at certain moments more visible than at others, but ever in danger of dying out: the emergence of the "state" as the sphere of the sacred and the new focus of loyalty. This idea was articulated and promulgated by the representatives of the Crown, and by the second half of the seventeenth century was absorbed by the collective mind of the nobility. At the same time, the meaning the "state" had for the authors of the idea, of an attribute and embodiment of the royal authority, and its virtual identity with the person of the king, came under attack. During the *Fronde* and the later years of Louis XIV's reign, the "state" was consistently redefined as the native population of France, or the French nation (in the neutral, literal sense of the word). In the early eighteenth century, spokesmen of the French elite joined to these elements of the indigenous tradition the value attached to the "nation" in England, where it had already become the ultimate source of authority and the object of supreme devotion (though without necessarily adopting the other aspects of the English idea). Thus upgraded, the state, alias nation, alias people of France, was finally freed from dependence on the king and became the symbol around which opposition to the Crown could rally and in the name of which the righting of wrongs could be legitimately and righteously demanded. This amalgam of native and imported concepts became the basis on which the unique idea of the *French nation* later developed.

The effect of the idea of the nation was analogous to that of the doctrine of Divine Right: like the latter, it both caused and signified a dramatic alteration in the meaning of French identity and soon changed the reality of the French polity. "Behind their faces I see other men and in the same realm another state. The form remains, but the interior has been renewed. There has occurred a moral revolution, a change of spirit." These words of Guez de Balzac, written when Richelieu first attempted to represent France as a polity, equally well describe its transformation into a nation. The change was striking and seemed to have come unannounced. "Suddenly," writes Simon Schama, "subjects were told they had become Citizens; an aggregate of subjects held in place by injustice and intimidation had become a Nation." [144] In fact, this process had been under way for close to a century, but it was tortuous, driven more by the desire to escape a certain condition than by a determination to reach a particular destination; and its final outcome was at no point predictable. The revolutionary idea itself was not entirely new. It was superimposed on and incorporated ideas that had constituted Frenchness earlier. The French identity, which in the eighteenth century became national, was a layered identity, and the elements that composed different layers were not necessarily consistent with each other. Moreover, the specifically national component of the French identity, namely the specific meaning attached to nationality in France, was itself a result of a compromise, or perhaps only a truce, between different conflicting tendencies.

### England as a Model

The concept "nation" was imported from England, but it was grafted on a body of indigenous traditions which gave it a unique twist and led the French nation away from the example on which it was initially modeled. The hybrid concept that resulted was further modified by a peculiar tension, a sense of inadequacy, in the incipient French national consciousness, introduced into it by the first nationalists who compared France with England and stressed the latter's superiority.

England was the only nation at the time, and it emphasized its nationality. It was also a country which offered the unusual spectacle of an almost instantaneous transformation from a peripheral, rather backward society torn by internal conflict into the greatest economic and political power in Europe, stable, proud, and enlightened, a formidable presence. For a while, around the middle of the eighteenth century, England was an object of general admiration in France, the state of affairs attested to by Voltaire's *Lettres anglaises* and other works, as well as by the popularity of English gardens and tea. The fashionableness of everything English was, with charming naïveté, expressed by Mlle de l'Espinasse, who confessed: "Il n'y a que la gloire de Voltaire qui pourrait me consoler de ne pas être née Anglaise." [145] The corollary of this admiration was unremitting self-criticism; some westward-looking Frenchmen found little if anything to be proud of in the country of their birth, so much so that sometimes they would rather not consider themselves a part of it. Inconsolate, they sought escape in cosmopolitanism.

The *philosophes* were above particularistic self-content and refused to allow an accident of birth to dictate to them what their commitments should be. Voltaire thought that "a philosopher has no *patrie* and belongs to no faction" and that "every man is born with the natural right to choose his *patrie* for himself." Abbé Raynal believed that "the *patrie* of a great man is the universe." Great men, explained Duclos, "men of merit, whatever the nation of their origin, form one nation among themselves. They are free of puerile national vanity. They leave it to the vulgar, to those who, having no personal glory, have to content themselves with the glory of their countrymen." [146]

And yet these were the architects of the French national consciousness, and it was the *nationality* of England, the "constitution" that made it a *nation,* the political culture and institutions of a free *people,* that excited the admiration of the *philosophes*. The foundations of English nationalism—the reinterpretation of the *people* which implied the basic equality of the great and the small, the glowing symbols of civil and political liberty—became the values of the French opinion-leaders who urged patriotism in the new, English sense of the word.

For a brief period England eclipsed classical antiquity as the model for France. England was the land of freedom. Even Rousseau, though but in a footnote and in conspicuous inconsistency with his general opinion of England, let slip from his pen that "the English of today . . . are nearer liberty than any one else." [147] In the eighth of his *Lettres anglaises,* "Sur le parlement d'Angleterre," the more consistent Voltaire hailed England as the paragon of civic virtues, whose constitution was infinitely preferable to that of Rome. The "essential difference between Rome and England, which gives the advantage entirely to the latter," he thought, was "that the outcome of the civil wars in Rome was slavery, while that of the troubles in England liberty. The English nation is the only nation upon earth that has been able to limit the power of kings by resisting them, and which, by joint efforts, has at last established that wise government where the prince is all-powerful to do good, and, at the same time, restrained from doing evil, where the nobles are great without insolence and without vassals, and where the people participate in government without confusion." Voltaire recognized that the liberty—and strength—of England rested on the respect for the *people,* the "plebeians," who in some crucial respect were treated as equal to the lords. His admiration was not devoid of an ulterior motive. The perceptive *philosophe* was particularly impressed by the consideration enjoyed by the English men of letters. He dwelt on this theme in several of his *Lettres anglaises,* noting that "this advantage is the necessary result of the form of their government," [148] and stressed the difference between the dignified position of English intellectuals and the unenviable-by-comparison state of their slighted brethren in France.

If Voltaire concentrated upon the civil liberty of the English citizens, Montesquieu emphasized their political liberty. His opinion of England was hardly unqualified praise; there is little that is unqualified in Montesquieu. But he did regard England as the model of the free state. The English constitution guaranteed political liberty because of the checks it placed on the exercise of power. This "beautiful system," he claimed, was of Germanic origin; it was "invented in the woods," and therefore originally was as much French as English. But in France it gave way to absolutism. The English, in distinction, had preserved it in its pristine form. This implied that the rights of the aristocracy in England were never infringed upon; respect for its privileges ensured its interest in the liberty of all. "In a state there are always persons distinguished by their birth, riches or honors: But were they to be confounded with the common people, and to have only the weight of a single vote like the rest, the common liberty would be their slavery, and they would have no interest in supporting it . . . The share they have therefore in the legislature ought to be proportioned to the other advantages they have in the state; which happens only when they form a body that has a right to put a stop to the enterprises of the people, as a people has a right to put a stop to theirs." This was exactly the situation in England. The unchallenged preeminence of the nobility did not prevent, but in fact was conducive to, the feeling of fellowship between it and the people. "Those dignities, which make the fundamental part of the constitution, are more fixed than else-where," Montesquieu thought; "but on the other hand, the great in this country of liberty, are nearer upon the level with the people; their ranks are more separated, and their persons are more confounded." Of course, the English had the advantage of an atrocious climate, which made them immune to the danger of enslavement. "Slavery," argued Montesquieu, "is ever preceded by sleep . . . But a people who find no rest in any situation . . . and feel nothing but pain, can hardly be lulled to sleep." [149] Less fortunate nations, like France, were an easier prey for tyrants. Nevertheless Montesquieu believed they ought to make an effort and follow the example of England, for, among other things, the life of the great in it was great, and this was worth a little cut in sleep.

The dignity of the elite, whether plebeian or patrician in origin; the strength of the state; and *nationality* appeared interrelated. And leaders of the French elite cast yearning glances at the greener grass of Albion and popularized the idea of the nation in hope that France would become a nation too. The example of England only accelerated the process of the symbolic elevation of the *people,* inspired by the structural changes within French society; but it was because of England that "nation," rather than "state" or *patrie,* the already charged concepts with a much longer history in France, became the name under which this rising deity was to be worshipped.

### Nationalization of Patriotism

The substitution of a national identity, whose source was membership in a civil society composed of citizens, for one derived from being a subject of the French king was a long and gradual process which proceeded by imperceptible stages. The inherited ideas died slowly. In 1715 the image of the king as the object of supreme allegiance, the embodiment of the sacred, and the state personified still seemed intact. "The king is the visible image of God on earth," asserted the Parlement of Paris that year. "The whole State is in him, the will of the people is enclosed in his will." Around 1750, wrote Daniel Mornet, the new ideas "had barely penetrated life . . . nothing seemed to have changed, or so very little." Yet, in 1754, the Marquis d'Argenson observed that "never before were the names of Nation and State evoked as often as today. These two words were never pronounced under Louis XIV, and one hardly knew what they meant." [150]

The new concepts that reflected the birth of a new spirit may be said to have finally entered the discourse. [151] The spirit manifested itself in print. Inspired perhaps by the translation of Bolingbroke's *Idea of a Patriot King,* anonymously published in French in 1750 under the title of *Lettres sur l'esprit de patriotisme et sur l'idée d'un roi patriote,* French writers busily wrote tracts which exhorted their countrymen to patriotism. The scale of values changed. In 1751 Rousseau devoted an essay to the subject of "virtue most necessary for heroes," in which he urged the French to abandon the vain pursuit of glory, and the show of bravery so characteristic of the noble code of conduct, for *l'amour de la Patrie,* which alone deserved to be considered a truly heroic quality. "The love of glory is responsible for a great deal of both good and evil; the love of the *patrie* is purer in its principle and surer in its effects, and while the world has been often oversupplied with heroes, nations will never have enough citizens . . . No, I will not grant the crown of heroism to the bravery of our fellow citizens who had shed their blood for their country, but to their ardent love for the *Patrie,* and to their invincible constancy in adversity." In his other writings, however, Rousseau saw patriotism and glory not as opposed but as inseparably connected. Grimm, too, regretted that "no germ of greatness, no idea of patriotism and true glory," was to be perceived in the young Frenchmen of his day. This appears to be a representative position. Glory, a legacy of the king's state, was becoming a French *national* characteristic. "Ah!" a citizen was to exclaim later, "how could one be French and not love it!" [152]

While some lamented the lack of patriotism among Frenchmen, a certain Basset de la Marelle, in a work entitled *Différence du patriotisme national chez les Français et chez les Anglais,* contended in 1762 that his countrymen were more patriotic than the English. Some years later C. A. Rossel, the patriotic lawyer, drew a similar comparison between France and Rome, and also concluded that love of country was more characteristic of the former. [153] The humiliating experience of the Seven Years' War stimulated the growth of national patriotism among the French elite and probably contributed to its deeeper penetration into the hardened hearts of lesser Frenchmen. In the literature, the sentiment was glorified. In comparison with it, less public virtues appeared banal. "I think that in establishing the hierarchy of virtues," wrote Condorcet to Turgot in 1773, "one has to put justice, charity, *l'amour de la patrie,* courage (not that of war, which is characteristic of all the farmyard dogs), hatred of tyrants, far above chastity, marital fidelity, sobriety." At about the same time, Rousseau, possibly with an eye to his own immortality, advised his Polish audience: "Imitate the magnanimity of the Romans . . . to shower proofs of their gratitude upon those who . . . had rendered

them outstanding services: foreigners, Roman subjects, slaves, animals even
. . . The men so distinguished should remain . . . the favorite sons of the
fatherland . . . even if they happen to be scoundrels." [154]

## Changes in Vocabulary

The change of sentiment was reflected in the change of vocabulary and was
noticeable as early as 1715. According to a limited but representative
sample of the ARTFL data-base of French literature, between 1710 and
1720, and then again between 1750 and 1760, there occurred a significant
increase in the employment of the related concepts *nation, peuple, patrie,*
and *état,* which signified the transfer of loyalty to the community and the
nationalization of discourse. [155]

Between 1700 and 1710, the word *nation* was used in the literature only
45 times, in 7 volumes out of a corpus of 20. In the next decade it was
employed 106 times, in 12 volumes out of 25. Its use steadily increased,
going up sharply between 1751 and 1760, when it appeared in 990 instances
in 43 out of 95 volumes, and thereafter remaining at this high level. [156] The
word *peuple,* which was used 376 times between 1701 and 1710 in 12 volumes, in the next decade appeared 1,782 times in 19 texts, and after 1760
became even more frequent. [157] The word *patrie* jumped from a low of 34
instances (used sparsely in 12 texts) per decade (1701–1710) to 279 in 14
texts between 1711 and 1720; between 1751 and 1760 it appeared 462
times, being employed in 48 volumes; there were 658 instances (in 61 texts)
between 1761 and 1770, and 806 (in 40 volumes) between 1781 and
1790. [158] A similar increase can be observed in the use of the word *état,* although in this case, owing to the multiple meanings of the word, plain numbers are less helpful. [159]

The four terms were used interchangeably, as near synonyms. In 1690, the
*Dictionnaire universel* of the Abbé Furetière defined *nation* as "a collective
name that refers to a great people inhabiting a certain extent of land, enclosed within certain borders, or under the same authorities." The examples
were the French, the Romans, the Cannibals. "Nation" thus was closely
akin to "people" and related to the state (government) and territory. Every
nation, according to Furetière, had a special character. The dictionary also
mentioned, among other meanings of the word, that of people belonging to
the same profession and "nations" of the university. The separate entry *national* defined it as "whatever concerns an entire nation." [160] The *Dictionnaire de Trévoux* of 1732 added to this definition but an example of "a nation of critics, well-known to every author," and an explanation that the
plural "nations" in the Scriptures refers to infidel peoples who do not recognize the true God. [161] The 1777 dictionary of the Academy, in its definition
of *nation,* emphasized the constitutive role of the state. This "collective

term," according to it, applied to "all the inhabitants of the same state, the same country, who live under the same laws, speak the same language, etc." However, it also defined as a "nation" "inhabitants of the same country, even if they do not live under the same laws, and are the subjects of different princes." [162] The *Nouveau dictionnaire françois* of 1793 reprinted the entry in the academic dictionary, but made an important addition to it. "In France," it noted, "one calls the *crime of lèse-nation* a conspiracy, a plot, or a criminal attempt against the laws and the constitution of the state." [163] Here "nation" was made exactly synonymous to the state and its laws. Interestingly, the illustrious *Encyclopédie,* that loudspeaker of the Enlightenment, in its treatment of *nation* followed Furetière's definition (of 1690) almost to the word, investing it with no particular significance and adding nothing new, [164] while the "historical and critical" *Dictionnaire universel des moeurs,* published in 1772, did not deem the concept important enough to be included in it at all.

The word *peuple* was ascribed two meanings by Furetière's dictionary— the general one, closely related to the concept of "nation": "the mass of persons who live in one country, who compose a nation"; and the particular meaning defined "by opposition to those who are noble, wealthy, and educated" (an implicit recognition of the three bases of elite status). The *Dictionnaire de Trévoux* affirmed this interpretation, paying more attention to the particular meaning and supporting it with a Latin translation, *plebs, vulgus,* and telling quotations from famous authors, such as: "There is a great difference between the *populus* in Latin, and *peuple* in French. The word *peuple* among us does not usually signify but what the Romans called *plebs,*" taken from Vaugelas, and the already mentioned opposition of the *peuple* to the elites of birth and culture by La Bruyère. It also cited several proverbs to the same effect, whose message it diligently spelled out: "Tout le monde n'est pas *peuple;* c'est-à-dire, tout le monde n'est pas sot, ou duppe." [165]

The article "Peuple" in the *Encyclopédie,* written in 1766, was a conscious attempt to vindicate the *people.* It began by stressing the respect for the *people* in classical antiquity and contemporary societies such as England and Sweden. "People," it stated, is "a collective name that is difficult to define since its meaning varies according to ideas, time, place, and the nature of government. The Greeks and the Romans, who knew much about men, greatly respected the people. In their midst the people made its voice heard . . . in all the affairs concerning the major interests of the country . . . in England the people chooses its own representatives to the House of Commons, and in Sweden peasants participate in the national assemblies." The author of the article (Jaucourt) obviously used the term "people" to refer to the rank and file of the population, rather than to the whole, thus staying close to the traditional pejorative meaning of the word. Moreover, following

Coyer (a treatise, "On the Nature of the People"), he observed that in France the application of the term was further narrowed to include only peasants and workers. But, while he accepted this definition, his essay did not share the contempt in which the people thus defined was held in France, but portrayed it as "sober, just, loyal and religious without caring about what it can gain from it . . . the largest and the most important part of the nation."[166]

In the academic dictionary of 1777, one notes that the emphasis had changed rather dramatically; the general, previously neutral, meaning of the word became unmistakably positive, while the particular, derogatory sense, which had been stressed in earlier dictionaries, all but disappeared. Here, "people" denotes "a multitude of men from the same country, who live under the same laws. (The Hebrew people, The Jewish people, The people of Israel, The Roman people) . . . Sometimes the term refers to a multitude of men that adhere to the same religion, whether they live in the same country or not. Sometimes it also refers to the least considered part of the population of a city or a country . . . In this sense one says "mean people" or "low people" [bas peuple] . . . It is often said The voice of the people is the voice of God, that is to say that ordinarily the common sentiment is founded on truth."[167] The entry in the New Dictionary of 1793 was identical. Both the explicit definition and the examples offered made the "people" an eminently respectable entity. It was constituted by law more than by anything else and was the source of truth.

If the people was made worthy of respect, patrie, now closely identified with the state, became an object of passionate devotion in which the members of the people were expected to share. Furetière's dictionary methodically recorded various conventional meanings of the word, without investing any one of them with a particular significance. It had no special relevance; in 1690 patriotism was a sentiment characteristic of the ancients. Thus the entry Patrie read: "the country where one is born, and it refers to a particular place as much as to the province and the empire or the state where one was born . . . the Romans and the Greeks were famous for their love of the patrie . . . It is sometimes figuratively said that Rome is the patrie of all Christians. Heaven is our true patrie, a philosopher is everywhere in his patrie. Patrie is the place where one feels good." By the 1770s this equivocal and tepid attitude was decidedly abandoned. The academic dictionary of 1777 ruled confidently: Patrie is "the country, the State where one is born." The examples of common usage it provided left no doubt as to the proper sentiments one was to entertain toward it. "France is our patrie. Love of the patrie. For the good of the patrie. In the service of the patrie. To serve one's patrie. To defend one's patrie. To die for the patrie. The duty to the patrie is one of the primary duties." The dictionary mentioned that the word was sometimes applied to provinces and cities and that the heavens could be referred to as the "céleste patrie." The 1772 Dictionnaire histo-

*rique et critique des moeurs,* on the other hand, omitted all the meanings the word had had in French earlier and, under the heading *Patrie (amour de la)* treated only the Roman virtue, newly reappropriated and held as a model to the recently-indifferent-to-it Frenchmen. Among other things, the editor of the dictionary linked patriotism to the condition of freedom. "Why," he asked, "did the Greeks triumph over the Persians at Salamis?" and answered, "On the one side was heard the voice of an imperious master driving his slaves to battle, while on the other—the name of the *Patrie* that inspired free men." [168]

It was this connection which was emphasized by the Chevalier de Jaucourt, who wrote the article "Patrie" for the *Encyclopédie.* A vulgar lexicographer, or a geographer not interested but in the location of one or another place, said the Chevalier, might define the *patrie* as a place of one's birth, but a philosopher would recognize that it expresses the significance we attach to the concepts of "*family, society, free state,* in which we are members, and of which the laws assure us our liberties and our happiness. There is no *patrie* under despotism."

Thus interpreted, the *patrie,* with its connotations of participation and liberty, appears to have acquired the meaning corresponding to that of the "free nation" in the English sense, although Jaucourt never made the connection; it seems to refer to the political system and community in which the nation, in the English sense, of the self-governing people, is able to exercise its nationality. The association of *patrie* and freedom could and did lead to universalistic, cosmopolitan attitudes. "The most perfect form of patriotism," wrote Jaucourt, "is to be so fully conscious of the rights of humanity, that one will want to see them respected for all the peoples on earth." [169] But at the same time, patriotism could be particularized. One sees this clearly in Rousseau's exaltation of national specificity: for this friend of humanity was as fervent a nationalist as any, without ever being a French patriot. Scores of lesser luminaries interpreted *amour de la patrie* as love of freedom *in France,* or even love for France without freedom. Furthermore, even when the primacy of liberty as such was emphasized, this notion of political community still took on meaning incompatible with the values implied in the English concept of "nation." In their devotion to the *patrie,* French patriots tended to forget about men. Rousseau excluded them from his definition altogether. "It is neither walls nor men that make a *patrie,*" he explained; "it is the laws, the mores, the customs, the government, the constitution, and the way of life that ensues from all this." [170]

A similar tendency—away from emphasis on the individual—was evident in the evolution of the concept of "state," to begin with much more emotionally charged in the French context. Furetière gives "Kingdom, country or an extent of land under the same authority" as the usual sense of *estat;* its other meanings, according to his dictionary, include "the manner of gov-

ernment in a particular nation," the different orders (estates) of the kingdom, "which were sometimes assembled to correct the disorders of the state,
to cure the troubles of the state." These "estates" are the Church, the *Noblesse,* and the Third Estate, which Furetière defines as *bourgeois notables.*
The word may also refer to assemblies of the Estates General and to "different degrees or conditions of persons distinguished by their functions, offices,
professions, or occupations." (Here Furetière adds an interesting note. "One
does everything," he says, "to sustain one's state, [that is] one's dignity, one's
rank. In France one cannot recognize the state [position] of a person by his
ways, or by his clothes. A comedian or a prostitute has the same dignity as
seigneurs or marquises.") According to the dictionary of the Académie Française of 1694, the word *estat* applied first of all to the "condition of a person, thing, affair"; among other meanings are found (in this order) dignity
or position, office, "government of a people which lives under the authority
of a Prince, or in a Republic," "the country itself which is governed by the
same authority," and finally, in France, "one calls *les estats* the three orders
of the Kingdom, that are the clergy, the *noblesse,* and the People [*nota bene*],
otherwise referred to as the Third Estate." The abridged edition of the *Dictionnaire de Trévoux* of 1762 also defines the "state" as "the empire, kingdom, province, or extent of territory under the same authority" and the
manner of government "of a nation" (adding disrespectfully in this connection: "the reason of state is a mysterious reason, invented by politicians to
authorize anything they might do without reason"), as well as government
personnel and the three orders. (The Third Estate is defined as *bourgeois
notables.*)[171] Curiously, the *New Dictionary* of 1793 adds to these neutral
and equivocal definitions very little. Its definitions of "state" as a polity, the
territory or population under the same government, the manner of government, and government personnel are borrowed from the 1694 academic dictionary. In this treatment there is no evidence of the dramatic change in political discourse, or, for that matter, of the Revolution, which in 1793 was
four years old. The article in the *Encyclopédie,* however, though written in
1756, reflects this transformation and demonstrates the collectivistic and
abstract character of the new French loyalties.

The Chevalier de Jaucourt, the author of the article "L'Etat" in the *Encyclopédie,* begins by discussing the concept in the sense of "the state of nature" and "primitive state of man." Since man is a free being, he can modify
this primitive state, creating thereby secondary states or *états accessoires.*
"There is no secondary state more important," he rules, "than the civil state,
or the state of civil society and government." Jaucourt proceeds to discuss
the "state" in its political sense. He defines it in general terms as "a civil
society, in which [or by which—*par laquelle*] a multitude of people are
united under the authority of one sovereign, in order to enjoy, thanks to his
protection and care, the security and happiness that are lacking in the state

of nature." Among the definitions likely to be known to his enlightened contemporaries, Jaucourt rejects that of Pufendorf, in which the state is confounded with the sovereign, and declares his preference for the one proposed by Cicero: "a multitude of people joined together by common interests and laws, to which they submitted by common accord."

From this Jaucourt jumps to the following momentous conclusion, saying: "We can consider the state as a moral person whose head is the sovereign, and whose limbs are the individual citizens: accordingly, we can attribute to this person certain specific actions and rights that are distinct from those of each citizen, and that no citizen nor group of citizens can arrogate to themselves . . . the state is a society animated by a single soul that directs all its movements in a consistent manner, with an orientation toward the common good. That is a happy state, a state *par excellence* . . . Thus it is from a union of wills supported by a superior power that the body politic, or the state, ensues; and without it a civil society is inconceivable." [172] This is a concept of a polity as an autonomous collective being, possessed of an independent will, different from and superior to the wills of the individuals who compose it and who constitute but cells in the larger organism. Like "nation" in England, it is a polity reinterpreted and glorified, but it is not a nation as an elite composed of rational individuals. It is a rational individual itself, a reification of such a nation, an abstraction.

## The Death of a King

At first it appeared that the community, which its champions named in the English manner a Nation, claimed only a portion in the sphere of the sacred and was content to share it with the king. Patriotism, as of old, was frequently confounded with devotion to the Crown. In 1767, Cardinal de Bernis as yet saw no contradiction between a faithful subject and a free and patriotic citizen. "The trust in the sovereign is the true mark of a patriot," he thought, "to obey and represent [the sovereign's will] with respect—here is the duty of a faithful subject and the way of a free and patriotic citizen." As late as 1787 Calonne still equated "la voix du patriotisme" with "le sentiment dû au souverain." [173] But the borderline between sharing with and the dispossession of the monarch was little by little obscured, and soon the king was expelled from the sphere of the sacred of which the Nation became the sole occupant.

The image of the sovereign Nation, partaking in authority alongside, rather than *in*, the king, which the now bold Parlements incessantly evoked in their remonstrances, presupposed rejection of the Divine Right theory. In vain did Louis XV fulminate against the arrogance of the *robins* during the dramatic *Séance de la flagellation* in March 1766, trying to reassert the principles of absolutism and insisting that "public order in its entirety emanates from me, and that the rights and interests of the nation, which some would make a body separate from the monarch, are necessarily joined with mine, and rest only in my hands." [174] It was to no avail. The Divine Right of kings made no sense to anyone anymore, and eight years later, when Louis XV's grandson acceded to the throne, even the new king did not believe in it any longer.

In the general *cahiers* of the nobility and the Third Estate only a tiny minority asserted the Divine appointment of the king. Those *cahiers* which discussed the question of the ultimate source of authority at all tended to place it with the nation. The *cahier* of the Third Estate of Barcelonette did call Louis XVI a God, but the epithet was used metaphorically, as a compliment rather than as an ontological statement, and was more than balanced by the praise of the Third Estate of Briey, who hailed him as "the most human of kings." The transfer of divinity from the king to the Nation was reflected in the use of the word "sacred" in the *cahiers*. A significant number of them concurred that "the person of the king is sacred," but an equally significant number also attributed this quality to the rights of the nation, of person and of property, as well as to the "security against arbitrary arrest," the "inviolability of the post," and the duty of justice that the king owed his subjects. The *noblesse* of Dourdan, which recognized the sanctity of the king, also demanded that a statement of the rights of the nation be "deposited in the treasury of the Church of Saint-Rémi in Rheims," the traditional place of coronation, with all the dignity of its God-sent and time-honored paraphernalia. [175]

The king who had been God was demoted to the post of the first magistrate of the nation, the foundation stone of the social edifice, then the citizen-king, and finally was deprived of membership in the nation, and consequently of life, as a born traitor. This last degradation was not inevitable; it was brought on by the logic (or rather the lack thereof) of events. But it was made possible by the slow transformation of consciousness responsible for the change in the identity of France and the enthronement of the Nation as the origin of all values. The Nation replaced the king as the source of identity and focus of social solidarity, as previously the king had replaced God. By the time of the Revolution the transformation was complete. "National" became the attribute of everything that had before been "royal"; there were *national* guards and *national* army, *national* assembly and *national* education, *national* domains and *national* economy, *national* welfare and *national* debt. *Lèse-nation* replaced *lèse-majesté* as the crime of high treason. [176] Yet, in a way, the nation France remained faithful to the principle of medieval and absolute monarchy which proclaimed that "the King never dies." It was only a man who expired on the scaffold on a January morning of the year 1793. The king's authority was transferred to the Nation, and with it came the attributes of the king's state—its unitary, abstract character, the indivisibility of sovereignty. The Nation became King.


## Nation, the Supreme Being

In some ways the enthroned nation resembled God even more closely than its deified predecessor. In distinction from the king, who was after all a concrete being of flesh and blood, the French nation—like God—was an abstraction. It was a supreme rational being, worshipped, but on the whole left undefined, and thus appropriately inscrutable. In a monotheistic, even though Catholic, society such as France the coexistence of two supreme deities was unthinkable. The erection of the new cult demanded that the old one be destroyed. And it is not inconceivable that the iconoclastic tendencies of the French elite before the Revolution, and specifically its intense anti-clericalism, had this imperative as their origin.

The concept of the "nation" was imported from England, but in the process was transformed. From a politically charged metaphor, a name for the association of free, rational individuals, it turned into a super-human collective person. In France, the "nation" inexorably tended toward abstraction and reification. To some extent this had to do with the sequence of the development of national consciousness there. If in England "nation" was a title given to a story, in France the title had existed long before the story was written. France (or at least its spokesmen) had wanted to be a nation long before it became one. The French elite adopted the idea of the nation not as an acknowledgment of the changes in social and political structure, which would necessitate or justify the application of the term to France (as this happened in England), but because such adoption might be instrumental in helping it out of its predicament. "We must have a nation for such a grand undertaking," exclaimed characteristically one enthusiast, "and the Nation will be born." [177] In other words, there was nothing in reality to constrain the imagination of the aspiring nationalists, no nation out there to impose its image on their consciousness; the concept was wholly negotiable, and it tended to remain abstract.

The nature of the needs that the idea of the nation was called upon to answer in the two countries determined the ideal relationship between the political community as a whole and the individuals of whom it was composed, and had important repercussions for the political culture it helped to create. In England, it was the dignity of the individuals who composed it that dignified the collective body (and justified calling it a "nation"). But in France it was the dignity of the whole that restored dignity to those who claimed membership in it. In England, it was the liberty of the individuals who composed it that made the nation free. In France, it was the liberty of the nation that constituted freedom of the individuals. In England, the source of authority was the individual, a thinking human being; individuals delegated their authority to representatives, and thus empowered the nation. In France, it was the nation from which authority emanated, and it empowered individuals.

### The Noble Nation and the Exclusion of Nobility

The first attempts to prove that the French nation was an empirical reality (an identifiable group of individuals that merited the title) were at the same time attempts of the nobility to monopolize nationality. According to the *thèse nobiliaire,* the nobility was the bearer of the sovereignty of the polity; it delegated authority to the king, who was subject to the fundamental laws or constitution of the kingdom, of which the nobility remained the guardian.[178] Absolutism was a usurpation of legitimate authority; it violated the rights (or liberties) of the nobility, and this violation implied infringement on the sovereignty of the polity, its enslavement. This identification of the liberty of the polity with the liberty of the nobility in it was rather commonplace at the time: since tyranny was defined as encroachment on the privileges (liberties) of those who traditionally enjoyed them, it followed logically that abstract liberty, its opposite, would be linked with respect to privilege. The nobility liked to see itself as the traditional, and therefore legitimate, governing part of the sovereign nation, and as the latter concept had the connotation of a community of citizens actively participating in government, rather than subjects devoid of will, it was easy to confuse and identify representatives with the entity that they represented. Montesquieu's compelling restatement of the *thèse nobiliaire* in the *Spirit of the Laws,* with its inclusive definition of the nobility that was acceptable to all of its many sectors, was a case of such identification, and the immense popularity of the *Spirit of the Laws* in its day was most probably related to this fact.

Montesquieu, who used the word "nation" throughout his work, both in the sense of a community of citizens and as a neutral term for polity, in several crucial passages made "nation" synonymous with the nobility. He defined it in this manner while discussing the "Origins and Revolutions of the Civil Laws among the French": "Under the two first dynasties, the nation, that is, the lords and the bishops, was often assembled; the common people were not yet thought of. [Sous les deux premières races on assembla souvent la nation, c'est à dire les seigneurs et les évêques; il n'était point des communes.]" Here the nation and the people were clearly distinguished. Occasionally, Montesquieu used the word "people," as well as "nation," as a neutral collective term, referring to the political community, but as a rule "people" was reserved for the lower classes.

.

An important feature of Montesquieu's notion of the nation, undoubtedly influenced by the fact that it was fashioned on the English experience, but also related to the confusion between the nation and the aristocracy, was its concreteness. It was not a reified concept, not the name of an abstract entity; rather, it referred to an identifiable association of individuals. "Their laws not being made for one individual more than another," wrote Montesquieu of the English perceptively, "each considers himself a monarch; and indeed the men of this nation are rather confederates than fellow-subjects [*concitoyens*]." [179] There was no nation beyond the individuals who composed it, and its will was a product of their wills.

In the torrent of pamphlets produced in the year and a half before the Revolution, there may be discerned a similar attempt to reserve nationality to the owners of property (perhaps also manifested in the later restriction— by the law of December 22, 1789—of electoral rights to higher classes of tax-payers). But the identification of the nation with the Third Estate was of an entirely different significance. [180] The Third Estate, as we have seen, could be defined both as "bourgeois notables" and as the People. The first definition might have led to the equation of the nation with the Third Estate, but would exclude from the nation both the nobility and the people. In distinction, the definition of the Third Estate as the People, paradoxically, allowed noblemen to identify with it (explaining the anomaly of aristocrats—deputies of the Third), and it was in its quality of the People that the Third Estate was eulogized and hailed as the Nation by its "bourgeois" members and nobility alike. Rousseau identified the Third Estate with "public interest." Rabaut-Saint-Etienne (or *de* Saint-Etienne) explained: "Take away by supposition the two hundred thousand churchmen in France. The nation still remains. Take away even all the nobility by further supposition. The nation still remains . . . But if you take away the twenty-four million Frenchmen known by the name of 'Third Estate,' nobles and churchmen will remain but no nation." [181]

The People worshipped, however, was not the same as the people actually existing; it was some other—quite imaginary—twenty-four million Frenchmen. And since both the term "people" in its new, lofty meaning and "nation" referred to an abstraction, rather than an empirical reality, the glorification of the People did not necessarily imply a belief in the equal dignity of all those who composed it, the masses and the elite alike. The tacit acceptance of fundamental inequality between them was perpetuated in the distinction made between people and Nation, which persisted, perhaps owing to some kind of linguistic inertia, the lingering memory of the pejorative connotations of the word "people," as late as the inauguration of the National Assembly, [182] and could be met with in the most unexpected contexts.

Who would expect to find contempt for the people, for example, in that harbinger of revolution, the *Social Contract?* And yet the liberty-loving

Jean-Jacques most certainly had no qualms in assigning the masses to the bottom of the social hierarchy, and no quarrel with hierarchy itself. "Thorough equality," he pronounced in the *Social Contract,* "would be out of place, as it was not found even in Sparta." By the social contract, citizens, to be sure, were all equal.[183] But, the oft-quoted definition to the contrary,[184] not every subject of a State was a citizen. In the *Government of Poland,* for instance, writing about "that one of the peoples of our day that [made him] feel closest to the men of old," whom Rousseau so much admired, he identified citizens with only the "active members of the republic, that is, those who are to take part in its government." The Polish Nation, the abstract Sovereign, it appears, was the Polish nobility: throughout most of the book Rousseau uses the two words as synonyms. "Take away the senate and the king," he says, "the knightly order, and thereby the state and the Sovereign as well, remain intact." The voice of the Polish nobility "is the voice of God on earth," for "the power to make laws belongs exclusively to the knightly order," and it is law, as we know, that is "the expression of general will," or "the will of the nation." [185]

This usage is not entirely consistent, it is true, and in several places Rousseau is reminded of "the most numerous part of the nation," that is, first of all, the enserfed peasants, and the burghers of Poland. He believes that to arouse their patriotism, to tie them to the *patrie* and to its "form of government by bonds of affection," would be a good idea. For this reason, he even suggests that Polish nobles think about emancipating their peasants. But he is by no means an unequivocal advocate of this measure. He is afraid "of the vices and slavishness of the serfs themselves"; he cautions: "[Do] not free their bodies before you have freed their souls" (and unless compensation is provided to the owners "by means of exemptions, privileges, and other benefits in proportion to the number of their serfs found worthy of enfranchisement"). Freed people would do better service to the Nation, but masses will always be different from masters. The distinctions of rank should be preserved. Consider Rousseau's reasons in the following remarkable paean to the virtues of physical education, which anticipates the patriotic exhortations of "Turnvater" Jahn:

> Because of firearms, bodily strength and skill now play a much lesser role in warfare than they used to, and so have fallen into discredit. But the result is that the man who possesses the advantage of good birth can now point to nothing within himself that sets him apart from other men and justifies his good fortune, no mark inseparable from his person that attests to his *natural right to superiority*—except for the qualities of mind and spirit, which are often open to dispute [and] turn up often in the wrong place . . . It is important . . . that those who are some day to exercise command over others should prove themselves, from early youth, superior to those others in every sense—or at least try to. More: it is a good thing for the people to be thrown with them frequently

on occasions set aside for pleasure, to learn to recognize them, to become accustomed to seeing them, and to share their amusements with them. *Provided only that distinctions of rank are maintained* and that the *people* never actually mingle with the *rulers* [emphasis everywhere added], this is the way to tie the former to the latter with bonds of affection, and to combine attachment to them with respect.

For Rousseau, thus, people remained "those others," who should be kept from mingling with the rulers who personified the nation. This attitude makes less surprising the explicit defense of slavery in the *Social Contract,* throughout which slave-holding societies of antiquity are presented as a shining model to modern nations, which Rousseau sees as degenerate: "Is liberty maintained only by the help of slavery? It may be so. Extremes meet . . . There are some unhappy circumstances . . . where the citizen can be perfectly free only when the slave is most a slave. Such was the case of Sparta. As for you, modern peoples, you have no slaves, but you are slaves yourselves; you pay for their liberty with your own. It is in vain that you boast of this preference; I find in it more cowardice than humanity." [186]

As the idea of the nation penetrated into the consciousness of educated Frenchmen and began to claim their allegiance as the incarnation of the sacred, nationality was reclaimed from the nobility, and before long the nobility was deprived of membership in the nation altogether and defined as the anti-nation. This followed logically from the abstract quality of the French concept and the tendency to reification, which made the nation as a whole, rather than its constitutive parts, the source of authority. For this clearly implied that any authority not immediately delegated by the people was a usurpation, that historical justification of privilege was inadequate, and a hereditary right to representation in principle impossible. Logical conclusions are not necessarily the same as the conclusions drawn, but in this case the implications were made explicit. In the first place, there was an interest on the part of a particular group to do so. Those who did not yet get a foothold within the elite, though seeking a place in it and believing themselves worthy to occupy it, or those who had barely got such a foothold, could save themselves the trouble of fighting for social acceptance if they defined the *people*, that is, their generalized selves, as the only locus of authority and rejected the claims of the nobility to represent the nation (and therefore its claims to a superior status) as illegitimate. [187] Perhaps even more important was the fact that many of the well-situated members of the elite took the idea seriously, spelling out its conclusions out of pure idealism. It is therefore not that surprising to find among the most fervent supporters of the Third Estate the youthful Comte d'Antraigues, who extolled it (earning the admiration of its electors in Paris, who thought of nominating the patrician for their list) while castigating the hereditary nobility whence he came as the scourge devouring the land of his birth. Gabriel Bonnot de Mably, a scion of a *parlementaire* (namely *robin*) family from Dauphiné, argued that the arrogation of the right of representation, and therefore privilege, by the nobility was a usurpation and "tyranny" equal in kind to the anti-national crimes of which he—and the nobility in general—accused absolute monarchy. Both he and d'Antraigues insisted that nobility, far from being the core of the nation, was an alien body, an impediment to the nation's freedom, a "sort of particular Nation within the Nation." The aristocracy endorsed and articulated an idea that doomed it. As was its habit in that century of frivolous enthusiasm, it "stepped out gaily on a carpet of flowers, little imagining the abyss beneath." [188]

In their selfless attack on the second order, the new noble nationalists were helped by the arguments supplied by those of their fellow-members who attempted to defend and strengthen it, and by zealots of modest birth who wished to see it annihilated. Abbé Sieyès, like Boulainvilliers, represented the nobility as a separate race of men, indeed the Germanic Franks, but drew from this the opposite conclusion. In *Qu'est-ce que le Tiers État?* he defined the nobility as a "people apart, a false people which, unable to exist by itself for lack of useful organs, latches on to a real nation like those vegetable growths which can only live on the sap of the plants they exhaust and suck dry," and asked, why does not the *real nation* "send all these families . . . back to the forests of Franconia?" Another son of the Gallic race, J. A. Delaure, in *The Critical History of the Nobility*, published in 1790, commiserated with his "unhappy people": "You have been trampled under the feet of barbarians whose ancestors massacred ours." The nobility, for him, were "all foreigners, the savages escaped from the forests of Germany." [189] They were not of the Nation, and there was no place for them within it.

### The Philosophical Basis of the French Idea of the Nation: Rousseau's *Social Contract*

The Nation was a hollow, but charged, concept. The image of its referent in the minds of its worshippers remained foggy, but it was obviously one and indivisible, the ultimate source of authority, with a claim on the unconditional and total loyalty of its members. (This loyalty was identified with patriotic virtue and made one eligible for nationality.)

"The Nation exists before everything, it is the source of everything," preached Sieyès in *Qu'est-ce que le Tiers État?* "All sovereignty resides essentially in the Nation. No body, no individual can exercise authority which does not explicitly emanate from it," read Article 3 of the Declaration of the Rights of Man and Citizen. [190] This revolutionary rhetoric drew on the ideas developed during several preceding decades; its idiom, specifically, was that of the *Social Contract*. This work remains the quintessential expression of the French nationalist vision on the eve of the Revolution, although Rousseau was not a French patriot and although the concept "nation" was never used there in its evocative sense, and it was not until later, in his advice to the Poles, that Rousseau translated the original terms "Sovereign" and "general will" into the language of "nation" and "the will of the nation."

The subject of the *Social Contract* is society as such. The contract is concluded by men when the preservation of the state of nature is no longer feasible, and society, or civil state, is its product. The clauses of the social contract, says Rousseau, "may be reduced to one—the total alienation of each associate with all his rights, to the whole community . . . alienation without reserve." As the personalities of the contracting parties dissolve, "at once, in place of the individual personality of each contracting party, this act of association creates a moral and collective body, composed of as many members as the assembly contains voters, and receiving from this act its unity, its common identity, its life, and its will. This public person, so formed by the union of all other persons, formerly took the name of city, and now takes that of Republic or body politic; it is called by its members State when passive, Sovereign when active, and Power when compared with others like itself. Those who are associated in it take collectively the name of people, and severally are called citizens, as sharing in sovereign power, and subjects, as being under the laws of the State." "Each of us," says Rousseau, "puts his person and his power in common under the supreme direction of the general will." The exercise of the general will, he defines, is Sovereignty.

The passage from the state of nature to the civil state is the source—and meaning—of morality. Society (body politic, Republic, State, Sovereign, or People) is law unto itself. All authority, all values emanate from it. It is, by definition, infallible. "The Sovereign, merely by virtue of what it is, is always what it should be," says Rousseau. "The general will is always right." A piquant corollary of this is Rousseau's acceptance of the "reason of state" argumentation: "There neither is nor can be any kind of fundamental law binding on the body of the people—not even the social contract itself." As Rousseau moves toward an essentially conservative and authoritarian position similar to that of the seventeenth-century advocates of the "reason of state" doctrine, he, like the latter, concludes that obedience is the proper characteristic of the citizen in his relationship with the Sovereign. Anything else is simply ruled out. "The Sovereign," says Rousseau, "being formed wholly of the individuals who compose it, neither has nor can have any interest contrary to theirs; and consequently the sovereign power need give no guarantee to its subjects, because it is impossible for the body to hurt all its members." And, as behooves a great mind, contemptuous of evidence (such as divers precursors of the guillotine), he insists that "it cannot hurt any [of its members] in particular" either. As to the individual members who fail to appreciate the state of bliss in which they exist, Rousseau's verdict is unequivocal: "Whoever refuses to obey the general will shall be compelled to do so by the whole body. This means nothing else than that he will be forced to be free."

The implications of this already alarming statement are even more disconcerting, since the general will, as we learn, is not necessarily unanimous, and while the "people is never corrupted . . . it is often deceived" as to what is good for it. "There is often a great deal of difference," cautions Rousseau, "between the will of all and the general will." While general will is the expression of common interest, the will of all is just a sum of particular interests. To ensure the expression of the former, rather than the latter, Rousseau advocates nothing less than a totalitarian state with no intermediate bodies between the central power and the mass of atomized individuals: "It is . . . essential . . . that there be no partial societies within the State, and that each citizen think only his own thoughts." It is not difficult to recognize in the obsession of the revolutionary era with *unity,* in the incessant calls for the erosion of distinctions between classes and provinces, precisely this concern of Rousseau.

Sovereignty—the authority of the collective being which is the State—is inalienable and indivisible, "for the will either is or is not general." For this reason, it cannot be proposed or even represented by any body which is smaller than the whole. Rousseau explicitly rejects the idea of representation as the invention of feudalism, "that iniquitous and absurd system which degrades humanity and dishonors the name of man." Yet, if no amount of particular wills constitute the general will, how is it to be known? To this Rousseau gives an answer which would satisfy the aristocracy, for it lets it in, appropriately defeudalized, through the back, yet capacious, door. First, he says, "the general will is always in the right, but the judgment which guides it is not always enlightened. It must be made to see objects as they are, and sometimes as they ought to appear to it . . . The individuals see the good they reject; the public wills the good it does not see. All stand equally in need of guidance. The former must be compelled to bring their wills into conformity with their reason: the latter must be taught to know what it wills . . . This makes the legislator necessary." The legislator, whose mission—legislation—"is at the highest possible point of perfection," is a special person, endowed with a "great soul" and reason "above the range of the common herd." He has the capacity to reveal to the multitude the general will ("law being purely the declaration of the general will") and in doing so is justified even in duping the people and presenting it in a religious idiom as divine revelation ("in order to sustain by divine authority those whom human prudence cannot move"). In the service of so great a cause anything is permissible, for, after all, "there are a thousand kinds of ideas which it is impossible to translate into popular language," and yet the dumb masses must be moved.

Second, while representation in legislation is unthinkable, the people may and should be represented in government. Government is "an intermediate body set up between the subjects and the Sovereign, to secure their mutual correspondence, charged with the execution of the laws and the maintenance of liberty, both civil and political." The government, like society or State, is also "a moral person endowed with certain qualities"; it is "on a small scale what the body politic which includes it is on a great one." The type of government most perfectly corresponding to the essence of society would be democracy, but perfection, unfortunately, is not the share of mortal men. "Where there is a people of gods," decrees Rousseau, "their government would be democratic. So perfect a government is not for men." The best *possible* government, he declares, is aristocracy. There are "three sorts of aristocracy—natural, elective, and hereditary. The first is only for simple peoples; the third is the worst of all governments; the second is the best, and it is aristocracy properly so called." The merits of aristocratic government are the following: "By this means uprightness, understanding, experience, and all other claims to preeminence and public esteem become so many further guarantees of wise government. Moreover, assemblies are more easily held, affairs better discussed and carried out with more order and diligence, and the credit of the State is better sustained abroad by venerable senators than by a multitude that is unknown and despised. In a word, it is the best and most natural arrangement that the wisest should govern the many." [191] So much for equality.

Rousseau's concept of society closely corresponded to the concept of the Divine Right "state" elaborated under Richelieu; it was its abstract and generalized descendant. The principles of the *Social Contract* were embraced by the pioneers of French nationalism lock, stock, and barrel; Rousseau himself, as was noted above, gave his theory a *national* flavor in the *Government of Poland*. By way of estrangement of a native idea and its return under a new name, the concept "nation" was brought and placed solidly within the fold of the French political tradition; and while the state was nationalized, the nation that emerged was destined to be profoundly etatist. Through the idea of the indivisible and sovereign general will—or the will of the nation—it was conceptualized as an autonomous entity, existing above and independently of the wills of its individual members and dominating their wills. This, in turn, changed the meaning of citizenship, which could no longer be understood as active participation in the formulation of the collective policy that presumably expressed the general will, but became limited to the willingness to carry it out. Good, that is, patriotic, citizens were those who served their Nation zealously, even if the only zeal its will allowed was that of servility. Above all, patriotism implied complete renunciation of self, the effacement of the private in front of the public. Civil liberty lost much of its meaning, while political liberty, which was emphasized, came to designate the unobstructed realization of the general will. In the *Social Contract*, Rousseau defined "civil liberty" by opposition to "natural liberty," which was closely related to "an unlimited right to everything [an individual] tries to get and succeeds in getting." The central characteristic of "civil liberty," by contrast, was that it was "limited by the general will." This limitation, however, only increased its value, making liberty "moral," which was liberty proper. "We might, over and above all this, add, to what man acquires in the civil state, moral liberty, which alone makes him truly master of himself; for the mere impulse of appetite is slavery, while obedience to a law which we prescribe to ourselves is liberty." [192] The will of the nation was to preserve itself. In the *Social Contract,* this self-preservation presupposed autonomy. But in the *Government of Poland,* liberty was more specifically associated with particularism, while the lack of *national* character fostered servitude.[193] The will of the Nation was to speak through an elite of virtue—the legislator and the elective aristocracy, whom Rousseau sometimes confused with the Nation itself—thus modifying the meaning of the concept of equality as well.

The concept of the elite of virtue, as well as that of intelligence—the select few to whom the objective laws of the natural and right social order were "evident"—were contributed to the French national tradition by Physiocrats and Neo-Physiocrats, the group that Tocqueville singled out as the quintessential example of the revolutionary ideology. Both notions appeared in Condorcet, in an essay written in 1788, "Sur la constitution et les fonctions des assemblées provinciales." Condorcet's verdict was unequivocal: the people could not be entrusted with managing its own affairs. "It's not in the least for the benefit of the superior classes, it's for the benefit of the people itself that one should not give positions of critical importance to those whom we call the bourgeoisie or the Third Estate, because the interests of the people are never defended with more nobility, moderation, and the least danger to the public tranquility, than when they are confided to men of a superior class. History offers innumerable proofs of this . . . In one word, it is for the good of all . . . to compose assemblies only of men whom education and personal consideration provide with the best means to do good." [194] In a nation conceived in this manner, equal right of opinion and participation made no sense. There was a fundamental inequality between the elite to which the will of the nation was revealed and the non-elite from which—owing to either insufficient virtue or ignorance—it was concealed. Equality thus acquired the meaning of uniformity of the populace, which was a condition for the unity of the nation, facilitated the expression of the general will, and therefore ensured its freedom. The apparently contradictory insistence of the intellectuals on natural equality and individual liberty, and characteristic pronouncements such as Turgot's "there is no greater enemy of liberty than the people," were not at all inconsistent, but formed a coherent authoritarian outlook.

## Competition with England and *Ressentiment*

The idea of the nation took root in France around 1750.[195] It became an integral, if not the central, part of the elite discourse and effected a profound change in mentality. Shortly thereafter it changed its original meaning. Two successive developments were chiefly responsible for this change. One was the reclamation of nationality from the nobility (itself, perhaps, a sign of the elite's impatience with the status quo and the unconscious substitution of the change in the cognitive *model* of reality for the much-more-difficult-to-achieve change of reality) and the redefinition of the nation, which made it much more inclusive, but eventually excluded the hereditary aristocracy and discredited the aristocratic position. The second development followed upon the success of the first. As the elite converted to national identity, the preoccupation with status and power struggle within the country was partially—and during the Revolution completely—eclipsed by the concern for international precedence.

The etatism of the French nationality was not a foregone conclusion. The idea of the nation, as imported from England, implied commitment to the values of individual liberty and equality. Within French political thought itself, etatism espoused and articulated by the agents of absolutism coexisted with the aristocratic (parliamentarian as well as "feudal") tradition of opposition to absolutism, which contained important libertarian elements. The abandonment of the noble order by its members and the attack on it by the actual or potential members of the elite who were not noble were partially responsible for the preference of the etatist over the libertarian current in the incipient French national consciousness. The factor which strongly reinforced this tendency and ensured the ascendancy of the etatist position was the competition with and changed attitude toward England.

After the death of Louis XIV it became clear that France had lost its preponderance in Europe. This was partly due to the policies of the late king, who had left the country in a sorry state, but was also highlighted by England's spectacular rise to centrality. France ceded to England the position of leadership it had held in the seventeenth century. As the elite came to identify with the political community as a whole, with France the nation, its members were increasingly bothered by this changed relationship. French national patriotism was expressed in the burning desire to restore to the nation the superior status it had lost to England and, with a typically French em-

phasis, win back its *glory*. This was the new meaning assumed by the concept of the "regeneration" of France, which nationalistic and patriotic
Frenchmen professed to be their goal.[196]

There were two ways to ensure the preeminence and glory of France: one
was to introduce liberal reforms and make France a nation similar to the
English; the other was to degrade this rival power. The first approach, espoused by, among others, some of the older *philosophes,* most notably
Montesquieu and Voltaire, and discussed earlier, was based on a firm confidence in the ability of France to implement what it had learned from England and, having done so, easily surpass its model and competitor. This confidence was at the basis of the mid-century popularity of England among the
educated French. Comfortable in their self-esteem, they held no grudge
against it, for they were sure that soon there would be no grudge to hold.
"We are in many things the disciples of England," wrote the staunchest An-
glophile of all, Voltaire; "we shall end by being equals of our masters." [197]
The task proved to be more difficult and promised to take much longer than
was expected. For that reason Anglophilia gradually gave way to Anglophobia.

The French aristocractic and intellectual elite in the second half of the
eighteenth century found itself in a position which was—from a sociological
point of view—a perfect breeding ground for *ressentiment*. Drawn into
competition with England by adopting the English national idea as its model
and by the desire to regain its glory, France lacked the social conditions necessary for the implementation of this model, thereby making equality with
(even less superiority over) England impossible. It was perceived as essentially comparable, equal to England, and at the same time was clearly inferior to it. And the aristocratic-intellectual elite in France—whose members now identified their status with that of France as a whole—was in the
position to be personally wounded by the superiority of England and to feel
*ressentiment* generated by the relative position of the country.

The early French nationalist thought, indeed, displays unmistakable characteristics of a philosophy of *ressentiment*. Significantly, these characteristics are more salient in the professedly liberal thought of the period than in
the conservative thought which simply rejected the English values and refused to admit that France was in any way comparable to its successful
neighbor.[198] The liberals resentful of England, in distinction, at least in name
shared the English values. France conceived of itself as a liberal nation. The
rejection of the English model was expressed in the transvaluation of its
values, but also in their emphatic appropriation. In the hands of the luminaries who forged the French national consciousness, the concepts of nation, liberty, and equality acquired an entirely different meaning, sometimes
diametrically opposed to the one they had in England, but remained tied to
each other and were idolized. They were affirmed in the "solemn" and ex-

plicit Declaration of the Rights of Man and Citizen, such as was never thought of in England, and this Declaration, with its proud slogan, "Liberty, Equality, Fraternity," became the symbol of France, replacing the Marian *fleur de lys*. The Nation France was committed to and worshipped its Holy Trinity as much as formerly France the community of the faithful worshipped another. But, as often as not, the idea of the nation was replaced by the ideal of national unity, which was called "fraternity"; equality exchanged for uniformity; and "liberty" for sovereignty or freedom of the general will from constraint by either another sovereign (whether presumed, such as the king, or real, such as another nation) or any of its members. Collectivity overshadowed the individual, and his rights, which never before had been articulated with such circumstance, were pushed into the background.[199]

Opinions that were both expressly liberal and Anglophobe became increasingly prevalent in the latter part of the century, counting among their advocates Rousseau, Mably, Diderot, d'Holbach, and Marat, and were especially influential in the 1780s. For this group of ideologues, England was no longer the land of freedom, and they found little to admire in its constitution. Mably explicitly disputed Montesquieu's authority in this matter, writing that English liberty was but tentative, a half-liberty at best. "Many writers, and the author of *The Spirit of Laws,* whose authority is so great, have lavished praises on this constitution; but can one examine it carefully and fail to see that liberty is only sketched there? . . . they enjoy only a half-liberty." England was justified in loving it, but it was wrong to regard it as "le modèle et le chef-d'oeuvre de la politique."[200] Rousseau was adamant that it should not be so regarded. The example of England should not be followed, he counseled his Polish audience; it should be "a lesson to the Poles" how not to behave: "Your constitution is superior to Great Britain." England "lost its freedom," he admonished. "I can only record my astonishment at the irresponsibility and lack of caution, the stupidity even, of the English: having lodged supreme power in the hands of their deputies, they place no limitation on the use these deputies will be able to make of their power through the seven long years of their mandate." This served England right, for, as Rousseau noted in the *Social Contract,* "the use it makes of the short moments of liberty it enjoys shows indeed that it deserves to lose them."[201]

The greatest obstacle for freedom in England was corruption, that "shocking evil . . . which transforms the organ of liberty into that of servitude."[202] England sold its liberty for thirty pieces of silver, bartered it away for luxury and monetary profits. Commercial interests ousted its sacred flame from the English hearts, and nothing but greed reigned therein. The verdict was clear. The aristocratic contempt for the *nouveaux riches,* which among the more methodical intellectuals turned into a consuming hatred of money as such, fused with resentment toward England. Though the judges might not use the phrase, England, that country which had only "des affections métalliques," in their view, was a *capitalist* society. It was irredeemable. Mably wrote: "Moved by the desire to augment their riches and extend their empire, [the English] consult nothing but their avarice and ambition . . . England, mistress of the seas, has nothing to fear from strangers. It is her own great power, her over-vast colonies, and her over-extended commerce that she has to beware of. Perhaps she needs to experience disgrace in order to conserve the greatest of her assets, that is, her liberty; but who can assure that it will know how to profit from a disgrace that will offend her avarice and her ambition?" [203] A capitalist society, a nation that was unjust, avaricious, venal, corrupt, and dominated by commercial interests was no fit model for France.

The resentment toward England that shaped the ideological foundations of the French national consciousness at this highest level of intellectual sophistication was present and contributed to its formation on more popular levels as well. The Seven Years' War of 1756–1763, we learn from the chroniclers of French nationalism, "aroused considerable national feeling." [204] In the popular literature of the time England was styled "les sauvages de l'Europe," "that abominable country, where reason, humanity and nature cannot make their voices heard." [205] This resentment was best reflected in the immensely popular *Le Siège de Calais*, a presentation of the traditional hostility between France and England in the form of a tragedy, which extolled the virtues of the former and stressed the vices of the latter. The author, Pierre de Belloy, was moved to write it by the urge to "instill in the nation a self-esteem and self-respect which alone can make it again what it was formerly," [206] that is, by the desire to see France "regenerated," but also by the perceived necessity to fight Anglophilia, which apparently still poisoned the mind of the theater-going public. Imitation of the English, including "their supposed independence," he insisted, could not even earn Frenchmen their esteem. Nevertheless, de Belloy admitted that something could be learned from perfidious Albion: patriotism. England was hated, but not ignored, and its enemies respected it in spite of themselves.

### French Involvement in the War of American Independence and Its Effects on the Character of French Nationalism

This resentment was also reflected in the enthusiastic support of the educated public for the American War of Independence, the French involvement in which—both military and emotional—had a profound effect on the subsequent development and character of French nationalism. The war was one of the important sources of inspiration for the Revolution,[207] and the passionate interest of the French elite in the conflict which, objectively speaking, had nothing to do with it may throw some light on the motives which led to the Revolution as well.

"The enthusiasm which the French people exhibited in the matter of the American War of Independence," wrote Aulard in the *Political History of the French Revolution,* "was born in part of their hatred of England, but also of their hatred of despotism in general." This diagnosis by the historian of French patriotism, revealing as it is, still seems to underestimate the share of Anglophobia in the French pro-American sentiments. The assessment of Abbé Morellet, when he wrote, in a letter of January 5, 1777, to Lord Shelburne, that enmity toward England was by far a stronger motive among the Parisian supporters of America than their love of American liberty, is, probably, more accurate.[208] In fact this moving sentiment was made quite explicit. For volunteers, such as Lafayette and Ségur, the chance to contribute to the humiliation of England was admittedly the paramount motivation.[209] These young men, on their own testimony, "burned with a desire to repair the affronts of the last wars, to fight the English and [in the last place] to fly to help the American cause." Lafayette was "persuaded that to harm England is to serve (dare I say revenge) my country" and advised involvement on the side of the colonists because of that. Upon his return from America he listed the primary reasons for "the part [he] took in the American cause" as "my love for my country, my desire to witness the humiliation of her enemies." The far more consequential motives of the War Minister, Vergennes, were apparently the same, except that he did not pay even lip service to Liberty, to which aristocratic volunteers declared themselves passionately attached.[210]

It was the relationship between England and France, rather than between England and America, that preoccupied the only seemingly altruistic supporters of the latter. It appeared clear that the secession of the colonies would weaken the "haughty islanders" and that this would be to the benefit of France. The *Journal de Genève,* a voice of the Establishment, asserted in 1778: "England in her days of splendour did not believe that her invasions and conquests must be limited; an immense trade contributed both to her natural pride and to the audacity born of her riches . . . finally worn out by her conquests, by her victories if you will, England thought to find in her colonies indemnities and inexaustible resources, a blind obedience that no vexation or the yoke of the heaviest despotism could alter. We have seen the falsity, the illusion, of this system: her tyranny abhorred, attacked, destroyed!" And at this very moment, as if it were some kind of see-saw, France "resumes her empire, her former preponderance, or at least returns to the place she should never have forfeited among the first powers of Europe." On the fringes, Brissot, in *Testament politique de l'Angleterre,* expressed confidence that France, "having embraced the cause of the persecuted colonists, would fall heir to the grandeur of her rival, who was in the last agonies." Significantly, it was not liberalism, but the nationalistic enmity toward England, to which appealed the propagandist journal *Affaires de l'Angleterre et de l'Amérique,* edited by, among others, Benjamin Franklin. It consciously played up Frenchmen's wishful thoughts of humiliating England and thus regaining the place which was properly their own. The support of America, insisted the journal in 1777, offered France the most favorable opportunity "ever given to any nation to increase its own wealth and power while humiliating and weakening the most formidable, the most insolent, and the most inveterate enemy." [211]

The American War of Independence eventually facilitated the identification of radicalism with nationalism in France and strengthened the appeal of the collectivistic (etatist)—and undemocratic—reinterpretation of the values of liberty, equality, and nation. The American War dissociated liberty, and with it equality, patriotism, and nation, from the English example. It seemed possible now to maintain these ideals without following England, and yet without giving up hope of triumphing over her on her own ground. This factual dissociation between the central values of the new canon and England added legitimacy to the theory of the general will in which such dissociation was already implied. The most explicitly anti-English works of its advocates, such as Rousseau's *Considérations sur le gouvernement de Pologne,* appeared in print in the 1780s;[212] the connection between their brand of liberalism and the self-assertion of France against England seemed obvious, and they were immensely popular. The cause of this liberalism was identified with the French national cause; and, as a result, this position was established as the dominant current within the French liberal tradition.

In addition, as Tocqueville pointed out nearly 150 years ago, the American War strengthened the rationalist tendency in French thought and modified this new tradition in a way which further removed it from its English source.[213] From the defensibility of disregarding the example of England, French thinkers derived the justification for disregarding history. American independence seemed to them to be the result of the right philosophy arrived at through a purely intellectual effort. Reason, in French thought, was not the ability of an individual, any individual in his right mind, to consider and choose betweeen different alternative ways to achieve the desired goals and between the goals to desire. From rather early on it had the meaning of the true philosophy. This view was consistent with and supported the theory of the general will and the belief in the existence of an elite, whether of virtue or intelligence, able to interpret it. Now, because of the American Revolution, this reason as the true philosophy, evident to a chosen few (and therefore the chosen few—the elite), became all-powerful. France could be changed, it could be made great again, it could surpass England and become free, if only it followed the advice of reason.

International competition altered the significance of the struggle for liberty. For the pre-revolutionary elite, as well as for the political leaders of the Revolution, at least one important reason for aspiring to it was the existence of England. Having gained liberty, which—given that France possessed the right philosophy—was an easy task, France would regain its position of leadership, which would instantly become clear to everyone, including its rival across the Channel. France would be the first to establish *real* liberty in Europe. Thus prophesied George Washington in a French play in 1791, while admonishing an Englishman:

> Peut-être le Français, objet de votre haine,
> Sera-t-il le premier qui brisera sa chaine.

Camille Desmoulins, too, in *La France libre,* expressed similar confidence: "How the face of this empire has changed! how we have advanced with a giant step toward liberty! . . . at present . . . the foreigners are going to regret that they are not French. We shall surpass these English, so proud of their constitution, who ridiculed our servitude."[214]

Liberty was to humiliate England and restore France to its rightful place. The elite transferred its vexation with the internal imperfections of French society, so far as it was concerned, to the threat to the country's external standing. Its efforts were redirected. The fight with absolutism became just a means to a far more glorious end. The sting of aristocratic reaction was displaced, and the anger that drove it became nationalism.

The surprising quality of French nationalism during revolutionary wars (which persisted for a long time after) was not so much the increased militancy of an embattled and threatened nation, as the violent and irrational Anglophobia which possessed it. Statesmen represented England as "les éternels ennemis de notre nation."[215] Poets believed no epithet sinister or grotesque enough to depict it. To Rouget de Lisle, England was "l'affreux brigand de la Tamise," the origin of all of France's afflictions ("de la France il fit tous les maux"), "artisan des malheurs du monde." Lebrun called it "the odious Insulary," "perfidious" and "drunk with fortune," "the greedy depredator of land and seas," and the destroyer of peace on earth. The mission of France was to rid the world of this monster. This was easier said than done, however, and patriotic frustration was poured into wishful and irate verse:

> Au livre des destins la vengeance est écrite;
> Albion expiera les maux de l'univers.
> Avant que la Tamise ait compté quelques lustres,
> Elle aura vu changer ses triomphes illustres
>> En sinistres revers.
> Vainement l'insolente à sa noble rivale
> Croit opposer des flots l'orageux intervalle;

La perfide s'épuise en efforts superflus.
Tremble, nouvelle Tyr! Un nouvel Alexandre
Sur l'onde où tu régnais va disperser ta cendre:
Ton nom même n'est plus.[216]

Given the moderation of England in relation to revolutionary France in comparison with other parties to the conflict, especially Prussia, such rage could be explained by the hostilities but to a minor extent. It reflected deeper motives, springing from the very core of the new French identity and consciousness.

## A Note on Non-Elite Nationalism

While the elite agonized, French people learned to read. The elite generalized its agony, transforming it into noble indignation with "tyrannies" of all sorts, and fiery patriotic idealism, and as it spared no effort in publicizing the results of these intellectual exercises, it gave the masses food for thought and forged the weapons with which they were to be armed. While the elite was drawn to nationalism, moved by interests peculiar to itself, the rest of at least the literate and semi-literate population in France, the groups that constituted the "bourgeoisie" or the middle class,[217] the denizens of the cities, were also growing more patriotic, realizing that their personal destinies depended on the existence of the nation and earnestly striving to help it on the way to happiness and greatness. But the idea of the nation appealed to the bourgeoisie for very different reasons.

If the nationalism of the elite originated in the belief that things had changed for the worse and the desire to arrest this development, to prop and refound their threatened, but still superior, status, that of the bourgeoisie was aroused by the unhoped-for possibility of improving their lot and acquiring a better status. In a nation, the bourgeoisie could be much more than it was allowed to be in the king's state and the society of orders. A new prospect of dignity opened before it. With the development of the ideology of nationality, the French middle classes found themselves in a potentially advantageous situation which made their members wish to take full advantage of it. They welcomed nationalization of identity. They were receptive to ideas of active membership in the political community, the guaranteed ability to exert influence on public policy which affected their lives, respect for themselves as individuals, liberty and equality in the English sense of these words. A nation defined as a unity of free and equal members both rendered legitimate these heretofore unthinkable bourgeois aspirations and made their realization possible.

The bourgeoisie eagerly joined the elite in demands for "uniformity of

taxation, equality in its assessment, political liberty, individual liberty."[218]
The English model, the system of values imported from England, appealed
to them and they subscribed to it willingly. In distinction from the aristocratic and intellectual elite, however, the interests of the bourgeoisie did not
lead it to identify with France as a whole; the middle classes concentrated
on conditions within France. As a result, the change of the relative standing
of France vis-à-vis other powers (or the other power) was at best of secondary importance for the middle-class nationalism, and it was much less fueled
by wounded pride and a desire to get even. This nationalism, as expressed
in pre-revolutionary pamphlets and especially in the *cahiers de doléances,*
from which the anti-English (and anti-foreign in general) sentiment was conspicuously absent,[219] was much closer to the English nationalism than to the
nationalism of the French aristocratic and intellectual elite. Since, unlike the
latter, bourgeois who remained bourgeois rarely articulated their views, we
know much less about what they really thought, but it is still possible to
venture some conjectures. What they read in the definitions provided by various primers in nationalism[220] was probably different from what was
stressed by the elite ideologues. The nation they envisioned and wanted to
become was unlikely to be the one emerging in the writings of Rousseau,
Mably, and their followers. But they were prone to welcome the identification of the nation with the Third Estate, that is, the people alone, against
those who still stuck to their privileges and were reluctant to recognize universal equality. (And yet many would be reluctant to carry this definition to
its logical conclusion and would rather restrict the "natural rights" of participation and active membership in a nation to the propertied classes.)

The writers of the bourgeois *cahiers* would agree that not another nation,
but the despotism in France, the class and provincial divisions and privileges, were responsible for its misfortunes, and that not the humiliation of
England, but the victory over and abolition of France's own deficiencies
would bring the nation happiness. This middle-class nationalism was
inward-oriented and fundamentally constructive. The national cause and
the cause of liberal individualistic reform were interdependent and seemed
identical. Only the elevation of everyone to the lofty position of members of
a nation, sharing in the same interests, brothers and equals, would ensure
the liberty and dignity of every individual Frenchman. And liberty and
equality would contribute to the development among Frenchmen of patriotism, "the secret resource which maintains order in the state, the virtue
which is most necessary for its preservation, its internal well-being, and its
external force and glory." The surest way to light this sacred fire in the hearts
of citizens was "to cater to their interests by rewards" and specifically to
offer them equality of opportunity.[221] The glory of France, according to this
line of argument, depended on the well-being of its members, not the other
way around.

The ideals upheld by elite nationalists, which in their arcane writings tended to assume a different meaning, easily lent themselves to this simple interpretation. Individual liberty could be regarded as "moral liberty found in obedience to general will" and equality as equality of citizens from which the masses of the people were excluded, but to find these notions convincing, one needed to be either very sophisticated (and able to understand them) or stupid (and thus susceptible to indoctrination), and the French bourgeoisie was neither. It consisted of a middling sort of people, smart enough to recognize a good opportunity. The elite forged and armed the middle classes with weapons it had not much use for itself. As the Revolution wrought havoc in the old social structure, and its elite succumbed to the guillotine or self-effaced to escape it, a new elite was recruited from the newly empowered middle classes and blended with the remnants of the old. Its notions were added to the national arsenal of ideas and assumed a prominent, though rarely dominant, place in it—to be used when the chance arose.

Tocqueville noted what he thought was the inconstancy of the love for liberty among his countrymen and was grieved by it. One could observe in France, he wrote, "the desire for freedom reviving, succumbing, then returning, only to die out once more and presently blaze up again," compelling Frenchmen now and again to try and "graft the head of liberty onto a servile body." [222] But one could argue that the love of liberty in France was a constant. It was a national trait, an element of the French national identity, only "liberty" meant different things to different Frenchmen, and frequently referred to its very opposite. The French national identity was of a mixed heritage; it was ambivalent. It was woven from threads which came from disparate sources and brought together independent—and sometimes contradictory—traditions and interests. The chief factor in the emergence of this encompassing ideology, which was to become the basis of the social and political solidarity in France and of the identity of every individual Frenchman, was the situation of the French nobility and later a modified part of it, the aristocratic *cum* intellectual elite—whose members were the main propagators of nationalism—in the course of the eighteenth century. The chief reason for the adoption of the idea of the nation in France was the fact that this French elite in the eighteenth century was in a state of crisis, and the idea of national patriotism offered a means of resolving it. French nationalism was born out of the grievances and frustrations of the most privileged groups of the society, the final form and channel of the aristocratic reaction. It was a result of appropriation by irritated lords of the idea of the state developed and disseminated by agents of the Crown, and its expansion and reinterpretation in such a manner that it could be turned against the latter. This idea elevated the selfish interests of the aristocracy, and turned their fight to protect their privileges into a moral crusade. It turned reactionaries into revolutionaries, transformed them, indeed, into ardent idealists, without making them reactionaries any less, or for that matter liberals—in the original sense of the word—any more.

Then as now liberal democracy was not the only alternative to despotism, and for a society wishing to exchange its "old regime" for a new one, it was a highly unlikely option. Despotism has many forms. The little man could be respected only in the name of the little man, but trampled upon, overtaxed, starved, guillotined, and otherwise mutilated in the name of thousands of lofty ideals; and when it came to this, the king's glory was as good as the glory of the state or the nation; the God of Christians as demanding and indifferent as the Supreme Being or abstract humanity. But then, the idea of the nation—the symbolic elevation of the people to the position of an elite—was imported from England, and there liberty meant liberty of the individual, and equality meant equality and not inequality. And there were a significant number of people in France to whom the arguments of ideologues made no sense, but these ideas appealed very much, and who in their sage innocence saw nothing but these ideas in the arguments of ideologues. They were pronouncing the same words, but proclaiming different principles. Yet the flame of French national patriotism burned in the breasts of them all.

And on top of this confusion there was the baggage of previous existences. France, the wandering soul, had moved from one domicile to another: from the temple of God, to the body of the king and his state, and then to that of the nation, and from each home she left, she took with her possessions that made her unique, some furnishings such as her elegant tongue, her brilliant culture, and her refined manners, her inextinguishable sense of election and love of glory.

Or perhaps she was a body, a chamber into which three souls came to dwell in succession, and as each one came, it found the arrangements left by the previous resident, which it made its own and rearranged, but not too much, and then left to the one that came to succeed it.

France the nation bore an unmistakable resemblance to France the king's state and France the Church. It was not the same—twice it had changed its identity—and yet it was France. But whether a wandering soul changing dwellings, or a body animated by different spirits, France, through its transmutations, acquired something of a split personality. In its new self the old traits persisted, which could only be understood as atavisms from its past identities. What was France the nation to do with them? What was the place of Catholicism in its national identity? And what significance was it to attach to the memory of its kings? There is no typically French answer to any of these questions, as there is no typically French answer to the question of whether France the nation stood for the liberty of man, as did England and

America, or for the deified State to which man's liberty was subjugated. (Or perhaps to each of them there are two mutually exclusive answers which are equally typical?)

But though the nation France, even as it first asserted itself as such, might be confused as to which gods it worshipped, it never doubted that its was the role of the high priest. It was not just a nation, it was the Great Nation, *la Grande Nation*, the most national of nations, which carried to perfection the virtues required by the new cult.[223] And in this, too, France remained faithful to her heritage. *La Grande Nation* was the reincarnation of *le roi très chrétien*. Like he of old, the eldest son of the Church, the defender of Christianity, who spread its message with fire and sword, she carried and spread the gospel of Nationality—liberty and equality—with fire and sword. The crusading nation succeeded the crusading king.

Only the heathen, pre-national world did not wait for France, and when she came she was met by converts to the new faith who would never forgive her this presumption.

# The Scythian Rome: Russia

A. Borodin

We too are men.
I. I. Nepluyev, 1725

We are better men than the Germans.
Denis Fonvisin, 1784

Russia is a European State.
Catherine the Great, 1767

Yes, we are Scythians,
Yes, Asians we are!
Alexander Blok, 1918

We are Europeans.
Michail Gorbachev, 1987

## *Perestroika* in the Eighteenth Century

Two autocrats can be held directly responsible for instilling the idea of the nation in the Russian elite and awakening it to the potent and stimulating sense of national pride: these were Peter I and Catherine II. It is not our task to pronounce whether Russia was fortunate or unfortunate in having been, within one century, subjected to two rulers of genius. It is a fact that it had. Though there is little doubt that in both cases their title "the Great" was due at least as much to the habit of open and slovenly flattery cultivated in their subjects as to the latter's unbiased recognition of their merit, both Peter and Catherine deserved the superlative designation by which they are known to posterity. Both were, unquestionably, people of ambition and energy far exceeding the average. They owed their greatness to natural intelligence and to the sheer strength of their personalities, and on their way to personal glory they dragged the reluctant, heavy, quailing Russian society farther than a moderate conviction in the role of the individual in history would lead one to expect.

The ability of Peter and Catherine to do so was, of course, dependent on the nature of the relationship between the autocrat and the subjects in Russia, which was the legacy of the Muscovite kingdom, and in which the subjects had neither a will of their own nor the ability to carry such will through if they had had it. But the direction in which the two monarchs eventually led this great mass, which they could mold and shape according to their wishes, was chosen by themselves. The direction was Westward, toward making Russia a European state to be reckoned with and respected. And the model was no longer Poland and Ukraine, as in the days of Peter's father, Tsar Alexis, but England, Holland, Germany, and later France: the Europe of progress, unlimited possibilities, and national identity, which for some time was to rule the future.

### The Transformation of Discourse under Peter I

It was Peter who, as is well known, "cut the window into Europe" and put Russia on the map of world politics. Why he chose to do so, why he was not satisfied with unlimited power within his great Eastern empire, but strove toward glory and recognition in the haughty, alien West, we shall never know for sure. This choice might have reflected his disgust with the Muscovite life, cultivated by the traumatic experiences of his childhood and youth; his fondness for the Moscow "German Suburb"; and the restlessness of his fiery spirit not to be soothed by an achievement less difficult. Perhaps it was only a game, a means to give vent to the playfulness of an energetic tsar, an autocrat who, within his domain, knew no limits to his wishes and was bored by the possibilities it offered him. A giant man with a colossal toy. At any rate, he decided to make Russia a European power.

The most thoroughgoing and radical changes of Peter's reign turned out to be those that had to do with culture, the way in which Russians were thence to think about themselves. Certainly, the tsar enjoyed the freedom and vitality of life in the "German Suburb" and later in the West: he understood and could appreciate the new values which were restructuring European societies. And yet he was no missionary; his aim was not to convert Russians into freedom-lovers; and he regarded the changes in ideas only as a matter of expediency, necessary for the achievement of his other, mainly military, goals. In this regard, the policy of the great Romanov was not much different from that of a Gorbachev. He set out to transform the way of his subjects' thinking in the same manner in which he approached their fashions: with threats of "cruel punishment" (not infrequently demonstrating what exactly he meant by that) and no regard for their own preferences, circumstances, or considerations. His methods were ruthless. He had none but slaves to rule over, and he treated them as slaves. His legislation, as one of his many admirers, though a moderate one, Pushkin, later characterized it, might have been written by a *knout* of an impatient and despotic landlord.[1] Peter wanted to create a new breed of servants—able to carry out his will with efficiency and eager to do so whenever called—not a new breed of men. The new Western learning he forced his subjects to acquire was practical; it was no *Bildung* he was after, but the training of specialists and technicians. But on occasion, the tsar made use of some of the broad values which made "the West" so different from the rest of the world to which Russia belonged, and slowly these values started to permeate the language of his decrees, and through them, the sleepy consciousness of the people whom he, *knout* in hand, tried to whip into feeling—or at least acting—like citizens. These values were all subsumed under the revolutionary, crucial idea of the nation, which implied the fundamental redefinition of the Russian polity (from the property of the tsar into a common wealth, an impersonal *patrie* or *fatherland* in which every member had an equal stake and to which everyone was naturally attached). The effect of this idea, in Russia as in other societies, was to transform the slaves into fellow-beings of the autocrat, elevating them by this implicit equality to breath-taking heights.

One can observe the gradual evolution of this revolutionary political discourse in the extensive corpus of Peter's decrees *(ukazy)*. One critical concept—*gosudarstvo*—changes its meaning, and two others—*otechestvo* and "general good" *(obshchee blago)*—appear and gain prominence, which results in the reinterpretation of the referent of service and loyalty. The transformation is tentative and, in the beginning of the Petrine period, at least, appears to be unintentional.

In the early years of the reign, Russia is defined consistently as the personal domain of the tsar. The service which the decrees demand, determining the manner and conditions under which it is to be rendered, is due to him personally, as "the Great Lord [*Gosudar'*], Tsar and Great Prince, the Autocrat of All Russias." The word *Gosudarstvo*, today the Russian for "state," in those early edicts appears uniformly in its original meaning, as "Lordship" or "Kingdom"—a derivation from *Gosudar'* (Great Lord or Ruler); it means either the Lord's (tsar's) personal government, the activity of governing, or his personal property, the domain over which he exercises his lordship. In this latter sense, *Gosudarstvo* is the synonym of *Tsarstvo* (tsardom); both are extensions of the person of the ruler and have no meaning apart from him. Gradually, however, the word changes its meaning and toward the second decade of the reign acquires the impersonal connotation of a polity which exists in its own right, a body politic, a state. Interestingly, this new concept, at that time already well established in European political discourse, and designated by no longer equivocal terms in English, French, and German, appears first in those Petrine edicts which are explicitly addressed to foreigners. For example, an edict of 1700 regarding a treaty between Peter and the Ottoman ruler Mustafa II speaks of an "independent and free Muscovite State [*Gosudarstvo*]" and uses "Muscovite people [*narod*]" as its synonym. In edicts addressed primarily to the Russian subjects of the tsar, the word *gosudarstvo* does not acquire this impersonal meaning of the body politic until the second decade of the eighteenth century. Since then, however, it is as a rule used in this new sense. The foremost duty of the subjects and the object of these decrees, service to "US the Great Lord and OUR Tsarist Majesty," is systematically represented also as service "to the State" and sometimes even replaced by this new requirement. At the same time, allusions to "state expenses," "state interests," and "state well-being" appear with increasing regularity. It is those "state," and therefore common, interests to which Peter appeals in the famous *ukaze* of 1714 regarding the order of inheritance, and which he uses to justify this very much opposed innovation.[2]

The first reference to the concept of "general good" in Petrine decrees is also met in an edict addressed to foreigners. This is the Manifesto of April 16, 1702: Regarding Invitation of Foreigners to Russia with the Promise to

Them of the Freedom of Religion. The original language of this Manifesto is Russian, but its idioms and tone are those of its intended Western European audience. It reads:

> It is sufficiently known in all the lands subjected by God Almighty to OUR Government, that since OUR accession to this throne, all OUR efforts and intentions tended to governing this State so that all OUR subjects, through OUR care for the general good, would more and more improve their situations; for this reason WE attempted to guard the internal quiet, protect the State from external attack and by all means improve and spread commerce. For the achievement of this goal, WE were compelled to perpetrate in the manner of government certain necessary changes tending to the well-being of OUR land, so that OUR subjects would with more comfort acquire that knowledge of which they are still ignorant, and become more skillful in all commercial arts. For which reason WE . . . with OUR unending mercy . . . issued and intend to issue in the future all the commands necessary for the cultivation of commerce with foreigners; since WE fear that these matters are not yet in the state WE wish to see them, and that OUR subjects cannot yet enjoy the fruits of OUR labors in perfect peace, WE thought of other means to secure OUR borders from enemy attacks and preserve the right and advantage of OUR State and general peace in Christendom, as is expected of a Christian Monarch. To achieve these worthy goals, WE cared above all to establish in the best way possible the Military Organization [*voennyi shtat*] as the stay of OUR State . . . but to perfect this further and to induce foreigners who can . . . be helpful in this perfection, together with other useful-for-the-State artificers, to come to US and stay both in OUR service and on OUR land, WE commanded to announce this manifesto with the clauses stated below everywhere, print it, and make it public in all of Europe.

Below this statement appear the clauses which promise foreigners entering Russian service complete freedom of conscience, remarkably tolerant (toward them) and libertine in tone.

The Manifesto is revealing in regard to Peter's goals, but deceptive in other respects. The native Russians of 1702 were not thinking in terms of "general good" and *their* welfare; nor did the autocrat at this point in time intend them to think in those terms. When addressing his subjects, Peter was unequivocal about the nature of "His Tsarist Majesty's" relationship to them, and this was not the relationship of people united in their concern for the "general good." In fact, not much earlier than the Manifesto which for the first time used this novel concept, in the same year 1702, Peter issued an edict "regarding the form of the requests addressed to the Supreme Lord," which instructed the more-often-than-not illiterate petitioners in the style of official writing and ordered them henceforth to end their letters with the eloquent formula: "Your majesty's lowliest slave Such-and-Such." [3] A monarch seeking to instill in his subjects the spirit of citizenship would hardly be likely to insist on such a cliché, habitually affirming their inferior status and lack of will.

This is not a political discourse in which the concept of "general good" could have any place or meaning, and this concept, contrary to the accepted opinion,[4] did not become "the stock-in-trade of the Russian Imperial Government" until later. It appears very rarely in Petrine edicts of the first decade of the eighteenth century, and almost exclusively in contexts which presuppose a foreign audience. Peter, undoubtedly, knew well and understood the nature of the political discourse in the societies he chose as models, but not until the second half of his reign did he begin to see in it a spiritual carrot to supplement the very tangible stick which could induce his native subjects to perform the tasks he set before them.

A similar pattern can be observed in the adoption by the tsar of other concepts, which by their very nature were changing the character of the political discourse in Russia and implanting the new way of thinking in those below him. Some of them, in the beginning, the tsar did not even wish his subjects to notice. For example, for the Russian public (if this designation had a referent at that time), Peter's title was modified to include the sonorous appellation of "Emperor" only in 1721, when he was humbly asked by the Senate to accept it and "according to his usual and admirable modesty and moderation for a long time rejected." However, he had been using this title with remarkable consistency since 1710 when addressing foreign and newly conquered European territories.[5] The imperial title stressed the formal similarity of the Russian autocrat to great European potentates and thus, conceptually, drew Russia closer to Europe.

The addition of the concept "fatherland"—*otechestvo, otchizna*—to the vocabulary of Peter's edicts was of utmost significance. The concept frequently appeared alongside the word "people"—*narod*—which had several meanings, but became the closest Russian synonym for "nation." The idea of "fatherland" made possible the exhortation to patriotism of individuals previously ignorant of suchlike sentiments.[6] In Petrine documents, again, "fatherland" seems to appear at first under special circumstances. It is encountered in the addresses to the Ukrainian, or Little Russian, troops when, under the leadership of Hetman Mazepa, they revolted against the tsar and sided with the Swedes, in 1708. In these documents Peter purports to represent Mazepa's intentions as anti-national (seeking to wrong "the Little Russian people") and anti-Christian, although Mazepa's breach of personal loyalty to the tsar is mentioned in the first place. Peter's own motives, by contrast, being those of altruistic concern for the well-being of the said "people," he exhorts them to think about the good of their "fatherland" and forget Mazepa, saying that Mazepa's action tended to the "injury of Russia" as a whole, "the Russian State."[7]

In later years, however, "fatherland" becomes a regular part of the vocabulary of the tsar's decrees and in the second half of his reign is met with increasing frequency. It too, like the impersonal State *(Gosudarstvo)*, denotes an impersonal referent of service and implies the existence of a body politic. Those who fail with due speed to conform to His Majesty's orders are called "traitors and betrayers of the fatherland" (for example, in #2315, where the period allowed the potential culprits to show their true nature is two weeks) and are to be punished accordingly. In the critical edict of 1722 on the Table of Ranks, of which we shall have more to say later, the only way to achieve a rank, and therefore status, is through service "to us and the fatherland." The Act of 1721, which offered "the Lord Tsar Peter I the title of the Emperor of All Russias," also asked to bestow on him the appellation of "the Great and the Father of the Fatherland [*Otets Otechestvia*]." The petitioners, members of the Senate and the Church Synod, explained their request in the following terms:

> . . . to show [His Majesty] their due gratitude for his high favor and Fatherly solicitude and care for the well-being of the State [*Gosudarstva*], which he had deigned to show during the whole duration of his most glorious government [*Gosudarstvovania*], and especially during the past Swedish War, thus bringing the State of All Russias into such strong and worthy state, and His subject people into such fame in the eyes of the whole world solely through this His guidance . . . the decision is made to ask His Majesty in the name of the entire Russian people to condescend and accept, as do others, the title: Father of the Fatherland, Emperor of All Russias, Peter the Great . . . of which appellations the Imperial title of Your majesty, has been applied to Your worthy ancestors since the days of most glorious Roman Emperor Maximilian for several centuries, and is given by many Potentates today. And the name of "the Great," according to Your Great deeds, is justly applied to You by many . . . As to the name of the Father of the Fatherland we . . . dare to apply [it] to You, according to the example of ancient Greek and Roman statesmen [*siglitov*], who applied it to their own, famous for their deeds and favor, Monarchs.[8]

The term "fatherland," for which the authors of the Act, inexperienced in national political discourse, chose a form of the word which was not destined to remain in the Russian political vocabulary (itself a sign of the novelty of the concept), was thus adopted in professed imitation of the classical model and, implying the notion of classical patriotism, meant *patrie*. This was as far as the discourse—if not yet the consciousness of all those who were encouraged to use it—advanced under Peter toward the idea of the nation. The transformation of the vocabulary was significant, and the new concepts would slowly filter into the minds of individuals constantly reminded that they were someone's "lowliest slaves."

Though Peter was aware of the existence of polities that were nations and had some direct experience of them, he did not think that Russia was a nation. He did not make any distinction between himself and his State, and this was so because the State for him was but an extension of his person. Not being a nationalist himself, he attempted to make nationalists of his subjects only to the extent that he believed this would increase their efficiency and zeal in his service. Perhaps because in carrying out this task he lacked the enthusiasm and determination which characterized his other endeavors, his success in it was moderate. There is indeed something pathetic in the discrepancy between Peter's insistence that his subjects serve the State, of which they were free-spirited, and therefore zealous, citizens, and their own firm conviction that they served nothing but Him, their merciful Father, the Great Lord, Tsar, and Autocrat.[9]

But, though Peter did not give his subjects the sense of individual dignity (fundamental to civic nationalism), he made them proud of being the subjects of such a strong and famous ruler and members—even if slaves—of a tremendously powerful empire. He gave them a cause for national pride which would be put to use by succeeding generations and provide the seedbed of a most passionate nationalism. His achievement was truly astonishing and could not fail to affect those who, under his orders, turned his fantastic plans into reality. Moreover, being justly proud of the success of his Herculean labors, Peter wished his subjects to be aware of what Russia owed him. He constantly drew their attention to his extraordinary exertions, and thus to the change in the situation of Russia. In this manner he fostered national pride—pride in the achievements of the polity—in his decrees, in the first Russian newspaper he started to publish in 1703, and in histories he commissioned of his and previous reigns. To one of the most important works of the period, *The Discourse on the Just Reasons of the War between Sweden and Russia,* by Pavel Petrovich Shafirov, Peter added a notably nationalistic conclusion, curiously reminiscent in tone and argument of the writings of later Russian and other nationalists. His aim in it, as in the work as a whole, which was written before the war was completed, was to justify the war's continuation primarily to his Russian subjects (although this was also a work of international propaganda, as we can judge from the fact that it was immediately translated into English and German), and to strengthen their commitment to his enterprise of raising the status of Russia in the eyes of Europe, in general. To achieve this, he stressed the difference in the situation of Russia under—and due to—him and before, and also the hostility toward it of the foreign powers, who wished to keep the Russian people in constant humiliation. He wrote:

> The past times are not like the present, for then the Swedes thought of us differently and considered us blind . . . And that not only the Swedes, but also other and remote peoples, always felt jealousy and hatred toward the Russian people, and attempted to keep the latter in the earlier ignorance, especially in the mili-

tary and naval arts. This is clear from . . . the histories of the past centuries [*seculov ili vekov*] . . . you may conclude what was the eternal hostility of these neighbors even at the cradle of Russia's fame . . . all the more now, when the Lord God [made Russia] so famous, that those, who, it seems, were the fear of all Europe, were defeated by us. And I can say, that no one is so feared as we are. For which one should thank God, while we, with his help raised onto such a lofty state (through the wise government and indefatigable labors of our All-merciful Tsar and Lord, who established and trained in Russia a regular army, which did not exist before, and built a navy, of which only a name was known in Russia in the past) instead of being indignant and weary, should patiently bear [this lofty state], and zealously strive, with his help, for a beneficial and secure completion of this war.[10]

How important Peter considered this argument is clear from the fact that, in the period when a usual printing of a book was two hundred to three hundred copies, the third edition of the *Discourse,* five years after it had first appeared, came out in the unheard of number of twenty thousand copies. Their fate underscored the lack of correspondence between the interests of the Emperor and the concerns of his people: only fifty were sold in the first three years, while the others were left to rot in the warehouse.[11] Yet, at least some of Peter's collaborators saw the point as well as he did, and few expressed it as clearly as Count Golovkin in a speech at the ceremony of the bestowal on Peter of his new title. "Only through your indefatigable labors and guidance," he said, "we, Your loyal subjects, are led from the darkness of ignorance into the theater of glory in front of the whole world, and, so to speak, *from non-existence into being,* and into the society of the political nations, as is known not only to us, but to all the world." [12]

The immediate successors of the great tsar Peter were hardly up to his measure, and for thirty-seven years Russia was ruled by monarchs who were, at best, mediocre. In their legislation they left us a revealing insight into the concerns that preoccupied their august minds. Anna Ioanovna gave some thought to hunting regulations and to overspeeding while driving sleds in the capital. Peter's daughter, Elizabeth, was more interested in fashions and thought an edict a proper means to record her wish to inspect personally all the imported "silver textiles" before they could be sold in her domain. Her heir, Peter III, the person responsible, so to speak, for giving Russia its second great ruler, occupied himself with military parades and painting sentries, also eternalizing his insights on these matters in the laws.[13] And yet the insignificant legislation of the years between the reigns of Peter and Catherine the Great preserved the new concepts; they appeared with great consistency, alongside the petty decrees, in the occasional edicts of importance which the monarchs were in one way or another talked into signing, and, invariably, in their Accession Manifestoes.

If anything, the novel, revolutionary conception of the polity, defined as a people or nation, in these documents grew stronger. Anna emphasized that she was "elected to the Russian Imperial Throne by the common wish and agreement of the entire Russian people." The Accession Manifesto of the Duke of Courland (who ruled for the infant Ivan VI) in 1740 repeatedly mentioned "interest of the State," "welfare of the State," and "unity of the State." Elizabeth, whose claim to the throne was securely based upon her filial relation to Peter, which she, understandably, stressed, nevertheless did not neglect to allude to the interest of the State either, and bid to represent her accession as necessary to it. Peter III also dwelt on the legitimacy of his succession by reason of kinship (to Peter I, who was his grandfather, and Elizabeth, his aunt, who explicitly designated him as her heir). But he, too, added to his Manifesto a declaration of his intention "to restore the well-being of loyal-to-US sons of Russia." [14] More eloquent was the language of the famous Manifesto on the Liberty of the Nobility, destined to have such a disconcerting effect on its beneficiaries. The fact that it almost certainly was not conceived or formulated by His Majesty himself, but by his courtiers and advisors,[15] does not diminish the importance of the choice of words, but, on the contrary, increases its significance. It provides some evidence that, in 1762, the language of "political nations" was no longer intelligible to the tsar alone, but was already finding its way into and affecting the thought of the nobility. The Manifesto freed the nobles from compulsory service to which they were obliged by Peter I, but characterized the regulation of the great tsar in sympathetic and patriotic terms. Peter I, it said "was obliged to suffer a great burden and great labors, solely for the good and advantage of his fatherland, pushing Russia to perfect knowledge of military and civic, as well as political, matters . . ." "Every true son of the fatherland," it insisted, "has to recognize that uncountable advantages followed [from compulsory service]," which educated the Russian nobility so that now "noble thoughts entrenched in all true Russian patriots boundless loyalty to US and love, great zeal, and worthy eagerness in OUR service." For this reason the need for it no longer existed. Those who would take the liberation too literally and indeed choose not to serve at all, however, were, under imperial orders, to be "despised and destroyed as such that do not care for the general good" by "all OUR true subjects and true sons of the fatherland" and, as a punishment for the lack of patriotism, would not be admitted at the Court.[16]

## The Contribution of Catherine the Great

Catherine II found her immediate predecessors unworthy as models and dissociated herself from them. In one of the accounts of the events related to her accession, she reminisced how on the fifth or sixth day upon her being proclaimed Empress she came to the Senate and learned about the "extreme paucity" of the Russian treasury. She wrote [in the third person]: "At the end of her life the Empress Elizabeth stocked as much money as she could, but kept it to herself, not using it for any of the needs of the empire; these needs were numerous; almost no one was paid. Peter III acted in a similar manner. When they were asked to give for the needs of the state, they grew indignant and would say: 'Find money elsewhere; but OUR savings belong to US.' Peter, like his aunt, distinguished his private interest from the interest of the empire. Catherine, learning about these financial difficulties, declared to the full assembly of the Senate, that as she herself belonged to the State, she wished that everything she had would belong to the State, and that no one would hence distinguish between her [personal] and its [general] interests . . . And Catherine supplied the needed funds." [17]

For such words (which in many, though not all, cases were accompanied by deeds) Catherine has been endlessly accused of hypocrisy. In fact, if one were to come up quickly with a cliché associated with her name in Soviet historiography, it would probably be "the hypocritical Empress Catherine II," and the Soviet scholars are not alone to arrive at this somewhat too obvious conclusion. Of course, Catherine was a shrewd ruler, with a cold and disciplined mind, and much of what she said and did, especially at the beginning of her reign, was calculated to endear herself to her subjects and justify the take-over for which there was no traditional legitimation. Her chief passion, like that of Peter the Great, was most certainly self-aggrandizement, and she must have greatly admired herself in that virtuous pose of *la reine patriote* and enjoyed the admiration this was supposed to (and did) arouse in others.[18] But all this does not imply that she did not believe what she said, did not intend to do what she promised, and carried out those intentions that she did reluctantly. On the contrary, she probably was quite sincere. What leads one to think so is not so much the words or even deeds of the Empress, but the conditions of the country where she uttered and performed them. For one has to realize that Catherine was a great innovator. She based her claim to the Russian throne on the arguments of modern national patriotism, which she learned from her friends the *philosophes,* as well as from other Western Europeans with whom she corresponded, whose books she carefully read and thoughtfully commented upon, and whose attention and approbation she constantly sought. It is true that she had little else to support her claims with; in actuality hers was a usurpation of the Russian throne. But it is also true that national patriotism made very little sense to most Russians, even within the nobility (it most certainly did not make any sense to the Guards, who made Catherine an Empress) and that Catherine took considerable risks in basing her appeal on it. Moreover, she continued to propagate its ideals consistently throughout her reign, when her position was already strong and the danger of deposition disappeared. Why would she do so, if she did not believe in it?

Unlike Peter I, Catherine quite probably was a convinced nationalist, and as such indeed marched in the avant-garde of the Continental intellectuals. She might not have loved Russia; she had few reasons indeed for such tender feelings toward a country where she was brought at the age of fifteen and spent eighteen years in humiliation, boredom, and unhappiness. Given these experiences, it is remarkable how little hostility and contempt toward Russia there is in Catherine's memoirs,[19] and equally remarkable are her diligence and earnest efforts to master its language, and her respect—at least outward—toward its religious traditions and customs at a time when the chances of her ever becoming its autocrat hardly existed at all. She might not have loved Russia, and therefore was not a nationalist by temperament. But she believed that the world was composed of nations, that Russia was a nation, that she, Empress Catherine II, therefore, was ruling over a nation, a body politic, a people in the lofty sense nationalism bestowed on this word, not over a piece of land. And she thought it a personal disgrace that Russians, her responsibility in the eyes of the enlightened world, were not behaving as a nation, and set out to correct this defect.

From one "Great" monarch to the other, the attitude of the tsars made a full circle, but with a difference. Peter I did not distinguish between himself and his State, because he saw the State as the extension of himself. His feeble successors thought, as Catherine II put it, that "the Great Lord has no need to meddle in the affairs of his Lordship (State) for it manages itself" and that "full-bodied and luxuriously dressed, in an armchair with elbow-rests and under a canopy," they fulfilled their role of monarchs perfectly. For the "general good" they could not have cared less.[20] Catherine II again identified her interests with the interests of the State. "The glory of the country," she declared, "creates my glory," adding in *Nakaz* (the Instruction): "God forbid! that after this Legislation is finished, any Nation on Earth should be more just and consequently should flourish more than Russia; otherwise the Intention of OUR Laws would be totally frustrated; an Unhappiness which I do not wish to survive." [21] But for her the ruler was the extension of the governed polity. In the concluding clause of *Nakaz,* she wrote: "All this will never please all those Flatterers, who are daily instilling this pernicious Maxim into all the Sovereigns on Earth, that their Peoples are created for them only. But WE think, and esteem it OUR Glory to declare, 'That WE are created for OUR People.'"

Catherine's tactics were likewise different from those of her venerated predecessor. Where he resorted to pulling out nostrils, she used her feminine wiles and fought, so to speak, with words. It was with rhetoric that Catherine tried to transform her Empire. The first rule of government, she jotted down in her private papers, was to "enlighten the nation which one governs . . . every citizen should be educated in the spirit of duty toward the Supreme Being, toward oneself, toward society." She set out to fulfill this mission as soon as she assumed the imperial power. Her Accession Manifesto appealed to "all direct sons of the Russian Fatherland" and spoke of the actions and intentions tending to the injury of the "Russian State" which moved her to support the *coup d'état* that led to the deposition of her husband. These included the threat to the "ancient in Russia Orthodox faith" and a possibility of its replacement by a foreign creed; a blow to the "Russian glory, raised high by its victorious weapons," caused by the peace treaty with the enemy of Russia, the Prussian king; and internal disorganization endangering the "unity of all Our Fatherland." The formula of the oath, customarily attached to the Accession Manifestoes, also contained a minor, but symbolically significant, alteration. All the previous formulations started from the emphatic assertion by the person taking the oath that he was His or Her Majesty's "slave." In Catherine's formula, although not altogether omitted, the expression appeared only toward the end of the oath, after the enumeration of civic responsibilities, and was much less conspicuous.[22] The Manifesto on Coronation carried the civic (one could almost say "republican") rhetoric to a further pitch. The reasons for Catherine's assumption of the imperial power, it said, were her "ardor in piety, and love for OUR Russian Fatherland, and in addition the zealous desire of all OUR loyal subjects to see US on this throne, in order to be delivered and protected, through OUR efforts, from all the wrongs and coming dangers to the Russian Fatherland." Thus, "WE accepted the Russian throne and liberated OUR Fatherland from all the above mentioned dangers."[23] The term "Fatherland" *(Otechestvo),* which was later to acquire all the Romantic overtones of "the land and the dead," for Catherine meant *la patrie,* the nation, as this was understood by the French. Very possibly, its sense was therefore limited in accordance with the definition of Catherine's avowed teacher, Montesquieu. But one must remember that even in this limited sense, the concept of the nation was revolutionary and almost visionary in Russia, of which, as of Walachia, one could say in the eighteenth century: "There is no Russian nation; there is only plebs."[24] The concept of *Otechestvo* (or Russian nation) had all the connotations of civic participation, liberty, and dignity the idea of the nation carried, and it is in this sense that it resounded through the documents of Catherine's reign. Again and again the addressees of her edicts were exhorted to show "true love and loyalty to the Fatherland and the Great Lady so devoted to it." In the famous Charter of 1785, the nobility was commended for its readiness "always to stand on guard over the Faith and Fatherland and . . . against the enemies of Faith, Monarch, and Fatherland" and was reminded that it entirely depended on "the security of the Fatherland and the throne."[25]

Catherine strove to instill in her subjects the elevating sense of national pride. Like Peter I, she missed no opportunity to draw their attention to the beneficial results of her own accomplishments which had raised the international prestige of Russia. Herself no less than *la passion dominante* of

Voltaire, Catherine succeeded indeed in making her—not so long ago bar-baric—realm the model state and a country of Light in the eyes of the French "rulers of opinion." [26] This was an achievement complementary to that of Peter the Great, and made Russia a European power in the cultural, as well as military and political, sense. However, Catherine looked for rea-sons to be proud not only about her own person and helped to propagate several themes which were to gain prominence in the incipient Russian na-tional consciousness. The Empress chose to start the 1785 Charter with the following preamble: "The All-Russian Empire in the World is distinguished by the expanse of the lands in its possession . . . comprising within its bor-ders 165 longitudes [and] 32 latitudes . . . in true glory and majesty of the Empire [WE] enjoy the fruits, and know the results of the actions of the obe-dient, courageous, fearless, enterprising, and mighty Russian people, OUR subject . . . [whose] labors and love of Fatherland together tend primarily to the general good." Why would the autocrat choose to open a Charter defin-ing the nature and privileges of the nobility by such a paean to the country and its people? She wanted to educate her captive audience, to teach it some-thing of which at that time it was, apparently, still not sufficiently aware. She did the same addressing other strata as well. A Charter on the Liberties of the Cities also opened with a lesson in national pride. It reiterated the du-bious, but agreeable to the national ego, argument on the origins of the name "Slavs": "The ancestors of the Russians, the Slavs, the name derived from their glorious deeds [from *slava*—glory], wherever their victorious hand reached, left their traces in cities they founded and adorned by names in the Slavic tongue." [27]

Those were only words. But one should not underestimate the weight such words might carry when spoken clearly and insistently, amidst what was at best a conceptual chaos, but, more probably, a primordial silence, and spoken by rulers who had unlimited power. Peter was the first one to speak these words. Catherine spoke them with passion and missionary zeal. And such are the possibilities of autocracy that these two individuals grew more closely to resemble the Original Author and Creator, God Almighty, than did any other contemporary monarch. It is indeed disconcerting to re-alize, when one thinks about the huge territory bearing the name of Russia today, and 150 million people seeing themselves as belonging to it in the deepest sense of the word, of deriving their very identity from it, that it all began with two people—a seven-foot-tall, wild-tempered Russian tsar and Sophia Augusta Frederika, a comely German princess—who started speak-ing words which few around them understood and drummed them into their subjects' heads.

These were remarkable words; they worked wonders. And yet one should not overestimate their power. The words would not sink into the conscious-ness of the people until the situations of many of them changed most substantially, making them responsive to the message, and learning these words became their vital interest.

## The Crisis of the Nobility

The Russian nobility differed substantially from the parallel strata in other European societies. Unlike these latter, it was not in its essence a landed elite, and for this reason its status was much less determined by lineage. Several scholars have drawn attention to such conspicuous facts of the Russian landscape and language as the absence of feudal castles and of signs of territorial connection in the family names of most Russian nobles: there was nothing like "de," "zu," "von," or "Lord of Such-and-Such" appended to the names of the nobility, and, with the exception of few ancient princely families, these surnames provided no clue as to their geographical origins. In contrast to the nobilities of other countries, the Russian nobility did not descend from a feudal elite. In fact, Russia hardly experienced feudalism at all; among the European societies, it was a site of a remarkably precocious absolutism. The Russian nobility was a service estate. It had been such at least since the late fifteenth century, when the Princehood of Muscovy under Ivan III subdued and incorporated most of the Russian principalities (or appanages). Ivan IV, the Terrible, who ruled for several decades in the middle of the sixteenth century, undermined the remaining power of the appanage princes and boyars who composed the hereditary land-owning estate, and built up an alternative service nobility.[28]

A sector of the land-owning elite originated as a service elite. Those were the *dvoryane,* so-called from their connection to the tsar's Court—*dvor.* The term first appears in the documents of the twelfth century, where it refers to people residing at the prince's Court, including menials and slaves. Already then, proximity to the central power, living "close to the favor" *(bliz milosti),* attracted to the ranks of the *dvoryane* the boyars and "boyar's children" *(deti boyarskie*—a slightly lower status). By the fifteenth century it was no longer possible to keep all the *dvoryane* physically at the Court, and as a result, they were allotted estates on the land of the prince, which they held on condition of service. In distinction from boyars and "boyar's children," whose estates were hereditary, the estates of the *dvoryane* were not, and they thus were entirely dependent on the prince for their livelihood. The appanage princes and boyars also owed service to the Grand Princes of Muscovy, but before the sixteenth century the conditions of their service differed considerably from those of the *dvoryane* in that it was "free," that is, they could freely leave it. This freedom was energetically fought by the Grand Princes and by the sixteenth century disappeared altogether. The hereditary estates (sing., *votchina*) of many were confiscated by the tsar and replaced by service estates (sing., *pomestie*), frequently in widely dispersed localities, which further severed the nobles' territorial connections. Everyone was obliged to serve, and the distinctions between *dvoryane* and other servitors were gradually obliterated. Around the same time, apparently, the designation *dvoryane* itself sank into oblivion, and the privileged service estate acquired the name of "serving men by right of inheritance" *(sluzhilye liudi po otechestvu)*, which name they had at the end of the seventeenth century when Peter I acceded to the throne. Thus, however wild a species the Russian aristocracy might have been otherwise, it had, in the sardonic phrase of S. N. Eisenstadt, been "domesticated" for several centuries prior to the reforms of the great tsar.[29]

Both the status and the material well-being of a nobleman (especially nearer to the Court) depended entirely on the extent to which the sovereign was satisfied with his service. Such dependence made the position of a nobleman highly unpredictable and resulted in a permanent sense of insecurity and anxiety among the nobility. Seeking to protect their status against possible changes of fortune, the aristocracy adopted the device of *mestnichestvo*, which linked rank in service to the degree of nobility of one's family, thus guaranteeing a modicum of stability in a constantly threatened situation. It is dubious that *mestnichestvo* was ever highly effective.[30] (Nevertheless it preoccupied those eligible to participate in *mestnichestvo* litigation to such an extent as to eliminate from their minds most other concerns, and it is possible that this exclusive preoccupation with the order of precedence within their ranks was responsible for the failure of the nobility as a whole to take advantage of the "time of troubles," when the central power was singularly weak, and check the unlimited authority of the tsars.) Apparently, it also ran counter to the efforts to increase military efficiency, for which reason Tsar Fyodor decided to abolish it in 1682. *Mestnichestvo*, however, must have provided a safety valve which enabled the aristocracy to vent its anxiety while keeping it out of mischief. The sense of insecurity among the nobility grew after the abolition of this arrangement. Several additional factors contributed to this development.

In the course of the seventeenth century the territory of Muscovy increased threefold. The growing need for service nobility inevitably led to the blurring of status distinctions. The nobility expanded. Only its top echelon (men holding Boyar Council and Moscow ranks) grew from 2,642 in 1630 to 6,000 in 1681. The aristocracy felt threatened by the advance of the newcomers and fought it. Simultaneously with this development, and also in response to the changing needs of the central power, an alternative hierarchy of military and civil service emerged. New military formations were organized under foreign command, according to Western European models, which by the late 1670s outgrew the traditional military organization in numbers and far surpassed it in importance. The waning of power and influence, however little of it there was (and because there was so little of it, it seemed so precious, and the slightest diminution in it was painfully felt), was a cause of considerable distress to the aristocracy, whose preserve the traditional military organization was, and it retaliated by denying the new formations social acceptance. The civil service also grew rapidly. Though the aristocracy continued to predominate at the top levels, there were enough newcomers to cause confusion and concern. Moreover, the aristocracy increasingly arrogated to itself positions at the lower levels of administration; there was, as Meehan-Waters put it, "a stampede to bureaucratic offices by the upper nobility." [31] All this resulted in a measure of integration of the numerous lower ranks of the nobility with the exclusive higher ranks. This integration was further promoted by the legal enserfment of the peasant population in 1649, which united the upper and middle echelons of the nobility who had the right to use serf labor, and by the gradual obliteration of distinctions between hereditary and service estates, which made it possible to redefine the nobility as the land-owning stratum. The swelling of ranks and simultaneous shifts in the bases of identity could not fail to add to the sense of precariousness and insecurity which was the more or less permanent lot of the Russian nobility.

Thus, when Peter I came to power, he found his aristocracy in a state of crisis, which was growing increasingly acute. Though the psychological tribulations of his fellow-beings could hardly concern him less, the effects of his actions were both to temporarily attenuate these tribulations, or rather move them to the background, and at the same time to aggravate the crisis and intensify this sense of insecurity. In addition, however, he unwittingly offered his suffering subjects the means which was eventually to lead them out of their predicament.

At the time of Peter's accession the elite segment of the Russian nobility consisted of the Boyar aristocracy and the service noblemen of Moscow *(Moskovskie dvoryane)*. The members of the Boyar aristocracy served in top positions in the army and administration and had the right to sit in the Boyar Council—the closest approximation to a supreme court with some advisory prerogatives; they were the descendants of the appanage princes and families which had served the Grand Princes and tsars of Muscovy (probably the ancient, original *dvoryane*) since the fourteenth century. The Moscow *dvoryane* formed the lower layer of this elite. The elite as a whole was separated from the rank and file of the stratum, the provincial nobility, although it was gradually becoming less exclusive, and enjoyed privileged access to positions of power and influence and to the source of all favors, the autocrat. The valuable study of Brenda Meehan-Waters shows that, in this respect, little had changed with the opening of the new era in Russian history. Though the titles of *boyarin* and *Moskovskii dvoryanin* might have become obsolete (while the collective designation *dvoryane* eventually returned), the top positions in the military and civil service, and the privileges which went with them, remained the preserve of their descendants. Peter "was more interested in retraining than in replacing the aristocracy." At the same time, the complaint of Kniaz' Kurakin, that "princely names were mortally despised and destroyed," [32] against which Meehan-Waters argues, and which helped to originate the view that the Petrine elite was created by the tsar from *novi homines* and eclipsed the traditional aristocracy, may have more truth to it than she is willing to grant. To those who lived through the experience of Petrine reforms, the situation most certainly looked as it did to Kurakin. For there is no doubt that the wild-tempered and determinate monarch degraded and terrorized his nobles to an unprecedented degree, although, and indeed because, he chose them as the chief means to carry out his plans. Not satisfied with their being "domesticated," Peter set out to civilize them, and in his determination knew no pity. He had no regard for their values and habits, for what they held dear and appropriate. He shaved their beards, groomed with care and worn with dignity, and under the threat of "cruel punishment" ordered them to give up their resplendent kaftans for funny, outlandish clothes, which made them feel naked and brought tears of shame to their eyes. He made them leave their dirty, cozy, and familiar homes in Moscow and move into the unhealthy climate of his new city, where, horrified of displeasing their Sovereign Lord, they built houses with walls "quite out of perpendicular, and ready to fall" [33] and wasted their wealth on necessities that would have cost them close to nothing in Moscow. He decreed that they entertain and pay visits in a civilized manner (the tsar and his head of police personally drew up the lists of guests and picked the hosts), talk, dance, and play cards, denying them even the liberty to pick their noses and ready to teach them manners in no uncertain terms. He sent them abroad to study and forbade them to marry before they had satisfied his requirements; if they half-heartedly clung to their chosen lives, in meek defiance of his commands, his wrath knew no limits, and he reduced them to nothing. He claimed the bodies and souls of their children, and early taught them the advantages of keeping a watchful eye over their neighbors, so that even in their homes and very beds they had no peace and kept shaking in fear. There was no end to the humiliation Peter's most privileged stratum experienced under the tsar whom they were moved to call "the Great," and the "domesticating" efforts of Ivan the Terrible, which won that other tsar his eloquent title, appeared lenient in comparison with the civilizing undertakings of his descendant.

Peter's policies aggravated the effect produced by his tactics. They carried the dependence of the nobility on the royal power to previously undreamed of degrees. This was achieved with the help of several successfully enforced path-breaking decrees. The 1714 Decree on Single Inheritance introduced into Russia the system of entail, which in a stroke deprived younger sons of the nobility of landed income and any means either to procure a living or to attain appropriate status outside state service. At the same time another edict explicitly forbade the purchase of estates by those who had not served, making it possible for others only on condition of having served for a lengthy period.[34] As scions of ancient families (who, in the case of titled families, inherited the titles of their fathers) were thus cut off from the land and made entirely dependent on service, the decree on single inheritance tended to sever the links to the land and again redefine the nobility as a whole, undermining its identity once more. For these reasons the entail decree was opposed with unusual determination and eventually rescinded by Anne in 1731.

Of far greater importance was the fateful *ukaze* #3890 of 1722, the Table of Ranks, which was never to be rescinded and whose implications were not to be easily obliterated. The Table of Ranks reinforced earlier laws of obligatory universal and permanent service and established two points of crucial consequence for the nature of the nobility and the existential situation it was to face after its appearance. The first point was that, with the exception of princes of the royal blood, everyone's social status was to be defined by, and inseparably linked to, rank in the service hierarchy, which one was able to achieve, and not by birth. The second point institutionalized ennoblement, automatically opening the doors and privileges of the nobility to people of low birth and to foreigners. In military service all ranks carried nobility, and in civil and Court service the eight upper ranks (out of fourteen) did so. Noble status acquired by a father in the ranks which carried hereditary nobility was passed down to the children. Ancient nobility—that is, descent from noble families of the pre-Petrine period—was also respected, but everyone had to begin at the bottom of the ladder and advanced according to achievement, not birth. People claiming precedence and deportment not in accordance with their service rank were to be fined, and although the nobles of the old stock enjoyed the cumulative advantage of better preparation for service and the all-important contacts (the fact that a father, uncle, or brother was personally acquainted with the Emperor helped), anyone achieving a certain rank was to be treated as "equal to the best ancient nobility in all dignities and advantages, even being of a low birth."[35]

The connection of status to rank separated it from and undermined the importance of lineage, which was thus stripped from all its worth as a basis of stability in the life of the nobles. The automatic ennoblement led to further swelling in the ranks of the nobility, and cut deeper into its insecure identity, destroying the boundaries between it and the outer world. Both effects served to aggravate the sense of insecurity among the nobles, exacerbate the protracted crisis of identity they had been experiencing, and secure their inescapable dependence on the central, personal power of the ruler.

This was not only a predicament of the old nobility, for the moment a low-born person became ennobled, he and his children faced the same vagueness of (a new) identity and the same insecurity with respect to the superior, and therefore most precious, status earned by hard labors. Of course, such a new nobleman could not have resented the Table of Ranks as did the old nobility, and had no ancestral honor to cling to and feel robbed of; indeed, there was a conspicuous difference in the way the two sectors of the nobility reacted to their predicament. But, on the whole, the anxieties of a new nobleman were similar to those of the class he joined as a whole: the moment one's identity was transformed into that of a noble, one lived in a crisis of identity.

The personality of the frightful and wonderful sovereign, the immediate dangers to life and possessions in which his closest collaborators and servants stood, and the very amount of the tasks they had to accomplish deprived Peter's nobles of the luxury of wallowing in the pain of and ruminating over the experience of status insecurity, alleviated its acuteness, and delayed the necessity of resolving the crisis. The reigns of Peter's feeble successors, on the other hand, made the crisis itself less urgent: the tsars and tsaritsas seemed gradually but consistently to give in to the clamor of their nobility and attend to its psychological needs. The participation of the nobility in the crises of succession, which became a permanent feature of Russian political life (its only feature, one might add) in the four decades between the death of Peter and the accession of Catherine the Great, when nobles seemed to hold the destinies of autocrats of All Russias in their own hands, might have also contributed to a false sense of stability among this permanently harried stratum.[36] The period was called that of the "gradual emancipation of the gentry." In 1731 Empress Anne, after graciously conceding to accept autocratic power over her people,[37] abolished the hated law of single inheritance; soon after, she established the Corps of Cadets, an exclusive educational institution which allowed noble children to enter the Guards as officers and skip service in the ranks. In 1736 she repealed the laws of permanent service for all and reduced it to twenty-five years after the age of twenty (under Peter it was for life and started at fifteen). In addition, if there were more than one son in a family, one of the sons could be freed from service entirely to attend to the needs of the family estate. Elizabeth, who professed devotion to the example set by her father, in practice followed the example of her cousin. She increased the economic privileges of the nobility and, having no taste for ruling herself, let the Senate augment its power. Finally, in 1762, Peter III, urged by love,[38] signed the already mentioned edict abolishing compulsory service altogether—although there still was no other way to prestige and position outside its ranks.

Catherine did not approve. She left a rather subdued account of the general reaction to, and her opinion of, this measure in her *Memoirs:* "Three weeks after the death of the Empress [Elizabeth] I went to the body for the funeral service. Passing the ante-chamber, I found Prince Michail Ivanovich Dashkov, who was crying and beyond himself with joy, and running to me, he said: 'The Sovereign [Peter III] deserves that we erect a statue of gold for him; he gave liberty to the entire nobility; and, with this, is going to the Senate to announce it.' I said to him: 'Is that so? Were you serfs before, to be bought and sold?' What did the liberty consist of? It happened to consist in that one could serve or not serve according to one's liking . . . All the *dvo-ryane* rejoiced about this permission to serve or not to serve and for that hour absolutely forgot that their ancestors acquired dignities and estates which they now use, through their service." [39] When her husband was deposed several months later, Catherine set out to correct the situation. Her efforts resulted in the intensification of the sense of crisis among the nobility. This time the chronic condition demanded treatment, and a powerful medicine existed which made some healing possible.

Notwithstanding the legal indulgences of the previous reigns, the crisis could grow more acute even before the accession of the great Empress. While the objective situation did not change, and even somewhat improved, there were significant changes in the subjective perception of it. In the sixty years between the first reference to the "general good" in a Petrine *ukaze* and the accession of the Empress for whom the discourse of the *Encyclopédie* was a natural language, the consciousness of the Russian elite underwent a transformation which paralleled the developments in its nature and position. The alien concepts which Peter the Great had imported from the West, alongside technical knowledge, models of military organization, and salted herring, were slowly but surely finding their way into the curves of the noble brains, where they gradually built up, transforming the way in which the members of the elite related to themselves. The great tsar's insistence that they were serving not only him personally, but something beyond him—the State, or Fatherland—his demand that they do this of their free will, his command to have such free will—all this was inconsistent with the sense of being somebody's (even the Great Lord's) slaves. There was something elevating in the sense of belonging to a State which one served of one's free will. There was something elevating too in the consciousness of belonging to a mighty, colossal power into which Peter had transformed Russia. Many members of his elite traveled abroad. Some were sent to European courts with diplomatic missions; they observed the respect with which the nobility was treated there and the dignity with which it carried itself; they had to carry themselves with similar dignity. Peter's rhetoric was retained and developed by each of his successors. In the reign of Elizabeth, Russia participated in the Seven Years' War. This, in the opinion of one historian, was "possibly the most important aspect of her reign, even from the point of view of the country's interior development . . . the officers of her victorious armies returned to Russia after experiencing at first hand the attractions of countries on a much higher material and cultural level. Since these officers were nobles, this episode meant in fact the introduction into the only educated class in society of new, not to say revolutionary ideas."[40] One may dispute that "from this date there begins the history of Russian intelligentsia," but it is indisputable that such firsthand experience by a mass of noblemen of eighteenth-century Europe must have had a shattering impact on their notions of social relations, in general, and the nature and rights of their own order, in particular. The permission to travel abroad freely, contributed to the body of Russian laws by Peter III, diminished the chance that the lesson they learned would be quickly forgotten. Finally, although to call the Russian nobility of the Elizabethan reign "an educated class" is an exaggeration, since the knowledge noblemen were required to and could acquire in the existing conditions was almost exclusively technical, and many of them in the second half of the eighteenth century were still illiterate, even the simple exercise of mental faculties made necessary by the requirements of service, and the exposure to the very minimum of Western mores and ideas in the preparation for it, had their importance. A literate person, able to dance a minuet, master some French or German on occasion, and talk about the "general good" or "duty to the Fatherland" was likely to find the possibility of corporal punishment more revolting than his bearded ancestor who did not know any better. This development of the mind and the self-respect accompanying it, the growing ability and the acquisition of the language in which to conceptualize this self-respect, and the new frame of reference tended to intensify the sense of crisis in spite of the improvement in the objective situation.

Corporal punishment was a real threat at the time of Catherine's accession. The Russian nobility was not exempt from it. In 1730 (!), we are told, there was some talk of treating nobility with more respect, and in 1750 Count Shuvalov *contemplated* including the exemption in the Russian law. In general, legal boundaries between the nobility and other strata were at the very best vague. If not bolstered by merit and individual achievement, nobility in fact meant exceedingly little and, raising the expectations of those who were born into it, as such offered nothing to satisfy them. Nobility derived its definition from the character of its service obligations, which were greatly elaborated in Petrine edicts. Noble privileges, in distinction, received little attention in them. As a result, the only thing that distinguished nobility as an order from the rest of the Russian people was "the nature of its burdens and bonds."[41]

Catherine took the plight of the nobility to heart. "I confess," she wrote, "that although I am free of prejudice and of a naturally philosophical frame of mind, I sense in myself a great tendency to respect ancient families; I suffer seeing that many of them are reduced to poverty; I would enjoy raising them up again." Many of Catherine's policies testify to the sincerity of her concern for the nobility (as well as to the exacerbation of the sense of crisis within it). Her period saw, in a sense, a "feudal reaction" (however inapplicable the word itself is to the Russian conditions) parallel to the "feudal reaction" in eighteenth-century France. Several already traditional avenues of ennoblement were curbed by decree. A 1765 edict regarding the recruitment of young noblemen into civil service ordered their preferential treatment over non-noblemen, "according to their dignity [merit]." A *ukaze* in 1766 forbade accepting soldiers' sons into positions of chancellery clerks; another edict in 1769 similarly limited the opportunities of children of clergymen.[42]

The noble estate was finally and conspicuously set apart from the rest of the population and became distinguished by characteristics other than the way it was expected to serve. The Legislative Commission of 1767–68 was invited to discuss the pressing question of who was to be considered a nobleman. (The identity of the nobility in the 1760s was so vague that even the Heraldmaster entrusted with the responsibility of keeping a record of the noble families could not answer it and did not know how many nobles there were in the country.)[43] The Charter of Nobility of April 21, 1785, granted the order significant personal, economic, and status privileges. In accordance with the Manifesto on Noble Liberty of 1762, the freedom of noblemen to serve or not to serve was confirmed, as was the right to enter the service of friendly European states and travel abroad for the purpose of study. Also confirmed was the exemption of the nobility from personal taxation. Personal taxation was introduced by Peter I, who thus sharply separated taxable and non-taxable classes. The service nobility was exempt from taxation; those nobles who were not able to serve, however, were not. Catherine made exemption from taxation contingent on the noble status itself. Nobles were declared exempt from corporal punishment and guaranteed inviolability of noble dignity: nobility could be lost only as a result of crimes "contrary to the foundations of the noble status," and that only after the conviction by peers, confirmed by the sovereign. Nobility was granted the right of possession of estates. This, again, had previously been contingent on service, but now became an unconditional privilege of the order. Moreover, only hereditary nobles could own populated estates—that is, had the right to own serfs. Henceforth, the nobility was protected from the confiscation of estates and guaranteed security of property; even upon the conviction of a nobleman in the case of a grave crime, the estate remained in the family. In addition, the Charter legally recognized the corporate rights of the nobility and encouraged its self-government.[44]

The definition of nobility in the Charter, though, retained the emphasis on merit and service. Nobility, it declared, was "the result of the quality and virtue of the men in positions of leadership in the past, who distinguished themselves by service and, turning the service itself into dignity, gained the title of nobility for their posterity." The Charter also did not limit access to nobility through the ranks (although as we have seen, access to the ennobling ranks was limited), and it added to the previously existing avenues of ennoblement—service and creation by the sovereign—new ones: certain decorations for merit were to confer nobility as well. Thus the Charter did not guarantee the exclusivity the nobility was clamoring for.

Not all the policies of the Empress favored the order she wished to elevate and set apart. She rejected the idea of a permanent council of nobles and strove to reduce the rather meager-to-begin-with powers of the Senate. In 1763 she called a commission to revise the Manifesto of Peter III on Noble Liberty on the grounds that it tended "to constrain the liberty of the nobility in a greater measure than may be required by the interest of the Fatherland," and encouraged voluntary service. Her Legislative Commission of 1767–68 included 160 noble deputies, but 207 representatives of other groups—possibly a reflection of Catherine's desire to build up a European middle class—and the early versions of the *Instruction*, we are told, "can be used to show that Catherine modified the views of her admitted model, Montesquieu, precisely on the point of the position of the nobility." If one adds to this the crisis in noble fortunes, which, whether or not connected to her policies, characterized Catherine's reign,[45] the period may appear as "the golden age" of this unfortunate order only if compared with other periods in its history. Regrettably, as so often happens, it was not such other periods with which Catherinian nobles cared to compare their situation.

By far the most pregnant transformation brought about by Catherine belonged to the sphere of consciousness. She accelerated the revolution in the subjective perception by the nobility of its situation and quickened the development of the sense of pride and dignity which made the vestiges of the humiliating practices and social arrangements (however little remained of them) and the continuing state of dependence on the royal power most oppressive. This was the "Tocqueville effect" again: the maddening itch of inconsistency, of the discrepancy between the possible and the existent, the frustrating apprehension of unfulfilled opportunity.

"Peter gave Russians bodies," wrote the gentleman-poet M. M. Kheraskov, "and Catherine—souls," and the age of learning dawned on Russia. Neither the benefactress nor the beneficiaries realized how dangerous was the gift. Catherine's efforts to provide Russia "with the most advanced laws, the best schools, and the most enlightened government," although not crowned with absolute success, resulted in an improvement of vast magnitude. The number of educational institutions increased significantly. The nobility grew more responsive to the need to be educated, and with the active support of the Empress, set out to conquer the existing institutions of higher learning. By the end of the 1770s, children of the nobility dominated the student population of Moscow University, which, since this was at the time the only university in Russia, amounted to the "ennoblement" or "aristocra-tization" of higher education as such. In 1765 Catherine personally assumed leadership over the St. Petersburg Corps of Cadets, the exclusive school where young noblemen prepared for military service, changing its curricu-lum to include civic and general education, so that it would serve "no longer only as a military school, but also as a political and civic school." [46] The circle of noblemen willing to acquire and encourage their children to acquire education widened. The status of learning and intellectual activities gained tremendously. More and more of the middle and lower provincial gentry were filling the ranks of aspiring intellectuals. Obligatory service being a matter of the past, members of the nobility were increasingly inclined to regard education as a possible basis for its privileges.

The Legislative Commission focused on matters of concern to the nobility, in spite of its being a minority among the deputies. Around 13 percent of the nobles who signed the instructions to the Commission were illiterate, the degree of literacy of the others left much to be desired, and the more fortu-nate foreigners regarded the whole affair as a bad joke. And yet participa-tion in it required nobles to think, discuss, have an opinion, and advise the sovereign regarding issues of national importance. This unique experience could not fail to bolster the budding self-respect of the order, while excep-tional examples, such as N. I. Novikov,[47] testify as to what an inspiration serving on the Commission could be for the more acute. The incipient, and immediately flourishing, periodical press, also more or less a creation of the indefatigable Empress[48] who fostered it with maternal care, augmented the effects of these educational measures and experiences. This development of the spirit was aided by the rousing language of dignity that Catherine used, her insistent allusions to the honor and virtue of the nobility in the service of the fatherland, the very belonging to which was elevating and ennobling. And this time the republican rhetoric of the autocrat of All Russias, who (before Radishchev) said: "Freedom—you [are] the soul of all," [49] was not wasted on her subjects: they were becoming culturally alert and acquired feelings and general sensibility, which had been unable to torment them in the past days of their innocence.

For, of course, this forced "civilization" could not fail to awaken those who were touched by it to the degrading inconsistency of their actual posi-tion with the principles of the noble status and their practical implementa-tion in the cases of their counterparts in other European societies. The poli-cies of Catherine were themselves inconsistent; they could not be consistent. On the one hand, she sincerely wished for the betterment of the nobility. She wanted to believe and prove to others that Russia was a European state and, therefore, wanted it to have a respectable European nobility. She was, or at least cared to pose as, a disciple of Voltaire, to whose views she exposed her loyal, but not quite awake of their primeval slumber, subjects. She sponsored the translation of the *Encyclopédie,* banned in France; she cultivated civic spirit. Yet she also believed that Russia could not do without autocracy. She was jealous of the nobles' timid efforts to interfere in her government. Ultimately, she was not ready and could not deliver what she had taught the nobility to expect.

Even the well-intended Charter of Nobility, which finally established this order as a privileged estate, given its timing, contributed to the intensification of the sense of anxiety within the nobility, instead of soothing it. The privileges of the nobility were confirmed exactly when it had lost the very basis for them: obligatory service, for which they were a just reward. True, education offered an alternative basis, but, unlike service, culture was not self-legitimating. The Russian *dvoryanstvo* under Catherine found itself in a situation analogous to that of the French *noblesse* in the early eighteenth century, and, like the French *noblesse,* it was turning into a cultural elite. As in France, not this would deliver it from its predicament.

### Preoccupation with the Crisis of the Nobility and the Turn to National Identity

The plight of the nobility was, undoubtedly, the first question seriously to preoccupy the inchoate Russian intellect. The sense of crisis was pervasive and manifested itself in many ways. The nobility could not make up its mind about service. On the one hand, it considered the freedom not to serve as its greatest privilege. On the other hand, it (at any rate, that sector of it which did not opt for non-existence and therefore was affected by the crisis) never used this freedom. Service, or rather rank earned in it, remained the main road to status until the end of the tsarist regime, and was the only such road at least until the 1820s. In 1786, a dramatist from the nobility, Ya. B. Kniazhnin, wrote: "People have all gone wild about ranks . . . And he who passes his dark life without rank does not seem to us a man at all." [50] The majority of the nobility, as is clear from the materials of the Legislative Commission, were concerned less with the necessity to serve as such than with the lack of guarantees for the distinctiveness of the nobility in service, which institutionalized its penetrability from below. Some even called for a return to obligatory service. The representatives of Kashin nobility instructed the Legislative Commission: "Every *dvoryanin* should serve his fatherland ten years without respite . . . because the first duty of the *dvoryanin* is to demonstrate his merits to his fatherland for all those advantages with which he is endowed by the sovereign." Alternately, noblemen expressed the wish for preferential treatment of the nobility when it came to promotions. While they were willing to serve, they were reluctant to share the privileges of service with others. A majority was opposed to the Table of Ranks and thought that service should not automatically ennoble. "As in all European states," wrote the representatives of Pustorzheva nobility, "non-nobles reaching the top ranks cannot without a grant of a diploma of nobility ascribe to themselves Von, De, Don, and similar nobility; in the like manner we also most humbly ask that the ancient *dvoryanstvo* . . . be distinguished . . . from non-*dvoryane*." [51] One way or the other, service remained essential for the definition of nobility.

Service was acquiring the connotation it had had within classical patriotism. The rhetoric of the tsars had caught on. The documents of the Legislative Commission are full of references to the "beloved fatherland." This is still little but rhetoric: the "fatherland" is incessantly reminded that it owes everything it is to the "blood and wounds" of its nobility, and the interests of the two are believed to be identical. The patriotic rhetoric, however, allowed the nobility to express its desperate craving for independence from the autocrat and at least to pose as an indispensable main element of the body politic. It gave them the possibility of expressing unthinkable, wishful thoughts, in which some later observers saw a move toward the idea of *Rechtstaat*. Whether this is what it was is debatable. At the Legislative Commission the mass of the nobility appeared to have but one concern: to distinguish itself as persuasively as possible from the lower strata and keep it that way.[52]

The position of the nobility as a whole was understandably conservative: the majority, who were essentially inactive, forsaking their own aspirations of high achievement, wanted to preserve their present status by preventing its devaluation, which would follow with the ascendancy of their inferiors. But, apart from the instructions to the Legislative Commission, the majority was not vocal. The opinion leaders who would soon fashion the ways Russia thought came from elsewhere. The vocal segment of the nobility, that is, the first Russian intellectuals, subscribed to two positions regarding the matter of the nature of nobility and, in particular, service. The first position was that of the ancient nobility. The other represented the views of "Peter's men"—those who owed their elevated status to the Table of Ranks and the spirit of reform. Intellectuals, even if they were of the ancient nobility, represented a novel type of personality in Russia; they were distinguished not only by their birth, and valued the distinctions which reflected their talent and education. Most of the intellectuals, however, came from the new or marginal nobility (such as the nobility of foreign stock), since, not having the honor of an indigenous ancient lineage to rely upon, they were more motivated to excel through their own efforts. Not unexpectedly, therefore, the position of the ancient nobility, which shared the fundamental conservatism of the majority, was a minority position in the case of the opinion leaders, and in addition was less systematically argued.

The most consistent representative of this conservative position was Kniaz' M. M. Shcherbatov, who showed himself to be the staunchest de-

fender of the exclusivist interests of the *dvoryanstvo* at the Legislative Commission. He too utilized patriotic rhetoric and justified his demands for the
preservation and protection of the privileges of nobility by the service it as
an order, and the ancestors of the present noble families, rendered the fatherland. For example, regarding the right of the nobility to own serfs, the
comparison of which to tyranny he found outright offensive, he argued:
"Did our fathers, who had the honor to marshal their service against common enemies and to defend the Orthodox faith, aspire to receive rewards so
that now their heirs would be compared to tyrants? Will such be your reward for the salvation of you and your souls?" Some of Shcherbatov's
works, which he carefully preserved for posterity, though they remained
largely concealed from his contemporaries, resound with republican pathos
the like of which can easily be found on the pages of Poynet or Hotman. In
his *Comments on the Great Instruction of the Empress Catherine II,* the
irreverent prince expressed himself directly: "Even though nations are subjected to the scepter of the monarchs, yet people belong to God, and God, as
their creator, never loses his right over His creation; and the monarchs are
nothing but magistrates placed [here] for the common good." Yet classical
patriotic outbursts such as this had no democratic overtones, and patriotism
was unquestionably subservient to the interests of the order. The "people"
Shcherbatov talked about was the ancient nobility. Whatever served its interests was patriotic; whatever did not—was despotism. "It is the clearest
sign of despotism," the Kniaz' wrote, recalling nobles who specialized in
jesting for the benefit of the royal audience, "that persons of most noble
families were reduced to such mean position." His identity, which was still
clearly determined by his order rather than nationality, was assaulted and
undermined, as he believed, by the upstarts, and it is against this that the
valiant Kniaz' fought. Nothing could be more "heinous and despicable," in
his opinion, than a merchant turned nobleman, which brought indignity on
the very names of "officer" and "nobleman"; he could not find another epithet for the desire of "almost all merchants to acquire ranks and nobility,"
confessed Shcherbatov, but that of a "wicked scourge" *(vrednaia zaraza).*
Shcherbatov's attitude toward service was logically consistent with his general outlook. Although service was an attribute of noble status, it was not
its primary basis; therefore, he rejected the Table of Ranks, which institutionalized ennoblement. He juxtaposed this arrangement to the times of
Ivan the Terrible, of which he wrote nostalgically: "Not only for the rank
were then noblemen respected, but also for their birth, and so the ranks gave
only positions, while birth brought dignity." [53]

Few went that far. More often the hesitant defenders of the old restricted
themselves to generalized expressions of elitism and conservatism, fulminat-
ing against upstarts and advising everyone to keep to one's place. Such were,
for example, the views of the famous Alexander Sumarokov, one of the first

Russian poets, "the father of the Russian theater," and a prominent defender of the interests of the nobility. Himself a nobleman of an old family, whose ancestors served under Tsar Alexis, Sumarokov scorned and feared *novi homines*. Nobility, the old nobility of birth, was for him the natural elite of the nation, and he found it absurd and unnatural that it could be challenged by people from below. In the preface to his play *Dmitri the Pretender*, he wrote: "A lowly clerk *(pod'yachii)* became the judge of the Parnassus and the arbiter of taste of the Moscow public! . . . Certainly the end of the world is coming." But nobility derived its superiority from its patriotism, and this—not birth as such—justified Sumarokov's conservatism. In fact, for Sumarokov, nobility and patriotism were synonymous; he called noblemen "sons of the fatherland." Even beyond that, Sumarokov's conservatism was not consistent. In the same preface to *Dmitri the Pretender*, he defined the concepts of "public" and "plebs" in a manner closely reminiscent of La Bruyère, thus: "The word 'Public,' as Mr. Voltaire also agrees, does not denote a whole society, but only a small part of it, namely people who are knowledgeable and have taste . . . The word 'Plebs' refers to the low people, not the word 'Mean people'; for mean people are convicts and other contemptible scum, and not artisans and agriculturists. We here give this name to everyone who is not noble. Nobility! big deal! . . . Oh, unbearable noble pride, worthy of contempt and lashing! The real Plebs are ignorants, even when they have a great rank, the wealth of Croesus, and count among their ancestors Zeus and Juno, who never existed, the son of Philip, the victor, or rather, ruiner of the universe, or Julius Caesar, who strengthened the glory of Rome, or rather destroyed it." He thus opposed formal nobility to the "public," and defined true nobility by culture and intellectual excellence. In a *Satire on Nobility*, he presented nobility as a reflection of service to the nation, although apparently he still considered people of noble stock the pool out of which such true noblemen were to be recruited:

> I bring this satire to you, *dvoryane!*
> I write for the first members of the fatherland . . .
> I should be honored, if I earned respect myself:
> And if I have no aptitude for office,
> My ancestor is noble, but I'm not.[54]

The position of the vocal majority—represented by noble intellectuals who owed their position in society to Peter's reforms—was that of unqualified support for the Table of Ranks. In it virtue—nobility of spirit and behavior, and especially service to the nation—was regarded as the basis of the noble status, thus giving this view an unmistakable tint of nationalism.[55] Prince Antiokh Kantemir, called "the first Russian writer to busy himself seriously with belles-lettres," was also among the earliest proponents of this position. Kantemir was the son of a Moldavian (or Wallachian) *hospodar'* who moved to Russia and became a Russian subject under Peter. The educated, intelligent young Antiokh was a protégé of the great tsar and could expect a bright future, but the tsar died when the youth was only seventeen. Kantemir, though of an ancient family, was left with no connections among the Russian nobility and, owing to circumstances in which he could see the hand of some Russian grandees, deprived of his inheritance. He began to write in the period of the temporary ascendancy of the ancient nobility and their assault against the "low-born" new nobility, which included newly ennobled natives, and foreigners now recognized as Russian nobles. His second satire (1730) was entitled "On the Envy and Pride of the Ill-Natured Nobles." Kantemir wrote in the preface: "I do not intend to disparage nobility, but to oppose the pride and envy of ill-natured nobles, by which means I defend nobility as such. In this satire I say that the advantage of nobility is honest, and useful, and glorious, if the nobleman has to his name honest deeds and is adorned by virtuous behavior, that the darkness of ill-nature eclipses the brilliance of nobility and that not the one whose name can be found in ancient scrolls deserves greatest distinctions, but the one whose good name is commended today; after that I show that pride is inappropriate to nobility and that it is base for a nobleman to envy the well-being of those of meaner birth, if they achieved honor and glory through their good deeds, and had to spend their time not in games and self-pampering, but in earning their glory with sweat and corns for the good of the Fatherland." [56]

More than half a century later "the singer of Catherine," Gavrila Derzhavin, "the first significant lyrical talent in the Russian literature of the eighteenth century," echoed Kantemir. He devoted to the subject a poem, "The Grandee," and, in it, wrote:

> . . . I wish to glorify the honor
> Which by themselves they would achieve
> As a reward for worthy deeds;
> Those who were not adorned from birth
> By famous names, luck, or position,
> But valiantly earned respect
> From their fellow-citizens.
> . . . What is nobility and rank
> But excellencies of our spirit?
> I am a prince—if spirit in me shines.
> A master—if I can control my passions;
> *Boyarin*—if I am a friend to tsars,
> The law, and Church, concerned
> About the good and welfare of all.
> A nobleman should be the one who has
> A healthy reason and enlightened spirit,

> The one who is a living proof
> Of that his rank is truly noble,
> That he is but a tool of power,
> The fundament of royal building,
> His every thought, his words, his deeds
> Are these—good, dignity, and glory.[57]

Derzhavin was a scion of a modest noble family who owed his position to his own efforts.

Whatever the position taken, the obsessive preoccupation with the definition of nobility was a sign of the status anxiety and insecurity which plagued its members. It continued to plague them until the annihilation of the order in the final debacle of 1917. The majority persisted in demanding to curb access to ennoblement, and in the nineteenth century their demands met with moderate success: the laws of 1845 and 1856 raised the level of ranks and decorations which carried nobility;[58] a *numerus clausus* for the nobility was introduced in the universities, which ensured their predominance in higher education. These alleviating measures were offset by the emancipation of the serfs, which signified the beginning of the speedy destruction of noble privileges, leaving the nobility a privileged order only in name, and thereby causing a sudden exacerbation of its chronic crisis. The implications of this fateful development, and their role in bringing about the Revolution, are not fully realized, but they form a subject for another book.

The protracted crisis of identity within the nobility, similarly to the development in other countries, rendered this elite stratum sympathetic to the nationalist ideas that had been forcefully promoted by Russia's energetic despots, Peter and Catherine the Great. For the great majority of the noblemen, even by the time of the Legislative Commission, the nationalist ideas were still nothing but rhetoric, which they used, as they would magical incantations, to appease their godlike rulers. Yet these ideas offered a most potent remedy for the malady with which the nobility was afflicted. Nationality elevated every member of the nation and offered an absolute guarantee from the loss of status beyond a certain—high—level. One could be stripped of nobility, but (unless one rejected it of one's own free will, a possibility which was not to be relevant for Russians) not of nationality. There was in nationalism the assurance of a modicum of unassailable dignity, dignity that was one's to keep. And so, Russian aristocrats were gradually turning nationalist; they were beginning to experience the therapeutic effects of national pride, and their identity as noblemen was giving way to the national identity of Russians.

It was exactly that sector of the nobility which felt its crisis most acutely—that is, the service nobility in the capitals, the elite, the aristocracy, which saw no solution besides total withdrawal and did not wish to withdraw—which was turning to nationalism. Among this elite rare was a man who, like Kniaz' Shcherbatov, did not escape into the soothing embrace of the new identity, but persisted in the desperate, hopeless efforts to salvage the old. There were some timid nationalists, the descendants of ancient families, who had too much to give up with their identity as nobles. They were quite satisfied with the idiom and limits of classical patriotism, in which the definition of the "nation" was narrow and in fact included only the nobility. This accounts for Sumarokov's use of the term "sons of the fatherland" as a synonym of *dvoryane*. But this notion could not aspire to longevity in Russia: the nobility there simply was not a "nation" in the sense given to the concept by Montesquieu, and such wishful thinking flew in the face of reality. For the nobility of service, however, classical patriotism was too tight, and they converted to the new, modern faith with abandon.

For at least half a century the new identity did not entirely eclipse the old, but existed side by side with it. How closely the two issues—the crisis of identity within the nobility and its nationalism—were connected is evident in most of the contemporary sources. But nowhere are this connection and the psychological entanglement of the noble nationalists expressed with greater clarity than in the famous "Questions" by Denis Fonvisin, answered by Catherine. Fonvisin belonged to a Lifland knightly family, but his ancestors, first captives of Ivan IV, settled in Moscow. The original faith of his family was Protestant, his name was spelled "fon-Visin," and thus, though in some way he could be considered of an old noble family, his ancient nobility was of a peculiar kind.[59] Fonvisin early became a Russian nationalist, and greatly contributed to the development of the national consciousness.

In his most famous play, *The Minor*, Fonvisin defines nobility through a protagonist, Starodum (Old Thinker), a man of Peter's time, who measures everything by the honest measure of those good old days. According to Starodum, nobility is earned in service of the fatherland and cannot be acquired simply by birth. He distinguishes between the true and formal nobility and says: "Honor! Only one sort of honor should be flattering—the spiritual one; and only that one deserves a spiritual honor who bought his rank not with money, and whose nobility is not just in the rank." "I reckon the degree of nobility according to the amount of services the grandee rendered the fatherland, and not according to the amount of affairs he grabbed because of his haughtiness." Starodum is distressed by the lamentable situation of Fonvisin's own time, when real nobility is undervalued and nobles only in name rule the day. If only people understood the significance of office, he says, "there would be no such noblemen, whose nobility, one may say, is buried with their ancestors. A nobleman unworthy to be a nobleman—I know nothing baser than that on earth." [60] But, alas, those considered noblemen do not behave like ones, and thus nobility is neglected. The vagueness and insecurity of the noble status which result from this are the focus of the "Questions."

In the form of open-ended questions Fonvisin, in fact, underscores the

chief symptoms of the evil and, by implication, points to the conditions that
should prevail instead. Question #4 is: "If nobility is the reward for service
(merit), and service (merit) is open to every citizen, why then are merchants
never ennobled, but only fabricants and monopolists?" The meaning is: if
nobility were indeed a reward for service, merchants would be ennobled
too; since they are not ennobled, nobility at present is not a reward for service, but is something corrupt. Another question (#9) is: "Why are notorious and evident idlers everywhere received with the same respect as are
honest people [people are, of course, nobility]?" The meaning is: unworthy
people are rewarded; we, the worthy ones, not they, should be preferred.
Another question (#13): "How can we raise the decaying spirit of the nobility? How can we ban from hearts the insensitivity toward the dignity of the
noble status? How can we make the honorable rank of a nobleman a doubtless proof of spiritual nobility?" The meaning is: the spirit of nobility is in
decay; the noble status has lost its dignity; the honorable rank of a nobleman (formal nobility) is not a reflection of spiritual (true) nobility. But what
is this formal nobility, and who are these idlers who ban the sensitivity toward the dignity of the noble status (thus threatening it) from the hearts of
the citizens? These are, of course, the representatives of the ancient families.
While Shcherbatov could not think calmly about the Table of Ranks, which
ennobled merit and thus assailed the exclusivity of the ancient nobility and
undermined it, the new nobility found it impossible to reconcile itself to the
respects still paid to the ancient nobility, for it could never hope to become
equal to the latter in birth and antiquity, and so long as those were legitimate
bases of the noble status, its own identity was insecure. However looked at,
the situation was unsatisfactory. Fonvisin clearly expresses this dissatisfaction and is unwilling to accept the situation as it is. He even rationalizes an
escape from it: nobility defined as it is, is corrupt, which is a good reason
for an honest, spiritually noble person not to belong to it. But escape where?
The two last questions (#20 and #21), on the face of it unconnected to the
points raised earlier, pose the alternative: nationality. And question #21
asks pathetically: "What does our national character consist of?"[61] It is a
most significant, urgent question. Here, Fonvisin is prepared to trade his
identity as a nobleman for that of a Russian, but what is it? This new entity,
Russian nationality, does not as yet exist.

## The West and *Ressentiment*

The other question—#20—reflected the instantly torturous character of
Russian nationalism and its frustrating, ambivalent, and ineluctable dependence on the West. For the first Russian nationalists found themselves between the hammer and the anvil. In a desperate bid to escape the psycholog-

ical agony of the crisis of identity, they threw themselves into the arms of *ressentiment*. Its poisonous vapors would cripple and mutilate their souls, and work wonders; they would create a fertile soil, a hothouse for the growth of national consciousness, and, melting old frustrations and aspirations, for long decades, incessantly, indefatigably fuel, nourish, and shape new passions. And so the Russian nation would be born. Fonvisin asked: "How can we remedy the two contradictory and most harmful prejudices: the first, that everything with us is awful, while in foreign lands everything is good; the second, that in foreign lands everything is awful, and with us everything is good?" [62] This was the dilemma on which the construction of the Russian national identity was predicated.

### The West as the Model

The awareness of the West was forced on Russia by Peter the Great, who, as in everything he did, allowed no time for getting prepared for the encounter: the confrontation was sudden and shocking, and evidently signified the beginning of a new era. While some *boyare* bewailed their beards that had to give way to the importation of Western customs, on the whole, the first reaction to this other world seems to be that of an undiluted admiration. The reminiscences of the first Russian travelers to the West, who were sent there by Peter, convey a sense of wonder, of meeting something—good—out of this world. *Stol'nik* Peter Tolstoy admired the temperance of Venetians, which evidently contrasted with the behavior of his countrymen. "Venetian people are clever, politic, and there are very many educated people; they do not appear affectionate, but are very hospitable [*zelo priyomny*] toward foreigners. They do not like to amuse themselves and do not go to each other for dinners and suppers, and they are all very sober; you will never ever see a drunken man here; and with that they have lots of beverages, lots of all kinds of excellent grape wines . . . but they do not use them much, but rather drink lemonades, coffee, chocolate [*kafy, chekulaty*], and others of this sort which cannot make a person drunk." A. A. Matveev, who visited France in 1705 (and thought that it "excels all European peoples"), noticed other things, but was similarly impressed. "Verily," he wrote, "it deserves to be mentioned with ineffable astonishment that not one person can be found of either male or female sex of noble family, who would not be honestly educated and taught." One could still find such expressions of unmarred admiration, some twenty years later, in the writings of most educated Russians, and V. K. Trediakovskii, also enchanted by France, devoted one of the very first verses in modern Russian to "the beautiful place, the dear banks of the Seine." [63]

At this early stage, the West was eagerly accepted as an absolute and incontestable model, the only possible standard of behavior. *The Honest Mir-*

*ror of Youth*, the Petrine manual of manners, contains some evidence of this attitude, uninhibited and un-self-conscious. Instructing its young readers regarding the appropriate manner of addressing one's parents, it advises: One should talk to them respectfully, "as if one happens to be talking to some important foreign person." Much later, Sumarokov, in the already quoted preface to *Dmitri the Pretender,* in an attempt to teach his audience respect toward Russian theater, dramatically asks: "You, travelers, who visited Paris and London, tell me! do people there crunch nuts while watching Drama; and when the performance is on the stage, do they whip drunken and quarreling coachmen, causing alarm to the floor, balconies, and the whole theater?"[64] (Of course, nothing of the sort happens in the civilized world.)

However, more revealing than such explicit references is the widespread unreflective imitation of Western ways in the everyday life of Moscow and St. Petersburg nobility, the extent of which can be gauged from the matter-of-fact descriptions of this life and even more so from the amount of criticism of which this imitative behavior became the focus.[65] The excitement with everything Western in Russia is reminiscent of the mass Anglophilia in France in the first half of the eighteenth century, and, if anything, is more enthusiastic.

The national idea itself is also, in some way at least, a sign of recognition of the West as a model, and the earliest expressions of Russian nationalism (in the sense of national patriotism and consciousness) have to do with comparisons of Russia with the West. Such comparisons remain an important element of the national lore, but later lose their originally unproblematic, confident character. The early representatives of Russian nationalism did not see the West as threatening. The achievement of Peter the Great and the change in the international position and, in many ways, internal image of Russia were so tremendous as to border on fantastic, which greatly contributed to the sense of confidence and pride of the first nationalists, all of whom were "Peter's men." Russia of their time was indeed a wonder in the eyes of the world, and they were justifiably proud of belonging to it. They were proud of Russia's greatness, but they defined it as similarity to Europe. Their confidence was the confidence that Russia was a European state, and this was the chief foundation of their *national* pride: they were proud to be up to the standard. A telling example of the prevalence of this view is the popular *Tale of the Russian Sailor Vasilii Koriotski and the Beautiful Princess Iraklia of the Land of Florence.* The tale dates to the early eighteenth century and belongs to the genre representing "the favorite reading of the average eighteenth-century reader."[66] Its audience is the literate Russian public— noblemen and burghers who, literally, can read. The tale is based on an earlier translated story, but is in significant ways a reflection of the Russian reality of the time. Vasilii is a poor nobleman who goes to St. Petersburg and becomes a sailor to earn himself a living and glory. From Petersburg he sails to Holland and Florence, is sent to study abroad, and eventually, after distinguishing himself in every possible way, becomes the king of the "land of Florence." While foreigners cannot find words to praise the remarkable "Russian sailor," Russia throughout the tale is called "Russian Europe" *(Rossiyskaya Evropia)*. The term has a peculiar sound and is never repeated in the later Russian literature, but whether it means the Russian part of Europe, or the European land of Russia, it clearly represents Russia as essentially a European state.

This early pride in Russia was frequently associated with the pride in its unusual monarch. Peter, however, was extolled for his part in increasing the prestige of Russia: its meteoric rise to equality with the ideal was believed to have been his doing. One can assume that the admiration for Peter was sincere, for it was expressed most forcefully when the tsar died, and the primary motive behind the trenchant panegyrics was likely to be grief rather than expectation of reward. The pioneers of Russian nationalism mourned their first and greatest patriot, the author of their glory.[67] In 1725, upon receiving the news of the tsar's death, the Russian ambassador in Constantinople, I. I. Nepluyev, wrote in his *Memoirs:* "I moistened the letter with tears . . . and, verily, was unconscious for more than a day and a night; and, of course, it would be sinful to behave otherwise: this monarch raised our fatherland to the comparison with others, taught to recognize *that we too are human* [emphasis added]; in one word, whatever you look at in Russia, everything has him as its beginning." [68] Feofan Prokopovich, a bishop and the foremost political propagandist of Peter's time, in his dramatic obituary *The Word on the Burial of Peter the Great,* was more ornate:

> The author of innumerable our advantages and joys, who resurrected Russia as if from the dead and raised it to such power and glory, or rather the one who gave birth [to] and educated [it], a veritable patriot [and] father of his fatherland [or: a veritable father to the patriots of his fatherland—*pryamoi syn otechestvia svoyego otets*] . . . This is your own, Russia, Samson, whom nobody in the world expected to appear in you, and when he appeared the world was astonished. He found in you but a feeble power and turned it into a strong one like a stone, adamant; . . . When he destroyed those who attacked us, he broke [the spirit of] those who wished us ill and *filling the lips of envy* [emphasis added], ordered the world to glorify himself . . . This is your first, O Russia, Jafeth . . . he spread your might and glory to the shores of the ocean, to the limits of your advantage . . . He left us, but not as paupers and wretched: the immense riches of his power and glory . . . remain with us. As he made his own Russia, so it will be . . . he made it glorious all over the world, and it will be glorious forever.[69]

The incipient national consciousness at the time of Peter utilized the proto-nationalist, Renaissance vocabulary developed mostly by the

Western-oriented Ukrainians and Poles at the Moscow Court of the seventeenth century. Already then, under the influence of Renaissance notions,
there appeared new concepts which identified "the land" and "the people"
and used as synonyms of both such new words and word combinations as
"Russia" (*Rossia,* which replaced *Rus'*), "Russian state," "Russian tsardom," "Russian realm." Already then, too, it is possible to find a few examples of poetic glorification of Russia as the extension of the monarch.
This glorification has a formal character and little, if any, relation to existing
reality: it extols Russia according to a Renaissance formula and for what
Russia should have been if it were a Western European state, but clearly was
not. In 1660, Simeon Polozki, the Court poet, wrote: "Russia increases its
glory/ Not only by her sword, but also/ By printing everlasting books." [70]
This—when in the course of the seventeenth century 374 books were
printed in Russia, of which only 19 were of a secular nature.

The nascent civic vocabulary and the borrowed formalistic traditions
were absorbed by the emergent national thought of Peter's reign, which,
spurred by the example of the great tsar himself, greatly augmented the former and changed the nature of the latter. In the writings of Prokopovich or
Pososhkov, existing civic terms appear with greater frequency and many
new terms emerge: "father of the fatherland," "glory of the fatherland,"
"Russian people," "sons of Russia." Shafirov, in the *Discourse,* introduces
the concept "son of the fatherland" as a synonym of "patriot," and Prokopovich, for the first time, uses the word "nation" *(nazia).*[71] Simultaneously
with the development of the vocabulary, instances of glorification and
expressions of pride in Russia—as a polity and/or a people—became more
frequent and acquired a measure of realism. Russia was belauded not for
printing books, which it did not do, but for what it really was or at the time
gave a reasonable promise of becoming. Such celebrated qualities were the
huge territory which Russia now possessed, and its miraculously increased
prestige—both to no small extent achievements of Peter. Not unexpectedly,
it was the Great North War which inspired many of these early expressions
of national pride. In 1709, Prokopovich, in the "Laudatory Speech on the
Glorious Victory over Swedish Forces," wrote: "Were someone to travel, or
rather fly in one's mind over [this territory], starting from our River Dneper
to the shores of the Black Sea . . . from there to the East to the Caspian Sea,
or even to the borders of the Persian kingdom and from there to the remotest
limits of the Chinese kingdom of which we have hardly heard, and from
there . . . to the New Land [*Novaya Zemlia*] and the shores of the Arctic
Ocean, and from there to the West to the Baltic Sea . . . and [back] to Dneper: those are the limits of our monarch." In another speech the eloquent
bishop turned to greatness of a different sort: "Oh, universal astonishment!
How suddenly and tremendously in this war Russia rose to glory and advantage! . . . and the whole world clearly perceived how the Russian people,

when many foretold its ruin, rose higher and as if ascended from disdain to praise, from contempt to fear, from weakness—to power!"[72]

The relevant other in these early panegyrics is "the West," which is clearly recognized as a model. Zhurovskii, in the drama *Russian Glory* (1724), represented Russia as favored by deities of the Greco-Roman Pantheon: Neptune, Mars, and Athena. While Russia before was miserable, now it is experiencing good times: Neptune offers it the seas—an allusion to the creation of the Russian fleet; Mars offers his help—a reference to its victorious weapons; but in Athena Russia promises to see a faithful friend—this is a recognition of the Western hierarchy of values, in which reason and its achievements represent a *sine qua non* of national excellency, and a bid to enter the competition with the West on its terms. The moment the West was recognized as a model—and this happened simultaneously with the first, tentative flirtation with national identity—the degree to which this identity was to be psychologically gratifying hinged on the outcome of the competition with the West.

### The Competition with the West and the Build-up of Ressentiment; The Stages of Reaction-Formation

That competition with the West was indeed the motive force behind the early achievements of Russian culture and the formation of national consciousness is attested by all of eighteenth-century Russian literature as well as life (and this is true, though in a less simple way, for subsequent centuries as well). In the late eighteenth century, Nikolai Karamzin, while still in the optimistic phase of his nationalism, explicitly pointed to the competition with the West—and a victory in it—as the main goal of Petrine reforms and the natural national motivation. In initiating his reforms, it was as if Peter had said to the Russians: "Look: become equal to them, and then, if you can, surpass them!" Like the reforms, contemporary attitudes were justified to the extent that they promoted the possibility of winning the competition. At this stage, Karamzin favored unabashed imitation of the West, for, he thought, "Shouldn't one first become equal in order to surpass?"[73]

This attitude, which, as we see, persisted until the end of the eighteenth century, very soon created a problem, and in the time of Karamzin, who several years later abandoned it himself, it was rarely encountered, at least in the literature, in such an uninhibited, untroubled form. For, after the death of the great tsar, whose unique personality and truly extraordinary achievement encouraged unbounded optimism, it became quite clear that Russia was not on a par with any of the European states it boldly and cheerfully bid to compare itself with, that it was not at all up to the standard it had appropriated, that it was, in fact, clearly, painfully, hopelessly inferior. Nationality saved Russian noblemen from the agony of the noble identity—

only so that their souls would burn in the consuming flame of the sense of national inadequacy.

The realization of the discrepancy between the Russian reality and its chosen ideal did not come as a shock: it developed gradually, with the growth of national consciousness itself. In fact, it was an integral part of the national consciousness. But it came early. Already in Pososhkov (1724) one finds a recognition of the superiority of the foreigners and a certain suspicion as to the effects of admiring them.[74] The recognition of the superiority of the West gave rise to increasingly complicated attitudes which eventually built up into *ressentiment*. The simplest reaction was the acknowledgment of the fact that comparison with the West in general was unflattering to Russia. It did not question the view of the West as a legitimate model, an ideal. One finds examples of this attitude throughout the eighteenth century. It is very well expressed in a 1763 poem by Sumarokov, "A Choir to the Upside-down World," which repeats the theme of "Overseas" as an idealized contrast with Russia:

> To the shore flew a bird, a titmouse
> From beyond the midnight sea
> From beyond the cold ocean:
> She was asked by those who met her here,
> What are the overseas customs?
> And the visitor-titmouse answered:
> Everything there is upside-down.
> Overseas, respectable scholars . . .
> Never cling to old superstitions,
> Never hypocrites, never flatter.
> Governors overseas are honest.
> Clerks there do not own teams of horses,
> Their wives do not display precious stones,
> Their children do not ask for gifts and presents.
> Overseas the scribes are not cheating . . .
> Overseas they are skilled in writing.
> Overseas the contracts are honored
> Farming revenues is not in fashion,
> So that the State does not suffer.
> They do not feed plaintiffs with "tomorrow."
> Overseas, honorable people
> Do not make it their habit to be haughty,
> And they do not ruin simple people.
> Money there is not buried in the ground.
> Peasantry is not despoiled there;
> Villages are not lost in card-games,
> Overseas they do not sell people.
> Women in their old age are not squeamish,

Although rosaries they there do not wear,
They do not backbite honest people.
And exorbitant rates on the money
Overseas are against law and order.
Overseas they do not steal the taxes.
Overseas, coquettes to the churches
Do not go to get into mischief.
Idlers overseas are not allowed
In the houses where live honest people.
They do not embarrass people overseas,
Do not wash dirty laundry in public.
Minds there are not drowned in hard drinking;
Those in power do not oppress others;
Overseas, grandees are not worshipped.
All the noble children go to school there;
Their fathers, too, are educated.
Even maidens overseas must have learning;
Overseas they are not prone to drivel
That a maiden has no need for reason,
That she only needs a skirt and be pretty . . .
Overseas they do not scorn their language,
Only those are scorned who destroy it,
Who, for no good reason, after travel
Fill their empty heads with foreign air
And then make with it turgid bubbles.
Orators there do not talk nonsense,
Poetasters do not make verses;
Writers overseas have clear thinking,
Speeches of the speakers are coherent:
Overseas, fools do not become writers,
Criticism is not full of poison.
People do not spy on each other,
Overseas the greatest merit is science,
It's loved better than chicanery there . . .
Merchants overseas are not deceivers.
Pride in those lands is hardly suffered,
Flattery is not to be heard there,
And there is no meanness overseas.[75]

"Overseas" is a Utopia, as is the generalized "West"; it is an ideal, a standard. And the sad fact is that Russia falls so conspicuously short of this ideal: in effect, it is the ideal turned upside-down.

Some of the themes in Sumarokov's poem were focal points in the growing nationalistic literature; one finds here the dissatisfaction with the haughtiness of the grandees, with honoring nobility without merit, with the attitude toward learning and the state of letters, with the attitude toward the native language and self-image, as well as—unexpectedly, for Sumarokov was a defender of serfdom—a condemnation of the habit of selling people. Yet the recognition of the discrepancy between Russia and the West in this case is diffuse; it does not focus on any one area where the discrepancy is most pronounced or postulate an organizing principle for it. Several important authors of the eighteenth century, more sensitive to the original meaning of the idea of the nation, regard the social and political conditions in the country (especially serfdom and the situation of the peasantry) as the essence of the difference between Russia and its ideal.

There are two reactions to the recognition of socio-political reality in Russia as the core problem: shame and denial. Shame is a rare reaction: given how singularly unpleasant this feeling is, it must be difficult to sustain it over a period of time of any length. As a result, this reaction is characteristic only of one important writer: Alexander Radishchev. Radishchev's genuine abhorrence of the barbarism of serfdom, and concern for the peasantry, his understanding and passion for liberty as a right of humans as such, make him an exception among the creators of the Russian culture. These qualities also make him the only possible representative of civic nationalism, which in Russia never took root. Radishchev is also unusual, though not unique, in that his Western model was not Europe, but the United States of America. Yet it is significant that even his abhorrence of and shame over this peculiar Russian reality is expressed and felt as an embarrassment in the presence of the West; it is a shame that Russia falls short of its Western ideal, as if the reason for it would disappear were Russia the only country in the world. Even with Radishchev, this is a matter of the relative position of Russia vis-à-vis the West. This pervasive "relativity" is at its most poignant in a passage from the chapter "Mednoe" in *The Voyage from Petersburg to Moscow*. There Radishchev tells about the harrowing experience of watching a family of serfs auctioned to separate buyers. Leaving the terrible scene in flight, Radishchev meets an American friend, to whose inquiry, "What happened? You are crying!" he responds: "'Return . . . do not be a witness of a horrible disgrace. You who cursed once a barbaric custom of selling black slaves in remote settlements of your fatherland. Return . . . do not be a witness of our derangement, and do not tell the story of our shame to your compatriots when talking to them of our customs.'"[76]

The usual reaction, however, was denial. In its early and simple forms it was very close to a conscious lie. A remarkable example of denial, and almost unbelievable in its naiveté and transparency, is Catherine's defense of Russia in a letter to Voltaire, where she writes that in Russia peasants live so well that there is no peasant family that does not have a chicken for dinner and some are so fed up with chickens that they now eat turkeys instead.[77] More interesting, among other things because of its precocity, is Antioch Kantemir's refutation of Locatelli's *Lettres moscovites*.

Kantemir was an ambassador in England when Locatelli's book appeared in Paris in 1735. It had two editions in France, and then was translated into English and published in London. For Kantemir, its contents were outright slander, and so he set out to write a refutation. In his letter of January 6, 1736, to Baron Osterman (another Russian patriot) in St. Petersburg, Kantemir wrote that he "never wanted to write more than on this occasion, having to defend the fatherland." He also mentioned his intention to write a refutation in an official dispatch, adding that he conceived of it as "a description, both geographical and political, of the Russian empire, similar to those which exist in all famous states under the title *'état présent.'*" The refutation was intended exclusively for the foreign audience and published in German, being ostensibly written *von einem Teutschen.*[78] In the treatise Kantemir stressed the huge territory of Russia, its enormous natural resources, and its momentous rise to prestige under Peter. He commended its economy, saying, for instance, that textiles manufactured in Ekateringof are so excellent that they are "almost as good as the Dutch." He drew attention to the national—unique—character of the Russian people (this is indeed one of the earliest attempts to define it) and stressed the unending patience of the peasants and their loyalty to the master. He also emphasized the thirst for knowledge characteristic of Russians and their extraordinary ability to learn, both demonstrated by their success in imitating the West during the period of Petrine reforms.

Of particular interest in the refutation of *Lettres moscovites* is Kantemir's depiction of the political values and civic conditions in Russia. He wrote: "Peter the Great and the gloriously reigning Empress Anne made tremendous reforms in Russia. [Now] urban artisans and the peasantry suffer no oppression from the supreme power," and brought eloquent examples to support his characterization. Indicative of the prevailing appreciation of liberty was a Petrine edict forbidding people to fall on their knees before the tsar, whom Kantemir quoted as saying—in the best tradition of European humanism—"I could never think without abhorrence, how much enslaved rational creatures must long, tremble and groan for freedom, if even creatures without reason, as is said in the Scriptures, when under subordination, passionately strive to be freed from it." The source of the quotation has never been located, but if Peter indeed had held such enlightened views, this certainly would have earned him the respect of those Westerners who, in the eighteenth century, were making such a fuss over freedom. For whatever insignificant relics of oppression there remained, Kantemir blamed, as one could expect, the ill-natured, unenlightened nobility, thereby killing two birds with one shot.

In all these innocent lies—and one is tempted to sympathize with them, for they were made in self-defense—the assumption that the West was the model remained unchallenged. The problem with lies, however, is that the liar knows that they are untrue, and thus, while they could, perhaps, convince some gullible foreigners, they were powerless to make the Russian patriots who circulated them believe that Russia was indeed equal to Europe. The next logical step in the development of the Russian national consciousness, therefore, was to present equality as undesirable, and the West as, for one reason or another, an unsuitable model for Russia. This attitude was clearly articulated toward the end of the eighteenth century. The exact nature of the reaction depended on the acuteness of the sense of discrepancy between Russia and the West, and the degree to which it was experienced as painful and reflecting Russia's inferiority.

If the self-dissatisfaction was not acute, the assessment of the West as an inappropriate model for Russia went hand in hand with the admiration of the West as such and produced a vague form of cultural relativism. As in Germany, this was a transient and therefore not a thoroughly argued position. In Russia it had no consistent representatives, and not even inconsistent ones similar to Herder. One finds expressions of cultural relativism interspersed with rudiments of other, contradictory positions in numerous writings of the formative period of Russian nationalism at the end of the eighteenth century. Karamzin's influential *Letters of the Russian Traveler* (1791–92) are characteristic.[79] The epigraph of the 1797 edition offers a psychological insight so accurate that it is hard to believe it was chosen unself-consciously. It reads: "Who with one's self can live in love and quiet,/ Will love and gladness find in countries all." Contentment with oneself increases one's ability to appreciate the merits of others. Karamzin left Russia in a happy mood, and his letters are indeed full of unqualified and uninhibited admiration of the West, which is astounding when compared with the morose defensive nationalism of his writings just a few years later. When he left Basel, for example, he "jumped out of the coach, fell on the blossoming shore of the green Rhein, and was ready to kiss the soil in rapture." Later, kissing soil became exclusively reserved for one's own soil. In the Alps the traveler experienced a fit of cosmopolitanism: "In this way on my own self I experienced the justice of what Rousseau has to say about the effect of the mountain air . . . Here a mortal feels his lofty destiny, forgets his earthly fatherland and becomes the citizen of the world."

Karamzin's cultural relativism is evident in his reaction to the *Russian History* by P.C. Levesque. Referring to it in a letter, he urges the creation of a *Russian History* by a Russian which would emphasize the uniqueness of Russia and show its equality to Europe not because it is like it, but because there is a distinctively Russian parallel to everything European of note. "What is not important we should cut down, as Hume did in his English history; but all the features which evince the uniqueness of the Russian people, the character of our ancient Heroes and famous people . . . describe vividly, strikingly. We had our own Charlemagne: Vladimir—our own Louis XI: Tsar Ioann—our own Cromwell: Godunov—and in addition such a Ruler, whose like is nowhere to be found: Peter the Great."

Karamzin's position in this letter (if what we find in it may be regarded as a coherent position) is complex. In accordance with the spirit of cultural relativism, he emphasizes the distinctiveness of Russia and subscribes to the Romantic—*avant le nom*—notion of the supremacy of inner understanding: only a Russian can truly understand Russia. At the same time, he believes that all nations follow the same path, that the West happens to be the leader and that Russia, therefore, should imitate the West. The firm confidence that it can do so, that it is very successful in doing so, allows Karamzin—without the anguish of self-contempt—to denounce characteristically Russian traditions which are inconsistent with or even irrelevant to universal progress: he has not as yet reached the point where what is peculiarly Russian becomes a synonym for moral good. This confidence in the ability of Russia speedily to catch up with the West also finds its expression in the admiration for the initiator of the process of catching-up, Peter the Great. In continuation of the quotation above, Karamzin writes:

> Is it not necessary to become equal in order to surpass? . . . Germans, Frenchmen, Englishmen, were in front of the Russians by at least six centuries: Peter moved us with his mighty hand, and we in several years almost caught up with them. All the pitiful Jeremiads about the alteration of the Russian character, about the loss of the Russian moral physiognomy, either are nothing but a joke or derive from the inadequacy of the well-founded thinking . . . Everything national is nothing in comparison with the human. The main thing is to be humans, not Slavs. What is good for humans cannot be bad for the Russians, and what Englishmen or Germans invented for the good and benefit of man is mine, for I am human! . . . *Il est probable*, says Levesque, *que si Pierre n'avait pas régné, les Russes seraient aujourd'hui ce qu'ils sont,* namely: even if Peter the Great didn't teach us, we would learn! By which means? By ourselves? . . . Russians were not predisposed, were not ready to become enlightened . . . Only the zealous, active will and unlimited power of the Russian Tsar could effect such a sudden, quick alteration . . . As Sparta without Lycurgus, so Russia without Peter, would not be able to become famous.[80]

It is clear from this passage that in this last decade of the eighteenth century, the belief in the salubrity of Peter's reforms, and the superiority of the West, was already far from universal. Many educated Russians were no longer "in love and quiet" with themselves; they were deeply troubled by the discrepancy between Russia and its model. When they resorted to cultural relativism, it was usually in a less cheerful manner than in the case of Karamzin: rather than believing that equal merit is to be found behind different appearances, they found solace in that different customs conceal behind them an equally grim reality. Fonvisin, for example, summarized his impressions of foreign travel in the following manner: "I saw that in all countries there is more bad than good, that men are men everywhere; that intelligent people are everywhere rare, that there are everywhere plenty of fools, and, in one word, that our nation is no worse than any other." [81] While Karamzin, in his eagerness to see Russia equal to the West, confident that it could easily become like it, thought Russian customs disposable and not worth keeping, many of his more pessimistic compatriots thought that these customs might as well be kept, for they preferred to see the West as not worth imitating. Karamzin himself, in 1810, in the *Memoir of Ancient and Modern Russia*, advised a more discriminating attitude: "Two states could be on the same stage of civic enlightenment and have different mores. A state may borrow from another useful information, without imitating the other's customs."

The inclination to seek solace in equality (whether of merit or misery) in difference was not sustained, for there was no equality. And so it gave way to *ressentiment*, the rejection of the West based on envy and the realization of the all-too-evident, and therefore unbearable, inferiority.

It was the recognition of the discrepancy between Russia and its ideal, and the inferiority of Russia, which led to *ressentiment*, not the "government of foreigners." [82] The anti-foreign sentiment before the reign of Catherine, and especially under Empress Anne and her German favorites, was essentially unrelated to the national sentiment. It was motivated by pragmatic group interests, rather than by a sense of an incipient national identity, and predicated on a specific, temporary situation. In conditions of general status insecurity and strife between the two sectors of the nobility—the ancient and the new, created by service—foreigners who were brought by Anne from Courland and gained immediate ascendancy at her Court represented another threat, not at all the main threat, but one on which the frustration of all could focus. Moreover, this threat, unlike the others, could be easily eliminated, and this ease, which created the illusion that with the elimination of foreigners the problematic situation would be resolved as a whole, increased the urgency of this elimination. In other words, this was not a generalized xenophobia, fired by the desire to protect Russia from what was not Russian, but an effort to ban a group of well-qualified competitors from access to the limited number of coveted-by-all positions. Such was the aim of Artemii Volynskii, who suffered for the cause and was posthumously canonized as a martyr of Russian nationalism, and such was the aim of the Frenchman Lestocq, who was a member of Volynskii's circle, and of two prominent Germans, like Lestocq personally invested in Russia, Ostermann and Muennich, to whom eventually belonged the honor of terminating the "German government" when they arrested its incarnation—Anne's favorite, Biron.

This anti-foreign sentiment was not long-lived. The reason for it disappeared, and it burned itself out in the sanguinary bout of the Guards who, whether from an overflow of patriotic feelings, a penchant for carnage which was not likely to be punished, or general playfulness, murdered their German officers. The sentiment was revived for a short period in 1762, during the reign of Peter III, who, being enamored with Prussia and deprived by this passion of the modest amount of good sense with which Nature had endowed him, threatened again to replace Russian nobles (including those of non-Russian origin) by Prussian soldiers. The Guards were eager to debauch, but the Princess of Anhalt-Zerbst, the clever Catherine, whom they made Empress, knew how to keep things under control, and the sentiment was heard of no more.

At the same time, already in the first half of the eighteenth century, the widespread hostility toward the foreigners who successfully vied with the Russian nobles for positions and favors now and then merged with and was used as a pretext for the expression of anti-foreign sentiments of a different nature. These were sentiments against the generalized foreigner, against the mythical foreign menace, against the world which, by its very existence, underscored Russia's inadequacy. When Archbishop Amvrosii of Novgorod accused the foreigners of conspiracy to keep Russia unenlightened and weak, saying: "They spared no means to convict a Russian experienced in the arts, an engineer, an architect, a soldier . . . to remove him by exile or execution, simply because he was an engineer or an architect, a disciple of Peter the Great,"[83] it is quite clear that the "German government" was the least of his concerns. Who were Russian engineers and architects in the 1740s?

It was this sentiment that persisted, for it so happened that the reason for it never disappeared. But it was not until the age of Catherine that it became ubiquitous and inescapable, and as a part of the cognitive reality of the Russian elite was able to shape other sentiments and determine the further development of the national consciousness. In the meantime, while the noble elite was otherwise engaged, the frail national sentiment found another abode: it grew and burgeoned in the hearts of the non-noble intellectuals in Petersburg and Moscow.

## The Laying of the Foundations
### The Contribution of Non-Noble Intellectuals

Unlike the nobility, the intelligentsia (which indeed appeared before its name) was created by Peter the Great from scratch.[84] Before Peter there were no secular schools in Russia, and the educational needs of the country were satisfied by theological seminaries. The most important of these were the Kiev Academy, founded in 1632, and the Slav-Greek-Latin Academy in Moscow, founded in 1687 by one of the Kiev graduates, Simeon Polozki. The Kiev Academy provided Russia with most of its high clergy well into the Petrine period. Not until the founding of Moscow University in 1755 did it lose its position as the largest and most important center of general education within the empire. Its students were recruited almost exclusively from the Ukraine, which resulted in the highly significant presence of Ukrainians among the clerical and, as we shall see instantly, secular intellectuals in Russia.

The first institutions of secular learning reflected Peter's preoccupation with technical knowledge. In the first quarter of the eighteenth century a school of mathematical and naval sciences was opened in Moscow, and an engineering and artillery school and the Naval Academy in St. Petersburg. At the Admiralty, in 1719, the so-called Russian schools were established for the children of peasants and artisans recruited to work in the shipyards. They provided instruction in Russian, arithmetic, and geometry.[85] Ten such schools existed between 1719 and 1734. In 1721, the War College (Chancellery) ordered the organization of schools attached to every one of the forty-nine garrisons then in existence, each of which was to provide education for fifty "soldiers' sons," who were divided into four groups according to abilities and inclinations. Similar schools were established for the children of those employed at the state stables. Large private schools, such as the one opened in 1721 by Prokopovich for "orphans and poor people of every condition," also started to appear. Many of the successful products of these modest schools later continued their education in other institutions.[86]

In 1732 the first Corps of Cadets was founded in St. Petersburg. This was, in principle, an educational establishment exclusively for the nobility, but children of soldiers and shipyard workers were accepted there in special classes for non-nobles. They were trained for positions of non-commissioned officers, and also as lower-grade teachers for the children of the nobility. The first medical school in Russia was opened in Moscow at the General Hospital in 1706 and trained 800 physicians and surgeons in the course of the century; three more schools were established in 1733, and by the end of the 1770s there were in Russia 488 physicians and 364 medical practitioners at a lower level (podlekari).

The Imperial Academy of Sciences started to function in 1725.[87] The institution consisted of the Academy proper and the University. A year later a gymnasium was added to the structure. The Academic gymnasium was the first secular secondary school with general educational purposes in Russia. Its curriculum consisted of languages, history, geography, mathematics, and natural sciences. The term of study was five years. The Academic University was the first secular institution of higher education. For about twenty years, mostly because of the lack of adequately prepared students, the institution lingered between life and death. In 1747 it was given a new reglement which provided for thirty state scholarships a year for the University and twenty for the gymnasium, to be given to "people of all sorts of ranks, according to abilities." In 1752 the number of scholarships was increased and was henceforth limited only by the quantity of academic funds. At the same time, everyone (from the nobility or *raznochinzy*) willing to study on his own account could do so. In 1748, there were 48 students in the gymnasium; in 1749, 62; in 1750, 70. In 1753, there were 150 students, one-third of them state stipendiaries. Between 1756 and 1765, 590 young people were educated there. Out of 429 of these, on whom background data are available, 80 came from noble, but mostly poor, families; 22 were children of merchants; 13, children of clergymen; 132 were "soldiers' sons"; more than 80, children of petty clerks; 50, children of artisans; 66 were freed serfs; fathers of 9 were medical assistants; 7, watchmen; 4, gardeners; 3, grooms; 2, free peasants; and 93 were children of foreigners. Most of the students at the Academy did not go further than the gymnasium, and upon leaving it, assumed various clerical and lower-grade teaching positions. Nevertheless, these people were among the most educated men of their country at the time, and an important part of the emerging intelligentsia.[88]

Finally, in 1755, the first Russian university proper was established in Moscow. The composition of the student population of Moscow University was similar to that of the Academy, with the difference that, under certain conditions, even serfs were admitted. Two gymnasia were attached to the University: one for the children of the nobility, the other for the *raznochinzy*. In the beginning each one had fifty students supported by state stipends; later their number increased. As in the Academy, many students, both in the University and in its gymnasia, paid their own way. In the first twenty years of its existence, 318 people graduated from the University. The University was divided into three faculties: law, medicine, and philosophy. The first two faculties had three professors each (of general law, Russian law, and politics; and of chemistry, natural history, and anatomy, respectively). The four professors of the philosophical faculty taught philosophy, experimental and theoretical physics, rhetoric, and general and Russian history. A remarkable feature of Moscow University was the lack in it of a theological faculty, a *sine qua non* in most European universities.

In 1758, on the grounds that foreign artists invited to Russia did not transmit their skills to the Russians, the Academy of Arts was founded in St. Petersburg. Its first students were transferred from Moscow University, and after twenty years of existence the institution could boast of 180 graduates.

These figures allow one to infer that, by the end of the eighteenth century, there were in Russia around four thousand people with a university education, about half of whom were physicians and sub-physicians, and a similar (perhaps somewhat larger) number of persons with advanced secondary education.[89] Although minuscule in a population of many millions, this number represented a dramatic improvement compared with the beginning of the century, when hardly more than half a score of people had a secular education of any level.

A significant proportion of these newly educated people—before the 1770s a majority—was of non-noble origin. This group, and not the nobility, was the first group in Russia which, as a whole, could be characterized as nationalist. The precocious nationalism of the non-noble intelligentsia, which manifested itself in the middle decades of the eighteenth century (1730s–1760s) was all the more remarkable because of the singular ethnic composition of this group. It is possible that as much as 50 percent of this first mass of Russian nationalists were Ukrainians.[90] In itself, this fact would not be significant, but in Russia, which was to move steadily toward becoming one of the model *ethnic nations,* the prominence of ethnic non-Russians does indeed add a touch of irony to the story.

The reasons for this odd phenomenon are simple. Through most of the eighteenth century, the chief educational institutions in Russia, in terms of their enrollment and impact, were still the clerical seminaries. Not only did their influence not diminish with the appearance of centers of secular learning, but for some time they continued to grow in numbers and importance. In the early 1740s there were seventeen clerical seminaries in Russia with a student population of twenty-five hundred; in 1764, twenty-six seminaries with six thousand students. The Kiev Academy remained the largest and the most important of the clerical schools. It also remained the center of learning for the Ukrainians. As such, it gained in importance with the growing deference toward education among the nobility and the formation of the Corps of Cadets, since the Ukrainian nobility, if not confirmed by the achievement of a nobility-carrying rank in the service, was not recognized as such, and therefore young Ukrainian noblemen were denied admission to these exclusive educational establishments. The Kiev Academy was the most advanced of the clerical schools: from early on, in addition to Latin and Greek, its students were taught modern languages, such as Polish and German, to which French was added in 1753. Since professors for the newly established medical schools, as well as for the Academy at St. Petersburg and Moscow University, were invited from abroad (mostly from Germany), and the teaching was conducted in Latin, the knowledge of languages was indispensable for the students of these secular institutions, and they could not acquire it outside the seminaries. The first cohorts of non-noble university students (who were not children of resident foreigners) were thus simply transferred from the seminaries. The Kiev Academy, from which, only in the fourteen years between 1754 and 1768, more than three hundred seminarists moved to Moscow and St. Petersburg, was the chief source of such recruits. Every seminarist willing to become a physician, for example, was offered ten rubles for travel and accommodation, and they went, either "moved by poverty" or because secular professions and sciences "were the only honest and advantageous way out [of the clergy] for everyone who felt indisposed to the priesthood." [91] In St. Petersburg and Moscow, literally in the front ranks of the nascent Russian intelligentsia, the humble youths from Little Russia forged the Great Russian national consciousness.

The non-noble stipendiaries of the Academic and Moscow universities were brought there to be trained for numerous positions which could not be filled with the existing human resources. An important minority of these positions carried with them nobility; almost all were new and, because of the novelty of secular education (and literacy in general) in Russia and the respect for this curious importation, had a certain prestige. For some poor seminarists and gymnasiasts the universities turned out to be the road to honors, wealth, and influence; they became the first Russian professors, academicians, high officials. Others spent their lives as copyists, translators, and petty clerks, more often than not in hopeless misery. All were transformed by education. Whoever they were before entering the universities they were no longer; they needed a new identity. They were a new stratum, and none of the existing definitions fit them. Even those whose social elevation was commensurate with their education and great efforts felt bitterly humiliated by the traditional definition of status, which, though embattled, persisted. Those whose status expectations, inflated by learning, were frustrated found the traditional definition unbearable.[92] They needed a perspective, an identity, that would confirm their sense of worth, justify their aspirations, and condemn the arrangements which left them unfulfilled. The idea of the nation could answer their needs, and they turned patriots.

Patriotism, the desire "to do service to the fatherland," to "demonstrate the zeal" of love for it, seems to be the chief motivation behind the studies and labors of the members of this group. A teacher, Stepan Nazarov, toiled "so that the Russian youth could derive benefit from this [his] modest effort." K. Florinskii translated "solely to bring some relief to the Russian youth ignorant of foreign languages and thereby do service to the fatherland." L. K. Sichkarev "devoted [his] life to literary labors for the sake of the fatherland." [93] The contribution of most of these people consisted in laying the foundations and preparing the soil for the future national culture. They compiled the first dictionaries and grammars; they translated and propagated the work of others. Only a few of them actually became *creators* of culture, but the first literary expressions of the Russian national sentiment came from these few.

The first one to *sing* of Russia as a nation, the author of the first lyrical verses in Russian inspired by the love of country, was V. K. Trediakovskii. The unmerciful editors of a pre-revolutionary anthology wrote that his poetry was but "the first babble of the new Russian muse," in which even "attentive and sympathetic criticism" was not able to discover "graceful taste and poetic talent." Yet, clumsy as his verses were, they resounded with genuine and deep feeling. In 1730, in Paris, Trediakovskii wrote the first lyrics of this kind, "Laudatory Verses to Russia":

> O mother Russia! My light excessive!
> Who would not know, in the wide world,
> The high nobility of your nature?
> You are nobility itself . . .
> All your people are orthodox
> And famous for their courage . . .
> Always ready to stand up for your defense.
> What plenty do you lack, Russia?
> Where did you not prove your strength?
> You are the treasury of every good,
> Ever bountiful, and thus ever glorious.
> . . . When I look at Russia from across remote countries,
> I need a hundred tongues
> To glorify all that I love in you.

The features that Trediakovskii admires in Russia, with the exception of the orthodoxy of the people, are observations of his inner eye, the figments of a loving imagination. This early poem articulates a sentiment which is not as yet focused on anything in particular. In a 1752 poem, "Laudations to the Izherskaia Land and the Reigning City of St. Petersburg," the earlier diffuse feeling is focused on a real achievement of Russia, so recognized by the relevant, that is, Western, world. It is on the basis of this achievement that Trediakovskii professes and prays for the future glory and superiority of his country:

> O charming shore! Amiable land!
> Where moves Neva its current to the ocean:
> O wilderness before, inhabited today
> We see in you a reigning city.
> O! you, Descendants coming after us,
> You are to hear laudations
> Which to this site the world will sing in raptures.
> Italian cities: Venice, Rome
> And Amsterdam of Holland; and the British
> City great London; Paris,
> The Queen or an ideal of all cities.
> All those are destinations of our journeys,
> The object of desires; their fame and beauty
> Attracts and tears us from native shores . . .
> But you will see, Descendants, from them all

> The visitors will come in immense numbers,
> To see and marvel at this city, and proclaim:
> This was an empty place, and now—a Paradise . . .
> O! Lord, please grant . . . for Russia's sake,
> That there be under the sun no equal
> Among all cities to the Peter's City.[94]

In this poem, Russia is glorified because it compares so well with—indeed in all likelihood promises to become superior to—the West, which is at present its model. This flattering comparison is due to the achievement of Peter, the creator of the new Russia.

By far the most prominent representative of the non-noble intelligentsia of the mid-eighteenth century was Mihailo Lomonosov, Russia's first chemist, physicist, grammarian, and significant poet—"this Pindar, Cicero, and Virgil, glory of Russians."[95] He was also the intelligentsia's most articulate nationalist. For Lomonosov, too, Peter was a "deity on earth," for the glory of Russia manifested itself only in comparison with the West, and it was Peter who made this comparison possible:

> [The Lord] to Russia sent a man
> Whose like the world has never seen;
> Through all the obstacles he raised
> The head that victories have crowned
> And Russia, by barbarity derided,
> He raised to glory with himself.

Yet, though Lomonosov recognized in Peter the source of Russia's fame, it is the nation, not the monarch, which is the object of his passion and devotion. Peter made Russia "a most [the most?—*vazhneishii*]" important member in the European system, Europe now looked to Russia for the establishment of peace, and its fame resounded throughout the world. Lomonosov's Russia is magnificent:

> To lofty mountains alike,
> Unshakable, it watches calmly
> The darkness of the world beneath.
> The wind is powerless to touch it,
> By frightful thunder it's unmoved
> High up in its serene abode
> Its feet are trampling upon clouds,
> It is contemptuous of storms
> And laughing at the bouncing waves.[96]

But Lomonosov takes pride not only in the military and political strength of Russia; his nationalism is frequently expressed in the glorification of the Russian people. Like noble patriots of the Petrine epoch, he marvels at the "abilities of our people, who achieved so much in the span of time hardly exceeding the life of one generation." The people, or nation, for Lomonosov, denotes the whole population of "native Russians"—"from peasants to the royal throne." Thus the nation is not limited, as it was for contemporary noble nationalists, such as Sumarokov, to a particular order in society; yet it excludes foreigners in Russian service, or Russians who are not "native." [97]

The democratic, inclusive of every order, definition of the nation was characteristic of the non-noble nationalist intellectuals in general. They came from the "people," and even those whose material ties with it were decisively severed would never—in the conditions of eighteenth-century Russia—be allowed to forget their origins. To ennoble themselves, therefore, the members of the intelligentsia needed to ennoble the "people," and they insisted indeed that there was no difference between the nobility and the plebs, that the very designation "plebs" was illegitimate. Translating from Latin, Lomonosov used the Russian word *narod* (people or nation) to render both *populus Romanus* and *populus vulgus,* although the latter would usually be translated—and meant—"rabble" *(chern').*[98] Other members of the group manifested a similar egalitarianism. The novelist F. A. Emin asked: "Can anything in the world be more noble and reasonable than the labor of a peasant?" N. G. Kurganov insisted: "We are all equal by nature, and there is not one who is to be honored more than another, because God loves us all equally." [99]

This democratic sentiment was also expressed in the stress on merit, particularly intellectual merit. Nikolai Popovskii, in a manner reminiscent of Sumarokov's definition of sons of the fatherland as nobility, simply identified intellectuals (lovers of science) with true patriots. Intellectual activity, learning, itself became a virtue. Lomonosov demanded that peasants be admitted to the universities and thought that "that student is more noble, who knows more, and whose son he is, there is no need to care." [100] The theme of learning (or science—*nauka*) was, understandably, one of the commonest themes in Lomonosov's poetry.[101] Lomonosov owed his position in society entirely to his academic achievement and constantly extolled science as the primary legitimate basis of social status. However, Lomonosov was mainly interested in learning for Russia, and not for its own sake. Even in his most esoteric scientific pursuits, the motivation was profoundly nationalistic, rather than purely academic. "For the well-being of sciences in Russia," he said, "if the circumstances will require, I am ready to sacrifice all my earthly well-being," and even more forcefully (sounding a precociously ominous note): "For the general good, and particularly for the establishment of sciences in the fatherland, I do not consider it a sin even to rise against one's own father." [102]

The non-noble intellectuals owed their elevation in Russian society to their education, yet this was not due to the prestige of learning as such, but to the function learning performed for the nation: with their learning they were better able to serve Russia. For this reason they demanded that Russia recognize them; and for this reason too, they believed that they had more rights to such recognition than did the foreign scholars in Russian universities. The purpose of developing scholarship in Russia was to prove Russia's equality to the Western nations. Only "native Russians" could prove that Russia was able to give birth to "Russian Columbuses," "Russian Platos," and "Russian Newtons." In the final analysis, it was "native Russianness" that justified the new status (or status aspirations) of the non-noble intellectuals, rather than their education. Their main contention was with the nobility, with the nature of social hierarchy in Russia. They could not forget (they were not allowed to forget) their origins. To achieve parity with the nobility—to be simply treated with the respect their education taught them to crave—it was essential for them to define the nation in such a way as to include in it both the nobility and the *populus vulgus*. By what right was the latter to be thus elevated? The only thing it ostensibly shared with the Russian nobility was its "nativity." This, as well as the preponderance of foreigners in the nascent Russian science, explains Lomonosov's bitter and unjustified hatred of German scholars at the Academy, and may help us understand the nature of "scientific" preoccupations and some tendencies of the Russian scientific ethos.

The intellectual pursuits of this first group of Russian men of letters seem to be motivated by the desire to aggrandize Russian culture and make it comparable to the cultures of Western Europe. The preoccupation with culture derives from the professional identity of these people; the stress on Russian—is an expression of the ascendancy of nationality in their overall identity. The efforts to develop the Russian language attest most tellingly to this motivation.

In the beginning of the eighteenth century Russia had two languages: the written Church-Slavonic, remote from everyday life and intelligible only to a chosen few, and the chiefly spoken language of the mundane—Russian. Both were inadequate for the expression of the new political and social reality; so much so that at some point Peter wanted to make Dutch the official language of his state. Having, apparently, given this idea up, the great tsar introduced, in 1700, a new, secular type *(grazhdanskaia azbuka)* and thus laid the foundations for modern literary Russian. His decrees and the writings of his close collaborators (for example, Shafirov) offer us a glimpse into the process of the forced, active formation of the new vocabulary: these documents are interspersed with foreign words with Russian endings and their explanations in parentheses or on the margins. (Soon, using russified foreign words, even for concepts for which Russian synonyms existed, became such a vogue that Peter actually ordered one of such linguistic neophytes among his high-placed servants to write all the official letters in pure Russian.) For at least half a century the infant language, devoid of agreed-upon orthography and limited in vocabulary, lingered waiting for proper care. But toward the 1750s it became the focus of attention and devotion of the non-noble intellectuals, for whom its successful development was a matter of personal honor.[103]

The contributions of Trediakovskii and Lomonosov to the development of literary Russian are well known. Trediakovskii was the one who proposed to make Russian rather than Church-Slavonic the language of Russian literature. He advocated phonetic orthography and (taking as his example Russian folk poetry) tonic verse. He was also the first to argue the superiority of Russian to other European languages. This argument, which went counter to some of his earlier assertions, was articulated in the "Three Discourses Regarding the Three Most Ancient Russian Antiquities: (a) On the Primacy of the Slavonic Language over the Teutonic, (b) on the Seniority of the Russians, and (c) on the Vikings, Russians of the Slavic Name, Nation [birth], and Language." The reason for the superiority of Russian was its derivation from Church-Slavonic. Unlike German or French, which were languages of the marketplace and politics, Church-Slavonic was a language of the spirit. "Why should we willingly suffer the bareness and narrowness of French," asked Trediakovskii, "when we have the varied richness and expanse of Slaviano-Russian?" Lomonosov, in "On the Usefulness of Church Books for the Russian Language," advanced a similar argument. He was aware of the newness of the expressive powers of Russian and its recent poverty: "In ancient times, when the Slavic people did not know the use of a written expression of its thoughts which were very limited for the reason of ignorance of many things and activities known to learned nations, then its language, too, could not abound in such a multitude of locutions and expressions of the reason, as we read today." At the same time, owing to the possession of its own Church language, the Slavic people, apparently, was always linguistically superior to European nations that used a foreign language in religious service. "German was very poor, simple and powerless all the time while Latin was the language of church service. But as the German nation began to read sacred books and perform religious service in its own language, its richness increased and there appeared artful writers. By contrast, in Catholic regions, where only Latin, and at that barbaric Latin, is used in service, we do not observe similar success in the purity of the German language." [104] The ultimate expression of Lomonosov's linguistic nationalism (and probably eighteenth-century Russian linguistic nationalism in general) is found in the *Russian Grammar* of 1755:

> Charles V, the Roman Emperor, was wont to say that one ought to speak Spanish to one's God, French to one's friends, German to one's enemies, and Italian with the feminine sex. Had he been versed in the Russian tongue, he would certainly have added that it is appropriate for converse with all of these. For he

would have found in it the majesty of Spanish, the vivacity of French, the firmness of German, the delicacy of Italian, and the richness and concise imagery of Greek and Latin . . . The most subtle philosophical speculations and concepts, the various phenomena and essences which express the visible structure of the world of nature and the world of human intercourse, all these find in Russian appropriate and expressive terms. And if something should be found incapable of expression, the fault is not that of the language, but of our own capacity.[105]

The lesser members of the intelligentsia spared no effort to make the Russian language correspond to this exalted image. A Ukrainian, D. S. Samoilovich, emphasized the necessity of creating a Russian medical vocabulary: "terms which are not even known in Russian"; at the same time, rather inconsistently with the recognition of the paucity of the language which this implied, he stressed the beauty and richness of Russian and quoted Lomonosov. Another Ukrainian and former seminarist of the Kiev Academy, Grigorii Poletika, compiled a comparative dictionary in six languages, juxtaposing Russian with the tongues "considered most famous and necessary for the sciences." In general, ethnic non-Russians from the Kiev Academy appear notable among the creators of the modern Russian language. When in 1762 the Senate requested people "artful in the purity of the Russian style and with a perfect knowledge of the Russian language," both persons who fulfilled these stringent and at the time unusual requirements, Nikolai Motonis and Grigorii Kozitskii, were at one time pupils in this ancient institution. But, of course, "native Russians" were equally devoted to the cause. K. I. Shchepin, the first Russian professor of medicine, resolutely lectured in Russian, though, as he confessed "to deliver ten lectures in Latin is easier than one in Russian."

The greatness of the nation hinged on the greatness of its language. The awareness of the pioneering nature of their efforts and the newness of the language which non-noble intellectuals tried to develop thus went hand in hand with an immense pride in it and an unshakable belief in its colossal potential. In 1773, Vasilii Svetov, the author of the *Study in the New Russian Orthography*, called the language he and his associates were forging "the new-Russian [*novorossiiski*] language" and dated it back only to the fifties or sixties of the century. But at the same time another member of the group, Nikolai Popovskii, confidently asserted: "There is not a thought which could not be expressed in Russian." [106] In the middle of the eighteenth century this was wishful thinking. But thanks to the efforts of these anxious dreamers, unwilling to put up with their inferiority, in just a few decades a magnificent language did in fact emerge. Equal to any, it was to be surpassed by none in beauty and power of expression. A newcomer to the world of literary creation, it was to be the language of some of the greatest writers of all ages, and when Russian patriots of later generations worshipped the "great Russian Word," it was no more a dream, but reality they worshipped.

Another preoccupation of the non-noble intellectuals was Russian history. "A half-educated Russian," wrote one of the first scholars to give this discipline systematic attention, a German historian, August Ludwig Schloezer, "takes to any reading with an unusual ardor; he particularly loves national history." [107] Although some Russian noblemen (notably Tatischev) were interested in history earlier in the eighteenth century, "the study and writing of history as a long-range enterprise . . . did not really begin in Russia until it was undertaken by German scholars who devoted themselves to it entirely." [108] The first Russian historical journal, edited by G. F. Mueller, whose early appearance (in 1732) is a sign of the centrality of history for the incipient national sentiment, was characteristically entitled *Sammlung Russischer Geschichte*. The efforts of the German historians, however, did not satisfy their Russian audience, and won them bitter reproaches and accusations rather than gratitude. History was expected to bolster national pride, while the pedantic scholars persisted in actually looking for facts. This difference of opinion regarding the definition of the discipline furnished the specific reason for Lomonosov's attacks on his German colleagues and eventually led him to devote part of his energies to the creation of Russian history as it should be. National history was "such a science through which one could best serve one's fatherland." It was "the most important science for a citizen." "If literature can move the hearts of men," said Lomonosov, "should not true history have the power to stir us to praiseworthy ends, especially that history which relates the feats of our ancestors?" "Native" Russian historians concentrated on those episodes in the national past which were inspiring and heroic. When there were no feats to report, this was not good history; and it was outright offensive if related by a Westerner. [109]

Patriotic historians were particularly upset by the so-called Norman theory of the origins of the Russian state, which had been corroborated by subsequent historical research. The theory pointed to Vikings, Scandinavians, as the founders of the Russian polity, underscoring both the recency of Russia's political existence (that is, the vexing newness of the Russian nation) and the central role of foreigners, Westerners, in its formation. Russian historians would rather see theirs as an original, ancient people, a conclusion to which they were led by the passionate desire to discover in the past the reasons for self-esteem which the present did not provide, and which they based on an ingenious but hard-to-substantiate linguistic analysis. It is therefore little wonder that they found the discoveries of German historians unsatisfactory. Mueller, reprimanded and reduced in rank for spreading such unflattering information, but wholly committed to his adopted fatherland, took his findings back. Schloezer, injured in his professional identity, uncommitted, and annoyed, did not, and showed no compassion for the sensitivities of his one-time compatriots. He represented the Russians before the Vikings as "savage, coarse, and dispersed" and wrote: "May patriots not be incensed, but their history does not go back to the Tower of Babel; it is not as old as that of Greece and Rome; it is younger even than that of Germany and Sweden. Before [the calling of the Varangians] all was darkness . . . they were a people without government; living like the beasts and birds of their forests, undistinguished in any way."[110] How could people whose status, whose very human worth, depended entirely on the image of their nation accept this humiliating portrayal? How could they, facing the evidence, however limited their respect for facts, deal with it at all? Eventually they found a remedy to relieve their mental agony. But, before its effects could be felt, for decades to come, anguish was the dole of Russian nationalists.

## The Incorporation of the Achievements of Non-Noble Intellectuals in the Incipient Nationalism of the Nobility

In the last third of the eighteenth century—because of the pro-noble policies of Catherine in education and service, and the fact that service as such was no longer an adequate basis for the noble identity—the nobility ousted and supplanted the non-noble intelligentsia in letters. For a long time to come culture and noble birth were to become entwined, and the Russian intelligentsia is believed to have originated in the nobility.[111] The appropriation of culture as an attribute of the nobility coincided with the eclipse of the estate identity by nationality, which immensely increased the significance of both culture in general and Russian culture in particular. In place of a trait separating blue blood from red, culture became the very bone of contention between Russia and its model (which it had chosen and now could not tear away from), all-important for the way in which Russians, noble and non-noble, could see themselves. The educated patriotic noblemen of the late eighteenth century devoted themselves to the task of elevating the cultural level of Russian society and developing Russian culture. In this they drew on the preparatory work of the non-noble intellectuals, taking pride in their achievements and thus appropriating both the fruit of their labors and the laborers themselves. The cultural elite of Russia, which was, since the time one may speak of it as a reality, predominantly noble, in principle did not distinguish between people of merit by family origins, and was open to talent. Radishchev's *Journey from Petersburg to Moscow* concluded with "A Word on Lomonosov." In it the representative of noble patriotism acknowledged the kinship and the debt of his generation of patriots to the son of a Northern peasant for his Herculean efforts in developing—in fact creating—the Russian language.[112]

Thus there occurred a merging and incorporation of the central ideas of non-noble intellectuals with and in the noble nationalism. If Sumarokov, however hesitantly, identified patriotism with nobility, and the humble graduates of the Academic and Moscow universities claimed this lofty virtue as an attribute of the "lovers of learning," the noble intellectuals of the late eighteenth century made all three—nobility, patriotism, and learning—synonyms. Culture existed to serve the fatherland; it had no other purpose. Novikov, commenting in his journal *The Painter* on the anonymous author of the comedy *Oh! Times* (actually Catherine), wrote: "Continue, sir, for the glory of Russia, for the honor of your own name and for the immense pleasure of your learned countrymen . . . to glorify your name with your compositions: your [Russian] pen is worthy of equality with that of Molière . . . You first are worthy to demonstrate that liberty given to the minds of the Russians is used for the good of the fatherland." In its turn, this patriotic interpretation of the role of culture justified the claims of the men of letters to the position of leadership in the nation, or their inclusion in (if not the exclusive right to be considered) the aristocracy. Fonvisin lectured on the subject in his journal entitled *The Friend of Honest People, or Starodum: A Periodical Dedicated to Verity* (1788). "I think that liberty to write such as is in our days enjoyed by the Russians," he wrote, "makes a person with talent, so to speak, the guardian of the general good. In a state where writers possess the liberty which was given us, it is their duty to raise their loud voice against the abuses and superstitions harmful to the fatherland, so that a man with talent can in his room, with a pen in hand, be a useful advisor to the sovereign and sometimes even the savior of his compatriots and the fatherland."

The belief that cultural creativity fulfilled a function of extraordinary importance for the nation early expressed itself in the celebration (including self-celebration) of the intellectual elite. One of the first actions of the newly formed Moscow University was the publication of the complete works of Lomonosov—the Russian equivalent of all that was glorious in Western letters. Derzhavin in 1796 prophesied his own immortality in one of the first Russian adaptations of Horace's *Exegi monumentum*. In it the poet linked his fame to the glory of the nation, confident that the former would live as long as the latter and thus implicitly defining culture (literature and his role in it) as the basis of national greatness:

> I shall not wholly die, but a large part of me
> Will live upon my death, and will escape decay,
> My glory will increase, without fading,
> So long as Universe will honor Slavic tribes.[113]

The idea of the *Monument* was soon to be eternalized in the splendor of Pushkin's verse, and this confidence in the centrality of letters and particularly of creative writing for the nation was to remain a pervasive theme in Russian thought.

Like their non-noble predecessors, the cultural elite of the late eighteenth century concentrated on language and history. Endorsed and supported by Catherine, their efforts led to the emergence of a culture whose resources and possibilities were truly awe-inspiring and whose very emergence in such a short time, and in place of a veritable desert, was nothing short of miraculous. Almost every writer of any stature wrote treatises on the Russian language. Significantly, many of them were not written in Russian, for they were intended for the persuasion of foreign audiences. Kheraskov, who, as the rector of Moscow University, made Russian the official language of instruction, wrote "Discours sur la poésie russe." Fonvisin prepared a lecture on the subject for the Académie Française. In 1783 a Russian equivalent of this illustrious French institution was formed. The first contributions of the Russian Academy to the common effort were the authoritative Russian explanatory dictionary in six volumes (published between 1789 and 1794) and a grammar (published in 1802). As with the non-noble intelligentsia, such acts of the actual creation of language, which implied some awareness of its incompleteness, were accompanied by expressions of unbounded pride in its qualities. Catherine herself echoed Lomonosov's introduction to the *Russian Grammar* (and, incidentally, Samuel Daniel's prophecy of the glory of English): "Our Russian language, uniting as it does the strength, the richness, and the energy of German with the sweetness of Italian, would one day become the standard language of the world." The most prominent writer of the end of her reign (and of the eighteenth century in general), Karamzin, writing on the English literature which he greatly admired, concluded his comment, surprisingly, with a panegyric to Russian, urging, "So let us honor and glorify Our language, which in its natural richness, almost without any alien admixture, flows like a proud, majestic river—roars, thunders—and suddenly, if need be, softens, murmurs like a tender brook and sweetly pours into one's soul, forming all the rhythms which may be contained in the falling and rising of a human voice." [114]

In 1803 Karamzin became the official historiographer and set out to work on the monumental *History of the Russian State*. In its preface he wrote: "History in some sense is the sacred book of nations, the most important, necessary one; the mirror of their being and activity; the record of revelations and rules; the behest of ancestors to their descendants; the supplement to and explanation of the present, and an example of the future . . . If any history, even unskillfully written, is pleasant . . . all the more so the national [history]. A true cosmopolitan is a metaphysical creature or such an exceptional phenomenon that there is no need to talk about him, to commend him or to condemn. We are all citizens [here—nationalists]—the personality of everyone is tightly linked to the fatherland; we love it, for we love ourselves . . . The world history by its great memories adorns the world for the mind; while Russian history adorns the fatherland where we live and feel." [115] The reign of Catherine witnessed extraordinary activity in historical research. Russian antiquities and records were studied, collected, and published. Yet it is revealing that Karamzin's *History*, the crowning event of this activity, and based on its achievement, provided an inspiration for the historical novel (Zagoskin, Lazhechnikov, Kukol'nik), rather than giving rise to a historiographical tradition and inspiring more interest in the study of historical facts. The past as it was, was not found sufficient for the nourishment of national pride and failed to satisfy the burgeoning national sentiment. It had to be rewritten as it should have been. Some Russian intellectuals tried that, and when rewriting history did not work, the Russians made history.[116]

### Transvaluation of Values: The Crystallization of the Matrix of Russian Nationalism

It was in the last third of the eighteenth century, when the abolition of compulsory service left noble identity hanging in the air, unjustified, undefined, even more insecure than it had always been, and when the noble elite turned to learning and national identity and claimed as its own the achievements of the non-noble intellectuals and their nationalism, that the matrix of the Russian national consciousness finally crystallized. The most important factor in this crystallization was *ressentiment*—the existential envy of the West— and the values which were to constitute the Russian national consciousness and later be embodied in the Russian national character were a result of the transvaluation born out of this *ressentiment*.

Intriguingly, initially *ressentiment* took the form of hostility toward those numerous Russians who were not as yet affected by it and persisted in their unashamed admiration of the West. The recognition of Russia's inferiority led the sensitive Russians among the educated elite (and those were the people who both experienced the crisis of noble identity most painfully and were the first to turn to national identity) to the realization that having the West as a model must inevitably result in self-contempt. Karamzin, endowed with an unusual talent for expressing what others perceived but dimly, after entirely reversing his opinion in regard to the role of Peter the Great, wrote in the *Memoir of Ancient and Modern Russia* (1810): "While eradicating ancient customs, presenting them as ridiculous, stupid, and introducing foreign ones, the tsar humiliated Russians in their own heart. Can self-contempt predispose a person and a citizen to great deeds?"[117] The Russians who naively admired the West were (or at least seemed to be) walking examples of such self-contempt and undermined the yet-uncertain national pride which, as a component of identity, was to substitute for the shattered individual self-esteem of the more thin-skinned members of the elite. "Russian Frenchmen," the "petimetry,"[118] became the chief objects of satire which derided them with varying degrees of cruelty, moral fervor, and wit. In satirical plays, poems, and sketches the imitation (and even admiration) of the West was represented as embedded in such qualities of character as to make anyone inclined to such imitation ashamed of himself and willing to nip it in the bud. The eighteenth-century Russian intellectuals taught themselves the social psychology of marketing and successfully marketed the rejection of the West.

The behavior of the complacent majority who actually enjoyed the proximity of the West, instead of being tortured by it, must have been a powerful irritant, for it provided constant inspiration for the best talents and served as the focus of some of the most entertaining works of the time. The hilarious *Misfortune from the Carriage* by Kniazhnin depicts its Francophile "heroes," the gentry couple Firiulins, as complete idiots, who carry empty-headedness to the level of high art; their idiocy, which is fortunately monitored by the fool of their small court, is shown to have potentially disastrous effects. In a scene from the second act, Firiulin and Firiulina exchange impressions from their native country to which they have just returned from a sojourn abroad:

> *Firiulin:* Barbaric people! Wild country! What ignorance! What vulgar names! How they insult the delicacy of my ears! . . .
> *Firiulina:* I am amazed, my soul! Our village is so close to the capital, and nobody here talks French; and in France even a hundred miles from the capital everyone does. [The fool sarcastically congratulates them on being so different from their own people.]
> *Firiulin* [responds]: Ah, even we, we, ah! are nothing in comparison to the French.
> *The fool:* You should have indeed traveled abroad to bring back only contempt, not solely toward your countrymen, but even toward your own selves.[119]

While lashing against their unconscientious compatriots, the committed nationalists launched an attack on the foreigners in Russia. Lists of protagonists in satirical plays usually included a German or French tutor, stupid and puffed up, with an appropriate name such as *Vral'man*.[120] This other object of derision also provided endless employment for the satirical journals. Young Novikov placed the following "communication" in *Truten'* ("The Bumble Bee"):[121]

> From Kronstadt: These days several ships from Bordeaux have arrived in this harbor: on board, besides most fashionable commodities, are twenty-four Frenchmen reporting that all of them are Barons, Chevaliers, Marquises, and Counts, and that, being unhappy in their fatherland, for all sorts of reasons touching upon their honor, they were reduced to such extremity that, seeking gold, instead of America, they were forced to come to Russia. In all these stories

they lied very little: for, according to reliable information, they are all natural Frenchmen, skilled in all kinds of crafts and professions of the third sort. Many of them lived in a great quarrel with the Paris Police, and for that reason it, out of hatred toward them, gave them a salutation which they did not like. This salutation consisted in the order to leave Paris immediately, unless they preferred to dine, sup, and sleep in the Bastille. Although this salutation was very sincere, these French gentlemen did not like it and for this reason they came hither, and intend to become tutors and Hoffmeisters of young people of noble birth. Soon they will leave here for Petersburg. Gentle compatriots, hurry to hire these aliens for the education of your children! Immediately entrust the future mainstay of the fatherland to these vagabonds and think that you have fulfilled your parental duty by having hired as tutors Frenchmen—without asking about their position or behavior.

Hostility toward the Russian admirers of the West, and Westerners in Russia, signified the rejection of this ideal geographical entity as a model. But it was veiled and not entirely consistent. Finally, the veil was dropped, and the rejection of the West was expressed candidly as the rejection of the West. Still, there were different levels of complexity. One—simple—modality of this attitude was that of undisguised and unreasoning hatred. The reaction was akin to that of a wounded beast, blinded by pain and moved by the desire to hurt back: nothing was good, everything was bad. Fonvisin's *Letters from Abroad,* especially his opinion of France, provide us with an illustration of what this was like.

The mood in which Fonvisin approaches Paris leaves little doubt as to the nature of the impressions he would derive from his visit. "Paris," he says upon entering the city, "this alleged center of human knowledge and taste. I have not yet had the opportunity to find my bearing here; but I can assure . . . that I try to spend every hour usefully, noticing all that can give me the most accurate idea about the national character." He makes an effort to judge with impartiality and notice both good and bad in the object of his examination. Fortunately, what he sees soon makes it impossible to follow this good intention. "One has to renounce all common sense and truth to say that there is not much of what is very good and deserving of imitation here. All this, however, does not blind me to the extent that I fail to see as much, or even more, of absolutely evil and such, from which God save us." For a moment, his conclusion appears to be cultural relativism. In France, he says, one learns very soon that "all the stories of the local perfection are lies, that people are everywhere people, that a really intelligent and worthy person is everywhere a rarity and that in our fatherland, however bad it can be sometimes, one can be as happy as anywhere else." But he does not stop there. France is not as bad as Russia, it is infinitely worse. Having prepared the ground by proposing a definition of the nation, which makes his analysis a foregone conclusion, Fonvisin writes:

My stay in this state greatly diminished its value in my opinion ... Good people, whatever their nation, compose between themselves one nation. Having excluded them from the French, I observed the qualities [of the latter] in general ... A Frenchman does not have any reason and would consider it a misfortune of his life to have one ... a Frenchman would never forgive himself if he ever missed an opportunity to cheat ... His God is money ... D'Alemberts, Diderots, in their own way, are as much charlatans as those I meet every day on the streets; all of them are cheating people for money, and the difference between a charlatan and a *philosophe* is only such that the latter to his greed adds an unparalleled vanity ... French nobility, for the most part, lives in extreme poverty and its boorishness has no parallels anywhere ... With the exception of the rich and the grandees, every French nobleman, with all his stupid pride, would consider it a great happiness to become a tutor to a son of our gentleman ... [Impartial foreigners] say that in their army there is no military spirit. Every soldier philosophizes, therefore, does not obey ... A cattle-yard in the holdings of our honest gentry is much cleaner than [streets] in front of the very palaces of the French kings ... If I found anything flourishing in France, those are, to be sure, their factories and manufactories. There is no nation in the world which would have such an inventive mind as the French, when it comes to arts and crafts pertaining to taste ... This gift of nature has tended greatly to the injury of their mores.[122]

So much for the poor French. Interestingly, Fonvisin was so annoyed by France, that, in passing, he would even pay a compliment to England, if this served to underscore the worthlessness of the chief object of his attention. "Equality," he said, "is a blessing when it, as in England, is based on the spirit of government; but in France equality is evil, because it comes from the corruption of mores." [123]

These passages are an expression of existential envy—pure and simple. This is *ressentiment*, to be sure, an unmistakable, typical case of *ressentiment*, but it is not as yet its creation. There is a certain pleasure in just saying things such as these aloud, but they can hardly add much comfort to one's existence. Hatred as such gave vent to the *ressentiment* of the first Russian nationalists, but it did not solve their problem. The final stage of this development—the construction of an identity with which one could live, the *flower of ressentiment*—was not undisguised hatred. It was a transvaluation of Western values, the creation of a new, this time in every sense imaginary model, and with it a new hope for Russia, a new image of Russia, a soothing, comforting image, able to serve as a basis for individual self-esteem. And this was the matrix of the Russian national identity.

At this point it might be helpful to recapitulate the stages in this complex evolution. The Russian elite was attracted to national identity because this identity could provide it with the basis for status and self-esteem that noble identity failed to provide. The ability of the national identity to do this depended on the successful development of national pride. But the growth of national pride, which initially built up so quickly because of the triumphant, miraculous rise of Russia to glory in the beginning of the century, was in later years impaired by the proximity—the very existence—of the West. Russians could not separate themselves from the West and return to the times when its existence was a matter of indifference to them. It was the West, the encounter with the West, that ushered Russia into the new era in which it became aware of itself as a nation; it was Russia's originally successful incorporation into the West which gave its patriots the first reasons for national pride, and it was before the West that they experienced it. The West was an integral, indelible part of the Russian *national* consciousness. There simply would be no sense in being a nation if the West did not exist. Russians looked at themselves through glasses fashioned in the West—they thought through the eyes of the West—and its approbation was a *sine qua non* for their national self-esteem. The West was superior; they thought it looked down on them. How could Russians overcome this obstacle and build up national pride in spite of the Western superiority?

There were basically three ways to do so. The first was to become like the West, to imitate it. The choice of this way was predicated on the optimistic belief that Russia could do this with relative ease, and most of the eighteenth-century creators of national consciousness subscribed to this position at one time or another. Equality proving impossible, it could be seen as unnecessary. The second response was to define the West as an inappropriate model for Russia, although it had merits of its own, because Russia was incomparable to it, unique, and went its own, unrelated-to-the-West, way. This was cultural relativism, a transient and inadequate position, because it defied the purpose which called it into being. To admit that Russia and the West were incomparable, that they were to be judged by different standards, amounted to relinquishing the hope of gaining the respect of the West—and there was no sense in being of value if it was not recognized by the significant other. In other words, national self-esteem depended on comparability to the West.

The response that proved the most viable was the rejection of the West because it was evil, or *ressentiment*. Like cultural relativism, *ressentiment* was based on a deeply pessimistic evaluation of Russia, on the recognition of its absolute impotence in the competition with the West, but unlike cultural relativism, it was a remarkably creative sentiment, capable of unending ramification, constantly generating and fermenting new sentiments and ideas, a seedbed of ideologies. Because Russians had few indigenous resources to provide them with building blocks, the rejection of the West as such, the pure *ressentiment* expressed in hatred, could not furnish the basis for national pride and contribute to the construction of a viable national identity. The Russians had left their pre-Western existence and would not go back to it. When in 1836 Chaadaev reminded them of this, his contemporaries were shocked and he was declared insane;[124] yet the creators of Russian national consciousness in the eighteenth century—Novikov, Fonvisin, Karamzin—faced, realized, and agonized over exactly this issue. And thus, unable to tear themselves away from the West, to eradicate, to efface its image from their consciousness, and having nothing to oppose to it, they defined it as the anti-model and built an ideal image of Russia in direct opposition to it. Russia was still measured by the same standards as the West (for it defined Western values as universal), but it was much better than the West. For every Western vice it had a virtue, and for what appeared as a virtue in the West, it had a virtue in reality, and if it was impossible to see these virtues in the apparent world of political institutions and cultural and economic achievements, this was because the apparent world was the world of appearances and shadows, while the virtues shined in the world of the really real—the realm of the spirit.

From the days of Kantemir, it was the political reality of Russia which Russian patriots found most embarrassing: the lack of liberty, equality, respect for the individual. It was this difference in the fundamental relation to Man, not economic or cultural under-achievement, which militated most conspicuously against the moral canon of the West, which Russia, eager to be incorporated in this luminary family of nations, nonchalantly embraced. It was also political reality which appeared most immune to change. This was the eighteenth century. The West for Russia was France of the Enlightenment. On the mental horizon vaguely loomed England, which France at this very time was determined to emulate and surpass, in the process giving its values the explicit and articulate expression they never had in the place of their birth. Other European countries, especially the neighboring Germany, were but imperfect reflections of France. America, the Land of Liberty, in the consciousness of eighteenth-century Russians, bordered on the imaginary, an ideal construction rather than real presence, an embodiment of a principle. But the principle was the same all along. The thinking individual—the common man endowed with reason, and thus partaking in the nature of the Deity was the measure of moral good. History had not yet revealed the failure of France and Germany to excel in the English values; the Russians could not have known that they were not alone in their shame. On the face of it, their reality did seem so much more repulsive. It was rationality, the reason of the thinking individual, which necessitated liberty and equality. Russia did not have liberty and equality, and so it revolted against rationality, rejecting both the thinking individual and the faculty that defined his nature. From the point of view of the eighteenth-century European elite, the Russian reality was not reasonable, and the first Russian nationalists found reason unpalatable. Reason as a faculty of the human mind referred to artic-

ulation, precision, delimitation, and reserve—they opposed to it life so full
of feeling that one could choke on it, the inexpressible, the unlimited, the
hyperbolic. Reason had to do with calculation, reflection, predictability—
they opposed to it spontaneity, the unexpectable, the unmeasurable. By their
very nature these qualities were vague, undefined. It was much clearer what
they were not, than what they were. They defied standards and were perfect
ingredients for the enigmatic Slavic soul.

The qualities of the Russian soul were arrived at through the mental exercise of posing antitheses to the existing Western virtues with regard to
which Russia was particularly deficient; and therefore in the beginning they
were as little present in Russia as anywhere else. But its possession was so
sweet, and its inventors or discoverers wanted so much to believe in it, that
this initially intangible entity materialized and, embodied in the national
character, became the most formidable and immutable component of the
culture that was emerging around it. Oh, how much did the enigmatic Slavic
soul store within itself! Nobody could see it, and yet it was irrefutable. Nobody could deny the Russian nation superiority which expressed itself in the
world beyond the apparent.[125]

The stages of this complex evolution (from the first realization of Russia's
inferiority, through optimistic acceptance of the challenge and different varieties of withdrawal from it—cultural relativism and pure *ressentiment*—
to the transvaluation of values) cannot be clearly separated and organized
chronologically. They coexist and overlap in various ways—and continue to
coexist and overlap beyond the eighteenth century, although in different
measures—and are frequently found on the same pages as a reflection of the
authors' struggle with the predicament faced by the Russian elite. These authors, the creators of the Russian national consciousness, oscillate between
the several positions, as if testing the powers of every possible remedy, but
they all eventually converge on the final stage of the transvaluation, as the
only viable solution to their problem. The rejection of reason runs through
all these searching writings, as it does, later, through assertions of the Russian national character.

At the end of the eighteenth century, this rejection is specific. The value of
"reason" is retained, but "reason" either is defined in a French way, as the
true philosophy, or becomes closely akin to the Hegelian *Geist*, the Spirit of
the Age or the Nation. What is rejected is the faculty of the human mind,
the ability that creates the individual. In the nineteenth century, it is the individual that becomes the central object of attack, but the eighteenth-
century pioneers concentrate on the pernicious attribute itself and oppose it
to the soul in comparison with which it is worthless. Fonvisin, in a detached
but loving description of himself, confesses with pride: "Nature endowed
me with a keen intelligence, but did not give me any common sense [*zdra-
vogo rassudka*]." "Ah!" exclaims Karamzin with evident self-satisfaction, "I

sometimes shed tears, and am not ashamed of them!" Elsewhere he advises aspiring authors: "They say that an Author needs talent and knowledge: acute, perceptive mind, vivid imagination, etc. [*i proch.*]. I grant this, but this is not enough. He must have also a kind, tender heart . . . I am sure that a bad man cannot be a good Author." Speaking through Starodum, Fonvisin articulates this position in *The Minor.* "My father repeated over and over again," he makes the worthy old man say, "have a heart, have a soul—and you will be a man always . . . Without it [the soul] the most enlightened sage is a pitiful nothing [*zhalkaia tvar'*]." Reason, on the other hand, is just a matter of fashion and can easily become outmoded. "What is there to be proud of in having reason, my friend? Reason, if it is only reason, is a veritable trifle." [126]

Perhaps the most articulate early image of the exuberant Russian soul, and the most explicitly contemptuous of the dull and cold reason of the West, belongs to the pen of a minor poet, N. A. L'vov. "The gigantic spirit of our ancestors," he writes, "appears in other lands to be an unnatural exaggeration. And how could it help being so? In foreign lands all goes according to plan, words are weighed, steps are measured. There one sits hour upon hour; then begins to think. Having thought, one rests. Having rested, one smokes a pipe. Then, thoughtfully, goes to one's work. There are no songs, no pranks. Among us, Orthodox, however, work is like fire under our hands. Our speech is thunder, so that the sparks fly and the dust rises in columns." [127] The majestic prose of the nineteenth-century writers would make the language of their predecessors sound like clumsy babble, but even such giants as Gogol would but embellish L'vov's succinct characteristic, adding nothing to the conception and in fact unable to conceive of the matter in any other way. The nineteenth-century Russians would internalize the fantasy of the eighteenth-century inventors.

The rejection of reason implied a reinterpretation of its corollaries in political culture: liberty and equality. While Russian nationalists agreed that the concepts denoted great moral virtues, they refused to see in Western institutions their true embodiment. Western liberty and equality were not *real* liberty and equality. These were something else. It was not entirely clear what they were, but the pivot of the reinterpretation is easily established. It was individual reason that was the source of all bondage: it stifled and constrained the inner forces of spirit. And every expression of this limiting rationality in economic or political institutions only exacerbated its deleterious effects. Real freedom receded into the soul; it became inner freedom, and political equality lost all meaning. Fonvisin was among the first to point to the crucial difference between the real and the apparent. In his letters to N. I. Panin (1778) he wrote: "Observing the condition of the French nation, I learned to discern liberty by law and real liberty. Our people does not have the first, but enjoys the latter in many ways. In contrast, the French, having the right of liberty, live in veritable slavery." But it was Derzhavin who, un-self-consciously, gave Russian liberty and equality a concise but articulate poetic definition. Blessed is the people, he said in "The Grandee," which, like the Russian people, sees "happiness—in unity/equality—in equity/and liberty—in the ability to control one's passions!" *(V edinodushii—blazhen-stvo/ Vo pravosudii—ravenstvo/ Svobodu—vo uzde strastei!).*[128]

One final step had to be taken before the transvaluation of the Western canon could crystallize as the Russian national consciousness. The back-wardness of Russia meant the immaturity and underachievement of its civi-lization by Western standards. The Russian patriots connected the abomi-nation of reason to too much civilization—a curse they were spared—and interpreted the latter as separation from vital, primeval forces, of which they had to spare. (While, in the course of the eighteenth century, it was many times emphasized that backwardness was not necessarily an obstacle on the road to greatness, this intellectual somersault, making virtue out of neces-sity, turned backwardness into a guarantee of greatness.) At this juncture the Russian nationalist elite discovered, or perhaps invented, the "people," which determined the criteria of membership in the nation and led to its definition as an ethnic collectivity. For they connected the spiritual virtues of the Russian soul: spontaneity and feeling, to these vital forces: blood and soil. The "people," which the elite eventually made the central object of col-lective worship, was a mental construct, the conclusion of a syllogism. The soul—the sign of Russianness—derived from blood and soil. The people in the sense of plebs, the toilers, animals uncontaminated by civilization, had nothing but blood and soil. Therefore their soul—their nationality—was the purest. A corollary of this conclusion was that those who were not of that blood and soil could not possibly have the Russian soul—the visible evidence being considered inadequate—and thus could not be Russian. The Ukrainians, Poles, and Germans, who contributed so much to the formation of the idea of the Russian nation, were by that time either dead or thor-oughly russified; Pushkin was able to disregard his Ethiopian, and Lermon-tov his Scottish, ancestors; and this racist verdict did not create a problem for those whom Russia wished to call her own.

It was *ressentiment,* not social concerns, that fueled Russian national con-sciousness, and it was *ressentiment,* not sympathy for the peasantry, that made the peasant a symbol of the Russian nation. The attitude toward real (that is, existing in the world of the apparent) people was hardly sympa-thetic and for a long time remained inconsistent with this tendency to see the peasantry as the standard bearer of nationality. Serfdom was not seen as contradictory to this idea, and not until the nineteenth century did the views appear which with any justification could be called democratic or egalitar-ian. The suffering and humiliation of the peasantry seemed to promote the development of the Slavic soul, and soon came to be themselves considered

its distinctive qualities, taking their place alongside spontaneity and hypertrophied feeling.

The image of the peasantry changed considerably with the evolution of
the national consciousness. In the beginning of the eighteenth century, *The
Honest Mirror of Youth* instructed its tender readers: "The serfs are by their
nature uncivil, obstinate, shameless, and proud: for this reason they should
be restrained, subdued, and humiliated." The young gentlemen were advised
to converse among themselves in foreign tongues to distinguish themselves
from peasants and "other ignorant blockheads," and also because peasants
were naturally untrustworthy, garrulous, and indiscreet, and it was wise to
keep them as little informed regarding the affairs of their masters as possible. In the late 1760s Novikov fought this attitude, lashing out against
landlords who treated their serfs inhumanely and did not respect them.
"Oh, foolhardy!" he addressed an imaginary culprit. "Did you forget that
you were created a human being, is it possible that you abhor your own self
in the image of the peasants, your slaves? Don't you know that between
your slaves and human beings there is more resemblance than between you
and a human being?" [129] The humanity of the simple people was glorified in
contemporary plays and journals. In their simplicity, they were more human
than their masters, who either persisted in barbaric cruelty and ignorance
unredeemed by suffering (like Prostakova of *The Minor*) or aped the cold-
hearted evil West (like the Firiulins of *Misfortune from a Carriage,*) and thus
they were more noble, they were truly noble, and more Russian than the
nobility. They had no manners, they did not speak French, they were spontaneous and knew no limits in love and suffering. Truly, when they loved or
suffered "dust was rising in columns." "Peasant women can love too," wrote
Karamzin in *Poor Liza,* a pivotal work which announced the age of the Russian novel, but one was made to understand that only peasant women knew
how to love. Interestingly, the image of the people was most exalted and
idealized in the works of writers like Karamzin, noblemen who wrote for
the noble elite. A *raznochinets,* M. D. Chulkov, who intended his collection
of freely interpreted folk stories for the barely literate merchants with firsthand knowledge of the "people," had a somewhat different view. "Envy and
hatred," he wrote in one of the stories, "are the same among peasants and
city dwellers, but as the peasants are more sincere than the city folk, these
vices are more conspicuous among the former." [130] Such realism was out of
place in the heat of the efforts to create the basis for the national identity.
The "people" was kind, long-suffering, endlessly patient, pure of heart,
never reasoning, and had a huge glorious soul which put the rest of the
world to shame. But it was best to keep it that way.

Already at the beginning of the nineteenth century serfdom was considered by many intolerable, but it is surprising how slowly this sensitivity developed. In the *Memoir of Ancient and Modern Russia,* Karamzin, con-

cerned about Alexander's dissatisfaction with serfdom (the young tsar took after his grandmother), wrote: "In the community of the state the natural right must give way to the civic right . . . [Freed peasants] will not have the land, which (indisputably) is the property of the nobility . . . [The tsar] wants to make peasants happy with freedom, but what if freedom interferes with the good of the state? And is it certain that the peasants will be happy, freed of their landlords, but sacrificed to their own vices, middlemen, and dishonest judges?" Fonvisin, who also had his share in the celebration of the "people," nevertheless considered any notion of equality (that would include it) as absurd. He reported from France, as a most curious incident, the following: "[The governor of Montpellier, Comte Périgord,] has a box in the theater. Usually there is a soldier on guard at its door, to show respect to the person [of the Comte]. Once when the box was full of the best people in the city, the guard, bored to stand at his place, left the door, took a chair, and, having placed it near the seats of all the noble persons, sat down to watch the comedy, holding the gun in his hands. A Chevalier of St. Louis, the major of his regiment, was sitting beside him. I was astonished at the impertinence of the soldier and the silence of his commander, and took the liberty to inquire of the latter: Why did the soldier join him like that? *C'est qu'il est curieux de voir la comédie,* answered he with such an expression as if he did not regard this as in any measure peculiar." [131] For the astonished Fonvisin this, evidently, was more than peculiar, and he was not an exception among his countrymen. In eighteenth-century Russia, the hierarchical view of society did not as yet interfere with the view of the "people" as the true nation.

With the "discovery of the people" the period of gestation of the Russian national consciousness ended. When the eighteenth century drew to a close, the matrix in which all the future Russians would base their identity was complete and the sense of nationality born. It was a troubled child, but the agony of birth was over, and the baby could not be pushed back. For the time to come, it would determine the course of Russian history.


## The Two-Headed Eagle

The ingredients of the Russian national consciousness, and the definition of the Russian nation, were already present by 1800. Between that date and 1917 the components of this living, self-proliferating whole were in many ways articulated, refined, reconceptualized, and acted out—but never essentially modified. I do not see one single exception to this generalization among the multitude of extraordinary, complex people who participated in this process. [132] The cognitive construct born out of the anguish and humiliation of the eighteenth-century elite became the identity of its nineteenth-century descendants; it defined them; they could no more escape it than jump out of their skin; and when it was not reflected in their writings, it was reflected in their lives.

The Russian national idea consisted in the following: The nation was (1) defined as a collective individual, (2) formed by ethnic, primordial factors such as blood and soil, and (3) characterized by the enigmatic soul, or spirit. The spirit of the nation resided in the "people," but, rather paradoxically, was revealed through the medium of the educated elite, who, apparently, had the ability to divine it. The rejection of the common thinking individual, which expressed itself in the glorification of his opposite, the community, also led to the emphasis on special, uncommon individuals, the prophets and divines of the national spirit, and as a result the adoration of the "people" frequently found its counterpart in elitism and contempt for the dumb masses. The special individuals, who knew what the "people" wanted, naturally had the right to dictate to the masses, who did not know. Russian nationalism was ethnic, collectivistic, and authoritarian.

Constructed in this manner, Russian national identity provided the ground for individual self-esteem; on the face of it, the comparison with the West was moved to a new plane where Russia, by definition, was in no way inferior. Unfortunately, the West remained the significant other for Russia and was still an absolutely necessary condition for the successful formation and sustenance of national pride; the paramount motivation within the framework of thus-defined national identity was still winning its approbation. Again and again, eager to prove its worth, Russia was forced to confront the West on its own ground, only to return, humiliated, to the world of inner glory, where it licked its wounds and thought of revenge. The very same drama was constantly reenacted; it is possible that it is being reenacted right now.

The Decembrist uprising of 1825 was the last dramatic and unadulterated expression of optimism and confidence that Russia could and would catch up with the West. Generated by the victory over Napoleon, in which Russia played such a prominent role, and an aspect of the general upsurge of nationalism and triumphant national pride in its train, this optimism expressed itself in the sense of urgency to close the gap—which at that moment appeared small and such that it could be easily closed—between Russia and Europe. This optimism was further inspired by the liberalism of the reigning monarch, Alexander I, who not only represented an object of national pride himself,[133] but seemed to encourage the boldest political aspirations of his subjects. "Emperor Alexander promised us much," wrote one of the Decembrists, Peter Kahovsky; in his testimony, "he, it could be said, enormously stirred the minds of the people toward the sacred rights of humanity. Later he changed his principles and intentions." The situation immediately leading to the uprising was a clear case of explosive frustration with reality resulting from inflated expectations, and the inability to tolerate what seemed to be the few remaining obstacles on the way to their fulfillment, an ominous psychological predicament described so well by Tocqueville in *Ancien régime*. The Decembrist uprising was indeed not unlike a mini–French Revolution. There was a fundamental similarity in motivation. The Russian rebels wanted to propel their country into equality with Europe in the same way the optimistic French wanted to wrestle the palm of world leadership from the hands of the English. In both cases the goal seemed easily achievable. "Napoleon invaded Russia and then only, for the first time, did the Russian people become aware of their power," wrote Alexander Bestuzhev to Nicholas I; "only then awakened in all our hearts a feeling of independence, at first political and finally national. That is the beginning of free thinking in Russia. The government itself spoke such words as 'Liberty, Emancipation!' . . . the military men began to talk: 'Did we free Europe in order to be ourselves placed in chains? Did we grant constitution to France that we dare not talk about it, and did we buy at the price of blood priority among nations in order that we might be humiliated at home?' . . . we, inspired by such a situation in Russia and seeing the elements ready for change, decided to bring about a *coup d'état*." There was also the similarity of models. The American Revolution, which from afar seemed to be the result of a successful divination of the Spirit of the Age, of which the Russian elite thought itself as capable as the French, and was a challenge to menacing Europe, went into the heads of the future rebels. Kahovsky wrote: "We are witnesses of great events. The discovery of the New World and the United States, by virtue of its form of government, have forced Europe into rivalry with [America]. The United States will shine as an example even to distant generations. The name of Washington, the friend and benefactor of the people, will pass from generation to generation; the memory of his devotion to the welfare of the Fatherland will stir the hearts of citizens." But Russia was no America.

"The story told to Your Excellency," protested Kahovsky in his letter to General Levashev, "that, in the uprising of December 14 the rebels were shouting 'Long live the Constitution!' and that people were asking 'What is Constitution, the wife of His Highness the Grand Duke [Constantin]?' is not true. It is an amusing invention. We know too well the meaning of a constitution and we had a word that would equally stir the hearts of all classes—LIBERTY!" [134] Yet, somehow the story refused to die, and even if it was just a cruel joke, we have learned since then that Russian jokes are not the least-accurate reflections of Russian reality. Russia was not ready for Liberty European-style; it fell dismally short of its ideal, and the confidence which inspired the Decembrists to wish equality with the West was buried together with their hopes.

The principal contribution of the nineteenth century to the Russian nationalist tradition was embedded in deep pessimism regarding Russia's ability to emulate and become equal to the West. This contribution was inherent in the matrix and represented its ramification or differentiation into what ostensibly were two opposing currents of thought, but were actually two sides of one current. Expanding the terms used to designate a pivotal instance of this differentiation, we may call these traditions Westernism and Slavophilism. These were to remain the chief alternating approaches to the confrontation with the West, or responses to its persisting superiority, until our day.

Facts do not speak; people do. And thus, Lenin notwithstanding, not the Decembrists and their failure awakened Herzen and with him all the others, but, according to Herzen's own testimony, "The First Philosophical Letter" of Chaadaev, which "rang like a shot in the dark night." Chaadaev, wrote R. T. McNally, "stands utterly alone in the history of Russian thought, a fascinating exception to almost any generalization that can be made about it."[135] This is true, although Chaadaev most certainly was a product of his native soil. Its influence was clearly evident in his major preoccupation, the place of Russia vis-à-vis the West; in his concept of the nation, "peoples are moral beings just as individuals are";[136] in his emphasis on the spiritual; and in his very intensity. Page after page of his long "Philosophical Letter" is a testimony to his profound concern for the moral image of his nation; he recognizes its inadequacy and is humiliated and pained by it. The letter is an indictment of Russian reality; it is an indictment of a passionate patriot, not unlike the indictments which can be found in the writings of other Russian patriots before and after him, and remarkably similar to Marx's indictment of the German reality in the "Introduction to the Contribution to Hegel's Philosophy of Right." Chaadaev's judgment is harsh, but his uniqueness lies not in that he lacerated the abscess, but in that he failed to provide an anesthetic. He did not believe in the possibility of a fast cure.

The picture of Russia Chaadaev paints is depressing:

> One of the most deplorable things in our unique civilization is that we are still just beginning to discover truths which are trite elsewhere . . . Placed, as it were, outside of the times, we have not been affected by the universal education of mankind . . . Our history experienced nothing remotely similar to this age of exuberant activity, this exalted play of the moral powers of the people . . . We have absolutely no universal ideals . . . Even in our glances I find that there is something strangely vague, cold, uncertain, resembling somewhat the features of people placed at the lowest rung of the social ladder . . . Alone in the world, we have given nothing to the world, taken nothing from the world, bestowed not even a single idea upon the fund of human ideas, contributed nothing to the progress of the human spirit, and we have distorted all progressivity which has come to us . . . One time, a great man wanted to civilize us, and in order to give us a foretaste of enlightenment, he threw us the cloak of civilization: we took

the cloak but did not so much as touch civilization . . . today . . . we do not amount to a thing in the intellectual order. I cannot stop being dumbfounded by this void and this surprising solitude of our social existence.

To this gloomy reality Chaadaev opposes Europe, its "ideas of duty, justice, law, and order." He dismisses the possibility of other ideals. "Do you believe," he asks, "that Abyssinian Christianity or Japanese civilization will produce the world order which I discussed before and which is the ultimate destiny of mankind? Do you believe that these absurd aberrations of divine and human truths will cause heaven to descend upon earth?" His Eurocentrism is uncompromising. "[The] sphere in which the Europeans live [is] the only one in which humanity can achieve its final destiny," he insists; "despite all that is incomplete, vicious, evil, in European society as it stands today . . . it is nonetheless true that God's reign has been realized there in some way, because it contains the principle of indefinite progress and possesses germinally and elementarily all that is needed for God's reign to become established definitely upon earth one day."

If it was to become morally acceptable, Russia had no choice but to follow in the steps of the West—to try, not to surpass, but to be like it. And there was no certainty that the goal would be achieved. Even though Chaadaev shared the missionary vision which characterized all European nationalisms, he remained pessimistic and uncertain. "We are one of those nations," he mused, "which does not seem to form an integral part of humanity, but which exists only to provide some great lesson for the world. The lesson which we are destined to provide will assuredly not be lost, but who knows when we shall find ourselves amid humanity and how much misery we shall experience before the fulfillment of our destiny?" [137]

It is for this—for this!—that Chaadaev was officially pronounced a madman. Only mental derangement could be the "reason for writing such nonsense." [138] So thought the chief of the Secret Police, and hardly anyone (including Herzen, who denied this) disagreed with him. For one could not live with the knowledge of such difficulty and insecurity. And it is in response to it—and to prove it wrong—that the two facets of the archetypal tradition of Russian nationalism that were to shape the ways in which Russians until our day relate to the world and themselves arose.

The Westernizer Herzen wrote upon the deaths of the Slavophils Khomiakov and Aksakov: "Yes, we were their opponents, but very strange opponents: we had *one love*, but *not an identical one*. Both they and we conceived from early years one powerful, unaccountable, physiological, passionate feeling, which they took to be a recollection, and we—a prophesy, the feeling of boundless, all-encompassing love for the Russian people, Russian life, the Russian turn of mind. Like Janus, or like a two-headed eagle, we were looking in different directions while a *single heart was beating in us.*" [139] One can comment on this formulation, but there is nothing to add to it. Slavophilism and Westernism were indeed the two sides of the same set of aspirations and sentiments, one facing an image of the past, and the other that of the future. The terms "Westernism" and "Slavophilism" were coined to characterize an intellectual feud; this feud, however, occurred between friends, people moved by the same concerns, who forever remained sympathetic toward the seemingly opposing views of their opponents. Westernism and Slavophilism were very much alike; they differed in emphasis and in mood more than in anything else. [140]

Both Westernism and Slavophilism were steeped in *ressentiment*. Both arose out of the realization of Russia's inferiority and a revulsion against its humiliating reality. In Slavophilism, this revulsion was transformed into excessive self-admiration. In Westernism, the very same sentiment led to the generalized revulsion against the existing world and to the desire to destroy it. Yet the difference was that of emphasis. Both were Westernisms, for as philosophies of *ressentiment* both defined the West as the anti-model. And both were Slavophilisms, for the model for them was Russia, which they idealized each in its own fashion, and whose triumph over the West both predicted. Westernism saw the fulfillment of the ideal (Russia as anti-West) in the future, following the destruction of the old world and beyond the present splendor of the West, but it still accepted the direction in which the West developed as the only way. Slavophils, on the other hand, placed their ideal outside Western development and, in fact, outside history. They did not have to go beyond the West to prove to it Russia's superiority. It was proven, whether revealed or concealed, by its very nature. There was nothing to do about this. Slavophilism contained a streak of escapism, and thus it could seem conservative. The Slavophils were not conservative; many of them were critical of the reality which concealed Russia's brilliant—holy—self behind Western appearances, but they did not think that Russia had to develop to fulfill its mission. Westernism, on the other hand, was activist. Even though the final triumph was guaranteed, Westernists were never averse to helping it on the way. In its activism and orientation toward the future, Westernism retained some of the optimism of the eighteenth century.

One observes a certain circularity in the intellectual and political movements of the nineteenth and early twentieth centuries, an attempt at political reform, failure, and withdrawal. And, though Westernism and Slavophilism cannot be clearly distinguished, they usually were found at the opposing points in the cycles of thought and unrest. Schematically, the cycle would start with the optimistic thrust to catch up with and surpass the West while following its direction—Westernism; with the failure of the attempted reform or the frustration of the aspiration, the cycle would reach its nadir;

then the pendulum would swing to a Slavophilic escape, revive national self-esteem by the loving contemplation of Russia's spiritual virtues, and lead to the upsurge of confidence, optimism, and Westernist activism again.

The solution that Slavophils proposed to the harrowing problem of the difficulty and uncertainty of catching up with the West, so poignantly formulated by Chaadaev, was simple. On the one hand, not only the equality, but the superiority of Russia was already clearly achieved (it was inherent in the nation), and on the other, the West was rotten to the core and did not deserve imitation. The days of the West were gone. "It is painful to see," wrote Ivan Kireevskii, "what a subtle, but inevitable and justly sent madness now drives the Western man. He feels his darkness, and, like a moth, he flies into the fire, which he takes to be the sun. He cries like a frog and barks like a dog, when he hears the Word of God. And this gibbering idiot they want to upbraid in accordance with Hegel!"

The superiority of Russia derived from the fact that it was *not* a Western nation; indeed it embodied the principle opposed to that on which Western civilization was based. This—Russian—principle represented the true aspiration of man (or should we say: his species-being?) and made possible true freedom; it was the principle of the individual's dissolution in community, and thus the one that expressed itself in true—perfect—nations. For the nation was, of course, a moral individual endowed with a unique spirit. The principle was manifested with particular clarity in the Russian—Ortho-dox—Church, Eastern Christianity, and in the peasant commune. Eastern Christianity, now preserved for the world by Russia, was the original, and therefore the true, Christianity. The Russian Church, in contrast to the Western Churches, which emphasized the individual, was characterized by *sobornost'*, which Khomiakov, the Slavophil theologian, defined as the expression of "the idea of unity in multiplicity." "The Church is one," he wrote; "her unity follows of necessity from the unity of God; for the Church is not a multitude of persons in their separate individuality, but a unity of the grace of God, living in the multitude of rational creatures, submitting themselves willingly to grace." It is hard not to be reminded of Marx, the religious context notwithstanding, when one reads the following lines: "A man, however, does not find in the Church something foreign to himself. He finds himself in it, himself not in the impotence of spiritual solitude, but in the might of his spiritual, sincere union with his brothers, with his savior. He finds himself in it in his perfection, or rather he finds in it that which is perfect in himself, the Divine inspiration which constantly evaporates in the crude impurity of every separate individual existence." The same redeeming qualities were found in the peasant commune. "A commune," wrote Aksa-kov, "is a union of the people who have renounced their egoism, their individuality, and who express their common accord; this is an act of love . . . in the commune the individual is not lost, but renounces his exclusiveness in favor of the general accord—and there arises the noble phenomenon of a harmonious, joint existence of rational beings (consciousness): there arises a brotherhood, a commune—a triumph of human spirit." Freedom was freedom to live this principle; of course it was inner, of course it had nothing to do with the outward world of politics. This enabled Slavophils to accept, in fact uphold, the autocracy. "Having understood after the conversion to Christianity that freedom is only of the spirit, Russia continually stood up for her soul . . . she knew that perfection was impossible on earth, she did not seek earthly perfection, and therefore she chose the best (that is, the least evil) form of government and held to it constantly without considering it perfect." The comparison between Russian and Western political structure underscored the idyllic character of the former: "In the foundation of the Western state: violence, slavery, and hostility. In the foundation of the Russian state: free will, liberty, and peace." [141] And since the Russian people expressed the essence of humanity itself, it was not a people like any other. Like Fichte of Germany, Aksakov spoke of Russia as a universal nation. "The Russian people is not a people; it is humanity; it is a people only because it is surrounded by peoples with exclusively national essences, and its humanity is therefore represented as nationality." [142] What an easy way out this was! There was no need to catch up with the West; it was this pitiful opponent who had some catching up to do; Russia was the opposite of the West and so much better for that. Russia contained the salvation of the world within herself; she preseved and held high the torch of humanity, and the West was to watch her in amazement.

The Westernizers rejected the West without transferring their loyalties outside it and without defining Russia as a non-Western nation, or an embodiment of principles opposed to those of the West. They rejected the West in its current, present state, which was the state of betrayal of its own lofty principles, a decadent, rotting, aging state—and to it they opposed the young, exuberant Russia destined to bring these principles to fruition. The West was the only repository of history, it was the world. "Following the paths of development which have been trodden by *all* [emphasis added] societies in historical times, with the exception of the patriarchal states of the East, it has proved impossible to escape a proletariat," wrote T. N. Granovsky, utterly oblivious of the fact that "all societies with the exception of the patriarchal states of the East" meant at the most three countries in Europe: England, France, and Germany. This embodiment of world history was now leaving its task to Russia, "the younger brother in the European family," opening before it "a great and splendid field of activity." But though Russia harbored great liberating forces, they were imprisoned within a distasteful reality. "The Russia of the future existed exclusively among a few boys," wrote Herzen, "yet in them lay the heritage of December 14, the heritage of the learning of all humanity as well as of purely national Russia." These boys, thought Herzen, included Slavophils as much as Westernizers. "The leading characteristic of them all was a profound feeling of aversion for official Russia, for their environment, and at the same time the urge to escape out of it." But in the form of escape the boys differed, for in some of them, the Westernizers, in addition to this urge there was "a vehement desire to change the contemporary state of affairs." [143] "Throbbing with indignation," the Westernizers lashed at the present imperfections of their nation. With a stupefying intensity, explained by consumption as well as the fiery Russian soul, "the furious Vissarion," Belinsky, sermonized in his *Letter* to Gogol, the traitor to the cause of progressive Russia:

> Yes, I loved you with all the passion with which a man, bound by ties of blood to his native country, can love its hope, its honor, its glory, one of the great leaders on its path to consciousness, development, and progress . . . [But] you failed to realize that Russia sees its salvation not in mysticism, nor asceticism, nor pietism, but in the success of civilization, enlightenment, and humanity. What she needs is . . . awakening in the people of a sense of their human dignity lost for so many centuries amid the dirt and refuse; she needs rights and laws conforming not with the preaching of the church, but with common sense and justice, and their strictest possible observance. [How could one rest content with] a country where there are not only no guarantees for individuality, honor, and propriety, but even no police order? . . . Proponent of the *knout*, apostle of ignorance, champion of obscurantism and Stygian darkness, panegyrist of Tatar morals—what are you about! . . . According to you the Russian people is the most religious in the world! This is a lie! . . . Take a closer look and you will see that it is by nature a profoundly atheistic people . . . mystic exaltation is not in its nature; it has too much common sense, and too lucid, and positive, a mind, and therein perhaps lies the vastness of its historical destinies in the future. [144]

Enlightenment and humanity, human dignity, law and common sense, guarantees for individuality, the lucid and positive mind of the people averse to mystical exaltation! One would think that the next minute Belinsky would start to speak English. But no. In his memoirs Herzen recalled an incident with Belinsky arguing his point. In a friend's house, in a conversation before supper, Chaadaev's *Letter* came up and a certain pedantic "Russian German" in blue spectacles expressed himself quite negatively in its regard. This irritated Herzen, and an unpleasant argument ensued in which Belinsky, enraged, intervened. "'In civilized countries,' replied the gentleman in blue spectacles with inimitable self-complacency, 'there are prisons in which they confine the insane creatures who insult what the whole people respects— and a good thing too.' Belinsky . . . terrible, great at that moment . . . looking straight at his opponent . . . answered in a hollow voice: 'And in still more civilized countries there is guillotine for those who think that a good thing.'" [145] So much for common sense, laws, and individuality.

Belinsky said different things at different times,[146] but Herzen and Bakunin rejected law with consistent vehemence. And there is little doubt that "common sense" for them was a profanity, the very sign of the "bourgeois mediocrity" of the present West, which so much insulted Herzen, and of the decadence of Europe in which, as he said, "there is no youth and there are no young men." The individualism of the Westernizers had nothing in common with Western—that is to say, Anglo-American—individualism: the commitment to the rights and liberty of the common man. Not for a moment did they doubt that "a nation is collective in its nature" and that real freedom is inner freedom. But the spirit of the nation and the principle of freedom needed great, special individuals to reveal them, and it was the individualism of these special uncommon individuals, men like themselves, and their freedom unlimited by law and common sense, that Westernizers craved. They wished the glory of Russia, but they despised the "masses." [147] And since the masses were expendable, the solution Westernizers proposed to the problem posed by Chaadaev, of the difficulty and uncertainty of catching up with the West, was that of a cataclysmic event, a purifying conflagration that would in one sweep destroy the West and the imperfections of Russian reality, and from which Russia, with its spirit finally liberated, would reemerge to enjoy its—crowning—share of historical greatness. The idea of a Revolution—not a Decembrist *coup d'état*—was the Westernizers' contribution to the Russian national consciousness. Undoubtedly, they were led to it by their activist, maniacal temperament. Unlike the Slavophils, they were unable to sit with their arms folded and tolerate the spectacle of Western superiority; and under the crafty influence of *ressentiment,* Revolution was the form taken by their wishful thinking. Six years before the appearance of the *Communist Manifesto,* in the *Deutsche Jahrbücher* in which Marx was to prophesy the inevitable leadership of Germany, Bakunin, under the *nom de plume* of Jules Elysard, announced the specter that was haunting Europe: "All peoples and all men are full of presentiments . . . Even in Russia, in that limitless and snow-covered empire, of which we know so little and which has before it perhaps a great future, even in Russia the dark storm clouds are gathering! The air is sultry, it is heavy with storms! And therefore we call to our brothers: Repent! Repent! The Kingdom of God is coming nigh." And he advised: "Let us put our trust in the eternal spirit which destroys and annihilates only because it is the unsearchable and eternally creative source of all life. The passion for destruction is also a creative passion!" Herzen was not at all certain what the results of the Revolution he welcomed would be. Most of the time he was only moderately optimistic. "The Chinese shoes of German make in which Russia has hobbled for a hundred and fifty years, though they have caused many painful corns, have evidently not crippled her bones, since whenever she has had a chance of stretching her limbs, the result has been the exuberance of fresh

young energies. That does not guarantee the future, but it does make it extremely *possible.*" Yet he could not live with uncertainty and would rather
have the end of the world than prolong it. In 1858, looking at Russia "from
the other shore," he wrote from London: "Where are we going? Very possibly toward a terrible *jacquerie,* toward a *mass rising of the peasants.* We
do not want this at all and state this, but, on the other hand, slavery and the
condition of excruciating uncertainty in which the country is at present are
even worse than a *jacquerie.*"[148] Of course, on the one scale were just thousands of human lives, while on the other lay the weighty matter of suffering
national pride.

Finding expression under the most diverse guises and names, the two traditions have formed the substance of Russian national sentiment ever since.
There was no clear demarcation in the minds of people between Slavophilism and Westernism. Before the split Ivan Kireevskii was a devoted admirer
of the West and edited a journal entitled *The European.* Herzen ended as a
Slavophil. Chernyshevskii was a Westernizer; *Narodnichestvo,* a reincarnation of Slavophilism, sprang out of his ideas. The first Russian Marxists—
the arch-Westernizers—were disillusioned Narodniks. The two currents,
united by the spirit of Holy Russia and the rejection of the West, were one.
They continued to exist side by side, upheld interchangeably in an unending
oscillation between hope and withdrawal. And in the best Romantic tradition of striving toward unity in multiplicity, one could be a Westernizer in
the morning, a Slavophil in the afternoon, and criticize after dinner.[149]

Westernism asserted itself in the conflagration of 1917. The fundamental
motivation of the Revolution, the imperative of Marxism, was the destruction of the world order that had betrayed its own first principles. However
unclear it might have been about the new world that would emerge from the
debris, the ideology guaranteed success in what mattered most—the destruction of the perfidious West; and if the price of that was self-destruction,
this was not too high a price. In the desperate bid to escape the anguish of
their inferiority (they believed, in an attempt to save the world), Russian
Westernizers were willing to begin with the destruction of the Russia that
was. So urgent was their desire for national self-esteem that for some time
they let their Russian identity be eclipsed by the sense of cosmic brotherhood Russia represented as a universal nation. "To the old world, the world
of national oppression, national squabbles, and national isolation, the
workers counterpose a new world of united working people of all nations,"
declared Lenin. I have no doubt that he sincerely believed that the mask of
proletariat, designed by Marx to cover the face of Germany when it sacks
what was "the West" for him, and now worn by the Bolsheviks, was not a
mask but their true face. But in his very advocacy of the sudden Russian
internationalism, Lenin clarified the national sentiment behind it. In the essay "On the National Pride of the Great Russians," directed against persist-

ing nationalists within and outside the revolutionary ranks, the leader wrote:

> It is unbecoming to us, representatives of the dominant nation of the East of Europe and a good deal of Asia, to forget about the enormous significance of the national question . . . Are we, the Great Russian socially conscious proletarians, devoid of national pride? Of course not! We love our language and our motherland; more than with anything else we are preoccupied with raising *its* working masses . . . to the self-conscious life of democrats and socialists. More than by anything else we are pained to see and feel what violence, oppression, and degradation our beautiful motherland had to suffer under the hands of the tsarist hangmen, nobility, and capitalists. We are proud that these oppressions have met with a rebuff from among us, the Great Russians, that *we* brought forward Radishchev, the Decembrists, the revolutionaries—*raznochintsy* of the 70s, that the Great Russian working class created in 1905 a mighty revolutionary party of the masses, that the Great Russian *muzhik* is becoming a democrat and starts to oppose the priests and the landlords . . . We are full of the sense of national pride, for the Great Russian nation *too* developed a revolutionary class, it *too* proved that it could show humanity great examples of struggle for liberty . . . "A people that oppresses other peoples cannot be free," so said the greatest representatives of systematic democracy of the nineteenth century, Marx and Engels . . . And we, the Great Russian workers, filled with the sense of national pride, want by all means the free, independent, autonomous, democratic, republican, proud Great Russia, building its relations with its neighbors on the human principle of equality . . . Exactly because we want it, we say: it is impossible in the twentieth century, in Europe (even if only Eastern Europe), "to defend one's fatherland" by other means than through the struggle with the monarchy, landlords, and capitalists of our *own* fatherland, that is, the worst enemies of our motherland.
>
>     . . . if history will judge to the advantage of the Great Russian capitalism, all the greater will be the socialist role of the Great Russian proletariat, as the main mover of the communist revolution . . . The interest . . . of the national pride of the Great Russians coincides with the *socialist* interest of the Great Russian (and all other) proletarians.[150]

Few explicitly nationalist arguments are more telling than these pathetically emphasized "we *too*."

One of several great poets of the epoch, Alexander Blok, understood the motives behind the Revolution in the same way and, in the poem "Twelve," gave it a mystical, deeply religious interpretation, evoking at once the fundamentally Westernist aspiration of Russia as the Third Rome and its Slavophil imagery. The twelve are a Bolshevik patrol, but their very number makes one think of the apostles of Christ. They are the representatives of the new world. The old world is likened to a hungry, homeless mongrel, who, together with the incarnation of the unjust past—the capitalist or *burzhui*—gloomily watches the twelve marching by, and then trots after them.

The dramatic ending of the poem carries the message to a soteriological pitch:

> . . . So they march with sovereign tread
> The hungry mongrel trots behind,
> At their head—with a blood-stained banner
> . . . At their head is—Jesus Christ.[151]

To gain self-respect Russia took upon itself the burden of the world's salvation. "We take pride in the fact," wrote Lenin, "that it fell to our happy lot to start the building of the Soviet state and thereby usher in a new era of history." The builders of the Third Rome set the most formidable empire on earth on fire, and burning in it, stretched out their hands to what they called "the West," and begged for approbation. Their desire shook the world. But the West, again, failed them. It was powerless to change *their* reality and relieve the sense of inadequacy which tortured them. And while the revolutionaries escaped into the busy work of destruction, the poet gave vent to despair. At the top of his voice he shouted: "To Hell With You!" He defied and threatened the West, and cursed it. He believed that should Europe open its eyes and recognize the achievement of Russia, the reality would transform. (And in the midst of threats and curses, he hoped against hope that Europe would indeed change its mind and gratify the desire of his nation.) In no other work of literature has the threat to and the defiance of the West by a Russian been expressed with such striking, distressing beauty as in Blok's "Scythians." [152]

As an epigraph Blok chose two lines from a poem by Vladimir Soloviev, "Pan-Mongolism": "Pan-Mongolism, though this is a wild name/ It does caress my ears." The poem itself developed the theme.

> There are millions of you, but multitudes of us.
> Come try and overcome us!
> Yes, we are Scythians! Yes, Asians we are
> With squint and lusty eyes!
> For you—the centuries, for us—one hour.
> Like slaves, obeying and abhorred,
> We held the shield between the warring breeds
> Of Europe and the raging Mongol horde! . . .
> For centuries your eyes were toward the East.
> Our pearls you hoarded in your chests,
> And mockingly you bode the day
> When you could aim your canons at our breasts.
> The time has come. Disaster beats its wings.
> With every day the insults grow.
> The hour will strike, and without ruth
> Your proud Paestums[153] be laid low!
> Oh, pause, old world! while life still beats in you

. . . Halt here, like wise Oedipus, in front
The Sphinx and its ancient mystery!
The Sphinx is Russia, exulting, grieving,
Oozing black blood,
It gazes, gazes, gazes into you
With hatred and with love!
Yes, you have long since ceased to love
As our blood loves! You have forgotten
That there is love on earth
That burns like fire and kills!
We love all things: cold numbers' burning chill,
The gift of sacred revelation.
We know all things: the Gallic reason
And the gloomy genius of the Germans . . .
We love the flesh, its color and its taste,
Its deathly, heavy, fleshy odor . . .
Are we to blame if the embrace
of our heavy tender paws will break your bones?
We are accustomed, seizing playing colts,
To break their mighty croups
And we are used to tame
Slave women unwilling to submit . . .
Come unto us! From horrors of the war
Come to our peaceful arms!
Sheathe the old sword, before it is too late,
Oh, comrades, let's be brothers!
If not, there's nothing we can lose.
We also know old perfidies! . . .
To welcome pretty Europe we shall spread
And scatter in the thickets of our forests!
And then we'll turn to you
Our ugly Asiatic face! . . .
For the last time, old world, we bid you come,
Come to the feast of labor and of peace,
For the last time to a happy feast
The barbarian lyre is calling you to come!

Ovid in *Tristia* described the Scythians as a terrifying, barbaric tribe: "They are scarce worthy of the name [of men]; they have more of cruel savagery than wolves. They fear not laws; right gives way to force, and justice lies conquered beneath the aggressive sword." [154] The Scythians were the negation of civilization, of all Rome stood for, the embodiment of the forces of darkness. The Russian intelligentsia of 1917 still knew its Ovid. Only in utter exasperation could Russians claim the name of this savage tribe. But even this act of defiance, against all rules of geography, implied that the light came from the West.

Moved by the restless spirit born out of the agony of its elite, Russia would never give in to despair completely. It would never give up hope to become the superior Western state, to fulfill the promise of France, to be the truly new New World; and in its bid for national greatness it continued to build its own—Scythian—Rome. Mandelstam called it "a Hyperborean plague." Fortunately, it is not a sociologist's task to pronounce judgment on history.

# The Final Solution of
# Infinite Longing:
# Germany

The concept of nation requires that all its members should form as it were only one individual.

Friedrich Schlegel

There is perhaps no country that deserves to be free and independent as Germany, because none is so disposed to devote its freedom so single-mindedly to the welfare of all. The German genius is among all nations the one which is least destructive, which always nourishes itself, and when freedom is secured Germany will certainly attain an outstanding place in every form of culture and thought.

Wilhelm von Humboldt

The German alone can . . . be a patriot; he alone can for the sake of his nation encompass the whole of mankind; contrasted with him from now on the patriotism of every other nation must be egoistic, narrow and hostile to the rest of mankind.

Fichte

I hate all Frenchmen without distinction in the name of God and of my people, I teach this hatred to my son, I teach it to the sons of my people . . . I shall work all my life that the contempt and hatred for this people strike the deepest roots in German hearts.

F. M. Arndt

National hatred is anyhow a peculiar thing. You will always find it strongest and most violent in the lowest stages of civilization.

Goethe

Fortunately, we Germans are not Scythians.

Karl Marx

T he development of German nationalism differed markedly from that of England, France, and Russia. German national consciousness emerged significantly later; it was born in the Wars of Liberation from Napoleonic domination in the early nineteenth century. In both France and Russia the sense of nationality was firmly embedded, and the idea of the nation dominated political discourse by 1800; in England national identity dated from the sixteenth century. The development of German national consciousness, however, was singularly rapid. One cannot speak of it before 1806; by 1815 it had come of age: it was a formidable presence and possessed all the characteristics by which the world would know it. This development, from birth to maturity, in other nations took a century. The architects of German national identity did not, as in other cases, come from the aristocracy and the ruling elite, but from a peculiar class of educated commoners, professional intellectuals. Their status was higher than that of the middle class in general (which, on the whole, in Germany had no status to speak of), but much lower than that of the higher classes, and thus they found themselves marginalized, suspended between different social strata in a society which did not, in fact, recognize anything between the middle classes and the nobility. When it finally emerged in the early nineteenth century, German national consciousness represented the culmination of a long and tortuous process of intellectual fermentation, continuously spurred on by the oppressive sense of status-inconsistency among those who eventually became the prime movers of German nationalism, and redirected at intervals by changing environmental constraints. Fundamentally a response to the social situation of the educated middle class in the last quarter of the eighteenth century, it was also the result of the confluence of several independent traditions, both imported (such as the philosophy of Enlightenment) and indigenous. The two most important of the indigenous traditions were Pietism—itself a product of the Reformation and the structural conditions of its spread in Germany—and early Romanticism, which was, among other things, an heir to both Pietism and Enlightenment. The complex genealogy of German nationalism and the overlapping stages in its formation are represented schematically in Figure 4.

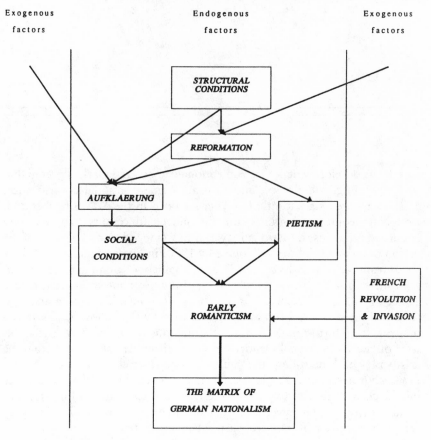

Exogenous factors          Endogenous factors          Exogenous factors

STRUCTURAL CONDITIONS

REFORMATION

AUFKLAERUNG

PIETISM

SOCIAL CONDITIONS

EARLY ROMANTICISM

FRENCH REVOLUTION & INVASION

THE MATRIX OF GERMAN NATIONALISM

*Figure 4*   Genealogy and stages in the emergence of German national consciousness

## I. The Setting

### The Conception and Miscarriage of Nationalism in the Sixteenth Century

The success of Protestantism in establishing itself as a legitimate Christian religion outside the Roman Catholic Church was a reflection of the disintegration of the centuries-old authority structure of European Christendom, known as *respublica Christiana*. It was this disintegration which provided the opportunity for national identities and nations to emerge. Nationalism and the Reformation, though springing from different sources, thus were made possible by the same development. They emerged within a short period of each other and, as the example of England clearly shows, developed together, Protestantism (however young itself, being a species of a familiar genus) sheltering nationalism during its first vulnerable century.

The German development, initially, was similar to that of England. In addition to the experience of the disintegration of the universal Church, Germany shared with England its exposure to the Italian Renaissance and was the home of an important Humanist movement. The concepts which went into the making of the idea of the nation, and the people able to articulate them, therefore, were present in Germany, too. By the beginning of the sixteenth century, several important social groups in Germany also had reason for dissatisfaction with the existing definitions of their social positions. They were experiencing a crisis which could make them receptive to the national identity. The success of the Reformation in Germany was to a considerable degree due to the fact that it touched upon and provided solutions to some of these pressing secular problems. That the sense of German nationality failed to take root in the sixteenth century is partly attributable to the notorious weakness of the central authority within Germany, but is largely explained by the fact that the crises of the groups that could promote nationalism had been resolved through unrelated developments already by the latter half of the century, thus eliminating the reason for the basic redefinition of the social and political collectivity and allowing the nascent national sentiment no time to develop.

The confusion and disenchantment of the Babylonian captivity (1305–1378) and the following Great Schism delivered the authority of the Papacy a blow from which it did not recover. It was permanently weakened, and the stronger among the secular potentates, long weary of the Holy See's intervention in their affairs, hastened to use this opportunity to weaken it further. The conciliar movement which challenged the monarchical authority of the Pope and opposed to it the ecclesiastical republic was one reflection of the spirit of the age. The establishment of the vote by "nations"[1]—the groups of representatives of secular and ecclesiastical princes—symbolized the disintegration of European Christendom and distinguished between its interests and those of individual territorial entities. After the Councils of Constance and Basel, the previously Holy Roman Empire was referred to as the Holy Roman Empire of the German Nation. Although, owing to conflicts between the "nations" at the Council of Constance, the Papacy was able to return to its old position, the rulers of England, France, and Spain in the fourteenth and fifteenth centuries were able to gain from it considerable concessions and secure a high degree of independence from papal intervention in their affairs. Germany was far less successful.

Germany at that time meant the territories loosely united under the name of the Holy Roman Empire. Since the middle of the thirteenth century and the demise of the Hohenstaufen dynasty, the imperial authority was unable to assert itself against the combined strength of the territorial rulers; and the latter grew increasingly aware of their own power. In their opposition to the central authority of the Emperor, by jealous preservation of the elective character of the imperial office, the princes inadvertently fostered the impersonal, modern concept of the polity (in this case empire) as a collectivity, rather than as the possession of the Emperor, which only later developed elsewhere, and claimed to be its representatives. The rift between Keiser and Reich widened even apart from the efforts of the princes. The dynastic successes of the Habsburgs led in 1519 to the election of Charles of Spain as the Emperor of the Holy Roman Empire of the German Nation. The "capitulation of election" which he had to sign sounded a nativist note: none but the native German nobility were to be employed in German imperial offices and only German and Latin were to be considered official languages.

While fearful of effective central power, the princes were equally unwilling to suffer the interference of Rome. The Golden Bull of 1356, called a "magna charta of German particularism," excluded the Pope from the election of the Emperor. The Pope negotiated with the most powerful of the territorial rulers, and Austria, Saxony, Brandenburg, and Jullich-Cleves obtained certain privileges through separate concordats. Yet, on the whole, papal intervention in the affairs of the Empire, including the territories of the privileged princes, remained much greater than in the territories of other European rulers, and this conspicuous discrimination added to the sense of heaviness of the actual burden. Since the Council of Constance in 1417, increasingly bitter complaints of the estates of the Empire against Roman injustice were recorded in the *Gravamina Nationis Germanicae* (The Grievances of the German Nation).

It is no wonder that German princes showed so little zeal in aiding the Roman Church to fight Lutheran heresy when it still could be fought. The spread of Lutheranism was eventually to put an end to Roman tutelage in all German territories, including those that remained Catholic, for with it the Papacy was no more the vicar of Christ on Earth. The princes welcomed this liberation, and it was a necessary condition for the emergence of national identity, but they were unwilling to form a unified polity which could serve as a framework for such an identity.

Another group—the general nobility, or the knights—was more sympathetic to the idea of a strong and united Germany. In the latter half of the fifteenth and the beginning of the sixteenth centuries, this general German nobility was in crisis. Several developments combined to bring it about. The military revolution of the fifteenth century had deprived the knights of their importance as the class of warriors. The significant loss of population and the depression of grain prices following the Black Death in the second half of the fourteenth century adversely affected those living off the land—the peasantry and the nobility. Conversely, the cities were enjoying increasing prosperity, the prices of industrial products rose, and, as a result, "in German history the age before and during the Reformation was more of a burghers' age than any other age before the nineteenth century."[2] The knights, as well as the peasants, resented the prosperity of the burghers and blamed their own misfortunes on the "monopolies" and other new economic practices dubbed *Fuggerei* (from Fuggers, the most powerful economic dynasty of the time), rather than on the Black Death. These practices were seen by the nobles as perverse in the religious sense (as "usury"), and as leading to the ruin of the "German nation."

Another development which had an adverse effect on the general nobility was the consolidation of power in the hands of the territorial princes. Toward the end of the fifteenth century many of the territories had permanent administrations in which officials, especially lawyers trained in Roman law, replaced the untrained nobility. The knights resented the lawyers as much as the merchants. They were also hostile to the centralizing policies of the princes. Their opposition had an effect similar to that of the opposition of the princes to the Emperor: the knights further promoted the modern concept of the polity as a collective enterprise oriented toward the common good, rather than as the patrimony of the ruler. Furthermore, the sympathies of the knights lay with the Emperor, for his strength would curtail the advances of the princes seen by the nobility as encroaching on its traditional privileges, unjust, and allied with burghers to ruin the nobility.

The knights, "as men concerned with the common welfare of the German nation,"[3] shared with the princes the latter's hostility to Rome. In combination with their "imperialist" aspirations, this insistence on the distinctiveness of German interests vis-à-vis those of the Church formed a variety of aristocratic nationalism, which was tinted by anti-capitalist resentment and opposition to the formal law, and in many ways resembled the modern German nationalism destined to emerge more than two centuries later. The ablest advocate of this precocious aristocratic nationalism was Ulrich von Hutten, who, at the outbreak of the Reformation, was the most influential writer in Germany besides Luther.

A Franconian knight himself, Hutten perfectly exemplifies the tight connection between the sense of insecurity and status-inconsistency of the nobility and nationalism at its inception, and the reinterpretation of the grievances of a class as those of the nation. Such reinterpretation, which identifies the plight of a specific group with that of the nation—a much larger entity—and thus renders legitimate the attempts to redress the situation, makes possible a solution to the problem in which the actual internal opponents of the nobility become its allies. Hutten starts by fighting princes, cities, and lawyers, but ends up calling on everyone to unite in the fight against Rome. Winning national freedom, rather than winning back the ancient privileges of the nobility, becomes the goal and the panacea to all private misfortunes. The foremost among those who represented the conflict with Roman Catholicism and Reformation as a struggle for national liberation, Hutten, parenthetically, associated national conflict with precociously racist connotations. He saw it as the continuation of the struggle between the Latins and the Teutons, which began with the attempts of the Caesars—luckily frustrated by Arminius the Cheruscan—to subjugate the virtuous Germanic tribes to their unholy rule.

Given the direct influence of the Councils of Constance and Basel on the perception of the imperial interests as distinct from those of the Church, which in the period under discussion was symbolized in the concept of the Holy Roman Empire of the German Nation, it is likely that the "nation" itself, when the concept was used by the nobility, had the conciliar meaning of the elite and thus excluded most of the population. The nobility had no reason to identify with and equate the "nation" with the "people." Their aim was to secure the consideration of the princes and to bar them and the cities from further encroaching on their privileges. Thus the knights, including, probably, von Hutten, stopped short of developing modern nationalism. For the most part, however, German nationalism in this period found spokesmen not among the knights, whom even Hutten regarded, acidly, as "centaurs," but—with the notable exception of Hutten himself—among Humanist scholars and poets who came from the lower strata of society and belonged to the "people." These German Humanists were among the earliest groups of professional intellectuals in Europe, who owed their considerable influence and standing in society not to inherited social position but entirely to their education and academic achievement.

The early existence of a significant number of such men was made possible in Germany, first of all, by its numerous universities, founded from the middle of the fourteenth century on to create indigenous clergy, loyal to the German rulers. Initially, theological faculties dominated the universities, and, since the nobility found the positions of lower clergy unattractive, it was chiefly the common people who were trained there. As a result, the prestige of academic training was not very high. During the second half of the fifteenth century, however, owing to the growing importance of Roman jurisprudence and the influence of the Italian Renaissance, the secular faculties of law and liberal arts markedly rose in status. The prestige of the academically trained lawyers grew enormously, paving the way, for some of them, to ennoblement, and this served to enhance the inherent worth of academic training. At the same time, the spread of Humanism from Italy, which saw in classical education an indispensable means for the development of a cultivated spirit, prompted liberal arts faculties, which previously had served the function of preparatory training for theologians, to assert their independence. The Humanists were supported by Emperor Maximilian, who crowned several of them (including Celtis, Bebel, and Ulrich von Hutten) poets laureate and appointed the first Court historian; this imperial recognition undoubtedly contributed to the favorable view of learning. But, similarly to what happened in England, France, and Russia, the chief reason for the increase in the self-esteem of the educated was education itself. Many important German Humanists came from simple peasantry,[4] yet they tended to regard themselves as a natural elite. In the controversy following the publication of Johannes Reuchlin's *Eyeglasses,* one could discern early examples of the juxtaposition of the *spiritual* aristocracy and the plebs, which cut across the existing social gradations, and which was to appear so often in later centuries (La Bruyère in France, Sumarokov in Russia). Humanists learned of the ideal of classical patriotism from the horse's mouth; they were likely to be patriotic in relation to the Holy Roman Empire of the German Nation, and likely to adopt the inclusive, modern definition of the object of their patriotism and equate the "nation" with the "people."

As elsewhere, identification with the polity turned the early patriots into zealous defenders of the honor of their nation—which in the conditions of conflict with Rome meant the defense of its honor against Rome. This defense took the form of the reinterpretation of the comparison between contemporary Italy and ancient Greece and Rome on the one hand, and Germany on the other; it was cultural, secular, and Rome, too, was defined not in religious, but in "national" (geographical, political, cultural) terms.[5]

Clearly, many academics and clerics of peasant origin outside the narrow Humanist circle, who had both the education and the reasons to advocate patriotism and define the German nation as its people, did not do so. The most important of them, Luther, had no feeling for modern nationalism with its democratic overtones. Luther's message was given a nationalistic interpretation by men such as Hutten, and the Reformer himself was not averse to national pride and predisposed at times to violently xenophobic fulminations. Yet he did not take the step that connected the separation from Rome to the definition of the polity as a people. The "German nation," for Luther, had none but the conciliar meaning of the princes and nobility of the Empire, and in this sense he used it in *An den christlichen Adel deutscher Nation.*[6] In his translation of the Bible, however, notwithstanding the frequent appearance of *natio* in the Vulgate, *Nation* appears but once, as the rendition of the Greek *ethnos,* in the Apochryphal *Stücke von Esther.*[7]

But national consciousness everywhere was initially limited to a tiny group of people. These carried it into wider sectors responsive to their message, and with the support of the latter, national identity would take root and develop. In Germany such responsiveness existed within the influential groups of princes and knights, and yet national sentiment failed to take root.

It was not the tremendous importance of religious sentiment at the time which prevented the growth of German nationality, for, as we saw in England, the rise of Protestantism was the single most important factor in ensuring the successful development of national identity. Still, this failure to develop did result in part from the course of German religious history. The religious struggle of the first half of the sixteenth century strengthened the centrifugal forces within the Empire and played into the hands of the territorial princes, transforming their territories into tiny empires of which they were the sovereign rulers. The nation-generating potential of Protestantism was spent and lost in the institution of *Landeskirchen*. There was no possibility of posing Germany united in its dissenting belief against the erring world, of saying that God put the Germans "in one commonwealth and church as in one ship together," and of defining Protestantism (or even Lutheranism) as a German national trait, and Germanity as Protestantism or Lutheranism. Instead of contributing to the creation of a stronger united Germany, the Reformation and the ensuing wars completed the process of its disintegration.[8]

Simultaneously the reasons for the possible responsiveness to the idea of the nation among princes and knights were eliminated. The attentions of Charles V, whose immense power and anticipated encroachment on the privileges of the German princes made the latter apprehensive, were engaged elsewhere. The German part of his possessions was left to itself, and eventually the imperial authority deteriorated further. The Empire became less of a concern for the princes, who wanted to weaken it, at the same time when it became less of a concern for the knights, who earlier had preferred to see it stronger, too. The position of the nobility in the territorial states strengthened in the latter half of the century, and *Ständestaat*, the dualistic state in which the princes and the estates shared authority, came into existence. The population increased and the prices of agricultural products, rising already since 1500, became very high and grew faster than prices for the products of urban industries. The economic hardships of the nobility were thus also resolved, and the decline of the cities in the period between 1550 and 1620 served to alleviate further the noble discontent.

Thus the conditions in which a change of identity might take place were no longer present, and the nascent nationalism of the Reformation period led to nought. This period left the future nationalists the cult of Arminius and the Teutonoburg Forest, and the language of Luther's Bible, but two centuries were to pass before this inheritance would be put to use.

## The Early Evolution of the Concept of the State

The severe restriction of the ability of the Church to interfere actively in the affairs of sovereign territories, which in England led to the transfer of sovereignty to those who claimed to represent the *nation*, in Protestant Germany, where viable national consciousness was absent, resulted in the emergence of absolutist governments; sovereignty was transferred to the princes.

The princes tended to regard the territories over which they ruled as patrimonies, and were combatted in this by the estates, which saw them as "a public trust to be administered for the common welfare."[9] Gradually, however, the princes adopted a new concept of "state" that was in greater accord with the wishes of the estates. This concept of state, exceptional in many respects and peculiar to Germany (for no concepts corresponding to it existed and no corresponding realities emerged, either in England and the United States of America or in France and Russia), was to have a profound influence on the character of German nationalism. The state was in effect defined as the prince's office, or calling. In it he was obliged to serve God as diligently as any shoemaker or peasant in theirs. He had to do so without consideration for his personal needs or wishes, and had no right to recoil from his responsibilities. Thus the state existed above the prince, and however closely it was initially associated with his person, it was impersonal. This notion had a special poignancy when the prince was a Calvinist, and, indeed, it is at the Calvinist Court of Prussia that one finds an exemplary model of this-worldly asceticism in government, embodied successively in the Great Elector, Friedrich Wilhelm I, and Frederick the Great.[10]

Frederick William I wrote to Prince Leopold of Anhalt that he himself was the "prime minister and the field Marshall of the King of Prussia." Whether he saw the "king of Prussia" as some abstract notion, the symbol of the state (as some historians tended to interpret this remark), or simply wished to say that he had no need for anyone to perform these functions for him since he performed them himself (which was indeed the reason for the letter), it is clear that he saw his kingship as a service to something far beyond his private interests. His son, who defined the king as "the first servant of the state," articulated the same idea. The eighteenth-century Hohenzollerns, no doubt, only carried to perfection the developments which had begun much earlier. "The first significant examples of the interventionist and regulatory *Polizeistaat*" are to be found in the second half of the sixteenth century, in such Protestant states as Saxony and Hessen, and "the system [of absolutism] reached an early and full expression, albeit on a small scale, in German states after the Thirty Years War."[11] The responsibilities of the prince were to ensure the spiritual and material welfare of his subjects, which were believed to be dependent on the state's power. The economic policies of cameralism and mercantilism, as well as the *dirigiste* efforts oriented toward increasing efficiency in every sphere of life, were the result of this definition.

The concept of state as the prince's office (in the sense of *Beruf*) had little in common with the idea of the nation; to the notion of individualistic civic nationalism, which presupposed citizenship in the sense of participation in collective decision-making, it was in fact opposed, for it implied the nonintervention of the subjects in the affairs of the state and their definition as an exclusive prerogative of the prince, whose calling the state, after all, was.

Yet the inherent absolutism of the original German idea of the state was compatible with and even congenial to particularistic national identity, as an identity whose source lay in the identification with a community. Unlike the French "state," which, once dissociated from the person of the king, became synonymous with the "nation," the German "state" remained a separate concept. But unlike the equally absolutist and interventionist Russian "state" (called, significantly, the "government"—*gosudarstvo*), which was never dissociated from the person of the autocrat—and later the very specific agency of the party—and never as such became an object of loyalty, the German concept implied such a dissociation and fostered the development of loyalty to an impersonal, secular political entity, the well-being or power of which, presumably, meant the common well-being.[12]

While the territorial state thus unwittingly paved the way for nationality, the lingering national consciousness, left-over from the days of the Reformation, in the seventeenth century favored the territorial state as the focus of *national*, that is, German, patriotism. This German national consciousness, unsupported by any significant segment of the population, lived on among the academics for whom nationality, being Germans—especially if the German nation could be proven to deserve the respect of others—promised more prestige than either their humble origins or their positions, earned by education and scholarly labors, could secure. These patriotic academics considered themselves Germans rather than Prussians, Hessians, or Hannoverians; they insisted that "Germany will live forever,"[13] and needed to reconcile this claim with the reality of the disintegrating Roman Empire and the growing independence of territorial states. This reconciliation was accomplished in a kind of legal history, for example, in Hermann Conring's *De Germanorum Imperio Romano* of 1643 and *De Finibus Imperii Romano-Germanici* of 1654, and in Pufendorf's *De Statu Imperii Germanici*, written in the 1660s, which presented the Empire as "a national institution vested not so much in the emperor as in the princes."[14] This view was also shared by another small group of seventeenth-century nationalists: the minor ruling princes, such as Count George Frederick von Waldeck. The privileges and the special position (above the territorial nobility and formally equal to that of the princes of significant territories) of this latter group were meaningful only within the framework of the Empire, and entirely depended on its preservation and viability. At the same time, the minor princes were as little willing to increase the power of the Emperor as their greater neighbors. The solution was the view of the Empire as distinct from the Emperor, the Empire without central authority but vested in its sovereign parts as an expression of a common (ethno-cultural or legal) essence and an entity larger than any of its parts.[15]

Apart from the lonely academics and rulers of tiny principalities, however, no groups in Germany felt the attraction of national identity as yet; by modern standards of nationality, to quote Leonard Krieger,[16] "early modern Germany shows . . . national semiconsciousness" rather than consciousness. The age of German nationalism did not dawn until much later. The important legacy of seventeenth-century thought for its development was the impersonal idea of the state and the fact that a nation split into several states was not considered a contradiction in terms.

### The Insouciance of German Nobility prior to the Nineteenth Century

Thus, ideas which went into the making of national identity had existed in Germany for a long time, but they failed to stir the people. The nobility, in particular, remained indifferent to their appeal, though in all other cases in this book, with the exception of the United States, where it did not exist, this stratum played a leading role in cultivating and molding the national consciousness. The passivity of the German nobility in this respect is especially striking, since after national consciousness developed in Germany, it was far more respectful toward the nobility than was the case in England, France, or Russia, and incorporated elements of the noble social code as those of Germanness itself. The German nobility kept its aloofness as late as the beginning of the reform period in the early nineteenth century and did so for the simple reason that it was comfortable, satisfied with its privileged lot, did not experience anything like the crises which ailed its counterparts in France or Russia, and was not made by the circumstances dynamic and open like its counterpart in England. In terms of its social position, for two and a half centuries between the end of the Thirty Years' War and the beginning of the Napoleonic Campaign, it enjoyed a period of uninterrupted and by comparison unusual stability. This stability, significantly, was not affected by the eclipse of the *Ständestaat* and the advent of absolutism. Politically, the estates were weakened and in effect deprived of a role in government. Yet, otherwise the nobility remained unchallenged, with the gulf between it and the rest of society as wide as ever.

It appears to be a matter of consensus that enlightened despotism, or absolutism, "as the *philosophes* envisioned it," and many social scientists still do, "could never exist [in Germany], even if the rulers were enlightened, because they were simply not 'absolute.'" The "despots" and the estates cooperated in forging the modern state, and in carrying out their reforms the rulers used existing frameworks and relied on the nobility.[17]

In Prussia the onslaught of absolutism was fairly vigorous. During the century between the end of the Thirty Years' War and the accession of Frederick the Great, the Hohenzollerns successfully augmented their authority, severely restricting the participation of the nobility as a corporate group in the affairs of state. By the middle of the eighteenth century, government became the exclusive prerogative of the king. The process of which this was the result was inaugurated by Frederick William, the Great Elector, in the middle of the seventeenth century. The conflict between the *Landsherr* and his first estate was resolved differently in different provinces, but ended everywhere with the victory of the former. Everywhere the nobility was compelled to acquiesce to the creation of the standing army and permanent civil service. In most provinces the jurisdiction of *Landtage* was severely restricted. On the whole, the nobility retained a measure of self-government only on the local level of the circles or counties, *Kreise,* which were defined as seigniorial corporations and in which local assemblies, *Kreistage,* continued to function.

The next great Hohenzollern ruler, "the father of Prussian bureaucracy," King Frederick William I, building on the achievements of his grandfather, stripped the nobility, which he considered the most dangerous class in society and of which his opinion was most unflattering ("dumb oxen, but as malicious as the devil"),[18] of several additional "liberties," encroaching even on their economic privileges. Determined to establish his authority against the stubborn nobles "as a rock of bronze," the king attempted to reform the system of taxation to redistribute its burden among the different strata more equitably. Only partially successful in some of these reforms, he formally abolished the long-since-useless military services of the nobility and turned the feudal estates, held on condition of availability for such service, into alodial possessions held in personal ownership. In return for this official recognition of a de facto situation, the king introduced a certain tax, converting *Lehnpferde*—a knight's duty of military service on horseback—into money, *Lehnpferdegeld.*[19]

The expanding responsibilities and regulatory capacities of the central administration under Frederick William I—the formation of the War and Domains chambers and the General Directory—further limited the influence of the provincial diets. Toward the end of the seventeenth century, the office of the representative of the local estates merged with that of the government war commissary, responsible for the recruiting and quartering of troops. This new office in 1702 was given the title of *Landrat,* county councillor. The *Landräte* were government officers, but they were selected from and by the local nobility. In certain provinces Frederick William interfered with this privilege and appointed *Landräte* without taking into consideration the preferences of the nobles who were to be represented by them. In addition, the king forbade his nobles to enter foreign service, discouraged them from attending foreign universities, and denied them the right to travel abroad except by special permission. At the same time, he did not neglect their training: to better prepare them for service in the Prussian officer corps, he established a "cadet house" in Berlin, and, perhaps inspired by the successes of Peter the Great, used gendarmes to remind some forgetful officers-to-be in the countryside of what was expected of them.

Yet, by comparison with either eighteenth-century Russia or the France of Louis XIV, the treatment of the nobility even in Prussia was lenient at the very least. Neither the Great Elector nor Frederick William I encroached on any of the *social* privileges of the nobility and in fact defended it from such encroachment on the part of the middle classes. Throughout the entire period of their reigns and into the nineteenth century remarkably few commoners were ennobled in all of Germany. Since the sixteenth century the avenues to ennoblement had narrowed. The new administrative and military elites, which on the face of it threatened to replace the traditional aristocracy, recruited their members predominantly from it. Fewer commoners were able to rise to a high administrative office in the seventeenth century than in the sixteenth; their situation, as we shall see, did not improve in the eighteenth century. Exclusive schools for the children of the nobility, *Ritterakademien,* providing "gentlemen's education" and preparing young gentlemen for positions in the government and the army, were founded in many Court towns. Everywhere in Germany the officer corps were the preserve of the nobility. In Prussia, the Great Elector insisted on his right to appoint commoners to positions of high command, but very few were in fact so appointed. Only some 10 percent of his officer corps came from the burgher class; the rest were noblemen: 10 percent foreigners from other German territories and Huguenots, and 80 percent native Prussian nobility. The non-noble officers were concentrated in the artillery and engineering troops, which enjoyed lesser prestige than other military units. Frederick William I believed that only noblemen could make good officers. His identification with the army, therefore, was at the same time identification with the nobility, and boosted its prestige.[20]

The position of the nobility vis-à-vis the peasants was strengthened; their seigniorial rights were confirmed and augmented. Since 1653 every peasant was assumed to be a serf, unless proven otherwise, which reinforced serfdom where it had existed and favored its spread in the territories earlier less affected by it. The introduction of the "canton" system of army recruitment further reinforced existing relationships in the countryside. Now nobles exercised double authority over the peasants: both as landlords and as officers. To emphasize this double bondage, soldier-peasants, even at home, had to wear at least one piece of their army uniform; this situation also found its reflection in the concept of "soldier-peasant desertion."[21] The Junkers were miniature kings on their estates.

The economic superiority of the nobility was hardly challenged by the absolutist policies of their rulers. While in Prussia they were expected to pay the *Lehnpferdegeld,* they could export the products of their estates and import basic provisions almost without taxes. At the local level, *Kreistage* regularly met, and no policy affecting the nobility was introduced without consultation with these county assemblies. Towns did not have similar representative bodies; it is in this sense that the Prussian monarchy, in the phrase of Hugo Preuss,[22] stood on one long and one short leg: while the government reached to every level and regulated every sphere of the burgher's existence, it stopped at the level of the county when it came to the nobility. Certainly, the peasantry was in an even less enviable position than the burghers. No other stratum enjoyed anything like the privileges of the nobility, which was defined, as earlier, exclusively by birth. Its standing in society was unchallenged, and its exclusion, as a group, from the affairs of the state, not combined with any threat to the personal status of its members, did not have the effect a similar exclusion—together with other factors—produced in France or Russia.

In the latter half of the eighteenth century, the position of the nobility was strengthened further and its superiority over the rest of society emphatically stressed. Frederick the Great identified with the aristocracy much more closely than did his father. This was reflected both in his opinion of its qualities, which differed drastically from those of Frederick William I, and in his policies. Instead of "dumb oxen," Frederick saw in the Prussian nobility "the fairest jewels of the crown," "the defenders of their country" of a stock "so good that it deserves to be preserved at all costs." Nobility, according to this enlightened monarch, was a species of men apart from the rest of humanity; only it possessed the sense of honor and responsibility necessary for command and only it could produce officers and high civil servants. In the political testament of 1752, Frederick declared the preservation of the nobility to be one of the chief goals of the monarchy. The exclusive right of noblemen to own manorial estates was confirmed by severe legal restrictions on their sale to commoners. Those burghers who were allowed to purchase noble land did not receive any of the seigniorial rights vested in it: they could not be represented in local assemblies and were denied the rights of personal jurisdiction and even hunting. Frederick discontinued his father's policy of requisitioning from the nobility lands formally belonging to the Crown or buying noble estates for the Crown. After the Seven Years' War he deferred the payments of all the debts due from noble land-owners for five years and established *Landschaften,* special credit institutions, to help noble owners in distress to keep their estates. The only limitation imposed by Frederick on the order of which he considered himself a member had to do with the economic and military necessity of keeping the peasants from depopulation and extinction: the nobles were prohibited from engrossing their estates at the expense of peasant holdings.[23]

Under Frederick, the rural assemblies regained their privilege of selecting candidates for the office of the *Landrat,* and the responsibilities of the office were expanded. The provincial courts *(Regierungen)* came under the control of the local nobility. The officer corps and high civil service, the preserve of the aristocracy since the days of the Great Elector, grew increasingly exclusive. The aristocratic character of the officer corps was especially emphasized. The prestige of military rank increased immensely, generals taking precedence over ministers of state in Court ceremonials; and while previously it was often economic incentives which attracted nobility to military service, now the chief attraction became social honor. The officer corps, which became a second name for the aristocracy, turned into a caste. Burghers had no place in the army, according to the soldier-king; Frederick would rather give commissions to foreign noblemen. If considerations of military exigency made recruitment of non-noble officers necessary, as they did during the Seven Years' War, they were still confined to regiments not considered integral parts of the army, and not aristocratic by nature, such as artillery and engineering. As a result, years after Frederick had died (in 1800) there were fewer burgher officers in the Prussian army than in the days of the Great Elector (9 percent), and in 1806 only 29 out of 1,106 senior officers were non-noble.[24]

The higher echelons of the civil service experienced similar aristocratization, though in this case the results were less dramatic. The representation of the nobility in the civil service grew proportionately to rank in the hierarchy; the nobility constituted at least one-third in the highest grades of the administration: in the War and Domains chambers and in the General Directory the higher posts were almost always occupied by nobles. The noble bureaucrats, it is true, had to be adequately educated and selected from a number of candidates according to established meritocratic criteria, but if qualified and admitted to service, they were assured of preferential treatment, quick promotion, and tenure. To achieve the latter they usually did not have to serve more than four to five years, which must have seemed a great boon in comparison with fifteen to twenty years for their middle-class colleagues.[25] The office, unlike the case in Russia, did not ennoble; on the contrary, it was the nobility which elevated the office by its incumbency. High officialdom, like the military, became an aristocratic vocation. And, while he put every obstacle in the way of commoners who would become officers or state servants, Frederick justified his preferential treatment of the aristocracy of birth by the services it rendered (and it alone was allowed to render) the state in the army and bureaucracy. "I have always distinguished [the nobility] and treated it with consideration," he wrote in 1768,[26] "because it provided officers for the army and suitable persons for all great offices of state. I have helped it to retain the ownership of its estates, and I have done my best to prevent commoners from buying up the properties of nobles. My reason for doing so has been that once commoners become landlords, they have a prescriptive right to office. Most of them have a vulgar outlook and make bad officers; they are not fit for any employment." This circular argumentation made the situation self-perpetuating; the old elite, strengthened in its traditional status and privileges, was at the same time becoming a new elite. It is small wonder, then, that at the time when both French and Russian nobilities, in an effort to protect their threatened, insecure positions, were changing their identity and their character, and transforming membership criteria in their societies, the Prussian aristocracy could watch them calmly, without for a moment considering their struggle its own. The potent ideas of nationality, which in this struggle were the main weapon, might have intrigued the Junkers, but they were irrelevant for them. The Prussian nobility was content. "There is no question," wrote Henri Brunschwig, "of any crisis in the Prussian nobility such as that which occurs in France at about the same date. Of all the orders of society the nobility seems to be the most stable and the most faithful to its traditions." [27]

This conclusion applies equally well to other states in Germany. While these states (with the exception of Austria, which was becoming less and less German) had neither armies nor bureaucracies as impressive as the Prussian, the position of the nobility in them was, on the whole, similar. Nowhere in Germany was the nobility's superiority challenged by any other group. The nobility retained its wide privileges; it stood apart from the rest of society and was looked up to by everyone. The traditional social hierarchy in Germany manifested remarkable stability by comparison with its neighbors. The ancient divisions between different strata remained sharp and clear. "Is there any other country in which the notion of quarterings of nobility has such a fundamental political and moral influence on ideas and culture as in Germany?" asked Knigge. "In what other country do the courtiers as a body form a completely separate class, within which only persons of particular birth and rank can make their career, as is the case in the entourage of most of our princes?" In fact, in Prussia merit mattered more than elsewhere: nobility had its privileges, but it was not allowed to forget its duties. In other states, duties did not necessarily accompany privileges. The gentleman's class "was in fact the only class in the state that was 'free' in the sense that nothing was demanded from it." [28] The acceptance of the high status of the nobility was universal, and Goethe, as well as Frederick the Great, found justifications for it.

For all these reasons, in the period of fermentation of the national sentiment in such great states as France and Russia, when nationalism as a pattern of discourse became ubiquitous and could be encountered everywhere, the German nobility remained completely unresponsive to it and passive. In the second half of the eighteenth century it was no longer in conflict with the absolutism of the princes, but reveled in it. (Like so many other forces in history, which we tend to treat as uniform, absolutism evolved, expressed itself, and affected different societies in entirely different ways.) The nobility was no longer a dangerous class. But another group had already emerged, humble and inoffensive on the face of it, which had since proved to be the most dangerous class of all. This group did not belong to the lower classes; the latter were not as yet believed to be threatening; neither was it the docile bourgeoisie, which seems never to have acquired this distinction. This new class was the "unattached" intellectuals. It was they who were destined to assume the leadership in urging and molding the German national consciousness.

## Bildungsbürgertum: The Dangerous Class

Among the European cases surveyed in this book, Germany is the only one which lends support to the view that nationalism is a middle-class phenomenon. Its leaders on the way to national identity came from the bourgeoisie rather than the aristocracy. This exception, however, serves to prove the rule, for the middle-class intellectuals, the visionaries and architects of German nationality, had as little in common with the bourgeoisie in general as they had with either the nobility, which looked down on them, or the peasantry, to which a significant number of them could trace their origins.

From very early on, in Germany, the secular middle-class intellectuals were a group apart, with its own ethos, and opportunities, aspirations, and frustrations peculiar to it. This group was a creation of the German universities, and to some degree owed its character to their nature and proliferation. German universities were unlike the universities in the rest of Europe in several respects. They were not a result of the spontaneous growth and incorporation of communities of scholars, but were imperial and princely foundations conceived as a means of training indigenous clergy and Court servants and as an assertion of the spiritual independence of the Empire from the Roman Church. In the sixteenth century numerous new foundations reflected the claim to sovereignty of the territorial states. The German universities thus were *instrumenta dominationis* of particularist governments, rather than *studium generale* serving all (at any rate within Christendom) who were thirsty for knowledge.

Two faculties were the stronghold of the university: theology and law. The other higher faculty—medical—remained numerically unimportant until the nineteenth century. The faculty of arts, or, as it was later called, philosophy, was originally a preparatory faculty for the more specialized studies in the other three, and provided a general education for those who had had too little of it in other frameworks. The theological faculty recruited its students predominantly, in Protestant Germany exclusively, from the poorer middle and lower classes. Such students also were the majority of those who studied philosophy. The faculty of law, in distinction, appealed to the better-off bourgeoisie and even the nobility.

The sharpening of class distinctions which had accompanied the increasing assertiveness of territorial rulers vis-à-vis the nobility led to the temporary abandonment of the universities by the nobility in the later seventeenth century, and as a result the prestige of the universities significantly decreased. At that time the universities had reached a low point in society's esteem for them, so that even famous scholars considered associating with them beneath their dignity. Leibniz, notoriously, thought the Court to be more congenial to the life of the spirit and the development of science and, while urging the formation of an academy to supplement it, relegated universities to the position of lower-level educational establishments. For those to whom the Courts were closed, the way out of this pit was to abandon the scholastic traditions with which the universities had been hitherto associated, and side with the moderns. This road was chosen by people like Christian Thomasius, a sometime professor at Leipzig, who became one of the founders of the University of Halle. He insisted on the inclusion of "gentlemanly education" (fencing, riding, modern languages, and sciences) in the curriculum and was the first professor to lecture in German instead of Latin. He also edited the first German monthly magazine. The university reform of the early eighteenth century and the adoption by the reformed universities of the *Aufklärung* can be in part attributed to this desire of some in the professoriate to escape the stigma of low esteem which came with university affiliation.

Since the early eighteenth century the prestige of academic training was on the increase. The reasons for that, for the most part, lay outside the universities. Learning was becoming popular among the European aristocracies, and at least in England and France—the main models for the Germanys—nobility came to imply cultural polish if not superiority. The merits of education and the educated were celebrated by the philosophy of Enlightenment. The University of Halle, which became a home to the *Aufklärung,* was attracting students of noble birth. At the same time increasing numbers of the nobility were seeing their vocation in the civil service of the territorial states and were flocking to the universities for this reason.

While some university education in Germany was considered necessary for entrance into the civil service, aspiring noble bureaucrats did not necessarily choose German universities. Many went to study abroad, or at least supplemented their training in a German university (usually Halle) by a stay in a foreign one. There, in the centers of new thinking, they were exposed to new sentiments and ideas—among them that of national pride. One of such future members of the German elite—the Hannoverian nobleman von Münchhausen—was bothered by this deference to things foreign, and the University of Göttingen (founded in 1737) was largely a result of his displeasure. According to the conception of its founder, Göttingen was to appeal to the nobility, including foreign nobility, whose presence among the students would in turn make the university visible and further increase its attractiveness. Münchhausen took care to find professors of great renown and, not unexpectedly, concentrated his attention on the law faculty, which was certain to be the choice of the great majority of the native nobility. "The kind of law taught at Göttingen reflected the resentment of many German nobles against the high-handed innovations of increasingly absolute rulers and was designed to reinforce their position and rights under the laws of the moribund empire, common law, and private law . . . more attention was paid to feudal law, German common law, German and European constitutional law, legal history, and trial law . . . than to the traditional Roman fare of the seventeenth century." [29] In this way, already in the middle of the eighteenth century, Göttingen unwittingly promoted nativist and historicist tendencies in jurisprudence, which were later to become important elements in German nationalist thought.

Yet another element contributed by Göttingen was to achieve centrality in the future German national consciousness. Münchhausen emphasized the importance of general learning, especially history, as the proper way to cultivate the mind of leisurely nobility (as against those preparing for service). This boosted the status of the philosophical faculty, inaugurating a transformation in the nature of German universities. In itself this was no major innovation, for the status of general learning was rising everywhere in Europe, and its importance for the nobility was increasingly recognized. What was an innovation was the shift of emphasis from the practical uses of education to its inherent value and significance for the development of the inner spirit, the *Bildung* of the personality, which came with this new respect. This recess into the depths of the inner world went against the this-worldly activism of the *Aufklärung*, yet both reflected the desire to dignify university education in Germany and were in a way related.

Already in 1740 Christian Wolff, brought back in triumph to Prussia by the philosopher-king, preferred a position in the university to the academy and the Court—a choice which contrasted with that of Leibniz several decades earlier. "At the close of the eighteenth century," wrote Friedrich Paulsen, "the German people regarded its universities as institutions from which, particularly, it expected to receive its impulses toward progress in all the departments of life, the same institutions which only a century before had called forth the derisive laughter of polite society." [30] In 1810, for the founders of the University of Berlin, university education as such—especially humanistic, not necessarily practical, education—was "noble." In this way, in Germany too, a concept of an alternative nobility emerged, a nobility based on culture rather than birth.

Significantly, all through the eighteenth century the vast majority of the educated came from the middle classes; the nobility supplied only a small minority of students. At Göttingen, the university most popular with the nobility, only 10 percent of the students in 1737, 8 percent in 1767, and 15 percent in 1797 were noble. The majority of them concentrated in law (55 percent, 45 percent, and 62 percent respectively, but as many as 79 percent in 1777).[31] The rest, that is, close to 100 percent in faculties other than law and universities other than Göttingen, were commoners. Overall enrollments in the universities in the eighteenth century were falling. Perhaps this reflected a perception of the decreasing marginal utility of academic training in finding appropriate employment in later years. In distinction from their aristocratic classmates, middle-class students, unless exceptionally wealthy, always attended the university with a view of finding such employment. The figures are: 9,000 students (in all universities) in 1700; 7,000 a year in the late 1760s; 6,000 a year between 1795 and 1800.[32] If we take 7,000 to be the average student population a year throughout the century (though it probably was larger), and four years as the period a student stayed in a university (though many spent only a year or two there), by the end of the century we get a population of 175,000 university-educated people, a great majority of whom were of middle-class origin. If we make an allowance for attrition by death, it does not seem unreasonable to estimate this population at any given point in the second half of the eighteenth century at 100,000.[33] This figure, small in comparison with the 20,000,000 of German population in 1800, is quite significant in comparison with the nobility, estimated as, at maximum, 2 percent of the whole.[34] These 100,000 university-trained commoners, and their families, are the "educated class," *Bildungsbürgertum*.

In the social hierarchy of German societies, *Bildungsbürgertum* stood above the middle class as a whole. The last *Kleiderordnung* (sumptuary law), in Frankfort-on-Main in 1731, divided the population of the city into five classes. Doctors of law and, notably, medicine were grouped together with the patricians and nobility in the first and most prestigious one.[35] Admittedly, in the middle of the century, the status of jurists, who to begin with came from better and wealthier families, was more elevated than that of theologians and philosophers. But, under the influence of the *Aufklärung* and the reinterpretation of learning which emphasized the significance of inner culture, the distribution of esteem among different degree holders became more equal. If anything, the philosophers enjoyed a larger share of it (the degree in philosophy grew more prestigious than the rest). In the reading clubs, which proliferated since the 1780s, the educated rubbed shoulders with the nobility, and the academic degree as such, as Mme de Stael noted later, "earned one the entrée"[36] into society. Education was the avenue of upward mobility.

For the first generation of non-noble university graduates or attendees, the inclusion in *Bildungsbürgertum* signified a move into a higher-status group and implied a significant increase in prestige. In the second half of the century, however, the educated class was already largely reproducing itself, and many students were coming from the families of *Bildungsbürger*. The marginal utility of university education for them was decreasing. At the same time, the growing respect for learning as such, and especially for humanistic, not occupationally oriented, education, increased the self-esteem of the educated, who were now expecting greater deference toward themselves on the part of the society at large. But the society did not defer to them to the extent they might have found satisfactory. More often than not it denied them entrance into the higher ranks and not for a moment let them forget their common origins. The name of the new class itself implied the inescapable bond to the commonality: while the intellectuals in France and Russia alike proudly referred to themselves as the aristocracy of the spirit, the alternative aristocracy, in Germany they were called the educated bourgeoisie, the alternative middle class. The *Bildungsbürger* identified with the aristocracy, which would not merge with them, and despised the bourgeoisie, to which they were inseparably tied. Elevated above the common lot, they remained a lower class nevertheless, and were vexed and made unhappy by their position in society. They, too, became the victims of status-inconsistency.

This frustration of the intellectuals was exacerbated by the condition of trained unemployability, which toward the end of the eighteenth century was becoming the lot of increasing numbers of them. The aura of moral loftiness which surrounded knowledge for its own sake had its uses for the middle-class intellectuals, but could not render such knowledge any more affordable for them. Their education remained fundamentally career oriented. Liberal professions were not yet seen as an appropriate employment in Germany, and middle-class students envisioned as the goal of their studies chiefly careers in the legal and administrative branches of the civil service, the Church, and university teaching. The opportunities open to *Bildungsbürger* in civil service—on the level which they would consider commensurate with their qualifications—appeared dwindling toward the close of the century, owing to the increased competition from the nobility. This competition was particularly strong in administration, where positions were fewer and more than a full third of the best positions were claimed by noble candidates.[37] The percentage of noble bureaucrats increased from 37.8 percent between 1770 and 1786 to 45.23 percent between 1786 and 1806, creating, according to Brunschwig, an impression of a small-scale feudal reaction. The legal branch, in distinction, was nearly monopolized by middle-class university graduates. There too, however, noble candidates successfully contended for the better positions, their percentage, which was slightly above 10 percent at the lower level, rising to a third in the higher grades. *Berlinische Monattschrift* in 1788 assessed: "The number of young men applying for posts in the civil service is so great that all the administrative services are overwhelmed. If you compare their number with the number of posts which, even if there were to be an epidemic of deaths, are likely to fall vacant, you can see that there is now no hope whatever of placing all, or even most, of them in any way that bears the slightest relation to the many sacrifices which their training has required of them." [38] Success in passing through this bottle-neck was not at all assured, and further hardship awaited after that passage: a middle-class official had to prepare for a long moratorium and could not expect to support himself until the age of twenty-seven.

The way to a clerical position was, if anything, even more arduous, even though the nobility found a clerical career entirely unattractive, and middle-class theologians, thus, had to compete only among themselves. Theological faculties continued to attract the mass of the poorer middle-class students, for they offered scholarships, and examinations by the consistory, in distinction from examinations in the civil service, were free. The Church, however, could accommodate only a minority of the aspirants: the annual average number of clerical appointments in Prussia, in the period between 1786 and 1805, was only 27.8, rendering a total of 584. But in 1786 alone, the theological faculty at Halle had 800 students (out of 1,156 at the university as a whole). Throughout Germany theological candidates, in anticipation of a brighter future, were becoming tutors to children of the nobility; just in Dresden they constituted as much as 20 percent of the city's population. A reporter reflected in 1785: "They hasten from house to house all day and barely earn enough from their lessons to eke out a miserable existence. All of them are withered, pallid, and sickly and reach the age of forty before the consistory takes pity on them and endows them with a living." [39]

Finally, university teaching could support only a tiny minority of exceptionally talented—and lucky—individuals. In 1758, in all German universities, with the exception of those in Austria, there were 244 full professors. The number rose to 658 in 1796, and, probably, more waited in the ranks as *Extraordinarien*.[40] The universities could not absorb the surplus of intellectuals they were producing, and those who were left in the cold had to look elsewhere for means to succor their bodies and apply their energies.

The unemployed academics were forming an army of "unattached," "free-floating" intellectuals (these terms, originally derived from German, fit them perfectly in more than one way). Many of them turned to free-lance writing, partly because they had no choice and partly seduced by the yet untapped resources which appeared to be hidden in the use of the printing presses and the appeal to the growing reading public, by examples of famous English and French writers, and by some suggestive ideas, of which we shall talk later. There were 3,000 writers recognized as such in Germany in 1771, and 10,650 by 1800.[41] If they saw in this profession a way to escape privation, they were wrong. The courts and the nobility, with a few exceptions, patronized French letters. And living off the yet undeveloped market was anything but easy. "The horde of famished poets is growing daily," observed Wieland, in *Der teutsche Merkur* in 1776; "the outcome . . . is still starvation. They grow sour and write satires against princes who have not aspired to imitate Augustus and act as wealthy patrons to them or poets who have a regular meal waiting for them on the table at home."

Wieland, who was born in 1733, was among the first German intellectuals to attempt the life of a professional man of letters. One of the most successful writers of his time, he was only partly successful and supported himself rather with his earnings as a town clerk in Biberach, a professor at Erfurt, and finally a tutor to Weimar princes. He was lucky, of course, to be offered these posts, which, however, he owed to his fame, and many of his younger compatriots embarked on the uncertain road of literary conquest in hope that it would lead them to a lucrative and above all secure official position. Wieland's contemporary, and another famous writer, Lessing, became a Court librarian in Wolfenbüttel. Two years before he accepted the post, in 1768, he wrote to his brother, who also aspired to become a writer: "Take my brotherly advice and give up your plan to live by the pen . . . See that you become a secretary or get on the faculty somewhere. This is the only way to avoid starving sooner or later."

Such reflections of the first generation of German writers rang true for the generations which came of age twenty and thirty years later. In 1791 Schiller concluded on the basis of his experience that it was still "impossible in the German world of letters to satisfy the strict demands of art and simultaneously procure the minimum of support for one's industry." [42] Writers of the end of the century assessed the situation similarly, although a change of tone is noticeable. In 1799, Wilhelm Schlegel compared the situation of writers in his country and in France: "Duclos notes that there are few noteworthy books which are not produced by professional writers. This Estate has long been treated with respect in France. Here a writer used to count for less than nothing if he was a writer and nothing else. Even today this prejudice still crops up here and there . . . The writer's trade is, depending on how it is plied, a stigma, self-indulgence, pure donkey work, a craftsman's job, an art or a virtue." [43]

The earnings even of a famous writer were meager. And though the payments rose steadily, they never amounted to an adequate income, and were not comparable to the earnings of equally famous authors in England or France. Sir Walter Scott is said to have earned more from literature in three years than Goethe, without a doubt the most successful writer of the century in all the Germanys, in all his remarkably long life. [44] In the security of his Weimar office, Goethe indeed remembered: "German poets . . . did not enjoy the smallest advantages among their fellow-citizens. They had neither support, standing, nor respectability, except in so far as their other position was favorable to them; and therefore it was a matter of mere chance whether talent was born to honor or to disgrace. A poor son of earth, with a consciousness of mind and faculties, was forced to crawl along painfully through life, and, from the pressure of momentary necessities, to squander the gifts which perchance he had received from the muses . . . a poet . . . appeared in the world in the most melancholy state of subserviency, as a jester and parasite; so that both on the theater and on the stage of life he represented a character which any one and every one could abuse at pleasure."

To some extent this situation was the result of the lack of copyright protection. The widely practiced "piracy," that is, unauthorized reprinting of well-selling works in cheap editions, made publishers reluctant to undertake publication of works which were not certain to sell and bring profits quickly. It also made them less willing to share these profits with the authors. Curiously, this tendency agreed with the authors. "The production of poetical works," reminisced Goethe in *Dichtung und Wahrheit,* in some contradiction of his assessment of the writers' condition above, "was looked upon as something sacred, and in this case the acceptance or increase of any remuneration would have been regarded almost as simony . . . The authors, who in addition to their talent were generally respected and revered by the public as highly moral men, had a mental rank, and felt themselves rewarded by the success of their labors: the publishers were well satisfied with the second place, and enjoyed a considerable profit . . . thus every thing stood in the most beautiful equilibrium." [45]

The view of literature as an activity of people who could afford not to be paid represented it as a "noble" occupation, which a person of standing could choose to practice without derogating himself. Thus the very unlikelihood of substantial earnings served to make literature more attractive for university graduates who liked to think mundane preoccupation with payments beneath their dignity. Some respectable authors in the mid-eighteenth century, such as Christian Fürchtegott Gellert, indeed did not want to accept money for their work. But they were hard pressed; however much they wished to believe otherwise, they had to make a living, and literature was the only means many of them had to do so.

As the reading market started to expand in the 1770s, an increasing number of men of letters were willing to redefine intellectual labor in a way which would make its remuneration expected, legitimate, and adequate. Klopstock's idea of the *Deutsche Gelehrtenrepublik* in 1772 was one expression of this changing attitude and the growing unwillingness of German authors to accept the destiny of honorable impecunity. The senior poet proposed to dispense with the services of the publishers-dealers and make subscription, the profits from which would go directly to the author, the way to finance and distribute publications. The appearance of the first and only part of the *Gelehrtenrepublik* was followed by a protracted debate over the nature of the book, which centered on the issue of the legitimacy of considering a work of literature the property of its author, for the production of which he could demand material reward. Many of the prominent authors of the time, among them Kant and Fichte, took part in the controversy and argued that such demands were indeed legitimate. Yet, though demanding to be paid for their services like other producers, the German writers as ever stressed that theirs was a special, lofty, "noble" calling. The idea of "genius" allowed them to reconcile these two apparently incongruous positions. It defined a work of *original* writing as one emanating from the inner resources of the author, and thus entirely his creation, which no craft, no learning alone, could make possible, and which used but did not depend on external observations. In this way, the work of original writing clearly appeared as its author's property, and since it was property, one could expect payment in exchange for it.[46]

The plight of the intellectuals was not only, or even mainly, economic. Even when desperately poor, they were oppressed more by the humiliation caused by poverty than by poverty itself. Their plight was the price they paid for upward mobility. It was, indeed, exorbitant. One has to keep in mind that Germany was essentially a static society in this period, which meant that it was composed of a given number of social strata, petrified in their traditional definitions, which stood in given, long-established relations to each other, immutably separated. In these conditions the nature and experience of upward mobility differed fundamentally from its nature and experience, for example, in sixteenth-century England, where the entire social structure was in flux and whole strata moved up and down the social hierarchy, changing their contours at the same time as they were changing their positions vis-à-vis each other, like the yet unformed continents in the time of primeval earthquakes. In eighteenth-century Germany upward mobility was the movement of exceptional individuals from lower toward higher strata. The possibility of reaching the coveted destination existed, but was in no way assured. Indeed, to reach it was the lot of only a few of those who ventured to travel this road. And in the nowhere land of in-between, the travelers found loneliness, degradation, and despair. It is no wonder at all that the experience left so many of them gloomy, misanthropic, and bitter.

More than from anything else they suffered from acute status-inconsistency, the painful discrepancy between their self-esteem, which they had acquired with and because of their education, and which was reinforced by the current philosophies they were only too well acquainted with, and the lack of respect for them in the society which obstinately graded its members according to official rank. They could not reconcile themselves with the criteria, but accepted the gradation; they shared the contempt for the strata from which they came and resented the nobility, as well as officialdom and the upper bourgeoisie, to which they could not gain admission. The *Bildungsbürger* could not become a part of the society of which they aspired to be a part. They did not dispute the superiority of the nobility (though their views of the reasons for it might sound rather academic: many, no doubt, believed with Goethe that only noblemen could attain to the "general cultivation" of personality, which was the goal of civilization itself). And they did not wish to be a part of the society with which they were in fact associated. "No one lacking wealth and leisure can enter 'good society,'" wrote Christian Garve. "But in the society of peasants, mechanics, journeymen, apprentices, shop-keepers, or students he will find that manners are coarse or loose and that their speech is incomprehensible." [47] They were suspended between two so-cial worlds, out of place everywhere and always in agony; it is this social isolation, the pain of it, its roots and the ways to escape it, not poverty, which is the constant preoccupation of eighteenth-century German litera-ture. What ailed them constantly and made their life a torment was "the feeling of humanity oppressed by its *burgher* condition." [48]

### Anton Reiser: A Story of Upward Mobility

The ordeals of *Bildungsbürger* did not start with graduation; rather they commenced with the very first steps they made in its direction, lured by the rewards it might bring and the unhappy "consciousness of mind and facul-ties." What misery it was to be a clever poor boy—and therefore upwardly mobile—in the Germany of that time we can learn from the many written testimonials left to us by those who were such. The *Gelehrten* naturally in-clined to self-analysis, and frequently, being unemployed, had nothing better to do than to put the results of it, and their experiences, into writing. These testimonials are unquestionably reliable, for, whether they form the very focus of an autobiography, a novel, a play for the stage or are un-self-consciously referred to in a diary or personal letters, the experiences of up-ward mobility recounted in them converge in the same pattern. Whatever part of Germany their authors came from, and whatever sector of the lower classes they left to move up, they shared the same structural situation, and therefore the very same misery.

Perhaps the most powerful of these testimonials is *Anton Reiser*. This "psychological romance" is in fact an autobiography, a description of the first twenty years in the life of its author, Carl Philipp Moritz. Historians of eighteenth-century German life have recognized in it a rich and valuable source, and in its own day the book was greatly esteemed by the author's contemporaries, its admirers including no lesser men than Goethe and Schiller. The description of the outward circumstances of Anton's life and of his inner development under the pressure of these circumstances indeed pre-sents before us a portrait of the formative years of several generations of intellectuals in Germany. The dry and dispassionate, as if tired, manner in which the story is told helps to underscore the depth of suffering that it describes. No embellishments of style are needed to drive home the point contained in the bare facts. This unadorned, almost pornographic frankness makes the book painful reading: one is allowed to look into such depths of unacceptable misery that it makes one recoil. And yet this suffering is only of the spirit.

Anton is the neglected child of poor and unhappily married parents. His father, a petty official in Hannover, is a Pietist of sorts, a follower of the doctrines of Madame Guyon.[49] In his eighth year, the father teaches Anton to read; the boy learns remarkably quickly, which brings him for the first time "some attention from his parents, still more from his relations." And, reading being his only pleasure, he is early driven "from the natural world of children into the unnatural world of imagination, where his spirit was put out of tune for a thousand joys of life which others can enjoy with a full heart." The teachings of Madame Guyon constitute some of his readings, and he learns to find solace in her hymns "of the blessed escape from self and the sweet annihilation before the source of existence." He has no other joys besides "that melancholy tearful joy" and to experience it more frequently imagines reasons for sadness even when no such reasons exist. He decides to emulate the behavior of saints of whom he reads and soon makes such progress on this path of piety that he is able to talk to God, who, as Anton has no other companions, becomes the only confidant and companion of this eight-year-old boy.

Reading makes Anton ambitious. After reading some romantic story, at the age of ten, he, for a long time, thinks of "nothing less than the idea of playing a great part in the world." He believes that learning provides the means to achieve this desire and has "a boundless respect for any one who had studied and wore a black coat, [regarding] such people as almost superhuman beings." The vocation of a preacher attracts him in particular: for some years "he could imagine nothing more noble or more attractive" than this profession. He is sent to a writing-master and later, in his twelfth year, to a private Latin class in the town Grammar School. He becomes the first of the class, but then, after two months, has to leave school. He tries to follow the studies of his schoolfellows, but is unable to keep up with them, and his unhappiness makes him a "bad" boy.

He is apprenticed to a master-hatter in Brunswick, who abuses him, and lives a life of real physical hardship. Yet this is a bearable life, and the hardship is interrupted at regular intervals by mealtimes, sleep, Sundays, and holidays. Others find joy in this, "but Anton's romantic ideas put him out of tune with this rhythm." He dreams of a Latin School and watches with sadness boys going in and out of it. It is these unfulfilled desires that torment him, while the hard life of an apprentice provides a refuge. His spirit is lifted when he is given a black apron, worn by other apprentices. "He now looked on himself as a person who was beginning to have a position of his own.

The apron brought him into line with others like him, whereas before he was lonely and isolated." [50]

Since his master regards "him as a tool, to be thrown out when worn out," he has to work in conditions which are harmful to his health. In winter his hands bleed, but even in this he finds a source of satisfaction, for his bleeding hands make him feel that he carries the burden with the rest. Hard work and discomfort eventually make Anton seriously sick, but they oppress him much less than what he perceives as humiliating tasks, such as having to carry a load on his back along a public street, while his master is walking in front of him.

At the age of fourteen Anton is discharged by the hatter and returns to Hannover. To be confirmed he must attend a school with some religious instruction for a while, and again wins general admiration by his excellent performance. He reveals to his teachers his desire to study further, and, on their recommendation, no less than the Prince of Mecklenburg-Strelitz decides to sponsor his education. The boy's fortunes suddenly become a matter of general interest and for the first time in his life he is treated with respect. This boosts his self-esteem and inflates his thoughts of future greatness: he already sees himself a preacher. This is where his real sorrows begin.

Education appears immensely attractive. Wide domains of knowledge lie before Reiser; his name is for the first time made to end in "us," "Reiserus," the Latin ending associated with the idea of dignity; and in addition, "the name High School, current among common folk, the expression 'High-School boys' which he often heard, [make] his prospects of going there more and more significant." People vie among themselves for the privilege of helping him, another proof of the high esteem in which education was held. But Anton is poor. His tuition is waived, and the Prince provides a *Reichstaler* for his maintenance, but his well-wishers decide to save this money for him, and, instead, several families, all of his own class—shoemakers, bandsmen, cooks—volunteer to provide for him one meal a week free of charge. He lodges, also free of charge, with another family, in the parlor. Some others give him "table-money" instead of meals, a few pence with which he has to make do for his breakfast and supper, and for dress an old, red soldier's coat is altered for him. As a result, instead of the pleasure he expected from his studies, his existence is embittered "by the crushing humiliations of his position." His ridiculous coat makes him conspicuously the worst dressed, "a circumstance which contributed not a little from the first to depress his spirits." All those who have offered him free meals feel they have the right to offer, in addition, advice, which he is expected to follow. They lecture him on the dearness of bread, and when the first excitement of righteousness and charity subsides, regret their hastiness and begrudge him every morsel. He is made to feel a burden and this depresses him; he is afraid to eat, to speak, even to cough. Telling of Anton's predicament here, Moritz, as a rare exception to his systematic abstention from judgment, says: "The position of the meanest artisan's apprentice is more honorable than that of a young man who is dependent for his studies on charity . . . if he is not capable of becoming servile, he will fare as Reiser did: he will get sullen and misanthropic as Reiser did, for he now began to find his chief pleasure in solitude." He shuns his schoolfellows because he is embarrassed, and at first imagines himself and then really is despised by them. This embarrassment makes him hate himself; it is unbearable. Again, Moritz comments:

> To be reduced to the extremity of shame is perhaps one of the most distressing feelings possible. More than once in his life Reiser experienced this feeling: more than once there were moments when he felt reduced to nothing in his own eyes . . . He always felt the deepest sympathy with any one in this position. He would have done more to save a person from shame than to save him from real misfortune, for shame seemed to him the greatest misfortune that can happen to any one . . . Shame is as violent an emotion as any, and it is surprising that its consequences are not sometimes fatal. The fear of appearing ridiculous was at times so appalling to Reiser that he would have sacrificed everything, even his life, to avoid it. No one perhaps ever felt more strongly than he the force of *Infelix paupertas, quia ridiculos miseros facit,* for to him to be ridiculous seemed the greatest misfortune in the world.[51]

Anton gradually loses all of his free meals but one, at the shoemaker's, and is given notice to move from his lodging. He moves to the house of the Rector of his school, where he is given a place to stay but nothing more. Although he now earns some money as a chorister, this is not enough. He starves. "The alluring pictures of his future status" help him to persist for a while in his diligence and resolve, and after only one year at High School he is promoted to the senior class. But before long he succumbs under the degrading pressures of his position. Cut off from where he came, he does not belong where he is: "he felt how it was always a matter of course that he came last in everything and yet he must regard it as a great honor." He is derided by his schoolfellows, who show him nothing but contempt, "which, apart from the general irrational antipathy, arose chiefly from his position which was humiliating or thought to be so, from his shy manner and his short coat." And so he shuts his eyes to the reality which is so repugnant to him. He withdraws into himself, and conceives a passion for the Stage, which offers him an escape from reality. "What he wanted was to have a powerful part, in which he could speak with strong emotion and transport himself into a series of moving scenes, which he loved, but could not have in the real world, where every incident was so poor and miserable." He also escapes into reading. Reading becomes a drug, able to "reduce the senses to a pleasant stupor"; he "read himself deep into debt . . . [for] reading took . . . the place of food and drink and clothing." The boy feels "forced to dream himself into another world where he was better off," entertains thoughts of suicide, loses all belief in himself and all interest in his own fortunes, being now solely preoccupied with the fortunes of the heroes of dramas and books he reads. As his reading is, for the most part, rather sad, he reads choking with tears, and revels in the "joy of grief," which is the only joy he has the opportunity to experience and which he enjoys all the more for that. Found incorrigible, he is expelled from the Rector's house.

In a novel he comes across the story of a nobleman turned peasant out of love for a peasant girl and finds the idea of becoming a peasant most attractive. His motives are revealing. "In the calling which Reiser had taken up he was now of no account at all, and it seemed impossible for him to work his way up again. But he had received far more education than is needed for a peasant, as a peasant he would be raised above his class while as a young man who devoted himself to study and should have prospects he found himself far below his class. The idea of becoming a peasant then became his ruling idea and drove out everything else." [52] But this new hope for a better future, however improbable, is soon driven away by hunger, which paralyzes Anton's mental abilities. He shares his lodgings with two other young men in similar circumstances, spending most of his time in bed. It is most significant that throughout the book we meet one character after another in situations very similar to that of Reiser; this is his story, but it is not at all unique.

After a spell of such existence, Anton, who is now sixteen, is promised forgiveness on the condition that he repents and abandons his "bad" ways: namely the reading of romances and the theater. He moves to live with the family of a tailor, sharing a room with many other people; his tastes change: he reads mostly philosophy and "scientific" books and learns French in a few weeks; his humiliations continue; he is still generally despised and suffers from want. He disgusts himself. "His self-consciousness, with the sense of being worthless and rejected, was as burdensome to him as his body with its feeling of wet and cold . . . That he must be unalterably himself and could be no other, that he was shut up in the narrow prison of self—this gradually reduced him to despair."

And then he discovers in succession Shakespeare and *The Sorrows of Young Werther,* which appear that year. These books provide him with the means to reinterpret and find dignity in his unbearable position. "After he had read Shakespeare in his spirit he was no longer an ordinary commonplace person, before long his spirit rose above all the outward circumstances that had crushed him and all the ridicule and scorn he had suffered . . . when he felt himself tormented, oppressed, and confined he no longer thought of himself as alone: he began to regard this as the universal lot of mankind. This gave a higher note to his complaints . . . the reading of Werther, like that of Shakespeare, raised him above his circumstances ... he was no longer the insignificant abject being, that he appeared in other men's eyes." [53]

The humiliations which are his lot in Hannover, "the unbearable sense of being unnoticed" in the multitude, make him hate the city in general, and human society, and he becomes a lover of Nature and solitude. (It was his troubles in a society which refused to change, not, it should be emphasized, industrialization or atomization brought by modernity, that caused these anti-urban sentiments.) He seeks Nature and solitude even after he no longer needs to escape from reality. For his fortunes suddenly take a turn for the better. Two poems of his own creation which he recited in class propel him to a position of general respect, so that "those who thought he would come to nothing began to think that perhaps he would come to something after all." The Prince, who is interested in Anton again, contributes toward a new coat for him, and "the new coat, which he regarded as putting him on an equality with his schoolfellows, from whom he had been so long distinguished by his shabby dress, inspired him with courage and confidence, and what was most remarkable, it seemed to win him more respect from others." Significantly, "Reiser nevertheless retained his melancholy humor, and found peculiar satisfaction in it." Being now a local celebrity, Anton is entrusted with composing and delivering a public address on the occasion of the Queen's birthday, the highest honor a High School student could achieve. According to custom, it is his right and duty to invite all the nobility and the high officials of the town in person, by all of whom he is received "with the most encouraging demonstrations of politeness." This unexpectedly acquired status brings him employment—private lessons—and therefore for the first time real income. His very poverty now becomes for him a matter of pride; "when, in spite of his humble dwelling, one of his rich and important fellow-students visited him, he felt a secret pleasure, that without attractive quarters or other external advantages he was sought out for his own sake."

But now his tragedy is reenacted in an up-scale version. Acting and creative writing take the place of preaching as the vocation of his dreams, and as did preachers in his childhood, so now actors and writers seem to him beings of a higher species. His poetic success, as earlier his learning abilities, make him aspire to become one of these beings. He wavers between poetry and the Stage, leaning toward the latter, because, he believes, theater would allow him quickly to "win fame and applause [which] had always been his dearest wish." In his aspiration he is not alone: the Stage was the rage of the whole generation. This "brilliant" career, explains Moritz, among other things, "did not require three years preliminary study at the University." [54] But Anton, still a High School student, does not even know how he can make it to the University, and instead of winning immediate applause enacting noble sentiments on the Stage, has to tutor less capable but more fortunate schoolfellows. This brings him income and new humiliations:

> A young nobleman, whom he was teaching, and with whom he was often to have some conversation in his room after the lesson, took leave of him without waiting for Reiser himself to take leave . . . his action struck Reiser as so strange and shocking that it completely upset him, so that when he left the house he stood still for a while and let his arms fall . . . He felt himself for some moments a nonentity, all his resources were paralyzed. The thought of being *de trop* even for a minute weighed on him like a mountain; he would have liked to rid himself at that moment of an existence which was so burdensome to an outsider . . . At bottom it was the feeling of humanity oppressed by its burgher condition which laid hold of him and made life hateful . . . What crime had he committed before birth, that he had not become a person, about whom a number of other men were bound to be attentive and concerned? Why was he assigned the part of the worker and another of the paymaster? If his circumstances had made him happy and content, he would have seen purpose and order everywhere; now all seemed contradiction, disorder, and confusion.[55]

The expenses of his now higher status exceed the income earned at the price of such humiliations. Finally, the petty debts and the abasements become too much for him and he leaves Hannover for Weimar (on foot, with one ducat of money, and a volume of Homer in his pocket), to join a stage company there.

Misfortune follows Anton in his travels. He pursues the company of his dreams unsuccessfully, feeding on raw turnips, for his money soon runs out, but feeling free and happy exactly because of this. He resolves to become a man-servant to Goethe, on any conditions. Starved and exhausted beyond all power to continue, he finds temporary refuge at the University of Erfurt, again thanks to his poetry and Latin, but the free board and lodging he is forced to accept there are unbearably humiliating to him and are worse than starvation. He decides to leave and is, finally, employed as an actor by another traveling company. Its Director, however, runs away with the money before Anton has a chance to perform. These misfortunes are multiplied by the effects of his earlier sufferings. He lives in a dual world: the inner one, of his imagination, and the world of external reality, frequently losing all touch with the latter. His imagination is morbid, but he seeks solace in morbidity, because "his nature had been attuned to this train of feeling by all the countless wounds and humiliations which he suffered from his youth up." He is driven into imaginary sufferings by his unwillingness to reconcile himself with his hated real self, with his place in reality, by his self-contempt "caused by the constant pressure of circumstances, for which chance was more responsible than men,"[56] and when the pressure of circumstances abates, he is no longer able to distinguish between what is real and what is not, or rather the world of his fevered brain becomes real to him.

We leave Anton Reiser, at the age of nineteen, with dreams of a stage career shattered, alone and penniless, and with no hope and prospects of a brighter future. Carl Philip Moritz eventually knew better days. He studied theology at the University of Wittenberg, obtained a post at the Gymnasium zum grauen Kloster in Berlin, published more than fifty works on language, psychology, and aesthetics, became a friend, rather than a servant, of Goethe, and died in 1793 (at the age of thirty-seven) as a *Professor der Theorie der schönen Künste und Alterthumskunde* in Berlin. But for many others like him happier days never arrived, and they, like Dr. Sauer, whom Anton Reiser met in Erfurt, "remained unnoticed and unknown" until their death, their spirit crushed by the incongruity of the dreams bred by their superior mental abilities and the petrified society which encouraged these dreams.

The exorbitant emotional toll levied by upward mobility into and within *Bildungsbürgertum,* and the social consequences of the perpetual sense of humiliation and exclusion of which the experience of it consisted, should not be underestimated. It crippled many a soul and left a lasting scar on the collective psyche, which it still disfigured more than a century later. It remained an open sore and was left, indeed made, to fester for generations, for "free-floating," suspended, and unhappy intellectuals made a profession of tinkering with it. Neither their impecunity nor their status-inconsistency was unique to the professional writers;[57] rather, they were the lot of *Bildungsbürgertum* as a whole. But the writers were, willy-nilly, left at leisure to ruminate on their misery and, by the nature of their vocation, became the spokesmen for the grievances of the class. Forced by necessity, they brought into being and controlled the German press. This control was never challenged: the nobility, with very few exceptions, did not consider writing—of whatever sort—a proper occupation. All who read German, therefore, inevitably became readers of the middle-class "unattached" academics and were exclusively exposed to their view of the society of which they believed themselves to be members, which meant their view of its scope and nature, as well as their specific perception of its imperfections and injustices and the solutions they proposed to ameliorate these. The German reading public in the second half of the eighteenth century was very small: a contemporary estimated it at two hundred thousand people;[58] but it grew steadily. This reading public consisted of "attached," namely employed, *Bildungsbürger*—officials, jurists, clergy, schoolteachers, and other professionals—of the educated nobility, also frequently lawyers and high-placed bureaucrats, and possibly a section of the non-academic middle class, who lived under different governments in more than three hundred German states. For this reading public the ten thousand free-lance frustrated intellectuals became the source of a common language. Through their publications they molded its way of thinking and seeing reality, and the reading public—the bureaucratic elite, the teachers, and the clergy—carried this naturally biased perspective further into the population that did not read. The way anguished, poor university graduates, unsuccessful in their own view, saw the world was becoming the *Weltanschauung* of most thinking Germans. It was, we may say, becoming the German mentality. This was one of the first manifestations of a new power later to be called *media*. The ten thousand people whom unkind destiny placed in its control were unknowingly acquiring a tremendous influence on their linguistic community. And so, inadvertently, trying to find an escape out of their particular predicament, the "unattached" intellectuals were laying the foundations of the German *national* consciousness.

## II. The Birth of the Spirit: The Preparation of the Mold for the German National Consciousness

### Aufklärung

In the last quarter of the eighteenth century the German *Bildungsbürger* found their position increasingly hateful and unsupportable. Many a man among them was familiar with Anton Reiser's disgust with his own self, diminished and degraded by his situation. Unable to escape their position, the intellectuals eventually arrived at a solution which was almost as good: they altered the image of their selves. National identity was the ultimate result of this transformation.

The idea of the nation belonged to the baggage of the Enlightenment. All German states prided themselves on being "enlightened," and some of them—Prussia, Austria, Saxe-Weimar—indeed set the tone in their dedication to the promotion of human progress and were considered epitomes of the age. Prussia was *the* exemplary "enlightened" state, a fact, widely recognized, that caused great satisfaction to Prussian subjects as well as to Germans in general. For German intellectuals, the Enlightenment opened a new era. It inaugurated the age of German letters with which intellectuals proper, secular intellectuals who saw in letters a professional calling, came into being. The vocation of the secular intellectual was its creation.

The age of Enlightenment in Germany triumphed in 1740—the year of accession of Frederick II, the Great, to the Prussian throne; "the age of enlightenment," believed Kant, was the same as "the century of Frederick." [59] In addition to the great philosopher, Frederick's generation included such men as Lessing, Mendelssohn, and Nicolai. It is during this period that the first professional writers, living off the market, were able to make their appearance, as well as the first widely (by the standards of the time) circulating literary and general intellectual journals, and numerous reading clubs and philosophical societies.

Like everywhere else, Enlightenment in Germany referred to the advance of rationalism: it achieved "an alternation in the range of human values, placing reason at the summit." [60] In "Was ist Aufklärung?" Kant defined Enlightenment as "man's release from his self-incurred tutelage" and as freedom, resolution, and courage to use one's own reason. But what did the German Enlightenment, *Aufklärung*, mean specifically? If we refer back to Kant's authoritative answer, we see that it consisted chiefly in the increasing ability of people "to use their own reason in religious matters," in other words, to doubt and criticize the established religious dogma. Lessing wrote angrily to Nicolai in 1769: "Don't talk to me of your liberty of thought and the press. It reduces itself to the liberty to let off as many squibs against religion as one likes. Let somebody raise his voice for the rights of subjects or against exploitation and despotism, and you will soon see which is the most slavish land in Europe." [61] Kant disagreed. "Our rulers," he emphasized, "have no interest in playing the guardians with respect to the arts and sciences," and the philosopher-king, so Kant believed, even saw "that there is no danger to his lawgiving in allowing his subjects to make public use of their reason and to publish their thoughts on a better formulation of his legislation and even their open-minded criticism of the laws already made." "Argue as much as you will, and about what you will, but obey!" was the king's admirable principle. But the focus of the criticism of the champions of reason nevertheless remained to them unreasonable established religion. The achievements of the *Aufklärung* in the sphere of religious toleration were impressive. Prussia was a haven to free-thinkers of all sorts and even in France was regarded as an example to be followed. At least in the minds of the educated, *Aufklärung* succeeded in thoroughly discrediting established religion, expelling it from their consciousnesses and hearts, and taking its place. This was a thoroughgoing change in mentality.

To be educated in the second half of the eighteenth century meant to be steeped in the values of *Aufklärung*. Aspiring intellectuals hardly had any choice in the matter, but they immersed themselves in its clear waters willingly, for the message of the *Aufklärung* was very attractive to them. It promised them dignity and advancement in life. "Was ist Aufklärung?" ends with an optimistic assertion that as the propensity for free thinking develops, it inescapably affects all the spheres of life, and men, "who are now more than machines," are treated "in accordance with their dignity." The belief in reason elevated those who were thought to possess it. Moreover, in Germany, it implied more than just dignity. German rationalism was very different from the English respect for common sense, which was the very basis of individualism: the belief in reason as the defining characteristic of the human species and therefore the belief in the reason of every human being. Rather, German rationalism was akin to French rationalism. It was the belief in human reason as the reason of those elect and superior humans who were able to arrive at the right philosophy, the cultivated reason, the reason of the educated, reason as a distinguishing characteristic among—rather than of—humans, and therefore an admission ticket to superior status.

As we have seen, *Aufklärung* did not fulfill its promise to the intellectuals. While the rulers' commitment to some of its principles, especially in Prussia, was sincere, and it was thus encouraged to penetrate certain areas of life, such as religion, and affected a most thoroughgoing transformation in the modes of thinking in general, *Aufklärung* did not attempt, and had it attempted would not be allowed, to affect the spheres of politics and of social relations. In these crucial areas of social existence, the philosophy was superadded to an unchanging society, immovable in its semi-feudal makeup. It added some gloss to it and highlighted its stubborn persistence in archaic ways blatantly inconsistent with the new outlook. The *Aufklärung* opened new vistas for the educated; it promised respect for the men of reason, and hinted that the future belonged to the university graduates. There were many more opportunities than before; education and intellectual merit were in demand and achievement could be highly rewarded. But exactly this was the problem. In accordance with the "Tocqueville effect," that iron law, a partial fulfillment was more disturbing than no promise at all. The stakes became higher, and the pain of failure intensified as a result. The demand for the educated increased, as did their prestige, but so did the competition, for the supply was greater than the demand. The possibilities—and glamour—of success grew simultaneously with the possibilities—and trauma—of failure. And those who failed, or those who were afraid to fail, turned away from the *Aufklärung* in dismay. It was the logical incongruity between the modern, officially sponsored philosophy and the inflexibly traditional social structure that was the chief source of the intellectuals' predicament. But the promise was that of the *Aufklärung*, and *Aufklärung*, not the tenacity of the social organism predating it, was seen as the immediate cause of their disappointment. The society they lived and struggled in—that was the site, the witness, and the cause of their humiliation—and the one they turned against was the "enlightened" society.

All the same, they remained the products of the *Aufklärung*. It furnished the language for their thoughts; their hopes and aspirations were formed by it. They were essentially "enlightened" themselves, and they could not escape measuring by its standards their performance, their success or lack of it, and the very means and devices they used to fight against it. *Aufklärung* was the basis on which the future German consciousness was built and one of the important ingredients of this consciousness.

Under the aegis of the *Aufklärung* the feeble voice of national patriotism, which was never silenced completely among the intellectuals, grew somewhat stronger. For the most part, the patriotism of the *Aufklärer* meant love for the noble ideals of liberty and equality, imported from England and France, and was critical of Germany (that is, the territories loosely integrated into the Holy Roman Empire), which, in this crucial respect, compared badly with the two model nations. Imperial conditions were not conducive to patriotism. "German patriots, who love the Empire as their Fatherland, where are they?" asked Wieland wistfully. Common patriotism was needed so that Germans "could at length say, We are a nation," and several able men endeavored to exhort their slumbering countrymen to awaken to this lofty sentiment. Since the Empire was beyond reform, some patriots focused on Prussia, whose monarch was an object of general admiration in Europe, and therefore "gave confidence and a sense of nationality to all Germans." [62] Frederick was glorified in poetry and prose. Even Goethe admitted to being a partisan of the brilliant Prussian in his youth.[63]

The moribund state of the Empire also provoked the first expressions of *ressentiment* against the West. The evident superiority of the model nations, England and France in particular, left a sour taste in the mouths of those who, despite themselves, sang their praise in Germany. Christian Schubart thundered in his *Deutsche Chronik* against excessive admiration of foreigners: "He who does not fling a curse across the frontier from the ruins of Heidelberg is no true German. And yet what is there that my countryman does not fetch from beyond the Rhine? Fashion, cuisine, wine, and even the language." England he found too commercial. Still, he admired English liberty and thought that "what [the Germans] might learn from the Frenchman with advantage is patriotism." [64]

A different kind of patriotism was preached and practiced by Klopstock. The senior poet turned his sight away from the age of Enlightenment, which illumined the decrepid and shameful condition of eighteenth-century Germany too brightly, and focused it instead on the glorious times when virtuous and youthful ancient Germans fought bloody battles against decrepid and shameless Rome, and were victorious. He was an inspiration to poets of lesser fame.

The predominant mood of the *Aufklärung*, however, was cosmopolitanism. In the age of reason, it coexisted peacefully with national patriotism. There was as yet no contradiction. The model nations, England, France, and certainly America, saw themselves as advanced, chosen, privileged parts of humanity, not as a different species. To be a good Englishman, Frenchman, or American, faithful to the ideals of one's nation, was tantamount to being a good citizen of the world. Having declared their membership in the enlightened world of England, France, and America, and having little to be proud of as Germans, the *Aufklärer* wished to be good citizens of the world.

For the spokesman of the *Aufklärung,* Nicolai, German nationalism was "a political monstrosity." Weishaupt, the founder of the secret society of *Illuminati,* believed that nationalism was comparable to despotism and, like it, prevented the spread of reason and happiness of humanity. Schiller was proud of his cosmopolitanism: "I write as a citizen of the world . . . I lost my Fatherland to exchange it for the great world."

Throughout the eighteenth century these varied sentiments intermixed in equally varied ways. Sometimes a person was in succession a cosmopolitan, a champion of the Prussian cause, a follower of Klopstock, a German patriot resentful of France, and then a cosmopolitan again—such was the case of Goethe. In other cases, cultural nationalism combined with political cosmopolitanism. Heinrich Heine called Lessing "our literary Arminius, who freed our theatre from the foreign yoke," and indeed the struggle against French letters was among Lessing's chief preoccupations. Yet he could confess with great satisfaction: "I have literally no conception of the love of the Fatherland (I am sorry to confess my shame), and it appears to me a heroic failing from which I am glad to be free." [65]

On the whole, cosmopolitanism (which often concealed the lack of any political sentiment) was a far more widespread attitude. The idea of the nation, long available, had no significant appeal in Germany until very late, at least by comparison with all the other cases in this book. It was an alien idea, which on the face of it seemed inapplicable to the Germany of the eighteenth century. Its psychological implications and potential were not recognized until the French revolutionary army drove the point home, and not until this idea underwent a profound transformation that made German national consciousness unlike any other. Ultimately, *Bildungsbürger* found national identity attractive because it implied an unassailable dignity for and automatically elevated members of the national collectivity, however lowly, putting them on a par with the most exalted nobility. It accomplished what the Enlightenment had failed to accomplish: it made them equal in human worth to any of their social superiors. And it did so in a manner which could not be offensive to the spirit of the Enlightenment, for it was a part of the Enlightenment itself, and the most advanced societies of Europe subscribed to it. Yet, as the national identity was adopted, it was adapted to the cultural soil to which it was transplanted. The meaning (and connotations) of nationality was reinterpreted in a way which rendered it familiar, comprehensible, and consistent with other dominant traditions of discourse, and the terms of these traditions were utilized in this reinterpretation.

## Pietism

The traditions which had this profound impact on the character of German national consciousness were Pietism and Romanticism. Pietism was the German counterpart of English Puritanism, a religious movement with a wide appeal and numerous converts within every class of society.[66] Like Puritanism, Pietism, an outgrowth of the Protestant Reformation, was opposed to the established orthodoxy and represented the adaptation of the dogma to the aspirations, situations, and constraints of the population that adopted it. It differed from Puritanism to the extent that these situations, constraints, and aspirations differed, and its effects, therefore, were essentially unlike those produced by Puritanism in England.

The source of fundamental difference between Puritanism and Pietism is that Puritanism was the religious ideology of upwardly mobile, ambitious, and confident groups in a dynamic society that experienced mobility on a mass scale, while Pietism was the religious ideology of a static society whose members were unacquainted with worldly success, but intimate with hardship and disaster, which fostered a fatalistic outlook. "[The] virtues favored by Pietism were more those on the one hand of the faithful official, clerk, labourer, or domestic worker," wrote Max Weber, "and on the other of the predominantly patriarchal employer with the pious condescension."[67] In other words, German Pietism was the form in which faithful officials, clerks, laborers, and so forth, appropriated Lutheran and, to some extent, Calvinist Protestantism, the manner in which they dealt with the dogma. In a way it fulfilled the same function which was later fulfilled by nationalism.

At the same time, Pietism was a variant of religious mysticism, which became a widespread phenomenon in Germany after the Thirty Years' War and was a response to the misery caused by it.[68] Under its proper name the movement emerged in 1675 with the publication by Philipp Jakob Spener of *Pia Desideria oder Wahren evangelischen Kirche*—the founding text of Pietism. Spener was a Lutheran, the son of a Hofmeister in Rappoltsweiler, and a university graduate. During travels undertaken to complete his education at the University of Strassbourg he became acquainted with and was deeply influenced by the spiritual leaders of Swiss mysticism. Later, in his capacity as preacher in many different cities, he was able to bequeath these influences to those who came in contact with him and, aided by his saintly personality and the general responsiveness to mystical tendencies, founded the Pietist movement within the established Church. Several other Lutheran leaders of the movement in the first half of the eighteenth century—such as the academic theologians August Hermann Francke and Gottfried Arnold—were personal acquaintances of Spener and were influenced by him directly. His impact on Count Nikolaus Ludwig von Zinzendorf—the founder of the Moravian Brethren community at Herrnhut, at whose baptism in 1700 Spener was a sponsor, was less direct but equally profound. These followers of Spener gave the spirit of Pietism body as well as prestige associated with the authority of the university and the status of the nobility, and carried it further in institutions such as the Halle Paedagogium (formed by Francke) and schools and communities of *Herrnhuter,* and in their writings. Their official positions ensured that what they had to say would be heard. The appointment of Gottfried Arnold as the first historiographer of Prussia was just one reflection of the high standing attained by the movement by the beginning of the eighteenth century in certain provinces. The main centers of Pietism were in Prussia and Württemburg, but the itinerant academics helped to spread it throughout Germany.[69] An extraordinary number of children were educated in Pietist institutions, and by the second half of the eighteenth century the movement had penetrated deeply and become influential in the Reformed Church as well.

The main source of Pietism, however, was Lutheranism, which adapted better to the needs of the various strata in Germany than did Calvinism. Pietism, like mysticism in general, was a by-product of the attempt to use the official religion as a practical philosophy: the means of rendering the existing order of things, in which suffering was the central element, both meaningful and livable. In the static world of faithful officials, laborers, and domestic workers, the emphasis on the doctrine of predestination would be psychologically untenable. In sharp contrast to their brethren in seventeenth-century England, their experience would be able to show them only that they were, indeed, eternally damned. And since, in their case, "the ascetic struggle for certainty about the future world" was bound to end in failure, they were led "to strive for the enjoyment of salvation in this world."[70] Rather than attempt to change their condition, which they were powerless to do, they interpreted it as a sign of grace. Their misery itself, the "humility and abnegation," which most of them could not escape if they tried, became a proof of *certitudo salutis,* and was freely chosen. Necessity was transformed into virtue.

The immediate knowledge of salvation, manifest in misery, not only led to passive acquiescence with fate, but was also actively sought after—in an unadventurous manner, to be sure, which involved no risk and guaranteed the success of the undertaking. Election could be proven by active piety— the *praxis pietatis*—and by the emotional experience of unity with Christ— Lutheran *unio mystica.* In the course of time the two ways of ascertaining one's salvation became confused, and piety came to mean chiefly the personal emotional experience of divine bliss.

Jesus was a real presence in the life of the Pietists, and the experience of personal contact with him was one of an unusual vividness and intensity. Count von Zinzendorf sometimes "wrote a little note to his beloved Savior, told Him in it how his heart felt toward Him, and threw it out of the window, in the hope that He would find it."[71] Anton Reiser, friendless and neglected, had talked to Jesus "on a footing of confidence" since his eighth year. Moreover, in the misery of his loneliness, he found a playmate in God's Child and amused him, giving him rides on an abandoned wheelbarrow. "He imagined a boy somewhat smaller than himself, and as he conversed so familiarly already with God himself, why should he not do so even more with this son of his? He trusted that he would not refuse to play with him and therefore would not object if he wished to wheel him about on the wheelbarrow. He prized it as a great piece of good fortune, to be able to wheel about so great a person and to give him pleasure in this way, and as this person was a creature of his own imagination he could do with him as he chose, and so made him find pleasure in riding for a longer or shorter time and even sometimes said, in all reverence, if he was tired of wheeling: 'I should be glad to give you a longer ride, but I cannot do it now.'" [72]

One can speculate how much of this intense intimacy could be attributed to the loneliness into which people like Anton Reiser were confined by their poverty and shyness, and by the inability or reluctance to form other—earthly—relationships. The experience of Gottfried Arnold could not have been much different from that of Moritz' hero: he too grew up in poverty humiliating for an educated youth and a son of a teacher in the Latin school, was forced to earn a living by giving private lessons at the age of thirteen, and yet went to a university. There, among students whose better fortunes underscored his misery and made it a source of constant humiliation, he did not make any friends and found no taste in the student life. Even later, when his exertions bore fruit and he was appointed a professor of history at the University of Giessen, an office he considered "truly divine," he could not fit in, but preferred to resign and went on to write his mystical works. [73] It is revealing that when these lonely souls did find a friend on this earth, their devotion was as fervent, and friendship as intense and all-consuming, as the love they, when still friendless, had felt for Jesus.

Emotionalism was the central characteristic of Pietism; it was *Herzenreligion,* and its counterpart was scorn for doctrine and theological learning. The knowledge of doctrine did not contain the certainty of salvation. On the contrary, it was often those who knew the least, or had the least *Kopfwissenschaft,* who were the best Christians, able truly to identify with the "blood and merit of the Lamb of God." The knowledge of doctrine also prevented the implementation of the principle of "priesthood of all believers." The emphasis on it was an additional reason for the appeal of Pietism to the numerous groups within the middle classes, for whom it provided a way to a loftier status and a basis for self-esteem, which they could not hope to find otherwise. Thus they agreed with Zinzendorf that religion was "not a question of formulas and ceremonies, nor of taking on certain customs . . . [but that of] the heart, in which all children of God are alike." [74]

The insistence on equality was soon transformed into preference for the humble and untutored as better able to serve and understand God. "Hidden wisdom," taught Gottfried Arnold, "is more surely found among the ignorant and the simple, content to seek their salvation in fear, than among learned theologians." [75] Simultaneously, the rejection of the established standards of religious virtuosity led to the formation of new standards of election and to a new religious aristocracy.

The deemphasis of dogma produced a pluralistic, individualized view of religion: it was the attitude of faith, rather than its content, that mattered, and so long as one believed in Christ, it was of little consequence what else and what exactly one believed. The 1740 declaration of the *Herrnhuter* Synod of Marienborn stated: "Unlike the Lutherans, we . . . construct no confession of faith which may not later be altered. We desire to retain freedom, that the Savior may from time to time enlighten our teaching." [76] This attitude necessarily and very soon led to the abandonment of traditional religious belief altogether and to a mystical pantheistic notion, which, as the *Herrnhuter* Schleiermacher was later aware, was indistinguishable from atheism. Two thoughts ran through his *Discourses on Religion:* "that all religious persons are priests, and that all are one," and he was certain the treatise would seem to the censor "little less than atheistic." "The true nature of religion," he asserted in this work, "is neither [the idea of the objectivity of God] nor any other, but immediate consciousness of the Deity as He is found in ourselves and in the world." For that reason, religion was "endlessly determinable." [77] What distinguished a genuinely religious person was the intensity of this consciousness. "Am I wrong," asked the widow of Schleiermacher's friend, whom he consoled and later married, "in calling those feelings religious which are awakened in me by the music in church? For I must confess that I feel quite differently when the service is not accompanied by music. I cannot describe to you how my soul is born aloft, as it were, by the tones; what a feeling of freedom is developed in me, what consciousness of the holy and the infinite seems to pervade me . . . But tell me, my Ernst, is it in accordance with pure Christian feeling, that anything *external* should produce such a powerful religious effect on me—that I require an *external* agency to enable me to lose myself in God?" "Dearest, be not over anxious," answered Schleiermacher, "and do not try to separate what God himself has intimately united. Religion and art belong together as soul and body . . . the heightened feeling with which [music] inspires the pious, is, no doubt, really religious." [78]

The characteristic of the new aristocracy of grace, when the abandonment of dogma led to the replacement of the old one, was thus emotional susceptibility, the ability to experience intense emotions. Passion took the place of scriptural learning as the highest religious—and moral—virtue. Pietist notions spread quickly and widely, and this change of standards could be felt on many levels. Emotionalism, as Weber, following Albrecht Ritschl, notes, was the reason for the appeal of Pietism to the nobility. It was "a religious dilettantism for the leisure classes." For the same reason it attracted the *Bildungsbürger,* in whom education and status-inconsistency had developed heightened sensitivity anyway, and for whom the cultivation of emotion provided an easier and surer way to enhance their sense of dignity than any other.[79]

A logical consequence of the view of religion as personal unity with God was a broad tolerance of the forms of Christian worship. Theoretically at least, all forms were legitimate, so long as faith was sincere, idiosyncrasy being in fact a sign of naturalness, sincerity of faith. The counterpart of this position on a collective level was a new respect for the forms of worship characteristic of ethnic communities (of Christians), and a novel, mystical idea of native language, the vernacular which, in Protestantism, replaced Latin as the medium of worship. This idea was reinforced by the greater regard for and increased preoccupation with the education of the lower classes and the instrumental emphasis on German. Like individual human beings, ethnic communities were unique, peculiar expressions of God's love and wisdom. It thus was a matter of Christian piety to preserve one's uniqueness. The mother tongue, in particular, acquired the dignity of the means through which God manifested Himself to a people, the peculiar, in-dividualized link between the Deity and a specific community. It was thus sanctified and acquired value beyond instrumental utility. This mystical idea of language as a peculiar bond with God first appeared in the thought of Jakob Boehme.[80]

The wide appeal of Pietism, its continuous applicability and relevance to the situations of many groups, and its diffuse therapeutic powers help to explain the sure hold religion enjoyed in Germany as late as the end of the eighteenth century. The nature of the movement, moreover, protected it from the direct assault of the *Aufklärung,* the brunt of which was borne by the doctrine. Rationalism chose the teaching of the established Church as its enemy and dismissed Pietism as hardly worth its learned attention. Pietism thus was able to provide an outlet for, and preserve, religious feeling in an anti-religious climate and to coexist with rationalism. Because of the nature of the movement, too, religious toleration, which was inevitably undermin-ing the credibility of coexisting yet mutually exclusive (by their very nature) doctrines, did not lead to religious indifference. Pietism abandoned doctrine, and was thus able to preserve faith.

And yet some of the elements of the religious creed, certain religious sym-bols, parts of the doctrine (or narrative), most congenial to be sure to the generally anti-doctrinal, mystical, and emotional nature of Pietism, were perpetuated and even reinforced in it manifold. Pietism did contain certain tenets of faith which combined into something like a doctrine of its own. Some of these tenets derived directly from the Pietist opposition to dogma and external symbols of faith. The rejection of doctrine and the insistence on *reine Innerlichkeit* necessarily led to an increase in the importance of the group, the community of like-minded, kindred spirits: an individual left en-tirely to his own spiritual resources and deprived of the sources of moral authority in the mind inevitably turns to the group for guidance. Indeed Pietism, which regarded the external organization of the official Church as unimportant, opposed to it a community of the faithful, the invisible Church of the elect. This Church was a reflection of each member's personal relationship with the Savior, yet it was impossible to achieve true unity with God outside the community. Since the way to God lay through "humility and abnegation," the community of the faithful consisted of individuals who renounced their particular interests and their very selves. It represented a diminutive Kingdom of God on earth and thus was the ideal community. It is not surprising, therefore, that Pietists had no sympathy for social structures in which individuals retained their selves and which allowed the existence of and even safeguarded particular interests, or that they regarded the principle of social contract, which evidently promoted impiety, as an aberration.

Furthermore, the Pietists strove to make the invisible Church visible. On the one hand, "the desire to separate the elect from the world could [and did], with a strong emotional intensity, lead to a sort of monastic community life of half-communistic character" in "conventicles removed from the world." [81] On the other, the same desire to establish God's Kingdom on earth expressed itself in missionary activity and proselytism. These paradoxically—if one considers Pietist withdrawal from the world—led to a revision of the nature of the State (the very embodiment of the mundane), which later acquired great significance. The aim of every Christian, including the great of this world, was the establishment of God's Kingdom. Everyone had to contribute to this in one's proper office; kings and princes were expected to dedicate to this goal the states over which they ruled. They were, in fact, expected to provide individual leadership in this pleasing-to-God process— possibly by analogy to the individual leadership of Jesus. The virtuous among these temporal rulers were seen by the Pietists as "angels of God" and "princes of the souls," and the State "from a simple utilitarian institution, as it was conceived by the rationalism of the seventeenth and eighteenth centuries, was transformed into an ideal entity, the instrument with which God raised and formed men in conformity with his supreme designs." [82] It was of no minor importance that it was the Prussian state and rulers that were so interpreted above all. The State was sanctified; it was increasingly viewed as the embodiment of the true Church, and this view, in combination with the Pietist idea of the community in which the personal individuality of each member dissolved in a true unity, was acquiring the unmistakable characteristics of totalitarianism.

Another crucial tenet of Pietist faith destined to have a long-lasting effect and to survive the decline of the faith itself was the cult of the Passion on the Cross. The physical agony of the Savior brought Him closer to the believers, made Him more human, and facilitated sympathy (in the Smithian sense) more than any other moment in the Biblical narrative. It is natural that in a religion which demanded personal contact, identification, and sympathy in exactly that sense, the Passion became the focal element. And so did the blood and the wounds which caused it, which soon became separated and stood—as religious values—on their own.[83] In turn, blood, wounds, and physical suffering added value to everything they were associated with: war, the profession of a soldier, death. Whether experienced or inflicted on others, they were sanctified, became the sublime signs of spiritual purity and strength and of moral righteousness, and paved the road to glory.

Gerhardt Kaiser traces the transplantation of the gory imagery of the Passion on the Cross from religious to secular contexts in the work of Klopstock. Klopstock is especially important for our purposes, for he was both the great religious—Pietist—poet of the century and the first famous author of secular patriotic poetry. The epithets applied to Christ's blood and suffering in the *Messiah* systematically reappear in the patriotic epic *Hermanns Schlacht* and in the *Odes*. Very frequently blood is associated with beauty. The day of crucifixion is characterized as a "precious, splendid, bloody day"; the day of the battle in the Arminius epic—as "the day of the combat to the death, beautiful and bloody." Christian martyrs are "covered with sublime wounds"; Germanic youths—"with beautiful wounds." The father of Arminius thinks that "blood will be a beautiful attire for the greying hair of an old man," and disciples in the *Messiah* want to "soak their greying hair in the blood of martyrs." Christ dies "the most beautiful death"; He is "beautiful with wounds" *(Schön mit Wunden)*. "Beautiful Blood" *(Schön Blut)* covers those dying for the Fatherland in patriotic *Odes*. What is most significant, blood of those one kills is as beautiful as one's own heroically shed blood. When Arminius returns from the battle "covered with sweat, with Roman blood and with dust of combat," Klopstock exclaims: "Never before was Arminius so beautiful!" Blood also works as an aphrodisiac: the sight of Roman blood on Arminius arouses Thusnelda's desire. "I want to see him dirty!" she cries. "His hair smeared with the blood of the Romans!"[84]

Others followed in Klopstock's steps. In the works of von Stolberg, Herder, Lavater, Arndt, and many more illustrious personalities of German letters, gory death, "death in blood," becomes a most desirable, glorious event, justified on both aesthetic and ethical grounds. Such sanctification of carnage, its elevation to the position of a supreme social value, which was a result of the emotionalism of Pietism, had never happened in any other society, and it may well be the element which did indeed make much of the more recent German history exceptional, unlike any other and unimaginable elsewhere, and was responsible for what so many wish to see as an incomprehensible aberration.

When one realizes how many of the late eighteenth-century intellectuals—the inventors of the German national consciousness—were at one point or another in their lives Pietists, as children of Pietist parents, students in Pietist educational establishments, it is easy to appreciate Pietism's role in the formation of German nationalism. Like English Protestantism in the sixteenth century, Pietism provided the language as well as the legitimation for the new identity, and as a result, while shaping it, was carried on in it. It is not that Pietism "planted the seeds" out of which nationalism developed:[85] nationalism was not a descendant of Pietism. But it provided the soil in which the seeds—brought from outside—could grow. And—here the biological analogy has to end—the soil, in a rather Lamarckian manner, changed the nature of the plant to live on in the fruit it bore.

Pietism exercised its influence on the character of German nationalism directly and in an indirect fashion—through Romanticism, another tradition of tremendous consequence for subsequent ages, which it helped to bring into being. A direct heir of Pietism, and at the same time a product of other influences opposed to it, Romanticism appropriated but secularized central Pietist notions, and in so doing was able to perpetuate them in an age which was becoming increasingly indifferent to religion.

## Romanticism

Romanticism is customarily associated with the domain of literature. While it is unquestionable that it was a literary phenomenon among other things, to define it as such necessarily minimizes its significance and hinders our understanding of it. Rather than originating in literature, as a solution to a problem in literary development, Romanticism was confined to literature in Germany by accident, because its creators had no other choice but to be men of letters, and in other countries—because the existential basis on which it grew in Germany was absent, and as a result, Romantic principles were applicable to and adopted only in art. The original—German—Romanticism was a movement of thought, a "mode of thinking" which found expression in almost every sphere of the social, political, economic, and cultural existence of the land of its birth and deeply affected its future development. Observing it from France, Henri Brunschwig saw it as "one of the most profound movements ever to affect Germany"; Ernst Troeltsch believed that "German thought, whether in politics or in history or in ethics, is based on the ideas of the Romantic Counter-Revolution"; and Friedrich Meinecke somewhat arrogantly proposed that it was "possibly the greatest conceptual revolution that the West has yet experienced." [86]

The *Weltanschauung* of Romanticism is older than its name. Its first significant manifestation was in the Storm and Stress of the 1770s, the *Genie* period. The unfortunate failure of the "geniuses" of the *Sturm und Drang* and related contemporary groups, such as the *Göttinger Hainbund,* to call themselves "Romantics"; the fact that the acclaimed leaders of the *Sturm und Drang* abandoned its principles and returned to the fold of the *Aufklärung* under the guise of German Classicism, as a result of which twenty years of Classicism separated *Sturm und Drang* from the "early" Romanticism of the very end of the eighteenth century in Jena and Berlin;[87] and finally the presence in the *Sturm und Drang* of Goethe (a genuine "genius" one might say, if the word did not have such a peculiar significance in the present context and was not so profoundly abused in it), an extraordinary individual, defying classification—all these necessarily obscure the fundamental similarity, almost identity, of the *Sturm und Drang* period and Romanticism. Nevertheless, they belong together. Their kinship does not imply that Romanticism proper was a development of the potentialities of the *Sturm und Drang,* and thus could not be possible without it. Though "early" Romantics were all deeply influenced by the work of the "original geniuses" of the 1770s, Romanticism could (and most probably would) emerge even if *Sturm und Drang* never existed. The two movements belong together because both were responding to the same structural situation and, in their response to it, used the same cultural resources: Pietism and Enlightenment. Differences between them certainly existed, but they were not greater than the differences between individual *Stürmer und Dränger,* between *Stürmer und Dränger* and other "original geniuses" of the 1770s, or between individual Romantics. In what follows I apply the term "Romantic" to all representatives of the Romantic *Weltanschauung,* whether before or after the adoption of the name.

Biographically speaking, all of the eighteenth-century Romantics began as rationalists; they were "enlightened" in every sense of the term, and their aspirations were formed by *Aufklärung.* Almost all of them, too, had to grapple with failure on their chosen path. Johann Georg Hamann, the great inspiration of the *Stürmer und Dränger,* was brought up in a Pietist family. His upbringing left his sensibilities "over-cultivated by devotional reading and practice" and himself with a heavy stutter which made him shy and uncomfortable in social intercourse. He went to the University of Königsberg to study first theology and then law, but quickly lost interest in both, devoted his time to the enthusiastic study of the French and English Enlightenment, and did not take a degree. Like so many other aspiring intellectuals, he earned his bread for a while as a private tutor, but then worked in the commercial firm of a friend who trusted him to go on a business mission to London. There, upset by the breakup of a homosexual affair, Hamann wasted the money entrusted to him and in despair turned to the Bible. Whether because what he read gave him courage, or because remaining in London any longer became impossible, he returned to Königsberg, but decided against resuming his job in the firm, although forgiven by his friend, and instead wrote his first anti-rationalist (and we may add—first Romantic) work, "Socratic Memorabilia."[88]

The chief theoretician of the *Sturm und Drang,* Herder, the son of poor Pietist parents, also attended the faculty of theology at the University of Königsberg. There he was influenced by Kant and studied the thought of the French and English Enlightenment with an enthusiasm at least equal to Hamann's. In 1769 he visited France and met some of the Encyclopedists, Diderot and Condillac leaving a particularly deep impression on him. His first works championed the cause of *Aufklärung,* and, as he later told Hamann, he only "narrowly escaped being a wit." Like many others he aspired to an academic career. He applied repeatedly for a chair of theology, but was as repeatedly denied it, among other reasons, because his theology was, as Nicolai sarcastically remarked, "very secular." At the age of thirty, when he became one of the leaders of the *Sturm und Drang,* Herder was already a frustrated and bitter man. Goethe, who had the opportunity to experience on himself the after-effects of his friend's unhappy past, wrote later: "Herder constantly embittered his finest days, both for himself and others, for he knew not how to moderate, by strength of mind in later years, that ill humor which had necessarily seized him in his youth."[89] He turned against the faith of his former days with the uncompromising passion of apostasy, and the earliest of his *Sturm und Drang* works were also the most violent in their rejection of the spirit he had professed just several years before.

Another one-time student of Königsberg University was Lenz, in whose person and broken life, if not necessarily works, the tortured and turbulent spirit of the *Sturm und Drang* found its most perfect embodiment. Lenz also had been brought up in a deeply Pietist environment and was studying theology. Like Herder under the influence of Kant, he found philosophy more attractive and interrupted his studies. To support himself he accompanied the brothers von Kleist to Strassbourg; his experience was similar to that of many other bourgeois tutors to young noblemen: he was and felt degraded and humiliated. He left his service in 1774 and joined Goethe's circle—never being able to resume his studies or find a proper employment.

The story of Klinger, who christened the movement, was, with but minor differences, that of Anton Reiser. For that reason, Guelfo, the hero of Klinger's *Twins,* became Anton's favorite part: "he found in Guelfo his own self-derision, self-hatred, self-contempt, and passion for self-destruction, but combined with force, Reiser delighted in the scene where Guelfo, after the murder of his brother, smashes the mirror in which he sees himself."[90]

To this pattern of frustrated hopes followed by apostasy, common to the *Stürmer und Dränger,* Goethe may appear a somewhat disconcerting exception. Goethe's exceptional abilities and personality, however, make him less of an exception than he would have to be considered were he an ordinary *Bildungsbürger.* Unlike other *Stürmer und Dränger,* Goethe came from an upper-bourgeois, patrician family, studied law rather than theology, read the Bible as a text in history and linguistics rather than as the word of God, and was only in the later years of his youth—by way of entertainment—exposed to Pietism. Moreover, in 1775, when he was snatched by the Duke of Weimar from the claws of the legal career to which he was predestined and which he heartily disliked, a turn of events that nipped his *Sturm und Drang* revolt in the bud, he was only twenty-six years old. Objectively, he had few reasons to fear and no time to experience failure. His youthful antagonism to the principles of *Aufklärung* is accounted for not by the misery of reality, but rather by the grandeur of his expectations. From very early on he recognized—and was fortunate to be encouraged in—his extraordinary abilities, and thus aspired to more than would satisfy his less richly endowed comrades. As a result, on the one hand, the discrepancy between expectations and reality in his case was as great as it might have been, for other reasons, in theirs. "The disparity between the narrow and slow-moving bourgeois sphere and the breadth and energy of my nature," he wrote later, "would have driven me mad." [91] He might have been apprehensive of a disappointment. On the other hand, setting his mind on greatness (not merely making a living) in letters put him in direct competition with the already great, all of whom at the time were champions of the *Aufklärung*. However subconsciously made, the choice of a different path might have been a product-differentiation strategy, a way to increase his chances of achieving greatness and reducing the risk of failure. Thus Goethe's situation, too, could have led to his youthful Romanticism, even if he had not arrived at Strassbourg, where *Sturm und Drang* originated, immediately after his short excursion into Pietism and had not been well versed in Pietist literature; and—while in Strassbourg—even if he had not been most profoundly influenced by Herder and had not written his *Sturm und Drang* works under the direct impact of the latter's views and personality.

The apprenticeship of the "early" Romantics of the end of the century was similar to that of the *Stürmer und Dränger*. Indeed, Henri Brunschwig sees the frustration of their hopes of obtaining a position within the institutions and in the spirit of the *Aufklärung* as the direct cause of their turning away from it. Their failure "casts doubt on the validity of the promises of the *Aufklärung*," and in rejecting it, they reject the "society which has proved incapable of absorbing them." Those acclaimed leaders of the "early" Romanticism who lived beyond the age of thirty—the brothers Schlegel, Schleiermacher, and Tieck—spent long years between one occasional employment and another, waiting for the position of their dreams. When Wilhelm Schlegel was finally appointed a professor (at the University of Bonn, in 1818), a position for which he had prepared all his life, he was fifty-one years old. Schleiermacher was only thirty-six, when, already a well-known author, and after years of obscurity and frustration as a private tutor, chaplain to the Charite Hospital in Berlin, and a pastor of Stolpe, he became a university preacher and professor of theology at Halle. But to him this seemed long overdue, and the position appeared so precious that the threat of Halle being closed by the French was one of the sources of that passionate national patriotism which made him famous in his later years. Friedrich Schlegel and Tieck ended their days in relative comfort, but to the end remained dependent on the personal patronage of the great of this world. Still, the "early" Romantics were closer to Goethe than to the other *Stürmer und Dränger,* for the discrepancy between expectations and reality in their case was more the result of their inflated desires than of the inclemency of objective circumstances. "There is a type of ambition which would rather be the first among the last than the second among the first," wrote Friedrich Schlegel. "That is the ancient kind. There is another ambition which would rather . . . be the second among the first than the first among the second. That is the modern kind." The Romantic was the modern ambition; even those who, like Wackenroder or von Kleist, could easily get a regular, respectable position in the civil or the military service would not settle for that. A whole generation younger than the *Stürmer und Dränger,* they not only carried on and perfected but were also formed by the mentality which is the subject of these pages. They wanted glory and fame, and aspired to positions of conspicuous leadership. That is why professorships and central preaching posts were considered so valuable. Seeing themselves as higher beings, they craved a tribune which would allow others to appreciate this.[92]

As a movement of thought, Romanticism was a response to the fears and frustrations of the *Bildungsbürger,* generated by the *Aufklärung.* The central value of the *Aufklärung* was reason, and it was rationalism that the Romantics revolted against. In reaction against the alleged source of their sorrows, the creators of Romanticism (or, as Henri Brunschwig rightly calls it, of the *"mentalité romantique"*) used available cultural resources to construct an alternative view. They were drawn to and drew upon Pietism, to the pervasive spirit of which all of them had been exposed and in which many of them had been steeped since their early childhood. Pietism had its own reasons to denigrate the powers of the intellect, which created a natural affinity between it and the Romantics, and possessed an additional merit consisting in that, unlike other alternatives to *Aufklärung,* it had escaped the discreditation by the latter. Romanticism, which was called "a kind of artistic and intellectual Pietism,"[93] thus transplanted Pietistic principles into the secular sphere and there articulated, amplified, and systematized them. Emptied of all specifically Christian content, these principles formed the infrastructure of a *Weltanschauung* which was infinitely more widely applicable, and in this form they exerted their most potent influence.

It is misleading to say that "Romanticism was an outgrowth and extension of pietistic principles or, more accurately . . . that pietism was only an early form of Romantic mentality, applied to the field of religion," as does Arlie Hoover,[94] for this presupposes an identity of source for the two traditions and implies that Romanticism was a result of the inner evolution of Pietism. This is as wrong as to attribute the nature of Romanticism exclusively to the fact that it was a reaction to Enlightenment or to Classicism, though this, among other things, it certainly was, and to represent it as the mirror-image of what it reacted against. It was the specific combination of the two traditions (rationalism, against which the Romantics were reacting, and Pietism, which they used in their reaction) brought together by their existential or structural situation and needs—by their fears, frustrations, and aspirations—which produced Romanticism, and it was these existential or structural situations and needs which provided the generative principle in this case, not either of the two traditions. Equally misleading, however, is the assertion of the otherwise remarkably suggestive and valuable study of Henri Brunschwig, that the Romantic mentality—in all its complexity—is a derivation from the structural position of the Romantics, which does not take into consideration the nature of the traditions which helped to shape their reaction. With different cultural resources the same structural situation would have produced a radically different result, but in the absence of this structural situation, the same cultural resources might not have produced anything and their potentialities might have been left unrealized.

The turn to Pietism as an alternative to rationalism in some—rare—cases was explicit and unreserved; it was in fact a return. A child of an earlier age, Hamann rejected reason because of its inadequacy as a medium of Divine revelation and, like other Pietists, opposed to it emotion, which made the immediate experience of Divine presence, of grace, possible and provided certainty of salvation. *Kopfwissenschaft,* abstract reasoning, was bad because it alienated man from Christ and prevented one from perceiving Him clearly; feeling was good, for it revealed His presence; so the "natural use of the senses" was to be "purified from the unnatural use of abstractions." And yet even Hamann secularized these orthodox Pietistic principles. Unlike "the normal pietist," he stressed the totality of human nature—the faculties of the body as well as the soul—as a proper medium of Divinity. "Nature works upon us through senses and passions . . . Every impression of nature upon man is not only a memorial, but also a pledge of the basic truth: Who is the Lord." [95] Any intense sensation—physical or spiritual—was to be interpreted as revelation and meant consciousness of the Deity. It was not its nature, but depth, spontaneity, and naturalness, which made it holy. Sexuality had a privileged place among the means God used to reveal Himself to man for Hamann, and one can speculate to what extent, in accordance with the principle that consciousness is determined by one's way of life, such sanctified sensuality reflected Hamann's own notorious libido. "Normal"

Pietists were made quite uncomfortable by this. Yet the fact remains that
Hamann felt bound to the fundaments of the Christian belief and saw Christianity as the basis of and ultimate justification for his preferences and actions. The younger generation dispensed with the justification and exulted
in sensualism, making it a supreme independent value, in fact a religion in
its own right.

Brought up in the atmosphere of *Aufklärung* at its most vigorous, the
members of the *Sturm und Drang* generation found the traditional Christian
belief—even if reduced, as in Pietism, almost entirely to the belief in the
person of Christ—intellectually offensive and could not accept it. Goethe, a
one-time "crazy scorner of religion," considered himself "a decided non-
Christian." "If only," he wrote in response to a discourse by Herder that was
still too orthodox for his taste, "the whole doctrine of Christ were not such
a mucky affair [*Scheissding*] that drives me crazy." Nor had he any patience
with Pietists "in their old state of inanition and stupidity without the least
sign of ever emerging out of it." Herder, who was after all a Lutheran clergyman, when it came to his views on religion differed from Goethe but little.
His preaching at Weimar led some to think he was "an atheist, a free
thinker, a Socinian, an enthusiast." He admitted that such suspicions were
not entirely without grounds. His sermons, as he wrote to his future wife,
had "nothing but the name in common with other sermons": "My sermons
are as little clerical as my person, they are human sentiments of a full heart."
With a chair of theology in mind, he did write a passionate tract defending
Genesis against the assault of modern science (*The Oldest Document of the
Human Race*, 1774), but at the same time thought that "the most sublime
name for God" was "World-Spirit" and openly preferred Spinozism. "I do
not recognize an extra-mundane God," he could say. "What is a God, if he
is not in you as an organ among his thousand million organs? . . . According
to [Spinoza] he is the being of beings, Jehovah. I must confess, this philosophy makes me very happy." Alternatively, bemoaning the demise of the
primitive Germanic society, for which he blamed the adoption of Christianity, he could reproach his forebears: "Was not Arminius good enough to be
a God for you?"[96]

The "early" Romantics were similarly unrestrained in their interpretation
of Christianity. "It's only prejudice and presumption that maintains there is
only a single mediator [namely, Christ] between God and man," states "Athenaeum Fragment" #234. "For the perfect Christian—whom in this respect
Spinoza probably resembles most—everything would really have to be a
mediator." "If God could be man," argues Novalis, "he can also be stone,
plant, animal, element, and perhaps, in this way, there is a continuous re-
demption in Nature." "What blindness to talk of atheism!" exclaims Friedrich Schlegel. "Are there any theists? Did any human mind ever encompass
the idea of divinity?" And in regard to the accusation that Fichte was an

atheist, he comments that since the essence of religion is "an interest in the world beyond the senses," Fichte's whole teaching is, in fact, "religion in the form of philosophy." [97]

While persevering in their "enlightened" anti-dogmatism, Romantics valued highly the emotional side of religious faith, and saw the experience of it as beneficial and even necessary components of a full life. As if attempting to appease both the *Aufklärer* and the Pietists in themselves, they redefined religion as the experience of faith, and in doing so elevated experience to the rank of religion. Goethe reflected in *Dichtung und Wahrheit:* "In Faith . . . every thing depends on the fact of believing: what is believed is perfectly indifferent. Faith is a profound sense of security in regard to both the present and the future; and this assurance springs from confidence in an immense, all-powerful, and inscrutable Being. The firmness of this confidence is the one grand point; but what we think of this Being depends on our other faculties, or even on circumstances, and is wholly indifferent. Faith is a holy vessel into which every one stands ready to pour his feelings, his understanding, his imagination, as perfectly as he can." [98]

Among the "early" Romantics this extension of the Pietist idea was most systematically elaborated by the theologian Schleiermacher in the famous *Reden,* the *Discourses on Religion.* The other members of the circle received this work with appropriate enthusiasm, and in their utterances on the subject more or less repeated Schleiermacher's maxims. "The Holy Ghost is more than the Bible," insisted Novalis. "This should be our teacher of religion, not the dead, earthly, equivocal letter." "The mind, says the author of the *Reden über die Religion,* can understand only the universe," approvingly quoted Friedrich Schlegel. "Let imagination take over and you will have a God. Quite right: for the imagination is man's faculty for perceiving divinity." He summarized this proposition differently in another "Idea": "The spirit of the moral man is everywhere suffused with religion; it is his element. And this bright chaos of divine thoughts and feelings we call enthusiasm." The chief merit of Christianity, accordingly, lay in that it was able to give rise to this view of religion: "In our age or any other, nothing more to the credit of Christianity can be said than that the author of the *Reden über die Religion* is a Christian." [99]

In this underemphasis of doctrinal content and stress on emotion the Romantics were still very close to Pietism. The step from this definition of faith as feeling to the definition of feeling as faith was small, hardly perceptible. And yet, in taking it, the Romantics decisively separated themselves from traditional religion of any kind. "Feel your heart with this feeling, great as it is," thus Faust urges Gretchen, enticing her to submit to his passion,

> And when you find full bliss in it,
> Give it whatever name you please,

> Call it rapture! heart! love! God!
> I have no name for it.
> Feeling is all;
> Name is noise and smoke
> Obscuring the glow of Heaven.[100]

Here it is no longer God that reveals Himself in feeling, it is feeling which *is* God. And while Pietism was an outgrowth of an old religion, this is the birth of a new one. The Romantics created a secular religion, and unknowingly opened a new era, for—and this is a fact which is not fully appreciated—it proved to be the seedbed of the secular religions of the nineteenth and twentieth centuries, which changed our lives.

All the basic propositions of Romanticism can be interpreted (and could be used) as defense mechanisms against the fear—or pain of experience—of failure in a society based on the rational principles of *Aufklärung*. The constitutive ideas of the ground layer of this way of thought, such as cultural relativism, totality, individuality, and the exaltation of emotion, provided psychological insurance and amortization of sorts. Denying the superiority of reason and posing equally legitimate alternatives to it, or denying reason legitimacy altogether, Romantics reduced the pain of the actual or possible failure to demonstrate such superiority and protected their self-respect from the actual or potential injury.

The ideas of cultural relativism, totality, and individuality were but different expressions of the notion that reason was not the only or the fundamental virtue, but just one of several fundamental virtues inherent in human nature, and that therefore there existed alternatives to it. This notion represented, logically and chronologically, the first stage of the Romantic devaluation of reason. These ideas were articulated already in the *Sturm und Drang* works of Herder—*The Oldest Document of the Human Race, Another Philosophy of History, To Preachers, On Knowledge and Perception in the Human Soul,* and the essays in *Von Deutscher Art und Kunst,* considered to be the *Sturm und Drang* manifesto. Herder's starting point in these works is cultural relativism. History, he says, is not a unilinear progression toward one ideal equally attractive for everyone: "Human nature is not the receptacle of an absolute, independent, unchanging happiness . . . it attracts everywhere as much happiness as it can . . . the ideal of happiness changes as circumstances and regions change—for what else is it but the sum of the fulfillment of wishes, of the purposes, and the gentle surmounting of wants, which all are transformed according to land, time, and place? So at bottom all comparison is out of place . . . Every nation has its centre of happiness within itself." [101] Thus it is impossible to consider reason the universal principle or standard of achievement, and to judge one culture by the standards adopted from another. Comparison is irrelevant; what matters is how "whole" the culture is, how true to its own nature, how harmonious with its—to use a later concept—*Wesenwille*, its "individuality."

The "totality" of a culture is its "individuality." The degree to which the culture expresses this individuality and fulfills itself is the only criterion by which it may be judged, as it is also its mission and purpose. Whatever its nature, the more fully it is acted out, the better is the culture. Wholesomeness becomes synonymous with moral soundness; onesidedness (and marginality), with unsoundness, corruption. The same principle applies to art, language, any part of culture, and—most important—to the individual himself. "Everyone's actions should arise utterly from the self, according to its innermost character," Herder wrote to Caroline, his bride; "to be true to oneself: this is the whole of morality." [102]

Such was the meaning of morality for the "early" Romantics as well. "A man should be unencumbered and move himself in accordance with his nature, without asking who is looking at him and how," wrote Schleiermacher in "Athenaeum Fragment" #336. In the *Monologen* he confessed: "To become ever more intensively that which I am is my only will. Every action is a special development of this one will. Come then what may!" Friedrich Schlegel combined the moral imperative of self-realization with the Romantic Spinozism: "Every good human being is always progressively becoming God. To become God, to be human, to cultivate oneself are all expressions that mean the same thing." [103]

This admiration for the inner, "natural" capabilities is close to the Pietist (and Hamann's) veneration of oneself as a creation, a vessel, a peculiar medium of God. For Herder, too, each culture had a religious meaning; it was an irreplaceable brick in the Providential construction. But on the whole Romantics dispensed with God: they dissolved the Deity in nature and made individuality and totality primary values. Very much like the Pietist God, Nature, thought Goethe, "seems to have made individuality her supreme purpose . . . She appears to everyone in a peculiar form." "Nature," wrote Schlegel in *Lucinde*, "wills that every individual should be perfect in himself, unique and new, a true image of supreme, indivisible individuality." (He added immediately after, possibly as a touch of Romantic irony, "Plunging deeper into this individuality, my reflection pursued such an individualistic turn that it soon ended and forgot itself.")[104]

Simultaneously, a criterion other than the degree of fulfillment of inner capabilities was applied to all cultures, as well as to parts of culture and individuals. This criterion was logically unwarranted (in fact inconsistent with respect to individuality as such), but answered understandable psychological needs and had recognizable historical origins—in Pietism. Cultures differed in the ways in which they provided possibilities of expression for the various faculties of man: his "undivided soul," the harmonious coexistence of feelings and senses alongside reason. In this context, "totality," in some disregard of "individuality," acquired the meaning of such an undivided soul, "the whole man"—which was to become one of the central ideals (or at any rate slogans) of Romanticism and to reappear in rather unexpected contexts throughout the nineteenth century. And, like Goethe's Nature, which made individuality her supreme purpose but "cared nothing for individuals," [105] Romantics, in redefining "totality" and "individuality," seemed to dispense with the actually existing—and naturally imperfect—human beings. Friedrich Schlegel declared: "Individuality is precisely what is original and eternal in man; personality does not matter much." "Individuals mean less to me than of old," confessed Hölderlin in 1793 to his brother. "My love is the human race—not, of course, the corrupt, servile, idle race that we too often meet . . . I love the race of the centuries to come." [106]

A bias, any bias apparently, whether a preference for reason or for emotion, was unnatural, for it injured totality. It was as "fatal to the spirit" as having or not having a system. The only solution in the latter case, insisted Friedrich Schlegel, was "to combine the two." [107] But to combine perfect rationality with equally perfect emotionalism was tricky. And indeed the impartiality of the Romantics was short-lived. Starting from the proposition that reason was but one natural endowment of humanity, a part of nature and a component of totality, they swiftly proceeded to viewing it as unnatural and an impediment to totality, the means of dissecting, compartmentalizing, the "whole man." It was, we might say, the weapon of alienation. Societies and cultures which were based on or highly valued reason institutionalized and promoted such crippling dissection. Cultural relativism was replaced by the new absolute standards of judgment.

The absolute devaluation of reason and exaltation of its opposite, the irrational, unthinking feeling, was the most characteristic and direct expression of Romantic rejection of the society which failed them. This was the establishment of a new orthodoxy; advocacy of the cause of totality and the "whole" man resulted—via defining these ideals in a certain way—in excluding a substantial chunk, in fact in a "decapitation," of human nature. The "whole" man was mutilated, his rational side was cut off as unholy, and "whole" now meant the unreasoning, "feeling" man. Reason was deadly; life came to be identified with lack of intellectual development. Lack of sophistication led to a superior culture. "The *wilder, i.e., the more living,* more fully active a people is," wrote Herder in the Ossian essay in *Von Deutscher Art und Kunst,* "the wilder, i.e., more living, more sensuous, freer, fuller of lyrical action must be its poetry." Primitive, simple people were incomparably more creative than the so-called civilized society. Learning, wrote Justus Möser, in addition to disrupting German society, "has weakened and perverted all human pleasures." Hamann thought that reason was "unnatural."

"You are right, dear Hamann," agreed Herder; "all learning is of the devil, like the lusts of the flesh." [108] (One wonders why Herder compared reason to the lusts of the flesh, since neither he nor Hamann thought that these latter were of the devil.) Emotion, however, came straight from Heaven. It was the expression of God, of Nature, of Life. It gave value to life, justified it, and was its purpose. It was all this because it was unthinking and natural; it reflected the innocence of the pains of reflection and of the burning, insatiable ambitions to which reflection gave rise; it expressed one's "natural" being and was the medium of totality and individuality. This was the source of the Romantic admiration for the *Volk,* children, and young, simple women, such as the Gretchen of Faust and the Lotte of Werther. They were, as Werther said of children, "so unspoiled [by civilization], so whole" *(so unverdorben, so ganz)*. This was also the source of the Romantic image of women in general, "the creatures of nature in the midst of human society, [who] alone possessed that childlike consciousness with which one has to accept the favors and gifts of the gods," and who had "less need for poetry of poets because their very essence is poetry." Unreflective emotion was an expression of *Wesenwille,* of being at peace with oneself and one's situation. In the simplicity and contentment of Gretchen or Lotte, their creations, later of women in general, or of peasants, whom in their naiveté they believed to be content, the Romantics constructed an image that was the opposite of their own marginality and alienation, which they thought were the products of reason. Unthinking emotion, thus, was both the expression of and the means to happiness. Faust, a prisoner of reason, tried to escape from it and fell in love with the unthinking simplicity of Gretchen:

> What plenty in this poverty!
> And in this prison cell what bliss![109]

They all longed for the "black apron" which had brought momentary contentment to Anton Reiser, unaware that the satisfaction it could afford them would also be at best fleeting.

So it was as the means to true happiness, as against the shallow gratification offered by *Aufklärung* (and denied them), that they glorified emotion. But, paradoxically, they considered every emotion worthy of glorification. It was the intensity, rather than nature, of emotion that was important. As in faith, the reasons for the "deep, irreplaceable feeling of being [*des Daseins*]," for *feeling,* mattered little. "I am delighted; I am happy!" recorded enraptured Goethe. "I feel it, and yet the whole content of my joy is a surging longing for something I do not have, for something I do not know." [110] Accordingly, since pain would arouse intense emotion most readily, Romantics celebrated pain. This attitude, again, though it did not derive from it, was closely reminiscent of Pietism, with the difference that the exaltation of pain here had no redemptory or penitential overtones.

Romantics welcomed pain. "My greatest sufferings are caused by my own heart," confessed Lenz, "and yet, in spite of all, the most unbearable state is when I am free of suffering." Goethe dreaded *Dumpfheit,* the dullness of soul, more than anything, and made it one of the sorrows of Werther, who would lament: "I suffer much, for I have lost the only joy of my life: the sacred, reviving force, with which I created worlds around me—it is no more." This joy—the fullness of feeling—was anguish; feelings tortured Werther. Yet he refused to be consoled and insisted on his right to suffer, to enjoy his suffering to the full, though not for a moment deceiving himself as to the nature of his experience: "Is it not the fate of man to suffer his fill, to drink his cup? . . . why should I pretend it tastes sweet?" A protagonist in *Lucinde* commiserated—somewhat condescendingly—with the meek in spirit: "Oh, these poor people who are afraid of suffering, and don't know what awareness is!" [111] They wanted to have their cake and eat it, too. Excessive, intense emotion was a substitute for self-fulfillment in the world, for the lack of objective rewards and satisfaction. It made their life, indeed, full, and gave it at least the sense of meaning, and so they reveled in this torment. There was a peculiarly perverse rationality in this celebration of irrationalism: they sought to maximize pleasure by maximizing pain.

The exaltation of feeling was a defense-mechanism in dealing with the fear or experience of failure in a world which prized rationality. But while it provided a means of coping with failure, it also increased its probability. It created a snowball effect. The sensibilities of these young men were over-cultivated; they were lured to abandon themselves, to succumb to shattering emotions. This reinforced the effects of competition for scarce resources among the university educated. Torn by their passions, they became really unfit for rational, worldly activity and were further marginalized by their inner life. Like Anton Reiser, they could escape this vicious circle in which they were all caught only by "dreaming themselves into" another reality—the creation of their fantasy. The certainty of failure grew together with the invention of ingenious ways to avoid its realization and the construction of alternative rewards and means of self-fulfillment.

These devices utilized and built on the hypertrophied sensibility of the Romantics—their distinguishing characteristic and the only skill they developed to perfection. The idea of "genius," the *Genie* which gave its name to the *Sturm und Drang* period and was inherited and carried on by the Romantics of the end of the century, was the most important of them. "Genius" denoted original, and thus ultimate, creativity, which turned its possessor into a God on a smaller scale and put him above ordinary mortals; it legitimated extreme sensibility, making feeling both the source and the sign of creative powers. The appeal of this idea was enormous; it gave several generations of unemployed and frightened intellectuals a reason to rejoice in their fate and be proud of themselves. In 1786 Moser noted: "Germany is suffering from an epidemia . . . This is the mania for genius." Goethe, in *Dichtung und Wahrheit,* reflected upon this revolution in values, which in the calm and serenity of his Weimar Classicism he considered an aberration, but to which in the earlier days he contributed perhaps more than any other individual:

> A new world seemed suddenly to come into being. The physician, the general, the statesman, and soon enough anyone who had any pretension to eminence in theory or practice was required to be a genius . . . The term "genius" became the key to everything, and as it was so frequently employed, people came to believe that what it ought to denote was tolerably common. Since everyone was entitled to demand that his neighbor should be a genius, he came to think that he was one too. It was a far cry from the time when it was believed as a matter of course that "genius" is the power with which man is endowed by the laws and regulations as a consequence of what he does. Quite to the contrary: it was displayed only by transgressing the existing laws and overturning regulations, for it openly claimed that there were no limits to its powers. So it was very easy to be a genius . . . If someone trotted around the globe with no great notion why he was doing it or where he was going, it was called a voyage of genius. To embark on a thing which had neither sense nor utility was a stroke of genius. Enthusiastic young men, some of them truly gifted, lost themselves in the infinite.[112]

The idea of "genius" espoused by the "early" Romantics corresponded rather closely to Goethe's mocking description. Genius was indeed thought to be something fairly common, something one had to be. "Though genius is not something that can be produced arbitrarily," declared Friedrich Schlegel, "it is freely willed . . . You should demand genius from everyone, but not expect it. A Kantian would call this the categorical imperative of genius." This was not too difficult a state to achieve: in many cases Romantics dispensed even with the effort to will it freely. According to Novalis, genius was the original state of man: "Instinct is genius in Paradise," he said, "before the period of self-abstraction." Genius was the good—the natural—aspect of man; thus everyone was, at least to some extent, a genius. "To have genius is the natural state of humanity," reads "Idea" #19. "Nature endowed even humanity with health, and since love is for women what genius is for men, we must conceive of the golden age as a time when love and genius were universal." But very few people remained true to Nature in the present, not golden, unnatural age. In it this lofty title could be claimed only by the virtuous, the select few. "Every *complete* [emphasis added] human being has some sort of genius. True virtue is genius."[113] Genius was, then, the expression of totality, of Nature, and thus the polar opposite of reason. "Athenaeum Fragment" #366 stated this polarity: "Reason [*Verstand*] is mechanical . . . genius is organic spirit."[114]

"People of genius have always been permitted to be ignorant and transgressors of the law," said Hamann. To be ignorant and transgress the law became the mark of genius. To be recognized, the inner workings of emotion had to be made manifest, and thus the adulation of genius reinforced the tendency toward overt expression of feeling; impulsivity, irregular behavior were highly praised. Originality was just another facet of this: it was expressed in doing what was not done, and what had not been done before. Genius was not to be learned. Johann Kaspar Lavater's outpourings on the subject, which read as a torrent of exclamations, no doubt should be considered expressions of original genius themselves. "Where there is activity," wrote this distinguished Pietist, "energy, deed, thought, feeling, which may not be learned or taught by men, there is genius! . . . Genius is not learned, not acquired, not to be learned, not to be acquired, it is our unique property, inimitable, divine, it is inspired. Genius flashes, genius creates; it does not arrange, it creates!" Genius, a human god, untutored and bending to no rule, was the opposite of artificiality and of alienation. He was as "whole" as a man could be, and therefore at one with nature, a "species-being" so to speak. "And I cry Nature! Nature! nothing so completely Nature as Shakespeare's characters," cried, on his own testimony, Goethe.[115] The excitement and dynamism of the Romantic prose was as accurate a reflection of what the writers meant to say as the actual words in which they put this intended meaning.

Genius sought fulfillment in basically two areas: art and personal life. The way in which it was translated into art was of paramount significance for the nature of modern art in general; the way in which it found expression in life was of significance not only for modern art.

In art genius became the medium and prophet of God, or—if God was dissolved in nature—of nature, of feeling, of the primeval source of all life. ("Many so-called artists," said Schlegel, "are really products of nature's art.") "Let us now hear the sum of my latest aesthetic," taught Hamann, "which is also the oldest: Fear God and give Him the honor." Since God in nature worked "through senses and passions," art had to be a faithful reflection of senses and passions in their intensity and irregularity. Rules were ruled out. "He who wants to abolish caprice and fancy from the fine arts is like an assassin, plotting against their honor and their life." Both art and artists were seen as divine in the literal sense of the word. The artist was a "human God" (or "God in Human form"—Lavater), a "dramatic God" (Herder), and it is in this sense that poetry was "the mother-tongue of the Human race"—the language spoken by God (Hamann). Art acquired fundamental religious significance: it became the form in which the rightly understood Deity could be properly worshipped, and the embodiment of the new cult of feeling. The authority of the artist was supreme, and his freedom unlimited. "Gods in human form!" screamed excitable Lavater. "Creators! Destroyers! Revealers of the mysteries of God and men! Interpreters of nature! Speakers of unspeakable things! Prophets! Priests! . . . Who is a poet?

A spirit who feels that he can create, and who does create, and whose creation does not only please himself as his work, but of whose creation all tongues must witness: Truth! Truth! Nature! Nature! We see what we never saw and hear what we never heard, and yet, what we see and hear is flesh of our flesh and bone of our bone!" [116] In a manner more reserved, but with equal presumptuousness, Herder exhorted the poet: "For you as a dramatic poet no clock strikes on tower and temple, but you have to create space and time; and if you can produce a world and it cannot exist but in time and space, lo, your measure of time and space lies within you; thither you must bewitch all your spectators, you must impose it on them, or you are—anything but a dramatic poet . . . It matters not how or where the dramatic poet carries you away; if he can carry you away, there is his world." [117]

The views on art and artists of the "early" Romantics—concisely expressed in Friedrich Schlegel's "Fragments"—differed from those of the passionate *Stürmer und Dränger* only in their authoritative tone and aphoristic obscurity. The rejection of all limits to the liberty of the artist is reflected in the attitude toward poetry. "People criticize Goethe's poems for being metrically careless," Schlegel noted ironically in "Critical Fragment" #6. "But are the laws of the German hexameter really supposed to be as consistent and universally valid as the character of Goethe's poetry?" In another "Fragment" he proceeded to define poetry. "Poetry is republican speech," he said, "a speech which is its own law and end unto itself, and in which all the parts are free citizens and have the right to vote." The famous "Athenaeum Fragment" #116 ("Romantic poetry is a progressive, universal poetry") contains the classical expression of this attitude: "[Romantic poetry] can be exhausted by no theory and only a divinatory criticism would dare try to characterize its ideal. It alone is infinite, just as it alone is free; and it recognizes as its first commandment that the will of the poet can tolerate no law above itself." Artists were elevated high above simple mortals. "What men are among the other creatures of the earth, artists are among men." This was so, again, because artists represented God on earth. "To mediate [between God and man, for instance, like Jesus Christ] and to be mediated are the whole higher life of man and every artist is a mediator for all other men." Making art, however, did not necessarily make one an artist, and many of those who were actually engaged in making it were not included, for they were not "creators" in a higher sense. Only a genius (as defined by the Romantics) apparently could be an artist. Schlegel insisted: "Not art and works of art make the artist, but feeling and inspiration and impulse." At the same time, similarly to the genius, anyone who wanted to acquire the exalted office of mediator between God and men could do so, for, Schlegel claimed, "everyone is an artist whose central purpose in life is to educate his intellect." [118]

These Romantic principles were put to practice without delay and were immediately evident in the style of its inventors. The tendency to write Fragments rather than completed and articulated works (for completion and articulation had a tint of reflection and artificiality); the violent, torrential rhythm of prose and the incessant use of exclamation signs in the *Sturm und Drang* writings; and the metrical structures of "early" Romantic (particularly Tieck's) poetry[119]—all elements that were adopted unconsciously—no less than the principled rejection of classical form, reflected the fundamental position of the Romantics, and derived ultimately from the mundane frustrations to which it was a response. The belief in the creative potentialities of the genius and deference to his freedom, which sprang from the same source, had long-ranging implications for the place of standards in art, for the hierarchy of different arts, and for the prestige of the artist and art in society.

Perhaps the greatest positive achievement of Romanticism, indeed an invaluable gift which German Romantic intellectuals (in their effort to will into being a world in which they would hold a place commensurate with their worth and denied them in reality) bestowed upon humanity, was the elevation of music to the position of "the most Romantic" and soon "the German" art. The reverence for music and the emergence of the composer as the quintessential genius followed naturally from the exaltation of emotion. Already in Luther one finds the perception of music as the most emotional art, as a divinely inspired form of speech, befitting angels (angels do not speak, they sing). Romantics secularized and amplified this view. Music was the immediate objectification of emotion and therefore partook of its divinity. It was this attitude which established Germany—already, and to no small extent due to the impact of Pietism and mysticism in general, a land of great composers—as the musical center of the world. Romantic music is a result of the internalized principles which constituted the Romantic mentality. Excerpts from Beethoven's letters and diary could easily find a place among the entries in the *Athenaeum;* one finds in them the idea of art as religion and the emanation of Nature, of the artist as a higher, special being, of the genius as a repository of unlearned, original creativity; his ideas are unmistakably those of a Romantic:

> I despise the world which does not intuitively feel that music is a higher revelation than all wisdom and philosophy.

> No metronome at all! He who has sound feeling needs none, and he who has not will get no help from the metronome . . .

> Artists are ardent, they do not weep.

> L'art unit tout le monde,—how much more the true artist!

> Only the artist, or the free scholar, carries his happiness within him.

> There have been thousands of princes and will be thousands more; there is only one Beethoven![120]

These words are naively arrogant, although no more so than Schlegel's "Fragments," and their pathos strikes the reader as pathetic; they never rise to the awe-inspiring grandeur of Beethoven's music. Yet this music would have been impossible had his ideas been different.

One should keep in mind that the view of art as religion was promulgated by intellectuals who since the end of the eighteenth century controlled the media. In the course of time, with their help, art was established as an activity of very high status, and it was because of this, and through art as the revealer of Truth, that many Romantic ideas penetrated and influenced our attitudes in areas of life far removed from intellectual and artistic pursuits.

Similar influence was exercised also in a more direct fashion, by the personal examples of the Romantics and especially by the examples of the very popular heroes of their works. The genius need not be an artist; his godlike qualities were equally evident in everything he did and expressed themselves in the very way he lived. The two types of Romantic heroes, for both of whom Goethe provided prototypes in the figures of Götz von Berlichingen and Werther—one the titanic man of action, the *Kraftgenie,* the other the hypersensitive soul whose existence consisted in intense feeling—exemplified the ways of living which were commensurate with the majestic, elemental nature of genius. So different on the surface, these two types shared one central, revealing characteristic. Though one was action personified, while the other—a plaything of exhausting emotions—was essentially passive, both were expressive rather than goal-oriented personalities, and sought fulfillment apart from the concerns of this world. Both, thus, were not of it, and in this otherworldliness reflected the plight of their creators. In the case of the heroes of Werther's type this is obvious. Emotion incarnate, Werther was consumed, wasted by his passions and "imaginary sufferings" which turned real. In him Goethe demonstrated the destructiveness of excessive sensibility. But the ceaseless activity of the *Kraftgenie* was no less wasteful and destructive. In the *Sturm und Drang,* such active heroes most often were warriors. War as such would provide them with intense experiences and thus was well suited to engage their characteristic powers and provide an outlet for their inner energies. With rare exceptions, such heroes did not fight for a cause; they had no cause; they fought to fight, for the violence of war made them feel alive. A protagonist in Klinger's play *Sturm und Drang* declared: "War is the only happiness I know." The author himself shared in this sentiment entirely. He wrote to a friend with evident contentment: "Where war is, there am I"; fondly referred to military service as "that slavery that flatters our ambition"; and in the end exchanged the laurels of an artist for a military position to live happily ever after. War was idealized; both for an individual and, significantly, for a state it was the proper way of being and self-assertion.[121]

The fact that war frequently led to and caused death did not deter the

Romantics: death was regarded as a thrilling, consummate living experience. "Life is [Nature's] fairest invention," rhapsodized Goethe, "and death
is the masterstroke by which she has much life." Lenz emphasized its sensual
qualities: death was erotic, similar to the consummation of love. Werther's
suicide was in a way a substitute for sexual fulfillment; and it was beautiful—no wonder that so many readers were tempted to experience such an
end themselves. The generation of "early" Romantics was raised believing
that "death can also be a sweet and beautiful thing," [122] in fact that it cannot
be but sweet and beautiful. Novalis glorified death in exquisite prose and in
the poetry of his *Hymns to the Night*—the chief symbol of death itself—
and, too, longed for it as if it were a beloved woman. This moribund poet
considered life a malady, "a disease of the spirit," in a way an abnormality,
for rest (death) was "the peculiar property of the spirit." [123] Therefore, the
closer to death, the better. "The idea of a perfect health is interesting only in
a scientific point of view. Sickness is necessary to individualization." This
friendliness to (in Novalis' case, preference for) death was related, of course,
to the Romantics' pantheistic view of the world. Death was not the end of
existence; it opened a new—and better—stage in it. Novalis proclaimed in
"Athenaeum Fragments": "Death is a triumph over the self that, like all self-
mastering, procures a new and easier existence." [124]

The view of death as a triumph over the self presupposed that it could be
legitimately self-inflicted. Suicide, indeed, held a prominent place in the
thought of the Romantics. Once Goethe started it going, "thoughts and visions of suicide had been such familiar companions" to the German youth
that, for the members of Schlegel's generation, they had already "lost all the
charm of novelty." The charm of novelty, however, was not suicide's only
charm. Suicide was the way "glorious," truly human people, the select, died.
In violently terminating their lives they achieved "freedom" and fulfilled
their destiny. That "mad little book," *Lucinde,* is interspersed with expressions of admiration for suicides. In the *Athenaeum* Schlegel taught: "It is
never wrong to die of one's own free will." [125]

Suicide or not, death became an experience worth living—and dying—
for. It promised the most exquisite sensual pleasure. "Like you I've already
learned to fuse the idea of death fearlessly with that of the highest bliss in
the daring and shamelessness of love," says Lucinde to Julius. [126] This orgias-
tic, erotic notion of death was at least one of the reasons behind the Romantics' peculiar return to Christianity in its Catholic form, in which, like
Goethe, but with different conclusions, they recognized a religion of death.
"Precisely because Christianity is a religion of death," philosophized Schlegel, "it could be treated with the greatest realism, and could have its or-
gies." [127] Thus beautified and tempting, death was invested with a religious
significance all its own. "Isn't every death," wondered Novalis, "a redemptory death? More or less, it goes without saying. And couldn't a number of

extremely interesting inferences be drawn from this?"[128] Such inferences surely could be drawn, and the time they were drew near.

In their veneration of death, especially violent, not natural, death (as in suicide), the Romantics were directly influenced by Klopstock and the Pietist tradition in general, in which death was also idealized, and continued the trend which had originated long ago. In their case all connections to the Passion on the Cross were at least temporarily severed (though they were presently re-established in their newly found Catholicism); the idealization of violence and death derived from a cult of human passions. Owing to the Romantic extension and secularization of this Pietist ideal, death became one of the central values of German secular culture in its very cradle. It was morally good, more than that, glorious, to die, to kill oneself. And since it is generally acceptable to do a good thing to another, it was acceptable to kill. The right to cause death was prudently limited to those who understood that this was a good thing. "Only someone who risks himself can risk others. So too only someone who annihilates himself has a right to annihilate another," advised the preacher Schleiermacher. But it was in the nature of Romanticism to despise prudence, and Romantics would not suffer limits in their desire to realize a lofty ideal. What a beautiful melancholy idea this was, an idea, too, "which no American mind can possibly reckon with." Assessing it in passing in 1913, an American critic, a rationalist, poor soul, reflected: "It is quite certain that 'this way madness lies.'"[129] And yet, how few people in his and later times realized its terrible significance.

For the authors of Romantic fiction, death served a valuable function: it provided a way out of the impasse in which their heroes inexorably found themselves. These heroes incessantly and intensely sought self-fulfillment, happiness, but could never find it. (Their creators knew that it was not to be achieved; that is why one of the names they gave to happiness was "the infinite.") Death put an end to their suffering. The great problem faced by the Romantic generations, which their lives reflected as faithfully as did the literary creations of the most talented among them, was that emotion, private life, however full of passion, and expressive activity such as fighting for no cause—which were after all substitutes for the attentions of the real world that were denied them—if they did not lead to death, led nowhere. So many of the celebrated Romantic ideals—friendship, love, marriage, as much as art and inner life—were substitutions for conspicuously successful public activity. In fact they represented an uninterrupted chain of substitutions: friendship substituting for love, love for infinity, and everything—friendship, love, marriage, sensuality, love of solitude, and so forth—for social acceptance.[130] These substitutions were designed to assuage the "unbearable sense of being unnoticed," to protect one from the pain of forced inactivity, the failure to fit, to participate in the life of the society, and to achieve *conspicuous,* recognized success in it, but they were not viable alternatives. Merely expressive activity, lacking direction, provided no marks with which achievement could be measured; the skills of Romantic intellectuals remained inapplicable and were made even more inapplicable by their hypertrophied sensibilities; the cultivation of feeling failed to satisfy the basic urge, the yearning for social status, it was intended to satisfy. It was only second best and at times seemed no good at all.

Moreover, in their attempt to elevate the source of their discomfort and present it as noble and befitting only the most lofty characters (which would allow them to see in their very misery a sign of election), they made the satisfaction of this very mundane desire virtually impossible. Though it is not difficult to gauge what it was that they felt deprived of from their private letters and diaries, they rarely went as far as Garve, who, in the introduction to his works—publicly—admitted to "a passionate love of the worldly" which "always governed and often troubled" his spirits, and "at all times weighed more than the desire for literary fame." [131] When Romantics transformed their experiences into art, or subjected them to philosophical analysis, they preferred to represent their privation as an in-principle insatiable yearning for something so ethereal and ideal that no earthly language could express it, and disguised its real nature under a series of either poetic or highly abstract euphemisms and allegories. They longed for a society that would accept them and give them their due, and they called it "The Blue Flower." [132] As in so many other respects, the situation of a generation (in fact generations) of young, educated people was similar to that of Anton Reiser, who was plunged into deep depression because of the humiliating lack of clean linen. ("He found it impossible to confess his want, which weighed on him most and was the chief cause of his gloom. He always attributed it to something else, for which he pretended to reproach himself, because the want of linen seemed too petty and unpoetical a subject.")[133] The function of this sublimation was similar to that performed for Anton— and numberless others—by Shakespeare and Werther; it "gave a higher note to their complaints." But at the same time it confined them to "the vacuum of universal enthusiasm." For how did one go about searching for "The Blue Flower"?

Having "no country to defend nor freedom to fight for," they had "nothing left save the pursuit of happiness." [134] And since private happiness was not what they wanted, this was not an easy task. One of the euphemisms for the fulfillment denied them was "action." They believed that their lives lacked it in spite of all their frantic activity. "Action is the soul of the world," wistfully commented Lenz. "God willed that man should be active." His existence was confined to imaginary sorrows, great sorrows conjured in the mind, and he was undone by them. Before he went mad, though, he gave a most explicit, poignant expression to the Romantic frustration. Perhaps he went mad because he could so clearly perceive that the flimsy devices they put so much energy into elaborating lacked the power to satiate their desires. In the review of Goethe's *Götz* Lenz wrote of emotions without "action":

> But can this be called being alive? can it be called feeling your existence, the spark of God? Ah, the attraction of life must be something better: for to be a plaything of others is a dismal, oppressive thought, an eternal slavery, an artificial, rational, but for that very reason all the more wretched brutishness. What do we learn from this? . . . This we learn: that action, action is the soul of the world, not enjoyment, not sentimentality, not ratiocination, and only so do we become images of God, who incessantly acts and incessantly rejoices over his works. This we learn: that [without action] all our enjoyment, all our feelings, all our knowledge are merely passive, merely a postponed death. This we learn: that this our active energy may not rest, may not cease to operate, to stir, to rage, before it has created freedom about us, room for activity, good God, room for activity, and even if it be a chaos that you have created, waste and void, but freedom would dwell therein, and then, like thee, we could brood over it till something emerged—Bliss! Bliss! a godlike feeling, that!

Had he known that in not more than thirty years his dream would come true, that there would be room for activity, and chaos, and waste, and void—enough for many generations of the likes of him to brood over—had he known all this, he would have persevered perhaps. But he could not know. He felt that his hands and feet were bound, and, like Schlegel and so many others a generation later, he turned to literature, for there was nothing better to do.[135] But this was not enough: literature only brought the discrepancy between the desires of the Romantics and the life they actually lived into focus; they dissected and articulated the feelings and the suffering of their heroes and were becoming still more acutely sensitive themselves. The higher they praised feeling, the worse they felt. They demanded satisfaction. In a poem called originally "My First Hymn," and then "Eduard Allwill's Only Hymn," Lenz addressed to the Deity a passionate, desperate plea to soothe his yearning:

> How the flame of life doth burn!
> God, it kindled at thy will.
> And thy love grants me in turn
> All the joy it may instill . . .
> Once I tasted, it is true
> Moments full of sheerest bliss.
> But in moments, God, so few,
> Thy reward should lie in this? . . .
> No, I cry—O Savior! Father!
> My heart's yearning must be stayed,
> Must be sated: if not, rather
> Smash the image thou hast made![136]

For the leaders of the *Sturm und Drang* it all ended well. The yearning of those who did not commit suicide (as did Merck) and did not become insane (as happened to Lenz) was sated. Both Goethe and Herder found their equivalent of the infinite at Weimar; Klinger had a successful military career in Russia. The geniuses went into service and left their rebellion behind as a memory of childhood, amusing, but unimportant. They were, to put it concisely, co-opted. Among those who helped to bring about the exquisite bloom of German Classicism, Duke Carl August of Saxe-Weimar should be thanked, perhaps, more than any other single individual.

For the change of fortune was followed by a change of heart, complete in the case of Goethe, wavering but unmistakable in that of Herder. Klinger left literature. How closely the two changes were connected, how closely they followed one upon the heels of the other, may be gauged by the comparison of Götz and Werther with Iphigenie and Wilhelm Meister, in whom duty and self-limitation replaced both unbridled rage of titanic energies which confused freedom with anarchy, and endless yearning. Goethe became reconciled with society; he accepted modernity and reason and wholeheartedly embraced the rationalistic French culture. Herder, as Goethe noted in *Dichtung und Wahrheit,* would never forgive the world his early humiliations and fears, and his hostility to modern civilization continued undiminished. Yet he too was no longer a champion of everything that was opposed to it.[137]

The prophets of "original genius" abandoned their God. But this did not happen to those numbers of humbler faithful whom they persuaded to believe in him. These did not relapse into Classicism, but carried the new faith further and further, until it penetrated deep into the mind of the people, and the Romantic way of thinking and feeling became the German way of thinking and feeling.

### Romantic Social Philosophy

Society and politics were not at the center of the Romantics' attention. Like Pietists, they saw these as mundane; to be preoccupied with the mundane was beneath them. "Don't waste your faith and love on the political world," advised Friedrich Schlegel, "but in the divine world of science and art, offer up your inmost being in a fiery stream of eternal creation."[138] Yet they laid the groundwork of a most portentous social philosophy.

Like everything else in the Romantic *Weltanschauung,* this social philosophy reflected the *Bildungsbürger*'s intense dislike of the society in which they were living and in which they felt neglected, and represented an embodiment of the principles of totality and individuality. Its basic tenets were first articulated by Herder. The individuality of each society, he argued in *Another*

*Philosophy of History* and elsewhere, arose out of its material conditions. By placing a society in a specific environment, God provided a particular principle around which the society was organized. The material conditions were not chosen; they were given, and the moral perfection of a society, like that of an individual, consisted in abandoning itself to its nature determined by these given circumstances. "The perfection of a thing is its reality," believed Herder after Spinoza; Goethe, too, thought that "the concept of existence and perfection is one and the same." [139] The Romantics concurred in this adulation of necessity. But, curiously, this principle did not apply to modern, that is, "enlightened," society—at the time represented by France, England, and Prussia. The fact that this society put a premium on reason was not interpreted as a reflection of its material conditions; the reality of the modern, rational society was not viewed as a sign of its peculiar perfection. Instead, modern society was considered an exception among human societies, an aberration. In contrast to past societies, which did not value reason, but were "organic," little affected by the division of labor, and in which community was cohesive and man "whole," the unholy effect of reason was to divide the community and to split man, making him a part, a sickly shadow of himself. Reason weakened emotions, "desire, instinct, activity"; it separated the heart from the head, the rulers from the people, and mental from physical labor. Community was replaced by fear and greed, and chimerical freedoms, such as in England, concealed real slavery. Modern, rational society was a catastrophe: "three parts of the world laid waste and controlled, and we ourselves depopulated, deprived of our manhood, sunk in luxury, exploitation, and death." [140]

It was specifically the plight of the man of letters which aroused Herder's sympathy. He knew from experience that the life of an intellectual in his day was burdened "by slavish expectations, timidly slinking diplomacy, and confusing premeditation." In early societies, Herder wrote in the "Essay on Knowledge and Perception in the Human Soul," men could be "everything, poets, philosophers, surveyors, legislators, musicians, warriors," but the division of labor created "half-thinkers and half-feelers; moralists who are not doers, epic poets who are not heroes, orators who are not administrators, artistic legislators who are not artists." [141] In modern society man became alienated, and the man of letters was the quintessential alienated man.

The Romantics' indictment of the "enlightened" society was a generalization of their personal experience in it. The unfulfilled promise of the *Aufklärung* to them—the unsuccessful intellectuals—which was responsible for their "unattached" state and turned them into pariahs, led them to think that reason separated man from community. A society that venerated reason forced men into painful isolation, and was unnatural and unhappy. To this unnatural society they opposed their image of an ideal *natural* community, which would put an end to isolation and exclusion, leave no one and nothing out, but gather all within its iron embrace. In short, they envisioned a totalitarian society.

As they were committed to fight rationalism on all fronts, they could not but scorn the methods of rational discourse. Clear definitions, the very notion of a concept, were anathema to them, and they welcomed confusion. Indeed, a double confusion supported the notion that totalitarianism was a natural state of man. In the first place, they failed to distinguish between a concrete society and social reality in general, and, second, they identified society, social reality, and the state. An attempt to grasp the unfathomable, lofty social reality with the help of analytical distinctions was nothing but sacrilege; an *idea* "that moves freely through all times and recognizes everywhere the nature of mankind, of right and of the state," [142] was needed instead. The specific *idea* in this context, which one finds throughout the writings of the Romantics, was in the early nineteenth century given an authoritative formulation by the political philosopher of Romanticism *par excellence*, Adam Müller, and consisted in the following:

The state (possibly owing to the influence of the Protestant, and especially Calvinist, concept of the office, decisively separated from the personality of the ruler and seen as an impersonal entity) was equated with social reality. The word "state" was used synonymously with "society," "social life," "civil life," "civil existence," and the like; it was "the total of the civil life itself." Man was a social being; to live within society was natural for man; human existence was impossible, had never been possible outside of society. "From the very beginning, nature has seen to it that there are always two humans and not just a single one." Naturally, there had never been an age in which the state did not exist. The state, in fact, was human nature itself. "The state is entirely autonomous; independent of human caprice and invention, it arises directly and immediately from where man himself comes from—from Nature—from God, the ancients said ... Man cannot be thought of outside the state ... man lacks everything, if he no longer experiences the bonds of society or the state ... the state is the embodiment of all the needs of the heart, the spirit and the body ... [man] is not conceivable other than in the state ... there is nothing human outside the state." [143]

If "the state" meant "social reality," this impassioned prose was but a tedious repetition of an innocuous sociological truism. Under the magical action of the Romantic logic, however, it was swiftly transformed into a justification for a moral and political imperative and acquired ominous connotations. To be true to one's nature, or individuality and totality, was the very purpose of human existence. Thus to be true to man's social nature became a matter of ethical conduct; a man who did not feel one with society was not an individual and was not "whole." And since "the state," or "society," meant at the same time a particular state, or society—the fatherland—nothing but complete fusion with the existence of a particular state answered the requirements of true humanity. Man's individuality was impossible without fusion with the state; his personality drowned in the individuality of the state. For states, too, were individuals. They were living, willing organisms. In fact, they were more individuals than people. "The state is not a mere factory, a farm, an insurance, institution or mercantile society, it is the intimate association of all physical and spiritual needs, of the whole physical and spiritual wealth, of the total internal and external life of a nation into a great, energetic, infinitely active and living whole," insisted Müller. "The state is a person like the individual. What man is to himself the state is to men," said Novalis; to his poetical imagination it appeared as "the beautiful great individual" whose spirit approached that "of a single exemplary man who has expressed forever one law only: be as good and as poetical as possible." [144]

The state did not exist for the good of men. It was a most unfortunate mistake to think of it in instrumental terms—a mistake which reflected man's alienation in a rational society, his loss of his true and whole self. The state "is too great, too alive to surrender itself exclusively and solely for one of those purposes [like freedom, security, right, and happiness], in conformity with the desires of the theoreticians," thought Müller; "it serves them all, it serves all purposes that can be imagined, because it serves itself." And what good was the good of men anyway? France exemplified the ridiculous pettiness of instrumental considerations. "The best of the French monarchs wished to make his subjects so rich that every peasant would have every Sunday chicken and rice on the table. But would not a government be preferable," asked Novalis, "under which a peasant would rather have a slice of moldy bread than a roast in another country, and yet thank God for the good luck of having been born in his land?" [145]

The purpose of the state was, of course, to preserve its individuality. If one understood the organic, living nature of the state, one could not conceivably desire to change any particular state. "If one regards the state as a great individual encompassing all the small individuals," believed Müller, "then one understands that human society cannot be conceived except as an august and complete personality—and one will never wish to subject the inward and outward peculiarities of the state, the form of its constitution to arbitrary speculation." Moved by its exalted purpose, the state, clearly, could not tolerate independence, indifference, or insufficient enthusiasm on the part of the smaller individuals who composed it. Toleration—that watchword of the *Aufklärung*—was generally scorned by the Romantics. To Novalis it was one of "the monstrous phenomena of the modern age," while Schleiermacher enigmatically declared: "Tolerance has no object other than destructiveness." On these grounds Müller defended the medieval state, justly intolerant of "anything which was exempted from its authority," and wondered, "How is it . . . possible . . . to tolerate . . . a domestic virtue which is entirely opposed to civil virtue . . . an inclination of the heart which is completely antagonistic to external obligations, a science whose work is contrary to all nationality, a religion of indolence, of cowardice and of isolated interest, which completely destroy the energetic spirit of political life? This is worse than the state within the state." There was to be no distinction between the private and public spheres, no corner where an individual could rest from the intensity of his civic life. The Romantics rested for too long. For too long they were reduced to a miserable, inconspicuous existence in a corner. They knew for a fact that life within the state "alone could be called truly life." [146]

The dreamy Romantic literati were not the only worshippers at the altar of "the increasing majesty of the state." It is important to remember that. Their nebulous effusions on the subject had an exact (in the sense of both very similar and rigorously argued) parallel within the bastions of scholarly learning. Venerable professors of philosophy (and not only Fichte and Schelling, personally involved with the Romantic coterie) who never openly renounced reason, but only redefined it out of existence, backed the collectivistic totalitarian view of the state with their formidable authority and fortified it with the iron, though somewhat idiosyncratic, logic that was the just foundation of their fame. While Kant's position on this matter was ambivalent, no ambivalence characterized Hegel's theory. For him the state was an organism, an "ethical totality," and the only vehicle through which the true individuality of any particular human being, that is, one's humanity, could be expressed. It was "the achievement of all, the absolutely accomplished fact, wherein individuals find their essential nature expressed and where their particular existence is simply and solely a consciousness of their own universality." [147] Like the Romantics proper, the Romantic Hegel advocated total integration of the interests of the individual with those of the collectivity: in a society or an age which allowed the existence of particular interests of any sort, the individual was split, he was *alienated* from his true (social) nature and thus from his own self.

Like people, states vied with each other and were moved by a "powerful striving for the possession of importance and splendour." This was natural. Natural, too, was the chief means they chose to satisfy this desire—war. Wars were "great institutions for the refinement of the idea" and reflected the "inner destiny of the human race." [148] In war the individuality of the state was revealed most forcefully, it showed itself as a totality, as one great beautiful *Kraftgenie*, while peace fostered discord and undermined its unity.

Corresponding notions of freedom, equality, and ideal political behavior were articulated simultaneously with this view of social reality. The Romantics had no understanding and no taste for the liberty of the individual— namely personal independence and freedom from coercion and arbitrary government. Freedom defined that way seemed alien to them, and they ridiculed it. "The subjects of several countries [that is, England and France]," noted Wilhelm Schlegel scornfully, "boast of having a great many freedoms, which would become wholly superfluous through the possession of freedom." [149] The real freedom *(jene uralte, lebendige Freiheit)* [150] which mercilessly underscored the pettiness and insignificance of all other notions of freedom was the freedom to fulfill the purpose of nature, to become "whole," that is, true to and fully conscious of one's individuality. Plainly put, it was the recognized necessity. The achievement of such full consciousness of individuality, for men, was possible only through fusion with the state, and thus freedom resulted from and was only possible because of the unconditional subjection of the individual to collective authority and the virtual dissolution of the individual personality within the state. The state was "nothing but the articulation of the concept of freedom," "that form of reality in which the individual [by definition] has and enjoys freedom; but on the condition of his recognizing, believing in, and willing that which is common to the Whole." Consequently, what the state demanded from its members as a duty was "eo ipso our right as individuals." [151]

While freedom was made to mean the total lack of independence, its corollary in Anglo-American and French political thought, equality, was rejected altogether. This rejection, however, was a result of the very same reasoning and also followed from the Romantic concern for individuality. Individuality, as was noted above, had two essentially incompatible meanings. They were used interchangeably, as the need arose, and owing to the confusion which was taken to be the sign of creativity and cultivated, added spice and pathos to the very same texts, without anyone being upset by the glaring contradiction between them. The original meaning was that of one's peculiar nature. It was certainly a carry-over from Pietism, which considered each human being a peculiar vessel of God. One's individuality in this sense, an irreplaceable brick, however tiny, in the Providential scheme, or alternatively a token of God's inscrutable wisdom, was sacred and to be jealously preserved. This peculiar nature apparently revealed itself in, among other things, one's calling, or position in life, which, too, thus partook of divinity. God willed the social world as it was; to desire to change it was impious. This was both a specific expression of and a reason for the Pietist acquiescence with the status quo. Hierarchy was sanctified. Most of the Romantics forgot about the theological justification for the celebration of heterogeneity, but since they had their own reasons to praise it (for it obfuscated the singular virtue of reason), they also considered individuality defined as peculiarity to be sacred. Nor did they need theological grounds for treating hierarchy as sacred, too. They believed that in a society where everyone kept his place, and was not lured away from it by empty promises, people were happier. Happiness was an expression of *Wesenwille,* of wholeness; people were happy in their place because they achieved individuality. Thus it was not only foolish but wicked to desire equality—it went against nature.

The other meaning of individuality was that of one's *human* nature. It contradicted the first, for it emphasized what one (allegedly) had in common with the rest of humanity, and not at all what made one unique. Nevertheless, in regard to equality, individuality as the expression of universality led to the same conclusion. The postulate that what was most sacred in every human being (his individuality) was his humanity, what he shared with the human species as a whole, contradicted not only the alternative postulate that what was most sacred in every human being (his individuality) was his peculiarity, but, on the face of it, also the demand that men forever remain unequal. The derivation of this latter conclusion from the first postulate demanded some philosophical doing. For a great mind such as Hegel's, however, this did not present any difficulties. He assumed that the self-consciousness (the consciousness of one's true individuality) that the individual acquired through the dissolution of his personality in the state, as it penetrated from the higher individual (the collectivity) down, stopped on the level of a "specific particularity," or, in other words, one's class or station. A human individual, therefore, could not acquire the consciousness of his individuality but as a member of a particular class. The preservation of distinctions between classes and stations became an indispensable means for the fulfillment of the highest good and the purpose of nature, as well as for human self-fulfillment, and thus a good in itself.

The intellectuals' dissatisfaction with their personal situation, their frustration with the principles of the *Aufklärung,* which was the direct, though not the main, cause of their predicament; their extrapolation from their experience to the experience of man in general in a society based on reason; and the ensuing humanitarian concern thus led to some rather disconcerting conclusions. To be free, it appeared, man had to renounce all independence; to be happy, he had to reconcile himself to the place assigned to him in the larger scheme of things and was never to will to change it. Not less disconcerting was the proviso that these conclusions applied only to other men; they did not apply to Romantic intellectuals themselves. For the Romantic rejection of the *Aufklärung* was incomplete. The intellectuals resented its failure to fulfill its promise, but clung to the promise itself: by hook or by crook the world had to belong to those with superior mental powers. Their claim to status in society rested on their intellect, and they were not willing to give this claim up. They magnified and deified the faculties that set them apart, and though they redefined the intellect and no longer meant by it the capacity for calm, analytical reflection valued by the *Aufklärung,* they nevertheless perpetuated the characteristic of the German- (as against Anglo-American-) "enlightenment" inclination to see in the intellect the ground for the inequality, rather than equality, of men.

Through the opening created by this insistence on the exceptional and superior nature of some individuals, the Romantic concepts of "genius" and "art" entered politics, where they acquired portentous significance. Artists were seers and oracles; they could divine history—that is, Providence—and thus could provide an alternative route to individuality for lesser men. "Artists make mankind an individual," wrote Friedrich Schlegel, "by connecting the past with the future in the present." They recognized necessity as, and better than, did other human beings, but their perspective on it was infinitely grander, and therefore their necessity was infinitely less limiting. In the eighteenth century the Romantics were apolitical and contemplative. They saw no place for themselves in politics, and reacted accordingly. Friedrich Schlegel, who seemed to be able to find virtue in any necessity, wisely advised: "The artist should have as little desire to rule as to serve. He can only create, do nothing but create, and so help the state only by making rulers and servants, and by exalting politicians and economists into artists." Quite innocently the Romantics proceeded to do just this. They defined political leaders as artists ("A true prince is the artist of artists," ruled Novalis) who spoke directly to God and owed respect to no human law. "What great men accomplish in enthusiasm, in which their whole being and the higher humanity in them raises and glorifies and reflects itself," asserted a character in a piece by the immensely popular Jean Paul Richter, "that is right for them and their fellows, but for them alone." "Yes," the author agreed with him, "there must be something loftier than mere law." [152]

This definition resulted in a new and sinister ideal of political leadership. The thorough collectivism and anti-individualism of the Romantics ruled out parliamentarian alternatives of government, and they, like the *Aufklärer* and the eighteenth-century German intellectuals in general, although for different reasons, tended to favor authoritarianism. The Romantic authoritarianism, the rule of a political "genius," was, however, essentially different from other varieties and, if implemented (as it eventually was), would be infinitely closer to absolute power than any exponent of enlightened absolutism could ever hope to be. For this was authoritarianism unrestrained by either tradition or reason and expediency—charismatic revolutionary leadership *par excellence,* unaccountable by nature and demanding unconditional devotion.

The social ideal of the Romantics reflected the intellectuals' dissatisfaction with their personal situation. It represented an inverted, upside-down image of social reality as they knew it. It was a remote ideal, similar to the infinite, and equally unattainable. This image against which Romantics measured reality remained constant. But sometimes it seemed to them that they perceived its features in the past, sometimes they saw it in the future, or in some distant lands. Examples to which they pointed lacked precision, and they were not particular about the terms they employed. "The revolutionary de-

sire to realize the Kingdom of God on earth," wrote Friedrich Schlegel referring to this ideal, "is the elastic point of progressive civilization and the beginning of modern history. Whatever has no relation to the Kingdom of God
is of strictly secondary importance in it." Since the location of the ideal in
time varied, the means believed to be necessary for its attainment and the
institutional forms of the values it embodied differed, too. Later, left and
right, radicals and conservatives, would adjust to this matrix equally well.
Most of the "early" Romantics, on the whole, preferred the past. But even
the fascination with the Middle Ages, so characteristic of the period that it
is frequently identified with the Romantic mode of thought, was not essential to their social philosophy. When regarded as an embodiment of the
Kingdom of God, the medieval society assumed the characteristics of this
ideal image, rather than molding this image in terms of its own historical
characteristics. And even the "early" Romantics did not always find this
retrospective vision satisfactory. The only thing Friedrich Schlegel found to
criticize in his "Critical Fragments" "about the model of Germany, which a
few great patriotic authors have constructed," was "its incorrect place-
ment." "It does not lie behind," he said, "but before us." [153]

Wherever it lay, the ideal society in which all the wrongs suffered by *Bildungsbürger* because of the unfulfilled promises of Enlightenment would be
corrected was the never-never land of the perfect Community. One can
understand and even sympathize with their yearning for it: they wanted to
escape a condition which caused them pain. But why have the intellectuals
of the West been so taken up by this fantasy? How could we take this creation of bitter and fevered imagination for a scientific description of a possible—and more than that, desirable—reality? Why have we for almost two
centuries admiringly followed those pied-pipers in their search for the Romantic dreamland (that terrible land of totally absorbing society, in which
the individual was sacrificed to the higher individuality and found freedom
and happiness in submission, and which was ruled by the unaccountable
and unrestrainable semi-divine men of "genius" whose power was absolute)? We must leave this question for another occasion, but it is worth pondering.

## III. The Materialization of the Spirit

### The Impact of the French Revolution

The social philosophy of the Romantics, like the Romantic mentality in general, developed as a response to the depressing situation of the *Bildungsbürger*. The intellectuals did not perceive any realistic way out of their predicament. Extraordinary abilities were developed in them which cried for public

expression and recognition. They were trained to become men of importance in their society, but were doomed to obscurity and scorn. Their imagination, the cause of many of their sufferings, was also their only protection. They dreamed their humiliation away, and convinced themselves that the neglect and alienation which they could not escape were the signs of election and true nobility, and were freely chosen. Love, friendship, marriage, titanic emotions, suffering, art, the yearning for the infinite, even "glorious inactivity" were so many ways they conjured to ennoble and justify their lack of success, of which they were ashamed, in achieving the social position of honor they had prepared themselves for—that is, the inactivity they in the depth of their soul felt as ignominious. The totalitarian Kingdom of God was another such device. The enlightened society was evil to the extent that it would be simply unnatural not to be alienated in it. The Kingdom of God, on the other hand, was so remote an ideal that it did not seem to be within human powers to bring it about—and one would be foolish to try to—and so it was quite enough, and a service to humanity, just to philosophize about it. The conception utilized the same building blocks of totality and individuality on which was predicated the rest of the Romantic worldview, and thus had its own momentum, and could develop regardless of external events. It was, also, initially unrelated to the development of the national consciousness. But, with the rest of Romanticism, and Pietism before and alongside it, this social philosophy prepared the mold, the very skin, bones, and muscle, for the migrant spirit of the national idea, and added essential finishing touches to the character nationalism was to acquire in Germany at the moment of its arrival.

Although this portentous development was mainly fueled from within, the last layers in the fundament of the German national consciousness took shape in the forty years (roughly from 1775 to 1815) under the shadow—or the brilliant light, as the case may be—of the French Revolution. This world-shaking event had such a confusing effect on the Romantic generation that for a time the latter found itself, almost unconsciously, back in the camp of the *Aufklärung*. When the mistake was discovered—in the very last years of the eighteenth century and very first ones of the nineteenth—both the *Aufklärer* and the Romantics abandoned the camp, and "enlightened" Germany was no more.

The story of the German educated reaction to the French Revolution is well known: unreserved rapture, with which it was met, gave way to equally unreserved repugnance and indignation; the final judgment on it was harsh. The initial excitement was due to several factors. The ideas of the Revolution, or at least its slogans, were familiar to the educated Germans who were taught by the *Aufklärung* to recognize in them desirable social goals. G. J. D. von Scharnhorst, the famous Hannoverian and then Prussian general in the wars against France, reminisced in his *French Revolutionary War*:

"When the French Revolution began . . . those who loved reading—that is, most of the educated classes—had already grasped the idea of a better constitution, which had long been seductively preached in novels and poems; and the ideas of liberty, equality, and independence had been thrown into circulation by the American War." [154] It seemed as if the promise of the *Aufklärung* had in fact come true. "It is glorious to see what philosophy has ripened in the brain and realized in the State!" exclaimed Forster. For the discontented middle-class intellectuals, this realization of ideals promised to be of great practical significance. The Revolution preached—and evidently practiced—the gospel of equality; for a moment it appeared that in Germany, too, undeserved privilege would be toppled and merit, intellectual merit in particular, would rise in its place. "The hatred of nobility" was recognized as one of the most common reasons for sympathy toward the French, when the war began, and the lower classes and, significantly, "the scholars" were generally considered the most likely sympathizers. In 1793 Fichte, in "Contributions to the Rectification of Public Opinion on the French Revolution," expressed the opinion of the intellectuals. Addressing the nobility, he wrote: "You fear for us the subjection by a foreign power, and to secure us against this misfortune, you prefer to subject us yourselves? Do not be so confident that we regard the situation in the same way as you do. It is easy to believe that you prefer to subject us yourselves than to leave it to somebody else; but what we cannot understand is why we should prefer it so much." H. Ch. Boie frankly suggested insubordination: "For whom are they calling upon you to fight, my good German people? . . . For the vile breed of princes and nobles and for the priestly vermin!" Hölderlin counseled his sister to pray for the French and wrote to his mother to take the war lightly: "Wherever it had penetrated in Germany, the good citizen has lost little or nothing and gained a great deal." [155]

The identification with France was made easier by the sense that it was no longer French. Since the German intellectuals saw in the Revolution the fulfillment of the *Aufklärung,* they found no difficulty in believing that the revolutionaries were moved by the plight of suffering Humanity, and that their concern for the French nation was of secondary importance. Cosmopolitanism, which, though widespread, had previously been more of an expression of diffuse indifference than of ardent feeling, turned into a passion, while the slowly brewing resentment against the French, which accompanied the yet unformed but already wounded national pride, retreated into the background. The letters of Joachim Campe, written from Paris in 1789, clearly reflected the new sentiment, as well as the sentiments it replaced. "Is it really true," the famous educator wrote in the first letter,

> . . . that I am in Paris? . . . I could have embraced the first people, who met us. They seemed no longer French . . . All national differences and prejudices

melted away. They had regained their long-lost rights, and we felt that we were men . . . Even before we reached Paris, I often asked myself, Are these really the people we used to call and think of as French? Were the shrill chattering dandies, the arrogant and brainless swaggerers who used to cross the Rhine and turn up their noses at everything they saw in Germany—were they only the dregs and scum of a nation of which on our journey we have not seen a single example? Or has their whole character so changed with their revolution that the noble elements which were underneath have now come to the surface, and vulgarity sunk out of sight? . . . the cleansing of [the French] national character in the purgatorial fires of liberty is a fact which has struck German and other observers who were here before the Revolution.[156]

No wonder that the "patriotic intoxication" of the Parisians on the night of August 4, noted by certain observers from Germany, perplexed and even disconcerted them. Still, in 1789, it failed to tint their opinion of the grand event. It was natural that, since all national differences and prejudices had melted away, the fact that Frenchmen had regained their long-lost rights made German intellectuals feel that they, too, were men, and they eagerly expected direct and personal benefits from the French upheaval.

But they were impatient. "My heart is heavy," complained Novalis to Friedrich Schlegel, "that the fetters do not already fall to pieces like the walls of Jericho." The welcome transformation tarried on the way, and the hope was abandoned. The consciousness that one was misled, that one hoped in vain, led to a drastic change of sentiment. The opinion of many a German intellectual about the French Revolution transformed overnight, yet this did not happen at the same time in every case. This lack of synchronization makes it difficult to attribute the disgust which replaced unqualified admiration to the shock to sensitivity caused by the revolutionary excesses, to which, in retrospect, many did attribute their about-face, an argument later backed by historians. Nursed as they were at the springs of Pietism, Klopstock, and *Sturm und Drang,* the Germans saw nothing wrong in violence. During the days of their short-lived revolutionary enthusiasm, they in fact had been rather annoyed when anyone pointed to the excesses and saw in them the reflection of the evil nature of the Revolution. "Blessed be its influence on nations and rulers," wrote Johannes Müller of the Revolution in 1789. "I am aware of the excesses; but they are not too great a price to pay for a free constitution. Can there be any question that a clearing storm, even when it works some havoc, is better than the plague?" Johanna Schopenhauer remembered later "the ardent love of liberty which burned in every young breast." "Murders and excesses committed," she wrote, "were regarded as inevitable incidents in a time of excitement." [157]

In some cases, at least, the decision, or rather the impulse, to change sides was directly related to the degree to which persistent hope in a better future interfered with the possibilities of a comfortable present, and the extent to which such possibilities were indeed open. The opportunities, after all, depended on those who could regard sympathy with the revolutionary cause as a personal affront. Thus Johannes Müller, employed as the secretary of the Elector of Mainz since 1788, seeing no sign that liberty would triumph in Germany by the spring of 1792, no longer felt inclined to sympathize with its cause. "People have told [the Elector] that I am a democrat and mixed up with the enemies of princes," he wrote at the time anxiously. "I am not . . . these cabals are a great worry to me." Indeed he turned into a sworn enemy of the Revolution, by which, as he saw it now, "all mankind was outraged in their deepest feelings," and did not lose an opportunity to stress that he, personally, was "for evolution, never for revolution." "Since the Elector ennobled him, made him his Councillor, and called him to his table," noted once an admirer of Müller's, Reichardt, "he is as zealous for the Emigrés and as hostile to the Constitution as he was previously enthusiastic for liberty and the rights of man." [158]

Young men, who could disregard the concerns of adult life, or men for whom no opportunities were open anyway, persisted much longer. Friedrich Schlegel, that eminently excitable young man, wrote to his brother in May 1796: "I am tired of criticism and shall work at revolutions with incredible enthusiasm. I shall also write something popular on republicanism . . . I do not wish to conceal from you that I have republicanism even more at heart than divine criticism or still more divine poetry." Even he, however, was aware of the danger such audacity might have presented for his advancement—had the new world he wished for failed to materialize—and he did not neglect to take the necessary precautions. In preparing the essay on "The Conception of Republicanism," which was published in 1796 in Reichardt's *Deutschland,* he chose to abide by the following rule (revealing both his anxiety and the spirit of Romantic science): "Because of the rigor of the scientific approach," he decided, "I shall refrain from any allusion to facts." He also comforted himself with the consideration that "the obscurity of abstract metaphysics will protect me. When one writes solely for philosophers, one can be incredibly daring without anyone in the police perceiving it, or even realizing how daring it is." After his hopes for a professorship were ruined, Henri Brunschwig tells us, Schlegel gained courage, and since there seemed nothing else for him to lose in this world, he put his faith in the prophets of the new one. In 1799, Dorothea, his wife, still hoped for salvation from the West: "The whole world is talking of Buonaparte. Can one not put one's trust in the fortunes of a truly great man?" That same year Caroline, Wilhelm Schlegel's, later Schelling's, wife, wrote to her daughter: "And now Bonaparte is here! Rejoice with me, or I shall have to think that you are not good for anything save romping and haven't a serious thought in your head." [159] The admiration for Napoleon among the Romantics was general.

Schlegel's circle, however, was among the very last champions of the revolutionary cause in Germany. And the mood was changing rapidly at the time even among Schlegel's familiars. The political works of Novalis distinctly sounded a new note. In *Die Christenheit oder Europa* (Christianity or Europe) he condemned the Revolution, the values it stood for, the nation that made it, and the age in which it occurred. Though a "Fragment," this essay represented an early self-contained statement of the *Weltanschauung* of mature Romanticism, and the arguments which first appeared in it were later to reappear again and again in German thought.

Novalis saw the Revolution as the final stage in the process of alienation and spiritual destruction started by the Reformation, a child of Reason, which undermined the pristine, wholesome world of Catholic Christianity. He wrote:

> With the Reformation Christendom was lost, and from that time onward it no longer existed . . . Modern Politics originated first during this period . . . religious hatred extended very naturally and consequently to all objects of enthusiasm, and denounced imagination and feeling, morality and the love of art, the future and the past as heretical, and gave man the highest place in the order of natural beings . . . One enthusiasm was generously left to the miserable human race and as a touchstone of the highest education was made indispensable to everyone thus concerned . . . France was so fortunate as to become the source and seat of this new faith, which was pieced together from mere knowledge . . . Light became their favorite subject on account of its mathematical obedience . . . and thus they named after it their great enterprise, enlightenment . . . They took pleasure in enlightening the common people and in training them to this cultured enthusiasm. Thus arose a new European guild of philanthropists and men of enlightenment. It is a pity that nature remained so wonderful and incomprehensible, so poetical and infinite, defying all attempts to modernize it. If anywhere there arose an ancient superstition about a higher world or something similar, alarm was immediately sounded on all sides and, if possible, the dangerous spark was suppressed by philosophy and wit; nevertheless, tolerance was the watchword of the educated, and especially in France it was synonymous with philosophy. This history of modern skepticism is the key to all the monstrous phenomena of the modern age, and only in this century and especially in its later half has it begun to grow to an immense size and variety . . . Shall the revolution remain the French Revolution, as the Reformation was the Lutheran reformation? Shall Protestantism once more be established contrary to nature as a revolutionary government? Is the letter without spirit merely to replace another letter without spirit?[160]

Novalis' answer to these burning questions is: "No!" Salvation will come and it will arrive from Germany, which "goes its slow but sure way in advance of other European countries." In this, too, he established a compelling pattern to be picked up by most unlikely followers in the years to come.

Friedrich Schlegel, in 1799, found the historical conception of *Die Chris-*

*tenheit oder Europa* "too arbitrary," its religiosity excessive; refused to publish the essay in the *Athenaeum;* and ridiculed it. In his case, as in several others of equal importance, it took a visit to France—at that time (in 1802) aglow with new national pride and aspirations—to effect a final conversion and to wean him irrevocably from the cosmopolitan and libertarian preoccupations of the *Aufklärung.* But by the beginning of the new century the transformation was complete. The revolutionary cause in Germany had only enemies. With the victorious advance of the French army, new, unexpected opportunities opened to the intellectuals, and with them the era of nationalism.

## The Birth of German Nationalism

It was the defeat of Prussia in the course of the French revolutionary wars that finally ushered German nationalism into the world. The emergence of the national sentiment was nothing short of miraculous. Notwithstanding the feeble and uncertain expressions of enlightened patriotism among the eighteenth-century *Gelehrte,* the conception in this case seemed to be immaculate and no visible pregnancy preceded the appearance of the infant. Yet, it emerged—endowed with healthy lungs and fists—and at its very birth acquired all the long-formed habits of its native land, to become the unexpected culmination of a century-long development of the German spirit.

For the unattached intellectuals, nationalism indeed was God-sent. It provided a practical, this-worldly solution to their problem, and put an end to their alienation. To Pietism and Romanticism it added directedness and activism—instead of persistence and acquiescence in the status quo, with its dubious emotional pleasures, it offered a goal for which to fight and a realistic possibility of changing the status quo and distinguishing oneself in the world, rather than through *reine Innerlichkeit*—and all this while remaining faithful to the Pietist-Romantic worldview and standards.

The conversion, the transformation of the Romantic mentality into nationalism, was sudden and unforeseen, for the glorious opportunities it offered were created all of a sudden, by an extraneous, unforeseeable event—the intervention and victorious advance of the French army. The idea of the nation was known in Germany throughout the eighteenth century; it was almost commonplace. But until the fall of Prussia and the dismemberment of the Empire, it did not ring a bell. It held nothing in store for the intellectuals marginalized by the unhappy inconsistency between the principles of the *Aufklärung* and the arrangements of the traditional society. Unlike the French and Russian aristocracies, the downtrodden German *Bildungsbürger* had no power to enforce the new definition of nobility and social honor which the idea of the nation implied. To demand it, to insist on the redistribution of prestige in open disregard of the class which controlled its distribution at present, would be inviting frustration and ridicule and was worse than a cry in the wilderness (and thus all sorts of escapism which the intellectuals practiced), for in this case one was certain to be heard. The news of the French Revolution, which inspired them with hope, moved them to do just that, but their optimism was short-lived and heavily tinted with cosmopolitanism. The tragedy of the *Bildungsbürger* was that their predicament was theirs alone. Without nobility and/or bureaucracy at their side, they had no chance whatsoever to change it, and for this the community of interest was lacking. The Napoleonic invasion created such a community of interest.

Whatever the effect of the invasion on the German population as a whole, the attack of the revolutionary army was explicitly directed against and intended to injure the representatives and beneficiaries of the "old order," the aristocracy and the bureaucracy. The intellectuals made the cause of the old order, which they christened the "German cause," their own. This identification allowed them to share in the common humiliation, the humiliation whose brunt was born by the most powerful and respectable members of society, the very groups whose acceptance the intellectuals so fervently desired, and into which this common experience finally afforded them the entry. This grand humiliation in which the *Bildungsbürger* had the privilege of sharing was far less humiliating than the "unbearable sense of being unnoticed" and the abject state of poverty and obscurity which contrasted so painfully with their self-esteem and was their singular dole. It was in fact elevating and filled them with noble sentiments. And for this reason they felt it all the more; they willingly let it eclipse the memory of all their private humiliations and concentrated solely on this collective misfortune. From this time on the pride and the self-esteem they strove to defend was national pride and self-esteem. They changed their identity and became, passionately and irrevocably, Germans.

Owing to the circumstances of its birth, the German national cause was from the start defined as the anti-French cause. This suited the influential groups who were directly affected by the invasion, and they lent a sympathetic ear to the nationalistic admonitions of the intellectuals. For the first time, the intellectuals were explicitly invited to participate in the experience and efforts of the highest ranks of society and were seen by them as valuable allies. Since the *Aufklärung* was irreparably stigmatized by its association with the French Revolution, the positive definition of the German national consciousness was left entirely in the hands of the Romantics. For several decades they vied successfully with the drier and less enchanting *Aufklärung* for the attentions of the German public. They were the voice of their people; they spoke to every German who could read through their novels, poems, and periodicals, and by this means furnished the terms in which their readers thought. Through their writings the Romantic *Weltanschauung* was already becoming the German *Weltanschauung;* their influence had been significant even before the war, though they were unaware of the degree of its significance. But this influence doubled and trebled now that their teaching had the weighty approbation of the upper classes and the governments of states behind it, and was elevated into the official gospel of the new public religion. The happy union of the intellectuals and the establishment lasted but briefly. The attachment was momentary, and with the end of the Wars of Liberation was over, leaving the most ardent of the *Bildungsbürger* "unattached" again. But in the ten years or so of the great collective effervescence in which they were allowed to play the central role, these intellectuals forged the national identity of the German-speaking people. German nationalism is Romantic nationalism. German national social philosophy is Romantic social philosophy, and the German national character is the Romantic character, for the ideal, the "true" German, expressing the individuality of his nation, is either the creature of nature, faithfully obedient to his *Wesenwille,* or the *Genie*—the man of titanic emotions and contempt for the peace and calm of the little men's lives—the creature of nature's art.

While Romanticism left a permanent imprint on the character of German nationalism, nationalism in turn reacted back on Romanticism. It broke the narrow circle of personal life and purely expressive agitation, which had constrained the expressions of the revolutionary inclinations of the Romantic spirit to futile rage about itself, and opened for it a room for activity, the one that Lenz had so fervently hoped for before he went mad. In this room, the spirit was let loose. It became imperative—and seemed possible—to establish the ideal state, instead of simply lamenting the perfidy of the existing reality. It became imperative to fight the holy glorious war, and receive and inflict real wounds, and meet and cause death, instead of simply imagining it and singing its praise. The "gloomy philosophy of quiescence" which Romanticism had inherited from Pietism was transformed into an unshakable belief that the infinite—the Kingdom of God—was within easy reach, and spurred the believers on to a frenzied activity to help in its realization. The Romantic spirit of the nineteenth and twentieth centuries was revolutionary in a way very different from that of the eighteenth: it was determined to be fulfilled in this world. The first expression of this reinvigorated Romantic mentality, and of the nascent German national consciousness, was the war against the French. This explains why German nationalism, which arrived on the stage so late, and almost unannounced, instantly became the most activist, violent, and xenophobic species of the phenomenon.

### First Expressions and Crystallization of German National Consciousness

This German nationalism, full-fledged and endowed with all the characteristics which made it unique, was quickly embedded in the soil which ten years before would have seemed a most unlikely place for its emergence. Friedrich Schlegel, who turned nationalist after his visit to France, and Ernst Moritz Arndt, who in 1802 wrote *Germanien und Europa*, were among the very first converts. But innumerable others followed in quick succession. Collections of folk songs and tales, expressive of the preoccupation with questions of national identity, began to appear in the first decades of the nineteenth century. Ludwig Tieck published his *Minnelieder aus dem Schwäbischen Zeitalter* in 1803, and pointed in the introduction to "the quick change which has occurred in so short a time, so that one is not only interested in the monuments of the [national] past but appreciates them." [161] The first collection of folk songs edited by Arnim and Brentano appeared in 1805, and the "folk-song fever" reached its peak in the next decade, when the brothers Grimm published their famous collections of tales. The patriotic zeal of poets and folklorists was supplemented by that of the scholars in established disciplines. The interest in German history revived. Anxious to foster this interest, Karl vom Stein sponsored the work on the *Monumenta Germaniae Historica*, a monumental collection of sources, which took more than a hundred years to complete, and which at the time of its completion, in 1925, numbered 120 volumes.[162]

It was clearly the preoccupation with the honor of the German nation which inspired the champions of liberal reform in Prussia—Stein, Hardenberg, Humboldt, and their counterparts in the military, such as Scharnhorst, Gneisenau, and Clausewitz. These leaders explicitly stated their motives. Stein wrote that the reforms were intended to create a "civic spirit" among Germans, to bring about "the revival of patriotism and of the desire for national honor and independence"; they aimed at imposing "the obligation upon the people of so loving king and fatherland that they will gladly sacrifice property and life for them." Clausewitz proclaimed fatherland and national honor two earthly deities he felt himself obliged to serve. The interests of Prussia were of secondary importance. "I have but one fatherland," wrote Stein, "and that is Germany . . . to it and not to any part of it, I am wholeheartedly devoted . . . my desire is that Germany shall grow large and strong, so that it may recover its independence and nationality." [163]

*Das Deutsche Volkstum* of "Turnvater" Jahn, published in 1810 and, along with Fichte's *Addresses to the German Nation* of 1808, that "bible of nationalism," recognized by the grateful compatriots as "one of the 'spiritual sponsors' of the new Germanness" and "one of the most precious products of the German spirit," [164] gave national sentiment an articulate ideological expression. In the electrifying sermons of Schleiermacher, who preached it from the pulpit of the Holy Trinity Church in Berlin, this sentiment was represented as a new religion, the true heir of the Reformation, and soon eclipsed the message of the Gospels, adulterated as it was already by the century-old labors of Pietists before him. In 1814, a Junker, F. A. L. von der

Marwitz, unsympathetic to popular nationalism and opposed to reform, which was one of its manifestations, admitted, in a letter to Hardenberg, that "the idea of a common German fatherland has taken . . . deep root. Whoever seizes upon this sentiment will rule Germany." [165]

The sudden conversion to nationalism was in many individual cases triggered by the collapse of Prussia in 1806. At least in some of the most important of these cases, an obvious connection existed between Prussian interests and the personal interests of the neophytes, which were directly affected by the defeat. One of the most influential propagandists of German nationalism, Johann Gottlieb Fichte, was before his conversion a principled cosmopolitan and sympathized with the French. As late as 1799, when, accused of atheism, he lost his professorship at Jena, he hoped for French victory in Germany, for nothing was more certain to him "than the fact that unless the French achieve the most tremendous superiority . . . in Germany . . . no German who is known for ever having expressed a free thought will in a few years find a secure place." Moved by this consideration, he asked to be employed by the French Republic, but then did find a secure place in Prussia. There, until 1805 faithful to his cosmopolitan credo, he remained indifferent to the fate of Germany and untouched by the nationalism to which some of his friends had already converted. The war of 1806 between France and Prussia, however, changed everything. There was no doubt in Fichte's mind that in this conflict France represented the forces of darkness and Prussia those of light, and he longed to be a soldier in its battle. In the absence of a sword, he wished "to talk swords and thunderbolts." [166] The *Addresses to the German Nation,* which were the product of this state of mind, indeed added a formidable weapon to the arsenal of the nation which he now proclaimed his own and through his attachment helped to create.

Similarly, the change in Schleiermacher was effected to a large degree by the fact that the French closed the University of Halle, where he was a professor. He described the circumstances that grieved him in this period of national humiliation in letters to Henrietta Herz,[167] enumerating his concerns in the following revealing order: "The sudden destruction of the school which I was in the act of founding here . . . the probable dissolution of the entire university . . . and added to this the precarious state of our fatherland . . . Dearest, you can hardly conceive how this affects me . . . The thought that it may be my fate for a long time to live only for and by authorship, is very depressing." "This much only is certain," Schleiermacher reflected on the vicissitudes of military fortune, "that as long as the war lasts, there is little likelihood that the university will resume its activity . . . Napoleon must have a special hatred for Halle." This terrible disaster, he concluded, meant that the rod of God's wrath fell on Germany, obviously for its past inability to fulfill the high mission for which it was destined. This paternal punishment was a sure sign of Germany's election. Its very degradation at present made it crystal clear that the triumph of Germany was willed by God, and that everyone had to toil without rest and do his part in helping to bring this triumph about. Patriotism was piety.

German nationalism brought together the Pieto-Romantic mentality, forged and hardened in the lasting predicament of successive generations of *Bildungsbürger,* which penetrated deeply into the souls of the Germans who could read, to become the way they thought and felt, and the idea of the nation, which, though long available, until then had had no appeal in Germany. When this idea was finally appropriated, it was inevitably interpreted in the light of Pieto-Romantic mentality and imbued with an entirely new meaning. At the same time, the Romantic ideals were "nationalized" and represented as the reality peculiar to the German people, language, and land. The German nation, which was now seen as the object of supreme loyalty, and which did not at the time exist as a united polity (or economy), assumed the characteristics of the true Church and the Romantic ideal community. Now it was the embodiment of true individuality, the moral totality, the eternal in this world. Only in the nation could an individual become a whole man, and therefore individuals did not live but for it. "The concept of nation requires that all its members should form as it were only one individual," declared Friedrich Schlegel.[168] In the Eighth Address, Fichte defined a nation less aphoristically. It is, he wrote,

a totality which lives and represents a definite and particular law of the development of the Divine . . . its distinctive characteristics . . . are the Eternal to which [the noble-minded individual] entrusts the eternity of himself and his continual influence, the eternal order of things in which he places his portion of eternity; he must will its continuance, for it alone is to him the means by which the short span of his life here below is extended into continuous life . . . his conception [of] his own life as an eternal life is the bond which unites first his own nation, and then, through his nation, the whole human race, in a most intimate fashion with himself, and brings all their needs within his widened sympathy until the end of time. This is his love for his people, respecting, trusting, and rejoicing in it, and feeling honoured by descent from it. The Divine has appeared in it, and that which is original [the source of all things] has deemed this people worthy to be made its vesture and its means of directly influencing the world; for this reason there will be further manifestations of the Divine in it. Hence the noble-minded man will be active and effective, and will sacrifice himself for his people. Life, merely as life, the continuance of changing existence, has in any case never had any value for him; he has wished for it only as the source of what is permanent [the Eternal]. But this permanence [eternity] is promised to him only by the continuous and independent existence of his nation. In order to save his nation he must be ready even to die that it may live, and that he may live in it the only life for which he has ever wished.[169]

This view of the nation did not differ from the Romantic concept of the state. Indeed, the words "nation" and "state" were frequently used interchangeably. Some difference in meaning did emerge, though, with the "nationalization" of Romantic concepts. "Nation," which was also synonymous with *Volk*, as distinct from the state, represented the inner unity and spirit of the people (designated by a variety of new concepts: *Volksgeist*, *Nationalgeist*, *Volkstum*, and others); it was the immediate embodiment of this spirit and unity, again reminiscent of the invisible Church of the Pietists, while the state represented its outward structure. The German *Volk* was preferred to *Nation*, which was of foreign derivation, but the two words referred to the very same concept.[170]

Since Germany was, apparently, one nation among many, a legitimate inference would be that it was also one individuality and one invisible Church among many. But this was not the inference made by the German patriots. In pre-nationalist Pietist and Romantic thinking, too, the original postulation of multiple equal individualities or expressions of Divinity inevitably gave way to the selection of only one of them as the true one, and the rejection of others as either incomplete or false. Thus, reason, initially conceived of as a part of nature and one way through which God manifested Himself to man, was rejected as unnatural, while irrational emotion became the sole venue of Divine revelation; and modern "enlightened" society was denied "individuality," its specific character being represented as the embodiment of alienation from natural will. Though no logical necessity commanded such conclusions (which were unequivocally *non sequitur* in each instance), the minds that conceived them were obviously unable to accept pluralism with equanimity and were driven to them by psychological necessity. When these logicians of Pietist and Romantic formation turned nationalists, therefore, they were immediately driven to abandon the inherently vexing position of cultural relativism, which presented Germany as one nation among many, for the much more satisfactory view that only Germany was a nation, or, which meant the same thing, that it was the only *true*, ideal, perfect nation in the world.

Germany was the perfect nation because it expressed humanity most fully, the most *human* nation of all. This was consistent with the ground rule that true individuality is the expression of the universal. For this reason, Germany was destined to play a great role in the world. The fate of Europe, or, alternately, of the entire world, depended on her. Every German personality of renown in the period of nationalist "awakening" expressed this belief in one form or another. Wilhelm von Humboldt reflected: "There is perhaps no country that deserves to be free and independent as Germany, because none is so disposed to devote its freedom so single-mindedly to the welfare of all. The German genius is among all nations the one which is least destructive, which always nourishes itself, and when freedom is secured Germany will certainly attain an outstanding place in every form of culture and thought . . . Other nations do not love their country in the same way as . . . we love Germany. Our devotion is maintained by some invisible force, and is far less the product of need or habit. It is not so much affection for a particular land as a longing for German feeling and German spirit." For Arndt, the German was "a universal man, to whom God has given the whole earth as a home," and Germany, consequently, "the greatest world-nation of the present earth." This view was most forcefully stated by Fichte in his Eighth Address, where he asserted that "only the German—the original man, who has not become dead in an arbitrary organization—really has truly a people and is entitled to count on one, and . . . he alone is capable of real and rational love for his nation." [171]

The reasoning behind this astounding claim testified to the remarkable single-mindedness beneath the apparent heterogeneity of Pieto-Romantic thought and reflected its unifying master-idea. True individuality was the expression of the universal; it strove toward the realization of the purpose of the universal. In "Der Patriotismus und sein Gegenteil," composed in 1806, Fichte explained that the will of the universal, "the dominant will," was "that the purpose of the existence of humanity be really achieved by humanity." He called this will "cosmopolitanism." Patriotism represented the individualization of the universal will; it was "the will that the purpose be first fulfilled in that nation of which we ourselves are members, and that the result shall spread from it to the whole of mankind." However, to will something necessitated first the knowledge of what to will. Therefore, patriotism, and consequently cosmopolitanism, could characterize only certain elite nations to whom such knowledge was revealed. In his as yet pre-nationalistic days, in the lectures on "Die Grundzüge des gegenwartigen Zeitalters" of 1804–5, Fichte maintained that at different ages different nations assumed the leadership of mankind on its way to the fulfillment of its purpose, and that the loyalty (or patriotism) of any reasonable person, whatever his nation of origin, was due to such leader-nations. "Which is the fatherland of the truly educated Christian European?" he asked, and responded: "In general it is Europe, in particular it is in each age that European state which had assumed the cultural leadership." [172] To use a more modern idiom, not all classes of humanity represented humanity equally; rather, it was represented in each age by one, ascending, class that was on its road to dominance fully justified by its universal role. The nation in which the knowledge of the purpose of humanity, or the true philosophy, was created was in a favorable position to perceive and follow this purpose. In Fichte's age such true philosophy was created by him, in Germany. Thus, in "Der Patriotismus und sein Gegenteil," he concluded that "the German alone, by possessing this knowledge and understanding the age through it, can perceive . . . the next objective of humanity."

It was but a short step to a further, and this time *non sequitur,* conclusion that Germany was a universal nation *par excellence,* that is, that, at all times, only it truly represented humanity and perceived its purpose: "The German alone can therefore be a patriot; he alone can for the sake of his nation encompass the whole of mankind; contrasted with him from now on the patriotism of every other nation must be egoistic, narrow and hostile to the rest of mankind." [173] A pan-human nation, Germany bore on its shoulders the destiny of humanity. "If there is truth in what has been expounded in these addresses," Fichte concluded his impassioned appeal to fellow-Germans, "then are you of all modern peoples the one in whom the seed of human perfection most unmistakably lies, and to whom the lead in its development is committed. If you perish in this your essential nature, then there perishes together with you every hope of the whole human race for salvation from the depths of its miseries . . . if you go under, all humanity goes under with you, without hope of any future restoration." [174]

Very frequently, the humanity which called for Germany's salutary intervention, however, was defined rather narrowly. The world for Germany was Europe, Western Europe, to be precise. It was European civilization that Germany represented to its thinkers, rather than the spirit of humanity, and they were concerned solely with the preservation of what they took to be this civilization. "The great confederation of European nations," prophesied Adam Müller, "will . . . wear German colors; for everything great, thorough and lasting in all European institutions is German." And Fichte warned: "Should the German not assume world government through philosophy, the Turks, the Negroes, the North American tribes, will finally take it over and put an end to the present civilization." There was no shadow of a doubt in the German educated mind that Western Europe, the perfidious world of enlightenment, was far superior to "the Turks, the Negroes, and the tribes of North America." Fortunately, Germany was the ultimate expression of the true spirit which Europe had betrayed, and while the latter decayed, it stood ready to uphold and reveal to the world God's will:

> Europa's Geist erlosch: In Deutschland fliesst
> Der Quell der neuen Zeit.[175]

German superiority was evident, first and foremost, in its thinkers, "the German mind." This understandably self-congratulatory attitude on the part of its representatives predated their wholesale and irrevocable conversion to nationalism, and was voiced frequently in the late eighteenth century by people otherwise professing cosmopolitanism. Friedrich Schlegel, for example, already in 1791 had discovered that the German people "has a very great character . . . There is not much found anywhere to equal this race of men, and they have several qualities of which we can find no trace in any known people." He saw this "in all the achievements of the Germans, especially in the field of scholarship," and foresaw (quite rightly, as it happened) "that things will happen among our people as never before among men." Time and again he returned to this point. Germanity was a specifically intellectual virtue—a superior degree of artistic sensibility and scientific spirit. "Not Hermann and Odin are the national gods of the Germans, but art and science . . . this spirit, this power of virtue, is precisely what differentiates the German from everyone else." [176]

In the nineteenth century, however, when the nation of whose superiority the excellence of the German mind was a sign was exalted by the triumphant nationalism as the incarnation of the Absolute and the Eternal, the praises of the German letters both increased in number and became louder, and its evident greatness was assigned a far greater significance. "The development of the scholarly mind in Germany is the most important event in modern intellectual history," announced Adam Müller. "It is certain that . . . just as German tribes have founded the political order of Europe, the German mind will sooner or later dominate it." The specific virtue of the German mind, and a reflection of its universality, was its ability to transcend itself and respect and appreciate the imperfect individualities of other peoples. Müller asserted that, apparently in spite of its natural humility, "the German mind is forced to ascribe to itself as an advantage over all other nations its obedient and pious understanding of everything alien, even if this prostration and understanding may sometimes degenerate into the idolatry of foreign habits and persons." "We find our own happiness," he concluded, "not in the suppression but in the highest flowering of the civilization of our neighbours, and thus Germany, the fortunate heartland, will not need to deny its respect for others when it will dominate the world by its spirit." Fichte commented on the German generosity of spirit in a similar vein, claiming that "this trait [was] so deeply marked in their . . . past and present, that very often, in order to be just both to contemporary foreign countries and to antiquity, they have been unjust to themselves." [177] Father Jahn thought that this generosity went too far. To him the alleged readiness to appreciate foreigners and to depreciate their own worth was the greatest vice of the Germans, rather than their virtue.

Driven sophists as were these *Erwecker zur Deutschland* could not, however, stop at asserting the superiority of their nation, but had to discover the deep and convincing-to-them reasons why this should be so. Their explanation derived from notions already present in Pietism. In distinction from all other nations (at least the Western European ones that counted), the German nation preserved its individuality unadulterated. For believing Pietists, this of course meant that Germany was the only God-fearing, pious people, for in its loyalty to its own ways it deferred to and acknowledged God's will. For those nationalists "of pietist formation" who no longer believed in God, (national) individuality nevertheless retained its ultimate value. The individuality—in this case the innermost unique character—of a nation was faithfully reflected in its language, and the German tongue differed from the rest in that it was not contaminated by borrowings from other languages, but remained pure. In Fichte's words, it was the *Ursprache*, the original language. It was directly related to Nature, and therefore, being whole (not alienated) in its humanity, was the only one capable of serving as a basis for a true Culture.[178] This admiration of individuality as a principled, adamantine impermeability to outward influences contradicted the belief in the universality of the German mind in which its spokesmen (such as Fichte) took understandable pride. But contradictions in a system of thought, for the Romantic mentality, were a merit rather than a fault.

During the period of German Liberation, German language became an object of worship. It was a favorite theme of patriotic poetry. Arndt's "Des Deutschen Vaterland," one of the most popular examples of such poetry, defined Germany as the realm of the German language (and, incidentally, also as the land where every Frenchman was called an enemy and every German a friend).[179] "Turnvater" Jahn, whose zeal for the perfectly German body did not lead him to neglect its spirit, but whose obsession with the necessity of combatting foreignisms in the German language might lead one to suspect whether its much advertized purity was not somewhat exaggerated, proclaimed in *Das deutsche Volkstum:* "A people is first made into a nation by its mother-tongue. Attention to the national vernacular has made victors and rulers . . . All foreign words are to be avoided. Only German family names should be permitted." The spirit of the people, he added, is reflected in its popular literature, one of the best examples of which he considered the collection of the Grimm brothers.[180] In the same work Jahn advised that the state should develop the teaching of the mother tongue and suggested that the knowledge of German be used as a qualification for citizenship.

Language was a reflection of the unique spirit of the people, of its *Volkstum*. With all due respect to higher realities, the champions of German nationality, "enlightened pietists [and Romantics]" as they were, refused to see this ethereal entity as the beginning of all things, and made it itself a reflection of material reality. The spirit of the nation, and therefore its language, reflected the body; ultimately nationality was based on blood. Again, the excellence of the German nation lay in the fact that its blood was pure, there were no foreign admixtures, the German was the *Urvolk*. Arndt put it rather bluntly: "The Germans are not bastardized by alien peoples, they have not become mongrels; they have remained more than many other peoples in their original purity and have been able to develop slowly and quietly from this purity of their kind and nature according to the lasting laws of time; the fortunate Germans are an original people." This was written in 1815, long before the word "race" acquired its specific meaning and assumed its honorable place in the German vocabulary, and long before racism, bolstered by the authority of science, became an articulate and presumably objective view. Nevertheless, German national consciousness was unmistakably and distinctly racist from the moment it existed, and the national identity of the Germans was essentially an identity of race, and only superficially that of language or anything else. The language, deeply revered as it was, was but an epiphenomenon, a reflection of race, "the indisputable testimony of common descent." In the mind of the architects of the German national consciousness, one could not exist without the other, and both represented the fundamental bonds of German nationality:

> Uns knüpft der Sprache heilig Band
> Uns knüpft ein Gott, ein Vaterland,
> Ein treues deutches Blut.[181]

Since the spirit and the language reflected the race, they could retain their originality—their *Ur*-character—only if the blood was kept pure. The founders of German nationality were utterly opposed to the blending of different nationalities. "The purer the people, the better," ruled Jahn. "For the benefit of the whole world as well as for the benefit of each individual nationality there must not be any universal union," stated Arndt. "It is much more appropriate to nature," decreed Schlegel, "that the human race be strictly separated into nations than that several nations should be fused as has happened in recent times." "Each state is an independent individual existing for itself, it is unconditionally its own master, has its peculiar character and governs itself by its peculiar laws, habits and customs." [182] National individuality, especially the individuality of the original and universal nation, was nothing to toy with.

German nationalism, like any other, symbolically elevated the masses and profoundly changed the nature of status hierarchy in German society. In its veneration of the people, specifically the peasantry,[183] the virtuous *Volk*, gloriously indifferent to the march of unnatural civilization and faithfully upholding its pristine purity, German nationalism, in fact, far surpassed its Western counterparts and, among the societies in this sample, was comparable only to nationalism in Russia. As in Russia, the internal political consequences of this outright adulation were insignificant. The people that was worshipped did not consist of living individuals, but represented a cognitive construct. Like "early" Romantics, who professed their passion for republicanism, their successors frequently declared themselves champions of democracy. In both cases this meant nothing but the total submersion of the individual within the collectivity (in the latter instance—the nation), renunciation of every particular interest, and unconditional service of the collective self by each in his proper place. "The rights of citizens," said Father Jahn in *Das deutsche Volkstum,* "are dependent upon the activity of such citizens.

That citizen loses his rights who deserts his flag, besmirches his Fatherland in foreign countries, or loses his reason." [184] What were the rights of citizens who did not defame themselves by a similar lack of patriotism or by cowardice, and remained sane, he did not deign to explain. This complete submission to the higher individuality could satisfy the craving for equality of a certain kind (and, naturally, one was to desire no other). However humble in his own state, each servant of the nation was equal to any other in its eyes, as the servants of God were all equal before God.

As to liberty, which was the watchword of the day and constantly on everybody's lips, the period of Liberation added to its definition a new meaning. This meaning was entirely consistent with the demand for dissolution of the person within the collectivity (and the abdication of the personal for the collective will) and reflected the belief in the salubrity and necessity of cultural and racial isolation. In addition to voluntary submission to recognized necessity, liberty came to mean freedom from foreign domination. Arndt defined it aptly: freedom he said, was a condition "in which no foreign executioner can order you around and no foreign slave-driver exploits you" [185] (native executioners and slave-drivers were apparently all right).

In this framework, foreign intervention was, by definition, the most heinous of crimes. It encroached upon the liberty of the people and threatened its individuality (which in the case of Germany was both universal and true, and therefore thrice sacred). No wonder that the French invaders were attacked with such vehemence and fought (at least by the minority of true believers) with such ardor. At the same time, there was more to the calls for war than the immediate need to expel the impudent foreigner. War was a good thing in itself. It was an ennobling, purifying rite which alone could assure true consciousness of nationality and the wholeness of human existence, which was impossible without the latter. Max von Schenkendorf gave this lofty thought a poetical expression:

> Denn nur Eisen kann uns retten
> Nur erlösen kann uns Blut.

Already after the war, on his return from vanquished Paris, Jahn dreamed: "Germany needs a war of her own. She needs a private war with France in order to achieve her nationality." "Germany . . . needs a war against Frankdom to unfold herself in the fullness of her nationhood [*Volkstümlichkeit*]." [186]

There was hardly an exception to this spirit among the German patriots of the Liberation period. Clausewitz argued that war was the most efficient means of politics and needed no further justification. But most of his contemporaries regarded it as an end in itself. Its virtues were expressive rather than instrumental. Peace was beneath German dignity; it was uniformly scorned. God spoke his word on the subject through Arndt: "Tell this lazy people: I am not the God of their perpetual peace; I am the God, the avenger, the terrifying, the destroyer who lusts for struggle and war. Otherwise all history which is my history would be a lie; for its beginning is war and its end will be war. Their peace is called death and rotting, my war is life and movement. To shed blood is always a horror, but not the blood which flows for liberty, for freedom and virtue. War and struggle, the live movement of live forces, that is my lust, thus my name is called, that is myself, I, God the Lord." [187] It is not surprising to find Arndt among worshippers of war, but to discover among them Wilhelm von Humboldt is somehow disheartening. Yet he, too, joined in singing its praises. "I recognize in the effect of war upon national character," he is reported to have said, "one of the most salutary elements in the molding of the human race. The possibility of war is required to give the national character that stimulus from which these [noble?] sentiments spring and thus only are nations enabled to do justice to the highest duties of civilization in the fullest development of their moral forces." [188]

Only several years earlier, in 1802, Friedrich Schlegel lamented the degeneracy of his nation with but a glimmer of hope that it would stand up to its former fame: "The poetry of former times has disappeared and with it virtue, its sister. Instead of the *furor tedesco* which had been mentioned so frequently by the Italian poets, patience has now become our first national virtue and beside it humility, in contrast to the formerly reigning mentality, on account of which a Spaniard who traveled with Emperor Charles V through Germany called the Germans *los fieros Alemanos*. But as far as we are concerned, we wish to retain firmly the image or rather the truth of the great times and not become confused by the present misery. Perhaps the slumbering lion will wake up once more and perhaps even if we should not live to see it, future world history will be full of the deeds of the Germans." [189] His hope was not in vain. The demonic spirit of the Romantics, long bottled within the tiny space of their personal existence and finally released, sought to avenge itself in destruction. Their passionate exhortations fell on attentive ears and set men's hearts on fire; their tireless efforts revived the *furor tedesco,* which swept around the world. The slumbering lion woke up time and again, history was full of the deeds of the Germans, and the lust of Arndt's terrifying God was, at least temporarily, quenched.

## The Finishing Touch: *Ressentiment*
### *The West as the Incarnation of Evil*

The belief that Germany, too, was a nation took root in the land only after it had been trodden by the victorious armies of the conqueror from the West;

France was ultimately responsible for the emergence of German nationalism. Its contribution to the development of the national spirit in the days of its fragile infancy, though incomparable in importance to the contribution of the Pieto-Romantic mold, was nevertheless inestimable. France gave Germans the Enemy, against whom all the strata of the disunited German society could unite, on whom everyone could blame their misfortunes and vent their frustrations. Hatred of France inspired the uncertain patriotism within the German breast; it provided this new and as yet flickering passion with a reason for existence and with a focus. Without the decade of collective effervescence and common effort, the vital enthusiasm which was sustained by the persistence of the French menace, German nationalism would not have survived its birth. The French victories preserved it through the first tender years, and, thanks to them, nourished by the incessant patriotic agitation which was its mother's milk, it could stand, in 1815, on its own.

France continued to stimulate German nationalism even after 1815. The Francophobia of the Wars of Liberation was aroused only in part by the aggression and the interference with the German order of things. It went much deeper. It was rather an expression of existential envy, *ressentiment*. Naturally, nothing but "total annihilation"—indeed demanded by Schlegel—could satisfy this sentiment; neither the temporary termination of the conflict nor even the German victory would put an end to it.

In the "German mind," that is, in the mind of its scholars and writers, Germany was never anything but a part of the Western world, to which it historically belonged. Much of German culture in the eighteenth century drew its inspiration from and developed in response to and in imitation of the "advanced" Western nations: France and England. *Aufklärung* was thoroughly Germanized, but Enlightenment was not a German invention. The nobility, insofar as it busied itself with culture at all, patronized French culture, Frederick the Great being only the most famous example of the utter contempt in which native genius was held. But even *Bildungsbürger,* determined to win for themselves, to the last person, the public justly appertaining to the universe of the German tongue, who since Lessing and *Sturm und Drang* had fought French culture in Germany—even they were encouraged to do so by the example of French and English men of letters and the imported spirit of Enlightenment, and, however reluctantly, saw in the countries west of Germany the model to be followed. The cosmopolitanism of the end of the century, so characteristic of German intellectuals, as well as the fight against foreignisms at the beginning of the new century (the very furiousness of which meant that there were foreignisms to fight indeed), betrayed the fact of the widespread acceptance of the West—that is, of France, first of all, and of England—as the model.

As everywhere, the satisfaction to be derived from national identity (adopted to satisfy the thirst for dignity which the traditionally defined society had failed to quench) depended on the ability to sustain and enjoy the elevating sense of national pride. National pride, in turn, depended on how well Germany measured against its significant other, and on the recognition of its merit by the latter. Thus with the conversion to nationalism, the psychological importance of the West for Germany increased. The arena of contest was political culture; for those who had any doubts on the matter, this had been clearly demonstrated just years ago by France in its explicit bid to outdo England. Political culture—with its three immovable pillars: reason, individual liberty, and political equality—defined the nature of the West and distinguished it from other societies. No special astuteness was needed to realize that, judged by these standards, Germany was inferior to its Western neighbors. German intellectuals only too clearly saw the truth in Mirabeau's indictment of German reality: "Your brains are petrified with slavery." [190] Thus the moment Germans turned to national identity and acquired national pride, this pride was wounded, and not by Napoleonic conquest alone, but rather by the miserable and laughable state of their society, rendered conspicuous by the proximity of the West. Their hatred toward the West was fed by the very fact that the West existed. The enemy could be driven out of the land and aggression stopped, but the springs of *ressentiment,* replenished as they were from within, would never dry out.

Even the heat of the Wars of Liberation was powerless to obscure French superiority. The borrowed idea of the nation was conceptualized with the help of specifically French importations: as in France, the emphasis was on unity and "regeneration." Though grinding their teeth, the Prussian reformers saw France as the model to be imitated. It is from France they learned that only a united nation could be strong, and only citizens could create a united nation. To be citizens people had to participate actively in their society; they could not remain slaves. The leaders of the Prussian state administration and the military understood and willed this as much as any—that is why, in the face of virulent and persistent opposition, accused of Jacobinism and lack of patriotism, they staunchly advocated the emancipation of serfs (Stein), the abolition of restrictions on economic activity (Hardenberg), the reorganization of the army along the lines of the *levée en masse* (the generals), in short, a revolution—from above—as thoroughgoing and radical as was the French Revolution. What was it, asked Stein's biographer, Lehmann, "that attracted these thoroughly German minds . . . to the revolutionary legislation of France, which they only approved with large reservations? The answer is that they desired to attain for their country the position of power which these laws had secured for France." [191] Liberal reforms were deemed necessary for the achievement of national unity, "regeneration," and strength.

This determined imitation, however, was very different from a genuine effort to become like the West, based on the acknowledgment of the West as the model. Of the three logically possible ways to deal with the sense of inferiority (see Chapters 2 and 3), this first one was ruled out from the beginning—by the native cultural tradition, the amalgam of Pieto-Romantic sentiments and concepts, which became the German character long before it was thought to be national. The second alternative, that of cultural relativism, which had been tried and abandoned by Herder, was never picked up by his successors. The Romantic mentality irresistibly impelled toward the remaining possibility: the definition of the West as the anti-model, the incarnation of evil, of all the values of *Aufklärung* that Romanticism rejected for its own reasons.

The choice of this third possibility as the archetypal response to the sense of inferiority was, as everywhere, prompted by *ressentiment*. In Germany *ressentiment* did not result in a transvaluation of values. The values which were to form the core of German national consciousness were already present and firmly embedded in the collective mind. The function of *ressentiment* in Germany was different. It fueled and directed, rather than defined, nationalism defined by indigenous cultural tradition. It allowed goal-oriented expression to the aimless Romantic spirit. Blended with the Romantic *Weltanschauung, ressentiment* focused its passionate but diffuse bitterness and hatred of the world. It eternalized both Germany's peril and its Enemy and not only explained the laughable present state of German society by the perfidy of the West and the fact that its malice and envy prevented Germany from attaining the greatness to which it was destined, but pictured the West as ever concerned about the possibility of such greatness in the future and ever ready to attack Germany again. A holy eternal war against this alien civilization and everything it stood for was the only way to cope with this situation.

The image of the West which resulted from its definition as the anti-model was not a reflection of empirical reality; it represented a projection of the ideal image of the evil world of the *Aufklärung,* an abstraction and generalization of the Romantics' personal experience, on the West. This projection was analogous to the "nationalization" of the image of ideal community, believed now to be represented by Germany. As a description of concrete societies, the image of the West was almost as far from reality as the Romantic image of perfect community was far from the real Germany. Whether this latter image was believed to exist in the past or in the future, the actually existing German society had to be changed to achieve the ideal. But in both cases Germany was much closer to it than the West, either because it was less estranged from the ideal past or because it was better prepared to make the leap into the ideal future. The values which the West, however imperfectly, embodied were unequivocally condemned.

The centrality of French letters in the German cultural life of the eighteenth century, the direct competition of the German intellectuals with the products of the French *philosophes* for the German public, and the Napoleonic invasion made France a natural choice for the personification of the imaginary "West." The rejection of Enlightenment, when first "nationalized," focused on this one country. By the second decade of the nineteenth century, Germany could boast of an established tradition of Gallophobia and possessed an impressive arsenal of clichés with which to express its sentiment.

In his essay on Strassbourg Minster, included in the collection *Von Deutscher Art und Kunst*—the manifesto of the *Sturm und Drang*—Goethe attacked "Frenchmen of all nations": French culture was the embodiment of the artificial, unnatural, dead rational thought. Unlike all other cultures, it was not "characteristic," not truly reflective of the being of the people which had created it (or perhaps this people was not worthy of being reflected?); it imitated classical antiquity and prescribed rational rules. But the rule for Romantics was no rules, and no imitation, and so the French culture was rejected. *Athenaeum,* "that journal which in a unique way represents the pure Romantic ideal at its actual fountain head,"[192] contains a whole gamut of the "early" Romantics' opinions on France: they range from judgments of the French superficiality to amazement at the French stupidity to the inevitable and grave conclusion of the worthlessness of the French culture as a whole. France is "a chemical" (as opposed to organic) nation; this explains its dominance in the "chemical" age. French tragedy "is merely the formula of a form"; "what can be more contrary to good taste than writing and performing plays that are completely outside nature?" The French language is a language "bound by conventions," French poetry is worth nothing, the philosophy is "pitiful." Even the famous "Fragment" #216, whose first line is so frequently quoted, aims in fact only at belittling the historical significance of the French Revolution. After the opening phrase—"the French Revolution, Fichte's philosophy, and Goethe's Meister are the greatest tendencies of the age"—it reads: "Whoever is offended by this juxtaposition, whoever cannot take any revolution seriously that is not noisy and materialistic [like the French], hasn't yet achieved a lofty, broad perspective on the history of mankind . . . many a little book, almost unnoticed by the noisy rabble at the time, plays a greater role than anything they did."[193]

The admiration for English literature, which was in great vogue among the *Bildungsbürger* in Germany throughout the second half of the eighteenth century, and later for some Spanish authors, owed a great deal to the general resentment of the still-unchallenged centrality of the French culture. Yet, in the judgment of the Romantics, England on the whole fared little better than France. In the "Athenaeum Fragments" it is attacked almost as frequently as France and with equal acerbity. English freedoms are worthless and will be made "wholly superfluous through the possession of freedom." Virtue, in England, can be bought and sold for money. "The notion that the English national character is sublime is . . . a by no means contemptible contribution to the science of sublime ridiculousness." The English are characterized by "pedantic bigotry"; they misunderstand Shakespeare. Even their Satan is not sufficiently Satanic in comparison with the German Satan, "to that extent one might say that Satan is a German invention." Besides the Germans, the French, and the English, the only other nation mentioned in the "Athenaeum Fragments" is the Dutch; characteristically, it is mentioned in a comparison. "Don't criticize the limited artistic taste of the Dutch," advises "Fragment" #179. "In the first place, they know exactly what they want. Secondly, they have created their own genres for themselves. Can either of these statements be made about the dilettantism of the English?" [194] England was a natural object of Romantic criticism, for it, like France, stood for rationality and represented the forces of "enlightenment."

During and after the Liberation period invectives against everything French increased in number and ferocity. The "odious French nation" was the "natural and hereditary enemy" of the Germans, an "impure, shameless, undisciplined race." "In no history," thought Stein, "does one find such immorality, such moral uncleanliness, as in that of France." "I hate the French as cordially as a Christian may hate anyone," he confessed when already an old man. "I wish they would all go to the devil." [195] With a passion of which the statesman was incapable, Arndt avowed the same sentiment: "I hate all Frenchmen without distinction in the name of God and of my people, I teach this hatred to my son, I teach it to the sons of my people . . . I shall work all my life that the contempt and hatred for this people strike the deepest roots in German hearts and that the German men understand who they are and whom they confront." To him, as to Romantics before him, the Frenchmen were "a talking, the Germans a thinking people." He failed to understand and refused to reconcile himself with the evident willingness of a still significant number of his compatriots to see in France the apex and fountain of civilization. "Can those men educate," he asked fervently, "who themselves are no men, who give you artificiality for nature, elegance for beauty, illusion for virtue, fashion for morality, and chatter for thought? Who understand and esteem nothing foreign? . . . Incapable of eternal ideas of deep enthusiasm, blissful ecstasy, human longing, for which they even lack words; making fun of the holiest and highest of mankind for the sake of wittiness." French language (which as any language "mirrored the soul of the people, molded and embodied its ideas, and therefore had a peculiar character corresponding to the quality of the people") indeed would hardly have words for anything worthy of expression. It was, wrote a German army volunteer from Paris in 1815, "not an orderly organic language" at all, but resembled "animal noises." The German tongue, which had words for everything, pinpointed the French bestiality with such apt epithets as *ein*

*Affenvolk* and, the animal world being unable to adequately express and sufficiently castigate its wickedness, offered some religious metaphors as well. To the learned Professor Heinrich Leo, whose creative mind it was that discerned the resemblance between the French people and the apes, the capital of that beastly nation was not a jungle, but rather "das alte Haus des Satans." [196]

In their rage against France, German patriots of the Liberation period were willing to go to any lengths, even as far as to consider England a paragon of virtue. Both Stein and Arndt, for example, admired England. His hatred of France, recalled Arndt, dated back to his childhood. Already then the story of that evil people had filled him with "distaste, even with repulsion" and he felt toward them "just like an Englishman." [197] To begin with, the English had the indisputable advantage of being of the same racial stock as the Germans; their Germanic blood was not contaminated by subhuman admixtures, as was that of the irresponsible Franks. In addition, England, like Germany, had fought Napoleon and was most instrumental in bringing about his downfall.

Yet with this downfall went the protection of the German economy from British competition. England could have been impeccably Germanic, but its economic might transcended the limits of good taste; it was too affluent for comfort. Now it, too, showed its true and ugly face. An admirer of British character, Friedrich List, the "apostle of German economic nationalism," clearly saw the treacherous ends that England pursued. "English national economy," he explained to his countrymen, "has for its object to manufacture for the whole world, to monopolize all manufacturing power, [and] to keep the world . . . in a state of infancy and vassalage by political management as well as by the superiority of her capital, her skill, and her navy." England was evidently opposed to Germany's economic greatness and would resist German unification.[198]

And what else could one expect of "perfidious Albion?" (Here the French had a point.) It was, after all, the country of Adam Smith, the prophet of capitalism, and capitalism was "the most general manifestation of that antisocial spirit, of that arrogant egotism, of that immoral enthusiasm for false reason and false enlightenment," [199] in short, the spirit of the West. It believed in reason, it upheld individualism—wicked, infamous notions—it was as irredeemably Western as France, and perhaps even more so. Herder recognized this in the eighteenth century, and Marx believed this in the nineteenth. In the middle of the nineteenth century the German opinion of the English nation was summarized by Treitschke. Wrote the famous historian: "The hypocritical Englishman, with the Bible in one hand and a pipe in the other, possesses no redeeming qualities. The nation was an ancient robber-knight, in full armor, lance in hand, on every one of the world's trade routes. The English possess a commercial spirit, a love of money which has killed every sentiment of honor and every distinction of right and wrong. English cowardice and sensuality are hidden behind unctuous, theological talk which is to us free-thinking German heretics among all the sins of English nature the most repugnant. In England all notions of honor and class prejudices vanish before the power of money, whereas the German nobility has remained poor but chivalrous. That last indispensable bulwark against the brutalization of society—the duel—has gone out of fashion in England and soon disappeared . . . This was a triumph of vulgarity." [200]

As the West was increasingly identified with capitalism, England eclipsed France and emerged as "the leader of the bourgeois world." Later still, the United States of America, "the land without a heart," [201] assumed its place by the side, and soon at the head, of the other two representatives of evil. The "German mind" justifiably regarded these three societies as faithful heirs of Enlightenment, and pinned on them the biased and exaggerated image of *Aufklärung,* generalized from everything it hated in it. This living anti-model, prosperous, proud in its freedom, and looked upon by the rest of the world as the center, kept alive the deepest grief of the *Bildungsbürger*—the "unbearable sense of being unnoticed"—with the difference that now they saw it as the unjust fate of their nation brought upon it by the malicious West, and spurred German nationalism to ever greater heights of xenophobic hysteria and ferocity. Yet the principal embodiment of Western degeneracy and the chief perpetrator of its treacheries was none of the actually existing Western societies. And not the actually existing West, forbidding in its might (though not so forbidding as to rule out the hope and eventually attempts of a just retribution), bore the brunt of Germany's rightful ire. Instead, it was "an Asiatic folk," the children of the bearers of an ancient religious creed, whose residence in Europe was but a sign of well-deserved Divine punishment—the eternal enemy of the Christian peoples, the scourge of humanity, the Jews.

### Anti-Semitism

How, through which mental gymnastics, Germany was led to this remarkable conclusion will forever remain obscure to the Western mind incapable of higher understanding. The Romantic psycho-logic, which ruled that a thing exists if it should exist (that is, if the "German mind," the representative of the Ego, the Individuality, and the Absolute, wills that it exist), undoubtedly helped. As a result of a double intellectual somersault through which the adjustment to the painful comparison between Germany and the "advanced nations" was in part accomplished, the Jew became the symbol of the West.

This portentous association was born together with German national consciousness during the years of Napoleonic invasion. In opposition to the liberal reforms of the "Jacobin" Hardenberg, high-minded patriots of noble birth and Romantic persuasion, von Kleist, von Arnim, and von der Marwitz, formed a *Christliche-germanische Tischgesellschaft,* from which they excluded the three enemies of virtue: "Jews, Frenchmen, and philistines." [202] In the wake of the Wars of Liberation, "the fire that burned . . . in patriotic hearts was fueled with hatred of the French and the Jews; the French who had invented Cosmopolitanism and invaded their sacred soil; the Jews who incarnated Cosmopolitanism and who, as born bloodsuckers and money-lenders, had profiteered by the French invasion. But the French were safely back home." [203] "Philistines" also got away lightly. In their rejection of the "enlightened" Western society, German intellectuals were led to compare Germany to the ideal community which personified the anti-West and anti-Enlightenment, and which for them was the "real" and true, not merely apparent, Germany. When they turned inward and searched for it in the Germany that existed, they were likely to find appalling those qualities in German life which represented points of similarity with, or reminded them of, Western values (and in which they could not but see a reflection of their hated selves that they wished to forget): the bourgeoisie, trade and industry, cities, science. Yet their attitude toward all these had to remain ambivalent: all these factors were absolutely necessary if Germany was not to forsake the hope of one day triumphing over the Western nations.[204] Jews represented all of these hated un-German values and they were not necessary.

The escalation of anti-Jewish sentiment after the Wars of Liberation was, Treitschke explained, an expression of a healthy German patriotism. "The powerful excitement of the War of Liberation," he wrote, "brought to light all the secrets of the German character; amid the general ferment all the old and profound hostility to everything Judaic once more made itself manifest." [205] But the hostility, which was indeed profound and harkened back to some very old traditions, was in effect rather new. So much militated against the Jews in the recent past and the present that their crimes of bygone days were all but forgotten. Their liberation was defended by the appeal to reason, and as reason became increasingly discredited toward the end of the century, to many Romantic minds it became increasingly indefensible. The Jews were further stigmatized by the determined French intervention on their behalf, and by the policy of emancipation conceived by the Prussian reformers who followed the French example. Jews, German patriots as they were in their infinite naiveté, did benefit from the *Aufklärung* which made German intellectuals suffer and from the French occupation which was a slap in the face of the German nation. It was clear that they were in a pact with the Devil.

To the honor of the German nation, it must be said that it did not invent the hatred and persecution of the Jews. These were Christian sentiment and pastime, as universal as Catholic Christianity itself. The Reformation in

Germany did not lead, as it did in Holland, England, and later the New World, to the tendency to recognize in Judaism the seedbed of the Christian tradition and in the Jews the first chosen people, steadfast in its covenant with God, which it held in common with Christian nations. This divergence, Heiko Oberman tells us, is related to the fact that in Germany the Reformation was not associated with the experience of diaspora.[206] German reformers, as well as reformed and unreformed German Humanists, even those who recoiled from Luther's sanguine fulminations against the Jews, retained in regard to them all the pre-Reformation notions and continued to dream of a "Jew-free prosperity." The German nationalists of the early nineteenth century inherited these notions; they did not create them. The traditional definition of the Jew as an evil and impure outsider, as wicked as he was defenseless, made him an exceptionally convenient peg on which to hang the blame for the innumerable frustrations which could not otherwise be soothed.

Still, it was not until "Christ and the tribal god Teut clasped hands"[207] that there appeared a sentiment one could call "anti-Semitism," and with its invention German nationalists who worshiped tribal gods should deservedly be credited. A mutant species of an old sentiment, anti-Semitism gave the traditional persecution a new significance and, much more important, a new lease on life, propelling and perpetuating it in an age that tended to forget religious differences. In 1879 its distinctive, racial rather than religious, character was recognized and asserted in a new German word, *Antisemitismus,* another creation of the German spirit which since then got international recognition. But the sentiment emerged long before the concept.[208]

When the age of Enlightenment dawned on Germany, German Jews formed the lowest rung of society, excluded from intercourse with the German culture, locked in filthy ghettos, and—on account of their filthy conditions, cultural exclusion, and lowly status, as well as religion—universally despised. In Prussia, at the end of the century, their lives were still regulated by "General-Privilegium und Reglement vor die Judenschaft," which expressed Frederick's views regarding Jewish nature and was, in the words of Mirabeau, a law "worthy of a cannibal."[209] Individual *Aufklärer,* Lessing and Prussian bureaucrats, such as Christian Wilhelm Dohm, fought this (unacceptable to them) situation in the face of unbending opposition. Although they achieved nothing like the emancipation they demanded, with their help individual Jews, men of extraordinary talents, were able to escape the unrelieved misery of the *Judengasse.* Like Moses Mendelssohn, "the German Socrates," they became "privileged Jews"—which meant that they were allowed to walk the streets walked by other human beings.[210]

These extraordinary individuals advanced where they were allowed: in finance, trade, and the professions. Most of them abandoned the faith of their fathers, and all enthusiastically embraced the burgeoning German culture. "To mix in good society without ceremony" one had to be introduced to Jewish salons. In these salons Jewish women provided the leadership, and their men the money. Their contribution to German literature of the period was inestimable. They filled the social void in the lives of the "unattached" intellectuals, made misanthropic by shyness; they introduced them to the society of women, and taught them sociability. Most important, the Jewish hostesses *noticed* these intellectuals when they were noticed by no one else. They pampered their egos and cultivated their talents. They were also trend-setters. Goethe-worship in German literature originated in the heart and home of Rahel Varnhagen. Goethe, no friend of the Jews himself, attested: "She was the first to understand and recognize me." [211] Schleiermacher's *Discourses* would have hardly been written at all were it not for the devotion and encouragement of Henrietta Herz.

Every person who was or aspired to be of note in letters sought to be among the visitors to the Jewish salons. Members of the free-thinking nobility, Alexander and Wilhelm von Humboldt and Achim von Arnim (as well as others with intellects less, but titles often more, brilliant) met there with the brothers Schlegel, with Fichte and Schleiermacher, Brentano, Chamisso, Fouqué, and Jean Paul. Tender friendships developed between hostesses and their guests. Ah, how Schleiermacher loved Henrietta Herz! She was too beautiful, and her "colossal, queenlike figure" too much an opposite of his fragile frame, which he thought neither colossal nor beautiful, for him ever to conceive of anything but a platonic relationship. But she admired his spiritual powers, and his platonic love was an ardent passion. To his sister Schleiermacher explained rather wistfully: "If it had so happened that I had married Henrietta Herz, I think we should have made a model couple, the only fear being that we might have been too united." [212] Friedrich Schlegel married Dorothea Mendelssohn; he was so proud of his achievement, of finally being able to find a woman who would love him and marrying her, that he commemorated the event in *Lucinde,* a novel that even shameless Romantics considered too indiscreet.[213]

On the whole, though, the German intellectuals were rather embarrassed by the fact that some of their best friends were Jewish. They objected to the taunts of the less enlightened, who sneered at their circle of acquaintances. But in defending it, they tried to justify to themselves the fact, which perplexed them no less than the others, that they found it acceptable. Friedrich von Gentz, a friend of Rahel Varnhagen, admitted that the society of the salons "always borders on *mauvaise société*"; the Jews were not good company. He thought, though, that among them "the women are . . . one hundred percent better than the men," and so continued to take pleasure in their hospitality. The Jews, in whose houses the German intellectuals were so rapturously received, never gained the wholehearted acceptance of their guests. Even eminent "friends of the Jews" regarded their advancement with rancor.

"I hear . . . that Varnhagen has now married the little Levy woman," recorded Wilhelm von Humboldt upon learning of the marriage of Rahel Levin to the Prussian of non-Jewish and even noble blood, Varnhagen von Ense. "So now at last she can become an Excellency and Ambassador's wife. There is nothing the Jews cannot achieve." [214] It piqued the German intellectuals when the Jews became too much like them, as if there were indeed no difference. When the opportunity arrived—and, in the dawning age of German nationalism, the German intellectuals gained entry into higher circles—they hastened to dissociate themselves from this embarrassing connection. And it was from these Jews, Jews who had relinquished Judaism and shared with them in the same culture, Jews who spoke the same language as they did (literally and metaphorically), Jews who fervently strove to participate in their sorrows and joys, Jews who loved the French when they did, and hated the French when they did, that the German intellectuals wished to dissociate themselves most emphatically.

The situation of the Jews who attempted to assimilate[215] was analogous to the situation of the *Bildungsbürger,* but in distinction from it, it was much more vulnerable, and as the German *Bildungsbürger* resolved their predicament, the predicament of the Jews worsened. For a while, before the advent of nationalism, Jews and German intellectuals shared in common misfortune. Both were outsiders, lured into and then forcibly alienated from the society to which they wished to belong; both were upwardly mobile and owed their advancement to individual merit, in a social system which frowned upon merit and was hostile to mobility. Like the *Bildungsbürger,* the Jews suffered from acute marginality, but their marginality was more profound and escape from it seemed less and less likely with time. "I have a strange fancy," wrote Rahel Varnhagen to a friend; "it is as if some supramundane being, just as I was thrust into the world, plunged these words with a dagger into my heart: 'Yes, have sensibility, see the world as few see it, be great and noble, nor can I take from you the faculty of eternally thinking. But I add one thing more: be a Jewess!' And now my life is a slow bleeding to death." This misery made her hate what she was, as it did Anton Reiser. "I wish nothing more ardently now than to change myself, outwardly and inwardly," she confessed passionately. "I . . . am sick of myself, but I can do nothing about it." [216]

While the *Bildungsbürger,* turning nationalists, were changing their so-hateful-to-them identity, they created for the Jews an identity far more hateful than before and nailed them to it as to a cross. Romantic nationalism brought racism in its wake, and made the cleft between Germans and Jews unbridgeable. In accordance with the materialistic twist of the Pieto-Romantic thought espoused by the unfaithful and yet indelibly "enlightened" disciples of the *Aufklärung,* the Jews, like the Germans, were defined as a race. Already Herder had insisted that the Jewish question was not a

question of "religious controversy," that religion was only an epiphenomenon, a reflection of Jewish history and individuality,of the fact that they
were "in Europe an Asiatic folk foreign to our continent." The Romantics
were likely to concur in this view, and at the turn of the century it became
an explicitly accepted notion. In 1803, in a pioneer publication in this respect, a patriotic lawyer, Grattenauer, denounced "elegant" Jews more than
others (for whom he had no sympathy either); they might talk about
Goethe, Schiller, and Schlegel, but still remained an "Asiatic, alien folk,"
and all intercourse with them was "highly reprehensible." The new racial
element made acceptance theoretically impossible. It did not, could not,
matter whether the Jews accepted everything German, subscribed entirely to
the ideals of the German culture, and rejected wholeheartedly their own. It
did not matter whether Jews were baptized or not. Or rather, it mattered
only for Jews. Years later, in 1862, Moses Hess, a one-time friend of Karl
Marx, felt compelled to stress: "The Germans hate the religion of the Jews
less than their race. Neither 'radical' reform . . . nor baptism, neither education nor emancipation completely unlocks for the German Jew the portals
of social life. They, therefore, seek to deny their origin." [217]

This was clear as day for several generations, but, to the last, not to the
Jews. Some Jews persisted in the belief that it was religion and nothing else
that divided them from the society to which they wanted to belong. Some
tried to reform their religion to bring it closer to Christianity. A great number converted to it. Heinrich Heine saw in baptism the "admission ticket to
European civilization"; the views of his critics proved beyond doubt that he
was wrong. There were no admission tickets. Since race was the issue, nothing but physical, biological conversion would make it possible for the Jews
to become Germans, and since this was impossible, there was no solution.
Fichte (who saw the Jews as "a powerful inimical State [within European
countries] which wars continually against all others and often succeeds in
bitterly oppressing their peoples") in 1793 put it this way: "The only way I
can see to give the Jews civil rights is to cut off their heads in a single night
and equip them with new ones devoid of every Jewish idea." [218]

The definition of the Jews as an alien race irrevocably changed the nature
of anti-Jewish sentiment. The fact that this alien race was identified with the
West, and therefore was the incarnation of all the evil in the world and of
everything to which Germany was opposed, added ferocity to this new and
already vigorous sentiment. This double modification of a moribund Christian tradition was predestined from the 1860s and 1870s to blossom and
still later bear a horrifying fruit. [219] Since German national identity was from
the outset defined as a racial identity, and as it was fueled by *ressentiment*
against the West, anti-Semitism was an integral part of this identity, and a
central element in it. The pervading presence and escalation of anti-
Semitism in Germany in the late nineteenth and the twentieth centuries has

been a subject of many detailed studies, and there is no need to dwell on its apparent but unnoticed madness, as it became increasingly widespread. Suffice it to stress again, as has been many times done, that a direct (though not "absolutely clear and unchallenged") line connected Hitler to the idealistic Romantic patriots of the Wars of Liberation.[220] In combination with the exaltation of violence and death, an equally fundamental element of German nationalism, racial anti-Semitism paved the way to the Holocaust. The possibility of the Final Solution was inherent in German national consciousness. While not inevitable, it was no accident and no aberration of German history; it was not a natural response to a historically immediate structural situation, and, given an identical situation, could not have happened elsewhere. A madman like Hitler was needed to hold a match, and certain immediate structural conditions were necessary to stimulate him and his audience, but the combination of racism, identification of a particular race as the incarnation of evil, and glorification of violence and brutality was highly combustible, and only Germany could produce Hitler and give this form to the response to structural conditions.[221] Germany was ready for the Holocaust from the moment German national identity existed. It is imperative to realize this. The simple Germans who obeyed orders obeyed them not simply because these were orders, but because these orders were within the range of orders they expected to be given (that is, accorded with their *Wesenwille*) and they were not outraged by them. One of the greatest sociologists of all times, Max Weber was a German, and he wrote that no lasting domination can rest on brute force alone, but is, instead, by necessity based on a realistic expectation that its orders will be obeyed, and thus on voluntary obedience, on willingness to obey on the part of those subject to it. This voluntary obedience—without which no social system can endure—is given in terms of the system's (of authority) claims to legitimacy, and because the subjects consider these claims persuasive. No system of authority, no society, exists for any length of time if it is not legitimate and cannot claim voluntary obedience from the mass of its subjects. The Nazis understood this as well as any. Perhaps they understood this better than most—for only to the inability or refusal to understand that a government as dependent on the cooperation of the mass of its population for the execution of its policies as was that of National Socialist Germany could hardly exist for a week without such cooperation, and therefore support, of this population can one attribute that dear to-the-West, persistent myth of Nazism as an unexplainable deviation from the course of otherwise virtuous German history, of which the majority of the German people were ignorant and innocent.

The anti-Semitic stereotype of the Jew reflected the symbolic substitution of the Jews for the West and bore striking resemblance to the image of the West in German thought. "Elegant" Jews of the cities spoke perfect German; the way they spoke it nevertheless betrayed their vile nature and genetic incapacity for feeling. It was as offensive to the musical ear of Richard Wagner as French and, like the latter, reminded him of animal noises. In *Judaism in Music*, directed against the annoyingly famous composers of Jewish descent Felix Mendelssohn and Giacomo Meyerbeer, the patriotic composer wrote: "The Jew speaks the language of the nation in whose midst he dwells from generation to generation, but he always speaks it as an alien. Our whole European art and civilization have remained to the Jew a foreign tongue. In this speech, this art, the Jew can only after-speak and after-patch—not truly make a poem of his words, an artwork of his doings [in this the Jews again were remarkably similar to the French]. In the peculiarities of Semitic pronunciation the first thing that strikes our ear as quite outlandish and unpleasant, in the Jew's production of the voice-sounds, is a creaking, squeaking, buzzing snuffle. This mode of speaking acquires at once the character of an intolerably jumbled blabber. The cold indifference of his peculiar blubber never by chance rises to the ardor of a higher heartfelt passion." [222]

Above all, the Jews, like the Western world as a whole, were revoltingly materialistic. They worshipped and represented the power of money. In the anti-Jewish polemic this was an old and tested line. It went back to the fathers of the Church. "The Jews," believed St. John Chrysostom, "live for their bellies, they crave for the goods of this world." This in the nineteenth century became a favorite theory of many respectable intellectuals. A philosopher, Professor Fries of Heidelberg, for example, in 1816 published a treatise, "On the Menace of the Jews to the Welfare and Character of the German," which was an instant success and in which the author claimed, among other things, that "Jews are a social pest which owes its rapid spread to money and is accompanied by misery, tyranny, and taxes." Wagner reiterated in 1850: "The Jew in truth is already more than emancipated: he rules, and will rule, as long as Money remains the power before which all our doings and our dealings lose their force." [223] But St. John Chrysostom's position was updated in accordance with the latest discoveries of science and philosophy. On the one hand, the Jews were now identified with the soulless and inhuman form of society, the generalized money principle—capitalism; on the other, Jewish reverence for money was attributed to their inner nature, race, rather than religion.

This view penetrated deep into the consciousness of Germany. Even Jews, among those who so fervently wished to be accepted as Germans, the great majority of whom were hard-working professionals or impecunious intellectuals, in complete disregard of all evidence of which they had immediate knowledge, shared in it. In fact, one of the exemplary expressions of this stereotype is to be found in the work of an author who was both Jewish and notoriously impecunious, Karl Marx.

The symbolic substitution of the Jews for the West is transparently clear in the "Essay on the Jewish Question." Marx's opinion of the Jewish religion—"contempt for theory, for art, for history, and for man as an end in himself"—which he considered to be the "real, conscious standpoint and the virtue of the man of money," is exactly the way Romantic nationalists pictured what for them represented "the West." Seeking the secret of Judaism "in the real Jew," materialistic Romantic as he was, Marx discerned in it "a universal *antisocial* element of the *present time*." "What is the profane basis of Judaism?" he asked, and answered: "Practical need, self-interest. What is the worldly cult of the Jew? Huckstering. What is his worldly god? Money." He could not repeat this more often: "Money is the jealous god of Israel, beside which no other god may exist . . . The bill of exchange is the real god of the Jew." Thus, the emancipation of the Jews was actually the emancipation of the world from Jews, and in fact, claimed Marx, "the Jew has already emancipated himself in a Jewish manner," for thanks to their financial power, Jews decided "the destiny of Europe." [224]

Anti-Semitism was an inherently frustrating and self-perpetuating sentiment. The identification of the Jews with and their symbolic substitution for the West made them the chief object of German *ressentiment*. The existential envy could be acted out on them, for, unlike the West, they were powerless to react. Paradoxically, the *ressentiment* did not diminish as a result, but instead grew, for it could not be acted out on its real object, for which the Jews were only a substitute. Whatever was the fate of the Jews, the West persisted in its infuriating superiority. Anti-Semitism, which relieved the psychological discomfort necessarily associated with *ressentiment,* also aggravated it. In so doing, it kept the consuming fire of this deadly sentiment burning, and nourished *furor tedesco*. A constant stimulant for German nationalism, it stimulated the worst in it.

## The Twin Blossoms of the Blue Flower

By the 1840s nationalism had "developed into an important emotional bond which absorbed the continuing loyalty of increasing numbers of individual Germans." [225] It was speedily becoming the framework of the deepest individual and collective identity, and as such informed contradictory political approaches. The matrix of German nationalism, which these approaches reflected and in various ways developed, was a product of anti-Western *ressentiment* injected into the complex system of Pieto-Romantic thought which had constituted the German consciousness before the latter became national, and included the following principles among its basic tenets: (1) the view of the modern—Western, capitalist—world as meaningless, worthless, and evil; (2) the view of modern man as fragmented, alienated from society and from his true nature; (3) the definition of social nature as the true nature of man and the belief that the real, objective man is possible only through a "fusion of individuality" in a collectivity, through the renunciation of all claims to particular autonomy, and through being essentially a member of a larger whole imbued with spirit; only the individual who became one with a community was considered to be his true self and thus both rational and free; (4) the yearning for the transformation of society that would make the real man possible, usually to be accomplished through a violent war or revolution; (5) the emphasis on the primacy of intellectuals in bringing about this transformation.

The insistent prophecy of Romantic intellectuals, however absurd and ridiculous in its arrogance, that the world would subject itself to the rule of the German mind, came true. In the century and a half that followed the birth of German nationalism, nothing had affected so many people so deeply as did two German traditions, one of the left and one of the right: Marxism and the Volkish tradition which culminated in National Socialism. One naturally recoils from admitting the kinship between the two, as indeed one would recoil from admitting the kinship of National Socialism to anything. Its crimes against humanity seem to stand apart from human history, as something that was not human at all, a sort of hellish apparition that could not have happened. The acronym "Nazism" conveniently obscures the fact that it denotes a variety of socialism. And the supposition that an internationalist doctrine, such as Marxism, conceived by a Jew and carried on by scores and scores of other Jews, which called on proletarians of all countries to unite, may have something in common with that most horrible variety of militant and xenophobic nationalism, for which anti-Semitism was the driving passion, seems utterly preposterous. Yet the two are close kin; they are, one can say, brothers—they come from the same parentage and are products of the very same upbringing. They are both elaborations of the matrix of German nationalism, a system of beliefs and aspirations, which was profoundly socialist, and while socialism, however obscured, is nevertheless a central element in National Socialism, so is nationalism (and very specifically German nationalism) a central element in Marxism.

It would be redundant to demonstrate the nationalist character of National Socialism. Its direct succession from the nationalism of the Liberation period has been many times traced, and there is no need to trace it again here. It added little to the already existing body of thought, but sharpened, articulated, brought into focus, and strengthened several central tendencies in it. It tended to represent modern Western reality in essentially economic, rather than political and cultural, terms (aspects of politics and culture being seen as reflections of the unnatural economic structure), and chose capitalism as the specific target of its attack on Western society. It represented the conflict between values (those of the West it opposed and the ones it opposed to them) which were embodied in the two antagonistic economies, Western capitalism and German socialism, as a reflection of a still deeper racial antagonism. It made the Jews its paramount enemy, anti-Semitism its principal motive, and liberation of the world from the Jews its ultimate goal. And, finally, it evoked the authority of science and brought science to bear upon and support the view of social reality it presented, as well as the moral message it derived from this presentation. Racism and specifically anti-Semitism were defined as disinterested, objective positions—imposed on one by stubborn, material reality—and anyone subscribing to these positions was absolved of all personal responsibility. Otherwise National Socialism preserved the Romantic matrix intact.

In Marxism, too, capitalism became the essential aspect of the evil modern reality. Its conclusions, too, were presented as scientific. It, too, as I shall attempt to show presently, retained the perspective and remained faithful to the aspirations of Romantic nationalism. And though it was neither racist nor explicitly anti-Semitic, racist anti-Semitism was almost certainly the central source of inspiration for it.

Shortly after the "Essay on the Jewish Question," in which Marx, among other things, attempted to dissociate himself from Jews and Judaism, he wrote an "Introduction to the Contribution to the Critique of Hegel's Philosophy of Right." This essay is one of the finest examples of the archetypal Romantic nationalist argument, almost identical in its structure to Novalis' *Christenheit oder Europa*. The essay starts with what was indeed the starting point of Romantic nationalism: comparison of Germany with the West and the realization that it is unfavorable. Early in the beginning of the essay Marx declares that it deals with Germany. He proceeds to describe the German situation: "If one were to begin with the status quo itself in Germany, even in the most appropriate way, i. e. negatively, the result would still be an anachronism. Even the negation of our political present is already a dusty past in the historical lumber room of *modern nations*. If I negate the German situation of 1843 I have, according to *French* chronology, hardly reached the year 1789, and still less *the vital center of the present day*." [226] This short passage reveals a number of points. There is an awareness that "the vital center of the day" lies outside Germany, somewhere among the "modern nations." Germany, accordingly, is not a modern nation. This realization and the comparison between Germany and the modern nations at the center are clearly humiliating.

Marx goes on to describe the unacceptable situation of Germany, rejects in passing the position of those who look for salvation in Teutonic forests, and declares war upon the state of affairs in Germany, because "this state of affairs is beneath *the level of history*." In order to give the nation courage to revolt against and change this state of affairs, he wants to make it terrified of itself and deny it an instant of illusion and resignation.

Germany, says Marx, will not change only for itself. "Even for the modern nations," he says, "this struggle against the limited character of the German status quo does not lack interest." Actually, Germany would be performing a world mission, "for the German status quo is the open consummation of the *ancien régime,* and the *ancien régime* is the *hidden defect of the modern state.*" Germany would be in effect curing the defect of other, modern nations, at the vital center of the present day. He names these nations; they are France and England.

Up to this point Marx lamented German inferiority in comparison with the advanced nations. Now he changes the direction of the argument and declares that this is not so much an inferiority as an advantage. Germany is, after all, not so bad—especially if compared with some less fortunate nations—and, in fact, its present backwardness and difference from the modern nations contains the guarantee of its future greatness. This turn of thought also was an element of the archetypal Romantic nationalist argument, and was present already in Pietism, which, compelled to seek salvation in misery, glorified misery as a necessary path to salvation. Marx's argument in this Pietist vein also reflected, alien to Pietism, but characteristic of Romantic nationalism, pride in the intellect and the tendency to see in German letters the essence of the nation. Marx wrote:

> If the whole of German development were at the level of German political development, a German could have no greater part in contemporary problems than can a *Russian* . . .
>
> Fortunately, we Germans are not Scythians.
>
> Just as the nations of the ancient world lived their prehistory in the imagination, in mythology, so we Germans have lived our post-history in thought, in philosophy. We are the philosophical contemporaries of the present day without being its historical contemporaries. German philosophy is the ideal prolongation of German history . . . The German philosophy of right and of the state is the only German history which is *al pari* with the *official* modern times. The German nation is obliged, therefore, to connect its dream history with its present conditions, and to subject to criticism not only these existing conditions but also their abstract continuation.

The German speculative philosophy of right, says Marx, was raised to the level of science. Its criticism, also science, would be both an extremely significant development in philosophy and a critical analysis of the modern (not German) state and of the reality connected with it. Why should one criticize this modern reality? Because it is fundamentally evil, much more so than the present German reality. The modern state, says Marx, which for Germany remains in the beyond, "leaves out of account the *real man,* or only satisfies the *whole man* in an illusory way."

Germany compares unfavorably with France and England, but the question for it, says Marx, is not whether it can catch up with these modern nations. These nations are corrupt, they disregard the real man, and their social flesh is degenerate. The question for Germany is: Can it overcome these nations? He asks rhetorically: "Can Germany attain a practical activity *à la hauteur des principes;* that is to say, a revolution which will raise it not only to the *official* level of the modern nations, but to the *human level* which will be the immediate future of these nations?"

Marx's answer to this question is: Yes, it can. Germany had already proved itself capable of such revolutions in the past, and in the past, too, it did so with the help, and under the leadership, of ideas. As it did in the Reformation, so will it lead the world again on its road to the revolutionary transformation of society now. It has what other nations lack—philosophy developed into science.

For a revolution to take place, however, there must exist a mass to carry through the prescriptions of the philosophy. "A class must be formed," says Marx, which will fight not for partial interests and benefits, as did revolutionary classes in advanced nations, but for the complete emancipation of man. This class is proletariat. It is only beginning to form itself in Germany, but since partially revolutionary classes cannot exist in Germany anyway, it will surely be formed in the nearest future. And "once the lightning of thought [German philosophy] has penetrated deeply into this virgin soil of the people [German proletariat], the *Germans* will emancipate themselves and become men . . . In Germany no type of enslavement can be abolished unless all enslavement is destroyed. The emancipation of Germany will be an emancipation of man." The essay concludes with an enigmatic statement: "The day of German resurrection will be proclaimed by the crowing of the Gallic cock." This statement recalls the urgent question in Novalis' *Christianity or Europe:* "Shall the revolution remain the French Revolution?" Marx, like Novalis, answers it in the negative. The French Revolution is merely a precursor, a herald of salvation brought to humanity by Germany.

This outburst of patriotism does not necessarily show that Karl Marx was a passionate German nationalist.[227] However, at the time of Marx's early adulthood nationalism had already acquired the character of a deeply embedded cognitive blueprint and in fact became a "convenient cultural frame"[228] for the expression of ideas in the most diverse areas. The fact was that Marx inherited the nationalistic attitude *in toto* and—far from being unaware of it, as his later writings were to suggest—shared in it fully. He accepted it unreflectively, without a shade of the skeptical "suspension of commitment."[229] No element of this perspective was for him as much as questionable; this was the very prism through which he to the end of his life saw and related to the world.[230] Nationalism, molded by the Romantic vision and widely shared, formed the foundation of Marx's thought, and if it was never mentioned as such but went unnoticed, perhaps it was that very fundamental, natural character of this vision, self-evident for Marx, that explained this lack of recognition.

Marx's early writings bear remarkable resemblance to the general spirit of the German letters of the first half of the nineteenth century, informed by Romanticism and *ressentiment* against the West. One finds in them the reiteration of all the essential elements of this spirit: the curious blend of chauvinism and cosmopolitanism in the vision of the German mission; the emphasis on the essentially social nature of man and collectivistic definitions of freedom and individuality; the emphasis on the *whole* man and the inability of the anti-social decadent West to allow his self-realization; the pride in German letters and the belief in the special salvational power of German philosophy. The differences which exist between Marx in his early writings and those of the Romantics proper amount to no more than differences in terminology. For example, the ideal society is called the "Kingdom of God on Earth" by Schlegel and "communism" or "socialism" by Marx, but both refer to the state of what Marx in *Economic and Philosophical Manuscripts of 1844* calls "transcendence of human self-alienation." Even this choice of vocabulary still may, and probably should, be interpreted as an expression of Marx's youthful patriotism. Friedrich Engels, in an article written in English for an Owenite newspaper in 1843, before he and Marx had become collaborators and friends, made it clear that communism had a special significance for the Germans. This was due to its centrality in German philosophy. The Germans, unlike the English and the French, explained Engels, arrived at the idea of communism by a philosophical path; it constituted the fulfillment of Hegel's philosophical principles. Hegel's philosophy was the crowning achievement of German philosophical thought, and philosophical thought was the pride of the German nation. To believe in and propagandize the idea of communism was the patriotic duty of a German. Engels wrote: "The Germans are a philosophical nation, and will not, cannot abandon communism, as soon as it is founded upon sound philosophical principles; chiefly as it is derived as an unavoidable conclusion from their *own* philosophy. And this is the part we have to perform now. Our party has to prove that either all the philosophical efforts of the German nation, from Kant to Hegel, have been useless—worse than useless; or, that they must end in communism; that the Germans must either reject their great philosophers, whose names they hold as the glory of their nation, or that they must adopt communism." [231] Communism thus took the place of the "Kingdom of God" without in the least changing the reasons for which this new form of society had to be advocated. It represented the "nationalized" infinite, was an updated name for the Absolute, that is all. Philosophy and national glory were connected, and to be a Hegelian philosopher in the 1840s implied being a German patriot in the same way as at the beginning of the century to be a Romantic poet implied being a German patriot.

After the 1844 *Manuscripts*, while the structure of the argument remained exactly the same, the idiosyncrasies evident in Marx's early writings (such as the idea of the proletariat, the alleged predominance of economic factors and motives over all others) developed into major propositions of the Marxist theory and gave it a look which on the face of it had little in common with Romanticism and the explicitly nationalistic (or Volkish) varieties of German political thought. The reason for this development away from an explicitly nationalistic problematic was, one is led to think, the racist and emphatically anti-Semitic character of mainstream German nationalism. Marx tried to take care of the problem this created for a German patriot of Jewish descent in the "Essay on the Jewish Question." For a while he seemed to be satisfied with the result; in his very next essay he—with a sense of liberation—could say: "We Germans." But Marx's passionate rhetoric appeared convincing to hardly anyone but himself: it was not enough to renounce one's Jewishness to be accepted as a German. Even the skin of an elephant would not be sufficiently thick to leave Marx unaware that the intellectual feat he had performed in "On the Jewish Question" could not be entirely effective, and that he never would become a real German in the eyes of those he considered to be real Germans.

Anti-Semitism made it impossible for Marx to remain faithful to the letter of Romantic nationalism. But through an ingenious turn of thought he succeeded in remaining faithful to its spirit, and retained the rest of its fundamental beliefs and aspirations without having to subscribe to the position which—at least in the eyes of the others—would define him as an alien, inferior being, excluded from participation in the victorious march of the superior race destined for glory. He ensured his own participation and escaped racism. This was achieved by the substitution of "class" for "nation."

As is well known, Marx arrived at the idea of the proletariat not through empirical study, but by way of philosophical speculation. In the "Introduction to the Contribution to the Critique of Hegel's Philosophy of Right" Marx postulated the need for a mass to carry out the teachings of German philosophy. The mass had to correspond to the character of this philosophy: in other words it had to be the material expression of the situation and destiny of Germany, in the same manner in which philosophy was its spiritual expression. This mass therefore had to embody the very antithesis of modern society, and to contain within itself the seeds of its overthrow. It was destined to become "everything," and therefore had to be as close to "nothing" as possible. A concept of a new class closely corresponding to these requirements was available in contemporary French socialist literature, which had been very fashionable in Germany since the 1830s. Already German philosophers tended to identify the proletariat with mankind in the same way in which since the beginning of the century they had identified Germany with mankind. The goal of German history—the overthrow of modern Western society—was in their opinion the goal of humanity. It was but a small step to the identification of the proletariat with Germany.

The concept of the proletariat and the phenomenon it corresponded to was analyzed in the Hegelian framework by Lorenz von Stein in his *Der Socialismus und Communismus des heutigen Frankreichs,* published in 1842. Von Stein viewed the proletariat as an entirely new class, emerging in the wake of the French Revolution. It was propertyless and tended to generalize its condition by creating a "community of goods." Thus it was the very antithesis of the modern Western society "founded on principles of property and personality." Moreover, the proletariat was not simply the mass of the poor; it was a special class of defiant propertyless people who resented their society and wished to transform it into a different one through a revolution. Marx was deeply influenced by von Stein's book, and adopted the concept of the proletariat developed in it.[232]

It is in this function, as the mass—the carrier of the German philosophical idea—that the proletariat appeared for the first time in Marx's "Introduction to the Contribution to the Critique of Hegel's Philosophy of Right." Later the idea of Germany's mission and leadership on the way to world revolution disappeared from his theoretical writings (though it reappeared now and then in letters and occasional newspaper articles), and the proletariat emerged as the sole savior and leader. The true philosophy—earlier a manifestation of the national spirit, the ideal projection of the real tendencies of national history—was incorporated in the idea of the proletariat; it was the true class consciousness, part and parcel of the proletariat's economic situation. At the same time, Capital—or capitalism—replaced the West, the "modern nations," England and France (which nevertheless were believed to represent it), as the anti-hero. While the proletariat was the metamorphosed Germany, Capital was the metamorphosed West. Both retained all the qualities of the forces of good and evil, respectively, of the Romantic nationalist scheme.

In Marxism classes took on all the characteristics of the Romantic nations. It is classes for Marx that are the actors of history; classes, not men, are the real individualities. Men are subsumed under them; they are nothing but their members in the biological, rather than sociological, sense of the word. The characters, abilities, behavior, and views of men are but reflections of the dispositions of classes, as they are of nations in the thought of German patriots of the period. Like nations (notably in Fichte), classes in Marxist theory are divided into partial and pan-human. The view of the proletariat as the universal class, in distinction from all other classes, reflects the idea of Germany as the pan-human nation in distinction from all other nations.

Thus most of the elements of the Romantic nationalist *Weltanschauung* were retained. Though it was Capital now, and not particular societies, which was evil personified, its characteristics were unmistakably the characteristics ascribed to the advanced, Western nations, and one therefore was justified in resenting these nations, for they were the historical embodiment or expression of Capital (in much the same way, one must note, in which Jews were its racial embodiment and expression within another tradition). The West was still seen as the doomed embodiment of evil; the role of the savior of mankind was to be played by the anti-West. As a result of the metamorphosis of nation into class, this vision, inherent in German nationalism, gained a source of universal appeal. While originally each nation vexed by the superiority of the West had to express its *ressentiment* in its own terms, with the role of the anti-model and savior performed for Germans by Germany, for Russians by Russia, and so on, and while therefore the battles fought by each nation and the enemies against which it fought were different in every case, the new Marxist version was acceptable to all nationalities struggling with the realization of their inferiority; in this sense it was indeed international.

In addition, Marxism had the form of an economic theory. Like the racism of the late nineteenth century, it ostensibly represented a scientific, objective, and therefore non-ethical position. To subscribe to it was no longer a question of moral choice, or of choice in general.[233] Those who were willing to subscribe to it were absolved from moral responsibility. Their sympathies and antipathies were now justified by science. They were doing what they wanted to do, but now they knew that they had to do this. In a way, they simply fulfilled orders. Here they stood and they could do no other. They were free—of doubts and pangs of conscience—for this was a state of recognized necessity.

Of course, in the conditions of nineteenth-century Germany, there was a choice to be made; it was a choice between two conflicting "scientific" doctrines. Since, whatever differences there were between them, their way of doing science and the notions as to what constituted it were pretty similar—in accordance with the Romantic redefinition of scientific pursuit, both had little regard for facts and concentrated on the exploration of reality beyond the apparent—this was a particularly difficult choice to make. It is hardly a wonder that in the end it was the circumstances of one's material existence (it should be granted, more often racial than economic) that determined one's consciousness, and not the scientific qualifications of either of the two theories.

In Germany, as elsewhere, Jews tended disproportionally in the direction of Marxism. It prophesied the disappearance of nations and promised to deliver them from a humiliating and oppressive identity. In Russia, Trotsky, when asked whether he would define himself as a Russian or a Jew, is reported to have replied, revealingly: "Neither. I am a Socialist."[234] Jews were likely to be firm and sincere internationalists and to see the transformation of the world, rather than of any particular nation, as the ultimate and truly significant goal of their activity. The idea of socialism in one country, by default National Socialism, appealed to them less; they were overrepresented among the supporters of permanent revolution.

In many central issues an admirable agreement existed between German Marxists and representatives of Volkish ideology who were also socialists (and therefore direct ancestors of National Socialism). The number of socialist nationalists was not insignificant, for German nationalism in general was inherently socialist, and it included some of the leaders of the German anti-Semitic movement.[235] Wilhelm Marr, the founder of the Antisemiten-Liga and the inventor of the term "anti-Semitism," declared that "anti-Semitism is a Socialist movement, only in nobler and purer form than Social Democracy." (One must admit that in the light of Marx's pronouncements in the essay "On the Jewish Question," such an assertion did sound rather plausible.) Marxists doubted the intellectual quality of their alleged kin, but recognized the kinship. Anti-Semitism, they admitted, was indeed socialism, but that "of the dumb" *(der Sozialismus des dummen Kerls)*.[236] German socialists agreed that insofar as anti-Semitism was anti-capitalist, which it emphatically was, it represented a "step forward in historico-political development" and compared well with liberalism, which was not anti-capitalist.[237]

Whether Marxists, the preachers of communist internationalism, or anti-Semites, the prophets of National Socialism, they came from the same stock, burned with the same desire, and fought the same enemy. Their mind was still that of Pietists and Romantics; they were driven by *ressentiment* and hatred of the West. Both were faithfully pursuing the national dream—the Blue Flower—looking for it, one on the right side of the road, the other on the left. When they found it, it appears, both discovered that its color was red.

# In Pursuit of
# the Ideal Nation:
# The Unfolding of
# Nationality in
# America

It is of great importance to begin well.

John Adams

The commonwealth of mankind, as a whole, was not to be constructed in one generation. But the different peoples are to be considered as its component parts, prepared, like so many springs and wheels, one day to be put together . . . In this great work our country holds the noblest rank . . . Our land is . . . the recipient of the men of all countries . . . Our country stands, therefore, more than any other, as the realization of the unity of the race.

George Bancroft

As it spread on the European continent, nationalism changed its character. The direction of its transformation was away from the original, English, individualistic principles of nationality—the very same principles, it is worth stressing, which the world has named, in a manner which conveniently obscures their *national* origins, "the ideas of modern democracy." Having followed their permutations at some length, we may find it useful to return to these principles and examine the conditions under which they were not only preserved in their original significance, but also developed and carried into new areas of social experience.

We have left English nationalism in the late seventeenth century. In that "unhappy age, when an universal deluge of tyranny [had] overpowered the face of the whole earth," liberty, together with equality and reason, constituted the core of English nationality. One of the foremost Whig philosophers of the time, the Third Earl of Shaftesbury, articulated the social and political implications of the English idea of the nation. "Of all human Affections," he wrote, "the noblest and most becoming human nature, is that of love to one's country. This . . . will easily be allowed by all men, who have really a Country, and are of the number of those who may be called a People, as enjoying the happiness of a real constitution and polity, by which they are free and independent." He explained in a note to the term "People": "A multitude held together by force, though under one and the same head, is not properly united: nor does such a body make *a people.* It is the social league, confederacy, and mutual concent, founded in some common good or interest, which joins the members of a community, and makes a People one. Absolute Power annuls *the publick;* and where there is no *publick,* or *constitution,* there is in reality no *mother*-Country, or Nation." The term "nation" referred to a "civil state," a union of men as "rational Creatures," not a "primordial" unit; the latter view Shaftesbury thought a misconception. He accounted for it with marvelous insight. "I must confess," he wrote, "I have been apt sometimes to be very angry with our language, for having denied us the use of the word Patria, and afforded us no other name to express our native community than that of country . . . abstracted from mankind or society. Reigning words are many times of such force as to influence us considerably in our apprehension of things. Whether it be from any such cause as this, I know not; but certain it is, that in the idea of a civil state or nation, we Englishmen are apt to mix somewhat more than ordinary gross and earthy. No people who owed so much to a constitution, and so little to a soil or climate, were ever known so indifferent towards one, and so passionately fond of the other." To derive national loyalty from the place of birth and residence was absurd. "Had it happened to one of us British men to have been born at sea, could we not therefore properly be called British men? . . . It may therefore be esteemed no better than a mere subterfuge of narrow minds to assign this natural passion for society and a country, to such a relation as that of a mere fungus or common excrescence, to its parent-mould, or nursing dunghill."

John Locke, in the second *Treatise on Civil Government,* also defined political community or "commonwealth" as a "civil state" or compact between rational beings, and not a mystic unity arising from common origins: "Nothing can make any man [a member of a commonwealth] but his actually entering into it by positive engagement, and express promise and compact." He did not use the word "nation," but the society of which he spoke, unquestionably, was one. Locke presented liberty and equality of men in society—that is, association of men in a nation—as required by the law of nature: "The *state of nature* has a law of nature to govern it, which obliges every one: and reason, which is that law, teaches all mankind, who will but consult it, that being all *equal and independent,* no one ought to harm another in his life, health, liberty or possessions." Man's liberty and equality to other men followed from "*his* having *reason,* which is able to instruct him in that law he is to govern himself by." [1] Given that men were rational beings, inequality and lack of liberty, or a society which was anything other than a nation, were, therefore, both unnatural and unreasonable.

These ideals were rarely disputed. But the gap between ideals and reality was wide and, in the eighteenth century, seemed to grow wider. The reason lay in part in what John Murrin calls the English "revolution settlement"— "the pattern assumed by a revolutionary regime after the turmoil itself is over," which for a long time to come determines the manner of the political and social evolution. In England, this "settlement," achieved between 1688 and 1721, following the Restoration, established *Court,* rather than *Country* (which stood for the original ideals of English nationalism) as the dominant force in British politics.[2] As a result, progress toward a closer alignment between the lofty principles, to which most professed loyalty, and reality was significantly slowed. The more general reason was the identification of the abstract idea of the nation with the actually existing institutions, the concrete and necessarily imperfect reality, and the gradual transfer of loyalty to the latter. This identification, the idea that England as it was, was the elect nation, had its origin in the ardent hope of the Elizabethans. Since that early time, therefore, English patriotism—devotion to the English nation—could refer both to the idealistic commitment to the values of liberty, equality, and reason (which is what Shaftesbury meant in speaking of the nation) and to the emotional attachment to the land, government, and ways of England. One was the original English nationalism, the other an updated particularism, clothed in nationalist rhetoric. One was inherently revolutionary, inevitably critical of the status quo so long as the embodiment of the ideals in it was imperfect; the other—conservative in the literal sense of the word: it cherished the actual. Shaftesbury was, of course, over-critical of his countrymen, perhaps because he lacked comparative perspective. When it came to the definition of the nation, Englishmen, on the whole, tended to be less rather than "more than ordinary gross and earthy," as the works of their eminent thinkers attested. Nevertheless, there was truth in his assessment. In Restoration England, tired of the revolutionary striving to attain the ideal, people found comfort in the thought that their destiny was not of their making, but was instead inherent in the "soil and climate," and were eager to be satisfied with the status quo. The author of the *Origines Britannicae* (1685), Edward Stillingfleet, argued sensibly that it was fortunate that men were "contented with the places of their habitations; for . . . now, since the true Paradise is lost, it seems to be most convenient for the world, that every nation should believe they have it at home."[3]

This sense of satisfaction with the existing state of society was expressed in the vague idea of and the admiration for the British constitution. In the eighteenth century, "constitution" as a rule referred not to the fundamental principles of a polity, but to "that assemblage of laws, customs, and institutions which form the general system according to which the several powers of the state are distributed and their respective rights are secured to the different members of the community"[4]; it was a term for the existing order of social and political relations. Of course, relatively speaking, and by comparison with other societies of the age, the state of the English society was rather satisfactory, and the desire to make it even more so did not revive on a significant scale until the nineteenth century, with the appearance on the political scene of new groups, heretofore denied the pleasure of experiencing such satisfaction personally.

But before it could regain momentum at the place of its birth, the promise of original English nationalism was carried much further toward its realization, and at a much swifter pace, than could have been possible in any part of Europe, with its age-old habits of doing things and thinking, by Englishmen on the other side of the Atlantic. The story of this development, a direct continuation of the process begun in England in the sixteenth century, is the story of the emergence of the American nation.

The conditions under which civic nationalism developed were unique, and although in matters of national identity exceptionalism is unexceptional, this makes the uniqueness itself of American nationalism peculiar. The *nationality* of American identity and consciousness does not demand an explanation. The English settlers came with a national identity; it was a given. They necessarily conceived of the community to which they belonged as a nation; the idea of the nation was an American inheritance. *National* identity in America thus preceded the formation not only of the specific American identity (the American sense of uniqueness), but of the institutional framework of the American nation, and even of the national territory, all of which—since we no longer follow Shaftesbury—are conventionally thought of as foundations of nationality. Because of this singular development, the symbolic nature of nationality and its essential autonomy from material or "objective" ethnic and structural factors are demonstrated here with particular clarity.

It has been the fate of the American nation, it is said, "not to have ideologies but to be one." [5] In a way this is true of every nation, for a nation is first and foremost an embodiment of an ideology. There are no "dormant" nations which awaken to the sense of their nationality existing due to some objective unity; rather, invention and imposition of national identity lead people to believe that they are indeed united and as a result to become united; it is national identity which often weaves disparate populations into one. Yet this applies more rigorously to America. For, in America, at the outset, ideology, the firm conviction that the American society (every objective attribute of which—territory, resources, institutions, and character— was as yet uncertain) was a *nation*, was the only thing that was certain. An explanandum in every other case, nationalism, in the American society, is an independent variable.

The idea of the nation emerged in an old, traditional society, very different from the ideal image the concept implied. Subsequently, in every case but British settlement in America, it was imported into social environments whose reality stood in flagrant contradiction to it. In the uneven battle between the nascent principle and long-established ways of life, it was the principle that had to adjust. But in America, to begin with, there was almost no social reality, other than the one the settlers brought with them in their own minds. (One could say that there were no structural constraints apart from the constraints of the symbolic structure.) To be sure, a society was soon formed. Economic opportunities, or their scarcity, bred interests and structural relations which had little to do with the ideal of national collectivity. But this ideal was nevertheless a given. While in older societies the novel idea was acting upon the obdurate reality, in America the new reality acted upon the stubborn inherited idea. The transformative effect of the national idea on reality has been great everywhere, but the idea which eventually had this effect was, in older societies, itself transformed by the counterpressure of institutions and traditions that were the legacy of their pre-national past.

The specificity of the American case lay in that the idea of the nation, nationality as such, although undoubtedly also modified by the independently emerging reality, was a much more potent factor in the formation of the national society. Contrary to the accepted opinion, then, in a certain, analytical, sense, the American nation is an ideal nation: the national element in it is challenged by the fewest counterinfluences; it is a purer example of a *national* community than any other.

Because of the strictly derivative character of the national identity in America, the conceptual problem presented by American nationalism is different from the one we confronted in the four previous cases, and the emphasis in the following pages will be different from the one in the rest of the book. Rather than seeking to explain how nationalism in America emerged (which is unproblematic), we address the question of how a unique society and its very geo-political framework were molded by the given of national identity, by the fact that the seed population, so to speak, to begin with consisted of citizens of a nation who brought the conviction of their nationality with them to a new continent. This process of formation, which began aboard the motley fleet carrying Englishmen to the New World, was not completed until after the Civil War between the Union and the Confederacy. Only then was the fundamental question settled of what was to be the concrete geo-political referent of the American national loyalty. The outcome of this conflict, another "revolution settlement," reconfirmed the commitment of the new society to the original principles derived from the old one, and determined that it would henceforth develop toward ever closer alignment with them.

## America as a New England

Examples of the developed, articulated nationalism of the Americans of the colonial period, and of the fact that theirs was English and then British nationalism, are not hard to find. Their loyalty found expression in many forms. Not the least eloquent were the names they gave to their settlements. Of these "New England" was just the most explicit. "Boston" and "Cambridge," which did not bother to stress their derivative character, or "Virginia," the "Carolinas," and "Georgia," which honored and commemorated English rulers rather than localities, reflected a similar sense of sameness— *identity* with England—nostalgia and desire to recreate the dear image and essence itself of the mother country on the foreign shores. This pattern of naming is not self-evident: it presents a striking contrast to the practice of Latin American colonies.[6] Where Spaniards encountered an alien country, Englishmen tended to discern similarities which made their "removal" across the ocean not much different from a regular change of residence. In

the preamble to the first New England sermon to be printed, Robert Cushman, one of the organizers of the *Mayflower* group, explained: "NEW-
ENGLAND, so called, not only (to avoid novelties) because Captain *Smith*
hath so entitled it in his Description, but because of the resemblance that is
in it, of *England,* the native soil of Englishmen; it being much what the same
for heat and cold in Summer and Winter, it being champaign ground, but no
high mountains, somewhat like the soil in *Kent* and *Essex;* full of dales, and
meadow ground, full of rivers and sweet springs, as *England* is. But principally, so far as we can yet find, it is an island, and near about the quantity of
*England,* being cut out from the main land in *America,* as *England* is from
the main of *Europe.*" Two generations later Cotton Mather, in *Magnalia
Christi Americana,* wrote similarly: "The Name of NEW-ENGLAND . . . has
been ever since [1614] allowed unto my Country, as unto the most *Resembling Daughter,* to the chief Lady of the *European* World." [7]

The motives for "removal" to America were diverse. The founders of Virginia, in the spirit of Elizabethan adventurers, sought earthly opportunities,
like the latter eager to honor England by the successes of their ventures.
These Cushman characterized as "mere worldlings . . . having their own
lusts carrying them . . . out of discontentment in regard of their estates in
*England;* and aiming at great matters here, affecting it to be gentlemen,
landed men, or hoping for office, place, dignity, or fleshly liberty." Still, he
did not deny legitimacy to materialistic motives altogether: they occupy a
central place in an apologia he published in England early in 1621, under
the title "Reasons and Considerations Touching the Lawfulness of Removing out of England into the Parts of America." Cushman undertook in it to
answer the question "how a man that is here born and bred, and hath lived
some years, may remove himself into another country." He started from the
premise that, though the home of a Christian "is nowhere but in the heavens
. . . now, as natural, civil and religious [pertaining to the religious controversies of the time] bands tie men, so they must be bound," and that, therefore,
legitimate reasons for leaving England should take these secular "bands"
into account. The removal should be as beneficial to England and people
remaining at home as to those who would endeavor it, he argued, even leaving aside the religious motives of the latter ("the bitter contention that hath
been about religion"). For now many an able-bodied person was forced to
"sit here [in England] with their talent in a napkin," since notwithstanding
the many blessings England enjoyed thanks to God's favor ("sweet delights,
and variety of comforts"), there was "such pressing and oppressing in town
and country, about farms, trades, traffick, &c.; so as a man can hardly any
where set up a trade, but he shall pull down two of his neighbours." "Let us
not thus oppress, straiten, and afflict one another," he called; "but seeing
there is a spacious land, the way to which is through the sea, we will end this
difference in a day." This solution was all the more natural because the spa-

cious land he was referring to was "proper to the king of England," as a result of "the ancient discoveries, contracts and agreements which our Englishmen have long since made in those parts," and was thus a part of the national patrimony.[8] Presented in this manner, "the practise of removal" was an act of true English patriotism.

The religious reason, for Cushman, was, of course, much more important. He was a Puritan, and on the whole, the Puritans identified with the ideal England which at the time they saw violated on the island where it had taken its earthly residence. Some stayed to fight for it at home; some left and carried it with them to the wilderness where it could not be assailed. Mather later described the reasons that drove Englishmen to America: "The Sum of the Matter is, That from the very Beginning of the REFORMATION in the *English Nation,* there hath always been a Generation of *Godly Men,* desirous to pursue the *Reformation of Religion* . . . And there hath been another Generation of Men, who have still employed the *Power* which they have generally still in their Hands . . . to stop the Progress of the Desired *Reformation* . . . Then 'twas that . . . Multitudes of Pious, peaceable Protestants, were driven, by their Severities, to leave their Native Country, and seek a Refuge for their Lives and Liberties, with Freedom, for the Worship of God, in a Wilderness, in the Ends of the Earth."

If the removal of the Virginians began as a business trip, the Puritans went into voluntary exile. In both instances, the prohibitive vastness of the ocean and the opportunities of the open continent transformed what could have been a temporary situation into a permanent one and redefined it. Had the Puritans gone no farther than Holland, they would probably have returned after the conditions at home became more to their liking. It is certain that the removal was not conceived as a renunciation of national allegiance; it was not expatriation or emigration. Indeed, with Cromwell's victory, many chose to return even from America, and one of the reasons why more resolved to stay was that America, for them, was a part of England. Recounting the story of the Plymouth plantation, Mather tells the following: The founders "had not been very long at *Leyden* before they found themselves encountered with many Inconveniencies . . . they were very loth to lose their Interest in the *English Nation;* but were desirous rather to enlarge their *King's Dominions.* These *Reasons* were deeply considered . . . and . . . they took up a *Resolution* . . . to REMOVE into AMERICA." There, "in the utmost parts of the Earth," they insisted that "we have changed only our Climate, not our mindes." They remained faithful both to the principles of the English government, "best agreeable to our English temper" and to English religion. In 1648, *The Cambridge Platform* asserted: "Wee, who are by nature, English men, doe desire to hold forth the same doctrine of religion . . . which wee see and know to be held by the churches of England."[9]

The men of Mather's generation, himself foremost among them, clearly also saw themselves as Englishmen. They spoke of "both Englands," professed that separation between them and the mother country was only spatial, and thought of England with heartfelt affection. Among the numerous merits of *Magnalia,* wrote John Higginson in the "Attestation to this Church-History of New England," was that it stressed the ties which united Englishmen in America and Europe and allowed "that the Little Daughter of *New-England* in *America,* may bow down her self to her mother *England* in *Europe* . . . assuring her, that tho' by some of her *Angry Brethren,* she was forced to make a *Local Secession,* yet not a *Separation.*" Mather himself referred to England as "the *Best Island* of the Universe," talked with pride about the discoveries of the "English Nation" in the New World, insisting on the chronological precedence of some of them over Columbus, and declared that "all the concern of this our History, is to tell how *English People* first came into America": the "Magnalia Americana" were the "wonderful works" "done since by Almighty God for the *English* in these Regions." [10] In the New as in the Old England, Puritans fused the English with the Protestant cause: they viewed their "removal" in terms of pilgrimage, an "errand into the wilderness." In America they saw the dream of England come true at the very same time as it was being frustrated on their native island, but they never lost sight of the fact that this was England's dream.

Whether or not religious liberty was the main motive for migration to America, it was early represented as such in the colonial lore and became a central element in the emerging sense of uniqueness and local—American—identity. This identity was formed in the process of systematic, though presumably not entirely intentional, selection of certain characteristics of the colonial way of life and careful weeding out of others, the result of which was a uniform and eminently positive image. The determination of the government of Massachusetts in suppressing criticism (by such unsavory means as cutting malcontents' ears, whipping, and otherwise convincing people to modify their opinions)[11] contributed to the establishment of the idea of the Godly Commonwealth of New England, which was later extended—at least for the outsiders—to include all of the British settlements in America, although New England remained the model of godliness. In *Magnalia,* Cotton Mather quoted George Weymouth as saying in regard to the early colonization "that one main End of all these Undertakings, was to plant the Gospel in these dark Regions of America." Mather agreed that this was the "main" end for them, indeed, but proceeded "to tell Mankind" about that one of the English plantations for which "this was not only a *main End,* but the *sole End* upon which it was erected." This was, to be sure, "that *English* Settlement, which may, upon a Thousand accounts, pretend unto more of *True English* than all the rest, and which alone therefore has been called *New-England.*" All the settlements considered themselves "true English";[12] however, eventually, as the discourse secularized and religious liberty became liberty as such, they accepted New England's lead in the interpretation of the English identity which in America was carried to perfection. It was through the Puritan mediation that love of liberty became the distinguishing characteristic of America. Thus, from very early on, American identity was New England's identity in more than one sense.

The formation of the sense of American uniqueness in no manner interfered with the loyalty of Americans to the English nation and their English national identity: the people of which they were members was still the English people, regardless of the place of residence. The place of residence, nevertheless—and naturally—generated emotions of local pride, not unlike the pride of an Englishman in Kent or Yorkshire. This pride in locality was all the more pronounced in the face of the actual hardship and disappointment the early settlers necessarily encountered; they had to think positive— this was a way to boost the fragile morale. Criticism aroused such violent reaction in the early colonies because, in the conditions they faced, objectivity was depressing and potentially destructive. Of course, death then did not bespeak the finality it does now, and for people who had already moved to one New World, a move to yet another one might not be such a frightening prospect, but the confidence of the surviving members of the Plymouth plantation, who had buried half of its population in the course of the first year, and still wholeheartedly subscribed to the "somewhat hyperbolic" [13] commendations of New England's abundance and felicity, nevertheless appears striking. The allegedly wholesome and plentiful natural resources of the new continent were a subject of constant celebration. As it happened, the expectations of prosperity based on the natural "excellency of the place" were soon fulfilled. In 1654 Edward Johnson (writing about the year 1642) told the reader of his *Wonder-Working Providence* of the "remote, rocky, barren, bushy, wild-woody wilderness . . . [that] through the mercy of Christ becom a second England for fertilness . . . [and] hath not only equalized England in food, but goes beyond it in some places." To him, this made America "the wonder of the world." [14] This prosperity was taken as a sign of God's favor and linked with the godliness of the people in the consciousness of American uniqueness. Common expressions such as "New-English Jerusalem," "American Jerusalem," "God's American Israel," "American Canaan" connoted both the superior virtue of the people of the colonies and their superior well-being, a sure sign of their election. If the English were God's own people, the American English were the elect of the elect.

When in the eighteenth century this sense of uniqueness received a more secular expression, the emphasis on the singular American prosperity was retained. The fact that it was general, so impressive in comparison with the wretched conditions of the masses in Europe, inspired most comments. After a tour in Ireland and Scotland, Benjamin Franklin wrote from London: "In those countries, a small part of the society are landlords . . . extremely opulent, living in the highest affluence and magnificence. The bulk of the people are tenants, extremely poor, living in most sordid wretchedness, in dirty hovels of mud and straw, and clothed only in rags. I thought often of the happiness of New England, where every man is a freeholder, has a vote in public affairs, lives in a tidy, warm house, has plenty of food and fuel, with whole clothes from head to foot." Another contented American, Hector St. John de Crevecoeur, opened his discussion of "the Situation, Feelings, and Pleasures of an American Farmer" with a philosophical remark to the effect that "it is strange that misery, when viewed in others, should become to us a sort of real good," and though he was "far from rejoicing to hear that there are in the world men so thoroughly wretched (Hard is their fate to be thus condemned to a slavery worse than that of our Negroes)," joyfully proceeded to enumerate the material, among other, blessings of the American whose lot compared so well with that of destitute humanity elsewhere.[15]

Bodily comforts generally enjoyed by Americans were related to equally if not more felicitous experiences of the soul, of which paramount was equality in liberty and dignity, which characterized the American society. As in England, godliness in the colonies gradually acquired a secular meaning, which by the eighteenth century became dominant and, even more than in England, expressed itself in devotion to the triad—liberty, equality, and reason. In "Information to Those Who Would Remove to America," Franklin wrote that in America individuals were respected for their merits and birth had no value. "The people have a saying, that God Almighty is himself a mechanic . . . and he is respected and admired more for the variety, ingenuity, and the utility of his handiworks, than for the antiquity of his family . . . According to these opinions of the Americans, one of them would think himself more obliged to a genealogist, who could prove for him that his ancestors and relations for ten generations had been ploughmen, smiths, carpenters . . . and consequently that they were useful members of society, than if he could only prove that they were gentlemen . . . living idly on the labor of others." This situation was a realization of an English ideal, yet Britain, at that time without doubt one of the most egalitarian societies in Europe, could not equal America in equality. British visitors were quick to notice the difference. Lord Adam Gordon in 1765 observed that inhabitants of Massachusetts "resemble much the people of Old England, from whence most of them are sprung." "But," he added, the "levelling principle here everywhere operates strongly, and takes the lead. Everybody has property, and everybody knows it." Crevecoeur, who, it is worth noting, was as firmly convinced of the Englishness of America as any American of British descent, mused about what could be going on in the mind of a visiting Englishman. He thought:

> He must greatly rejoice that he lived to see this fair country discovered and settled; he must necessarily feel a share of national pride [saying to himself,]

"This is the work of my countrymen . . . They brought along with them their national genius, to which they principally owe what liberty they enjoy and what substance they possess." Here he sees the industry of his native country displayed in a new manner . . . He is arrived on a new continent; a modern society offers itself to his contemplation, different from what he had hitherto seen. It is not composed, as in Europe, of great lords who possess everything and of a herd of people who have nothing. Here are no aristocratical families, no courts, no kings, no bishops, no ecclesiastical dominion, no invisible power giving to a few a very visible one, no great manufactures employing thousands, no great refinements of luxury. The rich and the poor are not so far removed from each other as they are in Europe . . . The meanest of our log-houses is a dry and comfortable habitation. Lawyer or merchant are the fairest titles our towns afford; that of a farmer is the only appellation of the rural inhabitants of our country. It must take some time ere he can reconcile himself to our diction-ary, which is but short in words of dignity and names of honor . . . We have no princes for whom we toil, starve, and bleed; we are the most perfect society now existing in the world.[16]

If earlier America had been identified with the Providential design, now, as the course of empire took its way Westward, it became in addition the end and fulfillment of history. American society was exemplary in its devo-tion to the English ideals: it turned them into reality. Liberty and equality, for Americans, became self-evident. "I need not spend any time to prove the equality of men, or the inalienable rights of humanity," wrote Samuel Dick-inson somewhat later; "you, my countrymen know the reality. They are a sacred deposit in the bosom of every American." (To point out that such was the reality for the white male population only would in our skeptical age be redundant, but it is worth emphasizing that for white male populations else-where such reality could not be but a dream.)

The sense of exemplary devotion to and implementation of English values was shared by the colonists everywhere and became a central element in the local American identity. Not only were they, indubitably, English, but they were better English than the English. Beyond this Americans of different colonies shared little, and the differences of locale, climate, and economic and social arrangements other than the basic equality of conditions among the white men led to the differentiation of the unique American identity into different local identities of specific colonies. As Englishmen, the colonists all belonged to one nation; as Americans, they inhabited different provinces. Their local pride as New Englanders, Pennsylvanians, or Virginians was fierce and their sentiments toward the other colonies only on rare occasions resembled brotherly love. New Yorkers styled New Englanders "Goths and Vandals," "contemptible to the extreme" on the revealing account of their "Levelling Spirit," and this sentiment was shared by other colonies. New Englanders regarded Virginians as "uncivilized Natives," and so on.[17]

In this the colonies were not different from rivaling provinces anywhere. The development of strong feelings of local patriotism was natural; in fact one would have to come up with an ingenious explanation had such sentiments failed to develop. But, generally, local patriotism was not exclusive; it was a sentiment of a different nature and in no way contradicted the British nationalism of colonial Americans. In fact it could be used as an argument for and an explanation of the persistence of British nationalism. British nationalism was both necessary and invincible, claimed Franklin in 1760, for, if the colonies "could not agree to unite for their defense against the French and Indians, who were perpetually harrassing their settlements, burning their villages, and murdering their people; can it reasonably be supposed there is any danger of their uniting against their own nation, which protects and encourages them, with which they have so many connexions and ties of blood, interest and affection, and which it is well known they all love much more than they love one another?" [18] Whichever colony Americans called "my country," their national allegiance was English, becoming, according to some colonial historians, still more, or more articulately, English by the second half of the eighteenth century.[19]

In *Candid Examination*, which he addressed to his "dear countrymen," Joseph Galloway adopted Burlamaqui's view of a nation as a "society animated by one soul, which directs all its motions, and makes all its members act after a constant and uniform manner, with a view to one and the same end, namely the public utility." It was in no way geography that defined such a nation. The British nation, to which the great majority of Galloway's compatriots before independence were absolutely loyal, in his view consisted of the two countries: England and America. He, too, called America "my country," but this in no way contradicted his nationality. Daniel Dulany urged: "Let it be demonstrated that the subjects of the *British* Empire in *Europe* and *America* are the same," revealingly juxtaposing not the British and the Americans, but the Europeans and the Americans of Britain. "Are we not one nation and one people?" asked Francis Hopkinson in 1766. "We in America are in all respects Englishmen, notwithstanding that the Atlantic rolls her waves between us and the throne to which we all owe our allegiance." [20] The distinction between Britain, or the British Empire (the terms "nation" and "empire" were used interchangeably), as a nation in which one was a member, and America, or a particular colony in America, where one happened to live, as "my country," was commonplace and reflected not a divided loyalty, but concentric circles of loyalty. No contradiction was perceived or existed between the two attachments as there is no contradiction in being a member of a family, a resident in a city, and a citizen in a state. John Adams disputed the applicability of the word "empire" to Britain, whose constitution he considered to be that of a quintessential republic. At the same time he did not question that Americans and the inhabitants of

Great Britain were one nation. The "quarrel between the British administration and the Colonies," on which he commented, was for him "the great *national* subject." Franklin's "affection to Pennsylvania" prevented him from accepting for his daughter an offer of marriage into a good family in England, for he did not wish to be separated from her by a great distance and "could not think of removing" there; yet he was most enthusiastic about England (to the extent, in fact, that he found criticism leveled on it by Englishmen in England too harsh). During the Seven Years' War he rejoiced over British victories, explaining: "And this is not merely as I am a colonist, but as I am a Briton"; considered the British Empire "the greatest political structure that human wisdom ever yet erected"; and insisted on the "true British spirit" which animated Americans.[21] Americans "exulted in the name of Britons." England for them was still "the finest country in the world," "the Eden of the world." They emphasized the natural, historical, and emotional ties connecting Americans to Britain and frequently used the highly charged metaphor of mother country and children colonies, forever beholden to her, to denote them. John Randolph, the Virginian, wrote in 1774: "The Americans are descended from the Loins of Britons, and therefore may, with Propriety, be called the Children, and *England* the Mother of them." "The Americans are properly Britons," insisted Charles Inglis. "They have the manners, habits, and ideas of Britons; and have been accustomed to a similar form of government." These ties were priceless and irreplaceable. If America separated from the mother country, speculated John Dickinson anxiously, "where shall we find another Britain, to supply our loss? Torn from the body to which we are united by religion, liberty, laws, affections, relation, language and commerce, we must bleed at every vein."[22]

American colonists considered themselves a part of the British nation. They were fully conscious of the nature of their loyalty and were deeply committed to it. In 1764 James Otis wrote in the "Rights of the British Colonies": "We all think ourselves happy under Great Britain. We love, esteem, and reverence our mother country . . . And could the choice of independency be offered the colonies, or subjection to Great Britain upon any terms above absolute slavery, I am convinced they would accept the latter."[23] Yet, within the next decade the definition of what constituted absolute slavery grew suspiciously inclusive, and the choice the colonists were put before grew far more difficult, urgent, and painful.


## The Separation

In January 1776, Thomas Paine opened *Common Sense* with the declaration of his awareness that the sentiments expressed in it were "not *yet* sufficiently fashionable to procure them general favor."[24] The documents of the period

bore out his impression. The soon-to-be architects of independence professed loyalty to Britain and stressed the British nationality of Americans as
vehemently and insistently as did future loyalists. Two months after the
Battle of Bunker Hill, Jefferson looked "with fondness toward the reconciliation with Great Britain"; a few months before the Declaration of Independence, the Continental Congress protested that it did not wish "to dissolve
that union which has so long and so happily subsisted between American
colonies and the mother country." To see in the conflict an attempt of a
colonized nation, conscious of its unity and uniqueness, to assert its sovereignty vis-à-vis a foreign power that had usurped it could not be more mistaken. Not that other colonized nations who in less distant times have indeed attempted to assert their sovereignty vis-à-vis foreign powers were,
prior to independence, invariably characterized by widespread awareness of
their unity and uniqueness, yet, in the case of such nations, at least, the
struggle for independence was preceded by a sometimes protracted period
of nationalist agitation by intellectual and other elites. No such agitation
took place in America. But, if Americans were loyal and proud Englishmen,
why did they seek independence from England? The answer to this question
is that they did so because their national identity was English.

To say this implies no paradox. A drive for secession was inherent in the
nature of the English nationalism which, furthermore, rendered it legitimate. English national identity, from its earliest days, provided for two types
of national loyalty: one was concrete and materialistic, for its referent was
a concrete reality, materialized in a territory, ways of life, and specific political institutions; and the other, the original one, was idealistic or abstract—
this loyalty was to the national values. The idealistic loyalty to national values, which could be and usually was as ardent a patriotism as the more
earthly love of country, was by its very nature a stimulus for disaffection and
revolt, for the more intense the commitment to the ideals, the more sensitive,
the more intolerant, one became to the imperfections in their realization. It
was this idealistic patriotism that in the seventeenth century had driven
some Englishmen to "removal" and others to rebellion; it was this patriotism that has bred discontent in England ever since. The central English
value—Liberty, embedded in reason, and in regard to which all rational
Englishmen were equal—was, at least since Milton, defined as "self-
government." [25] Another word for it was "independence." The logical consummation of the inherent tendencies of English nationalism, its fulfillment,
absurd as it sounds, was the absolute sovereignty, self-government, or independence of every individual; in other words, complete atomization and political anarchy. English nationalism, the cohesive force which held Englishmen together, was potentially self-destructive and propelled toward the
disintegration of the national collectivity. And so long as one was *consistently* devoted to the English national ideals (such consistency was necessar-

ily rare, because psychologically burdensome), one could not in good conscience object to this tendency. Thus, the colonists' very Englishness, which they took such pains to stress, served as a cause and a justification for the resistance of the colonies to the British government, which eventually transformed what had begun as but a "local secession" into a decided separation.[26]

As elsewhere, those modes of thought and sentiment fared best which were favored by the structural constraints of a given situation and could attach themselves to the interests they bred. For this reason, Englishmen in England tended toward the concrete or materialistic variety of patriotism, while in America the majority was attracted to the idealistic and abstract variety.[27] The idealistic nature of English patriotism in America was reflected in the modified notion of the "constitution," which, though a minority view in England, had become predominant in the colonies by the time of the Revolution. Rather than regarding the "consitution" as the character of a polity expressed in its institutions and ways of life, Americans tended to define it as a formal statement of the fundamental principles of the polity. "British constitution" referred to "a government of laws, and not of men," claimed John Adams in the *Novanglus* essays. *The Genuine Principles of the Ancient Saxon or English Constitution* in 1776 defined constitution as a "set of fundamental rules by which even the supreme power of the state shall be governed." These rules, and not the "variant, inconsistent forms of government which we have received at different periods of time,"[28] were the proper object of loyalty. This tendency to view "constitution," which conventionally referred to the actual community itself, and therefore also to view the community, in terms of basic principles was observable throughout the colonial period: the *Mayflower* and later "Compacts" and "Agreements" adopted by colonial governments were constitutions in exactly this sense.[29] But until the Revolution this novel view peacefully coexisted with the more traditional one.

Curiously, idealism in this context expressed itself in the appeal to self-interest, for the ideal and self-interest coincided in the idea of liberty. If some argued for unity with Britain on the basis of deep natural and emotional attachment, many more, and the same authors more often, defended this unity on instrumental grounds, as offering the surest safeguard of everyone's self-government. "He, who considers these provinces as states distinct from the *British empire*," argued John Dickinson in the second of the *Letters from a Farmer*, "has very slender notions of *justice*, or of *their interests*. We are but parts of *a whole*." "We are a part of the British dominions . . . and it is our interest and duty to continue so," granted John Adams. Otherwise in disagreement with *Novanglus, Massachusettensis* concurred with him on this point: "It is our highest interest to continue a part of the British empire."[30] In general, the argument ran: we are kept together by leaving each other alone, or, conversely, if addressed to the British administration: the more we leave each other alone, the stronger is our union.

Similar arguments were made in England. Edmund Burke, in his grand speech on conciliation with America, contended that loyalty to the British government could be secured only by eliminating the latter. He also accepted the American view on the nature of the bonds that held the British nation together and, in this speech at least, shared their notion of "consitution":

> Let the colonies always keep the idea of their civil rights associated with your government—they will cling and grapple to you, and no force under heaven will be of power to tear them from their allegiance. But let it be once understood that your government may be one thing and their privileges another, that these two things may exist without any mutual relation—the cement is gone, the cohesion is loosened, and everything hastens to decay and dissolution. As long as you have the wisdom to keep the sovereign authority of this country as the sanctuary of liberty, the sacred temple consecrated to our common faith, wherever the chosen race and sons of England worship freedom, they will turn their faces towards you . . . the more ardently they love liberty, the more perfect will be their obedience. Slavery they can find anywhere. It is a weed that grows on every soil . . . But until you become lost to all feeling of your true interest . . . freedom they can have from none but you. This is the commodity of price, of which you have the monopoly . . . Deny them this participation of freedom, and you break that sole bond which originally made, and must still preserve, the unity of the empire . . . It is the spirit of the English constitution which . . . unites . . . the empire.[31]

If it could be proven that the unity was detrimental to liberty, both the instrumental (and idealistic) and the natural attachment arguments easily lent themselves to inversion and became arguments for independence. This was later eloquently demonstrated by Thomas Paine.

The central issue in the controversy was the abuse, from the American point of view, of the liberties (all of which were aspects of self-government) to which colonists were entitled by birthright as Englishmen, which implied the violation of the British constitution. The latter altruistic concern of the colonists was articulated. John Hancock defined patriotism as opposition to unjust administration and, speaking of the possibility of a continental congress, saw its advantage and aim in that it would enable the colonists "to frustrate any attempts to overthrow our constitution; restore peace and harmony to America, and secure honor and wealth to Great Britain, even against the inclination of her ministers, whose duty it is to study her welfare." Similarly, Franklin, insisting that the Americans were to the last truly devoted to Britain (they were the "true *loyalists* . . . affectionate to the people of England, zealous and forward to assist in her wars . . . beyond their proportion"), qualified his assertion, adding: "But they were equally fond of what they esteemed their rights, and if they resisted when those were attacked, it was a resistance in favor of a British constitution, which every

Englishman might share in enjoying who should come to live among them; it was resisting arbitrary impositions that were contrary to common right and to their fundamental constitutions, and to constant ancient usage. It was indeed a resistance in favor of the liberties of England." It was a patriotic duty indeed to resist a government which betrayed the nation. Jonathan Mayhew, who argued so in 1750, merely echoed the English tradition of the sixteenth and seventeenth centuries. Such resistance was *national* in the strictest sense of the word, insisted another clergyman, and no different from lawful self-defense against a foreign invader: "[Americans] have as just a right, before GOD and man, to oppose king, ministry, Lords, and Commons of England when they violate their rights as Americans as they have to oppose any foreign enemy; and this is no more, according to the law of nature, to be deemed rebellion than it would be to oppose the King of France, supposing him now present invading the land." Conversely, John Dickinson's *Letters from a Farmer* compared the American colonies with other nations oppressed by native tyrants, such as England under James II. As England's resistance to James was a Glorious Revolution (in the sense of putting things right), so would be the American resistance to usurping British authorities.[32]

The entitlement of Americans to English liberties was incessantly stressed. This emphasis is, indeed, the most characteristic feature of the official declarations, petitions, and resolutions of the period immediately preceding independence. The members of the Stamp Act Congress, "with Minds deeply impressed by a Sense of the present and impending Misfortunes of the *British* Colonies on this Continent," esteemed it their duty to make the following declarations:

I. That his Majesty's Subjects in these Colonies, owe the same Allegiance to the Crown of *Great-Britain,* that is owing from his Subjects born within the Realm, and all due Subordination to that August Body the Parliament of *Great-Britain.*
II. That his Majesty's Liege Subjects in these Colonies, are entitled to all the inherent Rights and Liberties of his Natural born Subjects, within the Kingdom of *Great-Britain.*
III. That it is inseparably essential to the Freedom of a People, and the undoubted Right of *Englishmen,* that no Taxes be imposed on them, but with their own Consent, given personally, or by their Representatives . . .
VI. That all Supplies to the Crown, being free Gifts of the People, it is unreasonable and inconsistent with the Principles and Spirit of the *British* Constitution, for the People of *Great-Britain* [namely the Kingdom] to grant to his Majesty the Property of the Colonists.
VII. That Trial by Jury, is the inherent and invaluable Right of every *British* Subject in these Colonies.

After the repeal of the Stamp Act in 1766, Reverend William Smith, Provost of the College of Philadelphia, congratulated Americans on "asserting our pedigree and showing that we are worthy of having descended from the illustrious stock of Britain." [33]

In 1774 the deputies to the First Continental Congress denied that the colonies owed any subordination to the august body of the Parliament, but persisted in claiming for themselves the rights and liberties of Englishmen. Thus, "in the first place, as Englishmen, their ancestors in like cases have usually done, for asserting and vindicating their rights and liberties," they declared:

> 2. That our ancestors, who first settled these colonies, were at the time of their emigration from the mother country, entitled to all the rights, liberties, and immunities of free and natural-born subjects, within the realm of England.
>
> 3. That by such emigration they by no means forfeited, surrendered, or lost any of those rights, but that they were, and their descendants now are, entitled to the exercise and enjoyment of all such of them, as their local and other circumstances enable them to exercise and enjoy.
>
> 4. That the foundation of English liberty, and of all free government, is a right in the people to participate in their legislative council: and as the English colonists are not represented . . . in the British parliament, they are entitled to a free and exclusive power of legislation in their several provincial legislatures . . .
>
> 5. That the respective colonies are entitled to the common law of England . . .
>
> 6. That they are entitled to the benefit of such of the English statutes as existed at the time of their colonization.

Daniel Leonard, staunchly loyalist and arguing for submission to England even at the cost of some discrimination, summarized the argument of his opponents: "The principal argument against the authority of parliament, is this, the Americans are entitled to all the privileges of an Englishman, it is the privilege of an Englishman to be exempt from all laws, that he does not consent to in person, or by representative; The Americans are not represented in parliament, and therefore are . . . not subject to its authority." [34] To a very significant extent the conflict that was brewing was an internal struggle over the correct interpretation of the British constitution, in which both parties believed themselves faithful to the supreme values of the nation and had the good of the nation as their goal.

After 1763 the colonists were systematically treated by the British authorities as if their membership in the nation was of an inferior sort. Special regulations fettered colonial commerce and manufactures and interfered with their internal affairs. What made Americans particularly sensitive to this high-handed treatment, and added insult to the injury, was their sense that they were better English than the English. They had been long resentful of the condescending (as it appeared to them) attitude of their European fellow-nationals. Now, they felt not only materially threatened and infringed upon in their interests, but emotionally wounded by the actions of the metropolitan authorities who denied them the autonomy enjoyed by Englishmen elsewhere. Instead of allowing them fuller control of their own affairs—because of their superior capability to assume it and because they were different from the mother country and better acquainted with the peculiarities of their situation than the officials in London—or at least the control they had got used to before 1763, the English government tied their hands and treated them like children. They demanded recognition of their equality and grew firmer in the sense of their superiority. "Is there not something exceedingly fallacious in the commonplace images of mother country and children colonies?" asked vexedly John Adams. "Are we not brethren and fellow subjects with those in Britain, only under a somewhat different method of legislation and a totally different method of taxation?" [35]

Not everyone in Britain was oblivious to the virtues of the Americans. The Bishop of St. Asaph, in an eloquent commentary on the Bill for Altering the Charters of the Colonies of Massachusetts Bay in 1774, characterized America as "the only great nursery of freemen now left upon the face of the earth," the focus of "the fairest hopes . . . the last asylum of mankind." England, he thought, "ought to cherish [the colonies] as the immortal monuments of our public justice and wisdom; as the heirs of our better days, of our old arts and manners, and of our expiring national virtues." Others pointed to the contribution of the colonies (actual or potential) to the strength and wealth of the empire. Adam Smith envisioned the possibility of Parliament removing to America on account of the growing share of this contribution "to the general defense and support of the whole." [36] In America this idea was surprisingly common. Daniel Leonard used the prospect of the future centrality of America for the British nation as an argument for the continuing union with it in the present: "After many more centuries shall have rolled away . . . the colonies may be so far increased as to have the balance of wealth, numbers and power, in their favor, the good of the empire make it necessary to fix the seat of government here; and some future George, equally the friend of mankind, with him that now sways the British sceptre, may cross the Atlantic, and rule Great-Britain, by an American parliament." John Adams saw such an arrangement as nothing less than reasonable and demanded that steps be taken to implement it then and there: "A union of the colonies might be projected, and an American legislature; for, if America has 3,000,000 people, and the whole dominions 12,000,000, she ought to send a quarter part of all the members to the house of commons; and instead of holding parliaments always at Westminster, the haughty members for Great Britain must humble themselves, one session in four, to cross the Atlantic, and hold the parliament in America." [37] Even the most sympathetic British view of America hardly matched this sense of self-importance.

The growing realization of America's strength and resources further stimulated the brewing disaffection.[38] Franklin had warned already in 1767: "America, an immense territory, favored by nature with all the advantages of climate, soils, great navigable rivers, lakes, etc., must become a great country, populous and mighty; and will, in less time than is generally conceived, be able to shake off any shackles that may be imposed upon her, and perhaps place them on the imposers. In the meantime every act of oppression will sour their tempers . . . and hasten their final revolt; for the seeds of liberty are universally found there, and nothing can eradicate them." As in so many other cases, at least one reason for revolt was the perceived opportunity for attaining great power and prosperity, and increased expectations the speedy realization of which appeared curbed. This realization of strength threw a new light on the interests of Americans and made the connection with Britain seem superfluous. The extraordinary swiftness and ease with which the deep affection for Britain was transformed into indifference, hostility, and contempt are explained to no small degree by this beckoning of opportunity. As late as May 1775 Washington was reluctant to consider independence. Nine months later he wrote: "If nothing else could satisfy a tyrant and his diabolical ministry, we are determined to shake off all connexions with a state so unjust and unnatural." Granted that the impositions of the London authorities were taxing, their presumption annoying, and the Intolerable Acts truly intolerable, the dramatic leap to diabolical ministry and unjust and unnatural state still seems to be something of an overreaction. Only the confidence in the brilliant future of the offspring, and the opinion—which demanded justification on moral grounds—that continuing association with the mother country was not in its interest, could make the latter appear so unattractive. "When I consider the extreme corruption prevalent among orders of men in this old, rotten state [England]," wrote Franklin, "and the glorious public virtue so predominant in our rising country, I cannot but apprehend more mischief than benefit from a closer union." [39] He might have substituted the cause for the effect and vice versa, however. It was at least as likely that he tended to see England as rotten and corrupt, as well as to discern glorious public virtue in his own country so clearly, *because* he could not apprehend more mischief than benefits from the union.

On the whole, Englishmen understood this earlier than Americans. Moreover, they thought it *reasonable* that a part of the nation objectively capable of prospering on its own should seek political independence from the rest. Such thinking reflected the voluntary, rational character of the English idea of the nation. In 1767, Sir George Saville wrote to the Marquis of Rockingham: "In my opinion . . . it is the nature of things that sometime or other Colonies so situated must assume to themselves the rights of nature and resist those of Law, which is Rebellion. By *rights* of nature I mean advantages of situation or their natural *powers*." Captain William Evelyn, stationed with the British Army in Boston, also reflected on the matter and, rejecting the possibility that the Rebellion was plotted by "a few ambitious enterprising spirits," argued rather that "the true causes of it are to be found in the nature of mankind . . . it proceeds from a nation, feeling itself wealthy, populous, and strong; and being impatient of restraint . . . struggling to throw off that dependency which is so irksome to them." [40] "I have never met a man either in England or America," noted Paine in the fourth chapter of *Common Sense,* "who hath not confessed his opinion that a separation between the countries would take place, one time or other." This singular experience, no doubt, reflected the fact that, having arrived in these parts only in November 1774, Paine had not had the opportunity to meet many Americans. His observation on the state of opinion in England, however, was well founded. The British, not the settlers, writes John Murrin, "imagined the possibility of an independent America . . . British writers almost took it for granted that one day the American colonies would demand and get their independence." [41]

One also should not forget that the disorganized and ill-conceived actions of the British administration in the years after 1763 affected specific interests of certain influential groups. The reaction to the Stamp Act, in particular, was so violent because, by taxing paper, this act infringed on the rights and revenues of the most articulate segments of the population, such as printers and lawyers. The economic situation was volatile and exposed the authorities to attack: the post-war depression which affected broad sectors of the population in all the colonies made people willing to think in terms of conspiracies. The ills of the economy were attributed to the ill-will of the mother country, anyhow plotting to destroy the civil and religious liberties of the people. John Adams, indefatigable and unscrupulous in the service of the glorious cause, saw no wrong in speculations along these lines and commended printers on their "readiness and freedom" in publishing them. [42] The straitened circumstances of the large planters in the South, indebted to British factors, bred similar suspicions, and in addition made Southern gentlemen painfully sensitive to encroachments on their political authority, which, by way of compensation, they valued all the more the less prosperous they became. Neither would they, under the threat of impoverishment, accept with equanimity the restrictions imposed by London on speculation in trans-Allegheny lands. [43]

And yet, with so much against the British connection, independence was not a foregone conclusion. The unity of the nation had inherent value and Americans refused to believe that they wished to dissolve it. The illusion that the conflict was caused by Britain, that the provocation was such as not to leave the colonists any choice, persisted to the last. As late as 1775 Philip Freneau, soon to become an Anglophobe, pleaded:

> O Britain come, and, if you can, relent
> This rage, that better might on Spain be spent,

as if a calmer temper on the part of Britain would blind Americans to the opportunities which tempted them to independence. The Prohibitory Act of December 1775, which declared Americans rebels, was met almost with a sense of relief. "We cannot be Rebels excluded from the King's protection," reasoned Richard Henry Lee, "and Magistrates acting under his authority at the same time." Now they did not have a choice indeed. Independence, that "ill-shapen, diminutive brat,"[44] was forced on them.

But when it came, they were well prepared to accept it. The arsenal of arguments that would rationalize it was ready, and the justification of the separation existed before the fact. The popularity of *Common Sense* reflected the readiness of the public to be convinced as much as the ingenuity of Paine's propositions. The "weeping voice of nature" cried: "'TIS TIME TO PART," and its plea was backed by Providence itself. "Even the distance at which the Almighty hath placed England and America" proved that "the authority of the one over the other, was never the design of heaven."

Independence thus was a result of several factors. By far the most important was the fact that Americans had a national identity from the very start, and that this was the English national identity. It was the nature of the English nation which made the separation conceivable, possible, and legitimate. The English idea of the nation implied the symbolic elevation of the common people to the position of an elite, which in theory made every individual the sole legitimate representative of his own interests and an equal participant in the political life of the collectivity. It was grounded in the values of reason, equality, and individual liberty. The nation of an individual was the community within whose bounds he could realize his liberty and the right of participation, the community whose interests were fully one's own interests since one could influence them, and in which one had true membership. The inability to fulfill one's rights of citizenship within a particular geo-political sphere justified exit. An additional stimulus was provided by the fact that Americans excelled in the English values, that they believed to be and in many respects were more English than the English. The slightest degree of unfairness would offend people who believed they had the right to expect a greater than normal degree of respect. The lack of even such a modicum of recognition bred frustration and hurt feelings. Given that the attempts to change the attitude of the mother country did not succeed, separation was the way to deal with the problem. "Nations, in general, are not apt to *think* until they *feel*," argued John Dickinson perceptively in *Letters from a Farmer*.[45] This may be interpreted as an assertion of the priority of interest over ideology. But in bringing about independence, the two were so closely interwoven that it is not always possible to distinguish one from the other. Interests activated ideas, turning them into weapons in a battle, but ideas informed interests. The main interest of the colonists was their liberty—the control over their destinies (and purses)—which they felt was being treacherously snatched from them, but this was also the main tenet of their ideology.

Of course, the preservation of the spirit of English nationality was made possible in America by the specific social conditions prevailing there, and social conditions made it possible for the Americans to give vent to their sense of frustration. The unique equality of conditions made active participation of the people in the governance of local affairs both realizable and necessary. Americans could afford their pride because of the growing strength of the colonies and the awareness of their economic, political, and military possibilities, which, by increasing their expectations, motivated them to grasp for opportunities that appeared to be more accessible to them alone than to the British Empire.

The last, but probably not the least, factor that ensured commitment to the cause of independence was the success of the insurrection and its relative facility. Commenting on the colonial lack of preparedness and the dismal state of military discipline, Daniel Boorstin concluded that the most persuasive answer to the question "How could we account for the outcome of the conflict?" is not "that the Americans won but that the British lost—or perhaps that they simply gave up." This is plausible. The British, being British, were never completely convinced that their position vis-à-vis the colonies was morally defensible, and as to the British interest in keeping them, which might make it seem so, they were less and less certain that they had such an interest. *The Wealth of Nations* appeared in 1776, the year Americans declared their independence, and by 1783 the powers that be in Britain had ample opportunity to acquaint themselves with its argument regarding the costs of empire. Adam Smith wrote: "The rulers of Great Britain have, for more than a century past, amused the people with the imagination that they possessed a great empire on the west side of the Atlantic. This empire, however, has hitherto existed in imagination only. It has hitherto been, not an empire, but the project of an empire; not a gold mine, but the project of a gold mine; a project which has cost, which continues to cost, and which, if pursued in the same way as it has been hitherto, is likely to cost, immense expence, without being likely to bring any profit . . . If the project cannot be completed, it ought to be given up . . . it is surely time that Great Britain should free herself from . . . those provinces."[46] The British, like Thomas Paine, might have arrived at the conclusion: 'Tis time to part. And so America, almost by surprise, found itself on its own.

One peculiar feature of this short struggle for national self-determination, which had so many peculiar features, was the relative weakness and quick abatement of hostility to Britain. While the conflict lasted, this hostility performed the valuable function of justifying the resistance and supporting the wavering desire for independence. When it was over and this function disappeared, the sentiment, while not entirely dead, was no longer alive.[47] Un like the case in so many other nations, American national identity was not sustained by the hatred of the other; it knew no *ressentiment*. The free, and no longer British, Americans needed not and could not afford to brood over real or imagined offenses in the past; they had problems to attend to which were far more pressing.

## A Union Begun by Necessity

The American Prohibitory Act of December 22, 1775, was, in Max Savelle's apt, though—given its nature—oddly sexless, metaphor, "something like a childbirth, actually forcing the offspring out of the body of the parent." [48] The Declaration of Independence, the metaphor may be continued, cut the umbilical cord. Yet what was born was not the infant American nation, but the embryo; or rather, the nation was born so premature that for the next ninety years it existed only as a potentiality. The unformed American soul hung precariously to the undeveloped body, and the eventually firm union of the two was not a matter of certainty, but the result of a string of happy accidents.

In *Common Sense,* when the disaffected Englishman Thomas Paine set out to prove that Americans were not, and should have no desire to be, English, to begin, he disillusioned them *à propos* the "so much boasted" British constitution. On examination, it turned out "to be the base remains of two ancient tyrannies [the monarchical and the aristocratic], compounded with some new republican materials." He then proceeded to dispell the "myth" of the English descent of Americans, heretofore a matter of much pride, and claimed that "Europe, and not England, is the parent country of America. This new world hath been the asylum for the persecuted lovers of civil and religious liberty from *every part* of Europe . . . Not one third of the inhabitants, even of this province [conveniently, he resided in Pennsylvania], are of English descent. Wherefore, I reprobate the phrase of parent or mother country applied to England only, as being false, selfish, narrow, and ungenerous." Even were Americans descended from Britain, he continued, what would this amount to? His answer was: "Nothing. Britain, being now an open enemy, extinguishes every other name and title." American identity was of a far more universal (though appropriately qualified) sort: "We claim brotherhood with every European Christian, and triumph in the generosity of the sentiment." This expansive definition of the national community, which, in the understanding of the time, made Americans coterminous with humanity, led Paine, on the one hand, to claim that "a government of our own is our natural right," namely that self-government was Mankind's birthright, not an English liberty. On the other hand, it allowed him to identify the American cause with the cause of Mankind. Such ideas were not new: the identification of America with the best hope of humanity, and specifically with liberty, had a long tradition and was inherent in the early religious notions of "God's American Israel" and the superior Englishness of Americans.[49] What was new was the explicitness and unambivalent nature of their universalism, and this universalism was destined to become one of the hallmarks of the American national identity.

The separation from Britain implied universalization of English values. The ideal of liberty, which in the course of the sixteenth and seventeenth centuries, through long association, came to be seen as an English national characteristic, was dissociated from England. The "inalienable rights" evoked by the Declaration of Independence were no longer those guaranteed by the British constitution, but by "the Laws of Nature and of Nature's God," and the people of the United Colonies claimed them not by virtue of being Englishmen, but by virtue of being human. The significance of American independence, wrote Jefferson in what was probably his last letter, lay in that it opened the eyes of all "to the rights of man."[50]

Americans pledged themselves, far more explicitly and unambivalently than did the English before them, to universal liberty. The implication of this universalism was a pervasive individualism. Universal self-government meant the self-government—that is, the independence—of each individual (Christian European) man,[51] and this national commitment to the liberty of every individual man presented a formidable obstacle for the creation of a single American nation. It was not at all obvious why there should be only one American nation. In principle, to carry the ideal of self-government to its logical conclusion, every individual constituted a nation in his own right; in practical terms, at the moment of independence one could easily think of thirteen American nations. Thus the very nationality of the American identity, the uncompromising commitment of Americans to the purified principles of civic nationalism, for a long time to come was bound to hinder the formation of a consensus regarding the geo-political referent of American national loyalty, leaving open the question of what was, or whether there was, *the* American nation.

That nation-building on the (exclusive) basis of ideals of civic nationalism was a Herculean task was realized early in the process. However much some Americans wished to see the colonies united, they knew that as a matter of fact they were not one entity. We may never know whether Patrick Henry indeed claimed in 1774 that the distinctions between the colonies were no more and that he was not a Virginian but an American, or whether his electrifying and precociously triumphant unionist tirade was only the fruit of his biographer's fantasy; if he did, he certainly was talking of things that "have not yet gone through the formality of taking place."[52] The very frequency with which some enthusiasts in the years following independence insisted that America, the thirteen colonies together, was a nation leads one to suspect that there was an element of wishful thinking in it. John Murrin is undoubtedly right in proposing that "to repudiate Britain meant jeopardizing what the settlers had in common while stressing what made them different from one another." [53] While there existed an American identity—a sense that all Americans, be they from Virginia, Massachusetts, or elsewhere, shared certain characteristics (such as an exemplary love of liberty)—it was not accompanied by a sense that Americans constituted a unity. Only in later periods would some writers trace its emergence back to the early colonial period.[54] The habitual use of the collective designation "American" during the colonial period did not reflect the existence of an American collectivity. It was a purely geographical qualifier. Such use was to be expected. The term was employed to distinguish British citizens, Englishmen not in England. They were first called "English (or British) Americans," and then "Americans" for short. In this context it is significant that such a collective designation was more commonly employed at first by the British. Carl Bridenbaugh cites an English admiral's derisive reference to the Continental forces during the hostilities in 1741 as "Americans" as one of the first examples of such a collective designation. (The American response, revealingly, was to refer to the British troops, with equally derisive intent, as "Europeans.") Similarly, Merle Curti stresses that Burke used the expression "America" rather than "colonies" in his speech on reconciliation. Both Bridenbaugh and Curti seem to regard Franklin's characterization of himself in a letter from London as "an American" instead of "a Pennsylvanian" as a sign of a growing sense of American unity.[55] But it is not coincidental that Franklin was writing from England and, as he took care to make clear, it was in English eyes that he seemed "too much of an American." For England the colonies were "America" insofar as they were not European, not because of a presupposition of unity. It is probable that the English hardly knew the number or the names of all the colonies and cared even less. To see the term "American" as the reflection of an actually existing unity would be analogous to considering as such collective terms like "Africa," "the Third World," "Eastern Europe," or "the West."

One reason why many proud Americans failed to rejoice at the idea of independence was the widespread understanding that separation from England was likely to result in the total disintegration of the intercolonial unity. (Incidentally, those who were the least concerned were foreigners, such as Thomas Paine or Alexander Hamilton.) "The penman of the Revolution," John Dickinson, refused to sign the Declaration of Independence. On July 1, 1776, he explained the reasons for his caution, among them his fear that "it may weaken that Union (of the Colonies) . . . In bitterness of Soul [the people] may complain against our Rashness . . . A PARTITION of these Colonies will take place if Great Britain cant conquer Us. To escape from the protection we have in British rule by declaring independence would be like

Destroying a House before We have got another, in Winter, with a small Family . . . Not only Treaties with foreign powers but among Ourselves should precede this Declaration. We should know on what Grounds We are to stand with Regard to one another . . . Some of Us totally despair of any reasonable Terms of Confederation." He added almost prophetically: "I should be glad to know whether in 20 or 30 years this Commonwealth of Colonies may not be too unwieldy, and Hudson's River be a proper Boundary for a separate Commonwealth to the Northward. I have a strong Impression on my Mind that this will take Place." Yet John Dickinson was an American patriot who fervently desired the union of the colonies. It was he who composed the proud "Liberty Song," calling:

> Come, join hand in hand, brave Americans all,
> And rouse your bold hearts at fair liberty's call.

There, he insisted:

> No tyrannous acts shall suppress your just claim,
> Or stain with dishonor America's name.
> In freedom we're born and in freedom we'll live!

But this bright future was dependent on the existence of the union, which was not to be presumed as a given. The poem contained a well-known warning: "By uniting we stand, by dividing we fall." [56]

The Union of the States was proposed and defended on instrumental grounds, fundamentally for the same reasons that earlier were advanced in defense of the continuing association with Britain: it was argued that it served to promote and safeguard the self-government of its parts. Yet the end itself, to which the Union was supposed to be the means—self-government of the parts—was contradictory to its existence, for the Union necessarily presupposed a central government, and self-government implied decentralization. This was the issue of the controversy around the Constitution.

What was to be the nation of the Americans? Was a single nation (the union of the states) or several nations best suited to their national (and emphatically so) identity, most agreeable, as their seventeenth-century progenitors would have said, to their American temper? The architects of Independence were torn by these questions. There was no presumption of the existence of some metaphysical unity that made the formation of the political union natural and necessary. Americans held some things to be self-evident, but the Union was not among them. Its utility was clearly realized. Thomas Paine argued it with his usual rhetorical ability in the *Crisis* in 1783: "On this [the Union of the states] our great national character depends . . . It is through this only that we are, or can be, nationally known in the world; it is the flag of the United States which renders our ships and commerce safe on the seas, or in a foreign port . . . In short, we have no other national sovereignty than as United States. It would be fatal for us, if we had, for it would be too expensive to be maintained, and impossible to be supported . . . Our citizenship in the United States is our national character . . . Our great title is Americans—our inferior one varies with the place." Without the Union, thought Jefferson, America, "this heavenly country," would become "an arena of gladiators." Later he wrote regarding the motives for its formation: "It could not but occur to every one, that these separate independencies, like the petty States of Greece, would be eternally at war with each other, and would become at length the mere partisans and satellites of the leading powers of Europe. All then must have looked forward to some further bond of union, which would ensure eternal peace, and a political system of our own, independent of that of Europe." For such instrumental reasons, "these United States" were to be considered "as one nation" in all treaties concluded with foreign powers. In foreign relations, in other words, they were to conduct themselves *as if* they were one nation, although everyone at home knew that they were not. For, while Americans agreed that presenting a single national facade to the world had certain advantages, they were far from being persuaded that a single nation at home would promote the great cause of liberty. In fact, some argued, as did Samuel Bryan of Pennsylvania, that "if the United States are to be melted down into one empire . . . anything short of despotism could not bind so great a country under one government; and . . . whatever plan you might, at the first setting out, establish, it would issue in despotism." For this reason he urged to oppose the Constitution.[57]

Americans did not conceive of a nation, or a people, or a state, in terms of a unitary entity, a collective individual. None of these concepts were reified; they remained, as in England, but more conspicuously so, collective designations for associations of individuals. It is indeed a singular feature of the political language of revolutionary America that the word "people" in it is used, as a rule, in the plural. (For instance, in the Declaration of Independence: "Whenever any Form of Government becomes destructive of these ends [life, liberty, and the pursuit of happiness], it is the Right of the People to alter or to abolish it, and to institute new Government, laying its foundations on such principles and organizing its powers in such form, as to *them* shall seem most likely to effect *their* Safety and Happiness.") The location of sovereignty within the "people" in the plural divided sovereignty. A "nation," as in the original English conception, was a community of sovereign members. Its own sovereignty was composite, not unitary; it was derived from theirs. Thus any nation, in principle, was a *federal* structure, in the sense that it was based upon the good faith (from the Latin *foedus*—treaty, derived from *fides*—faith) of its members in one another, or a social contract. The moral primacy of the individuals, the parties to the contract, and the artificial character of societies (social compacts) were made explicit and insisted upon. Membership did not imply the dissolution of the individual in the community; while he exchanged some of his natural rights for civil protection, he in no way abrogated his sovereignty. In fact, he had no right to do so: "There are certain natural rights," stated Virginia legislators, "of which men, when they form a social compact, cannot deprive or divest their posterity." [58]

Because of the inherently contractual nature of the national collectivity, the size of an ideal society became an important matter for consideration. It could be reasonably argued that smaller societies, such as states, were better fit to be nations than a large society, such as the Union of the states. Yet, interestingly, because of the centrality of the issue of whether the states together did, could, or should consitute one nation, the concept became associated with the Union, acquiring a novel significance which has since influenced American thinking about nationality. Rather than refer to the inner structure of the collectivity, "nation" was increasingly taken to connote *generality*, commonality, and centralization of sovereignty. (By contrast, "state," seen in opposition to the Union, in the American context did not have such implications until much later.) How this transformation occurred could be observed in the resolutions proposed by Edmund Randolph on May 30, 1787, during the debates in the Federal Convention, and Gouverneur Morris' interpretation of them. That day, Madison reports:

> The propositions of Mr. RANDOLPH which had been referred to the committee being taken up, he moved, on the suggestion of Mr. G. MORRIS, that the first of his propositions,—to wit: "Resolved, that the Articles of Confederation ought to be so corrected and enlarged, as to accomplish the objects proposed by their institution; namely, common defence, security of liberty, and general welfare,"—should mutually be postponed, in order to consider the three following: "1. That a union of the states merely federal, will not accomplish the objects proposed by the Articles of Confederation—namely, common defence, security of liberty, and general welfare. 2. That no treaty or treaties among the whole or part of the states, as individual sovereignties, would be sufficient. 3. That a *national* government ought to be established, consisting of a *supreme* legislative, executive, and judiciary" . . . Some verbal criticisms were raised against the first proposition . . . which underwent a discussion, less, however, on its general merits than on the force and extent of the particular terms *national* and *supreme*. Mr. CHARLES PINCKNEY wished to know of Mr. Randolph, whether he meant to abolish the state governments altogether . . . Mr. GOUVERNEUR MORRIS explained the distinction between a *federal* and a *national supreme* government; the former being a mere compact resting on the good faith of the parties, the latter having a complete and *compulsive* operation. He contended, that in all communities there must be one supreme power, and one only. [59]

Curiously, the adjective "federal," though opposed by Morris to "national," by the same logic, through its association with the Union, soon became syn-

onymous with the latter term. In this framework, a "nationalist" or "federalist" position, which was originally that of the champions of self-
government, acquired the meaning of an advocacy of centralization.

## Federalists and Jeffersonians

"Every difference of opinion," argued Jefferson wisely in his First Inaugural
Address, "is not a difference of principle. We have called by different names
brethren of the same principle. We are all republicans—we are all federalists," all equally attached to "union and representative government."[60] The
"nationalist" Federalists held liberty as dear to their hearts as did their
states'-rights opponents. The difference in their views regarding the appropriate focus of American national loyalty reflected the opposing conceptions
they held of human nature and, as a result, of strategies necessary for the
preservation of liberty, not a difference in objectives or values. Federalists
were realists who tended toward pessimism. They were aware of the duality
of human nature, the coexistence in it of capabilities for both good and evil,
of the rational and the irrational. For them, as for the anti-Federalists, liberty was the right of rational creatures; its basis and justification was reason. But they thought that reason, that one side of the dual human nature,
unless supported by the committed-to-liberty government, was not to be
counted upon to sustain itself in the masses of men, and that, therefore,
liberty unsupported by government was in danger of being subverted. Liberty was not licentiousness; it was both a right and an obligation not to
encroach on the rights of others; it implied self-restraint. But to trust men
left to their own devices to restrain themselves was "to disbelieve history
and universal experience . . . to disbelieve Revelation and the Word of God,
which informs us that the heart is deceitful above all things and desperately
wicked." John Adams rejected such naiveté. He had a high opinion of the
American people, as distinguished from men in general, and thought that,
owing to the happy circumstances of their existence, they were reasonable,
"not subject to . . . those contagions of madness and folly which are seen in
countries where large numbers live . . . in dayly fear of perishing for want."
Yet he cautioned: "Remember, democracy [that is, a true, decentralized self-
government by the people] never lasts long. It soon wastes, exhausts and
murders itself."[61] Publius (either Hamilton or Madison) warned in the *Federalist #63*: "There are particular moments in public affairs when the
people, stimulated by some irregular passion, or some illicit advantage, or
misled by the artful representations of interested men, may call for measures
which they themselves will afterwards be the most ready to lament and to
condemn . . . liberty may be endangered by the abuses of liberty as well as
by the abuses of power . . . and . . . the former, rather than the latter, are
apparently most to be apprehended by the United States." The people, even

in America, where, the *Federalist* recognized, they were exceptionally judicious, had to be guarded "against the tyranny of their own passions." "It is the reason alone, of the public," insisted Publius in the *Federalist* #49, "that ought to control and regulate the government. The passions ought to be controlled and regulated by the government." Thus it was not the opposition to the republican form of government, but the awareness of "the dangerous propensities against which it ought to be guarded," [62] that prompted the Federalists' advocacy of restrictions on the popular democracy and the centralization of sovereignty in the *national supreme* government, as against leaving it, divided and endangered, in the hands of the local communities—the states.

By contrast, Jefferson believed in the essential, perennial rationality of men, which made a strong government unnecessary. He thought "that man was a rational animal, endowed by nature with rights, and with an innate sense of justice; and that he could be restrained from wrong and protected in right, by moderate powers, confined to persons of his own choice, and held to their duties by dependence on his own will . . . The cherishment of the people then was our principle, the fear and distrust of them, that of the other [Federalist] party." He thought that self-government was self-preserving and self-generating, that the best means to safeguard it was to let it be. "Where every man is a sharer in the direction of his ward-republic," he wrote, "or of some of the higher ones, and feels that he is a participant in the government of affairs, not merely at an election . . . but every day; when there shall not be a man in the State who will not be a member of some one of its councils . . . he will let his heart be torn out of his body sooner than his power be wrested from him by a Caesar or a Bonaparte." [63] Because states allowed fuller participation in the government, Jefferson favored states' rights.[64] In a society characterized by a unique equality of conditions and ruled by an indomitable leveling spirit (and this much more so in the Federalist East than in the Jeffersonian South), with opportunities which were indeed open and resources almost unbounded for those who would but see them, the masses would not accept tutelage, even such that was designed for their benefit. Watching Federalists in power allow their solicitude for unprotected liberty run amok and degenerate into paranoia persuaded them that it could not be for their benefit. The Jeffersonian position was more in harmony with dominant attitudes and concerns, and this position triumphed.

Ironically, it was this victory, which identified states' rights with liberty and thus with the American national purpose, that later allowed the slaveholding states of the South to claim and sincerely believe that they, and not the free states of the North, were the true champions of the American ideals. The irony went further. One cannot help suspecting that Jefferson's unwavering defense of a truly participatory democracy (to which New England with its notorious and resented-elsewhere "leveling spirit" came so close) was related to the fact that he had never experienced it. The good people of Virginia, by comparison with their unruly brethren farther North, were indeed a reasonable and docile lot. They knew that their betters knew better and trusted in them.[65] Jefferson showed perfect equanimity in the face of rebellion, whether in France or in Massachusetts, believing it to be "a medicine necessary for the sound health of governments" and holding that "a little rebellion, now and then, is a good thing, and as necessary in the political world as storms in the physical." "You never felt the terrorism of Shays' Rebellion in Massachusetts," John Adams reproached him later. "I have no doubt you were fast asleep in philosophical tranquility." [66]

Furthermore, Jefferson's belief in the incorruptibility of reason led him to approve of excesses and inhumanity perpetrated in its name and to rationalize irrationality (both in the sense of justifying it and presenting it as rational). He excused it as "the agonizing spasms of infuriated man, seeking through blood and slaughter his long-lost liberty." Speaking of the terror during the French Revolution he staunchly supported, he regretted the tragic death in it of his acquaintances and men he admired ("In the struggle which was necessary, many guilty persons fell without the form of trial, and with them some innocent"), but, he said, he regretted them "as I should have done had they fallen in battle. It was necessary to use the arm of the people, a machine . . . blind to a certain degree . . . My own affections have been deeply wounded by some of the martyrs to this cause, but rather than it should have failed I would have seen half of the earth desolated; were there but an Adam and an Eve left in every country, and left free, it would be better than as it now is." [67] How fortunate for America that its freedom did not have to be purchased at the price of depopulation. Such convictions on the part of a leader could be dangerous otherwise.

The final irony is, of course, that Jefferson, the tireless champion of the ideal participatory democracy, was a slave-owner. He was deeply troubled by the problem of men owning other men, though chiefly on the account of its effects on the owners.[68] After all, it was not difficult, in the framework of his view of human nature, to find a perfectly rational basis for slavery. The claim to liberty was based on reason. For Jefferson, reason was infallible and unassailable, perfect. This implied that there could be no degrees of reason: one either had it in its perfection, or did not have it. The Negroes, so Jefferson staunchly believed, were intellectually inferior to white men. This imperfection of their reason, which negated it altogether, excluded them from the race of men who were born equal and endowed by nature with an inalienable right to liberty. It was his firm conviction that man's reason was invincible, the very degree of his great respect for the rational man, which led Jefferson to acquiesce in this ultimate indignity inflicted by some men on others. The Federalists, on the other hand, did not have such respect for anyone; they thought all men, if unprotected by government, fallible, and it was much harder for them to justify a situation in which some fallible men had the right to own others.

The Constitution, as ratified, represented a compromise between the Federalist or nationalist position and the states'-rights attitude, which later became identified with Jefferson. The word "nation" was never once mentioned in the text;[69] the Constitution was of "these United States." The composite, contractual nature of the polity and the dispersion of sovereignty were reaffirmed. But at the same time the Constitution bound the states together in the shared loyalty to itself and thus by default created a unified inclusive polity—a nation in the American sense. Reverence for the Constitution, as earlier love of liberty, became the core of the American national identity. But, similarly to the love of liberty, the Constitution could not settle the question of what was to be the geo-political embodiment of this identity or the material, as against the symbolic, referent of national loyalty.

## The Tug-of-War: The Persisting Threat of Secession and the Development of National Unity

In 1780 Washington confessed in a letter to a delegate to the Continental Congress that he saw "one head gradually changing into thirteen." The adoption of the Constitution changed the situation but slightly. The Constitution did give significant powers to the central (federal or national) government, but it still was possible to interpret it, as did Jefferson in 1825, as "a compact of many independent powers, every single one of which claims an equal right to understand it, and to require its observance."[70] The separatist impulse was inherent in the very conception of the Union, as it was earlier in the conception of the English nation, and its legitimacy was much more explicit. The Union was in perpetual peril of dissolving, the materialization of which twice became imminent and was averted only owing to the fortuitous resolution of a military conflict, which was favorable to the preservation of the United States. In both cases thoughts of secession were provoked by a perceived threat to the economic or political interests of a particular region, which led its leaders to "calculate the value of the Union" and conclude that it did not pay off. This was, evidently, an easily comprehensible, natural response, and it highlighted the fact that the association of the states was regarded in instrumental terms. But in both cases the opposition to the Union was presented as a stand in defense of American—national—ideals, and there is no reason to doubt that this claim on the part of the advocates of disintegration was sincere.

It was the Federalist New England that threatened to secede first. The reason was the fear that the political influence of the Northern states in the

Union would be curtailed and their commercial interests hurt as a result of the Louisiana Purchase and the expansion of the agrarian West, which led to the War of 1812. "Admit this western world into the Union," argued Senator William Plumer of New Hampshire, referring to Louisiana, "and you destroy, at once, the weight and importance of the eastern states, and compel them to establish a separate and independent empire." When the war was declared on Britain by a narrow majority of votes in both the House of Representatives and the Senate, a Northern Confederacy was proposed and a union with Britain against the United States, and Gouverneur Morris confessed that he lost "all loyalty to the nation." Explaining their disaffection, citizens of Massachusetts assembled at a meeting in Springfield insisted on the elevated and general nature of their concern: "We consider the late act of the president unjust, unnecessary, and ruinous to the best interests of this country, as a war of aggression and conquest . . . we hold in utter abhorrence an alliance with France, the destroyer of all republics." [71] Altruism, which in the United States often informed self-interest, was at least as frequently motivated by it.

The secessionism of the South, which requires discussion at a later point, was similarly inspired by the perceived threat of Northern dominance. From the economic point of view, the practices of the rapidly industrializing North, on whose industrial production the South was dependent, indeed could be seen as "internal colonialism." The political weight of the South was also diminishing. In 1850, with the recently acquired Mexican lands in mind, the Charleston *Mercury* noted that "the South, for the first time, perceives the insecurity and ignominy of her situation in the Union," and advised "to don the casque and buckle the armor." Two years later, the people of the State of South Carolina, in Convention assembled, declared and ordained, very much in the spirit of 1776, "that South Carolina, in the exercise of her sovereign will," wished to secede from the "Federal Union," that this was her right, "without let, hindrance, or molestation from any power whatsoever," and that "for the sufficiency of the causes which may impel her to such separation, she [was] responsible alone, under God, to the tribunal of public opinion among the nations of the earth." [72]

Fortunately, the War of 1812 ended with a victory of the United States, and in the brief but healing "era of good feeling" that followed, both the noble indignation of the Northern states, whose fears were now allayed, and their intentions to secede vanished for lack of relevance. Likewise, fifty years later, after a much more brutal struggle, the Northern states, now fighting for the Union, prevailed, and Southern secessionism was subdued in its turn. Until 1865, however, it was unclear what the relationship between the many and the one in *E Pluribus Unum* should be, and entirely possible that the United States would disintegrate into several American nations.

The situation, however, was gradually changing, and as early as 1787 there existed important conditions that promoted the formation of the sense of unity which would not only increase the instrumental value of the Union, but render it a good and an end in itself. Throughout the period the secession impulse, as in England earlier, was held in check by the possibility of spatial separation. In 1780, owing to the self-interested obstinacy of Maryland, the unappropriated lands, to which individual states were entitled by their charters as colonies or otherwise, were ceded to the United States "for their common benefit."[73] This created a "national" or "public" domain, to be administered by the central government, and thus transformed the latter into the largest land-owner and the distributor of the most valuable resource. The opportunities available in the framework of the Union were multiplied, and the inability to realize them in a settled place did not generate disaffection, but simply encouraged one to move. It was a remarkable situation in which exit and voice were not the only ways to express dissatisfaction (in fact they were highly unlikely ways to do so), for loyalty did not imply staying where one happened to be born.[74] The marginal utility of secession for the people of the thirteen original states and the sheer number of possible motives for it were greatly reduced. At the same time the provident Northwest Ordinance of July 13, 1787, a true stroke of political genius, tamed the secession impulse of the Western settlers, which might have developed in the course of time, before it was born. It laid out the rules for the automatic ascent of a territory through the stages of increasing self-government to the status of a state and its admission to the Union on the footing of complete equality with its original members. The constitutional provision for a decennial census of the population guaranteed each new state political influence commensurate with the number of residents in it.[75]

The West, as is widely recognized, became a unifying factor of outstanding importance. This was not only because the major reasons for opposition to the Union had been eliminated from the start, but because it promoted the development of national—that is, general American—loyalty to a greater extent than was possible in the older states. To begin with, there were no competing loyalties capable of obstructing this development; local patriotism needed time to evolve. The emergent communities did not have a sense of their own particularity and did not tend to distinguish between their interests and the interests of the United States as a whole. Besides, it was the government of the United States which had obliged them with their land and on which they relied for the introduction of large-scale improvements, such as the construction of roads, that could not at that time be undertaken privately.[76] There was no Ohio or Illinois identity comparable to the identities of Massachusetts (or even Boston) or Virginia. And so the four-year-old Chicago, a town not yet incorporated, with a population of four thousand people, had a newspaper with a grand, capacious title: *The American*. (This was Chicago's second newspaper; the first one, founded a year earlier [1835], had an equally inclusive name: *The Democrat*.)

The West also, to a greater extent than the original states, promoted the sense of American uniqueness. If New England (taken in the comprehensive initial meaning of all the British settlements on the Atlantic coast) thought of itself as a better England, it still preserved the awareness of and cherished its Englishness; it stressed the fundamental sameness and the continuity between the mother country and its colonial progeny. But the West was no new England; it was essentially different. It was the West which led to the identification of America with a pioneering spirit, with the unpolished, but honest, independent, and self-confident individual who might have regarded the rules of spelling as "contrary to nature" (as did Davy Crockett), but knew the difference between right and wrong and was steadfast in his solid common sense.

The West reinforced the image of America as the land of opportunity and identified it with the promise of individual prosperity and advancement to a greater extent than was possible in the East. The opportunities of the Atlantic coast were many, but in the vast expanses of the West they appeared unlimited. "Everything was open to us," summarized William Larimer, the indomitable founder of failed cities, whose perseverance was eventually rewarded by the birth of Denver, Colorado.[77] The natural abundance of economic opportunities was complemented by the creation of a similar plenty in the political sphere. The unique American institution—the political party—with its focus on organization rather than issues, and its consequent geographical egalitarianism, furnished "an office for every man": so long as one wished to be politically involved, one could be politically involved.

Another factor which contributed to the formation of the sense of American unity was immigration. Even less than Western settlers did immigrants share in the divisive loyalties of the original states. Like Englishmen of earlier times, who had conceived of America as a unity long before such a thought entered the minds of the colonists themselves, immigrants were unlikely to be aware of internal distinctions among the United States. They came to "America," became "Americans" on arrival, and their loyalty was to the nation as a whole, which they tended to regard in much more cohesive terms than did the experienced native population. This attitude was supported by law: since 1740 a foreigner was granted rights of citizenship in all the colonies after seven years of residence in any one of them. The Naturalization Act of 1802, after some vacillation between two and fourteen years, fixed the residence requirement at five years, but the citizenship remained national. Although it was not spelled out until later, it was understood that "the immigrant is not a citizen of any State or Territory upon his arrival, but comes here to become a citizen of a great Republic, free to change his residence at will."[78]

Foreigners, unencumbered by unwieldy knowledge of regional specificities, were the first not only to conceive of American unity, but to perceive its uniqueness as well. It was Crevecoeur who gave an authoritative answer to the question: "What is an American?" It was Tocqueville who left us the anatomy of American society which is still used as a guide by its students. The perceptions by the sympathetic outsiders of what America was about helped to put its distinctiveness into a sharper focus for the Americans (there was a natural tendency to disregard the unsympathetic perceptions). In this manner the immigrants' impressions, too, aided in defining American identity.

The reasons for the immigrants' loyalty to America and the process in which it was formed allow one to make an important observation regarding the nature of national loyalty in general: the immigrants' commitment did not derive from the love of country; it derived from the uplifting, dignifying effects of liberty and equality, the exhilarating lure of opportunity, and the enjoyment or even the expectation of a greater prosperity. The love of country, allegedly a primary sentiment, was based on the national commitment, rather than generating it. In his perceptive analysis of the transformation of the European immigrant into an American, Crevecoeur underscored the essentially conceptual nature of national identity. European immigrants, he wrote, had no country before they came and could know no national feeling; they embraced American identity eagerly, because only as Americans were they elevated to the status of men. Prosperity, that is, having bread on one's table (or to be precise, "plenty of beefsteaks and onions," which according to the acid observations of Mrs. Trollope were the regular diet among the American poor), had its attractions for the hungry. Yet, even poverty in America appeared sweeter than elsewhere. "I think I would rather be poor here in America than in Blackenheim," mused a German immigrant in Wisconsin. "There one is obliged to do obeisance to the great, while here that is not necessary." An immigrant from Norway, in a letter to a friend, echoed Crevecoeur's analysis. "I have learned to love the country to which I emigrated more sincerely than my old fatherland," he wrote. "I feel free and independent among a free people, who are not chained down by any class or caste systems; and I am very proud of belonging to a mighty nation, whose institutions must in time come to dominate the entire civilized world, because they are founded on principles that sound intelligence must recognize as the only ones that are right and correct." [79] The immigrants shared and reinforced the sentiments felt by more experienced Americans. Both, the former and the latter, recognized equality in dignity as the essence of the United States. "She, that lifts up the manhood of the poor," James Russell Lowell characterized his country. It was this gift of dignity that the immigrants' awkward explanations reflected and because of which they were becoming ardent American patriots.

Of course, this was not so in every case, and with the immigration of the 1840s the general mood was altered significantly. The reason was the emergence of nationalisms in the countries from which the immigrants came.

Crevecoeur's assertion, that two-thirds of the Europeans did not have a country, in the eighteenth century was not a rhetorical device, but a statement of fact. In the middle of the nineteenth century this was no longer true. Some immigrants, specifically those from Germany, were coming with a competing national identity. Nationalism everywhere elevated the status of the indigenous *people,* and the respect immigrants got in America as individuals, for some of them, did not measure up to the outright adulation they had been growing used to as members of a group. For such immigrants with national identity, assimilation became much more difficult than it was for their countrymen without it. They had to give up comforting notions of this or that national character, on which were based their sense of self-esteem and pride. One dreaded to part with such notions; as a result, their loyalties for a long time continued divided. Still, at least until the late nineteenth century, European nationalisms affected chiefly the elites, and for the majority of simple men and women, America remained the only country where they could lead a dignified existence.

Immigrants and pioneers soon developed an attachment to the American *land,* both the specific plot on it where they happened to settle and the country as a whole. They eagerly appreciated its abundance and beauty, even in conditions where such appreciation required a certain imaginative effort. Somewhat like the original members of the Plymouth plantation, who sang praises to the salubrity of New England's air while burying their dead, the settlers admired Western sunsets, and believed, wherever they were and whatever difficulties were facing them in the present, that "never on earth did nature present a fairer field for the use of man, never one more beautiful for his eye to survey, or his heart to admire and love." [80] The possibilities inherent in the wilderness, which it was for them to realize, gave rise to the sense of proprietary pride: they loved the country because they had a stake in it. The pull of America's promise, inherent in the national commitment to equality, has always been stronger than the push of reality that failed—temporarily—to stand up to it. This explains why so few of the immigrants returned and so few of the native Americans (that is, Americans born in the United States) became expatriates. It was much easier to brave the difficulties with which one could meet anywhere, than to forgo the opportunity which was hardly conceivable anywhere else.

One indisputable virtue of the American land, on which the certitude of future prosperity to an extent rested, was its vastness. The sheer size of America early became one of its most endearing features and was celebrated in rapidly developing folklore as well as professional art. The bigness of the Western folk-heroes, says Boorstin, combined with the contempt for anything little, was quite without parallel in any other tradition. "The infant Davy Crockett was rocked by water power in a twelve-foot cradle made from the shell of a six-hundred-pound snapping turtle, varnished with rattlesnake oil, and covered with wildcat skins. According to the almanacs, he could 'walk like an ox, run like a fox, swim like an eel, yell like an Indian, fight like a devil, spout like an earthquake, make love like a mad bull.' His knife Big Butcher was the longest in all Kentucky, his dog Teaser could throw a buffalo." Works of professional art inspired by America's size were, if possible, even more astonishing. A New Yorker, John Banvard, "actuated by a patriotic and honorable ambition, that he should produce the largest painting in the world," set out "to paint a picture of the beautiful scenery of the Mississippi, which should be as superior to all others, in point of *size,* as that prodigious river is superior to the streamlets of Europe." The result of his efforts was "the Largest Picture ever executed by Man," three miles of ten-foot-high canvas, which the painter displayed piecemeal, helped by an ingenious device of revolving cylinders placed some twenty feet apart from each other. Banvard enjoyed great success and soon was imitated by other similarly inspired artists and patriots, who, being highly committed to realistic representation, produced still larger paintings. Bigness became American. For a long time to come in Chicago, that essentially American city "on the boundless prairie and the mighty lake," "'Big' was the word. 'Biggest' was preferred, and the 'biggest in the world' was the braggart phrase on every tongue. Chicago had the biggest conflagration 'in the world.' It slaughtered more hogs than any city 'in the world.' It was the greatest railroad center, the greatest this, and the greatest that. It shouted itself hoarse in *réclame.*" [81]

Like the West, immigration helped to put certain uniquely American qualities into sharper relief. It reinforced and gave a new meaning to the claim that America had a universal mission, and that the American nation itself was a universal nation, the nation of mankind. Its uniqueness was a result of a unique fusion of peoples, all of whom, so it was felt and so it was inscribed in the national consiousness, came hither in search of freedom, for America was the asylum for the oppressed. "Haste you to America," wrote a Jewish song-writer in Germany in 1848,

> Haste to greet the land of freedom,
> Free from prejudice, hate, and envy,
> Free from hangmen and tyrants!
> . . . think and make haste![82]

The scale and persistence of immigration reassured Americans of the superiority of their society; their government's and their own attitude of openness reinforced their sense of moral perfection. A speaker in the Congress, arguing for the reduction of the proposed two-year-residence requirement during the discussions of the 1790 naturalization bill, asserted confidently and, clearly, with pride: "It is nothing to us, whether Jews or Roman Catholics settle among us; whether subjects of Kings, or citizens of free States wish to reside in the United States," for here in America, "individuals of all nations" were "melted into a new race of men." [83]

This shining universalistic image was early tarnished by jealousy, suspicion, and wounding professions of religious and ethnic pride. There was opposition to other than English immigration as soon as it began. At different times it was opposed by Franklin, Jefferson, very strongly by the Federalists. DeWitt Clinton's boast that Americans had descended "from a superior stock" and his conjecture that the "extraordinary characters which the United States have produced" might be ascribed to the mixed blood of "those nations where civilization, knowledge, refinement have created their empire; and where human nature has attained its greatest perfection," may be interpreted both as an expression of somewhat biased and uninformed, or even tactless, universalism and as a statement of ethnic superiority, spiteful toward a good part of humanity. The later celebration of the Anglo-Saxon or, more generally, Teutonic roots of the American people could probably bear only the latter interpretation. Immigrants were seen as inferior and dangerous to the American community on religious or linguistic grounds, as well as on those of social and political unpreparedness. Zealous Protestants were concerned about the purity of manners and doubted the loyalty of Roman Catholics. The aristocratic sensibility of Henry James was offended by the proprietary irreverence of "the vast contingent of aliens whom we make welcome" toward his English language, which they made their own and handled like their own. But while in other countries ethnic chauvinism of this kind easily crowded out alternative attitudes and became a central element in the respective national identities, in America it always remained a marginal alternative to the national identity which was profoundly universalistic.

Nativism flared up when and where resources appeared scarce and there was a fear of competition for them. For this reason, organized labor was often hostile to immigration. The change in the structure of economic opportunities as a result of the inevitable exhaustion of the geographical frontier[84] was bound to make resources appear scarce. If before there was an opportunity and a reasonable hope to make good for everyone who was willing and able to work hard, now opportunities were in fact open only for those who had special access to them, either because of a singular acumen, the gift of resourcefulness which made Frederic Tudor the Ice King, or because of the initial possession of such auxiliary resources as contacts, education, and wealth. In other words, after the West was won, opportunities were no longer equal. The realization of this disappointing fact on the part of those who were not specially endowed in any way, which was the major reason for their fear and jealousy of immigrants, did not, however, promote disunity. Rather, by way of the reinterpretation of the fundamental American national values, it helped to foster a more unitary notion of the nation and thus contributed to the development of a sense of national cohesion.

In a society which sets great store by equality, economic inequality acquires a significance which goes beyond the effects of differences in material well-being. It is necessarily seen as unjust by the "have-nots" and is perceived as an affront to their dignity, because it belies the proposition that all men are created equal and have equal rights to life and happiness. Equality in liberty (that is, self-government) becomes less important in such situations. In fact, rather than being regarded as an absolute good, it is likely to be seen as a tool for the perpetuation and concealment of existing inequalities. Liberty is infinitely divisible; other goods are not. An increase in the liberty of another does not imply a proportional decrease in one's own; increase in another's share of a finite quantity of something, whether power or wealth, does. When these resources become scarce, the demand for equality of opportunity, dignity, and respect commensurate with one's abilities gives way to the demand for equality of result. It is clear that equality of opportunity, which does not provide for the equality of result, would appeal more strongly to those who have the qualifications necessary to realize the opportunities open to them. It is also clear that in the early American society, actually characterized by equality of conditions, equality of opportunity would be generally acceptable without special provisions for the equality of result simply because it would appear that the latter was implied, inherent in the former. But when actual equality of conditions no longer obtains, the provisions for equality of opportunity only (the legal equality of rights) must appear unsatisfactory. The transformation in the nature of desired equality began to be evident in America in the 1830s. It initiated the transformation in the perception of the functions of government: government as essentially a protective agency (guarding against encroachments on the people's rights by others) no longer appeared sufficient; there was a feeling that it should act as a distributive agency. This, in turn, affected the attitudes toward centralization, making it acceptable and even necessary.

One could observe this transformation in the labor disputes of the period and in the thought of labor leaders and spokesmen. They redefined national loyalty as commitment to equality seen as equal access of all classes of indigenous Americans to American prosperity, and claimed their share in the name of American ideals. As happened so often, in America as well as elsewhere, a particularistic interest was identified with the general, national one, and as a result, the general perception of the national interest was altered. Thus, Seth Luther, in an 1832 "Address to the Workingmen of New England," refused to see national interest in anything that did not promote the welfare of the workers, and interpreted appeals to the nation that did not take this welfare into consideration as thinly camouflaged attempts on the part of some Imperial and Kingly sympathizers to subvert the American national purpose. An attorney for the New York workers in a labor-conspiracy case in 1836 accused the employers of attempting "to keep any one class down . . . and thus exclude them from . . . the general prosperity." This was un-American, and he had no doubt that an end would be put to such treachery: "In our country the protection against such a partial operation of the laws, is to be found in our courts of justice, and though the remedy may be delayed for a while, the good sense and true patriotism which pervades our whole community, render it ultimately certain." But in practical terms protection was expected from the central government. It was to the Congress that Seth Luther appealed to restrict immigration in order "to protect the operative from foreign competition in the shape of importation of foreign mechanics and laborers, [which tends] to cut down the wages of our own citizens."[85]

With the rise of the mass political parties and the elimination of property requirements for voting in the Northern and Western states in the second and third decades of the nineteenth century, the working-men's perceptions as to what constituted the proper functions of government were bound to gain in influence. The demands of the rapidly organizing labor in the North for governmental patronage coincided with similar demands of the fledgling Western communities. Such demands were favorable to the concentration of authority (that is, sovereignty) in the hands of the federal government, thus contributing to a more unitary concept of the national community. Ironically, it was the Jacksonian commitment to decentralized, participatory democracy which made these demands heard and prepared the conditions for their eventual satisfaction.

While the settlement of the West, the massive immigration, and the changes in the economic profile of the settled population in the North worked clandestinely to form the sense of national unity, it was also forged consciously and explicitly by the intellectuals dedicated to the creation of a national ethos. Whether they were politicians and ideologues or belonged to the newer group of literati, American intellectuals from early on were disproportionately committed to the Union, which was for them a value in itself, and inclined to think in terms of a unitary American nation. Their frame of reference was larger; they thought in terms of the civilized world. Considerations of rank and honor figured more prominently among other matters that might have preoccupied them; their personal sense of status depended on the status of the community of which they were members; and the status of the United States—of America—promised in all conditions to be infinitely greater than that of any state in it. Many articulate Americans, therefore, with Daniel Webster, would redefine the hierarchy of American values, rejecting "those words of delusion and folly, 'Liberty first and Union afterwards.'" Theirs was the motto "Liberty *and* Union, now and forever, one and inseparable!" and they were dedicated to making it a "sentiment dear to every true American heart." [86]

Rather than seeing their personal interests as the national interest, such people were likely to internalize what they sincerely believed to be the interest of the nation (what would ensure its independence and augment its power and prestige) and make it their own. (Of course, since their inner well-being depended on the well-being of the nation, however defined, its well-being was clearly in their interest.) This solicitude for the nation formed the basis of the ideologies and programs of economic, political (territorial and pertaining to foreign relations), and cultural American nationalism.

A nation could not be powerful or well regarded if it was not independent. Independence, therefore—economic, political, and cultural—was the paramount concern of the nationalists. The aim of the economic program of Alexander Hamilton (including the protection of indigenous industries and the creation of the national bank) was to free the national government from dependence on the states and to ensure the economic self-sufficiency of America vis-à-vis foreign powers. Jefferson, who vehemently opposed Hamilton's economic centralism, recognized that he was moved by unselfish motives. "Hamilton," he wrote in "Anas," "was, indeed, a singular character. Of acute understanding, disinterested, honest, and honorable in all private transactions." Yet with all his good qualities he still held fundamentally, unforgivably mistaken views: he sacrificed the individual to the collective and was willing to compromise the ideals for which the American nation stood in order to assure its survival and strength. In his recollections of Hamilton's proposals regarding public credit and the bank, Jefferson recorded the following anecdote, which, he believed, spoke volumes. He had invited John Adams and Hamilton to dine with him, and at the dinner table "Mr. Adams observed, 'Purge [the British] constitution of its corruption, and give to its popular branch equality of representation, and it would be the most perfect constitution ever devised by the wit of man.' Hamilton paused and said, 'Purge it of its corruption, and give to its popular branch equality of representation, and it would become an *impracticable* government: as it stands at present, with all its supposed defects, it is the most perfect government which ever existed.'" Hamilton thought compromise of national principles a fair price for the welfare of the nation. This welfare was above the welfare of individuals who composed it (Hamilton was undaunted by the prospect of women and children "of a very tender age" [87] constituting the bulk of the industrial workforce he was advocating), and a little infringement on the rights or comforts of individuals did not necessarily hurt it. Jefferson thought it was Hamilton's Anglophilia which led him to such peculiar views.

Ironically, it was the steadfast Jeffersonians who, after the successful conclusion of the War of 1812, implemented the central tenets of the Hamiltonian program; Mathew Carey, who carried it on later, and who so impressed Friedrich List that he made Hamiltonian economic nationalism a pillar of German nationalism, was both a Republican and an Anglophobe, and so were many of his like-minded compatriots. Jefferson himself was not beyond compromising central values of the nation for the sake of its collective independence, though it is possible that he was not aware that he was doing so. The thrust of his territorial policy and of his isolationism in foreign relations was exactly that: to ensure the independence of the United States from outside pressures. The acquisition of Louisiana made possible enduring isolation, and isolationism betrayed the universalistic commitment of the American nation to the freedom of mankind. The claim that America, that oasis of liberty in the enslaved world, needed to withdraw from it in order to preserve itself and develop, so that it could serve it better as an example, was a clever excuse, but it did not square with the assertion that freedom was worth the reduction of human population to "but an Adam and an Eve left in every country." Apparently, the peace and prosperity of the United States of America were worth more. For Jefferson, too, whether he recognized it or not, the preservation of the nation became an end in itself.

Though some people wished to see the United States more independent, economically and politically, than they were, after the Revolution it was agreed that they were already essentially independent. In regard to cultural independence this was not at all clear. Until very late American intellectuals were tormented by a lingering suspicion that, culturally speaking, America was under-age, that it lacked a "national character," that there was no such thing as "American culture." This was a difficult thought to bear because, in the light of the new, German, theories of nationality, which became popular in the nineteenth century, the lack of a national culture raised the question as to the reality of the nation itself. But even before the wisdom of German Romantics caused American literati to realize the full significance of their cultural inadequacy, Noah Webster urged Americans to "unshackle [their] minds and act like independent beings." "You have been children long enough," he insisted, "subject to the control and subservient to the interests of a haughty parent [England]. You now have an interest of your own to augment and defend—you have an empire to raise and support by your exertions—and a national character to establish and extend by your wisdom and judgement." "The authority of foreign manners," he warned, "keeps us in subjection." [88] The plight of the intellectuals preoccupied with this problem was exacerbated by the general indifference of the population to it. When the American people felt an urge to commune with muses, which was rare to begin with, they were hardly bothered by the foreign inspiration of the latter. They contentedly read English books, and this not only demonstrated the low priority of cultural independence among their aspirations, but significantly complicated the situation of the native literary talent.

The question "Who reads an American book?" wickedly posed by an obviously self-satisfied Englishman, Sydney Smith, was a cause of anguish in the emerging literary community in America. Some thirty years later James Russell Lowell wrote: "The Stamp Act and the Boston Port Bill scarcely produced a greater excitement in America than [that] appalling question." Smith's judgment was devastating. "The Americans are a brave, industrious, and acute people; but they have hitherto given no indication of genius."[89] In 1823 William Ellery Channing gloomily reflected: "Literature is plainly among the most powerful methods of exalting the character of a nation ... Do we possess indeed what we may call a national literature? Have we produced eminent writers in the various departments of intellectual effort? We regret that the reply to these questions is so obvious." He added dejectedly: "It were better to have no literature than form ourselves unresistingly on a foreign one." "The American nation," conceded in 1838 James Fenimore Cooper, some time adamant in his optimism as to the cultural potentialities of his country, "is very far behind most polished nations on various essentials." Still in 1850, Herman Melville raged against American indifference to cultural independence: "You must believe in Shakespeare's unapproachability, or quit the country. But what sort of a belief is this for an American, a man who is bound to carry republican progressiveness into Literature, as well as into Life? Believe me, my friends, that Shakespeares are this day being born on the banks of the Ohio. And the day will come, when you shall say: who reads a book by an Englishman that is a modern?" His diagnosis of the present situation was as depressing as any other: "While we are rapidly preparing for that political supremacy among the nations, which prophetically awaits us at the close of the present century, in a literary point of view we are deplorably unprepared for it, and we seem studious to remain so."[90]

This insistence on the necessity, and anxiety over the continued lack, of cultural independence, much more than parallel demands in the economic and political spheres, presupposed a unitary interpretation of the national community. It implied the definition of the nation as a unity characterized by a uniform and unique manner of thinking and feeling, a collective personality. But, in America, such unitary notions have always had to compete with the contrary view, seeing the nation in composite terms, as an association of individuals, and before the Civil War they were characteristic only of a minority of thinkers even among the intellectuals preoccupied with such matters as literature.

In *Kavanagh*, a story which appeared at about the same time as Melville's review quoted above, Longfellow made a protagonist answer the claim that "if literature is not national, it is nothing" by a counter-claim: "nationality is a good thing to a certain extent, but universality is better." "It is only geographically that we can call ourselves a new nation," concluded Lowell, who reviewed the story. He felt no mortification, for, he thought, in culture nationality was "only a less narrow form of provincialism." The cultural independence of America was, like America itself, composite; it was a reflection of the individual independence of Americans in culture. This was the message of Emerson's "American Scholar." In the conclusion of the famous address Emerson unequivocally rejected the unitary concept of the national culture: "Is it not the chief disgrace in the world, not to be an unit;—not to be reckoned one character;—not to yield that peculiar fruit which each man was created to bear, but to be reckoned in the gross, in the hundred, or the thousand, of the party, the section, to which we belong; and our opinion predicted geographically, as the north, or the south? Not so, brothers and friends,—please God, ours shall not be so. We will walk on our own feet; we will work with our own hands; we will speak our own minds." The American nation was not a nation of Americans. "A nation of men," predicted Emerson, "will for the first time exist, because each believes himself inspired by the Divine Soul which also inspires all men." [91] The independence of the American Scholar rendered the whole issue of the cultural independence of America as a nation irrelevant. But, paradoxically, the very emphasis on the individual and the rejection of the unitary concept of the nation highlighted the uniqueness of American national consciousness and fostered the sense of national unity.

It is important to keep in mind that, until the Civil War settled the issue, the forces that could (and eventually did) bring the United States to the brink of disintegration were at least as strong as those which fostered unity. Therefore, while a few exceptional individuals were preoccupied with the essentialist issue of American national culture, many more were concerned with the cultivation of loyalty among the heterogeneous sectors of the American people. There was a conscious effort to forge a national consciousness that would admit of no doubt that the United States were indeed a nation, and a nation which more than any other deserved passionate commitment. Patriotism was taught through history, literary anthologies, national heroes and symbols, and even arithmetic.[92] Tocqueville noted in Democracy in America: "[Americans] are separated from all other nations by a feeling of pride. For the last fifty years no pains have been spared to convince the inhabitants of the United States that they are the only religious, enlightened, and free people . . . hence they conceive a high opinion of their superiority and are not very remote from believing themselves to be a distinct species of mankind." [93]

Such efforts continued well beyond the time he made this observation. The self-appointed apologists used numerous arguments to convince Americans (themselves often included) that they belonged together and were different from the rest of the world. One such argument was geographical. It was by the design of Providence, of Nature, or of both, it ran, that the United States were bound into an indissoluble union. A speaker in Charleston, in a Fourth of July Oration in 1820, demanded: "Do not our mountains, which run from North to South, bind us in indissoluble union, like the sacred chain in nature which links all her jarring elements in peace? Do not our rivers rise in one state and run into another, receiving the tributary streams of both, and fertilizing with their waters . . . the meadows of all through which they hold their majestic course, without distinction or regard to local prejudices?" What Madison called "the manifest indications of nature" were perceived as such in every geographical region of the country. When the South decided that, after all, they were not that manifest, Lincoln persisted in the belief. "Physically speaking, we cannot separate," he claimed. "We cannot remove our respective sections from each other, nor build an impassable wall between them." He argued: "A nation may be said to consist of its territory, its people, and its laws. The territory is the only part that is of certain durability. One generation passeth away, and another generation cometh, but the earth abideth forever." For this reason, the dissolution of the Union, which, territorially, was one flesh, was inconceivable. Political limits were determined, once and for all, by geography. Paradoxically, the very same argument was used to effect territorial changes, for geography, similarly to Nature and Providence, lent itself to a variety of interpretations. Those who saw America's "manifest destiny" in continental expansion (an expansion which was, of course, also justified by the fact that it increased the realm of freedom) regarded geography as their closest ally.[94] In this case, it must be recognized, contrary to the accepted view of the relations between territoriality and nationality, national loyalty *bred* territory. But those who opposed expansion relied on geographical arguments as well.

Patriots of a less mystical bent pointed to the intricate and expanding communication networks and the developing economic unity of the United States. However, not the material infrastructure, but the social relations and the values of American society were considered the most obvious reason for patriotism. Popular textbooks, such as McGuffey's *Eclectic Readers*, admonished schoolchildren that "America has furnished to Europe proof of the fact, that popular institutions, founded on equality and the principle of representation, are capable of maintaining governments . . . that it is practicable to elevate the mass of mankind, that portion which, in Europe, is called the laboring or lower class; to raise them to self-respect, to make them competent to act a part in the great right and great duty of the self-government. She holds out an example . . . to those nine-tenths of the human race, who are born without hereditary fortune or hereditary rank." Another author of children's literature, Samuel Griswold Goodrich, famous under the pen name of Peter Parley, wrote in a book on American history:

"There are doubtless other nations which surpass ours in certain refinements; but if we regard the general happiness of the great mass of the people, our country is without rival." [95] Such themes were harped upon endlessly, and the fact that they were harped upon in children's books ensured that the image of the American nation would be firmly tied with the notion of democracy in the consciousness of its citizens. When the young readers of Goodrich and McGuffey grew up, they were prepared to see their country with the eyes of Bancroft and Emerson, in whose magnificent tirades American national identity found its quintessential expression.

For George Bancroft, America was no longer the promise of man's self-fulfillment; it was the fulfillment of the promise. Unmindful of the internal contradictions of a democratic society, he did not perceive the discrepancies between American ideals and reality. In the reality of his country he saw the realization of the ideal, the end of the world's journey. His vision was formed already in 1821, when at the age of twenty-one he left for Europe, his bosom burning "with love for Freedom's western home." In his "farewell" poem to Rome two years later, he confessed his yearning for "Freedom's air and for western climes, where the brave, the generous, and the free dwelt," and exclaimed with relief and confidence: "O! there is Rome; no other Rome for me." This was a line in a poem, but no poetic exaggeration. Throughout his long intellectual and political career Bancroft emphasized the universal meaning of America, which, like Emerson, but in the very present, he defined as a "nation of men." It did not belong to a particular race or to an ethnic group that could be defined by religion or language; it was pan-human. In an oration delivered in 1854 he asserted the fundamental unity of humanity, which for ages had existed as a potentiality only but was finally being realized in the United States:

The commonwealth of mankind, as a whole, was not to be constructed in one generation. But the different peoples are to be considered as its component parts, prepared, like so many springs and wheels, one day to be put together ... In this great work our country holds the noblest rank ... Our land is not more the recipient of the men of all countries than their ideas. Annihilate the part of any one leading nation of the world, and our destiny would have been changed. Italy and Spain, in the persons of Columbus and Isabella, joined together for the great discovery that opened America to emigration and commerce; France contributed to its independence; the search for the origin of the language we speak carried us to India; our religion is from Palestine; of the hymns sung in our churches, some were first heard in Italy, some in the deserts of Arabia, some on the banks of the Euphrates; our arts come from Greece; our jurisprudence from Rome; our maritime code from Russia; England taught us the system of Representative Government; the noble Republic of the United Provinces bequeathed to us, in the world of thought, the great idea of the toleration of all opinions; in the world of action, the prolific principle of federal union. Our country stands, therefore, more than any other, as the realization of the unity of the race.

Arabia, India, Palestine, and Russia, in addition to the usual "leading nations of the world"—the desire to prove his point carried Bancroft far beyond the brotherhood of "Christian Europeans," which delimited the scope of American universalism in the popular imagination of his time. The image of America he helped to create expanded and gained in grandeur and significance in proportion to this liberal definition of mankind which it represented.

Universality was inseparably connected to liberty and equality. "As a consequence of the tendency of the race towards unity and universality," thought Bancroft, "the organization of society must more and more conform to the principle of FREEDOM." And as in America the historical tendency was brought to fruition, the organization of American society did so conform. In a still later address, "On the Life and Character of Abraham Lincoln," Bancroft reiterated: "Thousands of years had passed away before this child of the ages could be born. From whatever there was of good in the systems of former centuries [America] drew her nourishment; the wrecks of the past were her warnings ... The fame of this only daughter of freedom went out into all the lands of the earth; from her the human race drew hope."

The men whose nation America was and who found fulfillment in it were "common men"; freedom, which was self-government or government by the majority, was based on the recognition of the fundamental equality between them that reflected the universal diffusion of Reason, that "gracious gift to each member of the human family," existing "within every breast." Because of this universal endowment, Bancroft held,

> the common judgment in taste, politics, and religion is the highest authority on earth ... the nearest criterion of truth ... In like manner the best government rests on the people ... the sum of the moral intelligence of the community should rule the state ... [In America] free institutions ... have acknowledged the common mind to be the true material for a commonwealth ... The absence of the prejudices of the Old World leaves us here the opportunity of consulting independent truth; and man is left to apply the instinct of freedom to every social relation and public interest. We have approached so near to nature that we can hear her gentlest whispers; we have made humanity our lawgiver and our oracle; and therefore, the nation receives, vivifies and applies principles, which in Europe the wisest accept with distrust. Freedom of mind and of conscience, freedom of the seas, freedom of industry, equality of franchises, each great truth is firmly grasped, comprehended and enforced; for the multitude is neither rash nor fickle.[96]

Bancroft's contribution to the forging of the American national identity was gratefully acknowledged. Though his fame rests chiefly on the ten-volume *History of the United States,* which he wrote in the course of forty years, for his contemporaries he was more than a scholar. During his long life he was several times entrusted with high office and served his country as secretary of the navy, minister to England, and then to Prussia and Germany. When he died in 1891, he was mourned as a national hero.

Emerson, in distinction, could not count on the gratitude of the common man, because for him the common man was not an ideal. Or rather, he camouflaged his respect for the common man by exhorting every man to uncover the uncommon in himself; he extolled the individual and distrusted the multitude as such. Unlike Bancroft, he was a realist, intensely aware of the contradictions between principles and reality and painfully conscious of the failings of his society. His vision was critical, and for this reason he appealed to people who felt uneasy with Bancroft's complacent attitude. And yet Emerson had no doubt about the superiority of America over all other existing societies. With all its faults, it still came closer to the fulfillment of man's nature, because it was a universal nation and based on freedom and respect for the individual, and he was sure that with effort and perseverance it would correct the faults and realize the glorious ideals to which it was committed. This ideal state was in the future, but Emerson was certain that it was the future of his nation. In "Young American," he asserted: "We cannot look on the freedom of this country, in connexion with its youth, without a presentiment that here shall laws and institutions exist on some scale of proportion to the majesty of nature . . . it cannot be doubted that the legislation of this country should become more catholic and cosmopolitan than that of any other. It seems so easy for America to inspire and express the most expansive and humane spirit; new-born, free, healthful, strong, the land of laborer, of the democrat, of the philanthropist, of the believer, of the saint, she should speak for the human race. It is the country of the Future."

Emerson deplored the preoccupation with material goods which led men away from spiritual concerns and obscured for them the higher meaning of life and the true significance of American society. At the same time, he stressed the fundamentally beneficent effects of capitalism on society, which formed the basis not of equal prosperity, but of the dignity of man as such— a far greater good, in Emerson's eyes, and the distinguishing characteristic of the American nation. He wrote: "The philosopher and lover of man have much harm to say of trade; but the historian will see that trade was the principle of Liberty; that trade planted America and destroyed Feudalism; that it makes peace and keeps peace, and it will abolish slavery. We complain of its oppression of the poor, and of its building up a new aristocracy on the ruins of the aristocracy it destroyed. But the aristocracy of trade has no permanence, is not entailed, was the result of toil and talent, the result of merit of some kind, and is continually falling, like the waves of the sea, before new claims of the same sort. Trade is an instrument in the hands of that friendly Power which works for us in our own despite." Therefore, he concluded, "after all the deduction is made for our frivolities and insanities, there still remains an organic simplicity and liberty, which, when it loses its balance, redresses itself presently, which offers opportunity to the human mind not known in any other region." In Europe, and even in England, Emerson argued, "the aristocracy, incorporated by law and education, degrades life for the unprivileged classes." Americans could be only "too thankful for our want of feudal institutions." It was this that made America the leading nation of its age, standing for the interests of general justice and humanity. "Which should be that nation but these States?" Emerson asked rhetorically. To him, the answer was clear: he was confident that "if only the men are employed in conspiring with the designs of the Spirit who led us hither, and leading us still, we shall quickly enough advance . . . into a new and more excellent social state than history has recorded." For it was "plain for all men of common sense and common conscience, that here, here in America, is the home of man." [97]

## Inconsistencies and Tensions

The identification of the American nation with a democratic society whose members were free and equal, which was based on respect for the individual and in which humanity composed of individuals found its fulfillment, was universal. Whether or not one believed with Bancroft that America was such a society in reality, everyone agreed that this was what it should be. Much more than in England, the loyalty constantly cultivated was not to a particular stretch of land, sets of people, or political framework, but to the principles and institutions which embodied them. "Give the American his institutions, and he cares little where you place him," wrote Charles Mackay in 1837.[98] American nationalism was idealistic nationalism. As a result, the stronger it was, the more seriously did one take the ideals to which the nation was committed—the stronger was the potential for alienation from its reality. Often the very strength of American national loyalty tended to weaken the American nation.

### The "Stumbling Block"

It must be realized that individualistic-libertarian nationalism sets itself an impossible task. A nation, ideally, is a society composed of individuals equal in their human worth. But in fact such perfect equality cannot be achieved. The reality of an individualistic nation and its ideals are necessarily inconsistent, and this inconsistency breeds discontent and frustration. In *The American Democrat* (a book which its author wanted to call "Anti-Cant" to emphasize the dishonesty of treating the ideal image as if it were reality), a keen, though jaundiced, observer, James Fenimore Cooper, distinguished between the ideal equality and that imperfect approximation to it that, he thought, could exist in fact. Of *Leatherstocking* fame, Cooper is rarely remembered for his contribution to political analysis. Yet *The American Democrat* is one of the few works of that genre and period which are considered to be of lasting value.[99] The views expressed in it very likely represent the position of the patrician class in the North of the time, of which Cooper was a prominent member, and it is thus worth considering at length.

"Equality," Cooper wrote, "in a social sense, may be divided into that of condition, and that of rights. Equality of condition is incompatible with civilization, and is found only to exist in those communities that are slightly removed from the savage state. In practice, it can only mean common misery. Equality of rights is a peculiar feature of democracies." In societies of other types, he explained, "there exist privileged classes, possessed of exclusive rights . . . that are denied to those who are of inferior birth. All these distinctions are done away with in principle, in countries where there exists a professed equality of rights," though, he warned, "there is probably no community that does not make some distinctions between the political privileges of men." Rights in regard to which men were equal could be political or civil. Political rights referred to "suffrage, eligibility to office, and a condition of things that admits of no distinction between men, unless on principles that are common to all." Civil rights he defined as equality before the law, or "an absence of privileges." Equality of rights, Cooper insisted, was never absolute, and to prove this he brought up several apparently obvious examples. "Women," he wrote, "nowhere possess the same [civil] rights as men . . . Minors are deprived of many of their civil rights, or, it would be better to say, do not attain them, until they reach a period of life that has been arbitrarily fixed. Neither is equality of political rights ever absolute. In those countries where the suffrage is said to be universal, exceptions exist, that arise from the necessity of things, or from that controlling policy which can never be safely lost sight of in the management of human affairs. The interests of women being thought to be so identified with those of their male relatives as to become, in a greater degree, inseparable, females are, almost generally, excluded from the possession of political rights. There can be no doubt that society is greatly the gainer, by thus excluding one half its members . . . Men are also excluded from political rights previously to having attained the age prescribed by law . . . Thus birth-right is almost universally made the source of advantage."

The equality in America, he continued, "is no more absolute than that of any other country. There may be less inequality in this nation than in most others, but inequality exists, and, in some respects, with stronger features than is usual to meet with in the rest of christendom." "The rights of property being an indispensable condition of civilization . . . equality of condition is rendered impossible . . . Women and minors are excluded from the suffrage, and from maintaining suits at law . . . here as elsewhere. None but natives of the country can fill many of the higher offices, and paupers, felons and all those who have not fixed residences, are also excluded from the suffrage. In a few of the states property is made the test of political rights, and, in nearly half of them, a large portion of the inhabitants, who are of a different race from the original European occupants of the soil, are entirely excluded from all political, and from many of the civil rights, that are enjoyed by those who are deemed citizens."

Cooper did not bewail this situation (although he disagreed with some of its particulars), because he believed a certain degree of social inequality to be natural, and saw literal interpretation of the principle of human equality as both mistaken and dangerous:

The celebrated proposition contained in the declaration of independence is not to be understood literally. All men are not "created equal," in a physical, or even in a moral sense, unless we limit the signification to one of political rights. This much is true, since human institutions are a human invention, with which nature has had no connection . . . As regards all human institutions men are born equal, no sophistry being able to prove that nature intended one should inherit power and wealth, another slavery and want. Still artificial inequalities are the inevitable consequences of artificial ordinances, and in founding a new governing principle for the social compact, the American legislators instituted new modes of difference.

The very existence of a government at all, infers inequality. The citizen who is preferred to office becomes the superior of those who are not, so long as he is the repository of power, and the child inherits the wealth of the parent as a controlling law of society. All that the great American proposition, therefore, can mean, is to set up new and juster notions of natural rights than those which existed previously, by asserting, in substance, that God has not instituted political inequalities, as was pretended by the advocates of the Jus Divinum, and that men possessed a full and natural authority to form such social institutions as best suited their necessities.

There are numerous instances in which the social inequality of America may do violence to our notions of abstract justice, but the compromise of interests under which all civilized society must exist, renders this unavoidable. Great principles seldom escape working injustice in particular things.

Cooper believed himself to be "as good a democrat as there is in America," but his democracy was "not of the impracticable school." He wrote of himself in the preface: "[The author] prefers a democracy to any other system, on account of its comparative advantages, and not on account of its

perfection. He knows it has evils; great and increasing evils, and evils peculiar to itself; but he believes that monarchy and aristocracy have more. It
will be very apparent to all who read this book, that he is not a believer in
the scheme of raising men very far above their natural propensities." His
view of American ideals thus was instrumental. He wished to warn his countrymen against "notions that are impracticable, and which if persevered in,
cannot fail to produce disorganization, if not revolution," against "the idle
hope of substituting a fancied perfection for the ills of life." [100] He was a
conservative, in the sense in which loyalists were conservative, or Englishmen who loved England rather than the values for which it stood. But American nationalism was idealistic to the core, and many of Cooper's compatriots (at least as far as they personally were concerned) would settle for
nothing but perfection.

By the third decade of the nineteenth century, artificial invidious distinctions between men, which constituted the very fabric of European societies,
in America had been reduced to a minimum. There were no legal estates,
and neither wealth nor education was recognized as a legitimate claim for
superior status. The fundamental status categories that remained were related to natural differences, such as those of sex, race, and age, and to a
lesser extent to religion. That equality in American society had advanced
beyond anything imaginable elsewhere at the time cannot be disputed. But
the American society was also committed to equality to an extent that was
unimaginable elsewhere. Thus, while the reality in America in this regard
was incomparably better than in any other society, the gap between it and
its brilliant ideal was nonetheless wider.[101] Because equality was interpreted
literally, American inequality appeared to have "stronger features" than
usual. The problem with America, said Cooper in another work, was
"chiefly that it is lamentably in arrears to its own avowed principles." [102]

Twenty years later another earnest American addressed the issue of American inequality. Speaking on the Dred Scott decision, Abraham Lincoln said:

> I think the authors [of the Declaration of Independence] intended to include *all*
> men, but they did not intend to declare all men equal *in all respects.* They did
> not mean to say all were equal in color, size, intellect, moral developments, or
> social capacity. They defined with tolerable distinctness in what respects they
> did consider all men created equal—equal with "certain inalienable rights,
> among which are life, liberty, and the pursuit of happiness" . . . They meant to
> set up a standard maxim for free society which should be familiar to all and
> revered by all; constantly looked at, constantly labored for, and even though
> never perfectly attained, constantly approximated, and thereby constantly
> spreading and deepening its influence and augmenting the happiness and value
> of life to all people of all colors everywhere . . . Its authors meant it to be—as,
> thank God, it is now proving itself—a stumbling block to all those who in
> aftertimes might seek to turn a free people back into the hateful paths of des-

potism. They knew the proneness of prosperity to breed tyrants, and they meant when such should reappear in this fair land and commence their vocation, they should find left for them at least one hard nut to crack.[103]

While for Cooper, American principles were unrealistic even in their limited significance, and the inevitable inequality was the hard nut to crack, the stumbling block on the way to their realization, Lincoln, who accepted Cooper's limited definition of equality in the Declaration of Independence, believed that in regard to their rights men could and would be equal, exactly because inequality contradicted the American principles. This very inconsistency, he was convinced, would ensure the ultimate triumph of ideals over reality. However, while it certainly was the means for the solution, inconsistency also represented a greater part of the problem.

Inequality inherent in social reality was blatantly inconsistent with American national commitment. In a society which believed that "all men are created equal," the denial of equality meant that one was not human, was less of a human than others. If one chose not to or could not blind oneself to it, the experience must have been one of a crushing, unbearable humiliation, an indignity quite beyond that experienced by the lower classes in European societies which divided humanity into unequal groups to begin with, justified such division by its function in the Divine order of things, and consoled those at the bottom by their participation in the great chain of being.

That the degree of material deprivation and physical hardship associated with the denial of equality in America was relatively small is largely irrelevant in this context. The cliometric data of Fogel and Engerman in fact support the claims of Southern defenders of slavery that the material conditions of slaves' lives were better than those of free industrial workers in the North; their diet was nutritionally adequate, their health good, and as a result the slave population in the United States (and earlier in the colonies) rapidly increased.[104] The "anti-cant" American Democrat Cooper was undoubtedly right, writing of slavery, which he considered an evil, that it was "an institution as old as human annals" and "no more sinful, by the christian code, than it is sinful . . . to enjoy ease and plenty, while our fellow creatures are suffering and in want," and of American slavery, in particular, that "the African is, in nearly all respects, better off in servitude in this country, than when living in a state of barbarism at home . . . American slavery is mild, in its general features, and physical suffering cannot properly be enumerated among its evils . . . It is an evil, certainly, but in a comparative sense, not as great an evil as it is usually imagined. There is scarcely a nation in Europe that does not possess institutions that inflict as gross personal privations and wrongs, as the slavery of America."[105]

Indeed, what was peculiar or particularly cruel about the peculiar institution of some American states, was the fact that it existed in America. American slaves might have been better off than slaves elsewhere, but they were slaves in America, which made their slavery appear more oppressive, for they were slaves of people dedicated to freedom. Men, at least some of them, live not by bread alone, and however much America emphasized prosperity, it always placed greater emphasis on liberty and dignity. The deprivation from which slaves suffered was not primarily material, but psychological, and the suffering was most acute among those who might have been better off materially than others—the uncommonly intelligent, sensitive, and educated. The master to whom Nat Turner (the leader of the sanguinary slave revolt in 1831) belonged as a child remarked of him early in his life that he "had too much sense . . . and . . . would never be of any service to anyone as a slave." He learned to read and write; he was "discovered to be great" by his "fellow servants"; and Mr. Travis, the "kind master" who was his first victim and whose property he had been since 1830, placed "greatest confidence" in him. It is not surprising that, arriving to man's estate and being still a slave, Nat Turner began seeing "white spirits and black spirits engaged in battle" and believed that he was chosen by God to "slay [his white] enemies" and liberate black people.[106] It is surprising that slave revolts, similar to this, did not happen more often.

Perhaps this could be explained by the fact that, as Cooper put it, referring to the "personal restraints of the system," men do not "feel very keenly, if at all, privations of the amount of which they know nothing."[107] It was often the free blacks who felt "the weight of degradation" more. It was the insupportable, the intolerable contradiction between slavery and the national commitment to equality of men in liberty, not the cruelty of slavery in America, which tormented Nat Turner, driving him to his indiscriminate "work of death," and it was this contradiction which inflamed William Lloyd Garrison, moving him to increasingly radical abolitionist positions.

Still an advocate of gradual emancipation, which he was to renounce several months later, Garrison argued passionately on July 4, 1829: "Every Fourth of July, our Declaration of Independence is produced, with a sublime indignation, to set forth the tyranny of the mother country and to challenge the admiration of the world. But what a pitiful detail of grievances does this document present in comparison with the wrongs which our slaves endure! . . . Before God, I must say that such a glaring contradiction as exists between our creed and practice the annals of 6,000 years cannot parallel. In view of it, I am ashamed of my country. I am sick of our unmeaning declamation in praise of liberty and equality; of our hypocritical cant about the inalienable rights of man. I could not, for my right hand, stand up before a European assembly and exult that I am an American citizen, and denounce the usurpations of a kingly government as wicked and unjust . . . the recollection of my country's barbarity and despotism would blister my lips and cover my cheeks with burning blushes of shame." Similarly, Lincoln hated

"the monstrous injustice of slavery," "because it deprives our republican example of its influence in the world; enables the enemies of free institutions
with plausibility to taunt us as hypocrites; causes the real friends of freedom
to doubt our sincerity; and especially because it forces so many good men
among ourselves into an open war with the very fundamental principles of
civil liberty." [108]

For propaganda purposes, Abolitionists stressed the mistreatment of the
slaves by bad masters and their physical suffering, which easily aroused pity
and sympathy. This, on the whole, weakened their position, for slavery apologists could not only refute their claims, but point to the greater material
misery of the lower classes elsewhere (including the free states) and thus
accuse the Abolitionists in being inconsistent and, therefore, dishonest.[109]

Slavery was the ultimate betrayal of the national ideals—the "blackest
spot," "strictly a national sin." It was also the most conspicuous contradiction: it bore the name of the negation of freedom. The situation of women
contradicted American commitment less openly, but was equally inconsistent with it. In fact, if one accepts Orlando Patterson's interpretation of slavery (according to which the essential characteristic of the slave status is the
lack of "personal autonomy" and "honorable will," which makes a slave,
however thriving physically, "socially dead," rather than the legal definition
of a slave as a form of property), the position of women in nineteenth-
century America—as well as elsewhere—appears in significant respects
analogous to slavery. Women did not fail to perceive this analogy. Man,
claimed the authors of the "Seneca Falls Declaration on Women's Rights" in
1848, established "an absolute tyranny" over the woman, making her "civ-
illy dead." [110]

It may be claimed that American women on the whole had it better than
most of their European sisters, which is undoubtedly true. The independence of the "American girl" was notorious. Tocqueville duly acknowledged
that "nowhere are young women surrendered so early or so completely to
their own guidance." To a far greater extent than in Europe, they were "mis-
tresses of their own actions." One could expect—and accept—on the part
of an American girl liberties inconceivable and unforgivable on the part of a
European. Mr. Winterbourne (whom Henry James perhaps saw as a reflection of himself), hesitant whether or not to be shocked by Daisy Miller's
eccentricities, wrote them off to her nationality. But more experienced
Americans were shocked, and her independence was punished by death, for
there was no other resolution, the choice facing the American woman being:
live unfree or die.

According to Tocqueville and numerous others, the freedom of American
women ended (was "irrecoverably lost") with marriage. He thought they
loved it. "I never observed," he wrote, "that the women of America consider
conjugal authority as a fortunate usurpation of their rights, or that they

thought themselves degraded by submitting to it. It appeared to me, on the contrary, that they attach a sort of pride to the voluntary surrender of their own will and make it their boast to bend themselves to the yoke, not to shake it off." He believed the reason for such voluntary submission lay in the education of the American woman. Americans, he said, were of the opinion that a woman's mind was "just as fitted as a that of man to discover the plain truth, and her heart as firm to embrace it" and sought to "arm her reason." Thus, "while they have allowed the social inferiority of woman to continue, they have done all they could to raise her morally and intellectually to the level of man." What Tocqueville did not recognize in *Democracy in America* (and what he so persuasively demonstrated in his later book on France) was the "Tocqueville effect" produced by exactly this inconsistency. Cultivated, accomplished women, daughters, sisters, and wives of active men who insisted on the equality and liberty of intelligent beings, yet whose authority over them was unquestionable, women whose sensibilities and abilities were developed, overdeveloped given the prospects open to them, could not help feeling degraded. The Seneca Falls Declaration stressed this: "[Man] closes against her all the avenues to wealth and distinction which he considers most honorable to himself. As a teacher of theology, medicine, or law, she is not known . . . He has endeavored, in every way that he could, to destroy her confidence in her own powers, to lessen her self-respect, and to make her willing to lead a dependent and abject life." [111]

The profession of a woman, said Catharine Beecher, was to serve the men around her. The function that awaited a woman, the end of her development, was self-effacement. Not being a man, a woman had no right to happiness. No matter that, when Tocqueville wrote, there were few such women; there were more and more of them as years went by; they multiplied as the slaves multiplied in the prosperous United States, which could afford to cultivate those whom they would not care to recognize. The existence of a stereotype for what was such women's alternative to marriage, "Boston marriages," on which they expended their otherwise pent-up capacities which had gone sour for lack of expression, suggests that in the latter part of the century they were not uncommon, and that they were particularly common in places like Boston, "within sight of Bunker Hill and in the birthplace of liberty," where the inconsistency of their situation was most glaring. [112]

What is remarkable about all this is how long and how patiently the American public as a whole endured the gross inconsistencies in its midst. Different sectors of it might have been acutely aware of their own plight (if plight it was) and yet completely insensitive to the similar indignity inflicted on others. Contemporaries and observers of the same situation perceived in it different contradictions. Nothing, in fact, appeared "self-evident," least of all that all men were created equal, or, rather, that all those clamoring for equality were equally men. More often than not the adjective "self-evident" denoted the persuasiveness of positions which fit or served the interests of those who advanced them. While many Northern patriots during the Revolutionary conflict clearly understood the inconsistency of Negro slavery with the ideals for which they were fighting and spoke against it, John Dickinson believed the colonists had it much worse than the slaves of the South, for, he said, there was no "idea of slavery more complete, more miserable, more disgraceful, than that of a people where justice is administered, government exercized, and a standing army maintained at the expence of the people, and yet without the least dependence upon them." The stance of the Southern champions of liberty and equality was, of course, even more problematic. Later, Thoreau, the author of *Civil Disobedience,* seeking to escape from the philistine preoccupations of mid-nineteenth-century American society into the haven of self- and nature-watching, wrote in *Walden:* "I sometimes wonder that we can be so frivolous, I may almost say, as to attend to the gross but somewhat foreign form of servitude called Negro Slavery, [while] there are so many keen and subtle masters that enslave both north and south. It is hard to have a southern overseer; it is worse to have a northern one; but worst of all when you are the slave-driver of yourself." [113] For him, Negro slavery was an insignificant evil, compared with the socially and self-imposed subjection of the spirit in the pursuit of material things. Love of property, not treating men as such, truly contradicted the principle of liberty.

To white laborers protesting the employment of skilled "ebony" workers as masons and carpenters in the South, it seemed self-evident that white labor should always be preferred to black. A working-man wrote in the *Southern Banner* of January 13, 1838: "The white man is the only real, legal, moral, and civil proprietor of this country and state . . . By white man alone was this continent discovered; by the prowess of white men alone (though not always properly or humanely exercized [what an amazing qualification in this context]) were the fierce and active Indians driven occidentally. And if swarms and hordes of infuriated red men pour down now . . . white men alone . . . would bare their breasts to the keen and whizzing shafts of the savage crusaders—defending Negroes too in the bargain." "The right, then, gentlemen, you will no doubt candidly admit," appealed the author to the honorable public, "of the white man to employment in preference to Negroes, who *must* defer to us since they live well enough on plantations, cannot be considered impeachable by contractors." And he added: "I am surprised the poor do not elect faithful members to the legislature, who will make it penal to prefer Negro mechanic labor to white men's."

Some two months later forty thousand black citizens of Pennsylvania protested against their disenfranchisement by the decision of the state's supreme court. In their "Appeal to the People" they asked that "no man shall be excluded on account of his *color*," and explained: "When you have taken from an individual his right to vote, you have made the government, in regard to him, a mere despotism; and you have taken a step toward making it despotism to all. To your women and children, their inability to vote at the polls may be no evil, because they are united by consanguinity and affection with those who can do it." They were oblivious of the fact that the ties of affection, if not consanguinity, connecting masters and slaves were claimed by supporters of slavery in the South, thereby justifying the exclusion of blacks from citizenship; to the free blacks of Pennsylvania it appeared self-evident that only sex and age constituted legitimate bases of exclusion.

Henry James, the sensitive post-emancipation Bostonian, however inconstant, through whose eyes we see the drama of "The Bostonians," found the concerns of the feminists amusing, but had no sympathy for them. Olive Chancellor, the young woman—and yet "a signal old maid," "a spinster as Shelley was a lyric poet, or the month of August is sultry"—who represents these concerns, is an unattractive character. James describes her views with ironic exaggeration; his irony makes it embarrassing to agree with them. The author's sympathies lie with Basil Ransom, the irresistible Mississippian, whose idea of women's rights—the rights for gentlemen's condescension and protection—he evidently shared. (As it happened, the first feminists were also—and first—Abolitionists, which can be explained perhaps by the fact that the injustice of sexual inequality was even less self-evident than others and did not become a legitimate object of attack until later.)[114]

Of course, such egocentrism and selective indifference were not universal. Many disinterested men and women found the contradiction of American inequality intolerable and advocated the rights of minorities to which they themselves did not belong. There were male champions of sexual equality, while the Abolitionist sentiment in the free Northern states was notoriously strong and grew stronger. Thousands of Americans must have felt oppressed by the purely mental burden of inconsistency, demanding anxiously and impatiently, as the preacher Levi Hart demanded as early as 1775: "When, O when shall the happy day come, that Americans shall be *consistently* engaged in the cause of liberty?"[115]

Still, the fact that the great majority of those personally unaffected by a particular discrimination were blind to the plight of those who suffered under it, and did not perceive the denial of equality and freedom to others as inconsistent with the ideals of the nation, made the correction of any one inconsistency possible only if it connected to a powerful interest. In general one may describe the relationship between ideals and interests in the American case—and elsewhere—as follows. (The specificity of the American case consists in that we *start* from a pool of values, but otherwise the pattern is fundamentally the same everywhere.) Of the available ideals and their possible interpretations, only those are selected and upheld at any given period which correspond to significant interests operating at the time (namely the interests of groups that possess the necessary means for their realization, such as critical mass, influence, and so forth), while others are at least temporarily discarded or put aside. They may be picked up at a later point—when interests emerge that can be served by them. The selected ideals and interpretations are usually capable of further diverging ramifications; and again, some of these are selected and some are discarded in accordance with existing interests. Interests are frequently informed by the ideals and reflect them, but often they are formed by the existential, or structural, constraints of the actors. In the latter case, they are strengthened if they correspond to the ideals in the pool, and are rendered problematic if they contradict them, but may persist nonetheless. Arrangements inconsistent with ideals in the pool, therefore, may exist so long as there are either interests which support them or no interest that requires and has the requisite means for their elimination. However, when interests of the latter type do emerge and the inconsistencies in social arrangements are conceptualized as such, they quickly become indefensible and are likely to disappear more or less gradually. The ideals, therefore, to an extent prescribe the general direction for the development of the society, the general course it is to follow. Yet it is not at all inevitable that it will follow this course. At any point in time interests created by structural constraints unconnected to the ideals may emerge which could be incongruent with or even antithetical to the latter, and yet powerful enough not to give way under the pressure of inconsistency and opposing interests. Such interests may lead to the creation of a different pool of ideals which are consistent with them and, in the case of their success, arrest the previous development of society and divert it from its initial course.

In addition to these general reasons why systemic contradictions may continue unattended for long periods of time, there existed in America a particular reason which accounted for the persistence of arrangements inconsistent with American ideals. The gross inconsistencies of American society—the denial of equality of rights to particular groups of Americans—might not be perceived as such so long as liberty and equality were considered the prerogatives of rational beings, and reason was seen as the essence of humanity. In this framework, if it were possible to prove, for example, that blacks were significantly less rational than whites, and women similarly inferior to men, the denial of equality to these groups would, in fact, be consistent with the proclaimed ideals of the nation. Indeed, the intelligence of the blacks was the focus of the early debate around the issue of slavery, in which Jefferson committed himself so strongly to the view of black intellectual inferiority. (Less explicitly, but unambivalently, he supported the claim that women were no equals of men in the "masculine sound Understanding.") But it was a matter unsusceptible to proof, or rather, the ability to prove it one way or the other depended on one's desire and not on evidence which lent itself to various interpretations. Besides, the emphasis on group characteristics itself was inconsistent with the American respect for the individual. Thus reason was eventually discarded as a means of establishing group eligibility for partaking in the dignity of equality in liberty and abandoned by the defenders of both broad and narrow definitions of humanity endowed with inalienable rights. Already in 1789, the Maryland Abolition Society asserted that "the human race, however varied in color or intellects, are all justly entitled to liberty." Rights were dissociated from reason and became unconditional. Thus the only conceivable justification for inequality in the framework of American ideals was eliminated.[116]

### The Myth of Anti-Intellectualism

The American attitude toward reason was an element in yet another built-in tension in American society which stood in the way of the formation of national loyalty and made it waver. If the flaws in the realization of the ideal of equality bred frustration, so did the approximation to that ideal. The attitude toward equality is necessarily ambivalent: one wants to be equal to one's superiors, but does not desire equality with those seen as one's inferiors. The principle of equality of human worth works against one of the most important and ubiquitous social interests—that of status-seeking. The American ideals conflicted with and impeded status-achievement and status-display. All pretensions to inherent superiority among the white male citizens of the nation were rendered illegitimate, un-American. From a certain point of view, this was a systemic deficiency, and it particularly affected creative intellectuals, such as writers of fiction and other artists—people whose self-esteem and, in many cases, creative energy and *raison d'être* depended on the inner consciousness and general recognition of their very inequality, superiority to others, on the belief that there was within them some inherent quality which could be neither learned nor acquired otherwise, and which distinguished them from the rest of the human race.[117] While the imperfect realization of the ideal of equality bred disaffection among groups who were treated as inferior, the very desire to realize it formed the structural basis for the alienation of the intellectuals, because they were treated as equal to the rest. In both cases, discontent expressed itself chiefly in attempts to reform American society, and frequently intellectuals were found at the head of reform movements aiming at the achievement of a more perfect equality. At least in some such instances, it may be assumed that this was the result of the displacement of the frustration peculiar to intellectuals and of the rationalization of their vexation in terms that rendered it legitimate within the framework of American values. As often, however, this vexation was not displaced. It was experienced as the frustration of intellectuals, not of Americans, and this experience gave rise to the myth of the anti-intellectualism of American society, which connoted crass materialism and contempt for learning.

It is important to analyze this persistent misconception in the present context, for it is responsible for one distinctive feature of American patriotism: the fact that it is not, primarily, the province of intellectuals; patriotic effusions by prominent cultural figures in it are relatively—and by comparison with other nations, conspicuously—rare. Conversely, this phenomenon also explains, at least to the same extent as the structural inconsistencies of American society, the latter's unparalleled penchant for self-criticism. All societies tend to be self-congratulating. The self-congratulatory tendencies in America, therefore, do not make it in any way unique. But only in England, and for the same reasons, there exists a similar tendency to perceive and focus on the shortcomings not simply of the government, but of the nation as such. This social criticism is naturally articulated by the articulate segment of society—the intellectuals—and the built-in discontent within this articulate segment, indeed in accordance with the famous Marxist dictum, inevitably serves as a major source of inspiration for it.

The claim of anti-intellectualism was cultivated because of the systemic alienation of American intellectuals, but it also reflected an actual peculiarity of the American attitude toward culture, which was noticed even by the unprejudiced foreigners. Tocqueville opened his interview with Livingston with a statement: "It seems to me that American society suffers from taking too little account of intellectual questions." [118] This statement was in direct contradiction to many of his observations in *Democracy in America,* but only because it was imprecisely formulated. America was indeed characterized by a pervasive disrespect toward its creative intellectuals. It did not defer to them. In comparison with European societies, such as France (or Germany, or Russia), where intellectuals formed an alternative, if not the only, aristocracy, this was indeed striking. This noticeable lack of awe in regard to intellectuals was interpreted as lack of intellectual interests and contempt for culture. But, at least until the latter half of the nineteenth century, nothing could be further from the truth. American society was singularly receptive to culture; rather than repelling it, it absorbed it like a sponge, and therein, not in its cultural indifference, lay the reason for the intellectuals' distress.[119]

The general literacy of the population was another facet of the characteristic equality of conditions during the colonial period. In 1701 Governor Joseph Dudley was of the opinion that in New England "there are no children to be found 10 years old who do not read well, nor men of twenty who do not write tolerably." In 1722 Rev. Jacob Duche wrote of Philadelphia: "Such is the prevailing taste for books of every kind, that almost every man is a reader; and by pronouncing sentence, right or wrong, upon the various publications that come in his way, puts himself upon a level, in point of knowledge, with their several authors." Visitors were surprised by the high level of popular discourse in the country and the purity of English spoken in all walks of life. Common people were "well instructed in the knowledge of their Rights and Liberties"; toward the end of the eighteenth century, Edmund Burke noted that "in no country perhaps in the world is the law so general a study . . . all who read, and most do read, endeavor to obtain some smattering in that science." [120] It is no trivial detail that New England had a college when Massachusetts Bay colony was but six years old. The newness of America, sectarian enthusiasm, and the absence of legal fetters allowed colleges to proliferate. Because of the territorial dispersion, they competed for students and thus were not selective. In the eighteenth century, the cost of higher education, while not cheap, was comparatively low: ten to twenty pounds per year as compared with fifty pounds earned by a skilled carpenter. The colleges depended on the support of the community and were governed by it; their goal was the spread of learning rather than cultivation of "pure" knowledge. This was not conducive to the development of specialized education, but fostered an exceptionally high level of general literacy. Because general literacy was so widespread, intellectual monopoly was resented; priests, lawyers, and physicians were regarded as the "three great scourges of mankind," "Learned Gentlemen" unworthy to be maintained by the community. And yet, twenty-five of the fifty-six signers of the Declaration of Independence, thirty-one of the fifty-five members of the Constitutional Convention, ten of the twenty-nine first Senators and seventeen of the sixty-five Representatives in the first Congress were "lawyers," while the Constitutional Convention could be called "the first American brain trust" because so many of its members were college educated, and because it included first-rate (by the existing standards) scholars and scientists, two university presidents, and three college professors.[121] There was no contradiction here: educated men in colonial America did not constitute a separate estate.

Colleges continued to grow in numbers in the nineteenth century. In 1851 an enthusiast referred to the United States as "a land of colleges." In 1815 Hezekiah Niles bragged in a letter to William Cobbett: "There are no such men in the world as our independent farmers, who constitute the large majority of our people. Many of them have libraries, like your English lords, and what is more, they even understand the books they have." [122] No matter that he might have exaggerated, the fact that he considered the superior intellectual propensities of the mass of his countrymen a subject worthy of advertising is important in itself. Besides, Niles had some hard evidence to support his view: by 1819 his *Weekly Register* had more than ten thousand subscribers. Around the same time the most popular publication in Russia had three hundred.[123] "Although America is perhaps in our days the civilized country in which literature is least attended to," wrote Tocqueville circumspectly, "still a large number of persons there take an interest in the productions of the mind and make them, if not the study of their lives, at least the charm of their leisure hours . . . There is hardly a pioneer's hut that does not contain a few odd volumes of Shakespeare. I remember that I read the feudal drama of Henry V for the first time in a log cabin." [124] Those who know "when Russia learned to read" or when French peasants turned into Frenchmen will not doubt for a moment that odd volumes of Shakespeare (or Zhukovsky, or Racine) in a peasant hut in Central Russia or Provence in the 1830s (or 1850s, or 1870s) would be an utter impossibility, and that whatever might constitute the charm of leisure hours in those parts, it would not be, by any stretch of imagination, the productions of the mind.

The high-placed spokesmen for colonial and later national authorities in America consistently stressed the importance of education for the people.[125] Educational achievement was a condition of a happy and respectable existence. A popular rhyme urged children to take their alphabet seriously, for "he who learns his letters fair / Shall have a coach to take the air." This was an openly instrumental approach. Americans did not treat learning as an end in itself: both the needs and the opportunities of the country militated against such an attitude. "We want hands, my lord, more than heads," wrote William Livingston to the Bishop of Llandaff; "the most intimate acquaintance with the classics will not remove our oaks; nor the taste for the *Georgics* cultivate our lands." "So great is the call for talents of all sorts in the active use of professional and other business in America, that few of our ablest men have leisure to devote exclusively to literature or fine arts," Justice Story thought in 1819. "This obvious reason will explain why we have so few professional authors, and those not among our ablest men." [126]

In Europe, the view that learning was an end in itself was related to the traditional contempt for manual labor as the dole of inherently inferior classes—the mass of *laboratores*. Intellectual preoccupations, although originally less respectable than military ones, implied that one did not need to work to support oneself, but belonged to a superior leisure class. There was no American leisure class and, in general, in the beginning Americans had very little leisure, which allowed neither full-time gentlemanly dedication to intellectual pursuits that had no practical application on a scale of any significance nor the formation of a mass market that could support such dedication, turning it into a sort of business. Yet it would be wrong to assume that culture was valued less because it was considered practically indispensable. Some forms of culture—fiction, speculative theology or politics—were valued less. Lack of leisure implied both scarcity of time one could spend on reading for pleasure and less boredom and therefore need for entertainment. But indifference to fiction and speculation made inquisitive Americans only more earnest in the pursuit of learning and understanding that could be defined as useful. A writer in the *Atlantic Monthly* claimed in 1858 that nowhere but in America was "speculative interest so colored with the hues of practical interest without limiting its own flight; nowhere [were] labor's executive powers so receptive of pure intellectual suggestion." [127]

The American temper was not anti-intellectual; it was an intellectual temper of a certain kind. While intellectuals might have been slighted, intellect was highly esteemed. This attitude was uncongenial to imaginative and speculative writing, but it fostered empirical study. Nothing at the time could be a better rule for the development of science than Jared Eliot's irreverent maxim: "An Ounce of Experience is better than a Pound of Science." It was the profound respect for the intellect, the veneration of human reason, which lay at the basis of disrespect for professional intellectuals. Americans thirsted for learning, but they wished and thought they could learn by themselves. Theirs was the priesthood of all believers; they did not need authorities to interpret for them the mysteries of the universe. "Reading many Books is but a taking off the Mind too much from Meditation," William Penn advised his children. "Reading your selves and Nature, in the Dealings and Conduct of men, is the truest human wisdom. The Spirit of a Man knows the Things of Man, and more true Knowledge comes by Meditation and just Reflection than by Reading; for much Reading is an Oppression of the Mind." [128]

This philosophy (and this rejection of mediated knowledge was indeed "love of wisdom") was never better expressed than in an address delivered in 1837 before an audience of aspiring intellectuals at Harvard University. The orator challenged the intellectual to be "Man Thinking," not "mere thinker, the parrot of other men's thinking." He spoke of the education of the scholar by nature and by action, and had this to say of education by books:

> Each age . . . must write its own books . . . The books of an older period will not fit this . . . The sluggish and perverted mind of the multitude, slow to open to the incursions of Reason, having once so opened, having once received [a] book, stands upon it, and makes an outcry, if it is disparaged. Colleges are built on it. Books are written on it by thinkers, not by Man Thinking; by men of talent, that is, who start wrong, who set out from accepted dogmas, not from their own sight of principles. Meek young men grow up in libraries, believing it their duty to accept the views, which Cicero, which Locke, which Bacon, have given, forgetful that Cicero, Locke, and Bacon were only young men in libraries, when they wrote these books. Hence, instead of Man Thinking, we have the bookworm. Hence, the book-learned class, who value books as such; not as related to nature and the human constitution, but as making a sort of Third Estate with the world and the soul . . . Books are the best of things, well used;

abused, among the worst . . . They are for nothing but to inspire. I had better never see a book, than to be warped by its attraction clean out of my own orbit . . . The one thing in the world, of value, is the active soul. This every man is entitled to; this every man contains within him, although in almost all men, obstructed, and as yet unborn . . . it is . . . not the privilege of here and there a favorite, but the sound estate of every man.[129]

This diatribe against canonized culture, this rejection of the authority of professional intellectuals, pronounced by one of the most sensitive—and professional—intellectuals of the age, was at the same time an apotheosis of human intellect. This was Emerson's "The American Scholar," called "our intellectual declaration of independence."[130] Its message was the motto of Enlightenment, *Sapere aude.*

What were mere thinkers to do among people accustomed to seeing themselves as Men Thinking? What could self-appointed high priests of intellect aspire to in the priesthood of all believers? When professional intellectuals began to form as a group in the 1830s (those 1830s when odd volumes of Shakespeare could be found in pioneers' huts), it was immediately perceived that the society, the masses as well as the elites, were unresponsive to the intellectuals' demands for status and authority. Not that there were no opportunities for intellectual activity (including the most esoteric intellectual activity) in America, or that it was economically insupportable; there were, probably, more such opportunities than elsewhere. But the society did not particularly reward it; it did not bestow on intellectuals its high approbation and gratitude, as it did on successful men of action; it did not admit of the aristocracy of reason. It was neither indifferent to culture nor suspicious of the life of the mind, but it refused to admit that those who lived such a life had a claim on its unconditional respect, just because they chose to do so.

This lack of credit, the unwillingness to grant that the mere fact of being an intellectual implied authority, put American intellectuals in an unenviable position, both relative to their European counterparts and in absolute terms. In Europe—at least on the Continent—being an intellectual did constitute a legitimate claim to deference. In the nineteenth century in France, Germany, and Russia intellectuals were the acclaimed leaders of society; they were objects of national cults, worshipped alongside—and more than—military leaders and kings. The worshippers were mostly intellectuals or quasi-intellectuals themselves (by no means could they be considered representatives of the popular mood), but this did not detract much from the sense of the exalted status that they enjoyed as a result of this adulation. Yet this relative deprivation was the lesser of the problems troubling American intellectuals. In intellectual labor, status anxiety is an occupational hazard, and they were exposed to it, objectively, to an unusually high degree. Creative intellectual activity to a greater extent than most others constitutes a reward in itself, and intellectual occupations are often chosen because one feels irresistibly drawn to engage in them. At the same time, creative intellectuals are singularly susceptible to agonizing attacks of insecurity and self-doubt, and only social approbation can reassure them of the reality of their talent and the worthiness of their pursuits. It is rarely that the joy of thinking, writing, or working in the non-verbal arts sustains itself for long in the face of persistent lack of recognition. Because of the extraordinary respect for the intellectual abilities of the human individual as such, there was less sensitivity in America to extraordinary intellectual abilities, and its creative intellectuals were doomed to higher levels of insecurity.

As so often happens, three options were available to them: loyalty, voice, and exit. They could either accept their society as it was and adjust to whatever approbation and respect they got; try to change their society and make it love them more; or change their frame of reference altogether. The choice of the first option was implicit in the constantly growing number of American scholars and artists. The second was behind much of the rhetoric of American cultural nationalism. The third led to expatriation or internal exile. Those who chose the two latter options were a minority, but they were highly noticeable, both because they articulated the arguments behind their choice, while the first group—a majority—did not, and because, in the international context, they were unique.

In the already quoted essay of 1823, William Ellery Channing asserted: "The true sovereigns of a country are those who determine its mind, its mode of thinking, its tastes, its principles; and we cannot consent to lodge this sovereignty in the hands of strangers. A country, like an individual, has dignity and power only in proportion as it is self-formed." [131] The insistence that it was essential for the nation to assert its cultural independence rested on, among other things, the assumption (a presumption ridiculous in its absurdity in the American context) that intellectuals were its natural leaders. Perhaps nobody professed this intellectual megalomania with more conviction and passion than the great poet and American patriot Walt Whitman.

National spirit, or Soul, manifested itself in native intellectuals (Whitman, a poet, narrowed the definition of the intellectual to a Poet, or "literatus," but used "literature" as an inclusive term, sometimes subsuming under it science). Therefore, by cultivating its intellectuals, America cultivated itself. At the time of the first appearance of "Leaves of Grass" (1855) Whitman seemed to be optimistic. He trusted the nation was of one mind with him and did not seek to persuade, but only to reinforce in it the truths which appeared to him self-evident. He asserted the superiority of the poet and praised universal equality in the same breath, and his nation was to him a spectacle of perfection. "The Americans of all nations at any time upon the earth have probably the fullest poetical nature," he wrote. "The United States themselves are essentially the greatest poem ... Of all nations the

United States with veins full of poetical stuff most needs poets and will doubtless have the greatest and use them the greatest. Their Presidents shall not be their common referee so much as their poets shall. Of all mankind the great poet is the equable man." As it was not entirely clear what this meant, he explained: "He is the equalizer of his age and land . . . His brain is the ultimate brain. He is no arguer . . . he is judgment . . . As he sees the farthest, he has the most faith . . . he is the seer . . . he is individual . . . he is complete in himself . . . the others are as good as he, only he sees it and they do not."

The American poets found no problem with equality. "The messages of great poets to each man and woman are, Come to us on equal terms, Only then can you understand us, We are no better than you . . . Did you suppose there could be only one Supreme? We affirm there can be unnumbered Supremes . . . The American bards shall be marked for generosity and affection and for encouraging competitors. They shall be kosmos . . . hungry for equals night and day." The American poets were also champions of Liberty. "Liberty takes the adherence of heroes wherever men and women exist . . . but never takes any adherence or welcome from the rest more than from poets . . . to them it is confided and they must sustain it."

The poets were "a superior breed," a new order of men, the "interpreters of men and women and of all events and things." They were to arise in America, and America was ready to receive them. "America prepares with composure and goodwill for the visitors that have sent word . . . Only toward as good as itself and toward the like of itself will it advance half-way . . . The soul of the largest and wealthiest and proudest nation may well go half-way to meet that of its poets . . . There is no fear of mistake. If the one is true, the other is true. The proof of a poet is that his country absorbs him as affectionately as he has absorbed it." [132]

He soon learned, however, that America was insensitive to its great poets. In a letter to Emerson a year later, Whitman reproached his country for using "ready-made" English literature and failing to assert its cultural independence. "America, grandest of lands in the theory of its politics, in popular reading [nota bene], in hospitality, breadth, animal beauty, cities, ships, machines, money, credit, collapses quick as lightning at the repeated, admonishing, stern words, Where are any mental expressions from you, beyond what you have copied and stolen? Where are the born throngs of poets, literats, orators, you promised? . . . You are young, have the perfectest of dialects, a free press, a free government, the world forwarding its best to be with you . . . do strict justice to yourself. Strangle the singers who will not sing you loud and strong . . . Call for new great masters to comprehend new arts, new perfections, new wants. Submit to the most robust bard till he remedy your barrenness." [133]

But America did not go half-way to meet her poets; she did not recognize in them her masters; she hardly noticed them. Whitman lost his confidence in the intellectual promise of America. Or rather, he doubted that America held a promise for intellectuals, for he acknowledged the "plentiful intellectual smartness" of the people. His commitment to equality became qualified. He realized that what he loved in America (and he dearly loved America) was its potential and not its actuality. There was no intuitive understanding. He felt he had to argue his case, to persuade. He did so in "Democratic Vistas," a long prose essay, written at the end of the 1860s. In it the poet maintained that the greatness of America depended on the existence of great poets, that without them it was lost, worse than lost—worthless. "I would alarm and caution even the political and business reader," Whitman wrote,

> against the prevailing delusion that the establishment of free political institutions, and plentiful intellectual smartness, with general good order, physical plenty, industry, &c. . . . do, of themselves, determine and yield to our experiment of democracy the fruitage of success. With such advantages at present fully, or amost fully possess'd . . . society, in these States, is canker'd, crude, superstitious, and rotten . . . never was there, perhaps, more hollowness at heart than at present, and here in the United States . . . The depravity of the business classes of our country is not less than has been supposed, but infinitely greater . . . In business . . . the one sole object is . . . pecuniary gain[134] . . . I say that our New World democracy, however great a success in uplifting the masses out of their sloughs, in materialistic development, products, and in a certain highly-deceptive superficial popular intellectuality, is, so far, an almost complete failure in its social aspects, and in really grand religious, moral, literary, and esthetic results.

His faith in America was shaken, but his belief in the superhuman powers of the poet remained firm. Nothing equaled literature in importance. "Our fundamental want to-day in the United States . . . is of a class . . . of native authors, literatuses, far different, far higher in grade than any yet known, sacerdotal, modern, fit to cope with our occasions, lands, permeating the whole mass of American mentality, taste, belief, breathing into it a new breath of life, giving it decision, affecting politics far more than the popular superficial suffrage . . . accomplishing [that] without which this nation will no more stand, permanently, soundly, than a house will stand without a substratum . . . never was anything more wanted than, to-day . . . the great literatus of the modern. At all times, perhaps, the central point in any nation . . . is its national literature, especially its archetypal poems. Above all previous lands, a great original literature is surely to become the justification and reliance . . . of American democracy." He went further: "Should some two or three really original American poets, (perhaps artists or lecturers,) arise . . . together they would give more compaction and more moral identity . . . to these States, than all its Constitutions, legislative and judicial ties, and all its hitherto political, warlike, or materialistic experiences." His conclusion derived from this logically: "I demand races of orbic bards, with unconditional uncompromising sway. Come forth, sweet democratic despots of the west!" [135]

This was, of course, poetic license, but the recurrent terms Whitman used to refer to intellectuals—"despots," "masters," "Supremes"—are revealing. Intellectuals (and poets least of all) were nobody's masters in America; they were people with strange hobbies, addicted to exclamation points to which the public at large was averse. This was a wishful vocabulary. It was hard to be an American intellectual and an admirer of America at the same time. For this reason so many American intellectuals were not admirers of America.

Only few of them were as outspoken as the other great literary talent of the mid-nineteenth century, Edgar Allan Poe, who went straight to the root of the intellectual alienation and rejected the fundamental value of American society. "The founders of the Republic," he wrote scornfully, "started with a queerest idea conceivable, viz., that all men are born free and equal—this in the very teeth of the laws of gradation as visibly impressed upon all things both in the moral and the physical universe." All that this achieved was to replace acceptable tyrannies of natural superiors by "the most odious and insupportable despotism that ever was heard on the face of the Earth"—that of the MOB.[136] There is a tendency to explain the discontent of American intellectuals by the persistent failures of American society to stand up to its ideals, by the fact that the latter, like all ideals, so easily degenerate into cant, and that a correction of one inconsistency only makes the others more glaring. While this is true in numerous cases, there is no doubt that many intellectuals among those particularly mortified by the unexceptional position of cultural occupations in American society were bothered not by the inconsistencies between ideals and reality, but by the ideals themselves. What jarred their sensitivities was the unceremonious handling of culture by Americans, as if, indeed, it was everyone's domain! Henry James resented immigrants because they so soon claimed English as their tongue: "All the while we sleep the vast contingent of aliens whom we make welcome, and whose main contention . . . is that, from the moment of their arrival, they have just as much property in our speech as we have, and just as good a right to do what they choose with it—the grand right of Americans being to do just what he chooses 'over here' with anything and everything: all the while we sleep the innumerable aliens are sitting up (*they* don't sleep!) to work their will on their new inheritance and prove to us that they are without any finer feeling or more conservative instinct of consideration for it . . . than they may have on the subject of so many yards of freely figured oilcloth . . . that they are preparing to lay down, for convenience, on kitchen floor or kitchen staircase." [137] This still bothered him in 1905, when after twenty years of absence and forty years of living in Europe (most of them in Eng-

land of which in 1915 he became a naturalized citizen) he came to the
United States as a visitor.

Emigration is a measure of the degree of dissatisfaction with one's country; emigration from America, the land of immigrants, was exceptionally
rare. Even those whose experiences in this land of their birth were far from
idyllic, even blacks, whether former slaves or freeborn, who could remember little but indignity and degradation at the hands of white fellow-
Americans, did not wish to emigrate, but preferred to wait or to fight for
their rights in America, for bad as it was, the result of their inner calculus
must have been, it was worth staying. Yet intellectual expatriation (specifically, that of writers and artists, though not of scientists) was more characteristic of America than of many countries which supplied America with
immigrants. If a French or, more commonly, a German or a Russian writer
was frequently an exile, a fugitive from persecution at home, an American
intellectual left his home of his own accord, for he found it distasteful. A
French, a German, or a Russian writer might not object to being translated,
but wherever he lived, his primary audience remained that of his native
country; and though he knew that the great majority of his people would
never read his works, because they were illiterate or entirely devoid of interest in intellectual matters, he wrote, undaunted by such a state of affairs, for
his country. Conversely, an American intellectual, dismayed at the condition
of "*true* intellect" in his all-too-literate native land, would not uncommonly
be concerned more about "the general interests of the Republic of Letters"
than his country, as was Poe, and, with Poe, "insist upon regarding the
world at large as the sole proper audience for the author." [138] Only to a certain extent could this cosmopolitan bent be explained by the fact that American writers wrote in English; American artists expatriated much more often
than did German or Russian ones (France, being a center of artistic expatriation, had almost no experience of it itself); the expatriation of American
scientists, on the other hand, was, in the nineteenth century, at least as infrequent as that of scientists of any other nation.

The point of the above is not that the American public has been consistently characterized by a superior sensitivity to culture. What I am saying is
that the dissatisfaction of intellectuals in America with their society cannot
be explained by American indifference to culture (and has to be accounted
for by the specificity of the structural position of the intellectuals), simply
because in countries characterized by a comparable if not greater indifference to culture, intellectuals, placed in a different structural situation, do not
as a rule complain of anti-intellectualism.

In our century, the development of the complex network of modern universities, that great archipelago of ivory tower islands, has afforded disaffected intellectuals the comforts of internal exile. Although this development
lies beyond the scope of the book, it might be worthwhile to draw attention

to its effects on the intellectual profile of the American nation considered as a whole. Aided by the institutional growth, the charge of anti-intellectualism tended to become a self-fulfilling prophecy. The universities completed a series of successive bifurcations in American culture, which separated the culture acceptable to the intellectuals from that of other groups.

The first split in the series, as is often noted,[139] was a result of the Great Awakening and then the persistence of a strong evangelical sentiment in the mainstream American religion. Like Pietism in Germany, Quietism in France, and popular expressions of Russian Orthodoxy, American evangelism was mystical, emotional, and anti-intellectual in the literal sense of being irrational and anti-rational. Back country was its center; it was predominantly a rural phenomenon, and the urban society, especially that of Boston, opposed to it rational, practical, and unemotional *Unitarianism*, which became the intellectual orthodoxy and so irritated Henry Adams. *Transcendentalism* was an intellectual reaction to this cold orthodoxy, from which it differed primarily by the emotional fervor and intensity of its belief in reason and the individual as a rational being. In Germany and Russia the haloed Romantic movement intellectualized, exulted, and sanctified the irrationality of their respective *Völker*, thereby making anti-intellectualism an indelible part of the national high culture and inscribing it in the national identity itself. In distinction, the educated classes in the United States never gave their support to grass-roots mysticism and remained firm in their devotion to reason.

Another split was a result of the shared aspiration of the upper classes to dissociate themselves from the lower, all the more intense in a democratic society because the separation was not automatic. In their pursuit of status, the upper classes used and presented culture as a status-symbol, thereby presiding over its division into high-brow and low-brow, and creating what Richard Hofstadter calls a "mugwump" culture.[140] The appropriation of certain forms of art and literature by the members of the upper classes willing to go to considerable lengths to prove that they were not equal to the rest of society made the rest of society unwilling to associate with the forms of culture thus appropriated. The masses were anti-mugwump, which made them anti-intellectual. But mugwumps were not necessarily intellectuals, and for status-sensitive intellectuals the high-culture club they created was not exclusive enough. Toward the end of the century such sensitive intellectuals and high culture parted company. From the point of view of the former, the latter was almost as contemptible as the mass (lack of) culture. They dubbed it "cultural Establishment" and transferred their loyalties to the cultural forms that were anti-establishment.

This process, as we know from Simmel, could go on forever. But the universities provided an organizational framework which sheltered the intellectuals from the madding crowds and put a stop to their fraternizing advances.

Universities created a protective environment in which intellectuals driven by cultural interests could earn their living while pursuing them, and status-sensitive intellectuals could legitimately seek and display status, which was tightly connected to intellectual achievement. Universities thus formed an alternative society, an aristocracy of merit within a democracy, which did not recognize equality in human—at least intellectual—worth, and rewarded natural superiority with status. The formation of this alternative society resulted in the creation of a cultural vacuum in the society at large. While professional intellectuals satisfied their curiosity or aesthetic sensibilities, while they sought answers to the urgent questions that perplexed them, or busied themselves with trivial pursuits (of fame and place in the republic of letters), this vacuum was filled by what came to be known as "mass culture." Its enterprising creators sought to entertain rather than educate and in most cases, though not all, cared little for the life of the mind. They provided the American public with a digestible, but probably not very nutritious, cultural diet, and made the society used to it. The taste that they created confirmed the traditional intellectual verdict of the anti-intellectualism of American society, which, in this century, may have more truth to it than in the previous one. However, if the society is indeed anti-intellectual, this might at least in part be the fault and responsibility of American intellectuals. Universities deprived society of the beneficial leadership of its best minds. They isolated intellectuals from society and society from intellectuals. At the same time, it is possible that they greatly contributed to the stability of the American society. In other countries discussed in this book, frustrated intellectuals proved to be a dangerous group. In America, universities mitigated the frustration of intellectuals, perhaps saving the nation from its potentially destructive effects.

## The Trial and Completion of American Nationality

Thus status-sensitive intellectuals decried American anti-intellectualism, their spirit oppressed by the irresistible egalitarianism imposed by American ideals, and other groups nursed grievances generated by the imperfect realization of these ideals and suffered from the oppression of inequality, which in America was insufferable. In the meantime, the stability of the American nation was threatened by the inherent and, in the framework of American nationalism, legitimate secessionist impulse which was confounded with the view, never seriously challenged, that the right of self-government was vested in the individual states. In the Fourth of July oration in 1858, Rufus Choate, anxious to preserve the Union, pointed to the potential for disruption inherent in the original conception of the American nation. "It is," he said, "the great peculiarity of our system . . . that the affections which we give to country we give to a divided object, the states in which we live and the Union by which we are enfolded. We serve two masters. Our hearts earn two loves. We live in two countries at once and are commanded to be capacious of both . . . Have you ever considered that it was a federative system we had to adopt, and that in such a system a conflict of head and members is in some form and to some extent a result of course?"[141] Because of the persistence and legitimacy of the dual loyalty, the possibility of secession as a response to dissatisfaction with the nation was always present. Yet only a most serious grievance could justify it. Since the end of the 1840s the Southern states became increasingly persuaded that their grievance was serious enough. Their attempted secession led to the Civil War. In this conflict, the interest of the Northern or Union states was to preserve the Union. This powerful interest (powerful because it was buttressed by the government, the army, and the popular sentiment) connected to the issue of slavery, whose inconsistency with the national ideals was articulated. The Northern cause became identified with the cause of emancipation, and with its triumph the most jarring inconsistency of the American life was eliminated.

Matters of interest and of principle, and different principles, intertwined and fused in the Civil War and the interpretations of events which led to it at least as much as in any similar social cataclysm. The issue for the Northern states, clearly, was one of the territorial and political extent of the American nation, rather than its ideals. That "Union must be preserved" was a "shibboleth of [the Northern] faith." Lincoln considered the conflict a war to preserve the Union. Answering Horace Greeley, who was "sorely disappointed and deeply pained" by the President's policy "with regard to the slaves of the Rebels," he wrote: "I would save the Union. I would save it the shortest way under the Constitution . . . My paramount object in this struggle *is* to save the Union, and is *not* either to save or destroy slavery. If I could save the Union without freeing *any* slave, I would do it, and if I could save it by freeing *all* the slaves, I would do it . . . What I do about slavery and the colored race I do because I believe it helps to save this Union; and what I forbear I forbear because I do *not* believe it would help to save the Union."[142]

For many years before 1860 the existence of the nation was a value in itself. It was a value everywhere, but where, as in the North, it did not appear to interfere with the ability of the relevant population to enjoy life, it was a value which eclipsed all other values. In 1850, when the threats of Southern secession became common, the old Daniel Webster anxiously asked: "Why, what would be the result? Where is the line to be drawn? What states are to secede? What is to remain American? What am I to be? An American no longer?" It was his, and the others', very identity that was at stake. Everything was secondary to that. Rather than think of secession, Webster pleaded, "let us enjoy the fresh air of liberty and union." After all,

America offered so little cause for dissatisfaction. "No monarchical throne presses these states together; no iron chain of despotic power encircles them; they live and stand upon a government popular in its form, representative in its character, founded upon principles of equality, and calculated, we hope, to last forever. In all its history, it has been beneficent; it has trodden down no man's liberty; it has crushed no state. Its daily respiration is liberty and patriotism; its yet youthful veins are full of enterprise, courage, and honorable love of glory and renown." In the name of this felicity, Webster called upon the free states to honor the fugitive slave law ("their constitutional duties in regard to the return of the persons bound to service," he put it gently, "who have escaped into the free states"), and still perceived no contradiction between what he preached and what he advised to practice and condoned. Love makes men blind. No friend of slavery himself, he was never forgiven by its enemies for advocating the appeasement of slaveholders. But the great majority of Northerners would tolerate slavery if this was the price of keeping the nation intact. Even a principled opposition to slavery, as in Lincoln's case, did not necessarily imply endorsement of immediate (or for that matter gradual) emancipation. And most Northerners did not regard slavery in the South as problematic, simply because it was not their central concern.[143]

But if the North would take the Union with slavery, the South would not take it without. If the position of the North was: *Union at any price,* "under the Constitution," of course (which, however, provided few guidelines in regard to slavery), that of the South was: *either slavery or disunion.* The grievances of the South were many. Having lost their leadership in national politics, the Southern states felt increasingly deprived of influence, at the same time as they were treacherously excluded from their share in the common prosperity by the industrial and rapacious North. These sentiments became particularly widespread and grew more acute after the Mexican War, when the acquisition of new territories and the impending admission of California as a free state revived the question of the extension of slavery, heretofore believed to have been settled by the Missouri Compromise of 1820. In the debate over compromise resolutions proposed by Henry Clay, the "grand old man of the South" Senator John Calhoun stated the reasons for Southern disaffection. The great and primary cause of it, he said, was to be found in the fact that "the equilibrium between the two sections in the government [the North and the South], as it stood when the Constitution was ratified and the government put into action, has been destroyed . . . as it now stands, one section has the exclusive power of controlling the government, which leaves the other without any adequate means of protecting itself against its encroachment and oppression." This state of affairs was achieved with the help of inequitable legislation on the part of the North, starting with the Northwest Ordinance and ending with the Missouri Compromise. "By these several acts, the South was excluded from 1,238,025 square miles . . . I have not included the territory recently acquired by the treaty with Mexico. The North is making the most strenuous efforts to appropriate the whole to herself by excluding the South from every foot of it . . . To sum up the whole, the United States, since they declared their independence, have acquired 2,373,046 square miles of territory, from which the North will have excluded the South if she should succeed in monopolizing the newly acquired territories, from about three-fourths of the whole, leaving to the South but about one-fourth."

It should be noted that no individual was excluded by any of the ordinances from settling in the West, and that there was no attempt on the part of any of the Northern states to transplant there as a community. What Calhoun meant by the exclusion of the South was that, in distinction from individuals from the North who could move to the West with all their property and enjoy it there, there was a category of property peculiar to the South which could not be enjoyed in some of the new territories—the slaves. In Calhoun's opinion, the limitations on the extension of slavery represented an aggression of the North against the rights of the South, as a result of which "what was once a constitutional federal republic [was] converted, in reality, into one as absolute as that of the Autocrat of Russia, and as despotic in its tendency as any absolute government that ever existed."

The South thus tied all its grievances to the Northern dislike for its "peculiar institution." Its interests were identified with slavery, at the same time as they came to be seen as rights, and an attack on slavery thereby became an attack on its rights. In this process the Northern opposition to slavery was generalized in two ways: it was conceived of as hostility toward the South as such—toward all its interests and toward its way of life—and as an attitude characteristic of the North as a whole. Calhoun was convinced that "every portion of the North entertains views and feelings more or less hostile" to what he delicately referred to as "the relation between the two races in the Southern section." "Those most opposed and hostile regard it as a sin," he wrote, "and consider themselves under the most sacred obligation to use every effort to destroy it. Indeed to the extent that they conceive they have power, they regard themselves as implicated in the sin and responsible for suppressing it by the use of all and every means. Those less opposed and hostile regard it as a crime—an offense against humanity, as they call it—and, although not so fanatical, feel themselves bound to use all efforts to effect the same object; while those who are least opposed and hostile regard it as a blot and a stain on the character of what they call the nation, and feel themselves accordingly bound to give it no countenance or support." [144] Although this would make perfect sense, it was patently untrue that all, or the majority, or even the leadership of the North subscribed to such views. But Southerners did not conduct surveys; they believed that it was natural and inevitable that Northerners would think so (for in the depths of their souls they knew that owning property in persons was incompatible with being Americans, and that it was therefore fundamentally wrong, immoral, and shameful), and what they thought to be a matter of fact was in fact a projection of their fears and shame.

It was possible to believe that "all men are created equal," and yet be oblivious of slavery elsewhere or even concede that because of the practical difficulties involved in its abolition, it should be temporarily tolerated. But one could not *champion* slavery and uphold the ideal of equality in liberty at the same time. This was not simply inconsistent, this was schizophrenic. Having identified their vital interests with slavery, Southerners were driven to champion it. They, said Lincoln, exchanged the old faith, in which slavery was tolerated only by necessity, for the new one, "that for some men to enslave others is a 'sacred right of self-government.'" [145] Unable to reconcile this faith with the values that constituted the core of American nationality, they set out to reinterpret and adjust them to their situation. Although the words they used remained the same, their meanings were transformed. They were creating a new pool of values. The ideals which they saw the South representing, and which formed their identity, were no longer American. When they seceded, they were on the way to being a different nation.

It would be wrong to see the secession as in any way a result of Southern nationalism (namely the development of a specifically Southern identity, loyalty, and consciousness). Southern nationalism and secession were both responses to the unbearable inconsistency between American national ideals and slavery. In the framework of individualistic nationalism, secession was possible without the preceding development of a separate identity, as was so clearly demonstrated by the American Revolution itself. But the fact that North and South appeared as separate and antagonistic nations might have made the transition even less traumatic than it would have been otherwise. The nascent Southern ideology bears unmistakable resemblance to the Romantic ethnic nationalisms such as the German and Russian ones.[146] Since this baby was, literally, murdered in its infancy, its features never got the chance to develop, but there is no doubt that they would have been strongly racist, collectivistic, and authoritarian, that it would have been traditionalist, anti-capitalist, less calculating, and, therefore, less rational, and would have valued honor above wealth. In fact, the resemblance went so far that the infant, barely beginning to prattle, had already manifested a taste for abstract theory and metaphysics in politics. Astute Northerners, actually, called Southern political thinkers "metaphysical politicians." [147] To present slavery as a social ideal one indeed needed a very sophisticated argument.

Presenting slavery as a social ideal did not at all imply that Southern ideologists turned enemies of liberty. On the contrary, with the exception of slavery, nothing was so dear to their heart: liberty and slavery, one may say, were their twin passions. In the Civil War they fought for liberty, trusting that victory would be theirs, for while "our enemies rely on their numbers, we rely upon the valor of free men." They gloried in their freedom from public opinion; it was beneath the honor of a gentleman to bow to it.[148] Their chief concern in secession was to preserve their sacred right of self-government. While they were not the first to claim that slavery was requisite for the preservation of liberty, they claimed, in addition, that progress itself necessitated it. "To secure true progress" (which required chaining down mediocrity, as well as unfettering genius), George Fitzhugh, the spirited self-appointed sociologist, demanded: "Liberty for the few—Slavery, in every form, for the mass!"[149]

Fitzhugh was a particularly able and articulate apologist of slavery. In his defense of it, he placed his faith in sociology rather than in history, political theory, or what not, and his variety of sociology was "Marxist." Although it is highly unlikely that Fitzhugh was influenced by Marx, since his major works had appeared in 1854 and 1857, while *Capital* was published only in 1867, he was remarkably close to the master in reasoning and in tone, and—what is most surprising—in terminology. If Fitzhugh did not necessarily share Marx's sympathies, he did, unquestionably, sympathize with the latter's antipathies. His main argument in defense of slavery was that, whatever one could say of it, the free, capitalist society, based on division of labor and competition, was infinitely worse. Its boasted liberty was mockery; it was inconceivable how slavery could degrade men lower than they were degraded by freedom. Given the depths of misery into which the free society had reduced its lower classes, Fitzhugh approved of their socialist leanings. He differed from Marx in that he believed that the promise of socialism was realized in slavery. In *Sociology for the South, or the Failure of the Free Society*, he wrote:

> The poor themselves are all practical Socialists and in some degree pro-slavery men. They unite in strikes and trade unions and thus exchange a part of their liberties in order to secure high and uniform wages . . . Slavery to an association is not always better than slavery to a single master. The professed object is to avoid ruinous underbidding and competition with one another; but this competition can never cease while liberty lasts. Those who wish to be free must take liberty with this inseparable burden . . . A well-conducted farm in the South is a model of associated labor that Fourier might envy . . . Slavery protects the infants, the aged, and the sick . . . They are part of the family, and self-interest and affection combine to shelter, shield, and foster them . . . Socialism proposes to do away with free competition; to afford protection and support at all times to the laboring class; to bring about, at least, a qualified community of property and to associate labor. All these purposes slavery fully and perfectly attains.[150]

Thus slave society was "the best form of society yet devised for the masses."

Fitzhugh articulated his arguments in his other book, with the catchy title

*Cannibals All! or, Slaves Without Masters.* The indictment of the free capitalist society in it rested on the theory of surplus value, which our prescient sociologist elaborated in a language whose similarity to that of Marx in the yet unwritten *Capital* cannot fail to amaze the reader. North and South, claimed Fitzhugh, were engaged in the white slave trade, which was far more cruel than black slavery, because it exacted more from the slaves, and yet left them unprotected. In an eloquent passage Fitzhugh disclosed to his Northern reader the full significance of his actions: "What you have considered and practiced as a virtue is little better than cannibalism . . . Capital commands labor as master does the slave. Neither pays for labor; but the master permits the slave to retain a larger allowance from the proceeds of his own labor, and hence 'free labor is cheaper than slave labor.' You, with the command over labor which your capital gives you, are a slave owner; a master without the obligations of a master. They who work for you, who create your income, are slaves without the rights of slaves. Slaves without a master! . . . under the delusive name of liberty, you work [the laborer] 'from morn to dewy eve,' from infancy to old age; then turn him out to starve. You treat your horses and hounds better. Capital is a cruel master. The free slave trade, the commonest yet the cruelest of trades."

Clearly, Fitzhugh saw little value in liberty for the masses. He treated it as simply irrelevant to the comparison that he was drawing. As to equality, he rejected it altogether. "Men are not 'born entitled to equal rights!'" he insisted; the famous passage in the Declaration of Independence had no truth or meaning out of its specific context. Slavery was based on natural inequality and was thus itself natural. "It is, we believe, conceded on all hands," argued Fitzhugh (holding the following truths to be self-evident),

> that men are not born physically, morally, or intellectually equal; some are males, some females, some from birth, large, strong, and healthy, others weak, small, and sickly; some are naturally amiable, others prone to all kinds of wickedness; some brave, others timid. Their natural inequalities beget inequalities of rights. The weak in mind or body require guidance, support, and protection; they must obey and work for those who protect and guide them; they have a natural right to guardians, committees, teachers, or masters. Nature has made them slaves; all that law and government can do is modify, and mitigate their slavery. In the absence of legally instituted slavery, their condition would be worse under the natural slavery of the weak to the strong, the foolish to the wise and cunning. The wise and virtuous, the brave, the strong in mind and body, are by nature born to command and protect, and law but follows nature in making them rulers, legislators, judges, captains, husbands, guardians, committees, and masters.[151]

This argument was not obviously absurd, but its usefulness for the cause Fitzhugh was defending depended on the assumption that the inherent inequality of men derived from the inherent inequality of uniform groups to which they belonged, that it was, in other words, the inequality of collectivities, not of individuals. In the framework of American nationalism, the core element of which was individualism, it was untenable. Lincoln demonstrated how easily it could be turned around if the emphasis was transferred back to the individual. In his notebooks appear the following syllogisms: "You say A is white, and B is black. It is color, then; the lighter having the right to enslave the darker? Take care. By this rule, you are to be slave to the first man you meet with a fairer skin than your own. You do not mean color exactly? You mean the whites are intellectually the superiors of blacks, and therefore have the right to enslave them? Take care again. By this rule, you are to be slave to the first man you meet with an intellect superior to your own." [152]

But in the emergent Southern consciousness the group and rights of the group as such were consistently substituted for the individual and the rights of the individual. This was the fundamental alteration wrought in the American ideology, which underpinned other alterations. Racism was only a variety of collectivism, and authoritarianism was made possible only by it. Unity was no longer a plurality; the many in one were no longer associated but fused. Indeed, among the very few changes introduced by the Confederacy in the Constitution of the United States was the removal of the motto *E Pluribus Unum*, in the place of which was put *Deo Vindice*. The South and the North, which were but names of geographical sectors, the borders between which were established by convention and could be recharted, in the Southern consciousness became reified concepts, collective bodies possessed of antagonistic souls and pitted against each other as might be two warring persons. At least to the same degree to which specific states remained the focus of American loyalties after independence, the state, rather than the Confederacy, remained the focus of Southern loyalties. Had the Confederacy survived, the secession might have brought into the world several Southern nations, rather than one. But if the South was even less of a union than the United States, each Confederate state was a unitary state. It was this fundamental transformation in the definition of the relationship between the individual and the collectivity which allowed the reinterpretation of the principle of self-government, that is, liberty in its original American sense, which made it compatible with slavery. "Self-government" was the watchword of the South. Within the Union, Southerners clamored for the recognition of their inalienable right to it; because they felt that it was trampled upon, they seceded; and in secession they remained faithful to it, firmly believing that they were the true bearers of the supreme American ideal. In fact, they betrayed it and upheld its negation. "They call themselves Democrats," wrote Frederick Law Olmsted of the Southerners in 1854. "Call them what you will . . . they are not the legitimate offspring of democracy, thanks to God, but of slavery under a democracy." [153] Self-government could not be made into a communal right. It was the inalienable right of individuals, and only in this sense was it meaningful; the right of communities to self-government was but the composite liberty of its members. A collectivistic interpretation of this value was a distortion of its original—of its American—meaning. To demand the extension of slavery as a recognition of *the South's* right of self-government, thought Lincoln, was preposterous. "When the white man governs himself," he said, "that is self-government; but when he governs himself and also governs another man, that is more than self-government—that is despotism." [154]

The attempt of the South to found a new nation, which would be one very different from the American nation, was thwarted. At the price of thousands of lives, the Union (the association of thousands of individuals) was preserved. In 1865, the soul of the American nation, which had been before but a resident tenant in its vast territorial body, became its owner: the national identity finally achieved a geo-political embodiment. A nation of self-made men, America was a self-made nation. As a material reality, a country on a map, it, more than any other, was a creation of people who believed themselves Americans, and a product of their national identity and loyalty.

For many Americans, the Civil War marked the line between the dream of nationality and its realization, which was comparable to the significance of the Revolution and the Constitution for other generations. For many, it only then became, in the words of James Russell Lowell, "something more than a promise and an expectation." Their loyalty was justified and many times reinforced. "Before the War our patriotism was a firework, a salute, a serenade for holidays and summer evenings," wrote Emerson. "Now . . . it is real." "If among us in the earlier day there was no occasion for the word Nation, there is now. A Nation is born," asserted Charles Sumner in an 1867 address entitled "Are we a Nation?" [155]

The establishment of the geo-political referent of national loyalty completed the long process which brought into being the American nation as it exists today. Between then and now, to be sure, it has changed tremendously, for American ideals, or rather the inescapable inconsistency between them and reality and the tensions they bred, implied permanent revolution, but it has changed within the structure which emerged at the end of the Civil War and along the lines provided in it. At that crucial moment the rules of the game in American politics were redrawn and political action redirected. Since then the American revolution has been going on in a new framework.

The Civil War was fought because the Union was believed to be indivisible. Its preservation in the bloodiest struggle in the Western world before the era of world wars confirmed this belief, as it increased the value of and strengthened the commitment to national unity. A speaker addressing Yale alumni in 1865 stressed: "In this blood of our slain our unity is cemented and sanctified . . . We had not bled enough [before] to merge our colonial distinctions, and let out the state-rights doctrine, and make us a proper nation." Lowell exulted: "What costly stuff whereof to make a nation!" The Southern secession discredited the idea of states' rights; dual allegiance, to the state and to the nation, became inadmissible; the states were denied the right to compete for loyalty with the nation. "State rights, in all their denationalizing pretensions," declared Sumner, "must be trampled out forever." The government, he thought, should be national, not federal.[156] As a result, ironically, the triumph of American national ideals, the individualist principles associated with the Union, paved the way for the development of a unitary notion of the American nation which was not entirely consistent with them.

Hegelian ideas and ideas of political Romanticism which had been the standard fare of German thought for three-quarters of a century were discovered and enjoyed brief popularity. There appeared a tendency to reify the nation and see it as a living organism or a collective—and higher—individuality. It was indivisible and sovereign in its own right, it existed above and beyond men, and its members owed it natural allegiance. This organic theory of the nation, novel in America, was opposed to the traditional constitutional view, according to which a nation was a social compact, a voluntary association of free individuals, which derived its sovereignty from theirs. American Hegelians who thus apostrophized the nation, however, were patriots devoted to the ideals of *their* nation, and the organic theory was given a peculiar twist in their hands. Unruly, individualistic Americans would not dissolve in the higher individuality. In the best Romantic tradition, the nation represented an "Idea," but the "Idea" of the American nation was individual freedom. A prominent representative of this trend of thought, the German immigrant Francis Lieber, for example, asserted: "We belong to that race, whose obvious task it is . . . to rear and spread civil liberty over vast regions . . . We belong to that tribe which alone has the word 'Self-Government.'" Furthermore, in the German tradition nationality was interpreted in ethnic and ultimately racial terms. The unique national "Idea" reflected the ethnic and racial uniqueness of the nation. To a certain extent this interpretation was carried over into the American version of the organic theory and expressed itself in the emphasis on the Anglo-Saxon foundations of the American nation. Yet American Hegelians were emphatically universalistic. A nation, proclaimed the Hegelian Elisha Mulford, if it asserts as its ground "the rise of a race and not the rise of man," "has no longer a moral foundation, nor a universal end."[157]

The organic theory of the nation in America was not a coherent system of thought and it never had wide appeal. At the same time, its central proposition, though stripped of its Hegelian garb and brought down to earth, was shared by many, eventually becoming yet another "self-evident" truth. This proposition, that the United States were one nation, and that this nation was a unity, with no longer many, but one head, one tremendous body, and one soul, reflected the new reality. In 1874 Patrick Henry would indeed have reason to claim that "the distinctions between Virginians, Pennsylvanians, New Yorkers, and New Englanders, are no more," and that all were now, first and foremost, and unquestionably, Americans. (The regional differences that remained were secondary, and to regard them as fundamental was no longer legitimate.) Centralization of authority in the federal government aroused less suspicion and in many cases was welcomed or even demanded.

Yet, although America was now seen as a unitary polity, rather than as a federation of states, it differed significantly from unitary Continental nations in Europe, for it still was an association of individuals, and therefore a composite body, rather than a higher individuality. Underneath the nation in the singular, the original nation in the plural remained. In contrast to the European nations, where the primacy of the nation over the individual imposed general uniformity, the unchallenged primacy of the individual allowed—even guaranteed—plurality of tastes, views, attachments, aspirations, and self-definitions, within the shared national framework. Pluralism was built into the system. The united American nation did not become, in the phrase of Michael Walzer, "a jealous nation." [158] It tolerated multiple allegiances. Individual states no longer could serve as a major focus for loyalty, but circumstances and the climate of opinion soon combined to create a substitute for them. Indeed, it is entirely possible that the organic theory of the nation itself contributed to its formation. For the entity which took the place of a state in the heart of an American citizen, and which from then on, above any other factor, defined the identity of different *groups* of Americans and distinguished between them, was ancestral nationality, or, as it came to be defined, "ethnicity." [159] Dual identity thus remained typical, but Virginians, Pennsylvanians, and New Yorkers were replaced by hyphenated Americans. In the beginning of the twentieth century it was reasonable to assert that the United States was less a Union of states than of nations. [160]

America has been a nation of immigrants from the beginning, and from early on these immigrants have been coming from different countries. Yet the dual national, or "ethnic," identity of Americans is of a more recent origin. It dates only from the end of the last century. [161] As was already emphasized above, originally and primarily, Americans, with the exception of English Americans, were not recruited from nations. [162] They were recruited from various populations which, having some identity (in the case of the lower-class immigrants, as a rule, not well articulated), had not as yet developed a national identity. Only toward the end of the nineteenth century was the average immigrant likely to be a member of a nation before he arrived in America. The fact that more often than not the nation of which such immigrant was a member was an ethnic, rather than a civic, nation adds poignancy to the compound "ethnic American."

This momentous transformation in the populations from which Americans are recruited inevitably affects the ability of the immigrants to integrate and the character of the American nationality in which they partake. The psychological gratification which national identity affords to the humblest of nationals makes one hold on to it. The integration, therefore, becomes more difficult, because it requires at least some degree of conscious renunciation. Immigrants with national identity became the rule when immigration acquired its truly mass character. It is probable that of 1,100,000 immigrants admitted to the United States in 1906, the great majority had a sense of nationality. The view that nations represented indissoluble unities possessed of a unique spirit, which was the essence of the organic theory and was shared in some very fundamental way by such people as Woodrow Wilson (otherwise it is difficult to explain his championship of the rights of nations), prepared the receiving society for a high degree of tolerance toward the retention of original national identity among new Americans, or at any rate made it ambivalent in regard to such a possibility.

There were, of course, nativist movements and sentiments which opposed such retention and resisted the formation of dual loyalties even before the mass immigration and before the Civil War. Later, both Theodore Roosevelt and Wilson inveighed against hyphenated Americans. If America was not a "jealous nation," there were always plenty of jealous Americans. But, on the whole, nativist sentiments were not widespread and efforts to enforce uniformity on the part of the leadership were half-hearted. Exclusive loyalty was not insisted upon, and the void left by the discreditation of the states as major foci of group loyalty was filled by nationalities of origin without much or strenuous opposition. The toleration of ethnic pluralism was a functional equivalent of the Northwest Ordinance, when nationality of origin replaced a state as the chief competitor of the American nation for the attachments of its members. Acceptance of this other identity as legitimate tamed a potentially divisive force, prevented disaffection, and secured loyalty to the nation. Perpetuation of ethnic allegiance, and in many cases deliberate cultivation of an allegiance long forgotten, however, created a new source of tension; Americans again lived in two countries at once and were commanded to be capacious of both; conflict, therefore, in some form and to some extent, became a matter of course.[163]

As long as the geo-political framework of the nation remained ambiguous, one could choose among political secession, geographical separation, and internal reform as ways to deal with the discontent generated by the internal contradictions of individualistic nationalism. In the framework of unambiguously fixed geo-political boundaries, with group secession ruled out and geographical separation within the system no longer possible, this discontent was channeled toward internal reform, the only other option being withdrawal into privacy. Society itself became the new frontier. Instead of clearing forests, one group after another, and many groups simultaneously, have been attempting to carve out for themselves or even create new, heretofore unimagined social spaces. This has been hard labor, but the society is steadily becoming more inclusive and accommodates more interests than before.

The national commitment of America—to liberty and equality—remains the main source of social cohesion and the main stimulant of unrest in it. The rigidity of loyalty to these national ideals, as well as its laxity, endangers the nation; yet this loyalty preserves it. In America, the maxim "My country, right or wrong" is wrong: it betrays the ideals. But the alternative principle—"My country, right or wrong! When right, to be kept right; when wrong, to be put right!"—is unrealistic and sets one onto a frustrating project which may lead to disaffection. Compromise is inconsistent with idealism. Yet the ability to compromise has become a distinguishing characteristic of this intensely idealistic nation. To be an American means to persevere in one's loyalty to the ideals, in spite of the inescapable contradictions between them and reality, and to accept reality without reconciling oneself to it. "One has to live in the world and accept it in all its frightening implications," wrote an American idealist. "One has to to live consciously and self-consciously, in the involvement and the alienation, in the loyalty and the questioning, in the love and in the critical appraisal . . . At best we can live in a paradox." [164]

The uniqueness of the American nation consists in that in the course of its long existence, a *national* existence longer than that of any other society with the exception of England, it has remained faithful to the original idea of the nation, and come closest to the realization of the principles of individualistic, civic nationalism. It stands as an example of its original promise—democracy—a proof of its resilience and viability despite the contradictions inherent in it. It is because of this, not because of its newness or heterogeneity, that America is not a nation like all the others.

But, then, as this book has attempted to show, neither is any of the others.

# AFTERWORD

U ltimately, nationalism can be traced to the structural contradictions
of the society of orders. It was a response of individuals personally
affected by these contradictions to the sense of disorder they created. Many other responses were possible, and at other times tried and
found successful; the choice of nationalism was not inevitable. Neither (certainly not in the form it assumed and at the time it actually occurred) was
the dissolution of the old society. It was contingent on the nationalist response to its dysfunction. Once adopted, nationalism accelerated the process of change, channeled it into a certain direction, limited the possibilities
of future development, and became a major factor in it. It thus both acknowledged and accomplished the grand social transformation from the old
order to modernity. The old society was replaced with a new one, based on
the principle of nationality.

The inventors of nationalism were members of the new English aristocracy. Commoners by birth, they found the traditional image of society, in
which upward mobility was an anomaly, uncongenial and substituted for it
the idea of a homogeneously elite people—the *nation*. Had they concentrated, instead, on forging genealogies, a perfectly logical thing to do given
the circumstances, history could have taken an entirely different course.

As it was, the idea of the nation took root. The ascendancy of England
ensured its salience, but its appeal in circumstances different from those of
its emergence was due to its nature, rather than descent. Nationality elevated every member of the community which it made sovereign. It guaranteed status. *National identity is, fundamentally, a matter of dignity.* It gives
people reasons to be proud.

In the society of orders, pride and self-respect, as well as the claim to
status or the respect of others, was a privilege of the few, a tiny elite placed
high above the rest. The lot of the rest was humility and abnegation, which
they tried to rationalize and make tolerable in one way or another and
sometimes even managed to enjoy, but could never escape. Even the proud
elite was not safe from degradation. Its status depended on the preservation
of rigid distinctions between orders and the strict observance of the rules of
precedence; any breach in them threatened it, for status is entirely a matter

of social convention, it is socially constructed in its every element, and easily deconstructs if the convention is broken. Nationalism diminished the significance of invidious distinctions and, at the same time, secured everyone from ultimate degradation. Within a nation, status (and, with it, sense of pride and self-respect) can never be totally lost. One still can rise and fall, but never fall so low that it would break one's heart.

It would be a strong statement, but no overstatement, to say that the world in which we live was brought into being by vanity. The role of vanity—or desire for status—in social transformation has been largely underestimated, and greed or will to power are commonly regarded as its mainsprings. In all the five cases in this book, however, the emergence of nationalism was related to preoccupation with status. The English aristocracy sought to justify it; the French and the Russian nobility—to protect it; the German intellectuals—to achieve it. Even for the materialistic Americans, taxation without representation was an insult to their pride, more than an injury to their economic interests. They fought—and became a nation—over respect due to them, rather than anything else.[1]

The political, and even economic, realities of the modern world were to a significant extent shaped by nationalism born out of such preoccupation with status. In the former case, the influence of nationalism has been more direct. The basic framework of modern politics—the world divided into nations—is simply a realization of nationalist imagination; it is created by nationalism. The internal political structures of different nations reflect the original definitions of nationality in them, specifically whether it is defined as individualistic or collectivistic, and as civic or ethnic. The former definition gives rise to democratic, liberal societies; others—to various forms and degrees of authoritarianism. Foreign policies, which are of course dependent on the structure of international opportunities and the availability of means to carry them out, are motivated by the ideas of national missions or objectives, and by considerations of international prestige, which are also to a large degree defined by the image of the nation and of its standing vis-à-vis the others. Even the availability of the means to carry policies out is related to this. The reification of the nation in the framework of collectivistic nationalism increases the susceptibility of a nation to *ressentiment*. *Ressentiment* not only makes a nation more aggressive, but represents an unusually powerful stimulant of national sentiment and collective action, which makes it easier to mobilize collectivistic nations for aggressive warfare than to mobilize individualistic nations, in which national commitment is normally dependent on rational calculations.

The five nations on which this book focused have been major actors in modern politics. Their nationalisms were particularly important in defining the political structure of modernity, as they were in defining its cultural character. Each one of them left on it a unique, indelible imprint. Had any of the five nationalisms—English, French, Russian, German, or American—been different, the world would be a different place for all of us.

Economic reality is not constructed in the same sense and to the same extent as political reality. Imagination may be an important economic resource, but most economic resources (which determine structures of economic opportunities) have little to do with imagination. Moreover, similar economic systems exist in widely differing political and cultural environments. The impact of nationalism in the economic sphere is felt most where economic issues are interwoven with political and ideological ones. Nationalism affects economic behavior insofar as it creates a certain ethic (in this sense it is not different from Protestant or any other religious ethic, and similarly to the economic effects of dissimilar religious ethics, economic effects of various nationalisms differ); it affects attitudes toward money and money-making, toward various occupations, thereby determining the strengths and weaknesses of particular economies. It also affects the economic policies of governments, domestic as well as foreign. The economic ideological politics characteristic of this century, the central expression of which was the often victorious struggle against "capitalism" around the globe, are largely a product of nationalism, and specifically of the nationalist resentment against *politically* "advanced" nations. "Capitalism" was first associated with liberal society of the Anglo-American type in France (that first anti-Western nation); other nations resentful of the West (in which they before long included France) made this association into a dogma. And today the belief in it makes us rejoice at the resolve of the Soviet government, and of Eastern European nations recently liberated from the yoke of the Soviet government, to replace their defunct "socialist" economies with functioning "capitalist" ones. We interpret this for-a-change rational behavior as a sign of their desire to adopt—and capability to implement—liberal ideals and turn democratic. But if there is a necessary connection between capitalism and democracy, it exists only to the extent that a free society necessitates a capitalist economy. Capitalism (which allows a certain freedom, which is never absolute, to the play of market forces and is, therefore, always a mixed economy), on the other hand, can very well coexist with societies which are anything but democratic.

Marx to the contrary, there is no one-to-one correspondence between systems of production and ownership and systems of social and political relations. Economy does not define the nature of society. This is determined by the image the society has of itself or by its essential identity. A profound change in the structure of economic opportunities may lead to a modification of identity (as was the case of the American South), but does not guarantee it, and the introduction of a mixed economy may not result in a profound change of economic opportunities to begin with.

National identities which owe their origins to long-forgotten circumstances and needs which today can hardly be imagined persist because of the psychological rewards inherent in nationality, its status-enhancing quality. Nationality makes people feel good (and collectivistic and ethnic nationality on the whole makes them feel better than individualistic and civic national-ity, for the simple reason that individualistic nationalism merely affirms the dignity inherent in the individual, adding nothing to it, while collectivistic nationalism allows one to partake in the dignity of a far greater, stronger, and more perfect being, the brilliance of whose virtues has the power to blind one to one's own failings). Although groups whose interests every spe-cific nationalism was summoned to serve, and which in turn defined it, no longer exist, and their interests have lost all relevance, national identities still serve people's interests. These interests, which are served by particular national identities in their respective nations, however, in most cases would be equally well served by other national identities. No individual and no group of people are genetically bound to define themselves in one or another fashion, and as the original interests which gave rise to particular national identities disappear, a change of national identity is not impossible. Apart from deep changes in the economy, other structural changes—for instance ones brought on by the outcome of a war and occupation—may result in the redefinition of a particular national identity. (West German national iden-tity, for example, may be significantly different from the German identity that existed in the unified Germany, although careful research is necessary to establish in what ways exactly they differ. This new identity, in turn, may be affected by the reincorporation of Prussia and other Eastern provinces.) One has to admit, though, that such redefinitions are extremely rare.

So long as the national identity remains unchanged, the fundamental structure of motivations and, consequently, the fundamental nature of the national society remain unchanged, and patterns of behavior characteristic of it in the past should be expected. Of course, motivations are not always realized. Desire and ability alone do not determine the course of action; it also needs propitious conditions. Nevertheless, the potential for their real-ization exists. The power of nationalism to mold collective behavior makes it all-important to realize that nationalism is not a uniform phenomenon. There is no greater—and graver—mistake than to regard all nations as cre-ated equal. Men are created equal, but nations are not. Some are created as compacts of sovereign individuals and emphasize the freedom and equality of men; some are created as "beautiful great individuals" who may feed on man, and preach racial superiority and submission to the state. Rights of nations, which we now consider incontestable, to no small extent owing to American naiveté, have very different significance and implications in such different cases.

Images of social order, born out of the efforts of elites in the society of orders to escape its contradictions, are perpetuated in the laws, institutions, and cultural forms of modern societies. Our world is still the one they created. The continuity, however blurred, is unbroken. The age of nationalism has not ended; we have but entered the phase of neo-nationalism. At no other time has this been demonstrated more clearly than during these very days when regimes and ideologies crumble around us, and nationalism everywhere raises its head amid the rubble and confusion, as full of energy as ever. Forces shaped centuries ago continue to shape the destinies of mankind at the end of the twentieth century. Our ability to make sense of them and to deal with the reality around us depends on our understanding of their origins.

Nationalism is a historical phenomenon. It appeared in one age and it can disappear in another. But if it does, the world in which we live will be no more, and another world, as distinct from the one we know as was the society of orders that it replaced, will replace it. This post-national world will be truly post-modern, for nationality is the constitutive principle of modernity. It will be a new form of social being and it will change the way we see society; to understand it, we shall have to begin anew.

# Notes

## Introduction

1. The concept "style of thought" was coined by Karl Mannheim in his essay "Conservative Thought," in *Essays on Sociology and Social Psychology* (New York: Oxford University Press, 1953), pp. 74–165, and was based on the notion of style developed in art history. It encapsulated the idea that broad cultural currents, or traditions, similarly to artistic styles, cannot be characterized by any of their composing elements, each of which may be found in many other traditions, including those directly contradictory to the tradition in question, but only by the organizing idea, or principle, which brings these elements together in a distinctive configuration that imparts to each element a special significance it would lack in any other configuration. Obviously nationalism does not have the unity of a tradition such as Liberalism (though it is questionable whether Conservatism may be regarded as a unified tradition in the same sense). The concept "style of thought," therefore, may not be strictly applicable to nationalism, which, rather, represents a class of styles unified by the same fundamental idea, which, however, can be interpreted in a variety of ways.

2. Guido Zernatto, "Nation: The History of a Word," *Review of Politics*, 6 (1944), pp. 351–366.

3. (Ch.-L. de Secondat) Montesquieu, *De l'esprit des lois* (Paris: Librairie Garnier Frères, 1945), vol. II, p. 218. Zernatto ("Nation") quotes this definition on p. 361.

4. The concept comes to us from biology (see, for example, Samuel Alexander, *Space, Time and Deity* [London: Macmillan, 1920], and Michael Polanyi, "Life's Irreducible Structure," *Science*, 160 [June 1968], pp. 1308–12); and life is the paradigmatic example of emergence. Life cannot be reduced to the sum total of its inanimate elements, it cannot be explained by any of their properties; it is the relationship between the elements, unpredictable from these properties, which gives rise to it, and which in many ways conditions the behavior of the elements the moment they become elements of the living matter. The mystery of life lies in that we do not know its unifying principle: we do not know why inanimate elements form a relationship which gives rise to life. Because of our systematic inability to solve this mystery, the best strategy in the study of life has been considered to put this question aside and be content with the study of the mechanisms and expressions of life. In many other areas of study this is not the best strategy. In the case of emergent social phenomena,

which are structurally parallel to the phenomenon of life, we can answer the question of what brings elements together, and why, and can discover the unifying principle, if we choose to do so. A text, a simple sentence, is such an emergent phenomenon. A sentence is composed of certain elements which have definite grammatical, morphological, and phonetic properties. Yet, nothing in them can explain the existence of a sentence or why all these elements combine together to form it. This is explained by the idea of the author of the sentence, by what he or she wishes to express, by the significance of the sentence for him or her. Undoubtedly, the author is only able to construct a sentence within the boundary conditions formed by the grammatical, morphological, and other properties of the elements in a language he or she uses. But it is the idea which brings some of the elements together in a sentence and determines the role each of them is to play in it. It is the idea which creates out of existing elements a novel reality. Currents of culture, traditions, and ideologies are also emergent phenomena, though on a higher level of complexity. It was their emergent character that led Mannheim to refer to them as "styles of thought."

5. This political nature of nationalism does not necessitate statehood either as a reality or as an aspiration. It has to do with the definition of the ultimate source of authority which does not have to belong to the state, as religious believers among us so well know, although it may be in part delegated to it. As a result, nations without states of their own are in no way abnormal or incomplete, and the one-to-one correspondence between the two, while a fact or a desideratum in many cases, is not at all of essence in nationalism. In much of the scholarship on nationalism it is seen as such, however. (On the imperfect correspondence between states and nations, see G. P. Nielsson, "States and 'Nation-Groups': A Global Taxonomy," in *New Nationalisms of the Developed West*, ed. E. A. Tiryakian and R. Rogowski [Boston: Allen and Unwin, 1985], pp. 27–56.)

6. For discussion of "ethnicity," see Nathan Glazer and Daniel P. Moynihan, eds., *Ethnicity: Theory and Experience* (Cambridge, Mass.: Harvard University Press, 1975), especially the editors' introduction. A. D. Smith's *The Ethnic Origins of Nations* (Oxford: Basil Blackwell, 1986) emphasizes the role of ethnicity in nationalism.

7. David Laitin suggested in a conversation that in the two hundred years since this transformation took place, the meaning of the word "nation" could be further modified, and that the new nations of today may be "nations" in a sense not considered here. Theoretically, this is a possibility. But in practice, the nation as "a unique people" is so broadly defined and allows so many interpretations without the change of the concept that if such a change did occur, the idea of the nation would be defined out of the framework of nationalism altogether.

8. A recent book by Jeffrey Brooks provides us with a good example (*When Russia Learned to Read: Literacy and Popular Literature, 1861–1917* [Princeton: Princeton University Press, 1985], pp. 54–55). According to the data of several studies of schoolchildren (entering pupils, ages 8–11) conducted in Russia in the early twentieth century, a whole one-fifth of the children interviewed in rural areas could not tell their first names. Only about a half knew their patronymics or family names. Over a half of the Moscow children did not know that

they were living in Moscow. What was their identity? Clearly, the identity of the children who did not know what their first names were—and one shudders imagining the destitute, horrible existence they led—did not include these names. For themselves, they were nameless. Probably they realized that they were human, male, poor; this is as far as their identity went. Did these Russian children, who did not know that they were Russian, have national identity? (We can ask this question since in this case the sense of a unique Russian identity developed simultaneously and is inseparable from national identity.) The answer is: definitely not. And this is so even though they might have shared, and very likely did share, all those qualities which would characterize any self-conscious Russian and which, so nationalists believed, made a Russian. They were born in Russia of Russian parents and had, probably, the distinctive light-brown (in Russian—*rusy*) or fair hair; they spoke Russian; they crossed themselves in an Orthodox manner; if they could find it, they drank vodka. All these qualities, however, in no sense, with the possible exception of the legal, assured their nationality. In the legal sense, one should note, newborn babies have national identity, although they do not know that and although, clearly, in the psychological sense they have no identity at all. Such automatic categorization, so long as it is not realized and acknowledged by the person who is categorized in this fashion, is irrelevant to this discussion, for, obviously, while it can orient the behavior of others toward the person, it cannot orient and affect his or her actions in any way.

9. The existence of a supra-societal system, or shared social space, was a necessary condition for the spread of nationalism from the very beginning of the process. Borrowing presupposed the existence of a shared model, and such a model could exist only for societies which were explicitly relevant for each other. It is probable that initially such shared social space was created by Christianity and, perhaps, the Renaissance. Parenthetically, this may explain why, while individual proto-nations—namely societies held together by solidarities remarkably similar to national, although not called "nations"—were known in the ancient world, notably among the Jews and the Greeks, nationalism never spread beyond the borders of these individual societies. In distinction, Christianity did create in Europe the supra-societal social space which made such spread possible. This social space could contract or expand. The rise to dominance of the West continued the work of the Middle Ages, and ensured the expansion of this social space. The more it expanded, the more societies were drawn within the orbit of the influence of the "nation canon," until, in our day, it became shared by virtually the whole world.

10. This means that "reference societies" (Reinhard Bendix, *Kings or People* [Berkeley: University of California Press, 1978]) do not simply impose themselves, but are chosen as models by those whom they influence.

11. I use this concept in the sense it was originally defined by Durkheim in *The Division of Labor in Society* and in *Suicide,* and later developed by Robert K. Merton in "Social Structure and Anomie," as denoting structural inconsistency, and specifically the inconsistency between values and other elements of social structure.

12. Friedrich Nietzsche, "Genealogy of Morals," 1887, in *The Philosophy of*

*Nietzsche* (New York: The Modern Library, 1927), pp. 617–809; Max Scheler, *Ressentiment,* 1912 (Glencoe, Ill.: The Free Press, 1961).

13. Alexis de Tocqueville, *The Old Regime and the French Revolution,* 1856 (Garden City, N.J.: Doubleday Anchor Books, 1955); François Furet, *Interpreting the French Revolution* (Cambridge: Cambridge University Press, 1981). In some cases (for example, Germany) *ressentiment* was originally nurtured by the situation within the community that was to be defined as national, but the unsatisfactory internal situation was interpreted as the result of foreign influence, and a foreign country that had been the object of imitation became the focus of *ressentiment* all the same.

14. *Ressentiment,* which is a specific psychological state associated with the emergence of certain types of nationalism (ethnic, and to a lesser extent, collectivistic but civic), should not be equated with the psychological dimension of nationalism as such, which is much broader. A student of society cannot be oblivious to psychological processes. In the social process they perform the role of necessary conductors, mediating between social structures and cultural formations, and between social structures and cultural formations at different stages in social transformation. The final outcome at any stage is affected by the nature of the psychological processes involved. Every social phenomenon is, therefore, also psychological, and nationalism is no exception. But, since this in no way defines it, in this book the psychological dimension of nationalism is treated as given. Even *ressentiment,* it should be noted, which plays a specific role in the formation of certain nationalisms, does not generate nationalism in and of itself. Only in certain structural conditions *may* it do so, and only in confluence with very specific ideas *can* it do so. In other conditions, and in conjunction with other ideas, the very same psychological state may translate into entirely different phenomena, as well as vainly spend itself and have no effect at all.

While there is no justification for interpreting nationalism as the product of specific psychological states or needs (possibly in distinction from identity in general), neither is there any for considering it a psychological state. As do many other stimuli, nationalism arouses psychological responses, and therefore has psychological manifestations. These manifestations are not specific to it: other identities, as well as emotions of a totally different nature, may be similarly expressed. The specificity of nationalism (that which makes it what it is, a phenomenon *sui generis*) lies not in the specificity of the psychological responses it arouses, but in the specificity of the stimulus, which is cultural.

15. Max Weber, *Economy and Society* (Berkeley: University of California Press, 1978), vol. I, *Basic Sociological Terms,* specifically pp. 4, 24.

16. The two most important recent works representing the conventional view are B. Anderson, *Imagined Communities: Reflections on the Origin and Spread of Nationalism* (London: Verso Editions, 1983), and E. Gellner, *Nations and Nationalism* (Oxford: Basil Blackwell, 1983). This view is briefly discussed in my "The Emergence of Nationalism in England and France," *Research in Political Sociology,* 5 (1991), pp. 333–370. It is embedded in a materialist conception of social reality, in which "material," or "real," factors, through unspecified psychological mechanisms which they activate, cause symbolic, cultural, or

"ideal" phenomena. "Real" factors may be economic or political structures or processes, as well as common language or shared history. Contemporary sociology tends to accentuate the former, and as a result, in sociology, and in the discourse influenced by it, the materialist conception assumes the form of one or another variety (sociological, as distinguished from other kinds) of "structuralism." The premises of "structuralism" are rarely spelled out, and often the name connotes merely the belief in the explanatory primacy of social structures. The only rationale of such belief, nevertheless, is contained in these premises. This is a good example of an "ideal" factor—a theoretical position—turning into an "objective" force which affects the professional behavior and beliefs of individuals, yet the significance of which they no longer fully understand. It appears, indeed, impossible, on the basis of empirical evidence, to distinguish between "real" and "ideal" factors in society, for people's beliefs and ideas are real forces in their lives, and structures are always informed with meanings. The only distinction that would make sense is that between systems of meanings which are embodied in social relationships and exist as inherent parts of social structures (for the sake of brevity these may be identified with "structures"), and systems of meaning, equally objective, that exist, so to speak, in a disembodied form, as cultural traditions, beliefs, and ideas ("culture," for short).

17. The term is the counterpart of "models of" reality, which distinguish human thinking and form the building blocks of culture; Clifford Geertz, "Religion as a Cultural System," in his *Interpretation of Cultures* (New York: Basic Books, 1973), pp. 87–125.

18. Emile Durkheim, *The Rules of Sociological Method,* 8th ed. (Glencoe, Ill.: The Free Press, 1966), author's preface to second edition, p. xlvii, fn. 3.

19. Quoted in Daniel J. Boorstin, *The Americans: The National Experience* (New York: Vintage Books, 1965), p. 336.

## 1. God's Firstborn: England

1. Thomas More, in E. F. Rogers, ed., *St. Thomas More: Selected Letters* (New Haven and London: Yale University Press, 1967), Letter 53 to Cromwell, March 5, 1534, pp. 212–213; Letter 54 to Margaret Roper, April 17, 1534, pp. 221–222.

2. The few existing studies of English nationalism locate the emergence of the English national consciousness in the seventeenth or even eighteenth century: Hans Kohn, "The Genesis and Character of English Nationalism," *Journal of the History of Ideas,* 1 (January 1940), pp. 69–94; Gerald Newman, *The Rise of English Nationalism: A Cultural History, 1740–1830* (London: Wedenfeld, 1987). Kohn's work was most useful as a pointer to primary sources.

3. *Promptorium Parvulorum,* 1499 (Menston, Eng.: The Scolar Press, 1968).

4. Perez Zagorin, *The Court and the Country: The Beginning of the English Revolution* (New York: Atheneum, 1971), pp. 33–38.

5. Thomas Elyot, *Dictionary,* 1538 (Menston, Eng.: The Scolar Press, 1970); this was the first dictionary reflecting the influence of the "new learning."

6. Thomas Cooper, *Thesaurus Linguae Romanae et Britannicae*, 1565 (Menston, Eng.: The Scolar Press, 1969).

7. John Rider, *Bibliotheca Scholastica*, 1589 (Menston, Eng.: The Scolar Press, 1970).

8. Shakespeare, *Julius Caesar*, Act III, Scene II (Brutus); Marlowe, *2 Tamburlaine*, Act V, Scene I: 10–11 (Governour). Such examples can be multiplied endlessly. Shakespeare uses the word "country" (often in the same breath with related terms: "nation," "people," and others) hundreds of times, usually in its new meaning, although the word is clearly multivalent, and the detailed concordances of his work make possible an easy quantitative as well as qualitative assessment of the new prominence and significance of the new concepts.

9. Zagorin, *Court and Country*; Lawrence Stone, *The Crisis of the Aristocracy, 1558–1641* (Oxford: Oxford University Press, 1965), pp. 61–62 and passim. This also makes it easier to understand why the "Country" party, or Parliamentary opposition, was alternatively called the "Patriots."

10. The alteration in the meaning of this concept has been the subject of a heated controversy in twentieth-century Tudor historiography. In the early 1960s the view of G. R. Elton (expressed in *England under the Tudors* [London: Methuen, 1955]; "The Political Creed of Thomas Cromwell," *Transactions of the Royal Historical Society*, 5th series, vol. 6, 1956, pp. 69–92; and elsewhere) that this change could actually be seen to have taken place in the Act of Appeals, 1533, was attacked by some other scholars (particularly G. L. Harriss) on the pages of *Past and Present*, 25 (July 1963) and 31 (July 1965). As far as I know, no agreement has been reached on the matter. According to Neville Figgis, *The Divine Right of Kings*, 1896 (New York: Harper Torchbooks, 1965), England, on occasion, claimed to be an "empire" even before Henry VIII. See Chapter 2 on similar uses of the concept in France. The exhaustive work on the history of the term is R. Koebner, *Empire* (Cambridge: Cambridge University Press, 1961).

11. Elton, *England under the Tudors*, p. 161; G. L. Harriss, "A Revolution in Tudor History?" *Past and Present*, 31 (July 1965), pp. 87–94.

12. "Act of Appeals," *Statutes of the Realm, Printed by command of His Majesty King George III in pursuance of an address of the House of Commons of Great Britain* (London, 1810–1821, reprinted in 1963 by Dawsons of Pall-Mall, London), vol. III, 24 Henri VIII, cap. XII, p. 427. (*Statutes of the Realm* hereafter cited as *SR*.)

13. *Sermons and Homilies of Bishop of Lincoln, gathered by Abraham Flemming* (London, 1582); "Homily against disobedience and willful Rebellion."

14. Thomas Elyot, *The Boke Named the Governour*, 1531 (New York: Everyman's Library, 1907); ch. 1, "The signification of a Publike Weale, and why it is called in latin Respublica," p. 1.

15. Significantly, *civitas*, the closest approximation to what we understand by the "state" in Latin, is translated by Elyot as "a citie," and he explains: "Properly it is the multitude of cytesens gathered togyther, to lyue according to lawe and ryght." The fact that the modern political concept of the "state" appears in English so late, as well as that Latin in fact had no equivalent to it, may be well

worth pondering over by those social scientists who toil today to "bring the state back."

16. *SR*, vol. II, 11 Henri VII, cap. I, p. 568; 1 Henri VII, cap. I, p. 499. (Below the spelling is modernized.)

17. *SR*, vol. III, 26 Hen. VIII, cap. III, p. 493; 35 Hen. VIII, cap. I, p. 955; 31 Hen. VIII, cap. VIII, p. 726.

18. *SR*, vol. IV, 1 Edw. VI, cap. XII, p. 18; 3–4 Edw. VI, cap. III, p. 102.

19. *SR*, vol. IV, 1 Eliz., cap. I, p. 350; 13 Eliz., cap. I, p. 526; 27 Eliz., cap. I, p. 704; 43 Eliz., cap. XVIII, p. 991; 13 Eliz., cap. I, p. 527.

20. *SR*, vol. IV, 1 Jac., cap. I, pp. 1017–18.

21. *The Journals of the House of Commons*, vol. I, p. 243.

22. James I, *Workes* (London: Robert Barkes and John Bill, 1616), pp. 514, 525, 533.

23. "The 'Three Resolutions' Passed by the House of Commons in Defiance of the King's Dissolution of Parliament, 1629," in J. Rushworth, *Historical Collections* (London: T. Newcomb for G. Thomason, 1659), vol. I, p. 660; S. R. Gardiner, *The Constitutional Documents of the Puritan Revolution, 1625–1660*, 3rd ed. (Oxford: The Clarendon Press, 1906), p. 206, and ibid., "Specimen of the First Writ of Ship-Money," October 20, 1634, p. 105.

24. *Journals of the House of Lords*, vol. VI, p. 430; Gardiner, *Constitutional Documents*, "Heads of Proposals Offered by the Army," p. 321.

25. Nevertheless, the text continued, "neither such Lords as have demeaned themselves with honor, courage and fidelity to the Commonwealth, nor their posterities who shall continue so, shall be excluded from the public councils of the nation." From the heights of our historical experience, which, among other events, includes the French and the Bolshevik revolutions, this specification is at least as remarkable as the language in which it is expressed. (Gardiner, *Constitutional Documents*, p. 387.)

26. Ibid., "The Act Erecting a High Court of Justice," January 6, 1649, pp. 357–358; "The Act Abolishing the Office of King," March 17, 1649, pp. 385–386; "The Act Establishing Commonwealth," March 19, 1649, p. 388.

27. Edward Hall, *Chronicle: Henry VIII*, ed. Ch. Whibley (London: T. C. and E. C. Jack, 1904), vol. I, p. 154. According to Kohn ("Genesis," p. 73), one-third of the London population was foreign in 1550.

28. John Bale, *Chronicle of the Examination and Death of Lord Cobham (John Oldecastell)*, in *Select Works of Bishop Bale*, ed. for the Parker Society by Rev. Henry Christmas (Cambridge: Cambridge University Press, 1849), p. 8. Bale's opinion of Polydore's history stuck. John Foxe, undoubtedly aware of it, related in *The Acts and Monuments* in the year 1570 that he had heard that the unfortunate historian "also burned a heap of our English stories unknown" (John Foxe, *The Acts and Monuments*, ed. Rev. Stephen Reed Cattley [London: R. B. Seelby and W. Burnside, 1841], vol. III, p. 750).

29. Roger Ascham, *The Scholemaster*, 1570, in William Aldis Wright, ed., *English Works of Roger Ascham*, 1904 (Cambridge: Cambridge University Press, 1970), p. 293.

30. Ascham, *Toxophilus*, 1545, in *English Works*, p. 53; John Bale, *Examinations*

*of Anne Askew,* "Preface of her first examination," 1547, in *Select Works,* pp. 141–143.

31. Bale, *Select Works,* pp. 5–6.
32. Ascham, *Toxiphilus,* pp. xii, xiii, xiv; Elyot, *Governour,* "The Proheme," p. xxxi; Thomas Wyatt, "Tagus," in E. M. W. Tillyard, *The Poetry of Sir Thomas Wyatt: A Selection and a Study* (London: The Scholartis Press, 1929), p. 119; Thomas Starkey, *A Dialogue between Cardinal Pole and Thomas Lupset,* 1533–1536, K. M. Burton, ed. (London: Chatto and Windus, 1948), p. 22.
33. George Gascoigne, *The Steel Glas,* 1576, ed. E. Arber (Westminster: A Constable & Co., 1895), p. 78.
34. The evidence that Lawrence Stone brings to the contrary—such as excessive preoccupation with status, heightened sensitivity toward possible signs of disrespect from inferiors, as well as legislative efforts such as the first draft of the Statute of Uses of 1529, which intended to freeze the structure of aristocratic land-tenure, or the Act of Precedence of 1539, establishing ranks among court officials—only proves this. These were the signs of the crisis of identity within the nobility and the increasing inadequacy of the traditional definition of aristocracy, as a result of which it could not be left alone as unproblematic. Stone, indeed, is aware of this: "This ideological pattern and these measures designed to freeze the social structure and emphasize the cleavages between one class and another were introduced or reinforced at a time when in fact families were moving up and down in the social and economic scale at a faster rate than at any time before the nineteenth and twentieth centuries. Indeed it was just this mobility which stimulated such intensive propaganda efforts." Stone, *Crisis,* p. 36.
35. Bale, *Anne Askew,* p. 141; Christopher Marlowe, *Tamburlaine the Great,* pt. I, I, II, 34 (Lincoln: University of Nebraska Press, 1967), p. 15; Barnabe Googe, 1563, *Eglogs, Epitaphs and Sonettes, by Barnabe Googe,* a facsimile reproduction (Gainesville, Fla.: Scholars' Facsimiles and Reprints, 1968), 3rd Eclogue, p. 37; George Chapman, "Dedication from Ovid's Banquet of Sense," 1595, in H. E. Rollins and H. Baker, eds., *The Renaissance in England: Non-Dramatic Prose and Verse of the Sixteenth Century* (Boston: D. C. Heath & Co., 1955), p. 449; George Puttenham, *The Arte of English Poesie,* 1589, ed. G. D. Willcock and A. Walker (Cambridge: Cambridge University Press, 1936), pp. 59–60; Henry Peacham, *The Complete Gentleman,* 1622, ed. V. B. Heltzel (Ithaca, N.Y.: Cornell University Press, 1962), p. 28. Also see Lewis Einstein's very informative *Tudor Ideals* (New York: Harcourt, Brace and Co., 1921).
36. Zagorin, *Court and Country,* p. 23.
37. Elyot, *Governour,* vol. I, ch. 1, pp. 5, 6; ch. 12, pp. 49–50; vol. II, ch. 4, p. 30.
38. Ascham, *Toxophilus,* pp. xiv-xv; Peacham, *Complete Gentleman,* pp. 5, 4; Sir Philip Sidney, *An Apologie for Poetrie,* 1583, in G. Gregory Smith, ed., *Elizabethan Critical Essays* (Oxford: The Clarendon Press, 1904), vol. I, p. 205; Gascoigne, *Steel Glas,* p. 76.
39. Lawrence Stone, *The Causes of the English Revolution, 1529–1642* (New York: Harper and Row, 1972), p. 65. This process was actually started by the Yorkist kings; see W. T. MacCaffrey, "England: The Crown and the New Aristocracy, 1540–1600," *Past and Present,* 30 (April 1965), pp. 52–64.

40. Only two of the seven peers created between 1509 and 1529 were civil servants, but the latter constituted the majority of the much larger number created in subsequent years. MacCaffrey, "The Crown," p. 54.

41. This elimination was signaled by the replacement of Cardinal Wolsey by Sir Thomas More as Lord Chancellor in 1529.

42. Among the first of them were Thomas Cromwell, the first two Cecils, Nicholas Sidney, Francis Knollys, Henry Cary, John Russell, John Herbert, William Paulet, Ralph Sadler, William Petre, and Thomas Audley. MacCaffrey, "The Crown," p. 54.

43. This simile is borrowed from Joseph Ben-David and Randall Collins.

44. But while their situation predisposed the new elite to sympathize with the nationalist perspective, it did not necessitate it. Neither did the thorough immersion in the "new learning," as we can judge from the example of Sir Thomas More, prevent a complete lack of such sympathy.

45. Stone, *English Revolution*, p. 67, connects this to macro-economic and demographic changes: "The doubling of the population in the 120 years before the civil war is the critical variable of the period, an event the ramifications of which spread out into every aspect of the society and was causally related to the major changes in agriculture, trade, industry, urbanization, education, social mobility and overseas settlement. It gave a tremendous stimulus to agricultural output, which increased sufficiently fast between 1500 and 1660 to feed twice the number of mouths." The importance of these factors cannot be underestimated, but at the same time it is certain that social change cannot be explained in such a simple behaviorist fashion. It was lucky that the English economy could respond and adjust quickly to the dramatic accretion in the population, but such adjustment was not inevitable. Social mobility was not a reaction to the greater need in agricultural output.

46. Stone, *English Revolution*, p. 72.

47. Ibid., p. 95; Einstein, *Tudor Ideals*, p. 318.

48. Gascoigne, *Steel Glas*, p. 62; Starkey, *A Dialogue*, p. 94; John Bate, *Dialogue between a Christian and an Atheist* (London, 1589), p. 160.

49. Edward Lord Herbert, *The Life and Reign of King Henry VIII* (London, 1683), quoted in Stone, *English Revolution*, p. 59; ibid.

50. Einstein, *Tudor Ideals*, p. 202. Sixteenth- and seventeenth-century interpreters of the break from Rome, by the way, would not accept the view later advanced by Voltaire and voiced by lesser celebrities in their own day, that England opted for Protestantism because the king had fallen in love. John Foxe in the *Book of Martyrs*, a revolutionary conservative as he was, interpreted the separation as the return to "the old ancient church of Christ" (a gloss in the margin stated: "The Church of Rome revolted from the Church of Rome"—Foxe, vol. I, p. 9). William Haller, *Foxe's Book of Martyrs and the Elect Nation* (London: Jonathan Cape, 1963), commenting on his argument, summarized it: "The reformed Church had not swerved from Rome; Rome had swerved from itself" (p. 136). In 1665 Thomas Sprat argued in a similar vein: "It is false that our English Reformation began upon a shameful occasion, or from the Extravagance of a private Passion. I know he [Sorbiere] has the Famous Story of King Henry's Divorce to oppose to what I say; but I am not startled by that . . . The

Reformation to which we stand is of latter Date. The Primitive Reformers amongst us beheld the Reason of Men tamely subjected to one Man's Command, and the Sovereign Powers of all Christendom still exposed to be check'd and destroy'd by the Resolutions of his private Will: Upon this they arose to perform Two of the greatest Works in the World at once, to deliver the Minds of Christians from Tyranny, and the Dignity of the Throne from Spiritual Bondage. Whatever was the accidental, this was the real Cause of our first Reformation, and of their Separation from us, not ours from them." Thomas Sprat, *Observations on Mons. de Sorbiere's Voyage into England,* 1665 (London, 1709), pp. 101–180; 129.

51. "An Act Concernyng Restraynt of Payment of Annates to the See of Rome," 1532, *SR,* vol. III, 23 Hen. VIII, cap. 20, p. 386.

52. Harriss, "A Revolution," p. 85.

53. Regarding this and other issues in the history of the English Bible, see F. F. Bruce, *History of the Bible in English: From the Earliest Versions* (New York: Oxford University Press, 1978) and Haller, *Foxe's Book of Martyrs.*

54. The metaphor is Stone's.

55. This, clearly, was unintended too. How little Henry intended to revolutionize the doctrine may be seen in the Dispensation Act of 1534.

56. In sharp contrast to France, as we shall see later, a strong sense of a unique English identity failed to develop earlier. The two main reasons for such failure, especially after the Norman conquest, were the French connections and aspirations of the English aristocracy and royalty, on the one hand, and the unexceptional character of English Catholicism, on the other. The sixteenth century eliminated both.

57. The English text is: "The Kings have laid waste all the nations"; the Latin: "fe cerunt reges Assyoriorum terras et regiones earum." Isaiah 51.4, which in the original Hebrew has *am* and *leom* in the verse, is rendered in English: "Hearken unto me, my people; And give ear unto me, O My nation" (the use of "nation" here greatly increases the dramatic effect of the verse); the Vulgate text of the same verse reads: "Adtendite ad me, populus meus, et tribus mea me audite." The translation of the same verse in the Great Bible is also interesting: "Have respect unto me, the, o my people both high and lowe and laye thine eare to me." Nothing of the sort appears in Hebrew, and this is clearly an attempt to redefine a people in a nationalist vein, which downplays class and status distinctions and emphasizes the unity of various strata.

58. In Italy since 1471; France—1472; Holland—1477 (Old Testament).

59. W. K. Jourdan, *Philanthropy in England, 1480–1660: A Study of the Changing Pattern of English Social Conditions* (London: Allen and Unwin, 1959); Lawrence Stone, "The Educational Revolution in England, 1540–1640," *Past and Present,* 28 (July 1964), pp. 41–80.

60. Thomas Hobbes was of the opinion that the English Bible was not to a small degree responsible for the Puritan Rebellion, "for after the Bible was translated into English, every man, nay every boy and wench, that could read English thought they spoke with God Almighty, and understood what he said . . . The reverence and obedience due to the Reformed Church here, and to the bishops

and pastors therein, was cast off, and every man became a judge of religion, and an interpreter of the Scriptures to himself." Thomas Hobbes, *Behemoth: The History of the Causes of the Civil Wars of England,* ed. William Molesworth (New York: Burt Franklin, 1962[?]), p. 28.

61. Haller, *Foxe's Book of Martyrs,* p. 43.

62. Foxe, *Book of Martyrs,* vol. VII, p. 41; vol. VIII, p. 476.

63. Ibid., vol. VII, p. 53.

64. Quoted in Haller, *Foxe's Book of Martyrs,* p. 201.

65. John Poynet, *A Shorte Treatise of politike pouuer, and of the true Obedience which subjects owe to kinges and other ciuile Gouernours, with an Exhortation to all true natural Englishe men,* 1556, reprinted in W. S. Hudson, *John Ponet: Advocate of Limited Monarchy* (Chicago: University of Chicago Press, 1942), p. 61 of the original text.

66. Michele cited in Einstein, *Tudor Ideals,* p. 24. Later, after another transformation, Cardinal Allen eloquently wrote: "It is the turpitude of our nation through the world, whereas we blush before strangers that sometimes fall into discourse of such things, that in one mans memory and since this strange mutation began, we have had to our prince, a man, who abolished the Pope's authoritie by his laws, and yet in other pontes kept the faith of his fathers: we have had a child who by the like laws abolished together with the Papacie the whole ancient religion: we have had a woman who restored both againe and sharply punished Protestants: and lastly her Majestie that now is who by the like laws hath long since abolished both againe, and now severely punisheth Catholikes as the other did Protestants; and all these strange differences within the compasse of about 30 years." William Allen, *An Apologie of the English seminaries* (Mounds in Henault, 1581), f. 34. Religious pluralism breeds indifference. See Stone's caustic remarks in *English Revolution,* pp. 83, 109.

67. Paul Hughes and Robert Fries, eds., *Crown and Parliament in Tudor-Stuart England: A Documentary Constitutional History, 1485–1714* (New York, G. P. Putnam's Sons, 1959), comment on the Act Concerning the Improvement of Commons and Waste Grounds, 1550, p. 81.

68. "Typical of the multitude, is the anonymous writer who describes the queen's triumphal entry with King Philip into London, and Cardinal Pole's speech on the restoration of Catholicism. He relates how with many others he regretted his past conduct and repents for his religious sins, determining to make amends in henceforth practicing the 'most holy Catholic faith.'" Einstein, *Tudor Ideals,* p. 205.

69. MacCaffrey, "The Crown," p. 56.

70. Anthony Fletcher, *Tudor Rebellions* (Harlow, Essex: Longman, 1983), pp. 69–81.

71. Quoted by William Haller in "John Foxe and the Puritan Revolution," *The Seventeenth Century,* volume in honor of Robert Foster Jones (Stanford: Stanford University Press, 1952), p. 209.

72. Parker also was certain that God was English; in a letter to Lord Burghley, he wrote in connection to the pitiable situation of religion: "Where God Almighty is so much English as he is, should we not requite his mercy with some earnesty

to prefer his honour and true religion." Letter of March 12, 1572 or 1573, in *Correspondence of Matthew Parker, D.D.*, The Parker Society (Cambridge: Cambridge University Press, 1853), p. 419.

73. This is the title of the first English (1563) edition of the work.

74. An epistle attached to the edition of 1570. Foxe, *Book of Martyrs*, vol. I, p. 520.

75. From *A Booke of certaine Canons . . . Printed by John Daye*, 1571, quoted in Haller, *Foxe's Book of Martyrs*, p. 221.

76. William Harrison, "Description of England," in Holinshed's *Chronicles*, 1586 (London: J. Johnson et al., 1807), vol. I, p. 331. Harrison mentioned this as an example of England's love of learning: the books were provided "for the exercise of such as come into [the court]: whereby the stranger that entereth into the court of England upon the sudden, shall rather imagine himselfe to come into some publike schoole of the universities." Ibid.

77. The epithet is Richard Hakluyt's (*The Principal Navigations, Voyages and Discoveries of the English Nation*, 1589, dedication); the information about Sir Francis' pastime is from Haller, *Foxe's Book of Martyrs*, p. 221.

78. Hakluyt, *Principal Navigations;* Hakluyt mentioned Foxe alongside Bale and Eden.

79. Richard Hooker, *The Laws of Ecclesiastical Polity*, 1597, in John Keble, ed., *The Works of Richard Hooker* (New York: Burt Franklin, 1888, reprinted 1970), vol. III, p. 330.

80. Einstein, *Tudor Ideals*, p. 210.

81. Roger Cotton, in Edward Farr, ed., *Select poetry—Chiefly Devotional of the Reign of Queen Elizabeth* (London: The Parker Society, 1845), vol. II, p. 372.

82. Elizabeth's adulation "seems nauseating in its jingo ideology and its sycophantic flattery of the monarch." Stone, *English Revolution*, p. 88.

83. According to Haller, *Foxe's Book of Martyrs*, p. 90.

84. John Norden, *A Progress of Piety*, 1596 (London: The Parker Society, 1847), pp. 38, 44.

85. John Phillip, in Farr, *Select poetry*, p. 532.

86. Anthony Nixon, "Memorial of Queen Elizabeth," in Farr, *Select poetry*, p. 556.

87. Michael Drayton, *Poly-Olbion*, Song XVII, in J. W. Hebel, ed., *Michael Drayton: Tercentenary Edition* (Oxford: Basil Blackwell, 1933), vol. IV, pp. 337–338.

88. It is possible, however, that she sympathized with the national sentiment, for she was, after all, a tutee of Roger Ascham. She was certainly exceptionally well attuned to the spirit of nationalism and played the role assigned her by the zealots of the new—secular—faith very well. Among the signs of her sensitivity may be included both the fact that she referred to herself as "the nursing mother of Israel" and the replacement of the figure of Christ on the cross at parish churches by the royal coat of arms.

89. This view was consistently argued by Haller and disputed, for instance, by Paul Christiansen in *Reformers and Babylon: English Apocalyptic Visions from the Reformation to the Eve of the Civil War* (Toronto: University of Toronto Press,

1978) and K. R. Firth in *The Apocalyptic Tradition in Reformation Britain, 1530–1645* (New York: Oxford University Press, 1979).

90. Richard Crompton, *The Mansion of Magnanimity* (London: W. Ponsonby, 1599), ch. 12, sig. O; Walter Raleigh, "The Last Fight of the Revenge," p. 30, and Linschoten's "Account," p. 91, in E. Arber, ed., *The Last Fight of the REVENGE at Sea* (London: Southgate, 1871).

91. J. Rhodes, in Farr, *Select poetry*, pp. 269–270.

92. Haller, *Foxe's Book of Martyrs*, p. 214.

93. These authors were, for all intents and purposes, *raznochintzy*, though—for sociological rather than linguistic reasons—no equivalent term was ever coined in English.

94. William Shakespeare, *King Richard II*, Act II, Scene I (Gaunt).

95. William Webbe, *A Discourse on English Poetrie*, 1586, in Smith, *Elizabethan Critical Essays*, vol. I, pp. 240–242.

96. Gabriel Harvey, Letter to Spenser, *The Works of Gabriel Harvey*, A. B. Grosart, ed. (London: Hazel, Watson, and Viney, 1884), vol. I, p. 77.

97. Hakluyt, *Principal Navigations;* Raleigh, "The Last Fight of the Revenge"; William Harrison, *The Description of England*, in *Chronicles* of Raphael Holinshed, 1586 (London: J. Johnson et al., 1807), vol. I, p. 266; Peacham, *Complete Gentleman*, p. 115; regarding emblems, see the introduction by Heltzel in ibid., p. xi.

98. George Gascoigne, "The Making of Verse," 1575, in Smith, *Elizabethan Critical Essays*, vol. I, p. 50; Michael Drayton, *Poly-Olbion*, dedication, "To my Friends, the Cambro-Britains"; Francis Meres, *Palladis Tamia, wits treasury*, 1598, in Smith, *Elizabethan Critical Essays*, vol. II, p. 314; Thomas Nash, *A General Censure*, 1589, in ibid., vol. I, p. 318; Philip Sidney, *An Apologie*, vol. I, p. 152.

99. Thomas Nash, *The Unfortunate Traveler: or, the Life of Jack Wilton*, 1594, in H. E. Rollins and H. Baker, eds., *The Renaissance in England* (Boston: D. C. Heath, 1954), p. 794; Richard Carew, *Epistle on the Excellency of the English Tongue*, 1595–96, in Smith, *Elizabethan Critical Essays*, vol. II, p. 293; Meres, *Palladis Tamia*, pp. 313, 317; Nash, *A General Censure*, p. 318; John Weever, *Epigrams*, 1599, "Epigram 22," in Rollins and Baker, *Renaissance in England*, p. 467. Of course, authors are not the only ones to be adorned with such epithets and claimed—with a pronoun "our" and possessive pride—as the representatives of the nation. In Hakluyt, for instance, one naturally finds a reference to "our famous chieftan Sir Francis Drake." Nevertheless, it remains a fact that in the sixteenth century—in distinction from a later period—the authors, the people writing in English, are the focus of attention and collective veneration by the cultural elite.

100. Sidney, *An Apologie*, p. 152; Samuel Daniel, *Musophilus: Containing a General Defence of All Learning*, ed. R. Himelick (West Lafayette, Ind.: Purdue University Press, 1965), p. 86; Richard Stanyhurst, "On the translation of Virgil," in Smith, *Elizabethan Critical Essays*, vol. I, p. 138; Meres, *Palladis Tamia*, p. 319; Michael Drayton, "Henry Howard, Earl of Surrey, to Geraldine," from *England's Heroical Epistles*, 1598, in Rollins and Baker, *Renais-*

*sance in England,* p. 434. (Italian and French were the two languages most constantly evoked for comparison, while other contemporary tongues with which English was compared included German and Dutch.)

101. Carew, *Epistle,* pp. 285, 290, 292–293.
102. Daniel, *Musophilus,* p. 86.
103. Meres, *Palladis Tamia,* p. 316; Ascham, *Toxophilus,* p. 53; Ben Jonson, "Epigram to William Camden," 1616, in Rollins and Baker, *Renaissance in England,* p. 492; Peacham, *Complete Gentleman,* 1634 edition, sig. Cc2, quoted in Heltzel's introduction, p. x.
104. These are the numbers given by Haller, *Foxe's Book of Martyrs,* p. 227. The destinies of these Englishmen are discussed in Part 5.
105. Regarding this, see Mark H. Curtis, "The Alienated Intellectuals of Early Stuart England," *Past and Present,* 23 (November 1962), pp. 25–43; Christopher Hill, *Economic Problems of the Church* (Oxford: Clarendon Press, 1956).
106. Hooker, *Ecclesiastical Polity,* pp. 343, 357; Thomas Smith, *De Republica Anglorum* (London, 1635), pp. 48–49.
107. Joel Hurstfield summarized the situation: "Above all, by the end of the reign, Elizabeth had reached a stage in her relations with the Parliament when the increasingly urgent constitutional problems were insoluble within the existing framework of society. Through their control of direct taxation, the parliamentary classes made a bid for greater legislative power. Their wealth, relative to that of the queen, had sharply increased. They had also some pungent views on the political, religious, economic and diplomatic issues of the day, in which they felt that their interests were as much involved as were those of the monarchy." J. Hurstfield, *Elizabeth and the Unity of England* (New York: Harper and Row, 1960), pp. 212, 214; and Einstein, *Tudor Ideals,* p. 83.
108. William Camden, *Annales Rerum Anglicarum et Hibernicarum, Regnante Elizabetha,* quoted in Haller, *Foxe's Book of Martyrs,* p. 231.
109. Both quoted in Stone, *English Revolution,* pp. 100, 101.
110. Ibid., p. 99.
111. In the seventeenth century, at least, "Puritanism" appears to be at least as much a political term as a religious one. It referred to the opposition. According to Henry Parker (*A discourse concerning Puritans,* 1641, pp. 10–11), "by a new enlargement of the name, the world is full of nothing else but Puritans." "To be an honest man is now to be a Puritan," concluded the Commons (*Commons Debates,* 1629, p. 178). Both quoted in Zagorin, *Court and Country,* pp. 192, 191.
112. Christopher Hill and E. Dell, *The Good Old Cause, 1640–1660,* 1943 (New York: Augustus M. Kelley, 1969), p. 307; also from Hobbes: "The doctrines which to this day are controversed about religion do for the most part belong to the right of dominion" (p. 163).
113. Quoted in Stone, *English Revolution,* p. 81. Another manifestation of the switch was the patriotism of the English Catholics. Both at times of persecution at home and in exile they pleaded to be allowed to devote themselves to their "dearest, beloved countrie." Sir Thomas Copley, forced to accept service in Spain, begged Elizabeth for some employment "wherein a good Catholic Christian may without hazard to his soul serve his temporal prince," and con-

fessed that "though for a time I live abroad I cannot cease to be an Englishman and love this soil best" (*Correpondence,* ed. R. C. Cristie, London, 1897, p. 10—a Letter to the Queen, 1572; and p. 100—a Letter to Dr. Wilson, 1577). Cardinal Allen too, in *Apologie of the English Seminaries,* emphasized the devotion of Catholics to their country and pointed out that only very few of them—compared with the numbers of Calvinists in France—revolted in England.

114. This was succinctly put by Levellers, who thought that the issue of the Civil War was the question of to whom belonged the right to "exercise the supreme power" over the people. D. M. Wolfe, *Leveller Manifestoes of the Puritan Revolution* (London: T. Nelson and Sons, 1944), p. 237.

115. Gerard Winstanley, *An Humble Request to the Ministers of Both Universities and to All Lawyers in Every Inns-A-Court,* 1656, pp. 7–13, in Hughes and Fries, *Crown and Parliament,* pp. 243–244. Winstanley's position was, among other things, an early instance of the confusion between political and economic equality, that is, between equality in liberty, or right of self-government, and equality in prosperity, which would become a dominant demand in later periods in both England and America.

116. Oliver Cromwell, *The Letters and Speeches of Oliver Cromwell with Elucidations by Thomas Carlyle,* ed. S. C. Lomas (London: Methuen, 1904), Speech VIII, April 3, 1657, vol. III, pp. 30–31; Speech II, September 4, 1654, vol. II, p. 345; Speech III, September 12, 1654, vol. II, p. 388; Speech II, vol. II, p. 358; "Self-Denying Ordinance," December 9, 1644, vol. I, p. 187; Speech XVII, January 25, 1658, vol. III, pp. 172–173. See also Kohn, "Genesis."

117. Christopher Hill, *God's Englishman: Oliver Cromwell and the English Revolution* (New York: Harper Torchbooks, 1970).

118. H. Belloc, *Milton* (Philadelphia: Lippincott, 1935), p. 22.

119. John Milton, in F. A. Patterson, ed. *The Works of John Milton* (New York: Columbia University Press, 1931), *Areopagitica,* vol. IV, pp. 339–340, 341, 305; *Tetrachordon,* pp. 137, 117–118; *The Tenure of Kings,* vol. V, pp. 39–40. On the evolution of Milton's views see Haller, "Puritan Revolution," and *A Milton Encyclopedia,* ed. W. B. Hunter (London: Associated University Presses, 1978–79), especially the article "Areopagitica," vol. I, pp. 70–76.

120. Hill, *God's Englishman,* p. 265.

121. *The Book of Common Prayer* (London, printed by His Majestie's printers, 1662).

122. John Dryden, *The Works of John Dryden,* ed. W. Scott, revised by G. Saintsbury (London: W. Paterson, 1882–1893), vol. XV, pp. 273–377; vol. XII, pp. 59–60; *Annus Mirabilis,* vol. IX, p. 150. It should be remembered that Daniel's *Musophilus* was "a general defense of all learning," and that he, too, paid special attention to science and spoke of "these more curious times" (p. 83). In his time, though, science had not as yet acquired the specific meaning it had for Dryden's contemporaries. My argument regarding the connection between science and English nationalism was first presented in Liah Greenfeld, "Science and National Greatness in Seventeenth-Century England," *Minerva,* 25 (Spring–Summer 1987), pp. 107–122.

123. Sidney, *An Apologie,* p. 160.

124. Brian Tuke, preface to the 1532 edition of Chaucer's works, in *The Works of Geoffrey Chaucer and Others,* a reproduction in facsimile of the first collected edition 1532 from the copy in the British Museum, with an introduction by W. W. Skeat (London: De La More and Oxford University Press, 1905), p. xxii (p. 3 of the original).

125. Sidney, *An Apologie,* p. 182.

126. R. F. Jones, *Ancients and Moderns: A Study of the Rise of the Scientific Movement in England,* 1936 (New York: Dover, 1982), p. x. Also see L. I. Bredvold, *The Intellectual Milieu of John Dryden,* 1934 (Ann Arbor: University of Michigan Press, 1956).

127. Francis Bacon, vol. XIV, *Novum Organum,* and vol. II, *The New Atlantis,* in *The Works of Francis Bacon* (London: William Pickering, 1831, 1825).

128. Gabriel Harvey, in Grosart, *Works,* vol. I, p. 123.

129. This is the thrust of the famous thesis of R. K. Merton, *Science, Technology, and Society in Seventeenth-Century England,* 1938 (Atlantic Highlands, N.J.: Humanities Press, 1970).

130. Jones, *Ancients and Moderns,* p. 79, and, in general, "The Gilbert Tradition," pp. 62–87.

131. William Gilbert, *De Magnete,* trans. M. P. Fleury (New York: Dover, 1958).

132. A. Rupert Hall and Marie Boas Hall, eds., *The Correspondence of Henry Oldenburg* (Madison: University of Wisconsin Press, 1966–1973), vol. III, Letter 623, March 21, 1666 or 1667, p. 373.

133. H. W. Turnbull (ed. for the Royal Society), *Correspondence of Isaac Newton* (Cambridge: Cambridge University Press, 1955–1977), vol. I, Letter 29, January 2, 1671 or 1672, p. 73; Letter 41, August, 2, 1671 or 1672, pp. 107–108.

134. Ibid., Letter 95, September 24, 1672, pp. 242–243.

135. Ibid., Letter 309, July 5, 1687, pp. 481–482. These contemplations, Halley went on, should be pursued because they would be of "prodigious use in Navigation." This was only one of the numerous instances of promotion of inventions and scientific discourse because they were thought to be materially "advantageous to England." These can be interpreted as expressions of the utilitarian attitude to science, considered to be characterisitic of the seventeenth century, but in fact, it is very difficult to distinguish here between a purely utilitarian attitude and the desire for national eminence, in the framework of which utility is defined as service to the nation.

136. Letters of the most prominent scientists of this age, Boyle and Newton, are almost exclusively devoted to purely scientific matters. There is little else in them—virtually no discussion of the religious, political, or personal significance of science.

137. Newton, *Correspondence,* vol. II, Letter 248, January 1680 or 1681, p. 335.

138. *Correspondence of Henry Oldenburg,* vol. II, Letter 276, June 10, 1663, p. 65; Letter 401, August 21, 1665, p. 486.

139. Ibid., Letter 361, December 13, 1664, p. 337; Letter 364 (from Sachs) January 12, 1665, p. 345.

140. (Bernard le Bovier de) Fontenelle, *The Eulogium of Sir Isaac Newton* (London: J. Tonson, 1728), pp. 23–29. This is the original English translation of the French text.

141. Jones, *Ancients and Moderns,* pp. 221–222.

142. Thomas Sprat, *History of the Royal Society* (London, 1667), J. I. Cope and H. W. Jones, eds. of a facsimile edition (St. Louis: Washington University Studies, 1958), p. 2.

143. Sprat, *Observations,* p. 102.

144. Ibid., pp. 171–172, 178. Sprat is a true patriot, and would combat the arrogant foreigners wherever he perceived the need to do so. His defense of the English cuisine, insulted by Sorbiere, is as ardent as that of any other national characteristic. The cooking too brings forth the excellencies of the English nature: "I cannot but say to the Advantage of Boil'd Beef and Rost, that the English have the same Sincerity in their Diet which they have in their Manners; and as they have less Mixture in their Dishes, so they have less Sophisticate Compositions in their Hearts, than the People of some other Nations" (ibid., p. 175).

145. Sprat, *History,* pp. 114, 150, 78, 371–372.

146. Ibid., pp. 426–427; Joseph Glanvill, *Plus Ultra; or the Progress and Advancement of Knowledge Since the days of Aristotle* (London, 1668), p. 149.

147. Sprat, *Observations,* p. 179.

148. Bredvold, *Intellectual Milieu,* pp. 58–59; Jones, *Ancients and Moderns,* pp. 183–237.

149. The style of preaching changed dramatically during this period. While before the Restoration it was characterized by "affectations, fanciful conceits, metaphors, similes, plays upon words, antitheses, paradoxes, and the pedantic display of Greek and Latin quotations," after the Restoration its chief characteristics became plainness, directness, clarity—in short, the scientific ideal. (R. F. Jones, "The Attack on Pulpit Eloquence in the Restoration: An Episode in the Development of the Neo-Classical Standard for Prose," in *The Seventeenth Century,* p. 112.) The "vehement speech" of "horrid Metaphor-Mongers" (J. Eachard, *The Grounds and Occasions of the Contempt of the Clergy and Religion Enquired into* [an eloquent title], 10th ed. [London, 1696], p. 55) was opposed for "having too much affinity with madness and distortion" (Meric Casaubon, quoted in Jones, p. 113). For that reason Sprat, in a charming passage, proposed to banish eloquence "out of civil Societies, as a thing fatal to Peace and good Manners" (*History,* p. 111.).

## 2. The Three Identities of France

1. Collete Beaune, *Naissance de la nation France* (Paris: Gallimard, 1985), p. 207; Suzanne Citron, *Le Mythe national: L'Histoire de France en question* (Paris: Editions Oeuvrières, 1987), p. 123; Jean Lestocquoy, *Histoire du patriotisme en France des origines à nos jours* (Paris: Albin Michel, 1968), pp. 22–23.

2. Quoted in Beaune, *Naissance,* p. 208.

3. The French text is quoted in ibid., p. 209; the Latin original, in Marie-Madeleine Martin, *The Making of France* (London: Eyre and Spoffiswode, 1951), p. 103. It reads: "Christianorum sunt gentes et in varias sectas divisae quorum primi sunt Franci . . . et isti puri catholici sunt." Note that the Latin text does not use "nation."

4. Claude de Seysel, *La Grande Monarchie,* in Beaune, *Naissance,* p. 213.

5. Quoted in ibid., pp. 211, 215.

6. Quoted in Martin, *France,* pp. 88, 100–101.

7. "Miroir historial," cited in Beaune, *Naissance,* p. 214.

8. Citron, in *Le Mythe,* writes: "Au 15 siècle le lys royal et le lys marial sont confondus dans une même louange. Satan (l'Anglais) s'attaque au lys, Vierge et Roi, que Dieu a fait croître. Le lys est à la foi la vierge que tous doivent prier et le Roi qui, par ses vertus, accedera à la béatitude. La piété de Jeanne d'Arc ne pouvait les séparer" (p. 131). See also Beaune, *Naissance,* p. 246. Regarding the wavering loyalties of Jeanne d'Arc's contemporaries, see Martin, *France,* pp. 112–114.

9. This possibility is suggested by Beaune, *Naissance,* p. 229.

10. A. Tuetey, 1431, quoted in ibid., p. 221.

11. Lestocquoy, *Histoire du patriotisme,* pp. 64–69.

12. Jean de Montreuil, "L'Oeuvre polémique," Armagnac, and others quoted in Beaune, *Naissance,* pp. 295, 296; also ibid., pp. 291, 297; Citron, *Le Mythe,* p. 126; Code Michaud, Article 27, in F. A. Isambert, *Recueil général des anciennes lois françaises* (Paris: Belin-Leprieur, 1829), vol. XVI, p. 232.

13. J-P. Angleberme, 1517, quoted in Beaune, *Naissance,* p. 290.

14. Montreuil, "L'Oeuvre," quoted in Beaune, *Naissance,* p. 315.

15. Chansons de geste quoted in Martin, *France,* p. 83; Masselin, in Citron, *Le Mythe,* p. 136.

16. *Patrie* was used by Jean Chartier in 1437, Lestocquoy, *Histoire du patriotisme,* p. 31; for more on the history of the word, see Jacques Godechot, "Nation, patrie, nationalisme et patriotisme en France au XVIII siècle," *Annales historiques de la révolution française,* 206 (October-December 1971), pp. 481–501.

17. Ronsard quoted in Lestocquoy, *Histoire du patriotisme,* p. 47; Joachim Du Bellay, *Deffence et illustration de la langue françoyse,* édition critique par Henri Chamard (Paris: Albert Fontemoing, 1904), pp. 35, 169.

18. Quoted in Lestocquoy, *Histoire du patriotisme,* p. 48.

19. The work was written for the edification of the young François I, published in 1519, and "did little but present a theory which, in its main outlines, had long been accepted." See William Farr Church, *Constitutional Thought in Sixteenth-Century France: A Study in the Evolution of Ideas,* (Cambridge, Mass.: Harvard University Press, 1941), for its context, content, and importance. The quotation is from p. 23.

20. P. Charron, *De la sagesse,* Book I, ch. 51, "De l'estat, souveraineté, souverains" (Paris: Chasseriau, 1820, Collection de Moralistes Français), p. 376.

21. See Maurizio Viroli, *From Politics to Reason of State,* forthcoming, on a parallel development in the thought of Niccolo Machiavelli.

22. Quoted in Martin, *France,* pp. 139–144.

23. Ibid., p. 135. "Dialogue" is also analyzed by Church, *Constitutional Thought,* ch. 6.

24. Du Bellay, *Regrets,* 1559, canto IX (Paris: Sansot, 1908), p. 33.

25. Quoted in Lestocquoy, *Histoire du patriotisme,* p. 48.

26. The possibility of the correction of a ruler by a lesser magistrate is addressed

by Martin Bucer, and the Magdeburg Admonition of 1550 admits the legitimacy of resistance—by inferior magistrates—in the case of persecution of the true religion by a ruler. See discussion of Theodore Beza, *The Rights of Magistrates*, in Julian H. Franklin, ed., *Constitutionalism and Resistance in the Sixteenth Century (Three Treatises by Hotman, Beza, and Mornay)* (New York: Pegasus, 1969), p. 30.

27. *Francogallia*, pp. 47–96; *Vindiciae contra tyrannos*, pp. 137–199; in Franklin, *Constitutionalism*. The latter work has also been attributed to Languet.

28. *Francogallia*, p. 79.

29. Theodore Beza, *The Rights of Magistrates*, in Franklin, *Constitutionalism*, p. 109. John Neville Figgis, *The Divine Right of Kings*, 1896 (New York: Harper Torchbooks, 1965), stresses the feudalist character of the argument in the *Vindiciae*: "Its strange exaltation of municipal and provincial authority, seems to carry us back to the days of provincial sovereignty and semi-sovereign *communes*" (p. 116).

30. On the similarities between Huguenot and papist theories, see Figgis, *Divine Right;* on the reaction of moderate Catholic, and Huguenot, opinion to the populism of the League, see Church, *Constitutional Thought*.

31. *Dialogue d'entre le maheustre et le manant*, p. 544, quoted in Church, *Constitutional Thought*, p. 304.

32. Pierre Pithou, "Harangue de Mr. D'Aubray," in *Satyre Menippée de la vertu du Catholicon d'Espagne . . .* , revue sur le texte complet 1594 (Paris: Alphonse Lamerre, 1877; Genève: Slatkine Reprints, 1971), p. 187. "Nous voulons sortir à quelque prix que ce soit, de ce mortel labyrinthe," wrote the author. "Nous aurons vng Roy qui donnera ordre a tout, & retiendra tous ces tyranneaux en craintre & en devoir: qui chastiera les violents: punira les réfractaires: exterminera les voleurs & pillards . . . & conservera tout le monde en repos & tranquilité. En fin, nous voulons ung Roy pour avoir la paix." But, he added, "Nous demandons ung Roy & chef naturel, non artificiel: ung Roy desia fait & non à faire . . . Le Roy que nous demandons est desia faict par la nature, né au vray parterre des fleurs de liz de France." Ibid., pp. 185, 187.

33. Constant, *De l'excellence et dignité des rois*, 1598, French text quoted in Church, *Constitutional Thought*, p. 308, fn. 16; De Rivault, quoted in ibid., and meaning ascribed to the first maxim of Loisel's *Institutes*, p. 338. According to Figgis, certain elements of the theory existed before this period, but now it was "emphatically asserted" (*Divine Right*, p. 120).

34. Figgis, *Divine Right*, p. 123, and ch. 6 in general.

35. For a discussion of Loyseau's views, see Church, *Constitutional Thought*, pp. 315–335.

36. This opposition of political to religious loyalties was echoed in later centuries in the conflicts between *nationaux* and *sacerdotaux*, patriots and *clericaux*.

37. The statement of Charles H. McIlwain is referred to in the acknowledgment to William Farr Church, *Richelieu and Reason of State* (Princeton: Princeton University Press, 1972), as the inspiration for the book. Church lists and extensively quotes from the authors who contributed to the formation of the "reason of state" position in France under Richelieu. The discussion of these writings

here relies on this work and often utilizes Church's translations (©1972 by Princeton University Press; reprinted by permission of Princeton University Press).

38. J. Ferrier, "Lettre au roy," in Paul Hay du Chastelet, ed. *Recueil de diverses pièces pour servir à l'histoire* (Paris, 1643), pp. 84–85; J. Ferrier, *Le Catholique d'estat*, in ibid., pp. 91, 93. Church, *Richelieu*, pp. 129–132.

39. Du Chastelet, "Observation sur la vie la condamnation du Maréchal de Marillac," in *Recueil de diverses pièces*, pp. 840–841. Church, *Richelieu*, p. 230.

40. Ferrier, "Lettre au roy," pp. 85, 86; *Catholique*, p. 98; Church, *Richelieu*, pp. 130, 134; Balzac quoted in ibid., p. 257.

41. Church, in *Richelieu*, p. 14, writes about this period: "Unfortunately, for those who would trace the growth of the French state, the word *état* is ambiguous. Not only is the historic confusion between the king's "estate" and the "state" perpetuated by the single term for both; in this period it was also variously used to denote a territorial unit that was ruled by a single sovereign, the royal government with its vast apparatus of offices and powers, and community or nation at large. The most frequent and important usage was . . . the state as the governing organ that was animated and controlled by the sovereign power of the king."

42. J. Ferrier, *Response au manifeste du Sieur de Soubize*, in *Mercure françois* (Paris: Jean et Estienne Richer, 1626), vol. XI, pp. 242–243.

43. Richelieu, "Advis donné au roy après la prise de La-Rochelle," January 13, 1629, in *Lettres, instructions diplomatiques et papiers d'état du Cardinal de Richelieu* (Paris: Imprimerie Imperiale, 1858), vol. III, pp. 182, 195. The translation here is from Richelieu, "A Program for the King," pp. 29–34, in William Farr Church, ed., *The Impact of Absolutism in France under Richelieu, Mazarin, and Louis XIV* (New York: John Wiley and Sons, 1969), pp. 31, 33. This and subsequent quotations from the Church book are reprinted by permission of John Wiley & Sons, Inc.

44. Guez de Balzac, Letter to Richelieu, March 5, 1631, in *Oeuvres* (Paris: Jacques Lecoffre, 1854), vol. I, p. 199.

45. "Réponse du Roy à Monsieur," May 30, 1631, in *Mercure françois*, vol. XVII (1633), p. 262. Church, *Richelieu*, p. 209.

46. *Discours d'un vieil courtisan désintéressé sur la lettre que la reyne mère du roy a écrite à sa majesté après estre sortie du royaume*, in du Chastelet, *Recueil de diverses pièces*, p. 446; Church, *Richelieu*, p. 217; Sirmond quoted in ibid., p. 219; Mathieu de Morgues, "Advertissement de Nicocléon à Cléonville sur son advertissement aux provinces," 1632, pt. I, p. 91; Church, *Richelieu*, p. 221.

47. Ordinance of Villers-Cotterets, in Isambert, *Recueil Général*, vol. XII, pt. II, p. 590; also see Ordinance of Blois, Royal Declaration of 1610, in ibid., vol. XIV, p. 424; vol. XVI, pp. 6–8; Cardin Le Bret quoted in Church, *Richelieu*, p. 274; Code Michaud, Article 179, January 1629, in Isambert, *Recueil général*, vol. XVI, p. 275.

48. Richelieu, "Avis du Cardinal," in Richelieu, *Lettres, instructions*, vol. III, p. 665; Achille de Sancy, "Réponse au libelle intitulé 'Très humble, très véritable . . . ,'" in du Chastelet, *Recueil de diverses pièces*, p. 563.

49. Roland Mousnier, *Les XVIe et XVIIe siècles* (Paris: Presses Universitaires de France, 1954), p. 160.

50. Richelieu, *Lettres, instructions,* vol. II, p. 321; Guez de Balzac, Letter to Richelieu, December 25, 1625, in *Les Premières Lettres de Guez de Balzac* (Paris: Librairie E. Droz, 1933–34), vol. II, p. 21.

51. Mathieu de Morgues, *Très humble, très véritable et très importante remonstrance au roi,* 1631, in *Recueil de pièces pour la défence de la reyne mère du Roi Très Chrétien Louis XIII,* Anvers, 1643, p. 66.

52. The term did not exist then and for some time to come; when it was first employed as a self-standing noun in 1756, it meant the functions of "police"—the satisfaction of the everyday needs of the population. Roland Mousnier, *Institutions de la France sous la monarchie absolue,* vol. II, *Les Organes de l'état et la société* (Paris: Presses Universitaires de France, 1980), p. 34. On the organization of the governmental structure in the early seventeenth century, see ibid., ch. 3, "Chancelliers, conseils, ministres de 1598 à 1661"; Roland Mousnier, "Le Conseil du roi de la mort de Henri IV au gouvernement personnel de Louis XIV," *Etudes d'histoire moderne et contemporaine,* 1947, pp. 29–67; A. Lloyd Moote, *The Revolt of the Judges: The Parlement of Paris and the Fronde, 1643–1652* (Princeton: Princeton University Press, 1971), especially ch. 1, "French Government and Society in 1610."

53. Mousnier, *Institutions,* vol. II, pp. 149–52; also on the concept of "créature," see Orest A. Ranum, *Richelieu and the Councillors of Louis XIII* (Oxford: The Clarendon Press, 1963), ch. 2, "The Creatures of Cardinal Richelieu," pp. 27–44.

54. On possible reasons for Richelieu's identification with absolutism, see Orest A. Ranum, "Richelieu and the Great Nobility: Some Aspects of Early Modern Political Motives," *French Historical Studies,* 3 (1963), pp. 184–204.

55. Ranum, "The Great Nobility," pp. 201–202; *Councillors,* p. 22.

56. Mousnier, *Institutions,* vol. II, Book II, ch. 1, "Les officiers," pp. 47–66; Moote, *Revolt,* p. 6. In addition to Parlements, there were different lesser courts which adjudicated civil and criminal cases; *cours des aides* and lesser organizations to deal with taxes; *chambres des comptes* for accounting; and other corporations, which, in each province, composed a hierarchy. The Parlements, *cours des aides,* and *chambres des comptes* were, theoretically, sovereign courts, but they had no right to legislate and were subject to royal review.

57. Moote, *Revolt,* pp. 4, 32, and ch. 2, "The Reign of Louis XIII; Governmental Revolution and the Officiers"; Mousnier, *Institutions,* vol. II, pp. 487, 489–494.

58. Godefroi Hermant, *Mémoires sur la vie ecclésiastique du XVIIe siècle* (Paris: Plon, 1905–1910), vol. I, pp. 177, 178.

59. Church, *Impact of Absolutism,* p. 62. For general discussion, see Ernst H. Kossmann, *La Fronde* (Leiden: Universitaire Pers Leiden, 1954); and Louis Madelin, *La Fronde* (Paris: Plon, 1931).

60. Madelin, *La Fronde,* p. 338; Kossmann, *La Fronde,* pp. 259, 260.

61. Church, *Impact of Absolutism,* p. 45.

62. Claude Joly, "True Maxims of Government," in ibid., pp. 49, 46–52.

63. On kings' work, and particularly that of Louis XIV, see Mousnier, *Institutions*, vol. II, Book I, *Le Roi*, especially ch. 4, pp. 27–31.

64. C. Dreyss, ed., *Mémoires de Louis XIV* (Paris, Didier et Cie., 1860), vol. II, pp. 230, 403–405. (Passages from pp. 230–520 are translated in Church, *Impact of Absolutism*, pp. 69–73.)

65. Jean Domat, "The Ideal Absolute State," in Church, *Impact of Absolutism*, p. 78.

66. J.-B. Bossuet, "Sermon on the Duties of Kings," in ibid., p. 74. *Églises protestantes* quoted in Martin, *France*, p. 165. *Politique tirée de l'Écriture Sainte*, in J.-B. Bossuet, *Oeuvres choisies* (Paris: Hachette, 1868), vol. II, pp. 9, 21, 118, 122.

67. Pierre Corneille, *Horace*, Act II, Scene III, in *Théatre de Corneille* (Paris, 1765), vol. II, p. 49; J. Racine, *Esther*, Act I, Scene III, in *Théatre de J. Racine* (Paris: Librairie des Bibliophiles, 1842), vol. III, p. 189.

68. Pascal, *Pensées* (Paris: Editions Garnier, 1964), pp. 151, 152; La Bruyère, *Les Caractères*, "Du souverain ou de la république" (Paris: chez Lefèvre, 1843), vol. I, p. 348.

69. Georges Pagès, *La Monarchie d'ancien régime en France (de Henri IV à Louis XIV)* (Paris: Librairie Armand Colin, 1946), p. 186, and John Law, quoted in ibid., p. 186.

70. Charles Godard, *Les Pouvoirs des intendants sous Louis XIV, particulièrement dans les pays d'élections, de 1661 à 1715* (Paris: Librairie Sirey, 1901), p. 440.

71. Pagès, *La Monarchie*, p. 189. Sympathetic to the institution, Godard writes: "Through the power of centralization, Louis XIV's ministers and intendants assured the realm extraordinary development of national activity, suppression of brigandage and the worst abuses committed by the nobles and justices, the benefits of extraordinary justice without cost, severe control that won French administration its reputation for honesty, regular accounting in the cities and communities, and a notable decline of wrongs and vexations in matters of direct taxation . . . If the intendants had not been created, the French people . . . would have been abandoned to the capricious despotism of country squires, new nobles who held state offices, and urban oligarchies . . . In the absence of liberty, consistent despotism is preferable. [Here the historian agreed with Louis XIV.] There is always the possibility that administrative tutelage may be skillful and impartial, whereas it is much less likely that a local potentate will have both administrative skill and impartiality." Godard, *Les Pouvoirs*, pp. 443–444, as trans. in Church, *Impact of Absolutism*, p. 163.

72. *Les Soupirs de la France esclave, qui aspire après la liberté*, 1690, second memoir, in Church, *Impact of Absolutism*, pp. 102, 103, 104–105.

73. Saint-Simon, *Memoirs*, trans. B. St. John (Akron, Ohio: St. Dunstan Society, 1901), vol. II, p. 12. The religious nature of Jansenist teaching, to contemporaries at least, was not altogether clear. Saint-Simon thought this to be an "imaginary heresy," a fruit of Jesuit conspiracy. He wrote (ibid., pp. 86–87): "I need not dwell at any great length upon the origin and progress of the two religious parties, the Jansenists and the Molinists; enough has been written on both sides to form a whole library. It is enough for me to say that the Molinists were so called because they adopted the views expounded by the Père Molina

in a book he wrote against the doctrines of St. Augustin and of the Church of
Rome, upon the subject of spiritual grace. The Père Molina was a Jesuit, and it
was by the Jesuits his book was brought forward and supported. Finding, however, that the views it expounded met with general opposition, not only
throughout France, but in Rome, they had recourse to their usual artifices on
feeling themselves embarassed, turned themselves into accusers instead of de-
fendents, and invented a heresy that had neither author nor follower, which
they attributed to Cornelius Jansenius, Bishop of Ypres. Many and long were
the discussions at Rome upon this ideal heresy, invented by the Jesuits solely
for the purpose of weakening the adversaries of Molina. To oppose his doctrines was to be a Jansenist. That in substance was what was meant by Jansenism."

74. The repudiation of several propositions allegedly found in Jansenius' *Augus-
tinus* and declared by the Pope heretical.

75. On the education of Louis XIV, see Maurice Ashley, *Louis XIV and the Greatness of France* (London: Hodder and Stoughton for the English University
Press, 1946); and Mousnier, *Institutions,* vol. II, pp. 21–23.

76. Guy Chaussinand-Nogaret, *The French Nobility in the Eighteenth Century:
From Feudalism to Enlightenment* (Cambridge: Cambridge University Press,
1985), p. 1.

77. Mousnier, *Institutions,* vol. I, *Société et état* (Paris: Presses Universitaires de
France, 1974), p. 101.

78. Franklin L. Ford, *Robe and Sword: The Regrouping of the French Aristocracy
after Louis XIV* (Cambridge, Mass.: Harvard University Press, 1953), p. 31;
Mousnier, *Institutions,* vol. I, believes that many of these were heads of families, which would make the overall number much larger. Ford does not seem to
think so.

79. The opinion of contemporary historians is also divided. Mousnier (*Institutions,* vol. I, p. 121) tends to agree with Coyer, and claims that in the eighteenth
century the nobility represented 2 percent. Chaussinand-Nogaret (*French Nobility,* p. 30) goes to the other extreme; his assessment is 25,000 noble families
or 110,000 to 120,000 individuals in 1789. Ford (*Robe and Sword,* p. 31) believes d'Hozier's *Armorial,* if adjusted, to be the most reliable source; his figure
is, therefore, around 200,000 individuals, or 1 percent of the population in
1715.

80. Chaussinand-Nogaret, *French Nobility,* pp. 25–31.

81. Mousnier, *Institutions,* vol. I, p. 136; Ford, *Robe and Sword,* pp. 32–33.

82. Chaussinand-Nogaret, *French Nobility,* pp. 52–53; 58; 63.

83. Saint-Simon, *Memoirs,* vol. I, p. 255.

84. On duels and the government's efforts to prevent them, see Mousnier, *Institutions,* vol. I, pp. 114–120; and Ranum, "The Great Nobility."

85. La Roque, quoted in Mousnier, *Institutions,* vol. I, p. 103.

86. Ibid., p. 132.

87. Ibid., p. 125; Chaussinand-Nogaret, *French Nobility,* p. 30.

88. Lavisse, quoted in Ashley, *Louis XIV,* p. 80.

89. La Bruyère, *Les Caractères,* "De la cour," ch. 8, 63, vol. I, p. 301. He wrote
also: "Ceux qui habitent cette contrée . . . ont leur dieu en leur roi: les grands

de la nation s'assemblent tous les jours à une certaine heure, dans un temple
. . . les gens de pays le nomment Versailles" (pp. 305–306). Mme de Pompa-
dour, quoted by Chaussinand-Nogaret, *French Nobility,* p. 45, also referred to
the Court as "another country."

90. Ford, *Robe and Sword,* pp. 174–175; Mousnier, *Institutions,* vol. I, p. 126.

91. Saint-Simon, *Memoirs,* vol. I, pp. 66, 73; 31–35. The particular mistreatment
of the princes of the blood, as well as the reasons for it, are revealed in Saint-
Simon's characterization of the Duc d'Anjou, the second son of the Dauphin,
unexpectedly chosen by Charles II of Spain to succeed him on the Spanish
throne. "Younger brother of an excitable, violent, and robust prince, Philip V
had been bred up in submission and dependence that were necessary for the
repose of the Royal family. Until the testament of Charles II, the Duc d'Anjou
was necessarily regarded as destined to be a subject all his life; and therefore
would not be too much abased by education, and trained to patience and obedience. That supreme law, the reason of state, demanded this preference, for
the safety and happiness of the kingdom, of the elder over the younger brother.
His mind for this reason was purposely narrowed and beaten down" (p. 283).

92. *Mémoires de Louis XIV,* vol. II, p. 391.

93. Saint-Simon, *Memoirs,* vol. II, p. 125.

94. Chevigny, *La Science des personnes de la cour,* 1706, original text quoted in
Ford, *Robe and Sword,* p. 10; La Bruyère, *Les Caractères,* p. 303; Saint-Simon,
*Memoirs,* vol. I, pp. 295, 328.

95. La Bruyère, *Les Caractères,* "De la cour," 67, vol. I, p. 302. Saint-Simon, who
characterized La Bruyère as "a man illustrious by his genius . . . who died of
apoplexy at Versailles, after having surpassed Theophrastus in his own manner, and after painting, in the new characters, the men of our days in a manner
inimitable. He was besides a very honest man, of excellent breeding" (*Memoirs,* vol. I, p. 105), certainly thought him trustworthy.

96. Quoted in Chaussinand-Nogaret, *French Nobility,* p. 7.

97. Saint-Simon, *Memoirs,* vol. I, pp. 267, 268.

98. Mousnier, *Institutions,* vol. I, p. 112.

99. This was "the effort to exclude individuals enjoying some degree of independent, especially hereditary prestige from the sort of governmental functions
which might have made that prestige dangerous to the crown. This was no
innovation in royal policy, any more than noble opposition to it was a new
development. The Carolingians' *missi,* the medieval Capetians' *baillis* and *sé-
néchaux,* the intendants of the sixteenth century and even more under Richelieu, all had represented stages in the crown's long effort to retain control over
its officialdom by superimposing new administrative layers over previous
agents who had succeeded in converting into personal property their respective
segments of delegated sovereignty." Ford, *Robe and Sword,* p. 7. Also pp. 8,
35.

100. Saint-Simon, *Memoirs,* vol. I, p. 141. Also see Ranum, *Councillors,* p. 31.

101. Mousnier *Institutions,* vol. I, pp. 106–107; Ford, *Robe and Sword,* pp. 12–13.

102. Mousnier, *Institutions,* vol. I, p. 132.

103. It included members of the king's Council, Parlements, and other sovereign
courts—all in all, thirty-one corporations. In the first half of the eighteenth

century, the overall population of the *grands robins* was 2,000 to 2,300 persons. Ford, *Robe and Sword,* pp. 53–54.

104. Chaussinand-Nogaret, *French Nobility,* p. 35; Mousnier, *Institutions,* vol. I, p. 202. Nevertheless, it must be emphasized that financiers were not "bourgeois" by any criterion that would make sense of the term. Legally, they were more often than not members of the nobility, or were on the verge of ennoblement. They might have been born into the "middle class," but cut themselves off from it. They were a marginal and despised sector of the elite, but a sector of the elite nevertheless.

105. La Bruyère, *Les Caractères,* "Des grands," ch. 9, 40, vol. I, p. 335.

106. According to Mousnier, the merging took place late; Chaussinand-Nogaret and Ford seem to think that it both occurred earlier and was more complete.

107. Saint-Simon, *Memoirs,* vol. I, pp. 183–184. Marriages between men of the military aristocracy and daughters of rich magistrates were not infrequent; they provided the means for the families of the former, in the phrase of the period, to "manure their lands." Yet this reflected the tendency toward female hypergamy, rather than social acceptance of the nobility of the robe. Mousnier, *Institutions,* vol. I, p. 164.

108. Ford, *Robe and Sword,* pp. 177–178.

109. Quoted in ibid., p. 72. Ford cites "early in the Regency" as the date for the first quote.

110. Saint-Simon, *Memoirs,* vol. I, pp. 23, 170; a petition of the church nobles of 1748–49, quoted in Ford, *Robe and Sword,* p. 199.

111. Henri François d'Aguesseau, "L'Amour de son état," 1st mercurial, in *Oeuvres choisies* (Paris: Lefèvre, 1819), vol. I, pp. 92–93.

112. J. H. Shennan, "France, 1490–1715," pp. 472–483, in *Encyclopaedia Britannica,* 15th ed. vol. IXX, p. 473.

113. Chaussinand-Nogaret, *French Nobility,* pp. 82–83, rightly emphasizes this affinity.

114. G. A. de La Roque, *Traité de la noblesse,* preface, 1678, in G. Chaussinand-Nogaret, *Une Histoire des élites, 1700–1848,* vol. VI, *Le Savoir historique,* (La Haye: Mouton, 1975), p. 24; Boileau, *Satires,* "Satire V: La Noblesse," in *Oeuvres complètes* (Paris: Garnier Frères, 1870), vol. I, pp. 101, 102; La Bruyère, *Les Caractères,* "De quelques usages," ch. 14, 18, vol. II, p. 107.

115. Henri de Boulainvilliers, Comte de Saint-Saire, *Essais sur la noblesse de France* (Amsterdam, 1732), pp. 9–10, 11.

116. Abbé Gabriel Francois Coyer, *La Noblesse commerçante* (London and Paris, 1756), pp. 214–215; Philippe-Auguste de Sainte-Foix, Chevalier d'Arc, *La Noblesse militaire, ou Le patriote français* (Paris, 1756), pp. 40, 85, 86.

117. Chérin or Guyot quoted in Mousnier, *Institutions,* vol. I, p. 101.

118. Quoted in Chaussinand-Nogaret, *French Nobility,* p. 20.

119. Ibid., pp. 21, 60. D'Antraigues', said Simon Schama, in *Citizens: A Chronicle of the French Revolution* (New York: Alfred A. Knopf, 1989), was "the first and most famous of all aristocratic pronouncements of self-liquidation" (p. 121).

120. Quoted in Chaussinand-Nogaret, *French Nobility,* p. 6.

121. These regulations could be always overruled by the king, but this caused as

much annoyance to the *grands* as would have unlimited access to Court honors (for it was the expression of absolute power the king wielded over the nobility), and in addition must have irritated those of the not qualified to receive these honors, for whom no exception was made.

122. Ford, *Robe and Sword,* passim. The assumption of leadership by the robe is the focus of Ford's book.

123. Saint-Simon wrote of the Prince de Conti that he was very well educated "against the custom of those of his rank." *Memoirs,* vol. II, p. 75.

124. Chaussinand-Nogaret, *French Nobility,* pp. 65–85.

125. Alexis de Tocqueville, *The Old Regime and the Revolution,* 1856, trans. Stuart Gilbert (Garden City, N.J.: Doubleday Anchor Books, 1955), pp. 142, 145; Chaussinand-Nogaret, *French Nobility,* p. 73.

126. Maurice Reinhard, "Elite et noblesse dans la seconde moitié du XVIII siècle," *Revue d'histoire moderne et contemporaine,* 3 (1956), pp. 5–37, 20–24. Robert Darnton, in *The Literary Underground of the Old Regime* (Cambridge, Mass.: Harvard University Press, 1982), cites the income of Suard, a typical case of a successful *philosophe,* as being between ten thousand and twenty thousand livres a year, perhaps more. This compares well with the incomes of large sectors of the old nobility. An editor at the *Gazette de France,* Suard later took over its administration. The job provided him with an apartment where Mme Suard had a literary *salon* of her own (pp. 3–6). Much of the discussion of the changing position of middle-class intellectuals relies on ch. 1 in Darnton's book.

127. Chaussinand-Nogaret, *French Nobility,* p. 73. "Cultivation" is as characteristic of the eighteenth-century elite vocabulary as "creation" is of that of the seventeenth. This change of terms reflects a basic change of attitude. While "creation" implies making something out of nothing (or somebody out of nobody), only something worthy in itself deserves to be "cultivated." "Cultivation" refers to recognition of the innate merit of its object, and of the value of merit as such. It is a sign of substitution of universalistic criteria of social advancement for particularistic criteria, and of the transformation of an aristocracy of birth into a meritocracy.

128. Darnton, *Literary Underground,* p. 5.

129. Darnton, p. 3, quotes from Reinhard, "Elite," p. 21; the quotation is taken from John Nickolls (1754).

130. "There is the people opposed to the great, which is the populace and multitude. There is the people opposed to the wise, the clever, the virtuous; it includes the great as well as the small." La Bruyère, *Les Caractères,* "Des grands," ch. 9, 53, vol. I, pp. 345–346.

131. It is expressed, for example, in D'Alembert's *Essai sur les gens de lettres et les grands,* Duclos's *Considérations sur les moeurs de ce siècle,* Voltaire's "Gens de lettres," in the *Encyclopédie,* and "Gout," in the *Dictionnaire philosophique.*

132. *Turcaret* was first written in 1707 and bore a different title, *Les Etrennes.* Turcaret, the financier, is its central and most contemptuous character. "Le monde," by exalted members of which the play was sponsored, however, is not at all represented as noble and deserving of respect, but receives its share of ridicule.

133. Schama, *Citizens*, pp. 71–73.
134. According to ARTFL data, its first instance is found in Guillaume Thomas François Raynal, *Histoire philosophique et politique des établissements et du commerce des européens dans les deux Indes* (La Haye, 1776; written in 1770), vol. VI, p. 80. (ARTFL is a University of Chicago data-base, a comprehensive file of the important French texts published between 1600 and 1930. It does not include all the texts that were published, but seems to include every text of note.)
135. *L'Improvisateur français* (Paris: chez Goujon Fils, an xii, 1804), vol. III-IV, pp. 45–46.
136. Chaussinand-Nogaret, *French Nobility*, p. 35.
137. J. J. Rousseau, *Social Contract*, in *The Social Contract and Discourses*, trans. G. D. H. Cole (London: Everyman's Library, 1952, published by David Campbell Publishers), p. 77, and *Government of Poland*, trans. W. Kendall (Indianapolis and New York: The Bobbs-Merill Co., 1972), pp. 68–70.
138. "Noblesse," pp. 166–181, in *Encyclopédie*, vol. XI.
139. J. le Rond d'Alembert, *Histoire des membres de l'Académie Française morts depuis 1700 jusqu'en 1771* (Paris: chez Panckoucke et Moutard, 1779), vol. I, preface, pp. xxxii–xxxiii (Darnton's translation).
140. See Tocqueville's discussion, *Old Regime*, Book III, ch. 5.
141. Quoted in Chaussinand-Nogaret, *French Nobility*, p. 6.
142. Ford, *Robe and Sword;* Chaussinand-Nogaret, *French Nobility;* Patrice Higonnet, *Class, Ideology and the Rights of Nobles during the French Revolution* (Oxford: Oxford University Press, 1981); Schama, *Citizens*.
143. François Furet, *Interpreting the French Revolution* (Cambridge: Cambridge University Press/Editions de la Maison des Sciences de l'Homme, 1981), p. 183.
144. Balzac, *Le Prince*, p. 81; Schama, *Citizens*, p. 859.
145. Quoted in Hans Kohn, "France between Britain and Germany," *Journal of the History of Ideas*, 17:3 (June 1956), p. 283.
146. Voltaire, "Réflexions sur l'histoire," "Annales de l'empire," in *Oeuvres complètes*, vol. XXV, p. 170; vol. XIII, p. 513; Guillaume Thomas Raynal, *Histoire philosophique et politique des établissements et du commerce des Européens dans les deux Indes* (Geneve, 1775), vol. V, p. 10; Charles Pinot Duclos, *Considérations sur les moeurs de ce siècle*, in *Oeuvres diverses* (Paris: N. L. M. Dessesartes, 1802), vol. I, p. 10.
147. Rousseau, *Social Contract*, p. 13, fn. to ch. 6.
148. Voltaire, *Lettres anglaises* (Utrecht: Jean-Jacques Pauvert, 1964), Letter 8, pp. 49–50, and Letter 20, "Sur les seigneurs qui cultivent les lettres." There Voltaire continues: "Il y a à Londres environ huit cents personnes qui ont le droit de parler en public et de soutenir les intérêts de la Nation; environ cinq ou six mille prétendent au même honneur à leur tour; tout le reste s'érige en juge de ceux-ci, et chacun peut faire imprimer ce qu'il pense sur les affaires publiques. Ainsi, toute la Nation est dans la nécessité de s'instruire" (p. 127). The letter specifically devoted to the subject is "Sur la considération qu'on doit aux gens de lettres," where Voltaire writes: "Tel est le respect que ce peuple a pour les talents, qu'un homme de mérite y fait toujours fortune . . . Entrez à Westminster. Ce ne sont pas les tombeaux des Rois qu'on y admire; ce sont les

monuments que la reconnaissance de la nation a érigés aux plus grands hommes qui ont contribué à sa gloire" (pp. 140, 141). Voltaire's impressions echo Fontenelle's "Eulogium to Newton."

149. Montesquieu, *De l'esprit des lois* (Paris: Garnier Frères, 1945), Book XI, ch. 6 ("De la constitution d'Angleterre," pp. 163–174). The English edition used is the first American edition (Worcester: Isaiah Thomas, 1802); quotations are from vol. I, pp. 189, 191, 185; ibid., Book XIX, ch. 27, p. 341; English text, vol. I, p. 366, and Book XIV, *Of Laws Relative to the Nature of Climate*, ch. 13, "Effects Arising from the Climate of England," p. 252; English text, vol. I, p. 272.

150. Parlement quoted in Citron, *Le Mythe*, p. 150; Daniel Mornet, *Les Origines intellectuelles de la révolution française, 1715–1787* (Paris: Armand Colin, 1933), p. 23; and D'Argenson quoted in Jacques Godechot, "Nation, patrie, nationalisme et patriotisme en France au XVIII siècle," pp. 481–501, in *Annales historiques de la rèvolution française*, 206 (October–December 1971), p. 489.

151. Robert R. Palmer, "The National Idea in France before the Revolution," *Journal of the History of Ideas*, 1 (1940), p. 98.

152. J. J. Rousseau, "Discours sur cette question: Quelle est la vertu la plus nécéssaire aux héros; et quels sont les héros à qui cette vertu a manqué?" in *Collection Complète des Oeuvres* (Deux Ponts: chez Sansot et Cie, 1782–83), vol. XIII–XIV, pp. 10–11, 17–18. For comparison, see *Government of Poland*. Grimm quoted in Palmer, "National Idea," p. 105; the glory-loving citizen in Schama, *Citizens*, p. 127 (the occasion is the death of the aviator Pilâtre du Rozier).

153. Rossel, *Histoire du patriotisme français*, 1769.

154. Condorcet quoted in Lestocquoy, *Histoire du patriotisme*, p. 84; Rousseau, *Government of Poland*, p. 99.

155. The calculations are the result of a computer search for sentences with the words *nation, état, estat, patrie, peuple, France,* and combinations of them, by decade, between 1600 and 1800. There was a parallel, though not simultaneous, decrease in the use of *roi, royaume,* and *Couronne.* The number of times these words were employed dropped dramatically between 1720 and 1730, then rose again, possibly reflecting the strength of Louis XV's position, but started to decline steadily after 1770.

156. The numbers are: 1701–1710: 45 times in 7 out of 20 texts; 1711–1720: 106 times, 12/25; 1721–1730: 106, 15/31; 1731–1740: 156, 27/94; 1741–1750: 210, 25/62; 1751–1760: 990, 43/95; 1761–1770: 948, 46/118; 1771–1780: 837, 41/106; 1781–1790: 915, 68/97; 1791–1800: 530, 27/50.

157. 1701–1710: 376 times in 12 texts; 1711–1720: 1,782/19; 1721–1730: 418/16; 1731–1740: 1,584/41; 1741–1750: 628/40; 1751–1760: 1,643/49; 1761–1770: 2,003/68; 1771–1780: 2,026/47; 1781–1790: 2,175/43; 1791–1800: 1,542/35.

158. 1701–1710: 34/12; 1711–1720: 279/14; 1721–1730: 116/30; 1731–1740: 590/30; 1741–1750: 212/36; 1751–1760: 462/48; 1761–1770: 658/61; 1771–1780: 719/44; 1781–1790: 806/40; 1791–1800: 442/35.

159. The numbers for *état* are: 1701–1710: 491 instances; 1711–1720: 899; 1721–

1730: 453; 1731–1740: 2,647; 1741–1750: 1,441; 1751–1760: 3,561; 1761–1770: 3,640; 1771–1780: 2,303; 1781–1790: 2,371; 1791–1800: 1,306. This does not take into account the instances with the older spelling *(estat)*, which may affect the numbers for earlier decades. In any case, a textual analysis is indispensable for establishing when the word is used in any one of its political senses.

160. Abbé Antoine Furetière, *Dictionnaire universel, contenant généralement tous les mots français, tant vieux que modernes, et les termes de toutes les sciences et les arts* (La Haye: Arnout et Reinier Leers, 1690), vol. II, pp. 214, 215.

161. *Dictionnaire universel françois et latin vulgairement appellé Dictionnaire de Trévoux* (1732), vol. IV, pp. 32–33.

162. *Dictionnaire de l'Académie Françoise* (Lyon: Joseph Duplain, 1777), vol. II, p. 129.

163. *Nouveau dictionnaire françois, composé sur le dictionnaire de l'Académie Françoise, enrichi de grand nombre de mots adoptés dans notre langue depuis quelques années* (Paris et Lyon: J. B. Delamollière, 1793), vol. II, p. 140.

164. *Encyclopédie ou dictionnaire raisonné des sciences, des arts et des métiers, par une société de gens de lettres*, vol. XI (1756), p. 36.

165. Furetière, *Dictionnaire universel*, vol. II, p. 375; *Dictionnaire de Trévoux*, vol. IV, p. 784.

166. *Encyclopédie*, vol. XII, pp. 475–476.

167. *Dictionnaire de l'Académie* (1777), vol. II, p. 236.

168. Furetière, *Dictionnaire universel*, vol. II, p. 347; *Dictionnaire de l'Académie* (1777), p. 212; *Dictionnaire universel, historique et critique des moeurs* (Paris: J. P. Costard, 1772), p. 343.

169. Jaucourt, "Patriotisme," *Encyclopédie*, vol. XII, p. 181.

170. J. J. Rousseau, Letter to Charles Pictet, March 1, 1764 (No. 3162), in *Correspondance complète* (Banbury: The Voltaire Foundation, 1973), vol. XIX, p. 190.

171. Furetière, *Dictionnaire universel*, vol. I, p. 672; *Le Dictionnaire de l'Académie Françoise, dedié au roy* (Paris: Jean Baptiste Coignard, 1694), vol. I, pp. 402–403; P. Berthelin, *Abrégé du dictionnaire universel françois et latin, vulgairement appellé dictionnaire de Trévoux* (Paris: Libraires Associes, 1762), vol. I, pt. II, p. 141.

172. Jaucourt, "État," *Encyclopédie*, vol. VI (1756), pp. 18–19.

173. Quoted in Lestocquoy, *Histoire du patriotisme*, pp. 84, 85.

174. Quoted in Palmer, "National Idea," p. 104.

175. John Markoff, "Images du roi au début de la révolution," ed. Michel Vovelle, *L'Image de la révolution française*, vol. I (Oxford: Pergamon Press, 1989), pp. 237–245, 240, 239. The classic study of Beatrice Hyslop, *French Nationalism in 1789 According to the General Cahiers* (New York: Columbia University Press, 1934), also shows that the *cahiers* were not at all anti-monarchical.

176. Godechot, "Nation, patrie," p. 495.

177. Phillippe Grouvelle, *De l'autorité de Montesquieu dans la révolution présente* (Paris, 1789), p. 61.

178. See discussion in Ford, *Robe and Sword;* also Maurice Cranston, "The Sovereignty of the Nation," ch. 5, in *The French Revolution and the Creation of*

*Modern Political Culture,* vol. II, *The Political Culture of the French Revolution,* ed. Colin Lucas (Oxford: Pergamon Press, 1988).

179. Montesquieu, *Esprit,* Book XXVIII, ch. 9; English text, vol. II, p. 209; French text, vol. II, p. 218; Book XIX, ch. 27; English text, vol. I, p. 367; French text, vol. I, p. 342.

180. Boyd C. Shafer, "Bourgeois Nationalism in the Pamphlets on the Eve of the French Revolution," *Journal of Modern History,* 10 (1938), pp. 31–50, 35. In the pamphlets Shafer discerns a change in vocabulary which shows "a striking change in loyalties and psychology. More and more *la patrie* was used instead of *le pays, le citoyen* and *le concitoyen* instead of *le sujet,* and *la nation* instead of *l'état*" (p. 32). Representative titles included the *Catechisme national,* the *Essai du patriotisme,* the *Qu'est-ce que la nation? et qu'est-ce que la France?* and so on. Shafer stresses that the nation was never explicitly equated with property-owners. But he regards both the French Revolution and nationalism as "bourgeois" phenomena (a view which agrees neither with recent analyses of the Revolution nor with the conclusions of the present study) and therefore does interpret the identification of the nation with the Third Estate as such an equation.

181. Rousseau, *Social Contract,* p. 78; Rabaut-Saint-Etienne, *Considérations très importantes sur les intérêts du Tiers-État,* 1789, quoted in Shafer, "Bourgeois Nationalism," p. 38.

182. The notion of the nation as the elite of the population persisted well into the revolutionary decade, as did the derogatory meaning of the "people," though the idea of who constituted this elite had by then changed. The dispute over the proper name of what became the Assemblée Nationale and the rejection of the alternative title, Représentants de Peuple Français, proposed by Mirabeau, is a case in point. See discussion in Zernatto, "Nation," p. 365.

183. Rousseau, *Social Contract,* pp. 58, 80.

184. See p. 173.

185. Rousseau, *Government of Poland,* pp. 9, 89, 28, 29, 42. See also pp. 40, 51.

186. Ibid., pp. 29, 30, 97; 15–16; *Social Contract,* p. 80.

187. See Darnton's *(Literary Underground)* discussion of the literary underground and "low-life." Schama *(Citizens,* p. 121) quotes Grouvelle as saying: "O Montesquieu, you were a Magistrate, a gentleman, a rich man; you found it congenial . . . to demonstrate the advantages of a government in which you occupied an advantageous place."

188. D'Antraigues, quoted in Chaussinand-Nogaret, *French Nobility,* p. 21; Comte de Ségur, quoted by Schama, *Citizens,* p. 49.

189. Emmanuel Sieyès, *Qu'est-ce que le Tiers Etat?* (Paris: Quadrige/Presses Universitaires de France, 1982), pp. 30 (fn. 1), 32; Delaure quoted in Citron, *Le Mythe,* p. 146.

190. Sieyès, *Tiers Etat,* p. 67; Jacques Godechot, ed., *Les Constitutions de la France,* text of "Déclaration des droits de l'homme et du Citoyen du 26 août 1789," pp. 33–34. See Yehoshua Arieli, *Individualism and Nationalism in American Ideology,* for a comparison between the language of the Declaration and that of the American Constitution.

191. Rousseau, *Social Contract,* pp. 12, 13; 15, 23, 14; 15; 23; 20, 21, 78; 31; 33, 34, 79; 47, 49, 56, 57.

192. Ibid., p. 16. This magic trick by which less was made more also applied to property. "The State," said Rousseau, "in relation to its members, is master of all their possessions by the social contract." His endorsement of this state of things made Rousseau a socialist. But he believed that "the peculiar fact" about this dispossession which he called "alienation" was "that, in taking over the goods of individuals, the community, so far from despoiling them, only assures them legitimate possession" (pp. 17, 18), and this made him a very naive socialist.

193. Ibid., p. 14; *Government of Poland,* pp. 19–20.

194. "C'est, en un mot, pour le bien de tous, parce que c'est le seul moyen de parvenir, sans injustice, à ne composer les assemblées que des hommes à qui leur éducation et leur considération personnelle donnent le plus de moyens pour faire le bien." *Considération personelle* here may be interpreted as, on the one hand, "status," and on the other, "understanding" or "virtue." Marquis de Condorcet, *Oeuvres* (Paris: Firmin Didot Frères, 1847), vol. VIII, pp. 155–156.

195. Then, wrote Palmer, "the national idea came to life everywhere—in a government that gave help to patriotic tragedies and took over schools [from Jesuits], in theories of educational reform, in the Parlements and among their cohorts of adherents, in the minds of those philosophes who were still relatively young after 1750, and in the wide bourgeois circles where the philosophic ideas spread" ("National Idea," pp. 107–108). In the light of more recent studies, one might disagree with Palmer that the circles where the philosophic ideas spread were "bourgeois," but his dating of the formation of national consciousness is correct.

196. Originally "regeneration" referred to the return to the days when France was faithful to its fundamental laws and ancient constitution. It had "feudal"—and possibly certain Renaissance—connotations. It was not from the start a metaphor for winning back from England the position of centrality in Europe, but it is certain that in the course of the century this increasingly became its predominant meaning.

197. Voltaire to Mme d'Epinay, July 6, 1766, in *Correspondance complète* (Banbury: The Voltaire Foundation), vol. XXX, p. 299.

198. Frances Acomb, *Anglophobia in France, 1763–1789: An Essay in the History of Constitutionalism and Nationalism* (Durham, N.C.: Duke University Press, 1950), pp. 16, 26, 54. This book contains a very detailed and informative discussion of the varieties and development of the Anglophobe opinion in France.

199. At the same time, "liberty" in France retained an intensely individualistic, in fact egocentric, connotation, as unqualified in its rejection of all authority, and all limitations (including those imposed by the rights of other individuals), as liberty as an attribute of general will was in its submission to authority. Such libertarianism, a spirit of revolt for the sake of revolt, inconsiderate of others and unmindful of its own implications, was characteristic of Lafayette and expressed, for example, in the hero's youthful sympathy for man-hunting carnivores described by Schama (*Citizens,* pp. 26–27). The case of Lafayette makes it clear that the two "liberties," however contradictory in theory, could coexist in the very same person without ever making him aware of the contradiction between them.

200. Mably, "De l'étude de l'histoire" in *Collection complète des oeuvres de l'Abbé de Mably,* vol. XII (Paris: Desbrière, l'an III de la République [1794–95]), pp. 230, 233; 218.

201. Rousseau, *Government of Poland,* pp. 40–41, 36; 32, 36; *Social Contract,* p. 78.

202. Rousseau, *Government of Poland,* p. 36.

203. Mably, "De l'étude," pp. 238, 240. See also Holbach, *Ethnocratie, ou Le Gouvernment sur la morale.*

204. Palmer, "National Idea," p. 100. Schama also talks about the Seven Years' War as a stimulant of patriotic culture (*Citizens,* pp. xv; 33–34).

205. *Les sauvages de l'Europe* (Berlin, 1760); quoted in Palmer, "National Idea," p. 100.

206. Pierre Laurent Buyrette de Belloy, *Le Siège de Calais,* preface, p. v.

207. Schama put it strongly: "For France, without any question, the Revolution began in America." *Citizens,* p. 24.

208. Alphonse Aulard, *Histoire politique de la révolution française* (Paris: Armand Colin, 1901), p. 20; *Lettres à Lord Shelburne, depuis Marquis de Lansdowne* (Paris: E. Plon, Nourrit et cie., 1898), p. 110.

209. That is, if any motivation besides general restlessness is to be attributed to them. Lafayette's motto is reported to be "Why not?" Schama, *Citizens,* p. 42.

210. Ibid.: Ségur quoted on p. 25, Lafayette on pp. 25, 40, Vergennes on p. 49.

211. *Journal de Genève,* 1779, quoted in Acomb, *Anglophobia,* p. 77. (See also "Observations impartiales sur la guerre actuelle des Anglois avec leur colonies," in *Journal historique et littéraire,* July 15, 1777, pt. II. [vol. CXLVII], p. 418.) Brissot quoted in Acomb, p. 83. On Brissot as the denizen of the fringes, see Darnton, *Literary Underground,* pp. 21–22, 35–38, 41–70. *Affaires de l'Angleterre et de l'Amérique,* vol. I, no. 1 (1776), quoted in Acomb, p. 85.

212. This work, although completed in 1772, was first published in 1782.

213. Tocqueville, *The Old Regime,* p. 146; Acomb, *Anglophobia,* p. 101.

214. Louis Edme Billardon de Sauvigny, *Washington: ou, La liberté du nouveau monde* (Princeton: Princeton University Press, 1941), Act I, Scene V; Camille Desmoulins, *La France libre,* 1793 (Paris: Ebrard, 1834), p. 67.

215. Napoléon, Decree of October 26, 1806, quoted in Kohn, "France between Britain and Germany," pp. 283–300.

216. Rouget de Lisle, "Chant de vengeances," 1797, in *Poésies nationales de la révolution française, ou Recueil complet des chants, hymnes, couplets, odes, chansons patriotiques* (Paris: Michel Fils Ainé & Bailly, 1836), pp. 285–287; Ponce-Denis E. Lebrun, "Ode nationale contre l'Angleterre," *Poésies,* pp. 292–296.

217. On the internal differentiation of the French bourgeoisie before the Revolution, see Elinor G. Barber, *The Bourgeoisie in Eighteenth-Century France* (Princeton: Princeton University Press, 1955).

218. Le Brun, *La voix de citoyen,* 1789 (?), quoted in Shafer, *Bourgeois Nationalism,* pp. 34, 35.

219. See Hyslop, *French Nationalism.*

220. For example in *Catéchisme national,* 1789, p. 10 (quoted in Shafer, "Bourgeois Nationalism," pp. 35–36): "Une nation est une société d'hommes libres, qui

vivent sous un même chef, ou plusieurs chefs qu'ils se sont donnés volontaire-
ment, pour ne faire qu'une seul et même corps dont l'âme sont les loix par
lesquelles ils prétendent être gouvernés."
221. A. J. Rupe (Raup) de Baptestein de Mouliers, *Mémoire sur un moyen facile et
infaillible de faire renaître le patriotisme en France, dans toutes les classes des
citoyens, comme dans les deux sexes . . .* , 1789, quoted in Shafer, "Bourgeois
Nationalism," p. 33, and references in ibid., p. 47.
222. Tocqueville, *The Old Regime,* p. 209.
223. For connotations of *Grande Nation,* see Godechot, "Nation, patrie," pp. 499–
500.

## 3. The Scythian Rome: Russia

1. Referred to in N. I. Pavlenko, "Idei absolutisma v zakonodatelstve XVIII
veka," in N. M. Druzhinin, ed., *Absolutism v Rossii* (Moscow: Nauka, 1964),
p. 398.
2. *Polnoie sobranie zakonov Rossiiskoi Imperii s 1649 goda* (hereafter cited as
*PSZ*), 1830, #1752, vol. IV, pp. 8–10, and others; #1804, vol. IV, pp. 66–72;
#2789, vol. V, pp. 91–95. This evolution of the concept helps to explain why
the Russian State was, less than anywhere else, the State of this or that class,
but "the State's State." A. Gerschenkron, *Europe in the Russian Mirror: Four
Lectures in Economic History* (Cambridge: Cambridge University Press,
1970), p. 79. It was identical with autocracy, or rather, with each and every
ruling autocrat. This also explains why, in Russia, the State never became identified with the Nation, but could be so easily defined as something alien to and
superimposed on it. An informative and thoroughly documented piece on this
issue is James Cracraft, "Empire versus Nation: Russian Political Theory under
Peter I," *Harvard Ukrainian Studies,* 10 (December 1986), pp. 524–541.
3. *PSZ,* #1910, vol. IV, pp. 192–193; #1899, vol. IV, p. 189.
4. For example, N. V. Riasanovsky, *A Parting of Ways: Government and the Educated Public in Russia, 1801–1855* (Oxford: The Clarendon Press, 1976),
p. 12; Paul Dukes, *Catherine the Great and the Russian Nobility: A Study
Based on the Materials of the Legislative Commission of 1767* (Cambridge:
Cambridge University Press, 1967), p. 1. The source of this opinion is a somewhat hasty generalization in the otherwise informative review of *PSZ* by Pavlenko, "Idei absolutisma."
5. *PSZ,* #2287; #2298; #2301, vol. IV, pp. 543–545, 560–567, 575–577, and
so on.
6. This important word—*otechestvo*—originated in the fifteenth century and
originally applied to patrimony of the princes—the right coming to them from
their fathers and grandfathers *(po otechestvu i po ded'stvu)*. Whenever there
was a need, however, as under the attack from the khan Ahmat in 1480, to
arouse broader masses and inspire them to sacrifice their lives for the defense
of princely patrimony, it was represented as something in which these broader
masses too had a vital interest and for which they therefore were expected to
care deeply. In such cases what was generally regarded as the private property

of the overlord thus acquired the highly evocative connotation of the *patrie*. See L. V. Cherepnin, "Uslovia formirovania russkoy narodnosti do konza XV veka," p. 102, in *Voprosy formirovania russkoy narodnosti i nazii* (Moscow: Academy of Sciences, 1958), pp. 70–106.

7. *PSZ,* #2210, #2221, #2224 (vol. IV, pp. 424–425, 440–442, 444–448), and others.

8. *PSZ,* #2315, vol. IV, p. 588; #3890, vol. VI, pp. 486–493; and #3840, vol. VI, pp. 444–445.

9. Brenda Meehan-Waters, *Autocracy and Aristocracy: The Russian Service Elite of 1730* (New Brunswick, N.J.: Rutgers University Press, 1982), pp. 60, 69. See also Cracraft, "Empire."

10. P. P. Shafirov, *Rassuzhdenie o zakonnykh prichinakh voiny mezdu Shvetsiey i Rossiey,* 1717, reproduced along with the original English translation, with an introduction by W. E. Butler, in *A Discourse Concerning the Just Causes of the War Between Sweden and Russia: 1700–1721* (Dobbs Ferry, N.Y.: Oceana Publications, 1973), pp. 73–77. The text of the *Discourse,* and the conclusion in particular, is representative of Peter's efforts to create a new secular language, which are also evident in his decrees. Very frequently one meets there with Russian transliterations on foreign words, supplemented with an explanation, or a Russian equivalent in parentheses. Many of Peter's or his collaborators' importations took root; some, like *sekul,* did not.

11. Butler, *Discourse,* p. 32.

12. *PSZ,* #3840, 1721, p. 445, my emphasis.

13. Pavlenko, "Idei absolutisma," pp. 410–412.

14. *PSZ,* #5499, 1730, vol. VIII, p. 247; #8262, 1740, vol. XI, pp. 276–277; #8473, 1741, vol. XI, pp. 537–538; and #11.390, 1761, vol. XV, p. 875.

15. According to Prince Shcherbatov, *O povrezhdenii nravov v Rossii* (St. Petersburg: V. Vrublensky, 1906), p. 69, the fateful Manifesto owed its creation to the need of the Emperor for an alibi for his official mistress concerning the night which he planned to spend with an unofficial one.

16. *PSZ,* #11.444, 1762 vol. XV, pp. 912–915.

17. Catherine II, *Zapiski Imperatrizy Ekateriny Vtoroy* (St. Petersburg, 1907), p. 585.

18. W. F. Reddaway, ed., *Documents of Catherine the Great: The Correspondence with Voltaire and the Instruction of 1767 in the English Text of 1768* (Cambridge: Cambridge University Press, 1931), pp. ix–xxiii; F. de Labriolle, "Le *prosvescenie* russe et les lumières en France, 1760–1798," *Revue des études slaves,* 45 (1966), pp. 75–91.

19. In Catherine II's *Zapiski,* I found only one remark that could be interpreted as openly contemptuous of Russia; this is the story of a stupid lady-in-waiting, on p. 114, regarding whom Catherine writes: "In any other country, instead of sending such a person to the Court . . . the whole family would try to hide her in a far corner."

20. Catherine II, *Zapiski,* p. 601. The very fact that Catherine did not choose to follow these examples and limit her activity to luxurious dressing, sitting in an armchair, and enjoying life, which would be the traditional, quite appropriate, and easy option, but actually ruled her vast country, in itself, it seems, is a basis for a measure of admiration.

21. Catherine II, *Zapiski*, p. 626; and *Nakaz Yeio Imperatorskavo Velichestva Yekateriny Vtoroy* (St. Petersburg: Akademia Nauk, 1770). (This is a document on which the Empress studiously worked several hours a day for two years, and which also became a favorite object of attacks, this time on her lack of originality and tendency to quote thoughts of others verbatim without due acknowledgment—a tendency which she duly acknowledged.) The substitution of the personal *I* for the usual royal WE in this last passage of the document, which, kept as it was in every edition, could not have been a slip of tongue, is telling. It was Catherine's personal glory that was at stake in the glory of Russia.

22. Catherine II, *Zapiski*, p. 647, and *PSZ*, #11.582, 1762, vol. XVI, pp. 3–4. She abolished the term "slave" in 1786, and one of the poets, Kapnist, celebrated this historical occasion in exalted verse. "On the Abolition of the Term Slave," in Clarence A. Manning, ed., *Anthology of Eighteenth-Century Russian Literature* (New York: King's Crown Press, 1951), vol. II, pp. 67–68.

23. *PSZ*, #11.598, 1762, vol. XVI, pp. 12–13.

24. The story about Walachia is told by Zernatto, "Nation," pp. 362–363.

25. *PSZ*, #11.584, 1762, vol. XVI, p. 4, and others, and #16.187, 1785, vol. XXII, pp. 344–358, specifically, pp. 345, 348.

26. Labriolle, "Le *prosvescenie*," p. 75.

27. *PSZ*, #16.187, "Charter of the Rights, Liberties, and Privileges of the Russian Nobility," p. 344, and #16.188, 1785, vol. XXII, p. 358.

28. J. Blum, "Russia," pp. 68–97, in D. Spring, ed., *European Nobility in the Nineteenth Century* (Baltimore: John Hopkins University Press, 1977), p. 68; M. Beloff, "Russia," pp. 172–181, in A. Goodwin, ed., *The European Nobility in the Eighteenth Century* (London: A. & Ch. Black, 1953), p. 173.

29. "Dvorianstvo," *Enziclopedicheskiy slovar'* (St. Petersburg: Brokhaus and Evfron), vol. X, pp. 203–218; Meehan-Waters, *Autocracy,* p. 138. (In the seventeenth century, an average member of the Boyar Council, who belonged to the upper echelon of servitors, held estates in six provinces—Meehan-Waters, p. 6.) S. N. Eisenstadt, *The Political Systems of Empires* (London: Free Press of Glencoe, 1963), p. 182.

30. "Mestnichestvo," *Enziclopedicheskiy slovar'*, vol. XX, p. 332.

31. Meehan-Waters, *Autocracy,* pp. 9, 11.

32. Ibid., pp. 2, 36.

33. Algarotti; quoted in Beloff, "Russia," p. 177.

34. Meehan-Waters, *Autocracy,* p. 18.

35. *PSZ*, #3890, pt. 11, p. 491.

36. This is dubious, however. There is no sign of relief in the evidence we have: literature and occasional diaries (for example, Dolgorukaia). It is probable, though, that during these decades, the experience of the crisis itself stabilized on a certain level and was not aggravated.

37. The succession crisis of 1730 itself was a sign of the sense of insecurity and discontent among the nobility and an eloquent expression of the suspicions its two sectors—the ancient and the new nobility—had of each other.

38. See note 15.

39. Catherine II, *Zapiski*, p. 533.

40. Beloff, "Russia," p. 181.

41. A. V. Romanovich-Slovatinski, *Dvorianstvo v Rossii ot nachala XVIII veka do otmeny krepostnogo prava* (St. Petersburg: Ministry of Internal Affairs, 1870), p. 212. See also Dukes, *Catherine the Great and the Russian Nobility,* p. 6.

42. Catherine II, *Zapiski,* p. 626; *PSZ,* #12.465, vol. XVII, p. 319; #12.723, vol. XVII, p. 938; #13.306, vol. XVIII, pp. 898–899. Also see M. M. Shtrange, *Demokraticheskaia intelligentsia Rossii XVIII veka* (Moscow: Nauka, 1965), pp. 262–263.

43. Dukes, *Catherine the Great and the Russian Nobility,* p. 84.

44. *PSZ,* "Charter of Nobility," #16.187, 1785; M. Diakov, "Dvoryanstvo," *Enzyclopedicheskii slovar',* vol. X, pp. 206–208.

45. Regarding the Commission, see Dukes, *Catherine the Great and the Russian Nobility,* pp. 55, 61–62; the *Instruction*—Beloff, "Russia," p. 187; the crisis in noble fortunes—P. G. Liubomirov, "Kniaz' Shcherbatov i ego sochinenia," pp. vi–xi, in M. M. Shcherbatov, *Neizdannye Sochinenia* (Moscow: Works of the State Historical Museum, 1935).

46. Dukes, *Catherine the Great and the Russian Nobility,* pp. 189–217; Riazanovsky, *Parting of Ways,* p. 14; Shtrange, *Demokraticheskaia intelligentisia,* pp. 254, 267; 255.

47. Novikov served on the Committee as a secretary, after which, in 1769, at the age of twenty-four, he founded his first periodical, *The Bumble Bee.*

48. The first Russian newspaper appeared in 1703 and was published by Peter. Several periodicals of the Academy of Sciences, Moscow University, and the Cadet Corps followed. Sumarokov's *Busy Bee* was the first journal published by a private person, and it lasted only one year (1759). The coming of age of the periodical press did not occur until Catherine. Already in the first half of her reign twenty different journals circulated, and the number grew steadily. Catherine herself was an active contributer and sponsored several publications.

49. Catherine II, *Zapiski,* p. 627.

50. Ya. B. Kniazhnin, *Izbrannye Proizvedenia* (Leningrad: Sovetskii Pisatel', 1961), "The Boaster" *(Hvastun),* Act I, Scene IV, p. 318.

51. Quoted in Dukes, *Catherine the Great and the Russian Nobility,* pp. 158, 147. The discussion of the Legislative Commission here relies on this excellent study of the noble opinion in it.

52. See ibid., pp. 178–180; 129, 142, 174.

53. Ibid., p. 122; Shcherbatov, "Zamechanie na bol'shoi Nakaz Ekateriny," pp. 16–64, in *Neizdannye Sochinenia,* p. 16; *O povrezhdenii nravov,* pp. 47, 16; Liubomirov, "Kniaz' Shcherbatov," p. xxviii.

54. A. P. Sumarokov, *Polnoe Sobranie vseh Sochinenii* (Moscow: Novikov, 1781), vol. IV, pp. 61–62; G. P. Makogonenko, ed., *Poety XVIII veka* (Leningrad: Sovetsky Pisatel', 1958), vol. I, p. 38. (It is significant that Sumarokov identified patriots with noblemen; his definition of the nation was very similar to that of Montesquieu: the nation was, for him, the elite of the country, not the country as a whole; his was fundamentally an estate patriotism.) Sumarokov, vol. VII, pp. 356, 358.

55. One finds this view already in the first Russian manual of manners addressed to young noblemen, *The Honest Mirror of Youth (Younosti chestnoe zertsalo).* Among different useful instructions, such as "Don't glut like a pig and don't blow . . . to spatter everywhere" or "Don't clean your teeth with a knife," it

included the following assertions: "Not a famous family and high birth make a nobleman, but noble and commendable deeds" and "A peasant would be more respected than a nobleman who does not keep his noble word and promise: that's why it happens even today, that some rather believe a peasant than a nobleman." *Younosti chestnoe zertsalo*, pp. 8–9, 11, in A. Alferov and A. Gruzinsky, eds., *Russkaia literatura XVII veka: Hrestomatia* (Moscow: Shkola, 1915).

56. Antiokh Kantemir, "Na zavist' i gordost' dvorian zlonravnyh," in Alferov and Gruzinsky, *Russkaia literatura*, pp. 81–82. For characterization of Kantemir, see Manning, *Anthology*, vol. I, p. 35.

57. G. Derzhavin, *Sochinenia Derzhavina* (St. Petersburg: Academy of Sciences, 1868), vol. I, pp. 431–433. For characterization, see Alferov and Gruzinsky, *Russkaia literatura*, p. 410.

58. *Enzyclopedicheskii slovar'*, p. 207.

59. The orthography of fon-Visin's name was changed into "Fonvisin" in the mid-nineteenth century by Professor Tihonravov, but Pushkin thought the change advisable much earlier, for, in his opinion, it would make the name more "Russian" and thus emphasize the national character of the writer he considered "the Russian of arch-Russians" *(iz pererusskih russkiy)*.

60. Denis Fonvisin, *The Minor*, Act III, Scene II; Act IV, Scene II, *Pervoe Polnoe Sobranie Sochinenii D. I. Fon-Visina, 1761–1792* (Moscow: K. Shamov, 1888), pp. 125, 138–139.

61. Fonvisin, "Questions," *Pervoe Polnoe Sobranie*, pp. 812–814.

62. Ibid., pp. 813–814.

63. Piotr Tolstoy, "Puteshestvie," 1697–1699; Andrey Matveev, "Visit to Paris," 1705; V. K. Trediakovskii, in Alferov and Gruzinsky, *Russkaia literatura*, pp. 24, 37, 89.

64. "Younosti Chestnoe Zertsalo," #4, in Alferov and Gruzinskii, *Russkaia literatura*, p. 7; Sumarokov, *Polnoe Sobranie*, vol. IV, p. 63.

65. See discussion of this criticism in Hans Rogger, *National Consciousness in Eighteenth-Century Russia* (Cambridge, Mass.: Harvard University Press, 1960).

66. Alferov and Gruzinsky, *Russkaia literatura*, p. 39.

67. In one of the earliest panegyrical dramas, *The Sad Glory* by Zhurovskii, written on the death of the tsar, Eternity extolls Peter for his untiring patriotism. He was

> All the time in labors, not sparing himself
> And moved only by love toward fatherland . . .

Quoted in L. V. Krestova, "Otrazhenie formirovania russkoi nazii v russkoi literature i publizistike pervoi poloviny XVIII veka," pp. 253–296, in *Voprosy formirovania*, p. 264.

68. I. I. Nepluyev, *Memoirs*, in Alferov and Gruzinsky, *Russkaia literatura*, p. 19. Nepluyev's memoirs offer an insight into the specific reasons why the Emperor was so deeply admired and enjoyed such passionate loyalty from people whose lives he, objectively speaking, disrupted and rendered very difficult. One reason was the enormous personal investment of these people in his reforms; they were not unlike the Marines in some respect. "We, the disciples of Peter the

Great," wrote Nepluyev, "were led by him through fire and water" (p. 16). The other had to do with the truly remarkable personality of the monarch. When Nepluyev, sent abroad to study, returned to Russia, he was examined by the tsar himself and upon successfully passing the examination was rewarded with an office and the privilege to kiss the august hand. "The sovereign, turning his hand palm up, gave it to me to kiss and said: 'You see, brother, I am a tsar, but I have corns on my hands; and everything for this: to be an example to you and at least in my old age to see to myself worthy helpers and servants to the fatherland'" (p. 18).

69. Feofan Prokopovich, "Slovo na pogrebenie," 1725, in Manning, *Anthology,* vol. I, pp. 25–26.

70. Quoted in Krestova, "Otrazhenie," p. 254.

71. Shafirov, *Rassuzhdenie,* the page before "Dedication" (pagination starts with the latter); Krestova, "Otrazhenie," p. 259.

72. Quoted in Krestova, "Otrazhenie," p. 256.

73. Nikolai Karamzin, *Polnoe Sobranie Sochinenii* (St. Petersburg: Selivanovsky, 1803), vol. IV, pp. 285, 283.

74. "It is very dangerous to believe foreigners," he says; "they are not our great good-wishers; for this reason, one should not rely too much on their sciences too." Krestova, "Otrazhenie," p. 259.

75. Sumarokov, *Polnoe Sobranie,* vol. VIII, pp. 359–361. (The title in this edition is "Another Choir to the Upside-down World.")

76. A. N. Radishchev, *Puteshestvie Iz Peterburga v' Moskvu,* in *Polnoe Sobranie Sochinenii* (St. Petersburg: Akinfiev, 1907), vol. I, p. 189.

77. "Il n'y a pas de paysan, en Russie, qui ne mange une poule quand il lui plait, et . . . depuis quelque temps, il y a des provinces où ils préférent les dindons aux poules," July 3–14, 1769, p. 30, in Reddaway, *Documents of Catherine the Great.*

78. The full title of the refutation is: *Die so genannte Moscowitische Brieffe, oder die, wider die löbliche Russische Nation von einem aus der andern Welt zurück gekommenen Italiäner ausgesprengte abendtheuerliche Verläumdungen und Tausend Lügen aus dem französischen übersetzt, mit einem zulänglichen Register versehen und dem Brieffsteller sowohl, als seinen gleichgesinnten Freunden mit dienlichen Erinnerungen wieder heimgeschickt von einem Teutschen* (Frankfurt and Leipzig: Verlegts Joh. Leopold Montag Buchhändler in Regenspurg, 1738). This discussion relies on Krestova, "Otrazhenie," pp. 267–275.

79. The *Letters* were first published in Karamzin's *Moscow Journal,* the most popular periodical of the time, which, by comparison with others, had an extraordinary number of subscribers: three hundred. They appeared again in 1797. "Their numerous readers became inconspicuously educated in the traditions of the European civilization; they as if matured with the maturing of the young Russian traveler, learning to feel with his noble feelings, to dream with his beautiful dreams." Buslayev in Alferov and Gruzinsky, *Russkaia literatura,* p. 449.

80. Karamzin, *Polnoe Sobranie,* vol. III, pp. 60–61, 179–180; vol. IV, pp. 280–288.

81. Fonvisin, *Pervoe Polnoe Sobranie,* Letter of April 1778 (from Paris, to his sister), p. 963.

82. That it was the "government of foreigners" seems to be the argument of the most comprehensive treatment of Russian eighteenth-century nationalism— Rogger, *National Consciousness*.

83. Quoted in ibid., p. 30.

84. There were no "men of mental labor" *(liudi umstvennogo truda)* outside the clergy, and if we exclude the several Ukrainians and Poles imported in the seventeenth century to entertain the Moscow Court, in Russia before this time.

85. In the 1720s only one of the five St. Petersburg shipyards employed more than ten thousand workers.

86. The students in these schools were *raznochinzy*—they belonged to that residual category of people excluded from the taxable population (peasants, merchants, and artisans) who did not belong to the nobility or clergy, the two groups which composed the service sector. Admission to a school was regarded as entrance into state service and implied exclusion from the taxable category. Military draft had the same implication, and thus "soldiers' sons" born after their fathers were drafted were *raznochinzy* too.

87. It was formally founded by Peter, as an Academy of Sciences and Arts, in 1724.

88. The discussion of the emergent system of Russian education is based on Shtrange, *Demokraticheskaia intelligentsia,* and articles in the *Entsiclopedicheskii slovar'* of Brokhaus and Evfron and the *Great Soviet Encyclopedia.* All the figures are taken from Shtrange.

89. These figures refer only to secular education. For comparison, see the numbers in Dukes, *Catherine the Great and the Russian Nobility,* p. 244.

90. This calculation is based on the information in Shtrange, *Demokraticheskaia intelligentsia,* which does not at all focus on this remarkable circumstance. The number of Ukrainians among the non-noble intellectuals discussed by Shtrange is extraordinary; it is beyond doubt that they played a very prominent role in the activities of the eighteenth-century intelligentsia; at the same time, the figures have to be systematically checked before a reliable estimate can be arrived at. Fifty percent is an impressionistic assessment.

91. Quoted from Shumliansky and Znamensky by ibid., pp. 58, 22.

92. The growth of the sense of self-respect under the impact of education is illustrated by the tragic story of Nicholai Smirnov, a talented serf of the Golitsyns. His father, an able administrator who enjoyed the favor of his masters, with the help of hired tutors gave Nicholai an excellent education, which the boy continued in Moscow University, which he attended "privately," owing to an arrangement with the director, since without being freed by the masters, he could not be formally enrolled. He proved himself a brilliant student. But with the improvement of his education his sense of degradation (by his status as a serf) also grew. "The humiliating name of a serf made slavery appear to me as a heavy chain which oppressed me." He asked to be freed, his appeal was refused, and the youth decided to flee abroad. Caught, he was first condemned to hard labor, then made a soldier in Tobolsk and heard about no more (ibid., p. 207). The number of suicides among members of this group also attests to their uneasiness. See ibid.

93. Quoted in ibid., pp. 83, 99.

94. Trediakovsky, "Stihi pohval'nye Rossii," and "Pohvala Izherskoi zemle i tzarstvuyuschemy gradu Sanktpeterburgu," in Manning, *Anthology,* vol. I, pp. 41–

42. For characterization of the poet, see Alferov and Gruzinsky, *Russkaia literatura,* p. 89. In the *Enzyclopedicheskii slovar',* Trediakovskii is characterized thus: "A prominent Russian scholar of the eighteenth century and an unsuccessful poet, whose name became an adjective for the mediocre poetasters" (E. Lyatskii, vol. XXXIII, p. 750). Lyatskii adds that Trediakovskii was "one of the most educated people of the contemporary Russian society."

95. Derzhavin's characterization, quoted in Rogger, *National Consciousness,* p. 259.

96. M. V. Lomonosov, "Anniversary Ode of 1747," in *Sochinenia Lomonosova* (St. Petersburg: A. Smirdin, 1847), vol. I, p. 94; *Sochinenia* (St. Petersburg, 1891), vol. V, p. 143; vol. I, pp. 119, 135.

97. *Sochinenia,* vol. II, p. 252. This exclusion, apparently, applied only to Westerners; it seems Lomonosov considered Ukrainians to be "native" enough.

98. Krestova, "Otrazhenie," p. 282.

99. Quoted in Shtrange, *Demokraticheskaia intelligentsia,* pp. 107, 98. This egalitarianism was sometimes expressed in openly anti-noble attitudes, one conspicuous instance of which was the forged anti-noble decree found in 1764 in the Senate, where many of the graduates of the Academic and Moscow universities were employed as secretaries, copyists, and other clerical workers. Ibid., p. 117.

100. Ibid., p. 74 (regarding Popovskii), and M. V. Lomonosov, *Polnoe Sobranie Sochinenii* (Moscow: Academy of Sciences, 1957), vol. X, *Sluzhebnye dokumenty i pis'ma, 1734–1765 gg,* p. 55.

101. W. E. Brown, *A History of Eighteenth-Century Russian Literature* (Ann Arbor, Mich.: Ardis, 1980), p. 88.

102. Lomonosov, *Polnoe Sobranie Sochinenii,* vol. X, p. 497 (Letter to Shuvalov, November 1, 1753); p. 554 (Letter to Teplov, January 30, 1761). Science is valued as a condition and a component of the national greatness. This is so in the West, where great men of letters and scientists toil "to increase the pride" of their compatriots (Letter to Shuvalov, May 10, 1753); and so it should be in Russia, which as "clearly a [the?] most important member in the European system requires [cultural] splendor appropriate for and fitting its majesty and power" (*Sochinenia,* vol. V, p. 143). In letters to his noble patrons (for instance, Count Shuvalov), Lomonosov insists on this yet unfulfilled necessity and, comparing the situation of academics in Russia and the West, emphasizes the lamentable inadequacy of their support in Russia. In his poetry, however, perhaps as a rhetorical device, he represents his dreams as an established fact. The interrelation of science and national greatness is unambiguously expressed in the "Anniversary Ode of 1747." In it, Lomonosov depicts the reigning Empress, Elizabeth, as a great patroness of science, thereby exhorting her to become one. The poet exhorts Elizabeth: "Look at the high mountains / Look at your broad valleys / Where Volga, Dneper, and Ob' flow: / The secret riches of all these / Will be uncovered by science / Which flourishes due to your generosity," and says to the Russian scientists: "Oh, your days are blessed / Encouraged, dare now to show / With your assiduity that / the Russian land can bring to birth its own Platos and Newtons, swift of reason." (The translation of the last part of the sentence is Brown's, *A History,* p. 88.)

103. Noblemen such as Sumarokov also contributed to the development of the Russian tongue (see Rogger, *National Consciousness*, p. 104), but their individual efforts are less important than the collective effort of the intelligentsia.

104. Trediakovskii quoted in ibid., p. 99; Lomonosov, *Sochinenia*, vol. I, pp. 528–529.

105. Lomonosov, *Rossiiskaia grammatika* (St. Petersburg: Academy of Sciences, 1755), preface, pp. 6–7; the translation is Rogger's, *National Consciousness*, p. 103. Rogger justly emphasizes the similarity between this panegyric to Russian and Richard Carew's *Epistle;* the similarity is all the more striking, since it is certain that Lomonosov was unaware of minor English writers of the sixteenth century.

106. Shtrange, *Demokraticheskaia intelligentsia*, pp. 61, 84, 70, 171, 49.

107. Quoted in ibid., p. 214.

108. Rogger, *National Consciousness*, p. 194.

109. Bashilov, quoted in Shtrange, *Demokraticheskaia intelligentsia*, p. 158; Lomonosov in ibid., p. 157; Rogger, *National Consciousness*, p. 221. In general, see Rogger, pp. 202–220. Not only Germans, however, incurred Lomonosov's patriotic indignation. When another Russian patriot, a Ukrainian, as was so often the case, G. A. Poletika, wrote in 1757 a treatise "On the Beginning, Restoration, and Spread of Learning and Schools in Russia and on Their Current State," Lomonosov condemned the work, for the researcher failed to find any schools between the tenth and the seventeenth centuries to speak of (on the flimsy ground that there were none), and the treatise was not published. Shtrange, pp. 80–81.

110. Quoted in Rogger, *National Consciousness*, p. 220.

111. This opinion is justified, for there is a break in continuity between the non-noble intelligentsia of the mid-eighteenth century and that of the nineteenth, while the noble intelligentsia of the end of the century is directly connected to the nineteenth-century stratum for which the name was coined. See Marc Raeff, *Origins of the Russian Intelligentsia: The Eighteenth-Century Nobility* (New York: Harcourt, Brace and World, 1966).

112. "The Word of the Russian tribe, which was renovated in our time by you, will be carried in the mouth of the people over the boundless horizon of centuries." Radischev, *Puteshestvie*, p. 220.

113. Novikov, April 12, 1772, in Alferov and Gruzinsky, *Russkaia literatura*, p. 210; Fonvisin, *Pervoe Polnoe Sobranie*, p. 827; Derzhavin, "Pamiatnik," in *Sochinenia Derzhavina*, vol. I, p. 534.

114. Catherine quoted in Rogger, *National Consciousness*, p. 113; Karamzin, *Polnoe Sobranie*, vol. V, p. 346.

115. Karamzin, *Istoria gosudarstva rossiiskovo* (St. Petersburg: E. Evdokimov, 1892), vol. I, pp. xvii–xix. This is the same Karamzin who, breathing the mountain air in the Alps, talked about being a citizen of the world as the true destiny of man.

116. It is equally revealing that Karamzin became one of the most popular writers in Gorbachev's Russia.

117. Karamzin, *Zapiska o drevney i novoy Rossii*, ed. Richard Pipes (Cambridge, Mass.: Harvard University Press, 1959), p. 22. See the analysis of Karamzin's

ideas and their background in Pipes, *Karamzin's Memoir of Ancient and Modern Russia* (Cambridge, Mass.: Harvard University Press, 1959).

118. From the French *petit maître;* see the excellent discussion in Rogger, *National Consciousness,* p. 48 et passim.

119. Kniazhnin, *Izbrannye Proizvedenia,* "Neschastie ot karety," Act II, Scene V, p. 582.

120. *Vral'* means "a liar"; *man* is a German ending; "Vral'man"—the name of the German tutor in *The Minor.*

121. Novikov, *Truten',* p. xviii, August 11, 1769, in Alferov and Gruzinsky, *Russkaia literatura,* pp. 206–207.

122. Fonvisin, *Pervoe Polnoe Sobranie,* pp. 897–898, 903–909. The letters are addressed to Count P. I. Panin.

123. Incidentally, like many of Fonvisin's other aphorisms, this phrase is translated from Duclos.

124. Chaadaev was proclaimed insane by Nicholas II; his "First Philosophical Letter," published in 1836, was actually written in 1829.

125. Hans Rogger, in his sensitive description, presented the incipient national consciousness in eighteenth-century Russia as evolving in a series of antitheses, one element in each pair reflecting an aspect of Western society and culture as perceived by Russians, and the other, its opposite, upheld as a quality of Russian national character. These were antitheses, such as mind and heart, form and substance, age and youth. The list can be continued indefinitely, for the series is organized around one principle: every pair is but a variation on the theme of the rejection of reason.

126. Fonvisin, "Chistoserdechnoe priznanie v delach moich i pomyshleniach" in *Pervoe Polnoe Sobranie,* p. 856; Karamzin, *Polnoe Sobranie,* vol. VII, "O naukah," pp. 77, 20, 24; Fonvisin, *The Minor,* Act III, Scene I; Act IV, Scene I; pp. 121–122, 138.

127. Quoted in Rogger, *National Consciousness,* p. 270.

128. Fonvisin, *Pervoe Polnoe Sobranie,* p. 907; Derzhavin, *Sochinenia Derzhavina,* vol. I, p. 435.

129. "Yunosti chestnoe zerzalo," pp. 5–13, in Alferov and Gruzinsky, *Russkaia literatura,* #50, #27; Novikov, *Truten',* p. xxiv, October 6, 1769, in Alferov and Gruzinsky, p. 207.

130. M. D. Chulkov, "A Bitter Dole," from *Peresmeshnik ili Slavianskie Skazki,* pp. 110–114, in Manning, *Anthology,* p. 111.

131. Karamzin, *Zapiska,* pp. 72–74 (Russian text); Fonvisin, *Pervoe Polnoe Sobranie,* p. 908.

132. Isaiah Berlin, in "Herzen and Bakunin on Individual Liberty," pp. 82–113, in *Russian Thinkers* (London: Penguin Books, 1948), has forcefully argued that Alexander Herzen was such an exception; I attempt to show why I disagree with this.

133. Pushkin (in an unpublished letter to Chaadaev, quoted in Leonard Schapiro, *Rationalism and Nationalism in Russian Nineteenth-Century Political Thought* [New Haven: Yale University Press, 1967], p. 46), was to place him alongside Peter and Catherine the Great as another example of the Russian

genius—what other country could boast of such a pleiad of extraordinary, spirited people on the throne?

134. Kahovsky to General Levashev, in Thomas Riha, ed., *Readings in Russian Civilization* (Chicago: University of Chicago Press, 1969), p. 297; Bestuzhev in ibid., p. 299; Kahovsky in ibid., pp. 297, 298. Leonard Schapiro *(Rationalism and Nationalism)* wrote about Decembrists: "There can be no doubt . . . that national pride, far from being an incidental element in their outlook, was a dominant motive in determining their political attitudes. They were above all overwhelmed by strong feelings of resentment and humiliation because the military triumph of 1812 had not brought any commensurate political progress in its train" (p. 29).

135. R. T. McNally, ed. and trans., *The Major Works of Peter Chaadaev* (Notre Dame, Ind.: Notre Dame University Press, 1969), p. xvii.

136. Chaadaev in McNally, *Major Works,* "First Philosophical Letter," p. 32.

137. Ibid., pp. 27, 29–30, 35, 37, 38, 40; 42, 34, 44, 32.

138. Benkendorf, quoted by Riazanovsky, *Parting of Ways,* p. 171.

139. A. I. Herzen, *Polnoe Sobranie Sochinenii i Pisem,* ed. M. K. Lemke (Petrograd, 1915–1925), vol. XI, p. 11 (Letter 1539, 1861).

140. Schapiro, *Rationalism and Nationalism,* sees nineteenth-century political thought in Russia as split into traditions of rationalism and nationalism, Westernism being fundamentally rationalist, and Slavophilism representing nationalism. I do not think that this distinction is applicable to Russian thought in general; it certainly cannot characterize the differences between and the nature of Westernism and Slavophilism. Both were species of nationalism, and both were very far from rationalism, unless we assign the term a very peculiar, idiosyncratic meaning.

141. Kireevskii, Khomiakov, and Aksakov, quoted in Riasanovsky, *Parting of Ways,* pp. 183, 179, 193, 187.

142. Aksakov, in ibid., p. 192. In the nineteenth century the development of particular nationalisms was no longer autarchic, and nationalist ideas which fit in the matrix were freely borrowed from other countries and added to the inchoate indigenous traditions. The awareness of Western, particularly German, thought among the nineteenth-century Russian elite is ubiquitous, and almost every nationalist idea has a parallel—and a classic expression—in Fichte, Hegel, or their contemporaries and followers. Yet, in most instances, such parallels were cases of simultaneous invention, for they grew out of very similar matrices which indeed developed independently. Even in the cases of a wholesale borrowing, such as the adoption of Marxism, such borrowing was due to the perfect fit between the nationalist aspirations in Russia and the particular imported solution.

143. Granovsky, quoted in Schapiro, *Rationalism and Nationalism,* pp. 80; 79; Herzen, *Polnoe Sobranie,* vol. XII, p. 28 (*My Past and Thoughts,* pt. IV).

144. V. G. Belinsky, *Pis'mo k Gogolu* (Moscow: OGIZ, 1947), pp. 3–9.

145. Herzen, *Polnoe Sobranie,* vol. XIII, p. 26.

146. In the review of Zhukovsky's "Anniversary of Borodino," Belinsky eulogized autocracy: "Our *freedom* is in the tsar"; "Our unconditional obedience to the

tsar's authority is not only our benefit and our necessity, but also the highest poetry of our life, our *nationality,* if one is to understand by the word 'nationality' a merging of private individualities through a general consciousness of one's State personality and identity." See the discussion in Riasanovsky, *Parting of Ways,* pp. 213–216.

147. Herzen, *Polnoe Sobranie,* vol. XIII, p. 37; Granovsky, quoted in Schapiro, *Rationalism and Nationalism,* p. 76. Berlin's argument ("Herzen") regarding Herzen's exceptionalism hinges on the interpretation of Herzen's views as essentially libertarian and individualistic, which was indeed exceptional in Russia as well as in most of Continental Europe. But Herzen was a perfect Russian; he was such an attractive, fascinating, extraordinary personality because he was a perfect Russian, because he so fully imbibed the spirit of this beguiling culture; and for this reason he held no views that were not in this culture. Liberal individualism emphatically was not in it. Herzen was an elitist who held masses—and individuals who composed masses—in utter contempt; he did not uphold their liberty. The individual whose unlimited liberty he craved with all the passion of which he was capable, and the craving for which he expressed in that fiery, ardent language, the very power of which is the power to blind readers to its meaning, was himself, and people like himself, the special individual, the prophet and the leader. Herzen was no John Stuart Mill; Mill, also an elitist, cared for the masses and believed that they could and should be elevated by education. For Herzen, masses were irredeemable.

148. M. Bakunin, quoted in Riasanovsky, *Parting of Ways,* p. 218; Herzen, *Polnoe Sobranie,* vol. XIII, p. 37; Schapiro, p. 100.

149. It may be necessary to stress that the fact that the composition of the cultural elite changed in the course of the nineteenth century, and that at least since the 1860s *raznochinzy* predominated in it, did not fundamentally affect the nature of its concerns. These were inherited from the noble nationalists of the earlier period, appropriated, and developed. Far from being determined by "material" existence, this inherited consciousness of the Russian intelligentsia shaped life, defining people's aspirations and passions and channeling their energies in certain directions.

150. V. I. Lenin, *Polnoie Sobranie Sochineniy,* 1914, vol. XXVI, pp. 106–110.

151. I borrowed from the translation by C. E. Bechhofer (London: Chatto and Windus, 1920).

152. "Scythians" is another reminder that beauty has little to do with other virtues. This magnificent, majestic poem knows parallels only in music, of Borodin and Rimsky-Korsakov, written in the same mood (for in music one may express what one wishes without the fear of being taken at one's word). There is no possibility of doing it justice in translation. And yet it was written for this audience to hear. (The text is a significantly modified translation by Babette Deutsch and Avrahm Yarmolinsky, *Russian Poetry: An Anthology* [New York: International Publishers, 1927], pp. 187–189.)

153. For the sake of the rhythm Blok speaks of Paestums, but there is no doubt that it is the City Rome, the embodiment of Western civilization, whose destruction he foretells.

154. Ovid, *Tristia,* V, VII, 46. I am indebted for this reference to Rory Childers,

whose article "Mandelstam and Soviet Power," in L. Greenfeld and M. Martin, eds., *Center: Ideas and Institutions* (Chicago: University of Chicago Press, 1988), drew my attention to the pervasiveness of the theme of Rome vs. Scythians in Russian literature of the nineteenth and early twentieth centuries, and gave me the idea for the title of this chapter.

## 4. The Final Solution of Infinite Longing: Germany

1. On the meaning of *Nation* in German, and specifically on the conciliar meaning, see Joachim Ritter and Karlfried Gründer, eds., *Historisches Wörterbuch der Philosophie* (Basel and Stuttgart: Schnabe & Co. AG, 1984), vol. VI, pp. 406–414.
2. Hajo Holborn, *A History of Modern Germany*, vol. I, *The Reformation* (New York: Alfred A. Knopf, 1973), p. 57.
3. Gerald Strauss, trans. and ed., *Manifestations of Discontent in Germany on the Eve of the Reformation*, a collection of documents (Bloomington: Indiana University Press, 1971), p. 192.
4. Bebel, Celtis, Crotus Rubeanus, Eobanus, and Glareanus were peasant sons. Holborn, *Modern Germany*, p. 107.
5. "There was hardly a humanist writer who did not at one time or another charge that Germany's past history and present achievements were being shamefully concealed and flagrantly falsified by malevolent and covetous foreigners." Strauss, *Manifestations*, pp. 64–65.
6. Ritter and Gründer, *Historisches Wörterbuch*, pp. 407–408.
7. "Wie wir pflegen gegen alle Nation," p. 1947, *Stücke von Esther*, D. Martin Luther, *Die ganze Heilige Schrift Deutsch, 1545* (München: Rogner & Bernhard, 1972), vol. II. The English text (from the Standard Edition of the Bible, after the version of 1611) is "[the favor] that we show toward every nation." The location in the Greek text is Esther 8. 121 (p. 968).
8. This disintegration was symbolized in the formula "cujus regio ejus religio," and in the middle of the seventeenth century it was legalized and made a fact of international politics by the Peace of Westphalia.
9. Holborn, *Modern Germany*, p. 31.
10. In the sixteenth century the common meaning of *Staat* (state) was "status" or social position. Thus it is plausible that the modern German concept of the state represented the result of the reinterpretation of the prince's social position in the light of Protestant doctrine. It was a creation of Protestant doctrine, whether or not *Staat* as status was its point of departure. See *Adelungs Wörterbuch*, 1801, pp. 258–259; *Trübners Deutsches Wörterbuch* (Berlin: Verlag Walter de Grunter & Co., 1956), vol. VII, pp. 508–509.
11. Marc Raeff, "The Well-Ordered Police State and the Development of Modernity in Seventeenth- and Eighteenth-Century Europe: An Attempt at a Comparative Approach," *American Historical Review*, 80:5 (1975), p. 1222.
12. The growing needs of the state thus defined produced the first large group that developed such loyalty—the corps of the bureaucracy, which, although ideal-typical, was not typical at all, but also peculiar to Germany. These officials, no

matter where they came from, identified neither with the interests of the prince nor with those of their own social groups, but with the state.

13. Hermann Conring, *De Origine Juris Germanici,* 1643; quoted in Erik Wolf, "Idee und Wircklichkeit des Reiches im deutschen Rechtsdenken des 16. und 17. Jahrhunderts," in Karl Larenz, ed., *Reich und Recht in der deutschen Philosophie* (Berlin, 1943), pp. 111–113; also quoted by Leonard Krieger in "Germany," in Orest Ranum, ed., *National Consciousness, History, and Political Culture in Early-Modern Europe* (Baltimore: Johns Hopkins University Press, 1975), p. 85.

14. Krieger, "Germany," p. 85.

15. William Jannen, Jr., "'Das Liebe Teutschland' in the Seventeenth Century— Count George Frederick von Waldeck," *European Studies Review,* 6 (1976), pp. 165–195.

16. Krieger, "Germany," p. 71.

17. Charles Ingrao, "The Problem of 'Enlightened Absolutism' and the German States," *Journal of Modern History,* 58, supplement (December 1986), pp. 161–180; 170. Also see Charles Ingrao, "'Barbarous Strangers': Hessian State and Society during the American Revolution," *American Historical Review,* 87: 4 (1982), pp. 954–976, and Raeff, "The Well-Ordered Police State."

18. Quoted in A. Goodwin, "Prussia," in A. Goodwin, ed., *The European Nobility in the Eighteenth Century* (London: Adams and Charles Black, 1953), p. 88.

19. Ibid., pp. 85–87; Holborn, *Modern Germany,* vol. II, *1648–1840,* pp. 196–197. Goodwin discusses other examples of the economic encroachment on the nobility, specifically the conversion of royal estates into a family landed trust, which prevented the passing of these lands into the hands of the nobility, and encouraged the rise of middle-class estate-managers.

20. See Robert M. Berdahl, "The *Stände* and the Origins of Conservatism in Prussia," *Eighteenth-Century Studies,* 6:3 (Spring 1973), pp. 298–321; W. H. Bruford, *Germany in the Eighteenth Century: The Social Background of the Literary Revival* (Cambridge: Cambridge University Press, 1935); Goodwin, "Prussia," and Holborn, *Modern Germany,* vol. II.

21. Berdahl, "The *Stände,*" p. 301.

22. Quoted in Holborn, *Modern Germany,* vol. II, p. 203.

23. Goodwin, "Prussia," pp. 89–90, 94; Henri Brunschwig, *Enlightenment and Romanticism in Eighteenth-Century Prussia* (Chicago: University of Chicago Press, 1974; original French ed., 1947), p. 54; Berdahl, "The *Stände,*" p. 302; Holborn, *Modern Germany,* vol. II, p. 264.

24. Brunschwig, *Enlightenment,* p. 82.

25. Goodwin, "Prussia," p. 93.

26. Frederick II, *Political Correspondence,* quoted in Brunschwig, *Enlightenment,* pp. 51–52.

27. Brunschwig, *Enlightenment,* p. 53.

28. Bruford, *Germany in the Eighteenth Century,* p. 51.

29. Charles E. McClelland, *State, Society, and University in Germany, 1700–1914* (Cambridge: Cambridge University Press, 1980), pp. 37, 43–45.

30. Friedrich Paulsen, *The German Universities and University Study,* trans. F. Thilly and W. Elwang (New York: Charles Scribner's Sons, 1906), p. 48.

31. McClelland, *State, Society,* p. 46.

32. Ibid., p. 28. There were twenty-eight universities in Germany that year, not including the Austrian schools. Three more were added later in the century.

33. It was, most probably, larger than that: we lack some initial data and do not take into account the population, which must have been already significant, in 1700. A more accurate approximation may be 120,000.

34. McClelland, *State, Society,* p. 47; Bruford, *Germany in the Eighteenth Century,* p. 159.

35. Bruford, *Germany in the Eighteenth Century,* p. 193.

36. Mme La Baronne de Stael, *Oeuvres Complètes,* vol. X, *De L'Allemagne* (Paris: Treuttel et Wurtz, 1820), p. 109.

37. Henri Brunschwig sees trained unemployability in the late eighteenth century as a function, first and foremost, of the dramatic increase in population, the cause of the economic crisis in many areas and strata. This general increase in the population may partly account for the influx of the nobility into government service. Brunschwig (*Enlightenment,* p. 128) cites the yearly average of 13.2 appointments at the rank of *Referendar* in Prussia, as compared with 117 appointments of a comparable rank in the legal branch.

38. Quoted in ibid., p. 125.

39. *Der teutsche Merkur,* 1785, quoted in ibid., p. 135.

40. McClelland, *State, Society,* p. 80.

41. Martha Woodmansee, "The Genius and the Copyright: Economic and Legal Conditions of the Emergence of the 'Author,'" *Eighteenth-Century Studies,* 17:3 (Summer 1984), pp. 425–448, quoting from a contemporary catalogue; p. 433; Brunschwig's numbers are 3,000 in 1773, and 6,000 in 1787.

42. Wieland quoted in Brunschwig, *Enlightenment,* p. 140; Lessing, Schiller—in Woodmansee, "The Genius and the Copyright," pp. 431, 432.

43. *Athenaeum: Eine Zeitschrift von August Wilhelm Schlegel und Friedrich Schlegel* (Hamburg: Rowohlt), vol. I, p. 103, "Athenaeum Fragment" #20. Unless otherwise indicated, the translation is from the English edition, Friedrich Schlegel, *Lucinde and the Fragments* (Minneapolis: University of Minnesota Press, 1971). This quotation is from p. 163.

44. Bruford, *Germany in the Eighteenth Century,* p. 279.

45. Johann Wolfgang Goethe, *The Truth and Fiction Relating to My Life,* pt. II, Book X, in *Complete Works* (New York: P.F. Collier & Son, n.d.), vol. II, p. 9, and Book XII, pp. 108–109. Regarding authors' attitudes toward money, and the changing status of literary activity, see Levin Ludwig Schücking, *Die Soziologie der literarischen Geschmacksbildung* (München: Rosl, 1923).

46. See Martha Woodmansee, "The Genius and the Copyright."

47. Quoted in Brunschwig, *Enlightenment,* p. 151.

48. "Der durch bürgerliche Verhältnisse unterdrückten Menschheit," Karl Philipp Moritz, *Anton Reiser: Ein psychologischer Roman,* Mit den Abbildungen der Ausgabe von 1785, Insel Taschenbuch 433 (Frankfurt am Main: Insel Verlag, 1979), p. 315. All the quotations, unless otherwise specified, are given in P. E. Matheson's translation: Carl Philipp Moritz, *Anton Reiser: A Psychological Novel* (Westport, Conn.: Hyperion Press, 1978; reprint of 1926 Oxford University Press ed.). Matheson translates this sentence (p. 329) as "humanity oppressed by its *social* conditions"; this does not, however, transmit the meaning of *bürgerliche,* with its emphasis on middle-class, plebeian reality.

49. Mme Guyon was a Quietist; the tenets of her doctrine, however, on the whole closely resembled Pietism.

50. Moritz, *Anton Reiser*, pp. 9, 10–11, 26, 44, 73, 51, 55.

51. Ibid., pp. 130, 119, 129, 147, 149–151.

52. Ibid., pp. 163, 170, 176, 162, 178–179, 187, 199.

53. Ibid., pp. 236, 237–238, 264.

54. Ibid., pp. 247, 277, 274, 278, 289, 315, 319.

55. Ibid., pp. 328–329. Matheson's translation is modified here.

56. Ibid., pp. 295, 431.

57. See Brunschwig, *Enlightenment*, pp. 26–32; 132–135 on the plight of the teachers, clergy, and so on.

58. Nicolai in ibid., p. 141; Bruford, *Germany in the Eighteenth Century*, pp. 279–286, cites numbers of subscribers and buyers of various contemporary publications. They varied between a few hundred (for instance, for Goethe's *Works*, 1787–1790) and a few thousand (for Schiller's *Tell* or *Historische Kalendar für Damen*, to which famous writers contributed).

59. All quotations are from Immanuel Kant, "What Is Enlightenment?" in Kant's *Political Writings*, ed. H. Reiss (London: Cambridge University Press, 1970), pp. 54–60; 58.

60. Brunschwig, *Enlightenment*, p. 90.

61. G. P. Gooch, *Germany and the French Revolution* (New York: Russell & Russell, 1966), p. 5.

62. Wieland, Johannes Müller, Niebuhr, quoted in ibid., pp. 2, 4.

63. Goethe, *Truth and Fiction*, vol. I, Book II, pp. 39–40; 60.

64. Quoted in Gooch, *Germany*, p. 33.

65. Schiller, Lessing, quoted in ibid., p. 34.

66. "Le mouvement religieux le plus puissant en Allemagne depuis la Réforme." Gerhard Kaiser, "L'éveil du sentiment national: Rôle du piétisme dans la naissance du patriotisme," *Archives de sociologie des religions*, 22 (July–December 1966), p. 59.

67. Max Weber, *The Protestant Ethic and the Spirit of Capitalism* (New York: Charles Scribner and Sons, 1958), p. 139.

68. "Pietistic roots may be found in earlier mystical movements like those of Jakob Boehme, Valentin Weigel and Gichtel, in the earlier church poetry, particularly in the work of Paul Gerhardt, and the work of more emotional and moralistic theologians like Johannes Arndt, Theophilus Grossgebauer, Christan Scriver, and Balthasar Schuppius." Koppel S. Pinson, *Pietism as a Factor in the Rise of German Nationalism* (New York: Columbia University Press, 1934), p. 13.

69. "By 1700," says Pinson (ibid., p. 16) "there were about 32 cities in which the Pietists had attained to a position of great influence."

70. Weber, *Protestant Ethic*, p. 130.

71. Quoted from Spangenberg by Pinson, *Pietism*, p. 22.

72. Moritz, *Anton Reiser*, p. 18.

73. Pinson, *Pietism*, pp. 19–20.

74. Ibid., p. 24; Arlie J. Hoover, *The Gospel of Nationalism: German Patriotic Preaching from Napoleon to Versailles* (Stuttgart: Franz Steiner Verlag Wiesbaden GmbH, 1986), p. 8.

75. Quoted in Kaiser, "L'éveil," p. 68.

76. Quoted in Pinson, *Pietism*, p. 24. See Hoover, *Gospel of Nationalism*, p. 22, who relies on Ernst Troeltsch, *Protestantism and Progress: A Historical Study of the Relation of Protestantism to the Modern World.*

77. Friedrich Daniel Ernst Schleiermacher, *The Life of Schleiermacher as Unfolded in His Autobiography and Letters,* trans. F. Rowan (London: Smith, Elder & Co., 1860), vol. I, Letters to Henrietta Herz of March 27, and February 22, 1799, pp. 203, 189; and *On Religion: Speeches to Its Cultural Despisers* (New York: Ungar, 1955), pp. 82, 135.

78. Schleiermacher, *Life,* vol. II, Letter of November 8, 1808, from Henrietta von Willich to Schleiermacher, and Letter of November 27, 1808, from Schleiermacher to Henrietta von Willich, pp. 150–151; 157–158.

79. Weber, *Protestant Ethic,* p. 139. Moritz recalled how the landlady of little Anton's house, a shoemaker's wife, liked Anton to read to her from Carl von Moser's *Daniel in the Lion's Den,* "because it sounded to her so 'moral': which meant to her, so elevated; and of a certain preacher, who always preached in a very bombastic tone, she said she liked him because his sermons were so 'moral.'" This, Moritz adds in a footnote, is "another proof how careful we ought to be in books and talk with the people to refrain from such expressions as are not current among the people. In England even the most uneducated man knows what 'moral' means." Moritz, *Anton Reiser,* p. 32.

80. Kaiser, "L'éveil," p. 75. Zinzendorf spoke of "national religions" as specific forms chosen by God "to teach people, in accordance with their particular aptitudes and in accordance with the climate of their countries, the truth and the love of His Son" (ibid., fn. 73).

81. Weber, *Protestant Ethic,* pp. 131–132.

82. Kaiser, "L'éveil," p. 61.

83. "On en arrive," writes Kaiser, "de la sorte à un véritable culte du sang et des blessures analogue au culte de la Passion de Jesus-Christ tel que l'exerce le piétisme et, en particulier, le herrnhutisme" (ibid., p. 70). Some evidence of this effect of Christian mysticism, elements of which are present in Lutheranism, can be found in earlier periods and among Lutherans who were not Pietists as well: the exaggerated naturalism of Matthias Grünewald's Isenheim "Crusifiction," which knows no equal as a pictorial representation of physical pain, or the harrowing yet enthralling emotion of Bach's Passion Oratorios, which also have no parallels outside Germany, can be traced to the same idea. It is significant that Bach, like Luther, believed that music was the means of personal union with God and a superior medium of revelation; it differed from spoken sermon mostly in that it was by nature "divinely inspired" and made His Truth directly accessible. Luther's view of the special religious status of music as the most emotional speech testifies to the emotionalism of the Lutheran doctrine itself; Pietism inherited it, and made it explicit. Regarding Bach's philosophy of music, see Otto L. Bettmann, "Bach as Rhetorician," *The American Scholar,* 55 (Winter 1985–86), pp. 113–118.

84. See Kaiser, "L'éveil," pp. 70–73. Also see Hasko Zimmer, *Auf dem Altar des Vaterlands: Religion und Patriotismus in der deutschen Kriegslyrik des 19. Jahrhunderts* (Frankfurt am Main: Thesen Verlag, 1971).

85. Pinson, *Pietism,* p. 12.

86. Brunschwig, *Enlightenment,* pp. 247, 245; Ernst Troeltsch, "The Ideas of Nat-

ural law and Humanity in World Politics," in Otto Gerke, ed., *Natural Law and the Theory of Society, 1500–1800* (Cambridge, 1934), vol. I, p. 203; Friedrich Meinecke, *Die Idee der Staatsräson in der neueren Geschichte* (München und Berlin: Oldenbourg, 1925), p. 451.

87. The *Sturm und Drang* group consisted of Goethe, Herder, Klinger, Leizewitz, Lenz, Merck, Maler Müller, and Wagner. Among people associated with and sympathetic to it were Hamann, Klopstock, Justus Möser, Gerstenberg, Lavater, Jung-Stilling, Jacobi, Heinse, and Schiller. *Göttinger Hainbund* included Hölty, Voss, Bürger, and the brothers Stolberg. The "early" Romantics included the brothers Wilhelm and Friedrich Schlegel, Schleiermacher, Novalis (Friedrich von Hardenberg), Tieck, and Wackenroder. Closely associated with this group were the philosophers Fichte and Schelling and the novelist Jean Paul (Richter).

88. Roy Pascal, *The German Sturm und Drang* (Manchester, Eng.: Manchester University Press, 1967), p. 7; Frederick C. Beiser, *The Fate of Reason: German Philosophy from Kant to Fichte* (Cambridge, Mass.: Harvard University Press, 1987), pp. 19–20. My discussion of *Sturm und Drang* relies heavily on Pascal, and quotations from works discussed are often given in his translation.

89. Herder and Nicolai quoted in Pascal, *Sturm und Drang*, pp. 95, 94. Goethe, *Truth and Fiction*, vol. II, Book X, pp. 21, 13ff.

90. Moritz, *Anton Reiser*, p. 352.

91. Goethe, Letter of August 11, 1781, to his mother, in *Goethes Briefe* (Hamburg: Hans Christian Wagner Verlag, 1969), vol. I, p. 369.

92. Brunschwig, *Enlightenment*, p. 244; Schleiermacher, *Life*, pp. 64–75 especially; Schlegel, *Lucinde*, "Critical Fragments," #76, p. 152; Schleiermacher, *Life*, vol. I, p. 328: "Preaching is, in the present day, the only means of exercising personal influence over men in masses."

93. William J. Bossenbrook, *The German Mind*, p. 249, quoted in Hoover, *Gospel of Nationalism*, p. 11.

94. Ibid.

95. J. G. Hamann, "Kreuzzüge des Philologen," *Schriften* (Berlin: Reimer, 1821–1843), vol. II, p. 281 (quoted in Pascal, *Sturm und Drang*, p. 91); Pascal, p. 90; Hamann, in ibid., p. 283.

96. Goethe, Letters to Herder, May 12, 1775, and to Langer (in French), November 30, 1769, in *Briefe*, pp. 182, 97. Herder quoted from letters in Pascal *(Sturm und Drang)*, pp. 95, 94, 104, 102.

97. Schlegel, *Lucinde*, p. 194. Novalis, "Aphorisms," in *German Classics: Masterpieces of German Literature Translated into English,* (New York: The German Publication Society, 1913), vol. IV, p. 187. Schlegel, "Ideas," #118, #105, pp. 252, 251.

98. Goethe, *Truth and Fiction*, vol. II, Book XIV, p. 190.

99. Novalis, "Aphorisms," p. 186. Schlegel, *Lucinde*, "Ideas," #8, #18, p. 242; #112, p. 251.

100. Goethe, *Faust*, in *Werke* (Hamburg: Christian Wegnert Vergal, 1949), vol. III, p. 110. Pascal's translation, *Sturm und Drang*, p. 114.

101. Herder, *Auch eine Philosophie der Geschichte zur Bildung der Menschheit, 1774, Sämtliche Werke* (Hildesheim: Georg Olms Verlagsbuchhandlung, 1967), vol. V, p. 509. (Translation in Pascal, *Sturm und Drang*, p. 222.)

102. Herder, Letter to Caroline Flachsland, January 9, 1773, in *Herders Briefwechsel mit Caroline Flachsland* (Weimar: Verlag der Goethe-Gesellschaft, 1926–1928), vol. II, p. 325.

103. "Athenaeum Fragments" in Schlegel, *Lucinde,* p. 212; *Monologen* quoted in Oskar Walzel, *German Romanticism* (New York: Frederick Ungar Publishing Co., 1932), p. 50; Schlegel, "Athenaeum Fragments," #262, p. 200.

104. Goethe, "Die Natur," in *Gedenkausgabe der Werke, Briefe und Gespräche* (Zürich: Artemis-Verlag, 1949), vol. XVI, pp. 922, 924. Quoted in Pascal, *Sturm und Drang,* p. 208. Schlegel, *Lucinde,* p. 120. This moral imperative found an immediate expression in art theory, in the emphasis on the individuality of a work of art as its only value. Celebrating the Gothic architecture of the Strassbourg Minster, so irregular by classical standards, and so much better for it, Goethe wrote: "The only true art is characteristic art. If its influence arises from deep, harmonious, independent feeling, from feeling peculiar to itself, oblivious, yes, ignorant of everything foreign, then it is whole and living, whether it be born from crude savagery or cultural sentiment." Goethe, "Von Deutscher Baukunst," in *Gedenkausgabe,* vol. XIII, p. 24; translation—Pascal, *Sturm und Drang,* p. 265.

105. "She seems to have made individuality her supreme purpose and she cares nothing for individuals." Goethe, "Die Natur," p. 922.

106. Schlegel, *Lucinde,* "Ideas," #60, p. 247. Hölderlin in Gooch, *Germany,* p. 240, who quotes from Litzmann, *Hölderlins Leben in Briefen,* p. 169.

107. Schlegel, *Lucinde,* "Athenaeum Fragments," #53, p. 167.

108. Herder, "Briefwechsel über Ossian und die Lieder alter Völker," *Sämtliche Werke,* vol. V, p. 164, emphasis added. Analyzed and quoted by Pascal, *Sturm und Drang,* p. 253; and Letter to Hamann, August 1–25, 1772, in *Briefe an J. G. Hamann im Anhang Herders Briefwechsel mit Nicolai* (Hildesheim: George Olms Verlag, 1975), p. 70.

109. Goethe, *Sorrows of Werther,* in *The Complete Works,* vol. III, p. 29. (The translation here is not accurate: "their whole nature simple and unpolluted.") Schlegel, *Lucinde,* p. 99, and "Ideas," #127, p. 253. Goethe, *Faust,* p. 87.

110. Herder, "Ideen zur Philosophie der Geschichte der Menschheit," erster und zweiter Teil, *Sämtliche Werke,* vol. XIII, Book VIII, p. 337. Goethe, "Fragment eines Romans," in *Gedenkausgabe,* vol. IV, p. 266. This is not an entry in a journal, but a fragment of a future novel. Goethe's compelling descriptions of emotions in fiction, however, represent accurate descriptions of his own emotions: he had an exceptional ability for turning his personal experiences into art (as he indeed noted in *Truth and Fiction*).

111. Lenz quoted in Pascal, *Sturm und Drang,* p. 33. Goethe, *Sorrows of Werther,* pp. 75, 77. Schlegel, *Lucinde,* p. 138.

112. Moser quoted in Brunschwig, *Enlightenment,* p. 214. Goethe, *Truth and Fiction,* vol. II, Book IXX, p. 307. (The translation here, however, is from Brunschwig, p. 214; it is superior to Oxenford's.)

113. Schlegel, "Critical Fragments," #16, p. 144. Novalis, "Aphorisms," p. 188. Schlegel, "Ideas," #19, p. 242; "Ideas," #36, p. 244.

114. *Athenaeum,* German text, p. 177. The English translation in Schlegel, *Lucinde,* p. 221, of *Verstand* is "understanding"; in this context, however, "reason" is a more appropriate interpretation. In their ratiocinative early days, the leaders of

the "early" Romanticism deviated from the *Sturm und Drang* definition of genius as a force of nature expressed in the intense, non-reflective, irrational, and thus "true" feeling by adding to its characteristics the power of self-limitation. Later, however, they returned to the *Sturm und Drang* position. See Walzel, *German Romanticism*, who stresses the transient rationalism of the "early" Romantics and sees in it an important difference between Romanticism proper and *Sturm und Drang*. One should not forget, though, that *Stürmer und Dränger*, too, started as disciples of the *Aufklärung*.

115. Lavater quoted in Pascal, *Sturm und Drang*, pp. 154, 138. Goethe, "Zum Shäkespears Tag," in M. Morris, ed., *Der Junge Goethe* (Leipzig: Insel Verlag, 1909), vol. II, p. 140.

116. Schlegel, *Lucinde*, "Critical Fragments," #1, p. 143. Hamann quoted in Pascal, *Sturm und Drang*, p. 238. Pascal, pp. 138, 241—Lavater; p. 244—Herder; p. 237—Hamann. Lavater in Pascal, pp. 138, 241; translations slightly differ.

117. Herder, "Shäkespear," *Sämtliche Werke*, vol. V, pp. 227, 228, quoted in Pascal, *Sturm und Drang*, p. 244. This last sentence reflects an unbounded belief in the powers of human will. An artist could will a world into being—thus the prominence of miraculous occurrences in Romantic fiction and of the faith in miracles in Romantic philosophy and life. Novalis thought he could, and earnestly attempted to, will himself to die. Marx's belief that philosophy had the power to change the world, that classes would emerge just because they were necessary for the fulfillment of the philosophical mission ("a class must be formed"), was an expression of the same confidence in wishful thinking. The most remarkable thing about this is that they were right. Worlds were willed into being which could only have been conjured in a Romantic imagination, and which forever changed our views of human nature—not, unfortunately, for the better. Such was the power of genius.

118. Schlegel, *Lucinde*, "Critical Fragments," #6, p. 143; #65, p. 150; "Athenaeum Fragments," #116 (excerpt), p. 175; "Ideas," #43, p. 245; #44, p. 245; "Critical Fragments," #68, p. 151; #63, p. 150; "Ideas," #13, p. 242; #45, p. 245; #20, p. 243.

119. See ibid., "Athenaeum Fragments," #206 and #259. For an analysis of the metrics of Romantic poetry, see Walzel, *German Romanticism*, pp. 127–133.

120. Schlegel, *Lucinde*, p. 98. Walzel, *German Romanticism*, pp. 121–133, focuses on the "early" Romantics' attitudes toward music. To Thomas Mann, in 1910, it still seemed obvious that music was the German art, and that even literature could not compete with it for place in the national consciousness. See Thomas Mann, "Ein Brief zur Situation des deutschen Schriftstellers um 1910," *Thomas-Mann-Studien*, 3 (1974). On Luther's view of music, see Bettmann, "Bach as a Rhetorician." Beethoven, in Friedrich Kerst and Henry E. Krehbiel, eds., *Beethoven: The Man and Artist, as Revealed in His Own Words* (New York: Dover Publications, 1964; first published in 1905), pp. 13, 14, 39, 41, 51, 73.

121. F. M. Klinger, *Sturm und Drang*, Act I, Scene I, in *Dramatische Jugendwerke* (Leipzig: E. Rowohlt Verlag, 1913), vol. II, p. 269. Pascal, *Sturm und Drang*, pp. 51, 36 (quotations from Klinger's letters), 55.

122. Goethe, "Die Natur," p. 923: "Leben ist ihre schönste Erfindung, und der Tod ist ihr Kunstgriff, viel Leben zu haben." Schlegel, *Lucinde*, p. 118.

123. Novalis, "Aphorisms," p. 187. And, as if this statement were not enough as food for thought, he added, characteristically: "From the spirit comes gravitation."

124. Ibid., and Novalis in Schlegel, *Lucinde*, "Athenaeum Fragments," #292, p. 203.

125. Schlegel, *Lucinde*, p. 91; p. 60 (the characterization of his oeuvre is Schlegel's own); "Athenaeum Fragments," #15, p. 163.

126. Schlegel, *Lucinde*, p. 131.

127. Ibid., "Ideas," #138, p. 254. But, of course, Catholicism had many other merits to recommend itself: it was positively stigmatized by the hostility of Enlightenment; it was not Protestantism; it was the religion of the Middle Ages.

128. Novalis in Schlegel, *Lucinde*, "Athenaeum Fragments," #286, p. 203.

129. Schleiermacher in Schlegel, *Lucinde*, "Athenaeum Fragments," #328, p. 211. James T. Hatfield, "The Early Romantic School," pp. 48–70, in *German Classics*, vol. V, p. 66.

130. Uhland defined Romanticism as conscious, systematic substitution: "The spirit of man feeling, indeed, that it will never experience infinity in all its splendour and wearied by the vague groping of its desire, soon fixes its yearning upon temporal images in which there seems to be a dawning vision of the celestial . . . This mystic manifestation of our innermost feelings in an image, this projection of the world spirits, this incarnation of the divine, in a word: the presentiment of infinity in our perceptions is what is Romantic." Walzel, *German Romanticism*, p. 32. *Lucinde* is a very edifying story in this respect, for in it erotic exhibitionism alternates with passages of lucid and revealing self-analysis. Take, for example, this passage from "Apprenticeship for Manhood": "Women he actually did not understand at all . . . But he reacted to young men who were more or less like him with passionate warm love and a real rage for friendship. But that alone wasn't enough to satisfy him. He felt as if he wanted to embrace a world and yet couldn't grasp anything . . . He became sensual from spiritual despair, committed imprudent acts out of spite against fate, and was genuinely immoral in an almost innocent way . . . With this kind of personality, it was inevitable that he should often feel lonely in an even friendliest and loveliest society; and actually he felt least lonely when no one was with him. At such times he would intoxicate himself with images of his hopes and memories and intentionally let himself be seduced by his own imagination." "He was afraid of his passionate nature, and consequently devoted himself exclusively to friendships with other young men who, like him, were capable of being enthusiastic . . . Indeed, the whole group of his friends glowed with noble love, and many a great talent slumbered undeveloped in them. They would often utter . . . sublime things . . . particularly about the divine quality of male friendship, which Julius intended to make the true business of his life." Schlegel, *Lucinde*, pp. 78, 88.

131. Quoted in Brunschwig, *Enlightenment*, p. 151; also see Brunschwig's discussion in the chapter "Isolation of the Young Intellectuals."

132. "Die blaue Blume" of poetry, the quintessence of the ideal aspirations of the

human spirit, sought after by Heinrich von Ofterdingen of Novalis' unfinished novel of the same name. It became a symbol of Romantic idealism.

133. Moritz, *Anton Reiser*, p. 401.

134. Friedrich Schlegel, quoted in Brunschwig, *Enlightenment*, p. 161.

135. J. M. R. Lenz, "Über Götz von Berlichingen," in *Werke und Schriften* (Stuttgart: Neue Bibliothek der Weltliteratur, 1966), vol. I, pp. 378–379. (Translated in Pascal, *Sturm und Drang*, p. 148.) Lenz wrote: "We are, or at least would like to be, the first rung on the ladder of freely active, independent creatures, and since we see around us, here and there, a world that is the proof of an infinitely and freely active being, the first impulse we feel in our soul is the desire to do likewise. But since . . . we have to content ourselves with the things that are there, we do at least feel an accretion to our existence, happiness, by recreating its Creation on a small scale" (Lenz, "Anmerkungen übers Theater," in ibid., p. 333).

136. Lenz, "Eduard Allwills Erstes Geistliches Lied," ibid., pp. 95–96. (Translation—Pascal, *Sturm und Drang*, pp. 128–130.)

137. Herder's later works, and even later versions of earlier works such as the collections of folk songs and the "Essay on Knowledge and Perception in the Human Soul," are markedly different from those written during his *Sturm und Drang* period. It is nothing short of astounding to see the change in Herder's conception of "genius," which is completely reversed between the earlier and the later versions of the "Essay on Knowledge and Perception." While in the 1774 version of the essay, exuberance of feeling is considered the source and the sign of genius, in a later version people torn by passions are likened to the "hounds of Hell"; while not long ago intensity of emotions was the guarantee of their sincerity, this same intensity later makes Herder suspect that these emotions are "false." Genius now is characterized by cool reflection; those who succumb to feeling, by "eternal uneasiness, misanthropy, zealotry, envy and thirst for revenge in their hearts." "If this is genius," says Herder, who of all people certainly knew what he was talking about, "who would not cross himself against it?" Pascal, *Sturm und Drang*, p. 163.

138. Schlegel, *Lucinde,* "Ideas," #106, p. 251.

139. Quoted in Pascal, *Sturm und Drang*, pp. 220, 212.

140. Herder, "Auch eine Philosophie der Geschichte zur Bildung der Menschheit," in *Sämtliche Werke,* vol. V, p. 550. Herder's condemnation of the division of labor—before the publication in England of that great panegyric to it, Adam Smith's *The Wealth of Nations*—is of utmost significance for the understanding of the economistic opposition to modern society in the nineteenth century. His intense dislike of this ubiquitous—and, one must admit, indeed rational—device makes Karl Marx his direct descendant. Goethe found this hostility funny and depicted Herder as a satyr who, in an attempt to abolish the division of labor, would have people live on raw chestnuts. But this was exactly the ideal Marx envisioned in the *German Ideology,* when he eulogized the joys of hunting in the morning, fishing in the afternoon, reading Plato in the evening, and criticizing after dinner. There could be no totality if labor was divided; the division of labor destroyed the "whole" man.

141. Herder, "Übers Erkennen und Empfinden in der Menschlichen Seele," in *Sämtliche Werke*, vol. VIII, p. 261.

142. Adam Müller, "Elements of Politics," Lecture #2, in H. S. Reiss, ed. *The Political Thought of the German Romantics* (Oxford: Basil Blackwell, 1955), p. 155.

143. Ibid., pp. 144, 154, 155, 146.

144. Ibid., p. 150. Novalis, *Fragmente* (Dresden: Wolfgang Jess Verlag, 1929), #1532, #1541, pp. 487–488. Quoted in Hans Kohn, "Romanticism and German Nationalism," *Review of Politics*, 12 (1950), pp. 443–472, 448.

145. Müller, "Elements," p. 158. Novalis, *Fragmente*, #1583, p. 498 (quoted in Kohn, "Romanticism," p. 449).

146. Müller quoted in Kohn, "Romanticism," p. 466. Novalis, *Christendom or Europe*, in *The Political Thought of German Romantics*, p. 134. Schleiermacher in Schlegel, *Lucinde*, "Athenaeum Fragments," #349, p. 216. Müller, "Elements," p. 148. Von Eichendorff, "Politische Schriften," *Sämtliche Werke* (Regensburg: Verlag von J. Habbel, 1913), vol. X, p. 160.

147. Müller, "Elements," p. 146. Regarding Kant, see Leonard Krieger, *The German Idea of Freedom: History of a Political Tradition* (Chicago: University of Chicago Press, 1957), pp. 86–125. Hegel quoted in ibid., p. 132.

148. Müller, "Elements," pp. 160, 159, 158.

149. Wilhelm Schlegel in Friedrich Schlegel, *Lucinde*, "Athenaeum Fragments," #60, pp. 168–169.

150. "That ancient, living Freedom"; Eichendorff, in "Ahnung und Gegenwart," ch. 24, *Sämtliche Werke*, vol. III, p. 325.

151. Hegel, in Krieger, *The German Idea*, pp. 133, 132, 133.

152. Schlegel, *Lucinde*, "Ideas," #64, p. 247; #54, p. 246. Novalis, *Fragmente*, #1614, p. 514 (quoted in Kohn, "Romanticism," p. 449). Richter quoted in Gooch, *Germany*, p. 247.

153. Schlegel, *Lucinde*, "Athenaeum Fragments," #222, p. 192; "Critical Fragments," #38, p. 147.

154. Quoted in Gooch, *Germany*, p. 531.

155. J. G. Fichte, "Beiträge zur Berichtigung der Urtheile des Publicums über die Französische Revolution," 1793, in *Sämmtliche Werke* (Berlin: Verlag von Veit und Co., 1845), vol. VI, p. 95. Also see Hans Kohn, "The Paradox of Fichte's Nationalism," *Journal of the History of Ideas*, 10:3 (June 1949), p. 321. Boie quoted in Brunschwig, *Enlightenment*, p. 171; Hölderlin—in Gooch, *Germany*, p. 234.

156. Gooch, *Germany*, pp. 41–43.

157. Ibid., pp. 234, 47, 54.

158. Ibid., pp. 46–52.

159. Ibid., p. 232; Brunschwig, *Enlightenment*, pp. 176–177, 149, 177.

160. Novalis, "Christianity and Europe," pp. 131–136.

161. L. Tieck, *Minnelieder aus dem Schwäbichen Zeitalter*, "Vorrede" (Hamburg: Verlag Der Hamburger Presse, 1918), p. 1.

162. See J. G. Gagliardo, *From Pariah to Patriot* (Lexington: University Press of Kentucky, 1969), p. 147, and Louis L. Snyder, "Literature: Nationalistic As-

pects of the Grimm Brothers' Fairy Tales," pp. 44–74, in Snyder, *German Nationalism: The Tragedy of a People: Extremism contra Liberalism in Modern German History* (Harrisburg, Penn.: The Stackpole Company, 1952), regarding the explicitly nationalistic aspirations of the Grimms. Snyder's is a valuable book with a misleading title. German nationalism was, indeed, a tragedy, but it was a tragedy of peoples other than German in the first place.

163. Walter M. Simon, "Variations in Nationalism during the Great Reform Period in Prussia," *American Historical Review,* 59 (1953–54), p. 305; Friedrich Meinecke, *The Age of German Liberation, 1795–1815* (Berkeley: University of California Press, 1977), p. 80. Stein in Krieger, *The Idea of Freedom,* p. 148. Meinecke, p. 64. Stein (1812) quoted in Simon, p. 307; also see Simon regarding German orientation of other reformers.

164. Louis L. Snyder, "Pedagogy: Turnvater Jahn and the Genesis of German nationalism," pp. 21–43, in Snyder, *German Nationalism,* p. 32.

165. Quoted in Simon, "Variations in Nationalism," p. 312, fn. 29.

166. Kohn, "Fichte," p. 321, fn. 5; p. 327.

167. Schleiermacher, *Life,* vol. II, Letter of November 4, 1806, p. 66, and of November 21, p. 69.

168. Kohn, "Romanticism," p. 459.

169. Johann Gottlieb Fichte, *Addresses to the German Nation,* trans. R. F. Jones and G. H. Turnbull, reprint of the 1922 edition, published by Open Court Publishers (Westport, Conn.: Greenwood Press, 1979), pp. 134–136.

170. *Adelungs Wörterbuch* defines *Nation* in 1801 as "die eingeborenen Einwohner eines Landes, so fern sie einen gemeinschaftlichen Ursprung haben, und eine gemeinschaftliche Sprache reden, sie mögen übrigens einen einzigen Staat ausmachen, oder in mehrere vertheilet seyn . . . Ehe dieses Wort aus dem Latein entlehnet wurde, gebrauchte man *Volk* für *Nation*" (p. 439). The dictionary of the brothers Grimm interprets it as "das (eingeborne) Volk eines Landes, einer groszen Staatsgesamtheit" (p. 425). Ritter, in *Historisches Wörterbuch,* p. 406, writes: "Der Begriff ist nur selten eindeutig und ausdrücklich definiert; seine Bedeutung ist häufig schillernd und überschneidet sich mit der anderer Begriffe, besonders mit *Volk.*" See also *Trübners Deutsches Wörterbuch,* pp. 689–694, 697–698; and Campe's Dictionary of 1810.

171. Humboldt quoted in Simon, "Variations in Nationalism," p. 310; Arndt—in Hans Kohn, "Arndt and the Character of German Nationalism," *American Historical Review,* 54:4 (July 1949), pp. 787–803; 803. Fichte, *Addresses,* p. 130.

172. Fichte, "Die Grundzüge des Gegenwärtigen Zeitalter," Lecture #14, in *Sämmtliche Werke,* vol. VII, p. 212. See discussion in Kohn, "Fichte."

173. Quoted in Kohn, "Fichte," p. 326.

174. Fichte, *Addresses,* pp. 268–269. This flattering idea was not born during the Liberation period. It had been voiced already by Schiller, for example, in an unfinished poem "Deutsche Grösse," *Sämtliche Werke* (München: Carl Hanser Verlag, 1965), vol. I, pp. 473–478.

175. Müller, quoted in Kohn, "Romanticism," p. 471; Fichte—in Kohn, "Fichte," p. 327. Friedrich Schlegel, "An die Deutschen," 1800, in *Sämmtliche Werke* (Wien: Jakob Mayer, 1823), vol. IX, p. 16.

176. Schlegel, Letter to his brother, November 8, 1791, in O. F. Walzel, ed., *Briefe an seinen Bruder August Wilhelm* (Berlin: Verlag von Epner und Peters, 1890), p. 26; *Lucinde*, "Critical Fragments," #116, p. 157; "Ideas," #120, p. 252; #135, p. 254.

177. Müller in Kohn, "Romanticism," p. 467. Fichte, *Addresses*, p. 237.

178. Fichte, *Addresses*, specifically Address #4.

179. "Das ist des Deutschen Vaterland\ . . . Wo jeder Franzmann heisset Feind\Wo jeder Deutsche heisset Freund." Ernst Moritz Arndt, "Des Deutschen Vaterland," pp. 26–28, in *Deutsche Vaterlandslieder* (Leipzig: Insel-Verlag, 193[?]), Insel-Bucherei 154, p. 28.

180. Friedrich Ludwig Jahn, *Das deutsche Volkstum*, précis from the original edition (Lübeck: Niemann und Comp., 1810), trans. and printed in Snyder, *German Nationalism*, p. 37–38.

181. Kohn, "Arndt," pp. 791–792. Friedrich Schlegel in Kohn, "Romanticism," p. 460. Theodor Körner, "Jägerlied," 1813, in *Sämmtliche Werke* (Haag: Gebrüder Hartmann, 1829), p. 19. Fichte in the *Addresses*, however, did not see race as all-important, and believed there was no harm in admitting that the German-speaking people (that is, the German nation) was in fact a mixture of races.

182. Hans Kohn, "Father Jahn's Nationalism," *Review of Politics* 11 (October 1949), pp. 419–432; 428. Friedrich Schlegel, *Philosophische Vorlesungen aus den Jahren 1804 bis 1806* (Bonn: Eduard Weber, 1837), vol. II, pp. 358, 382 (quoted in Kohn, "Romanticism," p. 460).

183. See Gagliardo, *Pariah*, p. 172ff. Peasantry was the *Volk* in the original meaning; it merged with Germanness itself. This led to the idealization of agriculture through which man, allegedly, more than through any other activity, became a creator and therefore an active and free being, and reinforced the antipathy toward trade and industry (of which Germany anyway did not have much to show) and anti-urban sentiments. Efforts were made not to antagonize the bourgeoisie and to find a place for it within the German people. Yet this was done reluctantly; Arndt, for example, believed that burgher and peasant stood in "natural contrast" to each other. This, too, contributed to and in part accounted for the anti-capitalist, anti-bourgeois character of German nationalism.

184. Jahn, *Das deutsche Volkstum*, p. 37.

185. Arndt, "Katechismus für den deutschen Kriegs- und Wehrmann" (Leipzig: Verlag von Philipp Reclam, n.d.), p. 57.

186. M. von Schenkendorf, "Das Eiserne Kreuz," *Gedichte* (Berlin: Deutsches Verlagshaus Bong & Co.), p. 29. Jahn in Snyder, *German Nationalism*, p. 28. Jahn, inscription in the Wartburg guestbook, October 24, 1815, in *Werke* (Hof: Verlag von R. Lion, 1887), vol. II, pt. II, p. 1003.

187. Arndt, *Staat und Vaterland* (München: Drei Masken Verlag, 1921), p. 5, in Kohn, "Arndt," p. 800.

188. This is quoted by Snyder in "Militarism: The Development of War-Cult Extremism from Karl von Clausewitz to Ewald Banse" (pp. 227–254 in Snyder, *German Nationalism*) from Friedrich von Bernhardi, himself a notorious warmonger, and may not be entirely reliable.

189. Kohn, "Romanticism," p. 458.
190. Quoted in Gooch, *Germany,* p. 515.
191. Gagliardo, *Pariah,* p. 182; Gooch, *Germany,* p. 525. See discussion of reformers' attitudes in Gooch; Krieger, *German Idea;* Simon, "Variations in Nationalism."
192. Hatfield, *German Classics,* p. 51.
193. Schlegel, *Lucinde,* "Athenaeum Fragments," #426, #110, #141, #209, #210, #355, pp. 234, 174, 180, 190, 217.
194. Ibid., #60, #115, #199, #219, #301, #379, pp. 168, 175, 188, 191, 204, 223.
195. Stein and Carsten Niebuhr, quoted in Gooch, *Germany,* pp. 60, 520, 521, 523.
196. Arndt, *Schriften für und an Seine Lieben Deutschen* (Leipzig: Weidmannrsche Buchhandlung, 1854), vol. I, pp. 405, 412ff, quoted in Kohn, "Arndt," pp. 796, 795; army volunteer—in Kohn, "Arndt," p. 793; Professor Leo—in Hans Kohn, "France between Britain and Germany," *Journal of the History of Ideas,* 17:3 (June 1956), pp. 283–299; 295n. Significantly, at the very same time, France was apparently possessed by ardent Germanophilia *(Teutonomanie);* its enemy was England, while Germany was more than a friend, it was a "sister-nation." Contemporary French attitudes toward Germany and England are the subject of the very informative paper mentioned last in this note.
197. Quoted in Gooch, *Germany,* p. 63.
198. List was another patriot of the Liberation period denounced as a Jacobin and a Republican (but later vindicated by Treutschke as "a demagogue only in the noblest sense"), a friend of Lafayette, and a one-time denizen of the United States of America. See Snyder, "Economics: The Role of Friedrich List in the Establishment of Zollverein," pp. 75–100, in Snyder, *German Nationalism.* List in ibid., p. 87.
199. Adam Müller, *Ausgewählte Abhandlungen,* quoted in Kohn, "Romanticism," p. 466.
200. Treitschke, "Excerpts from Works," in Louis L. Snyder, ed., *Documents of German History* (New Brunswick, N. J.: Rutgers University Press, 1958), p. 262.
201. These were the titles of two books published in Nazi Germany in 1940 and 1942, respectively: *England: Leader of the Bourgeois World* and *America: The Land Without a Heart.*
202. Peter Pulzer, *The Rise of Political Anti-Semitism in Germany and Austria,* rev. ed. (London: Peter Halban, 1988), p. 31.
203. Marvin Lowenthal, *The Jews of Germany: A Story of Sixteen Centuries* (Philadelphia: The Jewish Publication Society of America, 1936), p. 230.
204. For an example of such ambivalence and the ways in which elements of Western civilization most obviously opposed to the German spirit were reconciled to it and incorporated in the German culture, see Jeffrey Herf, *Reactionary Modernism: Technology, Culture, and Politics in Weimar and the Third Reich* (New York: Cambridge University Press, 1984).
205. Lowenthal, *Jews of Germany,* p. 230.
206. "Once the homeless, fugitive Christians were compelled to share the destiny of the Jews, expulsion no longer bore the unambiguous marks of God-sent punishment. The destiny of worldwide diaspora, formerly the proof of the obsti-

nate Jew's guilt, was now the badge of faith of the avowed Christian. In the late sermons of Calvin, delivered in French . . . we encounter a growing sense of the hidden community of fate shared by Christians and Jews in their homeless state of persecution and diaspora.

This view of God's covenant as one held in common by Christians and Jews, utterly inconceivable from Augustin to Erasmus and Luther, now spread in two directions—by way of France and the Netherlands to England and Scotland, and eventually to North America." Heiko A. Oberman, *The Roots of Anti-Semitism in the Age of Renaissance and Reformation* (Philadelphia: Fortress Press, 1984; first published in German in 1981), p. 141.

207. Lowenthal, *Jews of Germany*, p. 231.

208. The inventor of the word is believed to be Wilhelm Marr, who also founded the *Antisemiten-Liga*. Both the word and the organization appeared in 1879. See the discussion in Pulzer, *Political Anti-Semitism*.

209. Lowenthal, *Jews of Germany*, p. 219.

210. Mendelssohn was made a "privileged Jew" by Frederick, who had no pro-Jewish sympathies otherwise. The philosopher-king was persuaded to do so by the Marquis d'Argens, who wrote on Mendelssohn's behalf: "A philosopher who is a bad Catholic begs a philosopher who is a bad Protestant to grant this privilege to a philosopher who is a bad Jew." This revealing story is recounted by Lowenthal, *Jews of Germany*, p. 203. He also relates the following: "In the year 1776—a date with other associations for Americans—Mendelssohn, then at the height of his fame as a European philosopher, had to pay at the gate of Dresden an entry-tax [as a Jew], a 'head-tax,' which as he remarked, was set at the same figure as for a 'Polish cow'" (p. 210).

211. Schleiermacher, *Life*, vol. I, p. 178; Letter to sister Charlotte, August 4, 1789. Goethe quoted in Lowenthal, *Jews of Germany*, p. 226.

212. Schleiermacher, *Life*, vol. I, pp. 249, 187.

213. "Indiscretion and shamelessness were phenomena of . . . Romanticism." Hanna Arendt, *Rahel Varnhagen: The Life of a Jewish Woman*, rev. ed. (New York: Harcourt Brace Jovanovich, 1974), p. 20.

214. Gentz and Humboldt quoted in ibid., pp. 33, 201. Commenting on Humboldt's reaction, Arendt says: "Here, as elsewhere, Wilhelm von Humboldt was the best, keenest and most malicious gossip of his age." She notes that "he did put the matter more crudely and more spitefully than was absolutely necessary."

215. One should keep in mind that the majority of the Jews, even in great cities such as Berlin, continued to live in the abject poverty and obscurity of the ghetto.

216. Arendt, *Rahel Varnhagen*, pp. 7, 13.

217. Herder in ibid., p. 29. Lowenthal, *Jews of Germany*, pp. 221–222. Pulzer, *Political Anti-Semitism*, p. 6. Moses Hess, *Rome and Jerusalem* (New York: Philosophical Library, 1943[?]), pp. 25–26.

218. Heine quoted in Gordon Craig, *The Germans* (New York: G. P. Putnam's Sons, 1982), p. 132. Fichte in Lowenthal, *Jews of Germany*, p. 229. See also Fichte, "Beiträge," in *Sämmtliche Werke*, vol. VI, pp. 149–150ff.

219. On the development of anti-Semitism in this period, see Pulzer, *Political Anti-Semitism*.

220. "Despite its claims of historical novelty in seeking to combine the waves of

nationalism and socialism, the Nazi movement in reality was stale and unoriginal. There was little new in naziism other than the fanatical and ferocious method of genocide used to implement its ideology." All the ideas in this ideology date back to the early nineteenth century or even earlier. Snyder, *German Nationalism*, pp. 18–19. See also George Mosse, *The Crisis of German Ideology: Intellectual Origins of the Third Reich* (New York: The Universal Library, 1964), on the absolute centrality of anti-Semitism in German consciousness in the late nineteenth and the twentieth centuries. Mosse's is the most systematic discussion of the perpetuation of the elements of Pieto-Romantic mentality, which he picks up around the middle of the nineteenth century and traces to Nazism, in the time following the period of its crystallization discussed here.

221. Those were still the same structural conditions, perpetuated in the course of more than a century, which frustrated the eighteenth-century *Bildungsbürger* and stimulated the emergence of German nationalism in the first place. Note the predominance of unemployed academics and frustrated intellectuals among the protagonists of Mosse's survey, *Crisis:* Lagarde, Langbehn, Hitler himself, and others.

222. Wagner, quoted in Snyder, "Music and Art: Richard Wagner and 'The German Spirit,'" in Snyder, *German Nationalism*, p. 163.

223. St. John Chrysostom quoted in Craig, *The Germans*, p. 127; Professor Fries in Lowenthal, *Jews of Germany*, pp. 231–232; Wagner in Snyder, *German Nationalism*, p. 162.

224. All quotations are given from the text in R. C. Tucker, ed., *The Marx-Engels Reader*, 2nd ed. (New York: Norton, 1978), pp. 26–52; italics everywhere are in the original. On the possible role of the "Essay on the Jewish Question" in the development of Marxist theory, see Liah Greenfeld, "Nationalism and Class Struggle: Two Forces or One?" *Survey*, 29:3 (Autumn 1985), pp. 153–174.

225. Krieger, *The German Idea*, p. 277.

226. The quotations are from the text in Tucker, *The Marx-Engels Reader*, pp. 53–65.

227. For some description of the passions that governed Marx's life, see Peter Demetz, *Marx, Engels and the Poets: Origins of Marxist Literary Criticism* (Chicago: University of Chicago Press, 1967); and Leopold Schwarzchild, *The Red Prussian: The Life and Legend of Karl Marx* (London: Hamish Hamilton, 1948).

228. Krieger, The *German Idea*, p. 327.

229. Robert C. Tucker, *Philosophy and Myth in Karl Marx* (New York: Cambridge University Press, 1961), p. 22.

230. This is not as surprising as it may seem. After all, Marx was a Romantic poet. On this point, see Leonard P. Wessell, Jr., *Karl Marx, Romantic Irony, and the Proletariat: The Mythopoetic Origins of Marxism* (Baton Rouge and London: Louisiana University Press, 1979).

231. Marx-Engels, *Collected Works* (Moscow: Progress Publishers, 1976), vol. III, p. 406.

232. Sidney Hook, *From Hegel to Marx: Studies in the Intellectual Development of Karl Marx* (New York: The Humanities Press, 1950). Tucker, *Philosophy and Myth*, pp. 114–116.

233. On this point, see Karl Kautsky, *Ethics and the Materialist Conception of History* (Chicago: Charles H. Kerr, 1907); Tucker, *Philosophy and Myth*, regarding Lenin; and Adam B. Ulam, *The Unfinished Revolution: An Essay on the Sources of Influence of Marxism and Communism* (New York: Vintage Books, 1960).

234. For similar reasons Jews were also attracted to Liberalism, which, however, was very weak in Germany, and to reformist varieties of Social Democracy. Trotsky quoted in Pulzer, *Political Anti-Semitism*, p. 255.

235. "Indeed a great many anti-Semites proclaimed themselves Socialists, and this becomes more comprehensible when we remember that, especially in Germany, many eminently conservative thinkers, inspired by a tradition of bureaucracy and mercantilism, were grouped in the school of Kathedrasozialisten" (ibid., p. 44).

236. Ibid., pp. 45, 262.

237. Here is, for example, how the two were compared by *Neue Zeit* in 1891 (quoted in ibid., p. 261): "Philo-Semitism [alias Liberalism] is no whit better than anti-Semitism. If the one claims to be fighting capitalism by persecuting the Jews, then the other claims to protect the Jews by defending capitalism through thick and thin ... As opposed to the brutalities committed by anti-Semitism, more in word than deed, against the Jews, we must not forget the brutalities committed by philo-Semitism, more in deeds than words, against all, be they Jews or Turks, Christians or heathen, who oppose capitalism."

### 5. In Pursuit of the Ideal Nation: America

1. John Trenchard, "An Argument Shewing that a Standing Army is inconsistent with a Free Government . . . ," 1697, in *A Collection of Tracts by the late John Trenchard, Esq., and Thomas Gordon, Esq.* (London: Cogan, 1751), p. 6. Anthony Ashley Cooper, Earl of Shaftesbury, *Characteristics of Men, Manners, Opinions, Times* (London: Basil, 1790), vol. III, *Miscellany III*, pp. 119, 119n., 124–125, 120–121. John Locke, *Two Treatises on Civil Government* (London: Butler et al., 1821), Treatise II, pp. 294, 191, 239.

2. John M. Murrin, "The Great Inversion, or Court versus Country: A Comparison of the Revolution Settlements in England (1688–1721) and America (1776–1816)," pp. 368–453, in J. G. A. Pockock, ed., *Three British Revolutions: 1641, 1688, 1776* (Princeton: Princeton University Press, 1980). An argument parallel to Murrin's is found in Lipset's illuminating comparison between the United States and Canada (Seymour Martin Lipset, *Continental Divide: The Values and Institutions of the United States and Canada* [Washington and Toronto: Canadian-American Committee, 1989]), whose differences, despite many similarities, Lipset relates to the different significance and legacy of the outcome of the American Revolution in the two cases.

3. Quoted in Sacvan Bercovitch, *The Puritan Origins of the American Self* (New Haven and London: Yale University Press, 1975), p. 85.

4. Charles Inglis, quoted in Bernard Bailyn, *The Ideological Origins of the American Revolution* (Cambridge, Mass.: The Belknap Press of Harvard University Press, 1967), p. 175.

5. Richard Hofstadter, quoted in Hans Kohn, *American Nationalism* (Westport, Conn.: Greenwood Press, 1957), p. 13.

6. Regarding comparison with Latin America, see Bercovitch, *Puritan Origins,* pp. 139–143.

7. Robert Cushman, "Sermon: The Sin and Danger of Self-Love," preached at Plymouth, in New England, 1621, printed in London, 1622, reprinted in Henry Wyles Cushman, *Historical and Biographical Genealogy of the Cushmans: The Descendants of Robert Cushman, the Puritan, from the Year 1617 to 1855* (Boston: Little, Brown, and Co., 1855), p. 42. (I am indebted to Thomas Cushman, a descendant of Robert Cushman, for making me aware of this document and putting it at my disposal.) Cotton Mather, *Magnalia Christi Americana,* Books I and II, ed. Kenneth B. Murdock (Cambridge, Mass: The Belknap Press of Harvard University Press, 1977), reprinted from the 1702 edition, p. 122.

8. Cushman, *Genealogy of the Cushmans,* pp. 56–57; and "Reasons and Considerations Touching the Lawfulness of Removing out of England into the Parts of America," pp. 31–38 in ibid.; pp. 33, 36, 34.

9. Mather, *Magnalia,* pp. 91, 125. John Norton; example of attitudes toward English civic principles; and *The Cambridge Platform* quoted in Daniel Boorstin, *The Americans: The Colonial Experience* (New York: Vintage Books, 1958), pp. 16, 22.

10. John Higginson, "Attestation . . . ," pp. 63–73, in Mather, *Magnalia,* p. 70. Mather, pp. 92, 120, 119. Mather's national identity, like that of his fellow New Englanders, was unquestionably and unproblematically English. It is as Englishmen that they faced the rest of the world. For example, Mather addressed to the Indians "An epistle to the Christian Indians, giving them a short account, of what the english desire them to know and to do, in order to their happiness. Written by an English minister, at the desire of an English magistrate," published in Boston, 1700.

11. On criticism and its suppression in early colonial Massachusetts, see David Cressy, *Coming Over: Migration and Communication between England and New England in the Seventeenth Century* (Cambridge: Cambridge University Press, 1987), ch. 1.

12. Mather, *Magnalia,* pp. 122, 120. In 1724, Rev. Hugh Jones wrote of Virginia that, by comparison with the other colonies, it "may be justly esteemed the happy Retreat of true Britons." Quoted in Boorstin, *Colonial Experience,* p. 123.

13. Thomas Dudley, quoted in Cressy, *Coming Over,* p. 16. Dudley thought such commendations pernicious and decided to set the record straight "lest other men should fall short of their expectations when they come hither, as we to our great prejudice did, by means of letters sent us from hence into England, wherein honest men, out of desire to draw over others to them, wrote somewhat hyperbolically of many things here."

14. Edward Johnson, *History of New England, or Wonder-Working Providence of Sions Saviour, 1628–1652,* ed. J. Franklin Jameson (New York: Scribner, 1952), pp. 209–210.

15. Benjamin Franklin, Letter to Joshua Babcock, January 13, 1772, in John Bige-

low, ed., *The Works of Benjamin Franklin* (New York: Putnam, 1904), vol. V, pp. 287–288. J. Hector St. John de Crevecoeur, *Letters from an American Farmer,* 1782 (New York: Penguin American Library, 1981), pp. 51–53.

16. Franklin, "Information to Those Who Would Remove to America," 1782, in *Works,* vol. IX, pp. 435–436. Lord Adam Gordon, "Journal," in Howard H. Peckham, ed., *Narratives of Colonial America* (Chicago: The Lakeside Press, 1971), p. 292. Crevecoeur, *Letters,* pp. 66–67.

17. These examples, among several others, are cited by Murrin, "A Roof without Walls: The Dilemma of American National Identity," pp. 333–348, in Richard Beeman, Stephen Botein, and Edward C. Carter II, eds., *Beyond Confederation: Origins of the Constitution and American National Identity* (Chapel Hill: University of North Carolina Press, 1987), pp. 343–344.

18. Franklin, "The Interest of Great Britain Considered, with Regard to her Colonies and the Acquisitions of Canada and Guadaloupe," 1760, in *Works,* vol. III, p. 321.

19. Murrin, "Roof," pp. 336–337.

20. Joseph Galloway, *Candid Examination of the Mutual Claims of Great Britain and the Colonies with a Plan of Accommodation on Constitutional Principles,* 1775 (New York: Research Reprints, 1970), p. 5. Daniel Dulany, "Considerations on the Propriety of Imposing Taxes in the British Colonies," 1765, in Bernard Bailyn, ed., *Pamphlets of the American Revolution, 1750–1776* (Cambridge, Mass.: The Belknap Press of Harvard University Press), vol. I, pp. 598–658, 649. Hopkinson quoted in Merle Curti, *The Roots of American Loyalty* (New York: Atheneum, 1968), p. 12.

21. John Adams, the opening sentence of the first *Novanglus* essay, January 23, 1775, in *Novanglus and Massachusettensis* (Boston: Hews and Goss, 1819), p. 9. Franklin, Letters to his wife, March 5, 1760; to Peter Collinson, May 9, 1753; and to Lord Kames, January 3, 1760, in *Works,* vol. III, p. 254; vol. II, p. 416; vol. III, p. 248; "The Interest of Great Britain," p. 294. Also see Franklin, Letter to David Hume, September 27, 1760, in *Works,* vol. III, pp. 337–338.

22. John Randolph, *Considerations on the State of Virginia,* n.p., 1774, quoted in Max Savelle, "Nationalism and Other Loyalties in the American Revolution," pp. 901–923, *American Historical Review,* 57:4 (July 1962), p. 912. Charles Inglis, "The True Interest of America Impartially Stated," 1776, pp. 62–69, in Richard Hofstadter, ed., *Great Issues in American History, 1765–1865,* a selection of documents (New York: Vintage Books, 1958), p. 67. John Dickinson, *Letters from a Farmer in Pennsylvania to the Inhabitants of the British Colonies* (New York: The Outlook Company, 1903), Letter III, pp. 32–33.

23. James Otis, "The Rights of the British Colonists Asserted and Proved," in Bailyn, *Pamphlets,* pp. 418–482, 458. "If I have one ambitious wish," confessed Otis, "'tis to see Great Britain at the head of the world, and to see my king, under God, the father of mankind" (ibid., p. 449).

24. Thomas Paine, *Common Sense,* in Bruce Kuklick, ed., *Political Writings* (Cambridge: Cambridge University Press, 1989), p. 2.

25. This definition was new and striking; it attracted the attention of those who, like Hobbes, could think of any number of alternative definitions. Hobbes

blamed the tendency of Milton and others to "extol popular government 'by the glorious name of liberty'" on excessive reading of the classics. Yehoshua Arieli, *Individualism and Nationalism in American Ideology* (Cambridge, Mass.: Harvard University Press, 1964), p. 53.

26. This is a point stressed by several authors. See ibid., p. 62; Murrin, "Roof," p. 340; Kohn, *American Nationalism*, p. 7; and others.

27. It was this idealistic nature of English nationalism in America which allowed Bernard Bailyn, in *The Ideological Origins of the American Revolution*, to characterize the latter as "above all else an ideological, constitutional, political struggle, and not primarily a controversy between social groups undertaken to force changes in the organization of society or the economy" (pp. vi, 18, and passim). But interests reinforced the ideals, and ideals themselves tended to be perceived as interests. By contrast, Savelle characterizes the differences of position between Whigs, who were soon to champion independence, and Tories, who were to remain loyalists, in America as "expediency versus loyalty, or British nationalistic idealism. The Tories were idealists; the Whigs were realists" (Savelle, "Nationalism and Other Loyalties," p. 914). I think that, analytically speaking, this was the other way around. It was the Whigs who defended the ideals of British nationalism irrespective of their current geo-political embodiment. The Tories, on the other hand, defended the embodiment, though cognizant of its failings in the realization of the ideals. The Whigs benefited from their position, while the Tories lost, and we can say, post factum, that the Whigs acted in their objective interest, while the Tories acted against their interest, but this should not obstruct our view of the fact that the Whigs, nevertheless, defended the ideals, and Tories—the status quo. The British could have persevered and won; who knows what the fate of the Whigs and Tories would have been then.

28. Adams, *Novanglus*, March 6, 1775, p. 84. *Genuine Principles*, William Hicks quoted in Bailyn, *Ideological Origins*, pp. 182, 181.

29. Arieli, *Individualism*, pp. 52–55, makes this point. In general, see Arieli and Bailyn, *Ideological Origins*, regarding the nature and evolution of the concept of constitution in colonial America.

30. John Dickinson, *Letters from a Farmer*, Letter II, p. 13; Adams, *Novanglus*, March 6, 1775, p. 94; Daniel Leonard, *Massachusettensis*, in Adams, January 9, 1775, p. 172.

31. Edmund Burke, Speech on conciliation with America, March 22, 1775, in Hofstadter, *Great Issues*, pp. 40–43.

32. Hancock quoted by Savelle, "Nationalism and Other Loyalties," p. 907. Franklin, Letter to Francis Maseres, June 26, 1785, *Works*, vol. XI, p. 66. Allen, "American Alarm" quoted in Bailyn, *Ideological Origins*, p. 305. Dickinson, *Letters from a Farmer*, Letter VI, pp. 62–66.

33. Stamp Act Congress, October 1765, Declarations. Smith quoted in Hans Kohn, *The Idea of Nationalism* (New York: Macmillan, 1944), p. 277.

34. First Continental Congress, Declaration and Resolves, October 14, 1774. Leonard, *Massachusettensis*, January 9, 1775, p. 170.

35. John Adams, "A Dissertation on the Canon and Feudal Law," 1765, in Charles Francis Adams, ed., *The Works of John Adams* (Boston: Little and Brown,

1851), vol. III, p. 461. (Adams continued: "But admitting we are children, have not children a right to complain when their parents are attempting to break their limbs, to administer poison, or to sell them to enemies for slaves? . . . will the mother be pleased when you represent her as deaf to the cries of her children?") See Bailyn, *Ideological Origins,* pp. 51–52, 202–204, and *The Origins of American Politics* (New York: Vintage Books, 1970), regarding circumstances which made Americans more capable than Englishmen of self-government.

36. Jonathan Shipley, *A Speech intended to have been spoken on the Bill for Altering the Charters of the Colony of Massachusett's Bay* (London: Cadell, 1782), pp. 31, 34, 33, 27. (The importance of this exceptionally sympathetic English view of America is slightly diminished by the possibility that its proponent—and the author of the speech—was Benjamin Franklin.) Adam Smith, *The Wealth of Nations* (Chicago: University of Chicago Press, 1976), vol. II, p. 140.

37. Leonard, *Massachusettensis,* January 9, 1775, pp. 172–173. Adams, *Novanglus,* March 6, 1775, pp. 90–91.

38. Carl Bridenbaugh, *The Spirit of '76: The Growth of American Patriotism before Independence, 1607–1776* (Oxford: Oxford University Press, 1975), devotes to this connection a chapter aptly entitled "Mounting Self-confidence and Gradual Alienation."

39. Franklin, Letter to Lord Kames, April 11, 1767, *Works,* vol. IV, p. 286. George Washington, Letter to Joseph Reed, February 10, 1776, in John Fitzpatrick, ed., *The Writings of George Washington* (Washington, D.C.: U.S. Government Printing Office, 1931–1936), vol. IV, p. 321. (On the development of Washington's sentiments, see Curti, *Roots,* pp. 16–17.) Franklin, Letter to Joseph Galloway, February 25, 1775, *Works,* vol. VI, p. 431. See also Kohn, *The Idea of Nationalism,* p. 272.

40. Quoted in Bridenbaugh, *Spirit of '76,* pp. 129, 146. It is worth noting that Evelyn here uses the word "nation" in the sense of a community capable of supporting itself.

41. Paine, *Common Sense,* p. 30. Murrin, "Roof," p. 339.

42. Adams, "Dissertation on the Canon and Feudal Law," p. 457.

43. According to Jefferson, planters became "a species of property, annexed to certain mercantile houses in London." Thomas Jefferson, "Answers by Mr. Jefferson to Questions of Mons. de Meusnier," 1786, *The Writings of Thomas Jefferson,* ed. A. A. Lipscomb (Washington, 1903), vol. XVII, p. 59. On such economic grievances, see Boorstin, *Colonial Experience,* p. 320; Bridenbaugh, *Spirit of '76,* passim; and Curti, *Roots,* pp. 17ff.

44. R. H. Lee, Letter to Patrick Henry, quoted in Arieli, *Individualism,* p. 70. The contemporary characterization of independence is quoted in Bailyn, *Ideological Origins,* p. 142.

45. Dickinson, *Letters from a Farmer,* Letter XI, p. 121.

46. Boorstin, *Colonial Experience,* p. 370. Smith, *Wealth,* vol. II, p. 486 (the closing sentences of the book).

47. At times, in the early decades, the government of Britain would be compared to "the powers of Hell," for being "equally hostile [with the latter] to the happi-

ness of mankind." Nathaniel Boileau, 1814, quoted in John Murrin, "Escaping Perfidious Albion," unpublished, p. 46. But there were at least as many of those who prayed: "Heaven bless America, and Britain,/May folly past suffice,/ Wherein they have each other smitten,/Who ought to harmonize." "Common Prayer for the Times," 1776, in Frank Moore, *Songs and Ballads of the American Revolution,* 1855 (reprint, Port Washington, N.Y.: Kennikat Press, 1964), p. 126. The opinion of the elite—this must be emphasized—was split already in the 1780s, a substantial number professing great respect and admiration for the oppressor and enemy of several years ago. This would have been inconceivable in Russia or Germany, and even in France. When the memories of the conflict faded, the anti-British sentiment all but disappeared; in other countries memories of conflicts persisted much longer.

48. Savelle, "Nationalism and Other Loyalties," p. 913.

49. Paine, *Common Sense,* pp. 1, 16, 30. John Adams held the same messianic view in 1765, when he asserted, in the often quoted passage from the "Dissertation on the Canon and Feudal Law," that the settlement of America was caused by "a love of universal liberty." Adams, *Works,* vol. III, pp. 451, 452n. Similar expressions were scattered in the writings of other colonial Americans given to expressing themselves in writing.

50. Jefferson, Letter to Roger C. Weightman, June 24, 1826, declining invitation to the celebration of the Fourth of July in Washington on account of ill health, *Writings,* vol. XVI, p. 182.

51. The narrowness of this original definition of humanity expressed itself not only in the exclusion of blacks and women, but also in allowing the State of New Hampshire, for instance, until 1877 to deny voting rights to the Jews.

52. A phrase of a nineteenth-century editor, referring to the unbridled enthusiasm of the nascent press in the West, quoted in Daniel Boorstin, *The Americans: The National Experience* (New York: Vintage Books, 1965), p. 127.

53. Murrin, "Roof," p. 341.

54. In 1853, George Burnap viewed the founding of the first American newspaper, in Boston in 1704, as the actual birthday of a specifically American nation. (Curti, *Roots,* p. 51.) But even the most outspoken contemporary advocate of this view, Carl Bridenbaugh, finds it necessary to qualify his belief in its existence before independence. He says: "The deep sense of a continental community—economic, social, and cultural, though not yet political—attained during the two decades 1740–1760—was . . . for the most part uncomprehended by the great body of the colonists of those years" (Bridenbaugh, *Spirit of '76,* p. 73).

55. Bridenbaugh, *Spirit of '76,* pp. 93, 107; Curti, *Roots,* p. 22. Franklin, Letter to a friend, November 28, 1768, *Works,* vol. V, p. 41. Bercovitch (*Puritan Origins,* p. 89), however, claims that the term "American" in its modern meaning first appears in Mather's *Magnalia.*

56. John Dickinson, "Arguments against the Independence of the Colonies," in Jack P. Green, ed., *Colonies to Nation, 1763–1789: A Documentary History of the American Revolution* (New York: Norton, 1975), pp. 295–296, and "The Liberty Song" (or "A Song much in Vogue in North America") in Moore, *Songs,* pp. 37–39.

57. Thomas Paine, *The American Crisis,* 13, 1783, in M. D. Conway, ed., *The Writings of Thomas Paine* (New York: The Knickerbocker Press, 1984), vol. I, pp. 374–375. Jefferson, Letter to Elbridge Gerry, May 13, 1797, and "The Anas," *Writings,* vol. IX, p. 385, and vol. I, pp. 266–267. "Instructions to the Ministers Plenipotentiary Appointed to Negotiate Treaties of Commerce with the European Nations," quoted in Arieli, *Individualism,* p. 32. Samuel Bryan, "Centinel," Letter I, in Herbert J. Storing, ed., *The Anti-Federalist: Writings by the Opponents of the Constitution* (Chicago: University of Chicago Press, 1985), p. 18.

58. Declaration of Independence, emphasis added. (See on this point Arieli, *Individualism.*) Regarding the original meaning of "federal," see Boorstin, *National,* p. 415. Preamble to the Virginia Bill of Rights, quoted in Arieli, p. 37.

59. James Madison, *Debates on the Adoption of the Federal Constitution in the Convention Held at Philadelphia in 1787; with a Diary of the Debates of the Congress of the Confederation,* ed. Jonathan Elliot (Washington, D.C.: Elliot, 1845), pp. 132–133.

60. Jefferson, "Inauguration Address," March 4, 1801, *Writings,* vol. III, p. 319.

61. John Adams, quoted in Fred Siegel, "Two Centuries of American Conservatism," in *Encyclopedia of American History,* and Adams, "Defence of the Constitutions of Government of the United States of America," Letter to John Taylor, April, 15, 1814, *Works,* vol. IV, pp. 489–490; vol. VI, p. 484.

62. Edward Mead Earle, ed., *The Federalist* (New York: The Modern Library, 1941), #63, pp. 410, 413; #49, pp. 331, 327.

63. Jefferson, Letter to William Johnson, June 12, 1823, advising him on the dispute and differences between Federalists and Jeffersonians, and Letter to Joseph C. Cabell, February 2, 1816, *Writings,* vol. XV, p. 441, and vol. XIV, p. 422.

64. I am aware that Jefferson's position on all those thorny issues was not entirely consistent and that at times he, too, was tormented by uncertainty. I do not see, however, that the thrust of his thinking, which is especially salient in comparison with that of the Federalists, can be mistaken.

65. See in this regard François Jean, Marquis de Chastellux, *Travels in North America in the Years 1780–1781–1782* (New York, 1827), p. 277.

66. Jefferson, Letter to Madison, January 30, 1787, and Adams, Letter to Jefferson, June 30, 1813, both in Jefferson, *Writings,* vol. VI, p. 65, and vol. XIII, p. 297.

67. Jefferson, "Inauguration Address," p. 319, and Letter to Wm. Short, January 3, 1793, *Writings,* vol. IX, p. 10. Jefferson opened the letter by reproaching Short for "the extreme warmth with which [his letters] censured the proceedings of Jacobins in France."

68. Regarding Jefferson's attitude to slavery, see Winthrop D. Jordan, *White over Black: American Attitudes Toward the Negro, 1550–1812* (Baltimore: Penguin Books, 1969), and John Chester Miller, *The Wolf by the Ears: Thomas Jefferson and Slavery* (New York: The Free Press, 1977).

69. Neither was slavery mentioned; in both instances a clever use of language allowed the avoidance of dealing with problematic issues.

70. Washington, Letter to Joseph Jones, May 31, 1780, *Writings,* vol. XVIII,

p. 453. Jefferson, Letter to Edward Livingston, March 25, 1825, *Writings,* vol. XVI, p. 113.

71. Plumer, Morris, and the Declaration of the Springfield meeting quoted in Kohn, *American Nationalism,* p. 95. In a footnote, Kohn cites other examples of the self-interested solicitude for the nation, and pro-British and anti-French sentiments during that period. On the same point see Curti, *Roots,* p. 45 and passim.

72. Charleston *Mercury,* July 4, 1850, quoted in Curti, *Roots,* p. 157. South Carolina Declaration—in Kohn, *American Nationalism,* p. 115.

73. Resolution of Congress on Public Lands, October 10, 1780, pp. 119–120, in H. S. Commager, ed., *Documents of American History* (New York: Appleton-Century-Crofts, 1963).

74. The options are those of Albert O. Hirschman, *Exit, Voice, and Loyalty* (Cambridge, Mass.: Harvard University Press, 1970).

75. The Constitution, Article 1, Section 2.

76. See Boorstin, *National,* the chapter on "Government as a Service Institution."

77. Ibid., p. 121.

78. President Grant, in a message to the Congress of May 14, 1872. "The immigrant is not a citizen of any State or Territory upon his arrival, but comes here to become a citizen of a great Republic, free to change his residence at will, to enjoy the blessings of a protecting Government, where all are equal before the law, and to add to the national wealth by his industry. On his arrival he does not know States or corporations, but confides implicitly in the protecting arm of the great, free country of which he has heard so much before leaving his native land ... I see no subject more national in its character than provision for the safety and welfare of the thousands who leave foreign lands to become citizens of this Republic." Quoted in Kohn, *American Nationalism,* p. 142.

79. Crevecoeur, *Letters,* pp. 69–70, 82–84. Frances Trollope, *Domestic Manners of the Americans,* 4th ed. (London, 1832), vol. I, *The Annals of America* (Chicago: Encyclopaedia Britannica, 1976), vol. V (1821–1832), p. 544. Immigrants' reflections quoted in Curti, *Roots,* p. 82, and Kohn, *American Nationalism,* p. 141. Translations vary slightly.

80. Pioneers' impressions quoted in Curti, *Roots,* pp. 36–41.

81. Boorstin, *National,* pp. 295, 237–239. Louis H. Sullivan, *The Autobiography of an Idea* (New York: Press of the American Institute of Architects, 1924), pp. 200–201.

82. Quoted in Lowenthal, *The Jews of Germany,* p. 250.

83. Curti, *Roots,* p. 73; also see F. George Franklin, *The Legislative History of Naturalization in the United States* (Chicago, University of Chicago Press, 1906); ch. 3 discusses the Act of 1790. Crevecoeur, *Letters,* p. 70.

84. The geographical frontier was not the only frontier, and other frontiers have not been exhausted so easily. See on this point David Potter, "Abundance and the Turner Thesis," pp. 109–134, in Don E. Fehrenbacher, ed., *History and American Society: Essays by David M. Potter* (New York: Oxford University Press, 1973).

85. Seth Luther, "An Address to the Cordwainers of the United States" (Philadel-

phia, 1836), p. 4; "Address to the Workingmen of New England" (Boston, 1832), p. 39; quoted in Curti, *Roots*, pp. 107, 80.

86. Daniel Webster, Speech delivered in the Senate, January 27, 1830 (second reply to Hayne), *The Annals of America*, vol. V, p. 355.

87. Jefferson, "Anas," *Writings*, vol. I, p. 279. Alexander Hamilton, "Report on the Subject of Manufactures," December 5, 1791, in Hofstadter, *Great Issues*, p. 172.

88. Noah Webster, in *American Magazine*, 1788 and 1787, quoted in Kohn, *American Nationalism*, p. 47, and Curti, *Roots*, p. 100.

89. James Russell Lowell, a review of *Kavanagh* by Longfellow, in *North American Review* (July 1849); see discussions in Kohn, *American Nationalism*, pp. 70–71, and in Perry Miller, *The Raven and the Whale* (Westport, Conn.: Greenwood Press, 1973), pp. 255–256. Sydney Smith was a famous critic and divine; his question appeared in an article in *Edinburgh Review* in 1820. The discussion here relies on Kohn, pp. 51ff.

90. William Ellery Channing, "Remarks on National Literature," 1823, *Works* (Boston: James Munroe, 1841), vol. I, pp. 248, 252, 261. James Fenimore Cooper, *Home as Found* (New York: Stringer & Townsend, 1852), preface, p. v. Melville, "Hawthorne and his Mosses," in Harrison Hayford, ed., *Melville* (New York: The Library of America, 1984), pp. 1161, 1164. "Let America then prize and cherish her writers," Melville implored; "yea, let her glorify them . . . And while she has good kith and kin of her own, to take to her bosom, let her not lavish her embraces upon the household of an alien . . . let America first praise mediocrity even, in her own children, before she praises . . . the best excellence in the children of any other land" (ibid.).

91. Henry Wadsworth Longfellow, "Kavanagh: A Tale," in *Kavanagh and Evangeline* (Philadelphia: McKay, 1893), p. 119. Lowell, a review of "Kavanagh," quoted in Kohn, *American Nationalism*, pp. 70–71, and in Miller, *Raven*, p. 256. Ralph Waldo Emerson, "The American Scholar," pp. 51–71, in Joel Porte, ed., *Essays and Lectures* (New York: The Library of America, 1983), p. 71.

92. Boorstin, *National*, pp. 327–390, and Curti, *Roots*, pp. 122–143.

93. Alexis de Tocqueville, *Democracy in America*, ed. Phillips Bradley (New York: Vintage Books, 1954), vol. I, p. 410.

94. Francis D. Quask, quoted in Curti, *Roots*, p. 43. Lincoln, *Complete Works*, ed. John G. Nicolay and John Hay (New York: Francis D. Tandy, 1894), vol. VI, p. 181, "The First Inaugural Address"; vol. VIII (the annual message of 1862), p. 110. John O'Sullivan, the editor of the *United States Magazine and Democratic Review*, who coined the phrase "manifest destiny," first used it in the context which emphasized Providence rather than geography: in an editorial urging the annexation of Texas (July 1845), he saw the latter as a step in "the fulfillment of our manifest destiny to overspread the continent alotted by Providence for the free development of our yearly multiplying millions." *The Annals of America*, vol. VII, p. 289.

95. William Holmes McGuffey, *Newly Revised Eclectic Fourth Reader*, 1853, and Goodrich quoted in Kohn, *American Nationalism*, p. 63. See also Goodrich, *A*

*History of the United States of America,* 4th ed. (Bellows Falls, Vt., 1824), introduction.

96. George Bancroft, *Poems:* "Expectations," June 1821; "Rome," July 1823 (Boston, 1823); "The Necessity, the Reality, and the Promise of the Progress of the Human Race," Oration delivered before the New York Historical Society, November 20, 1834 (New York, printed for the Society), pp. 28–29, 33–34; "Memorial Address on the Life and Character of Abraham Lincoln" (Washington, D.C.: U.S. Government Printing Office, 1866), pp. 4, 6; "The Office of the People in Art, Government, and Religion," oration delivered at Williamstown College, August 1835, in *The Annals of America,* vol. VI, pp. 128–136.

97. Emerson, "The Young American," in *Essays and Lectures,* pp. 217, 226, 221, 228, 229; 230, 226, 228.

98. Charles Mackay, *Life and Liberty in America,* quoted in Curti, *Roots,* p. 31.

99. George Dekker and Larry Johnston, introduction to James Fenimore Cooper, *The American Democrat* (London: Penguin Books, 1989), pp. 8, 45, and passim.

100. Cooper, *The American Democrat,* pp. 104, 105–109, 70, 69. *The American Democrat* was written in 1838, about the same time when Tocqueville postulated that equality of conditions—combined with prosperity—was the distinguishing characteristic of the American society.

101. This is Huntington's argument in *American Politics: The Promise of Disharmony* (Cambridge, Mass.: Harvard University Press, 1981).

102. Cooper, *Home as Found,* p. v.

103. Abraham Lincoln, Speech delivered at Springfield, Ill., June 26, 1857, *Complete Works,* vol. II, pp. 330–331.

104. Robert W. Fogel and Stanley L. Engerman, *Time on the Cross: The Economics of American Negro Slavery* (Boston: Little, Brown and Co., 1974). Those who, for propagandist purposes, present Southern slavery as in any sense comparable to the Holocaust miss the point (they diminish the enormity of the Holocaust and do no justice to slavery). It was a degrading, not a homicidal, arrangement, a way of life, however unacceptable, not of mass murder, and in order to comprehend its effects on those who experienced it, it must be understood as a way of life.

105. Cooper, *American Democrat,* pp. 220–223.

106. Nat Turner, "Confession" (dictated in prison and recorded by Turner's attorney, Thomas R. Gray), *The Annals of America,* vol. V, pp. 472–481.

107. Cooper, *American Democrat,* p. 222. There was undoubtedly more than a grain of truth, however awkward it is to admit this, in the pro-slavery argument of Thomas Dew that "all of us . . . are too prone to judge of the happiness of others by ourselves—we make *self* the standard and endeavor to draw down everyone to its dimensions . . . We might rather die than be the obscure slave that waits at our back—our education and our habits generate an ambition that makes us aspire at something loftier, and disposes us to look upon the slave as unsusceptible of happiness in his humble sphere, when he may indeed be much happier than we are." Thomas R. Drew, *The Pro-Slavery Argument* (1832), *The Annals of America,* vol. V, p. 510.

108. See the Address of the Negro Convention in Philadelphia, June 6–11, published

in *Liberator,* October 22, 1831 (*The Annals of America,* vol. V, pp. 424–426); William Lloyd Garrison, Address on "The Dangers of the Nation," July 4, 1829, *The Annals of America,* vol. V, p. 305; Lincoln, Speech on the Kansas-Nebraska Act, delivered in Peoria, October 16, 1854, *Complete Works,* vol. II, p. 205.

109. See, for example, George Fitzhugh, *Sociology for the South, or the Failure of Free Society,* 1854, four chapters reprinted in Harvey Wish, ed., *Ante-bellum: Writings of G. Fitzhugh and H. R. Helper on Slavery* (New York: Capricorn Books, 1960); and *Cannibals All! or, Slaves Without Masters,* 1857 (Cambridge, Mass.: Harvard University Press, 1960). Also see Edmund Ruffin, "Consequences of Abolition Agitation" (*De Bow's Review,* June–December 1857, *The Annals of America,* vol. VIII, pp. 466–475).

110. Orlando Patterson, *Slavery and Social Death* (Cambridge, Mass.: Harvard University Press, 1982). (Incidentally, Patterson rejects the usefulness of "defining slavery only as the treatment of human beings as property," because such definition "does not really specify any distinct category of persons. Proprietary claims and powers are made with respect to many persons who are clearly [in legal terms] not slaves"; specifically, wives and children may be considered as property of husbands and fathers. This again undescores the resemblance between the status of women and slaves.) "The Seneca Falls Declaration on Women's Rights," in *The Annals of America,* vol. VII, pp. 438–441.

111. Tocqueville, *Democracy in America,* vol. II, pp. 209, 223, 224, 211, 225. "The Seneca Falls Declaration," p. 439.

112. Henry James jotted in his *Notebook* that *The Bostonians* "should be a study of one of those friendships between women which are so common in New England." *The Bostonians* (Oxford: Oxford University Press, The World's Classics, 1984), p. 438. The quoted phrase is Garrison's, from the salutatory of the first issue of *Liberator,* for whose publication Garrison believed Boston to be the proper place, because the history and traditions of the place threw inequality into a sharper relief than those of any other place.

113. Dickinson, *Letters from a Farmer,* Letter IX, p. 98. Henry David Thoreau, *Walden and Civil Disobedience,* ed. Michael Meyer (New York: Penguin Classics, 1986), p. 49.

114. J. J. Flournoy, "Ebony Workers and White Workers," *Southern Banner,* January 13, 1838; "Appeal of Forty Thousand Citizens, Threatened with Disenfranchisement to the People of Pennsylvania," Philadelphia, 1838, *The Annals of America,* vol. VI, pp. 415–416; 417. James, *The Bostonians,* p. 32 and passim.

115. Quoted in Bailyn, *Ideological Origins,* p. 243.

116. Although one may add, tongue in cheek, that if the ability to reason is no longer invoked, there is no reason at all why Americans should deny their minors the rights enjoyed by people of age. For Jefferson's views on slavery and black intellectual inferiority, see *Notes on Virginia;* also, Jordan, *White over Black,* and Miller, *The Wolf by the Ears.* See Miller also for Jefferson's views on women. Maryland Abolitionists quoted in Jordan, p. 448.

117. Intellectuals working in areas with well-defined criteria of excellence are less affected by the lack of recognition, although undoubtedly it is always frustrat-

ing, because they are less dependent on it for the assessment of their abilities. The craving for status explains both the Unionist preferences of the intellectuals and their opposition to American ideals.

118. Alexis de Tocqueville, "Conversation with Mr. Livingston" (from *Journey to America*), *The Annals of America*, vol. V, p. 482.

119. I must disagree with the authoritative statement on this subject, Richard Hofstadter's *Anti-Intellectualism in American Life* (New York: Alfred A. Knopf, 1963). The vision of the book—an intellectual's response to McCarthyism—is obstructed by the author's sympathies and dislikes. Sharing in these sympathies should not prevent one from seeing the fallacy of the argument. Hofstadter defines anti-intellectualism as "a resentment and suspicion of the life of the mind and of those who are considered to represent it; and a disposition constantly to minimize the value of that life" (p. 7), thus confounding contempt for culture and disregard for professional intellectuals, and putting emphasis on the contempt for culture. He considers it, with certain largely perfunctory reservations, "a problem of more than ordinary acuteness here," a problem "of special urgency and poignancy" (p. 20), though willing to admit in passing that the situation in England might be almost as bad (he quotes a contemporary British intellectual, saying: "No people has ever despised and distrusted the intellect and intellectuals more than the British" [ibid.]). Hofstadter, however, provides no evidence whatsoever to support this claim. He admits in one sentence that "this is not, as it perhaps should be, a comparative study" (ibid.), but comparison is absolutely essential to his argument. When one claims that American society is anti-intellectual, the question necessarily must be asked: in comparison to what? If it is a tendency of societies as such, or of societies on a certain level of development, or of democratic societies, to be anti-intellectual, this claim, relative to American society, can only aspire to the status of exposition in a particular context of a general rule. For the claim of American anti-intellectualism to be a meaningful argument about the distinctiveness of the American society, American society should be proved to be markedly more anti-intellectual than other societies with a comparably developed culture. Moreover, it should be established that this is a characteristic general to the American population rather than, for example, to one or another of its elites, whose attitudes, given that this is a pluralistic society, might not be representative of the attitudes of society. Finally, it should be specified whether anti-intellectualism refers to a hostility to intellectuals or to a contempt for the intellect and its preoccupations—culture.

It is evidently not true that the masses of American society, historically, have been more hostile to intellectuals than, say, the masses of Russian or French societies. As to the intellect, they have, conspicuously, valued it more than their respective counterparts, although it cannot be said that they have uniformly valued all aspects and forms of culture. The elite sectors in European societies, however, are uniformly respectful both of intellectuals and of culture, which has not been so among American elites. Whatever they think of culture, American elites, in general, do not defer to intellectuals. The *intellectualism* of the European elites is explained in part by the fact that they are to a large extent composed of intellectuals, while in America professional intellectuals (rather than men thinking on their own time) have played a less prominent role in the leadership of society. In other societies national identity was created by intellectuals who made sure that it would henceforth be associated with their high status within the nation. In America, on the other hand, professional intellectuals as a group emerged significantly later than national identity and therefore they do not have the centrality within the consciousness of their compatriots enjoyed by intellectuals elsewhere.

What Hofstadter sees as "anti-intellectualism" is in fact an indifference to intellectuals. But to admit this would make the special interest of intellectuals deploring this phenomenon all too transparent. It is always safer to represent one's personal concern as a disinterested concern for the general good. The very frequency with which American intellectuals talk about the anti-intellectualism of their society underscores the existence of a special interest. In Russia the word "*intelligent*" is used by the people as a word of abuse, but one rarely encounters Russian intellectuals accusing Russia of anti-intellectualism.

Similarly, regarding the claim of the crass materialism of Americans, it must be admitted that the human race is deplorably materialistic. Consumer societies differ from those that are not so called by the fact that in them there are things to be consumed, not by the greater urge to consume or lesser spirituality. In fact, as the events of the last two years in Eastern Europe have shown us, consumer deprivation, if anything, makes people more rather than less materialistic.

120. Dudley quoted in Bridenbaugh, *Spirit of '76*, p. 27; Duche, Ezra Stiles, and Edmund Burke in Boorstin, *Colonial Experience*, pp. 316, 204, 201.

121. Boorstin, *Colonial Experience*, pp. 182, 172–184 passim, 205; Merle Curti, *American Paradox: The Conflict of Thought and Action* (New Brunswick, N.J.: Rutgers University Press, 1956), pp. 15–16.

122. Boorstin, *National*, p. 155. Hezekiah Niles, *Niles' Weekly Register*, November 11, 1815, quoted in Kohn, *American Nationalism*, p. 43.

123. See Chapter 3, fn. 142. A Russian visitor indeed noted the difference. Pavel Svin'in wrote in his *Opyt zhivopisnogo puteshestvia po severnoi Amerike* ("A Picturesque Voyage through North America," 1815, believed to be the first account of the United States by a Russian traveler): "You should not look for profound philosophers and celebrated professors in America; but you will be astonished at the correct understanding of the humblest citizen respecting the most abstract matters . . . Everyone studies the geography of his country, knows the rudiments of arithmetic, and has a general idea of other sciences. That is why every *muzhik* here not only would not be surprised by an eclipse of the moon or the appearance of a comet, but could discuss these phenomena with a fair degree of intelligence." Quoted in Abbott Gleason, "Pavel Svin'in," in Marc Pachter, ed., *Abroad in America: Visitors to the New Nation, 1776–1914* (Reading, Mass.: Addison-Wesley, 1976), p. 13.

124. Tocqueville, *Democracy in America*, vol. II, p. 58.

125. See Bernard Bailyn, *Education in the Forming of American Society* (Chapel Hill: University of North Carolina Press, 1960), pp. 26–27, on the laws concerning education, and in general on the importance and pervasiveness of education in colonial America.

126. Boorstin, *Colonial Experience*, pp. 242, 314–315. Bailyn (*Education*, p. 35), writes about Franklin's idea of education: "It was a subtle revolution too often interpreted as somehow peculiarly 'utilitarian.' Indeed, he did expect education to be useful, as who did not; but his revolution consisted in the kind of utility he had in mind. He wanted subjects and instruction that trained not for limited goals, not for close-bound, predetermined careers, but for the broadest possible range of enterprise. He had no argument with the classics as such. What he objected to was the monopoly of the higher branches of education which denied the breadth of preparation needed for the open world he saw."

127. David A. Wasson, *Atlantic Monthly*, October 1858, p. 527. Quoted in Curti, *Roots*, p. 72.

128. Jared Eliot, *Essays upon Field Husbandry in New England, as it is or may be Ordered* (Boston, 1760); Penn—quoted in Boorstin, *Colonial Experience*, pp. 264, 307.

129. Emerson, "The American Scholar," pp. 56–58.

130. By Oliver Wendell Holmes.

131. Channing, "Remarks," p. 261.

132. Walt Whitman, *Complete Poetry and Collected Prose*, ed. Justin Kaplan (New York: The Library of America, 1982), "Leaves of Grass," preface of 1855, pp. 5, 8–10, 14–15, 17, 24–26.

133. Whitman, *Complete Poetry*, "Letter to Emerson," August, 1856, p. 1328. "Leaves of Grass" was not recognized as a great masterpiece until the twentieth century. Whitman shared the fate of other now admittedly great literary figures of his time, such as Thoreau and Melville, whose genius, largely unnoticed at the time when they expected praise, was acknowledged only in retrospect.

134. Business early became the focus of intellectuals' criticism of American society; it was seen as the perfect embodiment of its failings. See Hofstadter, *Anti-Intellectualism*, pp. 233ff. Unlike the case in Europe, in America businessmen enjoyed the social consideration intellectuals would have liked to consider their own prerogative and felt deprived of.

135. Whitman, *Complete Poetry*, pp. 936–938, 932, 935, 974.

136. Edgar Allan Poe, "Mellonta Tauta," quoted in Kohn, *American Nationalism*, p. 45, and "Some Words with a Mummy, a Tale," in Poe, *Poetry and Tales*, ed. P. F. Quinn (New York: The Library of America, 1984), p. 820.

137. Quoted in Boorstin, *National*, p. 289. More to this effect can be found in Henry James, *The American Scene*, 1907.

138. Edgar Allan Poe, "Prospectus of the *Stylus*," *Essays and Reviews*, ed. G. R. Thompson (New York: The Library of America, 1984), p. 1035.

139. For example, Hofstadter, *Anti-Intellectualism*; Daniel Bell, "Resolving the Contradictions of Modernity and Modernism," *Transaction/Society*, 27 and 28 (Spring 1990).

140. Hofstadter, *Anti-Intellectualism*, pp. 400–404.

141. Rufus Choate, "American Nationality," *The Annals of America*, vol. IX, p. 56.

142. A Confederate opinion, quoted in Reid Mitchell, *Civil War Soldiers: Their Expectations and Their Experiences* (New York: Viking, 1988), p. 11. (See Mitchell on the participants' reasons for fighting in general.) Lincoln, Reply to the signed editorial in *New York Tribune*, "The Prayer of Twenty Millions," August 22, 1862, *The Annals of America*, vol. IX, p. 348.

143. Daniel Webster, Speech at the Senate, March 7, 1850, *The Annals of America,* vol. VIII, pp. 26–27, 25. See Mitchell, *Civil War Soldiers,* on the views of Northern soldiers regarding slavery.

144. John C. Calhoun, Speech at the Senate, delivered by James A. Mason, March 4, 1850, *The Annals of America,* vol. VIII, pp. 17–18, 19, 20.

145. Lincoln, Speech on Kansas-Nebraska Act, October 1854, *Complete Works,* vol. II, p. 246.

146. Consider, for example, the following pronouncements: "We must become national, nay, provincial, and cease to be imitative cosmopolitans . . . We want American customs, habits, manners, dress, manufactures, modes of thought, modes of expression, and language. We should encourage national and even State peculiarities . . . Take language, for instance. It is a thing of natural growth and development . . . It is never ungrammatical as spoken by children, but always expressive, practical, and natural. Nature is always grammatical, and language, the child of nature, would continue so but for the grammarians . . . The rules of art destroy art." This is not Friedrich Schlegel, but the American George Fitzhugh (*Cannibals All!,* pp. 59, 63).

147. Quoted in Boorstin, *National,* p. 218; see in general the chapter "Metaphysical Politics." Also see Arieli, *Individualism,* "The Great Debate on the Nature of the American Ideal."

148. The "battle cry of freedom" was that of the South as well as the North, as we learn from James McPherson, *Battle Cry of Freedom: The Civil War Era* (New York: Oxford University Press, 1988). See Mitchell, *Civil War Soldiers,* on the value of freedom among Confederate soldiers; Boorstin, *National,* pp. 215–218, on attitudes toward public opinion; the quotation is from Kohn, *American Nationalism,* p. 108.

149. Fitzhugh, *Cannibals All!,* p. 63.

150. Fitzhugh, *Sociology for the South,* pp. 68–71. *Sociology for the South* and another apology for slavery, *A Treatise on Sociology,* by the Mississippian Henry Hughes, which also appeared in 1854, were the two first American books to present themselves as sociological and to have the word "sociology" in their titles. It is interesting that Northern intellectuals at this time did not favor sociology. Lowell, for example, considered it a "fearful science" and found sociologists (who came from Europe) to be "hardest to bear." Lowell, "On a Certain Condescension of Foreigners," *Writings* (Cambridge, Mass.: Riverside Press, 1890), vol. III, p. 245.

151. Fitzhugh, *Cannibals All!,* ch. 1, "The Universal Trade," pp. 15–17, 20; *Sociology for the South,* pp. 249–250.

152. Lincoln, Fragment "On Slavery," July 1, 1854, *Complete Works,* vol. II, p. 186.

153. F. L. Olmsted, "Slavery in its Effects on Character, and the Social Relations of the Master Class," *New-York Daily Times,* January 12, 1854, *The Annals of America,* vol. VIII, p. 242. Olmsted noticed Southerners' tendency to reinterpret their principles in accordance with their interests, rather than abandon the former. "The South," he wrote, "endeavors to close its eyes to every evil the removal of which will require self-denial, labor, and skill. If, however, an evil is too glaring to be passed unnoticed, it is immediately declared to be constitutional, or providential, and its removal is declared to be either treasonable or impious—usually both; and, what is worse, it is improper, impolite, ungentle-

manly, unmanlike" (ibid., p. 239). Unlike Fitzhugh, Olmsted was not a sociologist, but a landscape artist. Yet he was evidently capable of sociological insight.

154. Lincoln, Speech on Kansas-Nebraska Act, p. 227.

155. Lowell, "Condescension in Foreigners," *Writings*, vol. III, p. 246. Emerson, *Journals*, quoted in Curti, *Roots*, p. 169. Charles Sumner, "Are We a Nation?" Address delivered on November 19, 1867, *Works* (Boston: Lee and Shepard, 1877), vol. XII, pp. 187–249, 193.

156. Yale address quoted in Curti, *Roots*, p. 171. J. R. Lowell, "Reconstruction," 1865, *Writings*, vol. V, p. 212. Sumner, *Works*, p. 191.

157. Francis Lieber, *Civil Liberty and Self-Government*, 1853, ed. T. D. Woolsey (Philadelphia, 1874), p. 295. Quoted in Kohn, *American Nationalism*, pp. 141–142. (Before he immigrated, Lieber was a German patriot and a disciple of Jahn. Invited to teach gymnastics in Boston, he soon taught political science first at the University of South Carolina and then at Columbia, and became the founder of the *Encyclopedia Americana*. On Lieber and organic theorists in general, see Kohn; Curti, *Roots*, pp. 174–179; Curti, "Francis Lieber and Nationalism," *The Huntington Library Quarterly*, 4 [April 1941], pp. 263–292.) Mulford quoted in Kohn, p. 127.

158. Michael Walzer, "What Does It Mean to Be an 'American'?" Paper delivered at the Institute for Advanced Study, Princeton, N.J., October 1989.

159. On the place of "ethnicity" in American society, see in particular Philip Gleason, "American Identity and Americanization," in Stephen Thernstrom, ed., *Harvard Encyclopedia of American Ethnic Groups* (Cambridge, Mass.: Harvard University Press, 1980).

160. Horace Kallen's *Culture and Democracy in the United States* (New York: Boni and Liveright, 1924) is an example of such early reinterpretation of dual identity in America. I am relying in this note on Gleason's ("American Identity") and particularly Walzer's ("What Does It Mean") reading of Kallen.

161. Consider the shock of Henry James upon discovering "ethnicity" in *The American Scene*.

162. The accepted view seems to be that they were. But it is based on a misunderstanding of the nature of national identity, and the projection onto the past of what to the present appear as self-evident truths.

163. Like any dual allegiance, that of "ethnic" Americans contains a potential for disunion. The perpetuation and cultivation of "ethnic" identities is at least as dangerous as the recognition of state sovereignties, particularly because most of these identities are essentially exclusive.

164. Daniel Bell, "Utopian Nightmare," review of *1984* by George Orwell, *New Leader*, 25 (June 1949), p. 8.

## Afterword

1. The right of control over one's property is a central element of the definition of liberty, and therefore status, in America, which gives a rather spiritual turn to its proverbial materialism. John Dickinson's "Liberty Song," quoted earlier,

contains some lines touching upon this. The first verse, calling on Americans to join hand in hand, ends with the following:

> Our purses are ready,
> Steady, Friends, steady,
> Not as *slaves,* but as *freemen* our money we'll give.

However dear they held their purses, it was not the necessity to part with some of their contents that incensed them, but the fact that they were deprived of the right to decide when and why to do so. Americans would rather go to war than be taxed without being represented, for

> To die we can bear,—but to serve we disdain,
> For shame is to freemen more dreadful than pain.

To draw a contemporary parallel, Sadam Hussein would be well advised to peruse the songs of the American Revolution before undertaking to dictate to the United States how much it should pay per barrel of oil. It is the indignity of accepting such dictation—the infringement on their liberty—not the expense of several more cents per gallon, which makes Americans willing to go to a far greater expense, and—much more important—to sacrifice their lives, to stop him. It is one thing to submit to the indifferent laws of supply and demand, a completely different one to suffer the imposition of somebody's will.

# Index